John A. Shtogren

The Structure of Competence

— the theories and facts about managing people

Chartwell Bratt
Studentlitteratur
Bratt Institut für
Neues Lernen

The Structure of Competence — the theories and facts
about managing people

Copyright © 1980 by Teleometrics International
All rights reserved. No part of this publication may
be reproduced or transmitted in any form or by any
means, electronic or mechanical, including
photocopy, recording, or any information
storage and retrieval system, without permission
in writing from the publisher.

First published in 1980 by:
Teleometrics International
The Woodlands, Texas

ISBN 0-937932-00-0
Library of Congress Catalog Number 79-93291
Printed in USA 1980

CIP-Kurztitelaufnahme der Deutschen Bibliothek

The Structure of Competence –

the theories and facts about managing people / ed. by John A. Shtogren.
— The Woodlands (Texas): Teleometrics Int[ernationa]l;
Bromley: Chartwell-Bratt, 1980; Lund (Sweden): Studentlitteratur;
Goch: Bratt-Institut für Neues Lernen.
    ISBN 0-86238-121-5 (Chartwell-Bratt);
    ISBN 91-44-00003-0 (Studentlitteratur);
    ISBN 3-88598-045-5 (Bratt-Inst.)

NE: Shtogren, John A. [Hrsg.]

Published in England 1980
by Chartwell-Bratt
ISBN 0-86238-121-5 (Chartwell-Bratt)

Published in Sweden 1980
by Studentlitteratur
ISBN 91-44-00003-0
Artikelnummer 1793

Published in Germany 1980
by Bratt-Institut
ISBN 3-88598-045-5

Managing Editor:
Robert K. Glasgow

Editorial Assistant:
Dorothy Anderson

Contents

Editor's Notes

One of the first hard facts of management consulting life I learned was, *be prepared to answer tough questions.* Managers taught me that lesson the very first time I stood up to offer a new strategy for working productively with people and, in my experience since, they have not changed their minds. Before managers are willing to try out new ideas, they want to know, *"Where has it worked before? What makes you think it will work here? Who is going to benefit?"*

My colleagues and I used the standards reflected in these questions from managers as we selected chapters for this collection—relevance, validity, and value were the chief criteria. I think we were successful. In my opinion, this book measures up to the standards managers hold important more than any other in the field of management development.

The key feature of the models for management you will find in this collection is that they are research based. They are not textbook theories waiting to be put into practice or war stories told by old veterans of corporate campaigns. These managerial strategies are distinguished from others you are likely to encounter by data, objectively gathered information from a variety of settings to insure relevance and validity. You will find an abundance of proof indicating that the models do in fact produce what they promise—high levels of worker satisfaction and productivity. But you will also find data of more personal value. Putting these models into practice will not only benefit your subordinates and organization but you as well. *The data show that managers who actually use these models experience much greater success in their careers than their colleagues who follow different paths.*

The data are also important from another point of view—so few promoters of managerial theories have bothered to take the time and expend the effort to collect data to prove or disprove their theories. For far too many, the rule in this field seems to have been, "If it sounds good, sell it!" And a lot of managers have been sold a lot of ideas that sounded good and they never quite understood why the ideas did not work and why nothing changed. Fortunately, there are some exceptions to this huckster's rule and I believe we have a high percentage of them represented in this book.

But, to begin, it would be instructive to take a look at how we got to where we are now.

PRODUCTION vs. EMPLOYEES: RESOLVING THE DILEMMA

Rensis Likert, [1] the distinguished theorist and practitioner from the Institute for Social Research at the University of Michigan, has discussed two major trends which have shaped management's thinking and practices since the turn of the century. "Scientific management" and the "human relations" movement both contributed to modern management but appeared to many managers to be mutually exclusive because of their different points of emphasis. Even today many managers feel they must make a choice between either scientific management's production orientation or the human relations concentration on employee morale. But neither choice is without drawbacks.

Scientific management, beginning with Frederick Taylor in the early 1900's, stressed a highly structured approach to planning, organizing, directing, and controlling work. By using such techniques as job simplification and specialization, span of control, and chain of command, managers could go so far as to dictate written instructions to employees on a daily basis. Such techniques unquestionably help raise production, but there are hidden costs involved. When efficiency becomes management's only quest, it is paid for with the workers' sense of self-worth.

As work becomes more systematized, workers begin to feel like disposable parts in a mechanical system called the organization. For today's worker such conditions are intolerable:

"Simplified tasks for those who are not simple-minded, close supervision by those whose legitimacy rests only on hierarchical structure, and jobs that have nothing but money to offer in an affluent age are simply rejected. For many of the new workers, the monotony of work and scale of organization and their inability to control the pace and style of work are cause for resentment which they, unlike older workers, do not repress." [2]

Soaring absenteeism, turnover, grievances, and scrap rates are some of the tangible results of the unrepressed resentment given rise to, in part, by too heavy an emphasis on scientific management techniques.

At the same time scientific management was coming of age, the Hawthorne studies at Western Electric Company began to challenge scientific management's basic assumptions about productivity. While assessing the effects of light, ventilation, and rest breaks on worker productivity, researchers were surprised to find that psychological conditions appeared to be more important than physical conditions. *Production was highest* in work groups where relationships were congenial and workers felt they were appreciated by their managers.

Based on these findings the human relations movement advocated an employee-centered approach at the opposite end of the spectrum from scientific management. Indeed many managers who experienced the negative effects of scientific management rode the pendulum to the opposite side, switching from a narrow focus on production to an equally narrow focus on employee morale. They soon found that a country club atmosphere produces equal parts of conviviality and complacency: Nothing much is accomplished but no one much cares.

In Likert's view it was essential to blend the strengths of scientific management and human relations in such a way that both production and employee morale could be maximized without the negative effects associated with the extreme use of either approach. It was clear to him that the manager's task was not to make work simple and effortless or to make the work group a surrogate family or social club. As research has shown since Likert first called for an integrated approach, managerial competence requires more than writing job descriptions and setting production standards, or "stroking" people and negotiating personal growth contracts. The competent manager, committed to high productivity, must have an integrated set of beliefs and skills relating to the way people interact on the job.

ORGANIZATION

This book is an attempt to provide structure for Likert's notion of an integrated approach to management. The intent is to present the reader with a conceptual framework and the research data that indicate which approaches to management are most likely to work. The organizing principle underlying the six sections in this book is that *competent managers utilize the competence of their subordinates*. In other words they take full advantage of available human resources, their subordinates' inherent willingness and ability to perform at high levels of productivity. To do so requires an integrated set of human skills drawn from the social sciences.

The structure of managerial competence rests on cornerstone assumptions about the human capacity for work and is comprised of a set of practices consistent with this philosophic outlook. The six sections build progressively toward managerial competence as they address key questions:

Managerial Philosophy — What is my view of work and workers and how does that impact on the way I relate to others?

Motivation — What is motivation and what can I do about it?

Involvement — How can sharing my managerial authority with subordinates make me more powerful as a manager?
Interpersonal Competence — What personal skills do I need?
Group Dynamics — Can groups really get the job done?
Managerial Competence — What about *my* goals, *my* life and *my* career—how do *I* benefit from all this?

Chapters in each section show the benefits of particular managerial practices for individual and group productivity. The final section presents clear, and I hope convincing, evidence to the manager which indicates that the best and the brightest managers in business and industry do indeed practice within this structure of competence.

MAKING THIS BOOK WORK FOR YOU

The goal of this book is straightforward—to help you attain the highest level of managerial competence. To do so may require you to trade in your current models for management, the ways you now conceive your role and pattern your actions. The exchange will seldom be an easy one. The tendency of most managers is to both protect and elaborate upon their personal models, thereby fostering a self-reinforcing, inbreeding of managerial philosophy and action.

Model changes begin when there are opportunities for introducing new elements so that new conceptual constructions may occur. The second step is to experiment with these new constructions in a "trying them on for size" manner to see how well they handle real data about the world and, finally, to validate the new models via objective feedback as to their ability to predict the impact and consequences of managerial acts. This book has been organized with these thoughts in mind. Your willingness to experiment with new ideas, to test out behaviors that are low risk but have a potential for high yield, will ultimately determine its value for you.

Although you can benefit from this book on your own, you can make it an even more meaningful learning experience by involving others. For example, ask several co-workers to read a section and make it the agenda for your next staff meeting or lunch date. Use your experiences within your organization as the context for assessing various models—"Is that the way we do things around here? If not, will it work here?"

Such discussions also provide an opportunity for further personalizing each model. Not only can you place each managerial model in the context of your organization's policies, practices and procedures, but you can examine the behavior of individual managers as well. Ask your colleagues for feedback on how they see your behavior in light of the models and their own behaviors as well. Share with them your perceptions and, if there are disagreements, find out why. This kind of self-other comparison can be an enormously rewarding experience in the pursuit of managerial competence.[3] As the poet Robert Burns pointed out, it is quite a gift to see ourselves as others see us—and it can free us from many a foolish notion.

Many of these chapters are tough reading. "Good things don't come easy" is a well-worn phrase, but it still stands up well. The introductions for each section will help you by describing the contents of that section. Furthermore, each section is followed by "Afterthoughts;" specific thoughts on how you might use what you have learned or additional information not covered in that section's chapters but pertinent to the ideas presented. I am confident your efforts can prove to be worthwhile for your co-workers and for your organization, but most of all, for your career. However, what you do with this material is your choice. I encourage you to read well and choose wisely.

REFERENCES

1. Likert, Rensis. "Patterns in Management", General Management Series No. 178, American Management Association, Inc., 1955.

2. *Work in America, Report of a Special Task Force to the Secretary of Health, Education, and Welfare.* Washington, D.C.: Ninety-third Congress, First Session, 1973, p. 16.

3. Learning instruments which facilitate such self-other comparisons within the framework of many of the models presented in this volume are available from Teleometrics International.

Section I.

Managerial Philosophy: The Cornerstone of Managerial Competence

Premise: *People respond to and treat the world as they construe it.*

Originating with the work of Gestalt and other cognitive theorists, this premise holds that much of what people do is determined by their attitudes, values and personal theories which come into play when deciding what is the most appropriate way to behave. This is no less true for managers. Philosophies of management—those assumptions about people in the workplace and their abilities and needs—are the foundation for managerial actions. They are the origins of managerial behaviors and, as such, are the logical point of departure for presenting behavioral models which promise to teach managers how to behave so that they and their organizations can function competently.

In this regard, the goal here is not just to increase understanding but is to provide an opportunity for personal appraisal which has the potential for constructive change. Since personal conceptions are the source of behavior, any change process must begin at that point. As George H. Kelly,[1] the noted clinical psychologist, has observed, *personal change may only be achieved once a change in personal constructs and awareness has been achieved.* Therefore, the first step in developing managerial competence is to gain a better understanding of those attitudes, values and personal theories which constitute an individual's philosophy of management. In other words, improved practices most probably will require a change in point of view.

MANAGERIAL SKILLS: WORK TECHNOLOGY VERSUS SOCIAL TECHNOLOGY

Robert L. Katz[2] has pointed out that managers at all levels need three distinct types of skills: 1) Technical—the ability to produce the organization's goods or services; 2) Human—the ability to work in groups as a leader or member; 3) Conceptual—the ability to see how organizational units and functions are integrated. Managers at different levels will require different proportions of two of the three skills, technical and conceptual. For example, lower level managers need more technical skills than upper level managers because they are making decisions and solving problems on the line where the work is actually being done. Conversely, top level managers need more conceptual skills since their task is to lead the total organization in the greater marketplace. However, managers at all levels need a high degree of human skills because people are the common element whatever the task. These human skills are the focus of this volume.

Some managers, comfortable with beliefs that are contrary to existing data, have found it more convenient to question the data rather than reexamine their own constructs. This is particularly true when such a reexamination might prove to the manager that certain past behaviors have been inappropriate. In these cases it is not uncommon for the manager to adopt the "We're different!" position which says that hard data can be overlooked because it was not derived from peers or colleagues in the same industry.

The human skills common across management levels are equally applicable in any formal organization. Organizations are different, of course, but their differences are a function of the technical and conceptual skills which form what can be thought of as an organization's *work technology*. Technical and conceptual skills in such areas as manufacturing, market analysis, or forecasting differ drastically in industries as diverse as automotive, banking, and communications. But the human skills comprising a *social technology*, the human interactions aspect of the work situation, are the same. *Here we are concerned with a social technology which managers can apply universally rather than the work technology which characterizes their individual enterprises.* Therefore, conclusions drawn from the social dynamics of women workers in pajama factories, scientists in medical research centers, or hard-core trainees should be seen as equally relevant—people are the common denominator. Rather than being a drawback, a variety of research settings is a major source of strength. No matter the setting the data converge to indicate that the application of the social technology has no apparent limits.

MANAGERIAL PHILOSOPHY: THE KEY TO BEHAVIOR AND PERFORMANCE

The way a manager perceives the relationship between people and work will determine the kind of organizational structures and management strategies thought to be the best way of getting the job done. Accurate perception is the key to behaving in the most productive manner, but perception can be an inexact process. In "The Managerial Lens: What You See Is What You Get!",

Jay Hall describes the dynamics of perception and how a manager's view of subordinates, shaped by personal assumptions about people and work, dictates the manager's behavior and how that behavior in turn influences others.

Douglas McGregor's analysis of managerial philosophies provides for a deeper look into the source of managerial actions. In his two chapters McGregor presents a broader view of the lens model at work in organizational settings as he describes two sets of managerial expectations called Theory X and Theory Y. The two theories, or philosophic points of view, show how perceptions about people at work drive particular kinds of managerial actions.

PERFORMANCE EXPECTATIONS AND THE SELF-FULFILLING PROPHECY

Albert Sidney King reports dramatic evidence from the industrial world about expectations and performance in "Self-Fulfilling Prophecies in Training the Hard-Core: Supervisors' Expectations and the Underpriviledged Workers' Performance." J. Sterling Livingston also probes the implications of the self-fulfilling prophecy for managers in business and industry in "Pygmalion in Management." He has documented the self-fulfilling prophecy phenomenon in numerous case studies and places the responsibility for employee development and productivity squarely on the manager's shoulders.

While studying the readings in this section a dominant theme should become clear; a theme that is unifying and optimistic. No matter what their managerial level in business, industry, or government, managers need to be adept in human skills. What they believe about people, whether they see their prospects for productivity as bright or dim, is the crucial factor in determining their ultimate level of managerial achievement. Having what might seem to be abnormally high expectations for subordinates is not the mark of a Pollyanna in the workplace but is, in fact, the cornerstone of managerial competence.

REFERENCES

1. Kelly, George A. *The Psychology of Personal Constructs*. New York: Norton & Company, 1955.

2. Katz, Robert L. "Skills of an Effective Administrator." *Harvard Business Review, Vol. 52*, 1974, pp. 90-102.

Chapter 1

The Managerial Lens: What You See is What You Get!

Jay Hall

Most managers have never heard of Egon Brunswik,[1] much less had the opportunity to examine his "Lens Model" of social perception. This is unfortunate because the concept of social perception is particularly important to individuals whose livelihoods are dependent on the effective functioning of other people. Management, as a process, literally begins with social perception: how we view others and make judgements about them are the origins of our efforts to manage them.

Brunswik's model, as it is presented here, is about being effective as a manager. It provides a conceptual framework for understanding how our own perceptions of other people affect our behavior toward them. It is a fundamental statement - a starting point from which to begin to explore the human aspects of managerial functioning.

Egon Brunswik was a professor of psychology. Born and educated in Austria, he came to the University of California at Berkeley in 1937. Although Brunswik had little first-hand experience with managers or the dynamics of business and industry, his ideas are universal and apply to any interpersonal setting. They are particularly important to managers who are concerned about the impact their relationships with subordinates have on their own personal productivity.

To begin with, Brunswik suggested that how we perceive others and how we interpret their actions determine how we will pattern our behavior toward them. This is a critical aspect of any interpersonal relationship and is of particular importance to managers who need to be aware of this when examining existing relationships or when establishing relationships with new subordinates or co-workers. What we *think* we see in others will determine, for the most part, how we will treat them and respond to them. The *accuracy* of what we think we see will dictate the appropriateness of the behaviors we utilize or the actions we take and the resulting productivity of the relationship.

THE LENS MODEL

The dynamics of Brunswik's lens model can be demonstrated by looking at social perception in its simplest form, the two person encounter. Figure 1 depicts the beginning of the process whereby the manager attempts to understand or to come to terms with an employee. Brunswik called this process "adaptation" and pointed out that its success depends on the manager's ability to gather accurate information about the employee and to interpret it appropriately. Interestingly, Brunswik equated successful adaptation, coming to terms with the nature of things, with personal achievement; a commodity of considerable concern for most managers. But to truly know another—to come to terms with the what and the who of the individual—is one of the most difficult tasks we face. Most of us do not even know ourselves as much as we would like to, much less others. And managers are no exception.

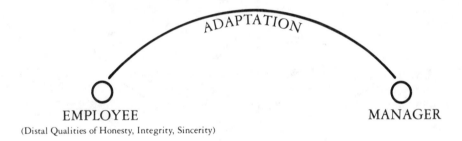

EMPLOYEE   MANAGER
(Distal Qualities of Honesty, Integrity, Sincerity)

Figure 1.

In coming to terms with others we are usually interested in their central dispositional characteristics, what they intend and their "goodness" or "badness" on a number of important dimensions. In deciding how to relate to others we make both conscious and unconscious judgements about their honesty, integrity, sincerity, loyalty, industriousness, creativity, perseverance and so forth. As important as they are, these all constitute highly intangible, internal, distant, or "distal" states which for all practical purposes are inaccessible to the manager or anyone else. For the most part they do not possess perceivable substance. Integrity cannot be seen, loyalty tasted nor creativity heard, yet the manager must somehow learn about the employee's real potential and motives.

Brunswik was aware of the dilemma in the perception—adaptation—achievement process caused by the inaccessibility of critical information. He noted that, as a result, symbolic representations of these traits and dispositional characteristics become the data from which inferences are drawn and upon which impressions are formed. The distal qualities must be *inferred* from more accessible "cues" which, according to our personal theories, are taken to represent in some way the traits we consider critical. Each of us, in a manner of speaking, learns to look for more obvious traits or characteristics which we believe "stand for" the quality we are interested in but cannot see. Brunswik called these self-selected indicators "proximal" cues and indicated that the perceiver feels—or consciously hypothesizes—that they are somehow representative of internal, distal characteristics. The use of such obvious and more controllable cues allows us to simplify the perceptual process, and to make interpersonal relationships more predictable and less anxiety producing.

Figure 2 shows some commonly used proximal cues for the distal qualities of honesty, integrity, and sincerity. The cues one selects—and there can be as many cues or cue systems as there are individuals making judgements—combine, according to Brunswik, to form a lens through which one views others.

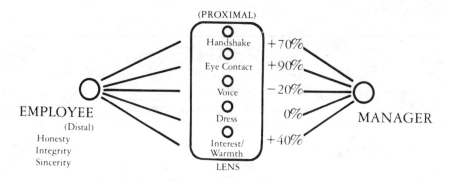

Figure 2.

Thus, the manager in this case believes there is some relationship between such cues and distal qualities as handshake and honesty, eye contact and integrity, or voice and sincerity, and so forth. Furthermore, each cue is weighted as to its importance or level of probability for predicting distal qualities. In this example the manager places more importance on eye contact than handshake, but both are nearly twice as significant as interest/warmth. Taken together they form the "lens" through which others will be viewed and according to which their worth as people will be judged. Needless to say, this is a most tenuous basis for making important social judgements. Yet most of us do just that.

Most people have implicit theories and preferences regarding the cues they attend to and the meanings they attach to them. This is a highly subjective process characterized by great individual differences. In effect, individuals weight cues in either positive or negative directions—that is, their presence is taken to mean that a trait of interest is either present (positive relationship) or absent (negative relationship). Weights attached, as statements of amount of emphasis placed on a given cue, really amount to statements of probability. For example, placing a lot of weight on "punctuality" as an indication that one is trustworthy is the same as saying "The probability is great that punctual people are also people worthy of trust!" Conversely, placing a lot of negative weight on male hair length as an indication of attitude is the same as saying "The probability is great that men with long hair have rebellious (or whatever) attitudes!" This process of using cues to build a probability model is a part of the human condition. Although we alter our models continuously, these alterations tend to be minor and, unfortunately, we tend not to concern ourselves much about the accuracy of our models once we become comfortable with them. In the final analysis, because the process is so subjective, the lenses we construct and the conclusions we draw as managers may tell more about each of us personally than about those whom we judge!

LENS ACCURACY

Since valid information is critical to the perceiver, lens accuracy is the central issue in perceiving and adapting effectively to others. First of all lens accuracy, as you might expect, is determined by the extent to which cues are actually related to particular distal qualities. Second, how closely the weights or importance given to cues by the perceiver coincide with the actual importance which exists in the objective world also affects lens accuracy.

The manager's cue system shown in Figure 2 can be used to demonstrate the liabilities of relying too heavily on subjective interpretations. Imagine the manager encountering an employee who displays all the proper cues. If the handshake is firm, eye contact is good and consistent, the voice is not too loud or overbearing, and the person displays genuine interest, the manager may see the employee as truly sincere, honest, and full of integrity. What, however, if the employee happens to have sociopathic tendencies—i.e., one who is sensitive to the cues others value and who adopts them consciously for purposes of misleading others? Or what if the employee has simply learned the organizational game so well that he knows how to play the system? In either event the manager, effectively seduced, would ultimately be proven wrong and probably at a point where it was costly.

Lens accuracy and the consequent accuracy of impressions and acts, is determined by the extent to which subjective expectations jibe with objective realities. The utility of cues and the accuracy of our lens systems may only be determined by testing out the left, or objective, side of the lens. One might find, as indicated in the following example, that the cues utilized do not, in fact, represent distal traits as anticipated:

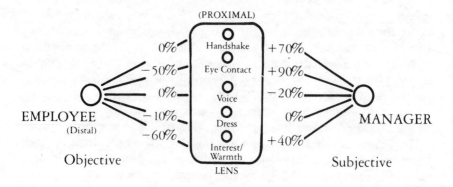

Figure 3.

In this example, the lens is quite distorted: a net distortion of 70% on hand-shake, 140% for eye contact, 20% for voice, 10% for dress, and 100% for interest/warmth. It follows that the impressions formed on the basis of such distorted lens perceptions will, themselves, be greatly distorted and lead to acts that are off target and inappropriate.

TENDENCIES TOWARD SUBJECTIVISM

Despite the obvious pitfalls to successful adaptation and personal achievement caused by relying on purely subjective cues, there is a strong tendency for individuals to remain subjective in making social judgements. We are, after all, human beings and it is easier and more comfortable to continue existing habits. If we have to defend our position occasionally, or even admit to error, that is still easier than taking the steps necessary to become more objective. Unfortunately, trusting completely in subjective cues leaves us open to surprises, some of which can be unpleasant. Moreover, constant reliance on the same cues can result in "lens rigidity," or stereotyping, and we begin using the same lens system to view all people in particular categories such as race, religion, or the region where they live. Although strongly resented when we are subjected to stereotyping, we apply it to others with incredible ease.

An interesting and important phenomenon of subjectivism is the interpersonal perceptual process called "the self-fulfilling prophecy." Rosenthal[2] recently noted that many times we make prophecies about the nature of other people and unconsciously use behaviors toward them which have the effect of confirming our original perceptions even though they were unfounded. For example, a manager might be talking to an employee and, perceiving the employee to be ill at ease, pointedly ask, "Why are you so defensive?" A predictable response from the employee would be a very defensive one—"What do you mean I'm defensive? I am not!" Upon hearing the response, the manager thinks, "I was right!", without realizing the part played by the question in producing the "defensive" response.

The flow of events in the self-fulfilling prophecy is as follows: 1) the perceiver is most sensitive to the cues which make up his or her personal lens; 2) the thus biased interpretation of proximal cues then dictates the actions taken toward another; 3) the actions elicit a reciprocal reaction; and 4) the reaction reinforces the original perception. The point is that the unconscious act of calling out behaviors in others severely limits the adaptation process.

Critical situations where information for decision making is not readily available also contribute to the tendency to remain subjective. Strangely, the more important a judgement is to a person, the more uncertain the situation and the less tolerant that person is of uncertainties, the greater will be that person's tendency to be purely subjective. Perceptions and impression formations will be narrowed, closing out additional information and refusing either to entertain alternative interpretations or to test out systematically the objective validity of the subjective lens and its resulting impressions. The following formula presents one way of looking at the contributing components to inflexibility and the closing off of new experiences and inputs:

$$\text{Subjectivism} = f\left(\text{Importance} \ \ X \ \ \frac{\text{Uncertainty}}{\text{Tolerance for Uncertainity}}\right)$$

At first the formula may seem implausible. Most of us like to think we are rational beings seeking out the necessary data to make solid decisions, especially when the stakes are high. However, we also know that it is not at all unusual for a manager who must select an employee for a critical assignment to trust "instinct." Even though little may be known about the task requirements and the necessary skills and abilities, the manager will quickly select the "best" candidate on the basis of a hunch.

On a larger scale Irving Janus[3] has documented numerous examples of subjective thinking and decision making when objective data were disregarded or discounted. The results were such fiascos as Pearl Harbor, the Bay of Pigs, and Vietnam. And, speaking in an organizational context, Douglas McGregor's[4] well-known Theory X-Theory Y proposition postulates that managers have personal theories about the nature of working man which form the basis for their individual management practices. Managers select practices which, in their minds, best account for—compensate, capitalize upon, etc.—the characteristics of the people supervised *as the individual manager perceives them.* These are all lens dynamics. Strategies, policies and procedures, therefore, are most often based on perceptions—not on objective reality.

Brunswik argued that programs should be undertaken to test out the objective realities—the true relationships between selected cues and distal characteristics. This book is intended as a step in that direction. Its objective is to stir and discomfit; to help the reader raise questions—about the reader. In addition, and perhaps more important, it supplies information about that critical yet elusive objective side of the lens. As a beginning Brunswik would have you acknowledge the fact that, as a human being, you operate every day with your own personal lens system. He would have you identify and become conscious of those cues you use and commit to checking out your own lens—to moving yourself from the subjective to the objective.

And, therein lies the ultimate answer. You are the key to your interpersonal behavior and you must be the source of questions raised about your existing lens systems. *You* are the key to your own managerial adaptation and achievement.

REFERENCES

1. Hammond, Kenneth R. (Ed.). *The Psychology of Egon Brunswik*. New York: Holt, Rinehart and Winston, Inc., 1966.

2. Rosenthal, Robert. "On the Social Psychology of the Self-fulfilling Prophecy: Further Evidence for Pygmalion Effects and Their Mediating Mechanisms." *Module 53*, 1973. New York: MSS Modular Publications.

3. Janus, Irving. "Groupthink." *Psychology Today*, Vol. 5, No. 6, November 1971, pp. 43-76.

4. McGregor, Douglas. *The Human Side of Enterprise*. New York: McGraw-Hill Book Company, Inc., 1960.

Chapter 2

Theory X: The Traditional View of Direction and Control

Douglas McGregor

Behind every managerial decision or action are assumptions about human nature and human behavior. A few of these are remarkably pervasive. They are implicit in most of the literature of organization and in much current managerial policy and practice:

1. *The average human being has an inherent dislike of work and will avoid it if he can.* This assumption has deep roots. The punishment of Adam and Eve for eating the fruit of the Tree of Knowledge was to be banished from Eden into a world where they had to work for a living. The stress that management places on productivity, on the concept of "a fair day's work," on the evils of featherbedding and restriction of output, on rewards for performance—while it has a logic in terms of the objectives of enterprise—reflects an underlying belief that management must counteract an inherent human tendency to avoid work. The evidence for the correctness of this assumption would seem to most managers to be incontrovertible.

2. *Because of this human characteristic of dislike of work, most people must be coerced, controlled, directed, threatened with punishment to get them to put forth adequate effort toward the achievement of organizational objectives.* The dislike of work is so strong that even the promise of rewards is not generally enough to overcome it. People will accept the rewards and demand continually higher ones, but these alone will not produce the necessary effort. Only the threat of punishment will do the trick.

The current wave of criticism of "human relations," the derogatory comments about "permissiveness" and "democracy" in industry, the trends in some companies toward recentralization after the postwar wave of decentralization—all these are assertions of the underlying assumption that people will only work under external coercion and control. The recession of 1957-1958

From *The Human Side of Enterprise*, McGraw-Hill Book Company, Inc., New York, 1960, chapter 3, pp. 33-44. Reprinted by permission of the publisher.

ended a decade of experimentation with the "soft" managerial approach, and this assumption (which never really was abandoned) is being openly espoused once more.

3. *The average human being prefers to be directed, wishes to avoid responsibility, has relatively little ambition, wants security above all.* This assumption of the "mediocrity of the masses" is rarely expressed so bluntly. In fact, a good deal of lip service is given to the ideal of the worth of the average human being. Our political and social values demand such public expressions. Nevertheless, a great many managers will give private support to this assumption, and it is easy to see it reflected in policy and practice. Paternalism has become a nasty word, but it is by no means a defunct managerial philosophy.

I have suggested elsewhere the name Theory X for this set of assumptions. . . Theory X is not a straw man for purposes of demolition, but is in fact a theory which materially influences managerial strategy in a wide sector of American industry today. Moreover, the principles of organization which comprise the bulk of the literature of management *could only have been derived from assumptions such as those of Theory X.* Other beliefs about human nature would have led inevitably to quite different organizational principles.

Theory X provides an explanation of some human behavior in industry. These assumptions would not have persisted if there were not a considerable body of evidence to support them. Nevertheless, there are many readily observable phenomena in industry and elsewhere which are not consistent with this view of human nature.

Such a state of affairs is not uncommon. The history of science provides many examples of theoretical explanations which persist over long periods despite the fact that they are only partially adequate. Newton's laws of motion are a case in point. It was not until the development of the theory of relativity during the present century that important inconsistencies and inadequacies in Newtonian theory could be understood and corrected.

The growth of knowledge in the social sciences during the past quarter century has made it possible to reformulate some assumptions about human nature and human behavior in the organizational setting which resolve certain of the inconsistencies inherent in Theory X. While this reformulation is, of course, tentative, it provides an improved basis for prediction and control of human behavior in industry.

SOME ASSUMPTIONS ABOUT MOTIVATION

At the core of any theory of the management of human resources are assumptions about human motivation. This has been a confusing subject because there have been so many conflicting points of view even among social scientists. In recent years, however, there has been a convergence of research findings and a growing acceptance of a few rather basic ideas about motivation. These ideas appear to have considerable power. They help to explain the inadequacies of

Theory X as well as the limited sense in which it is correct. In addition, they provide the basis for an entirely different theory of management.

The following generalizations about motivation are somewhat oversimplified. If all of the qualifications which would be required by a truly adequate treatment were introduced, the gross essentials which are particularly significant for management would be obscured. These generalizations do not misrepresent the facts, but they do ignore some complexities of human behavior which are relatively unimportant for our purposes.

Man is a wanting animal—as soon as one of his needs is satisfied, another appears in its place. This process is unending. It continues from birth to death. Man continously puts forth effort—works, if you please—to satisfy his needs.

Human needs are organized in a series of levels—a hierarchy of importance. At the lowest level, but preeminent in importance when they are thwarted, are the physiological needs. Man lives by bread alone, when there is no bread. Unless the circumstances are unusual, his needs for love, for status, for recognition are inoperative when his stomach has been empty for a while. But when he eats regularly and adequately, hunger ceases to be an important need. The sated man has hunger only in the sense that a full bottle has emptiness. The same is true of the other physiological needs of man—for rest, exercise, shelter, protection from the elements.

A satisfied need is not a motivator of behavior! This is a fact of profound significance. It is a fact which is unrecognized in Theory X and is, therefore, ignored in the conventional approach to the management of people. I shall return to it later. For the moment, an example will make the point. Consider your own need for air. Except as you are deprived of it, it has no appreciable motivating effect upon your behavior.

When the physiological needs are reasonably satisfied, needs at the next higher level begin to dominate man's behavior—to motivate him. These are the safety needs, for protection against danger, threat, deprivation. Some people mistakenly refer to these as needs for security. However, unless man is in a dependent relationship where he fears arbitrary deprivation, he does not demand security. The need is for the "fairest possible break." When he is confident of this, he is more than willing to take risks. But when he feels threatened or dependent, his greatest need is for protection, for security.

The fact needs little emphasis that since every industrial employee is in at least a partially dependent relationship, safety needs may assume considerable importance. Arbitrary management actions, behavior which arouses uncertainty with respect to continued employment or which reflects favoritism or discrimination, unpredictable administration of policy—these can be powerful motivators of the safety needs in the employment relationship at every level from worker to vice president. In addition, the safety needs of managers are often aroused by their dependence downward or laterally. This is a major reason for emphasis on management prerogatives and clear assignments of authority.

When man's physiological needs are satisfied and he is no longer fearful about his physical welfare, his social needs become important motivators of his behavior. These are such needs as those for belonging, for association, for acceptance by one's fellows, for giving and receiving friendship and love.

Management knows today of the existence of these needs, but it is often assumed quite wrongly that they represent a threat to the organization. Many studies have demonstrated that the tightly knit, cohesive work group may, under proper conditions, be far more effective than an equal number of separate individuals in achieving organizational goals. Yet management, fearing group hostility to its own objectives, often goes to considerable lengths to control and direct human efforts in ways that are inimical to the natural "groupiness" of human beings. When man's social needs—and perhaps his safety needs, too—are thus thwarted, he behaves in ways which tend to defeat organizational objectives. He becomes resistant, antagonistic, uncooperative. But this behavior is a consequence, not a cause.

Above the social needs—in the sense that they do not usually become motivators until lower needs are reasonably satisfied—are the needs of greatest significance to management and to man himself. They are the egoistic needs, and they are of two kinds:

1. Those that relate to one's self-esteem: needs for self-respect and self-confidence, for autonomy, for achievement, for competence, for knowledge

2. Those that relate to one's reputation: needs for status, for recognition, for appreciation, for the deserved respect of one's fellows

Unlike the lower needs, these are rarely satisfied; man seeks indefinitely for more satisfaction of these needs once they have become important to him. However, they do not usually appear in any significant way until physiological, safety, and social needs are reasonably satisfied. Exceptions to this generalization are to be observed, particularly under circumstances where, in addition to severe deprivation of physiological needs, human dignity is trampled upon. Political revolutions often grow out of thwarted social and ego, as well as physiological, needs.

The typical industrial organization offers only limited opportunities for the satisfaction of egoistic needs to people at lower levels in the hierarchy. The conventional methods of organizing work, particularly in mass production industries, give little heed to these aspects of human motivation. If the practices of "scientific management" were deliberately calculated to thwart these needs—which, of course, they are not—they could hardly accomplish this purpose better than they do.

Finally—a capstone, as it were, on the hierarchy—there are the needs for self-fulfillment. These are the needs for realizing one's own potentialities, for continued self-development, for being creative in the broadest sense of that term.

The conditions of modern industrial life give only limited opportunity for these relatively dormant human needs to find expression. The deprivation most people experience with respect to other lower-level needs diverts their energies into the struggle to satisfy *those* needs, and the needs for self-fulfillment remain below the level of consciousness.

Now, briefly, a few general comments about motivation:

We recognize readily enough that a man suffering from a severe dietary deficiency is sick. The deprivation of physiological needs has behavioral consequences. The same is true, although less well recognized, of the deprivation of higher-level needs. The man whose needs for safety, association, independence, or status are thwarted is sick, just as surely as is he who has rickets. And his sickness will have behavioral consequences. We will be mistaken if we attribute his resultant passivity, or his hostility, or his refusal to accept responsibility to his inherent "human nature." These forms of behavior are *symptoms* of illness—of deprivation of his social and egoistic needs.

The man whose lower-level needs are satisfied is not motivated to satisfy *those* needs. For practical purposes they exist no longer. (Remember my point about your need for air.) Management often asks, "Why aren't people more productive? We pay good wages, provide good working conditions, have excellent fringe benefits and steady employment. Yet people do not seem to be willing to put forth more than minimum effort." It is unnecessary to look far for the reasons.

Consideration of the rewards typically provided the worker for satisfying his needs through his employment leads to the interesting conclusion that most of these rewards can be used for satisfying his needs *only when he leaves the job.* Wages, for example, cannot be spent at work. The only contribution they can make to his satisfaction on the job is in terms of status differences resulting from wage differentials. (This, incidentally, is one of the reasons why small and apparently unimportant differences in wage rates can be the subject of so much heated dispute. The issue is not the pennies involved, but the fact that the status differences which they reflect are one of the few ways in which wages can result in need satisfaction in the job situation itself.)

Most fringe benefits—overtime pay, shift differentials, vacations, health and medical benefits, annuities, and the proceeds from stock purchase plans or profit-sharing plans—yield needed satisfaction only when the individual leaves the job. Yet these, along with wages, are among the major rewards provided by management for effort. It is not surprising, therefore, that for many wage earners *work is perceived as a form of punishment* which is the price to be paid for various kinds of satisfaction away from the job. To the extent that this is their perception, we would hardly expect them to undego more of this punishment than is necessary.

Under today's conditions management has provided relatively well for the satisfaction of physiological and safety needs. The standard of living in our country is high; people do not suffer major deprivation of their physiological needs except during periods of severe unemployment. Even then, social legislation developed since the thirties cushions the shock.

But the fact that management has provided for these physiological and safety needs has shifted the motivational emphasis to the social and the egoistic needs. Unless there are opportunities *at work* to satisfy these higher-level needs, people will be deprived; and their behavior will reflect this deprivation. Under such conditions, if management continues to focus its attention on physiological needs, the mere provision of rewards is bound to be ineffective, and reliance on the threat of punishment will be inevitable. Thus one of the assumptions of Theory X will appear to be validated, but only because we have mistaken effects for causes.

People *will* make insistent demands for more money under these conditions. It becomes more important than ever to buy the material goods and services which can provide limited satisfaction of the thwarted needs. Although money has only limited value in satisfying many higher-level needs, it can become the focus of interest if it is the only means available.

The "carrot and stick" theory of motivation which goes along with Theory X works reasonably well under certain circumstances. The *means* for satisfying man's physiological and (within limits) safety needs can be provided or withheld by management. Employment itself is such a means, and so are wages, working conditions, and benefits. By these means the individual can be controlled so long as he is struggling for subsistence. Man tends to live for bread alone when there is little bread.

But the "carrot and stick" theory does not work at all once man has reached an adequate subsistence level and is motivated primarily by higher needs. Management cannot provide a man with self-respect, or with the respect of his fellows, or with the satisfaction of needs for self-fulfillment. We can create conditions such that he is encouraged and enabled to seek such satisfactions for himself, or we can thwart him by failing to create those conditions.

But this creation of conditions is not "control" in the usual sense; it does not seem to be a particularly good device for directing behavior. And so management finds itself in an odd position. The high standard of living created by our modern technological know-how provides quite adequately for the satisfaction of physiological and safety needs. The only significant exception is where management practices have not created confidence in a "fair break"—and thus where safety needs are thwarted. But by making possible the satisfaction of lower-level needs, management has deprived itself of the ability to use the control devices on which the conventional assumptions of Theory X has taught it to rely: rewards, promises, incentives, or threats and other coercive devices.

The philosophy of management by direction and control—*regardless of whether it is hard or soft*—is inadequate to motivate because the human needs on which this approach relies are relatively unimportant motivators of behavior in our society today. Direction and control are of limited value in motivating people whose important needs are social and egoistic.

People, deprived of opportunities to satisfy at work the needs which are now important to them, behave exactly as we might predict—with indolence, passivity, unwillingness to accept responsibility, resistance to change, willingness to follow the demagogue, unreasonable demands for economic benefits. It would seem that we may be caught in a web of our own weaving.

Theory X explains the *consequences* of a particular managerial strategy; it neither explains nor describes human nature although it purports to. Because its assumptions are so unnecessarily limiting, it prevents our seeing the possibilities inherent in other managerial strategies. What sometimes appear to be new strategies—decentralization, management by objectives, consultative supervision, "democratic" leadership—are usually but old wine in new bottles because the procedures developed to implement them are derived from the same inadequate assumptions about human nature. Management is constantly becoming disillusioned with widely touted and expertly merchandised "new approaches" to the human side of enterprise. The real difficulty is that these new approaches are no more than different tactics—programs, procedures, gadgets—within an unchanged strategy based on Theory X.

In child rearing, it is recognized that parental strategies of control must be progressively modified to adapt to the changed capabilities and characteristics of the human individual as he develops from infancy to adulthood. To some extent industrial management recognizes that the human *adult* possesses capabilities for continued learning and growth. Witness the many current activities in the fields of training and management development. In its *basic* conceptions of managing human resources, however, management appears to have concluded that the average human being is permanently arrested in his development in early adolescence. Theory X is built on the least common human denominator: the factory "hand" of the past. As Chris Argyris has shown dramatically in his *Personality and Organization,* conventional managerial strategies for the organization, direction, and control of the human resources of enterprise are admirably suited to the capacities and characteristics of the child rather than the adult.

In one limited area—that of research administration—there has been some recent recognition of the need for selective adaptation in managerial strategy. This, however, has been perceived as a unique problem, and its broader implications have not been recognized. As pointed out in this and the previous chapter [of *The Human Side of Enterprise*], changes in the population at large—in educational level, attitudes and values, motivation, degree of dependence— have created both the opportunity and the need for other forms of selective adaptation. However, so long as the assumptions of Theory X continue to influence managerial strategy, we will fail to discover, let alone utilize, the potentialities of the average human being.

REFERENCES

Allen, Louis A.: *Management and Organization.* New York: McGraw-Hill Book Company, Inc., 1958.

Bendix, Reinhard: *Work and Authority in Industry*. New York: John Wiley & Sons, Inc., 1956.

Brown, Alvin: *Organization of Industry*. Englewood Cliffs, N.J.: Prentice-Hall, Inc., 1947.

Fayol, H.: *Industrial and General Administration*. London: Sir Issac Pitman & Sons, Ltd., 1930.

Gouldner, Alvin W.: *Patterns of Industrial Bureaucracy*. Glencoe, Ill.: Free Press, 1954.

Koontz, Harold, and Cyril O'Donnell: *Principles of Management*. New York: McGraw-Hill Book Company, Inc., 1955.

Maslow, Abraham: *Motivation and Personality*. New York: Harper & Brothers, 1954.

Urwick, Lyndall: *The Elements of Administration*. New York: Harper & Brothers, 1944.

Walker, Charles R.: *Toward the Automatic Factory*. New Haven, Conn.: Yale University Press, 1957.

Whyte, William F.: *Money and Motivation*. New York: Harper & Brothers, 1955.

Zaleznick, A., C.F. Christensen, and F.J. Roethlisberger: *Motivation, Productivity, and Satisfaction of Workers*. Cambridge, Mass.: Harvard University Press, 1958.

Chapter 3

Theory Y: The Integration of Individual and Organizational Goals

Douglas McGregor

To some, the preceding analysis will appear unduly harsh. Have we not made major modifications in the management of the human resources of industry during the past quarter century? Have we not recognized the importance of people and made vitally significant changes in managerial strategy as a consequence? Do the developments since the twenties in personnel administration and labor relations add up to nothing?

There is no question that important progress has been made in the past two or three decades. During this period the human side of enterprise has become a major preoccupation of management. A tremendous number of policies, programs, and practices which were virtually unknown thirty years ago have become commonplace. The lot of the industrial employee—be he worker, professional, or executive—has improved to a degree which could hardly have been imagined by his counterpart of the nineteen twenties. Management has adopted generally a far more humanitarian set of values; it has successfully striven to give more equitable and more generous treatment to its employees. It has significantly reduced economic hardships, eliminated the more extreme forms of industrial warfare, provided a generally safe and pleasant working environment, *but it has done all these things without changing its fundamental theory of management.* There are exceptions here and there, and they are important; nevertheless, the assumptions of Theory X remain predominant throughout our economy.

Management was subjected to severe pressures during the Great Depression of the thirties. The wave of public antagonism, the open warfare accompanying the unionization of the mass production industries, the general reaction against authoritarianism, the legislation of the New Deal produced a wide "pendulum swing." However, the changes in policy and practice which took place during

From *The Human Side of Enterprise*, McGraw-Hill Book Company, Inc., New York, 1960, chapter 4, pp. 45-57. Reprinted by permission of the publisher.

that and the next decade were primarily adjustments to the increased power of organized labor and to the pressures of public opinion.

Some of the movement was away from "hard" and toward "soft" management, but it was short-lived, and for good reasons. It has become clear that many of the initial strategic interpretations accompanying the "human relations approach" were as naïve as those which characterized the early stages of progressive education. We have now discovered that there is no answer in the simple removal of control—that abdication is not a workable alternative to authoritarianism. We have learned that there is no direct correlation between employee satisfaction and productivity. We recognize today that "industrial democracy" cannot consist in permitting everyone to decide everything, that industrial health does not flow automatically from the elimination of dissatisfaction, disagreement, or even open conflict. Peace is not synonymous with organizational health; socially responsible management is not coextensive with permissive management.

Now that management has regained its earlier prestige and power, it has become obvious that the trend toward "soft" management was a temporary and relatively superficial reaction rather than a general modification of fundamental assumptions or basic strategy. Moreover, while the progress we have made in the past quarter century is substantial, it has reached the point of diminishing returns. The tactical possibilities within conventional managerial strategies have been pretty completely exploited, and significant new developments will be unlikely without major modifications in theory.

THE ASSUMPTIONS OF THEORY Y

There have been few dramatic break-throughs in social science theory like those which have occurred in the physical sciences during the past half century. Nevertheless, the accumulation of knowledge about human behavior in many specialized fields has made possible the formulation of a number of generalizations which provide a modest beginning for new theory with respect to the management of human resources. Some of these assumptions were outlined in the discussion of motivation [beginning on page 12]. Some others, which will hereafter be referred to as Theory Y, are as follows:

1. *The expenditure of physical and mental effort in work is as natural as play or rest.* The average human being does not inherently dislike work. Depending upon controllable conditions, work may be a source of satisfaction (and will be voluntarily performed) or a source of punishment (and will be avoided if possible).

2. *External control and the threat of punishment are not the only means for bringing about effort toward organizational objectives. Man will exercise self-direction and self-control in the service of objectives to which he is committed.*

3. *Commitment to objectives is a function of the rewards associated with*

their achievement. The most significant of such rewards, e.g., the satisfaction of ego and self-actualization needs, can be direct products of effort directed toward organizational objectives.

4. *The average human being learns, under proper conditions, not only to accept but to seek responsibility.* Avoidance of responsibility, lack of ambition, and emphasis on security are generally consequences of experience, not inherent human characteristics.

5. *The capacity to exercise a relatively high degree of imagination, ingenuity, and creativity in the solution of organizational problems is widely, not narrowly, distributed in the population.*

6. *Under the conditions of modern industrial life, the intellectual potentialities of the average human being are only partially utilized.*

These assumptions involve sharply different implications for managerial strategy than do those of Theory X. They are dynamic rather than static: They indicate the possibility of human growth and development; they stress the necessity for selective adaptation rather than for a single absolute form of control. They are not framed in terms of the least common denominator of the factory hand, but in terms of a resource which has substantial potentialities.

Above all, the assumptions of Theory Y point up the fact that the limits on human collaboration in the organizational setting are not limits of human nature but of management's ingenuity in discovering how to realize the potential represented by its human resources. Theory X offers management an easy rationalization for ineffective organizational performance: It is due to the nature of the human resources with which we must work. Theory Y, on the other hand, places the problems squarely in the lap of management. If employees are lazy, indifferent, unwilling to take responsibility, intransigent, uncreative, uncooperative, Theory Y implies that the causes lie in management's methods of organization and control.

The assumptions of Theory Y are not finally validated. Nevertheless, they are far more consistent with existing knowledge in the social sciences than are the assumptions of Theory X. They will undoubtedly be refined, elaborated, modified as further research accumulates, but they are unlikely to be completely contradicted.

On the surface, these assumptions may not seem particularly difficult to accept. Carrying their implications into practice, however, is not easy. They challenge a number of deeply ingrained managerial habits of thought and action.

THE PRINCIPLE OF INTEGRATION

The central principle of organization which derives from Theory X is that of direction and control through the exercise of authority—what has been called ''the scalar principle.'' The central principle which derives from Theory Y is that of integration: the creation of conditions such that the members of the organization can achieve their own goals *best* by directing their efforts toward the success of the enterprise. These two principles have profoundly different implications with respect to the task of managing human resources, but the scalar principle is so firmly built into managerial attitudes that the implications of the principle of integration are not easy to perceive.

Someone once said that fish discover water last. The "psychological environment" of industrial management—like water for fish—is so much a part of organizational life that we are unaware of it. Certain characteristics of our society, and of organizational life within it, are so completely established, so pervasive, that we cannot conceive of their being otherwise. As a result, a great many policies and practices and decisions and relationships could only be—it seems—what they are.

Among these pervasive characteristics of organizational life in the United States today is a managerial attitude (stemming from Theory X) toward membership in the industrial organization. It is assumed almost without question that organizational requirements take precedence over the needs of individual members. Basically, the employment agreement is that in return for the rewards which are offered, the individual will accept external direction and control. The very idea of integration and self-control is foreign to our way of thinking about the employment relationship. The tendency, therefore, is either to reject it out of hand (as socialistic, or anarchistic, or inconsistent with human nature) or to twist it unconsciously until it fits existing conceptions.

The concept of integration and self-control carries the implication that the organization will be more effective in achieving its economic objectives if adjustments are made, in significant ways, to the needs and goals of its members.

A district manager in a large, geographically decentralized company is notified that he is being promoted to a policy level position at headquarters. It is a big promotion with a large salary increase. His role in the organization will be a much more powerful one, and he will be associated with the major executives of the firm.

The headquarters group who selected him for this position have carefully considered a number of possible candidates. This man stands out among them in a way which makes him the natural choice. His performance has been under observation for some time, and there is little question that he possesses the necessary qualifications not only for this opening but for an even higher position. There is genuine satisfaction that such an outstanding candidate is available.

The man is appalled. He doesn't want the job. His goal, as he expresses it, is to be the "best damned district manager in the company." He enjoys his direct associations with operating people in the field, and he doesn't want a policy level job. He and his wife enjoy the kind of life they have created in a small city, and they dislike actively both the living conditions and the social obligations of the headquarters city.

He expresses his feelings as strongly as he can, but his objections are brushed aside. The organization's needs are such that his refusal to accept the promotion would be unthinkable. His superiors say to themselves that of course when he has settled in to the new job, he will recognize that it was the right thing. And so he makes the move.

Two years later he is in an even higher position in the company's headquarters organization, and there is talk that he will probably be the executive vice-president before long. Privately he expresses considerable unhappiness and dissatisfaction. He (and his wife) would "give anything" to be back in the situation he left two years ago.

Within the context of the pervasive assumptions of Theory X, promotions and transfers in large numbers are made by unilateral decision. The requirements of the organization are given priority automatically and almost without question. If the individual's personal goals are considered at all, it is assumed that the rewards of salary and position will satisfy him. Should an individual actually refuse such a move without a compelling reason, such as health or a severe family crisis, he would be considered to have jeopardized his future because of this "selfish" attitude. It is rare indeed for management to give the individual the opportunity to be a genuine and active partner in such a decision, even though it may affect his most important personal goals. Yet the implications following from Theory Y are that the organization is likely to suffer if it ignores these personal needs and goals. In making unilateral decisions with respect to promotion, management is failing to utilize its human resources in the most effective way.

The principle of integration demands that both the organization's and the individual's needs be recognized. Of course, when there is a sincere joint effort to find it, an integrative solution which meets the needs of the individual *and* the organization is a frequent outcome. But not always—and this is the point at which Theory Y begins to appear unrealistic. It collides head on with pervasive attitudes associated with management by direction and control.

The assumptions of Theory Y imply that unless integration is achieved *the organization will suffer.* The objectives of the organization are *not* achieved best by the unilateral administration of promotions, because this form of management by direction and control will not create the commitment which would make available the full resources of those affected. The lesser motivation, the lesser resulting degree of self-direction and self-control are costs which, when added up for many instances over time, will more than offset the gains obtained by unilateral decisions "for the good of the organization."

One other example will perhaps clarify further the sharply different implications of Theory X and Theory Y.

It could be argued that management is already giving a great deal of attention to the principle of integration through its efforts in the field of economic education. Many millions of dollars and much ingenuity have been expended in attempts to persuade employees that their welfare is intimately connected with the success of the free enterprise system and of their own companies. The idea that they can achieve their own goals best by directing their effort toward the objectives of the organization has been explored and developed and communicated in every possible way. Is this not evidence that management is already committed to the principle of integration?

The answer is a definite no. These managerial efforts, with rare exceptions, reflect clearly the influence of the assumptions of Theory X. The central message is an exhortation to the industrial employee to work hard and follow orders in order to protect his job and his standard of living. Much has been achieved, it says, by our established way of running industry, and much more could be achieved if employees would adapt themselves *to management's definition* of what is required. Behind these exhortations lies the expectation that of course the requirements of the organization and its economic success must have priority over the needs of the individual.

Naturally, integration means working together for the success of the enterprise so we all may share in the resulting rewards. But management's implicit assumption is that working together means adjusting to the requirements of the organization *as management perceives them*. In terms of existing views, it seems inconceivable that individuals, seeking their own goals, would further the ends of the enterprise. On the contrary, this would lead to anarchy, chaos, irreconcilable conflicts of self-interest, lack of responsibility, inability to make decisions, and failure to carry out those that were made.

All these consequences, and other worse ones, *would* be inevitable unless conditions could be created such that the members of the organization perceived that they could achieve their own goals *best* by directing their efforts toward the success of the enterprise. If the assumptions of Theory Y are valid, the practical question is whether, and to what extent, such conditions can be created. To that question the balance of this volume is addressed.

THE APPLICATION OF THEORY Y

In the physical sciences there are many theoretical phenomena which cannot be achieved in practice. Absolute zero and a perfect vacuum are examples. Others, such as nuclear power, jet aircraft, and human space flight, are recognized theoretically to be possible long before they become feasible. This fact does not make theory less useful. If it were not for our theoretical convictions, we would not even be attempting to develop the means for human flight into space today. In fact, were it not for the development of physical science theory during the past century and a half, we would still be depending upon the horse and buggy and the sailing vessel for transportation. Virtually all significant technological developments wait on the formulation of relevant theory.

Similarly, in the management of the human resources of industry, the assumptions and theories about human nature at any given time limit innovation.

Possibilities are not recognized, innovating efforts are not undertaken, until theoretical conceptions lay a groundwork for them. Assumptions like those of Theory X permit us to conceive of certain possible ways of organizing and directing human effort, *but not others*. Assumptions like those of Theory Y open up a range of possibilities for new managerial policies and practices. As in the case of the development of new physical science theory, some of these possibilities are not immediately feasible, and others may forever remain unattainable. They may be too costly, or it may be that we simply cannot discover how to create the necessary "hardware."

There is substantial evidence for the statement that the potentialities of the average human being are far above those which we typically realize in industry today. If our assumptions are like those of Theory X, we will not even recognize the existence of these potentialities and there will be no reason to devote time, effort, or money to discovering how to realize them. If, however, we accept assumptions like those of Theory Y, we will be challenged to innovate, to discover new ways of organizing and directing human effort, even though we recognize that the perfect organization, like the perfect vacuum, is practically out of reach.

We need not be overwhelmed by the dimensions of the managerial task implied by Theory Y. To be sure, a large mass production operation in which the workers have been organized by a militant and hostile union faces management with problems which appear at present to be insurmountable with respect to the application of the principle of integration. It may be decades before sufficient knowledge will have accumulated to make such an application feasible. Applications of Theory Y will have to be tested initially in more limited ways and under more favorable circumstances. However, a number of applications of Theory Y *in managing managers and professional people* are possible today. Within the managerial hierarchy, the assumptions can be tested and refined, techniques can be invented and skill acquired in their use. As knowledge accumulates, some of the problems of application at the worker level in large organizations may appear less baffling than they do at present.

Perfect integration of organizational requirements and individual goals and needs is, of course, not a realistic objective. In adopting this principle, we seek that degree of integration in which the individual can achieve his goals *best* by directing his efforts toward the success of the organization. "Best" means that this alternative will be more attractive than the many others available to him: indifference, irresponsibility, minimal compliance, hostility, sabotage. It means that he will continuously be encouraged to develop and utilize voluntarily his capacities, his knowledge, his skill, his ingenuity in ways which contribute to the success of the enterprise.[1]

1. A recent, highly significant study of the sources of job satisfaction and dissatisfaction among managerial and professional people suggests that these opportunities for "self-actualization" are the essential requirements of both job satisfaction and high performance. The researchers find that "the wants of employees divide into two groups. One group revolves around the need to develop in one's occupation as a source of personal growth. The second group operates as an essential base to

Acceptance of Theory Y does not imply abdication, or "soft" management, or "permissiveness." As was indicated above, such notions stem from the acceptance of authority as the *single* means of managerial control, and from attempts to minimize its negative consequences. Theory Y assumes that people will exercise self-direction and self-control in the achievement of organizational objectives *to the degree that they are committed to those objectives.* If that commitment is small, only a slight degree of self-direction and self-control will be likely, and a substantial amount of external influence will be necessary. If it is large, many conventional external controls will be relatively superfluous, and to some extent self-defeating. Managerial policies and practices materially affect this degree of commitment.

Authority is an inappropriate means for obtaining commitment to objectives. Other forms of influence—help in achieving integration, for example— are required for this purpose. Theory Y points to the possibility of lessening the emphasis on external forms of control to the degree that commitment to organizational objectives can be achieved. Its underlying assumptions emphasize the capacity of human beings for self-control, and the consequent possibility of greater managerial reliance on other means of influence. Nevertheless, it is clear that authority *is* an appropriate means for control under certain circumstances—particularly where genuine commitment to objectives cannot be achieved. The assumptions of Theory Y do not deny the appropriateness of authority, but they do deny that it is appropriate for all purposes and under all circumstances.

Many statements have been made to the effect that we have acquired today the know-how to cope with virtually any technological problems which may arise, and that the major industrial advances of the next half century will occur on the human side of enterprise. Such advances, however, are improbable so long as management continues to organize and direct and control its human resources on the basis of assumptions—tacit or explicit—like those of Theory X. Genuine innovation, in contrast to a refurbishing and patching of present managerial strategies, requires first the acceptance of less limiting assumptions about the nature of the human resources we seek to control, and second the readiness to adapt selectively to the implications contained in those new assumptions. Theory Y is an invitation to innovation.

---

the first and is associated with fair treatment in compensation, supervision, working conditions, and administrative practices. *The fulfillment of the needs of the second group does not motivate the individual to high levels of job satisfaction and . . . to extra performance on the job.* All we can expect from satisfying (this second group of needs) is the prevention of dissatisfaction and poor job performance." Frederick Herzberg, Bernard Mausner, and Barbara Bloch Snyderman, *The Motivation to Work.* New York: John Wiley & Sons, Inc., 1959, pp. 114-115. (Italics mine.)

REFERENCES

Brown, J.A.C.: *The Social Psychology of Industry*. Baltimore: Penguin Books, Inc., 1954.

Cordiner, Ralph J.: *New Frontiers for Professional Managers*. New York: Mc-Graw-Hill Book Company, Inc., 1956.

Dubin, Robert: *The World of Work: Industrial Society and Human Relations*. Englewood Cliffs, N.J.: Prentice-Hall, Inc., 1958.

Friedmann, Georges: *Industrial Society: The Emergence of the Human Problems of Automation*. Glencoe, Ill.: Free Press, 1955.

Herzberg, Frederick, Bernard Mausner, and Barbara Bloch Snyderman: *The Motivation to Work*. New York: John Wiley & Sons, Inc., 1959.

Krech, David, and Richard S. Crutchfield: *Theory and Problems of Social Psychology*. New York: McGraw-Hill Book Company, Inc., 1948.

Leavitt, Harold J.: *Managerial Psychology*. Chicago: University of Chicago Press, 1958.

McMurry, Robert N.: "The Case for Benevolent Autocracy," *Harvard Business Review,* vol. 36, no. 1 (January-February), 1958.

Rice, A.K.: *Productivity and Social Organizations: The Ahmedabad Experiment*. London: Tavistock Publications, Ltd., 1958.

Stagner, Ross: *The Psychology of Industrial Conflict*. New York: John Wiley & Sons, Inc., 1956.

Chapter 4

Self-fulfilling Prophecies in Training the Hard-Core: Supervisors' Expectations and the Underprivileged Workers' Performance [1]

Albert Sidney King

It is now generally accepted that attitudes and beliefs about a disadvantaged group's behavior serve to a strong degree in determining the way in which its members behave.[2] Traditional stereotypes and attitudes about the low ability and apathy of underprivileged persons can act as self-fulfilling sources of their poor status. Where such persons are reminded they are indolent and not realistically trusted to perform responsible social roles, interpersonal relations arise which provide authority figures with confirmatory evidence of their beliefs. Clark spent years observing the ghettos and noted that Negroes could not succeed unless their white dominant group believed they could learn.[3] Recent evidence by Rosenthal has shown that teachers' high expectations have favorable effects on underprivileged students' intellectual developments.[4] Increasingly, evidence is emerging from the sociological and psychological literature as well as from medical research, management training, and experimental studies which suggests the operation of what has been termed interpersonal self-fulfilling prophecies.[5] In each case, the effects of interpersonal self-fulfilling prophecies have been observed to be a variant of the same general principle: that in the interaction between two or more persons, one person's expectation for the behavior of another can come to be self-confirming.

The purpose of this discussion is to examine the proposition that managerial expectations may significantly influence the adjustment and skill-development of disadvantaged workers in the industrial job role. Evidence of interpersonal self-fulfilling prophecies has been discussed and debated in greater detail elsewhere,[6] and will not be summarized here.

Recognizing that disadvantaged personnel do not have the required aptitudes, experience, and education to fulfill regular job requirements, many employment standards have been waived, dropped, or even banned altogether.[7]

From *Social Science Quarterly*, Vol. 52, Sept. 1971, pp. 369-378. Reprinted by permission of the author and the University of Texas Press.

Undeniably, tests and other employment standards have been found to be irrelevant and needlessly discouraging to the disadvantaged because of unrealistic assumptions and requirements.[8] However, it is doubtful that many programs in attempting to improve the skill level and status of the disadvantaged have completely taken into account the impact of these changes in employment standards, particularly on the attitudes of supervisors toward disadvantaged workers. Those managers who have adjusted to the dilemma of hard-core employment are confronted with some crucial questions concerning the establishment of employment standards and expectations for marginal workers. To what extent have these personnel been shaped in their work performance by expectations that their supervisors have for them? Have personnel and training organizations anticipated their poor performance and thus, in effect, trained and conditioned them to fail? If so, it seems reasonable to expect that disadvantaged workers can be motivated to perform appreciably better when their managers hold higher expectations for them.

METHODOLOGY

In order to test for the operation of interpersonal self-fulfilling prophecies, it is necessary to isolate the separate effects of expectations based on observed past performance and those which are instrumental in influencing it. Otherwise, if one simply observes that those who are low achievers are expected by supervisors to show substandard performance, it is not possible to answer the key question of whether the supervisor's expectation was the self-fulfilling cause or an accurate appraisal of observed past performance.

It was possible to explore the effects of expectations by creating conditions in which supervisors were falsely led to believe at the beginning of disadvantaged training programs that certain of their trainees could be expected to show considerable training improvement during the course of employment. Supervisors had no knowledge about the past behavior of the trainees and were told that predictions as to an individual's probable work-training performance could be based on a "specially developed aptitude test for the disadvantaged" which was administered at the beginning of the training period. Only the immediate supervisors had access to the fabricated test score results and they were asked not to discuss these with anyone.

For obvious ethical reasons, it was not desirable to investigate whether lowered expectations led to failure in trainee performance. It was only possible to suggest the impact of such low expectations on underprivileged workers' job development. Supervisors were explicitly told that all of their trainees had performed satisfactorily and should show progress in the future. Less emphatically, they were told that those designated as having "high aptitude" had performed remarkably well and could be expected to show exceptional gains from the training they were about to receive.[9]

More specifically, supervisors were told that further validation was needed for a new kind of test designed to predict high achievement potential among underprivileged workers. An ordinary mechanical aptitude test, G.K. Bennett's Mechanical Comprehension Test (low level) was used instead.[10] Actually, those designated as having "High Aptitude Potential" were chosen at random with their selection bearing no relation to actual test results. From 17 presser, 20 welder, and 19 mechanic trainees entering the program with common job histories and educational backgrounds, 4 presser, 5 welder, and 5 mechanic trainees were randomly designated to serve as the high aptitude personnel (HAPs). Supervisors were told they could be expected to show unusual training improvement and skill development during the period. Thus, differences in training performance between these trainees and the undesignated others making up the control group could be explained as the result of role-set expectations existing only in the minds of their supervisors.

These experiments covering five, six, and nine months for pressers, welders, and mechanics, respectively, were conducted in cooperation with state employment and educational agencies sponsored by the Manpower Development Training Act.

RESULTS

Table 1 compares the pretraining status and performance results between test (HAPs) and control (undesignated) trainees for the three occupations.[11]

Since members of experimental groups were randomly assigned without the use of pretraining indicators of status or aptitude test scores, we might suspect with such small group sizes that chance would not have operated to make the two groups equivalent to begin with. Examination of Table 1 reveals, however, that this suspicion is not confirmed. There were no significant differences between test and control trainees' ages or educational backgrounds. All of the presser trainees had previously held jobs as waitresses, housemaids, or were unemployed. Trainees going into welder and mechanic programs had previously been unskilled laborers, farm workers, or unemployed. None of the trainees had previous knowledge or experience for presser, welder, or mechanic training. Note that there were no substantial differences between HAPs' and undesignated members' scores on the "special test" of high aptitude. The Mechanical Comprehension Test was not intended as a yardstick against which to measure actual performance. The test served to create a plausible basis for arousing higher expectations for the HAPs. However, as far as testing aptitude among the disadvantaged goes, it serves as a costless bonus, providing an additional measure of pretraining aptitudes and status of trainees before the experiments began. In short, we can be quite sure that the experimental groups were about as equivalently matched as the design would allow.

At the end of each program, supervisory evaluations of those completing the courses were obtained. Ratings followed a standard form using eight criteria to indicate the degree of adjustment to training ("has improved," "no change," or "gone back"). Ratings for those designated HAPs were uniformly higher and more favorable in the direction of supervisors' expectancies. HAPs were rated as being more knowledgeable about jobs, producing better volume of neat and accurate work, showing greater ability to learn new duties, having more initiative, giving better cooperation, exerting more logic in job tasks, and generally showing the best performance. Of course, this could be accounted for by surrounding Hawthorne and/or "halo" influences caused by the experimental manipulation. Not so easily explained are the remaining differences in trainee group performances shown in Table 1.

Major differences between test and control groups occurred with respect to peer ratings—a difference which is difficult to explain theoretically. Near the end of the scheduled training periods, trainees were asked to rank those trainees that they would (1) most like to work with, (2) most like to be with, (3) judge as having shown the best overall performance. Total points for each trainee were used to rank each individual. Individual ranks were then averaged to yield the figures in Table 1. Differences as to whom trainees would prefer being with on task and social activities as well as who they rated highest on actual work performance indicate that trainees also held more favorable evaluations for the HAPs. The question immediately arises, how did trainees themselves come to evaluate HAPs more highly? Clearly, none of the trainees had been exposed to the experimental inducement, nor had any of the supervisors revealed to them the purpose or results of the "special test" for high aptitude. This point will be discussed below but preliminary explanations would be inconclusive without first examining the more objective measures of trainee performance.

In light of the emphasis placed by MDTA program directors on policies for controlling absences and separations, these measures represent remarkably important indicators of trainee performance. With respect to absences among welders and certainly with regard to separations for all three training contexts, Table 1 reveals some very tangible consequences of favorable expectations for HAPs.

In the program for welders, concrete evidence was available to indicate expectancy advantages for HAPs. In the second month of the program, a one week block of instruction was given on "Mechanical Methods for Testing Welds." Trainees took a series of practicals in making a specimen weld as many times as necessary until it passed the "root and face bend" test.[12] Table 1 shows the average number of times for HAPs to pass the test was substantially less than for the others. The large and significant differences between the two groups suggest the immediacy and strength of expectancy advantages for HAPs through their fundamental effects on objective measures of skills acquired. More subjective, but nonetheless important, HAPs independently assessed themselves as requiring less time to learn the fundamentals of welding. In the final week of training, welders and mechanics took written tests in which further differences were noted. These tests required no special preparation or

Table 1. Differences in pretraining status and training performance.

Variable	Pressers Test N	Test Mean	Control N	Control Mean	P	Welders Test N	Test Mean	Control N	Control Mean	P	Mechanics Test N	Test Mean	Control N	Control Mean	P
Age	4	23.5	13	25.4	N.S.	5	28.4	15	27.0	N.S.	5	20.8	14	23.1	N.S.
Education	4	8.3	13	8.9	N.S.	5	7.4	15	7.3	N.S.	5	8.8	14	8.0	N.S.
Mechanical Comprehension Test Score	4	21.8	13	17.8	N.S.	5	30.6	15	25.8	N.S.	5	26.6	14	29.8	N.S.
Supervisory Rating	4	26.5	8	22.0	N.S.	5	37.8	7	24.6	.05	5	28.6	6	11.8	.001
Peer Rating[a] Work with	4	71.3	11	115.0	.05	5	68.2	7	99.7	.05	5	91.0	7	146.3	.01
Be with	4	70.4	11	112.4	.05	5	71.8	7	92.4	.10	5	99.4	7	142.4	.05
Overall	4	56.5	11	114.6	.05	5	47.2	7	109.3	.001	5	70.0	7	151.1	.001
Absences	4	1.25	13	1.92	N.S.	5	.4	15	8.9	.001	5	1.4	14	2.9	N.S.
Separations	4	0	13	.38	.01	5	0	15	.53	.001	5	0	14	.57	.001
Root and Face Bend Test[b] (Times)						5	1.4	7	5.4	.001					
Weeks to Learn Fundamentals						5	6.0	7	10.0	.001					
Essentials Test						5	98.0	6	88.3	.001	5	77.2	4	59.5	.01
Average Rank[a]	4	5.0	11	9.2	.05	5	3.6	7	9.4	.001	5	4.3	7	9.8	.01

[a]Lower score represents more favorable performance.
[b]Average number of trials necessary to successfully test specimen weld.

study, but only knowledge gained through training and practice. In both training organizations HAPs averaged significantly higher than the others.

In an effort to recapitulate the degree of consistency for differences in performance between test and control groups, the average rank shown in Table 1 summarizes these results. Performance on measures of peer rating, absences, and training tests were ranked and then averaged to give each trainee an average rank. Overall, those individuals from whom supervisors expected better performance showed an average rank significantly higher than the other trainees.

MECHANICAL APTITUDE AND TRAINEE PERFORMANCE

Irrespective of random assignments to test groups, in the presser and welder organizations HAPs averaged slightly higher aptitude scores on the mechanical comprehension test. This inequality might imply that the aptitude test was a better predictor of performance than the experimental inducement, since those that made higher scores may have performed better. In order to assess the extent to which differences in trainee performances were the result of aptitude, rather than expectancy, comparisons were made between mechanical aptitude test scores and all other measures for trainee performance. Table 2 shows that

Table 2. Comparison of aptitude test scores and average rank performance.

Training Organization	Test Group	N	Control Group	N	Total Trainee Group	N
Pressers	—.67[a]	4	—.14	11	—.04	15
Welders	—.87[b]	5	—.12	7	—.23	12
Mechanics	—.23	5	—.66[c]	7	—.21	12

[a]P .05
[b]P .01
[c]P .05
Remaining coefficients (NS)

Spearman rank correlations between aptitude test scores and average rank performance for test, control, and total trainee groups were negative. Correlation coefficients for the remaining measures of performance, including those for undesignated control members quitting the training were also computed and are so similar to these findings that we can be confident that aptitude was not an important variable in the results.[13]

IMPORTANCE OF EXPECTANCY INFLUENCE

These results strongly suggest that disadvantaged personnel from whom supervisors expected greater training performance actually showed such performance. When trainees who were not especially expected to show similar outstanding skill development did not do so, they might have seemed "typical hard-core," or "not too special"; at least they were evaluated by supervisors as not meeting similar standards. For undesignated members of control conditions there may have been real disadvantages from not being identified as having "high aptitude potential." In terms of their higher separation rates, there were substantial hazards in their unpredicted performance.

It appears that if disadvantaged workers are to become quickly integrated into the mainstream of modern industrial organizations, higher and more favorable expectations must be planned for them to do so. Disadvantaged employees cannot be assessed against industrial work standards which they are not expected to fulfill. Haphazard, informal, and perfunctory plans and expectations for their ascribed status are products of the past which should not be allowed to sweep training programs into the future.

MEDIATION OF EXPECTANCY INFLUENCE

How do supervisors' expectations determine workers' performance? This is the crucial and unanswered question challenging contemporary investigations. Emerging research has stressed the covert and unintentional means by which expectancy effects are mediated in interpersonal relations. It is not enough to think in terms of a little black box into which high expectations are fed at one end and out of which high performance comes at the other. What happens inside the box? What are the essential cues and symbols serving to mediate and communicate the effect? In the welder and mechanic experiments conducted here, information was available to suggest that expectations are likely communicated in numerous possible ways ranging from simple to incredibly subtle and complex mechanisms.

Supervisors likely revealed their high expectations of HAPs in ways for which the actual cues and symbols were so slight and undetected that trainees could not even begin to articulate them. Post-experimental interviews with trainees served to dramatize this subtle and unintentional effect. A pair of seemingly identical photographs were used to determine how visual cues might serve to mediate the supervisor's message of high expectancy. Two pictures of their supervisor were shown to trainees in the combination welder training program. These two photos were identical except that one was modified to make the pupil-size of the supervisor's eyes much larger than the other. Both HAPs and undesignated control members were asked the same set of questions: (a) Do you see any differences in these pictures of your supervisor? (b) Whether you see any difference or not, can you select the photo that shows how you usually see the supervisor looking at you?

None of the trainees noticed that the photos were different. Most of them shrugged their shoulders, picking a photo for the second question without specifying their reason. Surprisingly, all five trainees who had been designated experimentally to the supervisor and who had shown the most marked performance in training selected the photo with the enlarged pupils. Five of the seven undesignated trainees chose the other photo. Since all of the trainees indicated that there was no difference between the two photos, why did members who had been designated as having and subsequently showing high performance uniformly select the photo with the larger pupil-size? One highly persuasive psychological explanation is that large pupil-size serves to convey more favorable attitudes and expectations.[14] The basic principle is quite simple. With respect to pupil-size, there is a continuum of responses that range from large dilation for favorable attitudes to extreme contraction or "pinpoints of hate" for unfavorable feelings toward another person. Clearly, eye contact in face-to-face relations is likely to serve as an unintentional, but nevertheless remarkable indicator of the attitude, interest, and expectations supervisors hold for subordinates. Most likely, expectations are communicated without any awareness by either supervisor or subordinate. Although trainees were not aware of the subtleties involved, these, as well as other complex and unnoticed cues operating in interpersonal relations with supervisors may have come to shape their own attitudes, motivations, and job performance.

Expectancy did not produce the desired effect only through highly subtle psychological means. In ongoing organizational relations for welders and mechanics the possibility that supervisors gave closer attention and preferential treatment to those earmarked for better performance could not be ruled out. If teachers at the high school where these training sites were located would buy the materials, they could have all the furnace covers, auto tune-ups, and so forth that trainees could produce. Not too surprisingly, HAPs were the first to be assigned to these mounting job orders. This, as well as other, anecdotal evidence was reported by the school's mechanical shop and vocational teachers who knew nothing about the experiments. While such subjective interpretations cannot be counted as complex mediating cues in the sophisticated social psychological sense, their common-sense consequences must be acknowledged. With more demanding assignments to skill developing tasks, HAPs had every reason for sensing a greater involvement in, and responsibility for, their roles as workers.

The implication that HAPs were subjects of more favorable attention by supervisors may have led to other indirect and subtle incentives for their success. While supervisors' evaluations could be attributed to "halo" and/or Hawthorne effects, the fact that HAPs were estimated more highly by their fellows is not so easily explained. Trainee evaluations of each other were known to be uncontaminated by attitudes and beliefs belonging to supervisors when the training programs began. How then, did trainees themselves come to hold higher evaluations for the HAPs? Since none of them had any knowledge of the aptitude test results, differences in their evaluations cannot be attributed to any ascertainable bias or ''halo.'' Possibly, supervisors' expectations for HAPs' individual performance were communicated to the group as a whole. Thus any change that involved the HAPs'may have alerted others to hold higher expectations and evaluations for their improved performance. Indirectly, supervisors' expectations likely benefited the HAPs by influencing group-made norms, perceptions, and evaluations of their behavior. Such collective predictions could serve to reinforce the HAPs' individual motivations for achievement and raise their individual expectancy for success. Admittedly, however, this explanation has been developed *post hoc*; only further research will make these interpretations less equivocal.

Upon completion of the studies, supervisors showed a substantial sensitivity and skeptical curiosity to the experimentally created expectations. Post-experimental interviews revealed their accuracy in recalling the names of those designated months earlier as HAPs. When debriefed about the nature of the study and deception involved, supervisors expressed no disenchantment concerning ethical issues of their deception. Supervisors did, however, insist that the notion of self-fulfilling prophecy was much ''too theoretical.''

There should be little wonder that people with an orientation toward applied behavioral knowledge become somewhat skeptical with the theoretical notion of interpersonal self-fulfilling prophecies. But no matter how ingenious the circumlocutions which may have been raised, an acceptable substitute for the concept remains to be found. For the proposition must ultimately play a critical role in any probing behavioral study.

CONCLUSIONS

In consequence of these findings, a serious reexamination of the process of leadership behavior and specifically of the role of supervisors and managers in organizations is required. Other studies have suggested information which corroborates the experimental evidence found here:

> ... his (the supervisor's) confidence in subordinates leads him to have high expectations as to their level of performance. With confidence that he will not be disappointed, he expects much, not little.[15]

This view of the requirements for changing underprivileged workers' habits, ambitions, and willingness to seek and assume responsibility may not be fully recognized by industrial relations practices in many firms. In order to motivate underprivileged workers to seek more responsibility on jobs, organizations must expect that disadvantaged workers are capable of more than has been realized. The underprivileged can be convinced not only by seeing personnel like themselves gaining responsible, secure jobs and opportunities for development, but also by feeling that this is to be expected.

Despite many doubts and the speculative nature of knowledge on how to approach employment problems of the hard-core, managers need not allow these characteristics to be conveyed in concealed premises and expectations for the underprivileged worker's status and performance. A major implication of this study holds that searching for explanations of low-level goals and social status by observing the inner-directed motivations of underprivileged workers has limited value. Studies might have been seeking to find in the worker what should have been sought in the supervisor.

Hopefully, this description of supervisors' expectations as determinants of underprivileged workers' performance will serve as a reminder that human resource potential, performance and development are the combined products of external social as well as of internal psychological motives. Failure to recognize the social basis of differences between human resource potential and performance is to limit understanding to half of reality.

REFERENCES

1. The Office of Manpower Administration, U.S. Department of Labor, presently provides grant support for this research under the provisions of Title I of the Manpower Development Act, PL 87-415, as amended.

2. For more precise analyses substantiating this point with special relevance to minorities, see, for example, Robert K. Merton, "The Self-fulfilling Prophecy," *Antioch Review,* 8, 1948, pp. 193-210, and Gunnar Myrdal, *The American Dilemma*, New York: Harper and Brothers, 1944.

3. Kenneth B. Clark, *Dark Ghetto,* New York: Harper and Row, 1965, pp. 131-132.

4. Robert Rosenthal and Lenore Jacobson, *Pygmalion in the Classroom,* New York: Holt, Rinehart and Winston, 1968.

5. Robert Rosenthal, *Experimenter Effects in Behavioral Research,* New York: Appleton-Century-Crofts, 1966.

6. Theodore X. Barber and Maurice J. Silver, "Pitfalls in Data Analysis and Interpretation," *Journal of Psychology,* monograph supplement, 70:6, Part 2, 1968, pp. 1-29, 48-62. See, also, the reply by R. Rosenthal in the same supplement, "Experimenter Expectancy and the Reassuring Nature of the Null Hypothesis Decision Procedure," pp. 30-47.

7. Peter Doeringer, *Programs to Employ the Disadvantaged*, Englewood Cliffs, N.J.: Prentice-Hall, Inc., 1969.

8. Harold I. Mathis, "The Disadvantaged and the Aptitude Barrier," *Personnel and Guidance Journal,* 47, January 1969, pp. 467-472.

9. Important limitations arise regarding the precise form in which expectancies were induced into the training situations. Supervisors possibly dichotomized their thinking about trainee groups into designated and undesignated,

corresponding to expectations for superior and inferior performance. This, however, was an uncontrollable consequence. For an analysis of the impact of rigorous research restrictions and their undesirable effects on field settings, see, for example, N. Friedman, *The Social Nature of Psychological Research*, New York: Basic Books, 1967.

10. Test forms were obtained from The Psychological Corporation, New York. Standardization, validation, and general features of the test are discussed in the first edition of the manual. For further information concerning validity and reliability see G.K. Bennett and R.A. Fear, "Mechanical Comprehension and Dexterity," *Personnel Journal*, 22, 1943, pp. 12-17.

11. Data supporting the significance of these comparisons, standard deviations for experimental and control groups and computations of students' *t* with degrees of freedom for each measure are available on request from the author.

12. This procedure for mechanically testing welds is described in any standard manual on welding. See, for example, *Mechanical Methods for Test Welding*, American Welding Society, 1942, pp. 14-15.

13. Additional information discrediting the validity and reliability of the "Special Test" was available in the welder and mechanic studies to make this more evident. Welders and mechanics were readministered the same form of Mechanical Comprehension Test in their final week of training. HAPs showed average individual gains compared to average losses for their undesignated counterparts on this second test. Moreover, correlation measures of retest reliabilities for test, control, and total trainee groups revealed no reliable relationship between pre-test and post-test scores.

14. Eckhard H. Hess, "Attitude and Pupil Size," *Scientific American*, 212, April 1965, pp. 46-54.

15. Rensis Likert, *New Patterns of Management*, New York: McGraw-Hill, 1961, p. 101.

Chapter 5

Pygmalion in Management

J. Sterling Livingston

Pygmalion was a sculptor in Greek mythology who carved a statue of a beautiful woman that subsequently was brought to life. George Bernard Shaw's play, Pygmalion (the basis for the musical hit, "My Fair Lady"), has a somewhat similar theme; the essence is that one person, by his effort and will, can transform another person. And in the world of management, many executives play Pygmalion-like roles in developing able subordinates and in stimulating their performance. What is the secret of their success? How are they different from managers who fail to develop top-notch subordinates? And what are the implications of all this for the problem of excessive turnover and disillusionment among talented young people in business? Such are the questions discussed here. The title of the article was inspired by Pygmalion in the Classroom, *a book by Professor Robert Rosenthal and Lenore Jacobson that describes the effect of expectations on the intellectual development of children.*

In George Bernard Shaw's *Pygmalion*, Eliza Doolittle explains:
"You see, really and truly, apart from the things anyone can pick up (the dressing and the proper way of speaking, and so on), the difference between a lady and a flower girl is not how she behaves, but how she's treated. I shall always be a flower girl to Professor Higgins, because he always treats me as a flower girl, and always will; but I know I can be a lady to you, because you always treat me as a lady, and always will."

Some managers always treat their subordinates in a way that leads to superior performance. But most managers, like Professor Higgins, unintentionally treat

Author's note: This article is a condensation of my forthcoming book, *High Expectations in Management*, to be published by the Sterling Institute Press.

their subordinates in a way that leads to lower performance than they are capable of achieving. The way managers treat their subordinates is subtly influenced by what they expect of them. If a manager's expectations are high, productivity is likely to be excellent. If his expectations are low, productivity is likely to be poor. It is as though there were a law that caused a subordinate's performance to rise or fall to meet his manager's expectations.

The powerful influence of one person's expectations on another's behavior has long been recognized by physicians and behavioral scientists and, more recently, by teachers. But heretofore the importance of managerial expectations for individual and group performance has not been widely understood. I have documented this phenomenon in a number of case studies prepared during the past decade for major industrial concerns. These cases and other evidence available from scientific research now reveal:

•What a manager expects of his subordinates and the way he treats them largely determine their performance and career progress.

•A unique characteristic of superior managers is their ability to create high performance expectations that subordinates fulfill.

•Less effective managers fail to develop similar expectations, and, as a consequence, the productivity of their subordinates suffers.

•Subordinates, more often than not, appear to do what they believe they are expected to do.

IMPACT ON PRODUCTIVITY

One of the most comprehensive illustrations of the effect of managerial expectations on productivity is recorded in studies of the organizational experiment undertaken in 1961 by Alfred Oberlander, manager of the Rockaway District Office of the Metropolitan Life Insurance Company.[1] He had observed that outstanding insurance agencies grew faster than average or poor agencies and that new insurance agents performed better in outstanding agencies than in average or poor agencies, regardless of their sales aptitude. He decided, therefore, to group his superior men in one unit to stimulate their performance and to provide a challenging environment in which to introduce new salesmen.

Accordingly, Oberlander assigned his six best agents to work with his best assistant manager, an equal number of average producers to work with an average assistant manager, and the remaining low producers to work with the least able manager. He then asked the superior group to produce two thirds of the premium volume achieved by the entire agency the previous year. He described the results as follows:

"Shortly after this selection had been made, the men in the agency began

---

1. See "Jamesville Branch Office (A)," METOO3A, and "Jamesville Branch Office (B)," METOO3B (Boston, Sterling Institute, 1969).

referring to this select group as a 'super-staff' since, due to the fact that we were operating this group as a unit, their esprit de corps was very high. Their production efforts over the first 12 weeks far surpassed our most optimistic expectations...proving that groups of men of sound ability can be motivated beyond their apparently normal productive capacities when the problems created by the poor producer are eliminated from the operation.

"Thanks to this fine result, over-all agency performance improved 40 percent and stayed at this figure.

"In the beginning of 1962 when, through expansion, we appointed another assistant manager and assigned him a staff, we again utilized this same concept, arranging the men once more according to their productive capacity.

"The assistant managers were assigned...according to their ability, with the most capable assistant manager receiving the best group, thus playing strength to strength. Our agency over-all production again improved by about 25-30 percent, and so this staff arrangement was continued until the end of the year.

"Now in this year of 1963, we found upon analysis that there were so many men...with a potential of half a million dollars or more that only one staff remained of those men in the agency who were not considered to have any chance of reaching the half-million-dollar mark."[2]

Although the productivity of the "super-staff" improved dramatically, it should be pointed out that the productivity of men in the lowest unit, "who were not considered to have any chance of reaching the half-million-dollar mark," actually declined and that attrition among these men increased. The performance of the superior men rose to meet their managers' expectations, while that of the weaker men declined as predicted.

Self-Fulfilling Prophesies

However, the "average" unit proved to be an anomaly. Although the district manager expected only average performance from this group, its productivity increased significantly. This was because the assistant manager in charge of the group refused to believe that he was less capable than the manager of the "super-staff" or that the agents in the top group had any greater ability than the agents in his group. He insisted in discussions with his agents that every man in the middle group had greater potential than the men in the "super-staff," lacking only their years of experience in selling insurance. He stimulated his agents to accept the challenge of out-performing the "super-staff." As a result, in each year the middle group increased its productivity by a higher percentage than the "super-staff" did (although it never attained the dollar volume of the top group).

It is of special interest that the self-image of the manager of the "average" unit did not permit him to accept others' treatment of him as an "average"

2. "Jamesville Branch Office (B)," p. 2.

manager, just as Eliza Doolittle's image of herself as a lady did not permit her to accept others' treatment of her as a flower girl. The assistant manager transmitted his own strong feelings of efficacy to his agents, created mutual expectancy of high performance, and greatly stimulated productivity.

Comparable results occurred when a similar experiment was made at another office of the company. Further confirmation comes from a study of the early managerial success of 49 college graduates who were management-level employees of an operating company of the American Telephone and Telegraph Company. David E. Berlew and Douglas T. Hall of the Massachusetts Institute of Technology examined the career progress of these managers over a period of five years and discovered that their relative success, as measured by salary increases and the company's estimate of each man's performance and potential, depended largely on the company's expectations of them.[3]

The influence of one person's expectations on another's behavior is by no means a business discovery. More than half a century ago, Albert Moll concluded from his clinical experience that subjects behaved as they believed they were expected to.[4] The phenomenon he observed, in which "the prophecy causes its own fulfillment," has recently become a subject of considerable scientific interest. For example:

☐ In a series of scientific experiments, Robert Rosenthal of Harvard University has demonstrated that a "teacher's expectation for her pupils' intellectual competence can come to serve as an educational self-fulfilling prophecy."[5]

☐ An experiment in a summer Headstart program for 60 preschoolers compared the performance of pupils under (a) teachers who had been led to expect relatively slow learning by their children, and (b) teachers who had been led to believe their children had excellent intellectual ability and learning capacity. Pupils of the second group of teachers learned much faster.[6]

Moreover, the healing professions have long recognized that a physician's or psychiatrist's expectations can have a formidable influence on a patient's physical or mental health. What takes place in the minds of the patients and the healers, particularly when they have congruent expectations, may determine the outcome. For instance, the havoc of a doctor's pessimistic prognosis has often been observed. Again, it is well known that the efficacy of a new drug or a new treatment can be greatly influenced by the physician's expectations—a result referred to by the medical profession as a "placebo effect."

---

3. "Some Determinants of Early Managerial Success," Alfred P. Sloan School of Management Organization Research Program #81-64 (Cambridge, Massachusetts Institute of Technology, 1964), pp. 13-14.

4. Robert Rosenthal and Lenore Jacobson, *Pygmalion in the Classroom* (New York, Holt, Rinehart, and Winston, Inc., 1968), p. 11.

5. Ibid., Preface, p. vii.

6. Ibid., p. 38.

Pattern Of Failure

When salesmen are treated by their managers as supersalesmen, as the "super-staff" was at Metropolitan Rockaway District Office, they try to live up to that image and do what they know supersalesmen are expected to do. But when salesmen with poor productivity records are treated by their managers as *not* having "any chance" of success, as the low producers at Rockaway were, this negative expectation also becomes a managerial self-fulfilling prophecy.

Unsuccessful salesmen have great difficulty maintaining their self-image and self-esteem. In response to low managerial expectations, they typically attempt to prevent additional damage to their egos by avoiding situations that might lead to greater failure. They either reduce the number of sales calls they make or avoid trying to "close" sales when that might result in further painful rejection, or both. Low expectations and damaged egos lead them to behave in a manner that increases the probability of failure, thereby fulfilling their managers' expectations. Let me illustrate:

☐Not long ago I studied the effectiveness of branch bank managers at a West Coast bank with over 500 branches. The managers who had had their lending authority reduced because of high rates of loss became progressively less effective. To prevent further loss of authority, they turned to making only "safe" loans. This action resulted in losses of business to competing banks and a relative decline in both deposits and profits at their branches. Then, to reverse that decline in deposits and earnings, they often "reached" for loans and became almost irrational in their acceptance of questionable credit risks. Their actions were not so much a matter of poor judgment as an expression of their willingness to take desperate risks in the hope of being able to avoid further damage to their egos and to their careers.

Thus, in response to the low expectations of their supervisors, who had reduced their lending authority, they behaved in a manner that led to larger credit losses. They appeared to do what they believed they were expected to do, and their supervisors' expectations became self-fulfilling prophecies.

POWER OF EXPECTATIONS

Managers cannot avoid the depressing cycle of events that flow from low expectations merely by hiding their feelings from subordinates. If a manager believes a subordinate will perform poorly, it is virtually impossible for him to mask his expectations, because the message usually is communicated unintentionally, without conscious action on his part.

Indeed, a manager often communicates most when he believes he is communicating least. For instance, when he says nothing, when he becomes "cold" and "uncommunicative," it usually is a sign that he is displeased by a subordinate or believes he is "hopeless." The silent treatment communicates negative feelings even more effectively, at times, than a tongue-lashing does. What seems to be critical in the communication of expectations is not what the boss says, so much as the *way he behaves*. Indifferent and noncommittal treatment, more often than not, is the kind of treatment that communicates low expectations and leads to poor performance.

Common Illusions

Managers are more effective in communicating low expectations to their subordinates than in communicating high expectations to them, even though most managers believe exactly the opposite. It usually is astonishingly difficult for them to recognize the clarity with which they transmit negative feelings to subordinates. To illustrate again:

☐The Rockaway district manager vigorously denied that he had communicated low expectations to the men in the poorest group who, he believed, did not have "any chance" of becoming high producers. Yet the message was clearly received by those men. A typical case was that of an agent who resigned from the low unit. When the district manager told the agent that he was sorry he was leaving, the agent replied, "No, you're not; you're glad." Although the district manager previously had said nothing to the man, he had unintentionally communicated his low expectations to his agents through his indifferent manner. Subsequently, the men who were assigned to the lowest unit interpreted the assignment as equivalent to a request for their resignation.

☐One of the company's agency managers established superior, average, and low units, even though he was convinced that he had no superior or outstanding subordinates. "All my assistant managers and agents are either average or incompetent," he explained to the Rockaway district manager. Although he tried to duplicate the Rockaway results, his low opinions of his men were communicated—not so subtly—to them. As a result, the experiment failed.

Positive feelings, on the other hand, often do not come through clearly enough. For example:

☐Another insurance agency manager copied the organizational changes made at the Rockaway District Office, grouping the salesmen he rated highly with the best manager, the average salesmen with an average manager, and so on. However, improvement did not result from the move. The Rockaway district manager therefore investigated the situation. He discovered that the assistant manager in charge of the high-performance unit was unaware that his manager considered him to be the best. In fact, he and the other agents doubted that the agency manager really believed there was any difference in their abilities. This agency manager was a stolid, phlegmatic, unemotional man who treated his men in a rather pedestrian way. Since high expectations had not been communicated to the men, they did not understand the reason for the new organization and could not see any point in it. Clearly, the way a manager *treats* his subordinates, not the way he organizes them, is the key to high expectations and high productivity.

Impossible Dreams

Managerial expectations must pass the test of reality before they can be translated into performance. To become self-fulfilling prophecies, expectations must be made of sterner stuff than the power of positive thinking or generalized confidence in one's fellow men—helpful as these concepts may be for some other purposes. Subordinates will not be motivated to reach high levels of productivity unless they consider the boss's high expectations realistic and achievable. If they are encouraged to strive for unattainable goals, they eventually give up trying and settle for results that are lower than they are capable of achieving. The experience of a large electrical manufacturing company demonstrates this; the company discovered that production actually declined if production quotas were set too high, because the workers simply stopped trying to meet them. In other words, the practice of "dangling the carrot just beyond the donkey's reach," endorsed by many managers, is not a good motivational device.

Scientific research by David C. McClelland of Harvard University and John W. Atkinson of the University of Michigan[7] has demonstrated that the relationship of motivation to expectancy varies in the form of a bell-shaped curve, like this:

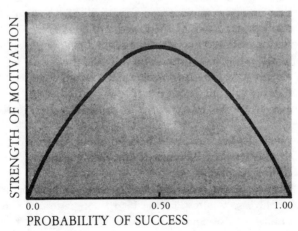

The degree of motivation and effort rises until the expectancy of success reaches 50%, then begins to fall even though the expectancy of success continues to increase. No motivation or response is aroused when the goal is

7. See John W. Atkinson, "Motivational Determinants of Risk-Taking Behavior," *Psychological Review*, Vol. 64, No. 6, 1957, p. 365.

perceived as being either virtually certain or virtually impossible to attain.

Moreover, as Berlew and Hall have pointed out, if a subordinate fails to meet performance expectations that are close to his own level of aspirations, he will "lower his personal performance goals and standards, his...performance will tend to drop off, and he will develop negative attitudes toward the task activity or job." [8] It is therefore not surprising that failure of subordinates to meet the unrealistically high expectations of their managers leads to high rates of attrition; such attrition may be voluntary or involuntary.

Secret Of Superiority

Something takes place in the minds of superior managers that does not occur in the minds of those who are less effective. While superior managers are consistently able to create high performance expectations that their subordinates fulfill, weaker managers are not successful in obtaining a similar response. What accounts for the difference?

The answer, in part, seems to be that superior managers have greater confidence than other managers in their own ability to develop the talents of their subordinates. Contrary to what might be assumed, the high expectations of superior managers are based primarily on what they think about themselves—about their own ability to select, train, and motivate their subordinates. What the manager believes about himself subtly influences what he believes about his subordinates, what he expects of them, and how he treats them. If he has confidence in his ability to develop and stimulate them to high levels of performance, he will expect much of them and will treat them with confidence that his expectations will be met. But if he has doubts about his ability to stimulate them, he will expect less of them and will treat them with less confidence.

Stated in another way, the superior manager's record of success and his confidence in his ability give his high expectations credibility. As a consequence, his subordinates accept his expectations as realistic and try hard to achieve them.

The importance of what a manager believes about his training and motivational ability is illustrated by "Sweeney's Miracle," [9] a managerial and educational self-fulfilling prophecy:

☐James Sweeney taught industrial management and psychiatry at Tulane University, and he also was responsible for the operation of the Biomedical Computer Center there. Sweeney believed that he could teach even a poorly educated man to be a capable computer operator. George Johnson, a black man who was a former hospital porter, became janitor at the computer center; he was chosen by Sweeney to prove his conviction. In the morning, George

8. David E. Berlew and Douglas T. Hall, "The Socialization of Managers: Effects of Expectations on Performance," *Administrative Science Quarterly*, September 1966, p. 208.

9. See Robert Rosenthal and Lenore Jacobson, op. cit., pp. 3-4.

Johnson performed his janitorial duties, and in the afternoon Sweeney taught him about computers.

Johnson was learning a great deal about computers when someone at the university concluded that, to be a computer operator, one had to have a certain I.Q. score. Johnson was tested, and his I.Q. indicated that he would not be able to learn to type, much less operate a computer.

But Sweeney was not convinced. He threatened to quit unless Johnson was permitted to learn to program and operate the computer. Sweeney prevailed, and he is still running the computer center. Johnson is now in charge of the main computer room and is responsible for training new employees to program and operate the computer.

Sweeney's expectations were based on what he believed about his own teaching ability, not on Johnson's learning credentials. What a manager believes about his ability to train and motivate subordinates clearly is the foundation on which realistically high managerial expectations are built.

THE CRITICAL EARLY YEARS

Managerial expectations have their most magical influence on young men. As subordinates mature and gain experience, their self-image gradually hardens, and they begin to see themselves as their career records imply. Their own aspirations, and the expectations of their superiors, become increasingly controlled by the "reality" of their past performance. It becomes more and more difficult for them, and for their managers, to generate mutually high expectations unless they have outstanding records.

Incidentally, the same pattern occurs in school. Rosenthal's experiments with educational self-fulfilling prophecies consistently demonstrate that teachers' expectations are more effective in influencing intellectual growth in younger children than in older children. In the lower grade levels, particularly in the first and second grades, the effects of teachers' expectations are dramatic.[10] In the upper grade levels, teachers' prophecies seem to have little effect on a child's intellectual growth, although they do affect his motivation and attitude toward school. While the declining influence of teachers' expectations cannot be completely explained, it is reasonable to conclude that younger children are more malleable, have fewer fixed notions about their abilities, and have less well-established reputations in the schools. As they grow, particularly if they are assigned to "tracks" on the basis of their records, as is now often done in public schools, their beliefs about their intellectual ability and their teachers' expectations of them begin to harden and become more resistant to influence by others.

10. Ibid., pp. 74-81.

Key To Future Performance

The early years in a business organization, when a young man can be strongly influenced by managerial expectations, are critical in determining his future performance and career progress. This is shown by a study at American Telephone and Telegraph Company:

☐ Berlew and Hall found that what the company initially expected of 49 college graduates who were management-level employees was the most critical factor in their subsequent performance and success. The researchers concluded: "The .72 correlation between how much a company expects of a man in his first year and how much he contributes during the next five years is too compelling to be ignored." [11]

Subsequently, the two men studied the career records of 18 college graduates who were hired as management trainees in another of the American Telephone and Telegraph Company's operating companies. Again they found that both expectations and performance in the first year correlated consistently with later performance and success. [12]

Berlew and Hall summarized their research by stating:

"Something important is happening in the first year.... Meeting high company expectations in the critical first year leads to the internalization of positive job attitudes and high standards; these attitudes and standards, in turn, would first lead to and be reinforced by strong performance and success in later years. It should also follow that a new manager who meets the challenge of one highly demanding job will be given subsequently a more demanding job, and his level of contribution will rise as he responds to the company's growing expectations of him. The key...is the concept of the first year as a *critical period for learning,* a time when the trainee is uniquely ready to develop or change in the direction of the company's expectations." [13]

Most Influential Boss

A young man's first manager is likely to be the most influential person in his career. If this manager is unable or unwilling to develop the skills the young man needs to perform effectively, the latter will set lower standards for himself than he is capable of achieving, his self-image will be impaired, and he will develop negative attitudes toward his job, his employer, and—in all probability—his career in business. Since his chances of building a successful career with his employer will decline rapidly, he will leave, if he has high aspirations, in hope of finding a better opportunity. If, on the other hand, his

---

11. "Some Determinants of Early Managerial Success," pp. 13-14.

12. "The Socialization of Managers: Effects of Expectations on Performance," p. 219.

13. Ibid., pp. 221-222.

manager helps him achieve his maximum potential, he will build the foundation for a successful career. To illustrate:

☐With few exceptions, the most effective branch managers at a large West Coast bank were mature men in their forties and fifties. The bank's executives explained that it took considerable time for a man to gain the knowledge, experience, and judgment required to handle properly credit risks, customer relations, and employee relations.

However, one branch manager, ranked in the top 10% of the managers in terms of effectiveness (which included branch profit growth, deposit growth, scores on administrative audits, and subjective rankings by superiors), was only 27 years old. This young man had been made a branch manager at 25, and in two years he not only improved the performance of his branch substantially but also developed his younger assistant manager so that he, in turn, was made a branch manager at 25.

The man had had only average grades in college, but, in his first four years at the bank, he had been assigned to work with two branch managers who were remarkably effective teachers. His first boss, who was recognized throughout the bank for his unusual skill in developing young men, did not believe that it took years to gain the knowledge and skill needed to become an effective banker. After two years, the young man was made assistant manager at a branch headed by another executive, who also was an effective developer of his subordinates. Thus it was that when the young man was promoted to head a branch, he confidently followed the model of his two previous superiors in operating his branch, quickly established a record of outstanding performance, and trained his assistant (as he had been trained) to assume responsibility early.

Contrasting records: For confirming evidence of the crucial role played by a person's first bosses, let us turn to selling, since performance in this area is more easily measured than in most managerial areas. Consider the following investigations:

☐In a study of the careers of 100 insurance salesmen who began work with either highly competent or less-than-competent agency managers, the Life Insurance Agency Management Association found that men with average sales aptitude test scores were nearly five times as likely to succeed under managers with good performance records as under managers with poor records; and men with superior sales aptitude scores were found to be twice as likely to succeed under high-performing managers as under low-performing managers.[14]

☐The Metropolitan Life Insurance Company determined in 1960 that differences in the productivity of new insurance agents who had equal sales aptitudes could be accounted for only by differences in the ability of managers in the offices to which they were assigned. Men whose productivity was high in relation to their aptitude test scores invariably were employed in offices that had production records among the top third in the company. Conversely, men

14. Robert T. Davis, "Sales Management in the Field," HBR January-February 1958, p. 91.

whose productivity was low in relation to their test scores typically were in the least successful offices. After analyzing all the factors that might have accounted for these variations, the company concluded that differences in the performance of new men were due primarily to differences in the "proficiency in sales training and direction" of the local managers.[15]

☐ A study I conducted of the performance of automobile salesmen in Ford dealerships in New England revealed that superior salesmen were concentrated in a few outstanding dealerships. For instance, 10 of the top 15 salesmen in New England were in 3 (out of approximately 200) of the dealerships in this region; and 5 of the top 15 men were in one highly successful dealership; yet 4 of these men previously had worked for other dealers without achieving outstanding sales records. There seemed to be little doubt that the training and motivational skills of managers in the outstanding dealerships were the critical factor.

Astute Selection

While success in business sometimes appears to depend on the "luck of the draw," more than luck is involved when a young man is selected by a superior manager. Successful managers do not pick their subordinates at random or by the toss of a coin. They are careful to select only those who they "know" will succeed. As Metropolitan's Rockaway district manager, Alfred Oberlander, insisted: "Every man who starts with us is going to be a top-notch life insurance man, or he would not have received an invitation to join the team."[16]

When pressed to explain how they "know" whether a man will be successful, superior managers usually end up by saying something like, "The qualities are intangible, but I know them when I see them." They have difficulty being explicit because their selection process is intuitive and is based on interpersonal intelligence that is difficult to describe. The key seems to be that they are able to identify subordinates with whom they can probably work effectively—men with whom they are compatible and whose body chemistry agrees with their own. They make mistakes, of course. But they "give up" on a subordinate slowly because that means "giving up" on themselves—on their judgment and ability in selecting, training, and motivating men. Less effective managers select subordinates more quickly and give up on them more easily, believing that the inadequacy is that of the subordinate, not of themselves.

15. Alfred A. Oberlander, "The Collective Conscience in Recruiting," address to Life Insurance Agency Management Association Annual Meeting, Chicago, Illinois, 1963, p. 5.

16. Ibid., p. 9.

DEVELOPING YOUNG MEN

Observing that his company's research indicates that "initial corporate expectations for performance (with real responsibility) mold subsequent expectations and behavior," R.W. Walters, Jr., director of college employment at the American Telephone and Telegraph Company, contends that: "Initial bosses of new college hires must be the best in the organization."[17] Unfortunately, however, most companies practice exactly the opposite.

Rarely do new graduates work closely with experienced middle managers or upper-level executives. Normally, they are bossed by first-line managers who tend to be the least experienced and least effective in the organization. While there are exceptions, first-line managers generally are either "old pros" who have been judged as lacking competence for higher levels of responsibility, or they are younger men who are making the transition from "doing" to "managing." Often, these managers lack the knowledge and skill required to develop the productive capabilities of their subordinates. As a consequence, many college graduates begin their careers in business under the worst possible circumstances. Since they know their abilities are not being developed or used, they quite naturally soon become negative toward their jobs, employers, and business careers.

Although most top executives have not yet diagnosed the problem, industry's greatest challenge by far is the underdevelopment, underutilization, and ineffective management and use of its most valuable resource—its young managerial and professional talent.

Disillusion And Turnover

The problem posed to corporate management is underscored by the sharply rising rates of attrition among young managerial and professional personnel. Turnover among managers one to five years out of college is almost twice as high now as it was a decade ago, and five times as high as two decades ago. Three out of five companies surveyed by *Fortune* magazine in the fall of 1968 reported that turnover rates among young managers and professionals were higher than five years ago.[18] While the high level of economic activity and the shortage of skilled personnel have made job-hopping easier, the underlying causes of high attrition, I am convinced, are underdevelopment and underutilization of a work force that has high career aspirations.

The problem can be seen in its extreme form in the excessive attrition rates of college and university graduates who begin their careers in sales positions. Whereas the average company loses about 50% of its new college and university

17. "How to Keep the Go-getters," *Nation's Business,* June 1966, p. 74.

18. Robert C. Albrook, "Why It's Harder to Keep Good Executives," *Fortune,* November 1968, p. 137.

graduates within three to five years, attrition rates as high as 40% in the *first* year are common among college graduates who accept sales positions in the average company. This attrition stems primarily, in my opinion, from the failure of first-line managers to teach new college recruits what they need to know to be effective sales representatives.

As we have seen, young men who begin their careers working for less-than-competent sales managers are likely to have records of low productivity. When rebuffed by their customers and considered by their managers to have little potential for success, the young men naturally have great difficulty in maintaining their self-esteem. Soon they find little personal satisfaction in their jobs and, to avoid further loss of self-respect, leave their employers for jobs that look more promising. Moreover, as reports about the high turnover and disillusionment of those who embarked on sales careers filter back to college campuses, new graduates become increasingly reluctant to take jobs in sales.

Thus, ineffective first-line sales management sets off a sequence of events that ends with college and university graduates avoiding careers in selling. To a lesser extent, the same pattern is duplicated in other functions of business, as evidenced by the growing trend of college graduates to pursue careers in "more meaningful" occupations, such as teaching and government service.

A serious "generation gap" between bosses and subordinates is another significant cause of breakdown. Many managers resent the abstract, academic language and narrow rationalization typically used by recent graduates. As one manager expressed it to me: "For God's sake, you need a lexicon even to talk with these kids." Noncollege managers often are particularly resentful, perhaps because they feel threatened by the bright young men with book-learned knowledge that they do not understand.

For whatever reason, the "generation gap" in many companies is eroding managerial expectations of new college graduates. For instance, I know of a survey of management attitudes in one of the nation's largest companies which revealed that 54% of its first-line and second-line managers believed that new college recruits were "not as good as they were five years ago." Since what a manager expects of a subordinate influences the way he treats him, it is understandable that new graduates often develop negative attitudes toward their jobs and their employers. Clearly, low managerial expectations and hostile attitudes are not the basis for effective management of new men entering business.

CONCLUSION

Industry has not developed effective first-line managers fast enough to meet its needs. As a consequence, many companies are underdeveloping their most valuable resource—talented young men and women. They are incurring heavy attrition costs and contributing to the negative attitudes young people often have about careers in business.

For top executives in industry who are concerned with the productivity of their organizations and the careers of young employees, the challenge is clear: it is to speed the development of managers who will treat their subordinates in ways that lead to high performance and career satisfaction. The manager not only shapes the expectations and productivity of his subordinates, but also influences their attitudes toward their jobs and themselves. If he is unskilled, he leaves scars on the careers of the young men, cuts deeply into their self-esteem, and distorts their image of themselves as human beings. But if he is skillful and has high expectations of his subordinates, their self-confidence will grow, their capabilities will develop, and their productivity will be high. More often than he realizes, the manager is Pygmalion.

"O the despair of Pygmalion, who might have created a statue and only made a woman!"[19]

---

19. Alfred Jarry, 1873-1907, *L'Amour Absolu*

Afterthoughts

After reading and reflecting on these chapters, you should ask yourself the question, "How do *my* beliefs compare with the research findings on the reasons why people work and the extent of their capabilities?" You may find that your personal theories compare quite favorably. If not, the data will hopefully lead you to reassess and modify your beliefs. Until your managerial philosophy is aligned with the actual characteristics of most workers, you will find it difficult to accept and put into practice the models for management presented in this volume.

The implication of Hall's chapter is that you should check out the validity of the cues you use to determine the capability of your co-workers—how well do they correlate with reality? Moreover, you should look behind your lens system to find out more about the beliefs that cause you to see things as you do.

In reflecting on Theory X and Theory Y, Charles R. Holloman[1] warned that McGregor's work may appear simple but is actually quite subtle and complex. Too often Theory X is equated with "hard management" and Theory Y with "soft management." Theory Y seems hopelessly naive to many tough-minded managers who learned how to behave in the school of hard knocks. Holloman underscored McGregor's position that Theory Y is actually the tough reality-centered management view. It provides for flexible solutions to dynamic problems rather than the narrow, more limited Theory X approach.

A good question for you to ask about Theory X and Theory Y is, "Which one is right—which theory best describes the way people really are at work?" Since both theories are statements of probability regarding the nature of working man, there is not a simple "yes" or "no" answer, but behavioral science research can shed a great deal of light on which is most correct.

A composite of findings from over one thousand studies of human behavior presents a clear profile of an average person in our culture—bright, flexible, self-directed, social, ambitious, and committed to peers and organization.[2] In short, most people, *more than two-thirds*, are in fact consistent by nature with

Theory Y assumptions. Only about ten percent are indeed the lazy, ineffective individuals described in a Theory X view. The key point to remember here is that if your practices are based on a Theory Y set of expectations you will be right on target most of the time, with seven out of ten individuals. However, the data show that if your practices emanate from a Theory X philosophy *they will be inappropriate almost ninety percent of the time!*

The data presented on the validity of Theory X and Theory Y may be hard to accept for some managers. A manager may well say, "More than ten percent of the people in my shop won't work unless I tell them exactly what to do!" However, the way people appear is not necessarily the way they are, only the way they have *learned* to behave. If workers behave in ways best described by a Theory X negative view, it is highly probable that they are reacting against coercive and demeaning organizational structures and managerial practices. The manager making such a statement may have unwittingly helped create the poor worker attitude and performance described. On the brighter side, Theory Y expectations can have just the opposite effect in bringing out in workers the highest levels of performance of which they are capable.

In Greek mythology Pygmalion was a sculptor who was able to transform a statue of a woman into a living breathing beauty. The moral for managers in the self-fulfilling prophecy is that an individual can, by force of will, lead another to transcend his or her current state despite what seems to be insurmountable odds. Recent research has proven that this phenomenon of interpersonal transactions is not a myth at all. In laboratory, classroom, and business and industrial settings one person's expectations of another consistently come to serve as a self-fulfilling prophecy.[3]

The conclusion that can be reached is that if a manager views subordinates as the creative, committed and competent people described by McGregor's Theory Y, and manages accordingly, with high expectations for their performance, both the manager and the subordinates will reap the rewards of the self-fulfilling prophecy.

REFERENCES

1. Holloman, Charles R. "What McGregor Really Said." *Business Horizons*, December 1974, pp. 87-92.

2. Berelson, B. and Steiner, G.A. *Human Behavior.* New York: Harcourt, Brace, and World, 1967.

3. Rosenthal, Robert. "On the Social Psychology of the Self-Fulfilling Prophecy." MSS Modular Publications, New York, 1974, Module 53.

Section II.

Managing the Motivation Process: Human Needs and Working Conditions

Although one of the most basic components of human behavior, motivation is one of the most frequently misunderstood behavioral topics. For years managers have felt that one of their prime responsibilities was to "motivate" their subordinates, to get them to do things they would otherwise avoid. In extreme cases motivating subordinates became a major factor in managerial performance appraisal. A good manager could motivate subordinates while those of lesser abilities could not.

Motivation has even become an industry in itself. Any company can, for a nominal fee, have well-known personalities who ride the lecture circuit drop in and deliver a "motivational" message at their annual meeting. If a live performance is not desired, there are literally hundreds of "motivational" films available. There are even organizations which do nothing but provide "motivational" incentives—everything from key chains and paper weights to exotic vacation trips. Prizes for performance!

But questions about these approaches to motivation remain. If these are truly motivational, why is the effect so short-lived? Is it that motivation is an episodic, short-term phenomenon? Or is it that these approaches do not really address motivation and, therefore, have no chance for sustained, long-term impact? What is motivation and what is it not? And what can managers really do about it?

MOTIVATION AND MANAGERS

Abraham H. Maslow's "A Theory of Human Motivation," provides a theoretical base from which to begin to explore the concept of motivation. As a personality theorist and clinical psychologist, he concluded that most behavior exists to accomplish some end. That is to say that behavior itself is motivated—we behave in a certain way for a reason. In general, behavior occurs in response to some internal tension state or discomfort, a condition created by the existence of an active or unsatisfied *need*. As shown in Figure 1 the behavior that results functions to reduce the tension or discomfort, to satisfy the existing need. Thus, needs or need systems serve as the source of motivation: they goad, energize and guide behavior toward the goal object which will satisfy the existing need. In this sense then, motivation is an internal process that occurs within a human being and is not instigated by outside forces.

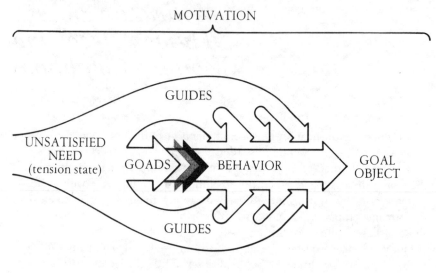

Figure 1.

So, where do managers enter this process? What part of it can they influence? Certainly, managers cannot create needs in their subordinates. A manager can capitalize on an existing need within an employee by creating opportunities for it to be fulfilled—but, if the need does not exist in the first place, the employee will not take advantage of the opportunity. The point is that managers really control only the goal objects. Managing the motivation process becomes a matter of recognizing the kind of need that drives a subordinate and matching it with goal objects in the workplace so that it can be satisfied. Indeed, managers must carefully consider what kinds of goal objects they offer to their employees and the potential for them to satisfy the needs that exist. Maslow's classification of needs makes such considerations more concrete for the manager.

In "Adult Life Stages: Growth Toward Self-Tolerance," Roger Gould discusses how adults feel about themselves and perceive their circumstances and how these are apt to change over time. Although the field of adult development is relatively new, the data suggest a re-cycling through the need hierarchy at different ages. Managers must be aware of the influence of these changing need cycles since related goal objects will change qualitatively: a goal object which will satisfy a particular need for individuals in one age group may not be at all desirable for younger or older individuals experiencing the same need.

Frederick Herzberg, along with Bernard Mausner and Barbara Block Snyderman, addresses the question, "What is motivation on the job and what is not?" in "Motivation versus Hygiene." Herzberg explains that some aspects of work have the potential to satisfy high order needs in employees and others do not. He differentiates between "motivator" factors which are directly related to the accomplishment of work and "hygiene" factors which are only peripheral. More importantly, he explains how managers can make the distinction also. His conclusions are thought-provoking and will be surprising to managers who have not yet challenged traditional views on motivation.

"A Basic Incongruency between the Needs of a Mature Personality and the Requirements of Formal Organization" was written by Chris Argyris in the mid-1950's. As he looked at the future, he saw workers as a whole becoming more mature and increasing their demands for work which met their need for feelings of self-worth. Unfortunately, he did not see organizations as being very well equipped to adapt in such a way as to capitalize on these needs. The new social values and personal awareness that emerged from the tumult of the 60's and 70's have reinforced Argyris' observations and concern. As William Glasser stresses, members of today's "identity society" make great demands on their jobs and, thus, their managers.

> "First, one has to love and be loved—to be involved with people whom one cares for and respects. Second, one must do a worthwhile task that increases his sense of self-worth and usually helps others do the same. Whether the person is a teacher or a manufacturer who gives others jobs, whether in a hobby or in volunteer work, the task must have a goal that reinforces a sense of worth."[1]

The manager's role in managing the motivation process has never been so demanding nor has the need for human skills been so great. Today's employees may not be, in fact, physically or mentally different from those of the past but they are more demanding and do have more options available to them— options which they will quickly pursue if their demands are ignored. Organizations whose managers continue to attempt to "motivate" employees in traditional carrot and stick ways will not succeed over the long run. What is required is a new social technology to deal effectively with today's work environment and today's employee.

REFERENCES

1. Glasser, William. *The Identity Society.* New York: Harper & Row, 1972.

Chapter 6

A Theory of Human Motivation

A. H. Maslow

I. INTRODUCTION

In a previous paper (13) various propositions were presented which would have to be included in any theory of human motivation that could lay claim to being definitive. These conclusions may be briefly summarized as follows:

1. The integrated wholeness of the organism must be one of the foundation stones of motivation theory.

2. The hunger drive (or any other physiological drive) was rejected as a centering point or model for a definitive theory of motivation. Any drive that is somatically based and localizable was shown to be atypical rather than typical in human motivation.

3. Such a theory should stress and center itself upon ultimate or basic goals rather than partial or superficial ones, upon ends rather than means to these ends. Such a stress would imply a more central place for unconscious than for conscious motivations.

4. There are usually available various cultural paths to the same goal. Therefore conscious, specific, local-cultural desires are not as fundamental in motivation theory as the more basic, unconscious goals.

5. Any motivated behavior, either preparatory or consummatory, must be understood to be a channel through which many basic needs may be simultaneously expressed or satisfied. Typically an act has *more* than one motivation.

6. Practically all organismic states are to be understood as motivated and as motivating.

7. Human needs arrange themselves in hierarchies of prepotency. That is to say, the appearance of one need usually rests on the prior satisfaction of

From *Psychological Review*, vol. 50, pp. 370-396, 1943. Copyright © 1943 by the American Psychological Association. Reprinted by permission.

another, more prepotent need. Man is a perpetually wanting animal. Also no need or drive can be treated as if it were isolated or discrete; every drive is related to the state of satisfaction or dissatisfaction of other drives.

8. *Lists* of drives will get us nowhere for various theoretical and practical reasons. Furthermore any classification of motivations must deal with the problem of levels of specificity or generalization of the motives to be classified.

9. Classifications of motivations must be based upon goals rather than upon instigating drives or motivated behavior.

10. Motivation theory should be human-centered rather than animal-centered.

11. The situation or the field in which the organism reacts must be taken into account but the field alone can rarely serve as an exclusive explanation for behavior. Furthermore the field itself must be interpreted in terms of the organism. Field theory cannot be a substitute for motivation theory.

12. Not only the integration of the organism must be taken into account, but also the possibility of isolated, specific, partial or segmental reactions.

It has since become necessary to add to these another affirmation.

13. Motivation theory is not synonymous with behavior theory. The motivations are only one class of determinants of behavior. While behavior is almost always motivated, it is also almost always biologically, culturally and situationally determined as well.

The present paper is an attempt to formulate a positive theory of motivation which will satisfy these theoretical demands and at the same time conform to the known facts, clinical and observational as well as experimental. It derives most directly, however, from clinical experience. This theory is, I think, in the functionalist tradition of James and Dewey, and is fused with the holism of Wertheimer (19), Goldstein (6), and Gestalt Psychology, and with the dynamism of Freud (4) and Adler (1). This fusion or synthesis may arbitrarily be called a "general-dynamic" theory.

It is far easier to perceive and to criticize the aspects in motivation theory than to remedy them. Mostly this is because of the very serious lack of sound data in this area. I conceive this lack of sound facts to be due primarily to the absence of a valid theory of motivation. The present theory then must be considered to be a suggested program or framework for future research and must stand or fall, not so much on facts available or evidence presented, as upon researches yet to be done, researches suggested perhaps by the questions raised in this paper.

II. THE BASIC NEEDS

The "physiological" needs. The needs that are usually taken as the starting point for motivation theory are the so-called physiological drives. Two recent lines of research make it necessary to revise our customary notions about these needs, first, the development of the concept of homeostasis, and second, the finding that appetites (preferential choices among foods) are a fairly efficient indication of actual needs or lacks in the body.

Homeostasis refers to the body's automatic efforts to maintain a constant, normal state of the blood stream. Cannon (2) has described this process for (1) the water content of the blood, (2) salt content, (3) sugar content, (4) protein content, (5) fat content, (6) calcium content, (7) oxygen content, (8) constant hydrogen-ion level (acid-base balance) and (9) constant temperature of the blood. Obviously this list can be extended to include other minerals, the hormones, vitamins, etc.

Young in a recent article (21) has summarized the work on appetite in its relation to body needs. If the body lacks some chemical, the individual will tend to develop a specific appetite or partial hunger for that food element.

Thus it seems impossible as well as useless to make any list of fundamental physiological needs for they can come to almost any number one might wish, depending on the degree of specificity of description. We can not identify all physiological needs as homeostatic. That sexual desire, sleepiness, sheer activity and maternal behavior in animals, are homeostatic, has not yet been demonstrated. Furthermore, this list would not include the various sensory pleasures (tastes, smells, tickling, stroking) which are probably physiological and which may become the goals of motivated behavior.

In a previous paper (13) it has been pointed out that these physiological drives or needs are to be considered unusual rather than typical because they are isolable, and because they are localizable somatically. That is to say, they are relatively independent of each other, of other motivations and of the organism as a whole, and secondly, in many cases, it is possible to demonstrate a localized, underlying somatic base for the drive. This is true less generally than has been thought (exceptions are fatigue, sleepiness, maternal responses) but it is still true in the classic instances of hunger, sex, and thirst.

It should be pointed out again that any of the physiological needs and the consummatory behavior involved with them serve as channels for all sorts of other needs as well. That is to say, the person who thinks he is hungry may actually be seeking more for comfort, or dependence, than for vitamins or proteins. Conversely, it is possible to satisfy the hunger need in part by other activities such as drinking water or smoking cigarettes. In other words, relatively isolable as these physiological needs are, they are not completely so.

Undoubtedly these physiological needs are the most prepotent of all needs. What this means specifically is, that in the human being who is missing everything in life in an extreme fashion, it is most likely that the major motivation would be the physiological needs rather than any others. A person who is lacking food, safety, love, and esteem would most probably hunger for food more strongly than for anything else.

If all the needs are unsatisfied, and the organism is then dominated by the physiological needs, all other needs may become simply non-existent or be pushed into the background. It is then fair to characterize the whole organism by saying simply that it is hungry, for consciousness is almost completely preempted by hunger. All capacities are put into the service of hunger-satisfaction, and the organization of these capacities is almost entirely determined by the one purpose of satisfying hunger. The receptors and effectors, the intelligence, memory, habits, all may now be defined simply as hunger-gratifying tools. Capacities that are not useful for this purpose lie dormant, or are pushed into the background. The urge to write poetry, the desire to acquire an automobile, the interest in American history, the desire for a new pair of shoes are, in the extreme case, forgotten or become of secondary importance. For the man who is extremely and dangerously hungry, no other interests exist but food. He dreams food, he remembers food, he thinks about food, he emotes only about food, he perceives only food and he wants only food. The more subtle determinants that ordinarily fuse with the physiological drives in organizing even feeding, drinking or sexual behavior, may now be so completely overwhelmed as to allow us to speak at this time (but *only* at this time) of pure hunger drive and behavior, with the one unqualified aim of relief.

Another peculiar characteristic of the human organism when it is dominated by a certain need is that the whole philosophy of the future tends also to change. For our chronically and extremely hungry man, Utopia can be defined very simply as a place where there is plenty of food. He tends to think that, if only he is guaranteed food for the rest of his life, he will be perfectly happy and will never want anything more. Life itself tends to be defined in terms of eating. Anything else will be defined as unimportant. Freedom, love, community feeling, respect, philosophy, may all be waved aside as fripperies which are useless since they fail to fill the stomach. Such a man may fairly be said to live by bread alone.

It cannot possibly be denied that such things are true but their *generality* can be denied. Emergency conditions are, almost by definition, rare in the normally functioning peaceful society. That this truism can be forgotten is due mainly to two reasons. First, rats have few motivations other than physiological ones, and since so much of the research upon motivation has been made with these animals, it is easy to carry the rat-picture over to the human being. Secondly, it is too often not realized that culture itself is an adaptive tool, one of whose main functions is to make the physiological emergencies come less and less often. In most of the known societies, chronic extreme hunger of the emergency type is rare, rather than common. In any case, this is still true in the United States. The average American citizen is experiencing appetite rather than hunger when he says "I am hungry." He is apt to experience sheer life-and-death hunger only by accident and then only a few times through his entire life.

Obviously a good way to obscure the "higher" motivations, and to get a lopsided view of human capacities and human nature, is to make the organism extremely and chronically hungry or thirsty. Anyone who attempts to make an emergency picture into a typical one, and who will measure all of man's goals and desires by his behavior during extreme physiological deprivation is certainly being blind to many things. It is quite true that man lives by bread alone—

when there is no bread. But what happens to man's desires when there *is* plenty of bread and when his belly is chronically filled?

At once other (and "higher") needs emerge and these, rather than physiological hungers, dominate the organism. And when these in turn are satisfied, again new (and still "higher") needs emerge and so on. This is what we mean by saying that the basic human needs are organized into a hierarchy of relative prepotency.

One main implication of this phrasing is that gratification becomes as important a concept as deprivation in motivation theory, for it releases the organism from the domination of a relatively more physiological need, permitting thereby the emergence of other more social goals. The physiological needs, along with their partial goals, when chronically gratified cease to exist as active determinants or organizers of behavior. They now exist only in a potential fashion in the sense that they may emerge again to dominate the organism if they are thwarted. But a want that is satisfied is no longer a want. The organism is dominated and its behavior organized only by unsatisfied needs. If hunger is satisfied, it becomes unimportant in the current dynamics of the individual.

This statement is somewhat qualified by a hypothesis to be discussed more fully later, namely that it is precisely those individuals in whom a certain need has always been satisfied who are best equipped to tolerate deprivation of that need in the future, and that furthermore, those who have been deprived in the past will react differently to current satisfactions than the one who has never been deprived.

The safety needs. If the physiological needs are relatively well gratified, there then emerges a new set of needs, which we may categorize roughly as the safety needs. All that has been said of the physiological needs is equally true, although in lesser degree, of these desires. The organism may equally well be wholly dominated by them. They may serve as the almost exclusive organizers of behavior, recruiting all the capacities of the organism in their service, and we may then fairly describe the whole organism as a safety-seeking mechanism. Again we may say of the receptors, the effectors, of the intellect and the other capacities that they are primarily safety-seeking tools. Again, as in the hungry man, we find that the dominating goal is a strong determinant not only of his current world-outlook and philosophy but also of his philosophy of the future. Practically everything looks less important than safety (even sometimes the physiological needs which, being satisfied, are now underestimated). A man, in this state, if it is extreme enough and chronic enough, may be characterized as living almost for safety alone.

Although in this paper we are interested primarily in the needs of the adult, we can approach an understanding of his safety needs perhaps more efficiently by observation of infants and children, in whom these needs are much more simple and obvious. One reason for the clearer appearance of the threat or danger reaction in infants is that they do not inhibit this reaction at all, whereas adults in our society have been taught to inhibit it at all costs. Thus even when adults do feel their safety to be threatened we may not be able to see this on the surface. Infants will react in a total fashion and as if they were endangered, if they are disturbed or dropped suddenly, startled by loud noises, flashing light, or other unusual sensory stimulation, by rough handling, by general loss of support in the mother's arms, or by inadequate support.[1]

In infants we can also see a much more direct reaction to bodily illnesses of various kinds. Sometimes these illnesses seem to be immediately and *per se* threatening and seem to make the child feel unsafe. For instance, vomiting, colic or other sharp pains seem to make the child look at the whole world in a different way. At such a moment of pain, it may be postulated that, for the child, the appearance of the whole world suddenly changes from sunniness to darkness, so to speak, and becomes a place in which anything at all might happen, in which previously stable things have suddenly become unstable. Thus a child who because of some bad food is taken ill may, for a day or two, develop fear, nightmares, and a need for protection and reassurance never seen in him before his illness.

Another indication of the child's need for safety is his preference for some kind of undisrupted routine or rhythm. He seems to want a predictable, orderly world. For instance, injustice, unfairness, or inconsistency in the parents seems to make a child feel anxious and unsafe. This attitude may be not so much because of the injustice *per se* or any particular pains involved, but rather because this treatment threatens to make the world look unreliable, or unsafe, or unpredictable. Young children seem to thrive better under a system which has at least a skeletal outline of rigidity, in which there is a schedule of a kind, some sort of routine, something that can be counted upon, not only for the present but also far into the future. Perhaps one could express this more accurately by saying that the child needs an organized world rather than an unorganized or unstructured one.

The central role of the parents and the normal family setup are indisputable. Quarreling, physical assault, separation, divorce or death within the family may be particularly terrifying. Also parental outbursts of rage or threats of punishment directed to the child, calling him names, speaking to him harshly, shaking him, handling him roughly, or actual physical punishment sometimes elicit such total panic and terror in the child that we must assume more is involved than the physical pain alone. While it is true that in some children this terror may represent also a fear of loss of parental love, it can also occur in completely rejected children, who seem to cling to the hating parents more for sheer safety and protection than because of hope of love.

Confronting the average child with new, unfamiliar, strange, unmanageable stimuli or situations will too frequently elicit the danger or terror reaction, as for example, getting lost or even being separated from the parents for a short

1. As the child grows up, sheer knowledge and familiarity as well as better motor development make these "dangers" less and less dangerous and more and more manageable. Throughout life it may be said that one of the main conative functions of education is this neutralizing of apparent dangers through knowledge, *e.g.*, I am not afraid of thunder because I know something about it.

time, being confronted with new faces, new situations or new tasks, the sight of strange, unfamiliar or uncontrollable objects, illness or death. Particularly at such times, the child's frantic clinging to his parents is eloquent testimony to their role as protectors (quite apart from their roles as food-givers and love-givers).

From these and similar observations, we may generalize and say that the average child in our society generally prefers a safe, orderly, predictable, organized world, which he can count on, and in which unexpected, unmanageable or other dangerous things do not happen, and in which, in any case, he has all-powerful parents who protect and shield him from harm.

That these reactions may so easily be observed in children is in a way a proof of the fact that children in our society feel too unsafe (or, in a word, are badly brought up). Children who are reared in an unthreatening, loving family do *not* ordinarily react as we have described above (17). In such children the danger reactions are apt to come mostly to objects or situations that adults too would consider dangerous.[2]

The healthy, normal, fortunate adult in our culture is largely satisfied in his safety needs. The peaceful, smoothly running, "good" society ordinarily makes its members feel safe enough from wild animals, extremes of temperature, criminals, assault and murder, tyranny, etc. Therefore, in a very real sense, he no longer has any safety needs as active motivators. Just as a sated man no longer feels hungry, a safe man no longer feels endangered. If we wish to see these needs directly and clearly we must turn to neurotic or near-neurotic individuals, and to the economic and social underdogs. In between these extremes, we can perceive the expressions of safety needs only in such phenomena as, for instance, the common preference for a job with tenure and protection, the desire for a savings account, and for insurance of various kinds (medical, dental, unemployment, disability, old age).

Other broader aspects of the attempt to seek safety and stability in the world are seen in the very common preference for familiar rather than unfamiliar things, or for the known rather than the unknown. The tendency to have some religion or world-philosophy that organizes the universe and the men in it into some sort of satisfactorily coherent, meaningful whole is also in part motivated by safety-seeking. Here too we may list science and philosophy in general as partially motivated by the safety needs (we shall see later that there are also other motivations to scientific, philosophical or religious endeavor).

Otherwise the need for safety is seen as an active and dominant mobilizer of the organism's resources only in emergencies, *e.g.*, war, disease, natural

---

2. A "test battery" for safety might be confronting the child with a small exploding firecracker, or with a bewhiskered face, having the mother leave the room, putting him upon a high ladder, a hypodermic injection, having a mouse crawl up to him, etc. Of course I cannot seriously recommend the deliberate use of such "tests" for they might very well harm the child being tested. But these and similar situations come up by the score in the child's ordinary day-to-day living and may be observed. There is no reason why these stimuli should not be used with, for example, young chimpanzees.

catastrophes, crime waves, societal disorganization, neurosis, brain injury, chronically bad situation.

Some neurotic adults in our society are, in many ways, like the unsafe child in their desire for safety, although in the former it takes on a somewhat special appearance. Their reaction is often to unknown, psychological dangers in a world that is perceived to be hostile, overwhelming and threatening. Such a person behaves as if a great catastrophe were almost always impending, *i.e.*, he is usually reponding as if to an emergency. His safety needs often find specific expression in a search for a protector, or a stronger person on whom he may depend, or perhaps, a Fuehrer.

The neurotic individual may be described in a slightly different way with some usefulness as a grown-up person who retains his childish attitudes toward the world. That is to say, a neurotic adult may be said to behave "as if" he were actually afraid of a spanking, or of his mother's disapproval, or of being abandoned by his parents, or having his food taken away from him. It is as if his childish attitudes of fear and threat reaction to a dangerous world had gone underground, and untouched by the growing up and learning processes, were now ready to be called out by any stimulus that would make a child feel endangered and threatened.[3]

The neurosis in which the search for safety takes its clearest form is in the compulsive-obsessive neurosis. Compulsive-obsessives try frantically to order and stabilize the world so that no unmanageable, unexpected or unfamiliar dangers will ever appear (14). They hedge themselves about with all sorts of ceremonials, rules and formulas so that every possible contingency may be provided for and so that no new contingencies may appear. They are much like the brain injured cases, described by Goldstein (6), who manage to maintain their equilibrium by avoiding everything unfamiliar and strange and by ordering their restricted world in such a neat, disciplined, orderly fashion that everything in the world can be counted upon. They try to arrange the world so that anything unexpected (dangers) cannot possibly occur. If, through no fault of their own, something unexpected does occur, they go into a panic reaction as if this unexpected occurrence constituted a grave danger. What we can see only as a none-too-strong preference in the healthy person, *e.g.*, preference for the familiar, becomes a life-and-death necessity in abnormal cases.

The love needs. If both the physiological and the safety needs are fairly well gratified, then there will emerge the love and affection and belongingness needs, and the whole cycle already described will repeat itself with this new center. Now the person will feel keenly, as never before, the absence of friends, or a sweetheart, or a wife, or children. He will hunger for affectionate relations with people in general, namely, for a place in his group, and he will strive with great intensity to achieve this goal. He will want to attain such a place more than anything else in the world and may even forget that once, when he was hungry, he sneered at love.

3. Not all neurotic individuals feel unsafe. Neurosis may have at its core a thwarting of the affection and esteem needs in a person who is generally safe.

In our society the thwarting of these needs is the most commonly found core in cases of maladjustment and more severe psychopathology. Love and affection, as well as their possible expression in sexuality, are generally looked upon with ambivalence and are customarily hedged about with many restrictions and inhibitions. Practically all theorists of psychopathology have stressed thwarting of the love needs as basic in the picture of maladjustment. Many clinical studies have therefore been made of this need and we know more about it perhaps than any of the other needs except the physiological ones (14).

One thing that must be stressed at this point is that love is not synonymous with sex. Sex may be studied as a purely physiological need. Ordinarily sexual behavior is multi-determined, that is to say, determined not only by sexual but also by other needs, chief among which are the love and affection needs. Also not to be overlooked is the fact that the love needs involve both giving *and* receiving love.[4]

The esteem needs. All people in our society (with a few pathological exceptions) have a need or desire for a stable, firmly based, (usually) high evaluation of themselves, for self-respect, or self-esteem, and for the esteem of others. By firmly based self-esteem, we mean that which is soundly based upon real capacity, achievement and respect from others. These needs may be classified into two subsidiary sets. These are, first, the desire for strength, for achievement, for adequacy, for confidence in the face of the world, and for independence and freedom.[5] Secondly, we have what we may call the desire for reputation or prestige (defining it as respect or esteem from other people), recognition, attention, importance or appreciation.[6] These needs have been relatively stressed by Alfred Adler and his followers, and have been relatively neglected by Freud and the psychoanalysts. More and more today however there is appearing widespread appreciation of their central importance.

Satisfaction of the self-esteem need leads to feelings of self-confidence, worth, strength, capability and adequacy of being useful and necessary in the world. But thwarting of these needs produces feelings of inferiority, of weakness and of helplessness. These feelings in turn give rise to either basic discouragement or else compensatory or neurotic trends. An appreciation of the necessity of basic self-confidence and an understanding of how helpless people

---

4. For further details see (12) and (16, Chap. 5).

5. Whether or not this particular desire is universal we do not know. The crucial question, especially important today, is "Will men who are enslaved and dominated inevitably feel dissatisfied and rebellious?" We may assume on the basis of commonly known clinical data that a man who has known true freedom (not paid for by giving up safety and security but rather built on the basis of adequate safety and security) will not willingly or easily allow his freedom to be taken away from him. But we do not know that this is true for the person born into slavery. The events of the next decade should give us our answer. See discussion of this problem in (5).

6. Perhaps the desire for prestige and respect from others is subsidiary to the desire for self-esteem or confidence in oneself. Observation of children seems to indicate that this is so, but clinical data give no clear support for such a conclusion.

are without it, can be easily gained from a study of severe traumatic neurosis (8).[7]

The need for self-actualization. Even if all these needs are satisfied, we may still often (if not always) expect that a new discontent and restlessness will soon develop, unless the individual is doing what he is fitted for. A musician must make music, an artist must paint, a poet must write, if he is to be ultimately happy. What a man *can* be, he *must* be. This need we may call self-actualization.

This term, first coined by Kurt Goldstein, is being used in this paper in a much more specific and limited fashion. It refers to the desire for self-fulfillment, namely, to the tendency for him to become actualized in what he is potentially. This tendency might be phrased as the desire to become more and more what one is, to become everything that one is capable of becoming.

The specific form that these needs will take will of course vary greatly from person to person. In one individual it may take the form of the desire to be an ideal mother, in another it may be expressed athletically, and in still another it may be expressed in painting pictures or in inventions. It is not necessarily a creative urge although in people who have any capacities for creation it will take this form.

The clear emergence of these needs rests upon prior satisfaction of the physiological, safety, love and esteem needs. We shall call people who are satisfied in these needs, basically satisfied people, and it is from these that we may expect the fullest (and healthiest) creativeness.[8] Since, in our society, basically satisfied people are the exception, we do not know much about self-actualization, either experimentally or clinically. It remains a challenging problem for research.

The preconditions for the basic need satisfactions. There are certain conditions which are immediate prerequisites for the basic need satisfactions. Danger to these is reacted to almost as if it were a direct danger to the basic needs themselves. Such conditions as freedom to speak, freedom to do what one wishes so long as no harm is done to others, freedom to express oneself, freedom to investigate and seek for information, freedom to defend oneself, justice, fairness, honesty, orderliness in the group are examples of such preconditions for basic need satisfactions. Thwarting in these freedoms will be reacted to with a threat or emergency response. These conditions are not ends in themselves but they are *almost* so since they are so closely related to the basic needs,

---

7. For more extensive discussion of normal self-esteem, as well as for reports of various researches, see (11).

8. Clearly creative behavior, like painting, is like any other behavior in having multiple determinants. It may be seen in "innately creative" people whether they are satisfied or not, happy or unhappy, hungry or sated. Also it is clear that creative activity may be compensatory, ameliorative or purely economic. It is my impression (as yet unconfirmed) that it is possible to distinguish the artistic and intellectual products of basically satisfied people from those of basically unsatisfied people by inspection alone. In any case, here too we must distinguish, in a dynamic fashion, the overt behavior itself from its various motivations or purposes.

which are apparently the only ends in themselves. These conditions are defended because without them the basic satisfactions are quite impossible, or at least, very severely endangered.

If we remember that the cognitive capacities (perceptual, intellectual, learning) are a set of adjustive tools, which have, among other functions, that of satisfaction of our basic needs, then it is clear that any danger to them, any deprivation or blocking of their free use, must also be indirectly threatening to the basic needs themselves. Such a statement is a partial solution of the general problems of curiosity, the search for knowledge, truth and wisdom, and the ever-persistent urge to solve the cosmic mysteries.

We must therefore introduce another hypothesis and speak of degrees of closeness to the basic needs, for we have already pointed out that *any* conscious desires (partial goals) are more or less important as they are more or less close to the basic needs. The same statement may be made for various behavior acts. An act is psychologically important if it contributes directly to satisfaction of basic needs. The less directly it so contributes, or the weaker this contribution is, the less important this act must be conceived to be from the point of view of dynamic psychology. A similar statement may be made for the various defense or coping mechanisms. Some are very directly related to the protection or attainment of the basic needs, others are only weakly and distantly related. Indeed if we wished, we could speak of more basic and less basic defense mechanisms, and then affirm that danger to the more basic defenses is more threatening than danger to less basic defenses (always remembering that this is so only because of their relationship to the basic needs).

The desires to know and to understand. So far, we have mentioned the cognitive needs only in passing. Acquiring knowledge and systematizing the universe have been considered as, in part, techniques for the achievement of basic safety in the world, or, for the intelligent man, expressions of self-actualization. Also freedom of inquiry and expression have been discussed as preconditions of satisfactions of the basic needs. True though these formulations may be, they do not constitute definitive answers to the question as to the motivation role of curiosity, learning, philosophizing, experimenting, etc. They are, at best, no more than partial answers.

This question is especially difficult because we know so little about the facts. Curiosity, exploration, desire for the facts, desire to know may certainly be observed easily enough. The fact that they often are pursued even at great cost to the individual's safety is an earnest of the partial character of our previous discussion [*sic*]. In addition, the writer must admit that, though he has sufficient clinical evidence to postulate the desire to know as a very strong drive in intelligent people, no data are available for unintelligent people. It may then be largely a function of relatively high intelligence. Rather tentatively, then, and largely in the hope of stimulating discussion and research, we shall postulate a basic desire to know, to be aware of reality, to get the facts, to satisfy curiosity, or as Wertheimer phrases it, to see rather than to be blind.

This postulation, however, is not enough. Even after we know, we are impelled to know more and more minutely and microscopically on the one hand, and on the other, more and more extensively in the direction of a world philosophy, religion, etc. The facts that we acquire, if they are isolated or atomistic, inevitably get theorized about, and either analyzed or organized or both. This process has been phrased by some as the search for "meaning." We shall then postulate a desire to understand, to systematize, to organize, to analyze, to look for relations and meanings.

Once these desires are accepted for discussion, we see that they too form themselves into a small hierarchy in which the desire to know is prepotent over the desire to understand. All the characteristics of a hierarchy of prepotency that we have described above seem to hold for this one as well.

We must guard ourselves against the too easy tendency to separate these desires from the basic needs we have discussed above, *i.e.*, to make a sharp dichotomy between "cognitive" and "conative" needs. The desire to know and to understand are themselves conative, *i.e.*, have a striving character, and are as much personality needs as the "basic needs" we have already discussed (19).

III. FURTHER CHARACTERISTICS OF THE BASIC NEEDS

The degree of fixity of the hierarchy of basic needs. We have spoken so far as if this hierarchy were a fixed order but actually it is not nearly as rigid as we may have implied. It is true that most of the people with whom we have worked have seemed to have these basic needs in about the order that has been indicated. However, there have been a number of exceptions.

1. There are some people in whom, for instance, self-esteem seems to be more important than love. This most common reversal in the hierarchy is usually due to the development of the notion that the person who is most likely to be loved is a strong or powerful person, one who inspires respect or fear, and who is self confident or aggressive. Therefore such people who lack love and seek it, may try hard to put on a front of aggressive, confident behavior. But essentially they seek high self-esteem and its behavior expressions more as a means-to-an-end than for its own sake; they seek self-assertion for the sake of love rather than for self-esteem itself.

2. There are other, apparently innately creative people in whom the drive to creativeness seems to be more important than any other counterdeterminant. Their creativeness might appear not as self-actualization released by basic satisfaction, but in spite of lack of basic satisfaction.

3. In certain people the level of aspiration may be permanently deadened or lowered. That is to say, the less prepotent goals may simply be lost, and may disappear forever, so that the person who has experienced life at a very low level, *i.e.*, chronic unemployment, may continue to be satisfied for the rest of his life if only he can get enough food.

4. The so-called "psychopathic personality" is another example of permanent loss of the love needs. These are people who, according to the best data

available (9), have been starved for love in the earliest months of their lives and have simply lost forever the desire and the ability to give and to receive affection (as animals lose sucking or pecking reflexes that are not exercised soon enough after birth).

5. Another cause of reversal of the hierarchy is that when a need has been satisfied for a long time, this need may be underevaluated. People who have never experienced chronic hunger are apt to underestimate its effects and to look upon food as a rather unimportant thing. If they are dominated by a higher need, this higher need will seem to be the most important of all. It then becomes possible, and indeed does actually happen, that they may, for the sake of this higher need, put themselves into the position of being deprived in a more basic need. We may expect that after a long-time deprivation of the more basic need there will be a tendency to reevaluate both needs so that the more prepotent need will actually become consciously prepotent for the individual who may have given it up very lightly. Thus, a man who has given up his job rather than lose his self-respect, and who then starves for six months or so, may be willing to take his job back even at the price of losing his self-respect.

6. Another partial explanation of *apparent* reversals is seen in the fact that we have been talking about the hierarchy of prepotency in terms of consciously felt wants or desires rather than of behavior. Looking at behavior itself may give us the wrong impression. What we have claimed is that the person will *want* the more basic of two needs when deprived in both. There is no necessary implication here that he will act upon his desires. Let us say again that there are many determinants of behavior other than the needs and desires.

7. Perhaps more important than all these exceptions are the ones that involve ideals, high social standards, high values and the like. With such values people become martyrs; they will give up everything for the sake of a particular ideal, or value. These people may be understood, at least in part, by reference to one basic concept (or hypothesis) which may be called "increased frustration-tolerance through early gratification." People who have been satisfied in their basic needs throughout their lives, particularly in their earlier years, seem to develop exceptional power to withstand present or future thwarting of these needs simply because they have strong, healthy character structure as a result of basic satisfaction. They are the "strong" people who can easily weather disagreement or opposition, who can swim against the stream of public opinion and who can stand up for the truth at great personal cost. It is just the ones who have loved and been well loved, and who have had many deep friendships who can hold out against hatred, rejection or persecution.

I say all this in spite of the fact that there is a certain amount of sheer habituation which is also involved in any full discussion of frustration tolerance. For instance, it is likely that those persons who have been accustomed to relative starvation for a long time are partially enabled thereby to withstand food deprivation. What sort of balance must be made between these two tendencies, of habituation on the one hand, and of past satisfaction breeding present frustration tolerance on the other hand, remains to be worked out by further research.

Meanwhile we may assume that they are both operative, side by side, since they do not contradict each other. In respect to this phenomenon of increased frustration tolerance, it seems probable that the most important gratifications come in the first two years of life. That is to say, people who have been made secure and strong in the earliest years, tend to remain secure and strong thereafter in the face of whatever threatens.

Degrees of relative satisfaction. So far, our theoretical discussion may have given the impression that these five sets of needs are somehow in a step-wise, all-or-none relationship to each other. We have spoken in such terms as the following: "If one need is satisfied, then another emerges." This statement might give the false impression that a need must be satisfied 100 per cent before the next need emerges. In actual fact, most members of our society who are normal are partially satisfied in all their basic needs and partially unsatisfied in all their basic needs at the same time. A more realistic description of the hierarchy would be in terms of decreasing percentages of satisfaction as we go up the hierarchy of prepotency. For instance, if I may assign arbitrary figures for the sake of illustration, it is as if the average citizen is satisfied perhaps 85 per cent in his physiological needs, 70 per cent in his safety needs, 50 per cent in his love needs, 40 per cent in his self-esteem needs, and 10 per cent in his self-actualization needs.

As for the concept of emergence of a new need after satisfaction of the prepotent need, this emergence is not a sudden, saltatory phenomenon but rather a gradual emergence by slow degrees from nothingness. For instance, if prepotent need A is satisfied only 10 per cent then need B may not be visible at all. However, as this need A becomes satisfied 25 per cent, need B may emerge 5 per cent, as need A becomes satisfied 75 per cent, need B may emerge 90 per cent, and so on.

Unconscious character of needs. These needs are neither necessarily conscious nor unconscious. On the whole, however, in the average person, they are more often unconscious rather than conscious. It is not necessary at this point to overhaul the tremendous mass of evidence which indicates the crucial importance of unconscious motivation. It would by now be expected, on a priori grounds alone, that unconscious motivations would on the whole be rather more important than the conscious motivations. What we have called the basic needs are very often largely unconscious although they may, with suitable techniques, and with sophisticated people become conscious.

Cultural specificity and generality of needs. This classification of basic needs makes some attempt to take account of the relative unity behind the superficial differences in specific desires from one culture to another. Certainly in any particular culture an individual's conscious motivational content will usually be extremely different from the conscious motivational content of an individual in another society. However, it is the common experience of anthropologists that people, even in different societies, are much more alike than we would think from our first contact with them, and that as we know them better we seem to find more and more of this commonness. We then recognize the most startling differences to be superficial rather than basic, *e.g.*, differences in style of hair-dress, clothes, tastes in food, etc. Our classification of basic needs is in part an attempt to account for this unity behind the apparent diversity from culture to culture. No claim is made that it is ultimate or universal for all cultures. The claim is made only that it is relatively *more* ultimate, more universal, more basic, than the superficial conscious desires from culture to culture, and makes a somewhat closer approach to common-human characteristics. Basic needs are *more* common-human than superficial desires or behaviors.

Multiple motivations of behavior. These needs must be understood *not* to be *exclusive* or single determiners of certain kinds of behavior. An example may be found in any behavior that seems to be physiologically motivated, such as eating, or sexual play or the like. The clinical psychologists have long since found that any behavior may be a channel through which flow various determinants. Or to say it in another way, most behavior is multi-motivated. Within the sphere of motivational determinants any behavior tends to be determined by several or *all* of the basic needs simultaneously rather than by only one of them. The latter would be more an exception than the former. Eating may be partially for the sake of filling the stomach, and partially for the sake of comfort and amelioration of other needs. One may make love not only for pure sexual release, but also to convince one's self of one's masculinity, or to make a conquest, to feel powerful, or to win more basic affection. As an illustration, I may point out that it would be possible (theoretically if not practically) to analyze a single act of an individual and see in it the expression of his physiological needs, his safety needs, his love needs, his esteem needs and self-actualization. This contrasts sharply with the more naive brand of trait psychology in which one trait or one motive accounts for a certain kind of act, *i.e.*, an aggressive act is traced solely to a trait of aggressiveness.

Multiple determinants of behavior. Not all behavior is determined by the basic needs. We might even say that not all behavior is motivated. There are many determinants of behavior other than motives.[9] For instance, one other important class of determinants is the so-called "field" determinants. Theoretically, at least, behavior may be determined completely by the field, or even by specific isolated external stimuli, as in association of ideas, or certain conditioned reflexes. If in response to the stimulus word "table," I immediately perceive a memory image of a table, this response certainly has nothing to do with my basic needs.

Secondly, we may call attention again to the concept of "degree of closeness to the basic needs" or "degree of motivation." Some behavior is highly motivated, other behavior is only weakly motivated. Some is not motivated at all (but all behavior is determined).

---

9. I am aware that many psychologists and psychoanalysts use the term "motivated" and "determined" synonymously, *e.g.*, Freud. But I consider this an obfuscating usage. Sharp distinctions are necessary for clarity of thought, and precision in experimentation.

Another important point[10] is that there is a basic difference between expressive behavior and coping behavior (functional striving, purposive goal seeking). An expressive behavior does not try to do anything; it is simply a reflection of the personality. A stupid man behaves stupidly, not because he wants to, or tries to, or is motivated to, but simply because he *is* what he is. The same is true when I speak in a bass voice rather than tenor or soprano. The random movements of a healthy child, the smile on the face of a happy man even when he is alone, the springiness of the healthy man's walk, and the erectness of his carriage are other examples of expressive, non-functional behavior. Also the *style* in which a man carries out almost all his behavior, motivated as well as unmotivated, is often expressive.

We may then ask, is *all* behavior expressive or reflective of the character structure? The answer is "No." Rote, habitual, automatized, or conventional behavior may or may not be expressive. The same is true for most "stimulus-bound" behaviors.

It is finally necessary to stress that expressiveness of behavior and goal-directedness of behavior are not mutually exclusive categories. Average behavior is usually both.

Goals as centering principle in motivation theory. It will be observed that the basic principle in our classification has been neither the instigation nor the motivated behavior but rather the functions, effects, purposes, or goals of the behavior. It has been proven sufficiently by various people that this is the most suitable point for centering in any motivation theory.[11]

Animal- and human-centering. This theory starts with the human being rather than any lower and presumably "simpler" animal. Too many of the findings that have been made in animals have been proven to be true for animals but not for the human being. There is no reason whatsoever why we should start with animals in order to study human motivation. The logic or rather illogic behind this general fallacy of "psuedo-simplicity" has been exposed often enough by philosophers and logicians as well as by scientists in each of the various fields. It is no more necessary to study animals before one can study man than it is to study mathematics before one can study geology or psychology or biology.

We may also reject the old, naive, behaviorism which assumed that it was somehow necessary, or at least more "scientific" to judge human beings by animal standards. One consequence of this belief was that the whole notion of purpose and goal was excluded from motivational psychology simply because one could not ask a white rat about his purposes. Tolman (18) has long since proven in animal studies themselves that this exclusion was not necessary.

Motivation and the theory of psychopathogenesis. The conscious motivational content of everyday life has, according to the foregoing, been conceived to be

---

10. To be discussed fully in a subsequent publication.

11. The interested reader is referred to the very excellent discussion of this point in Murray's *Explorations in Personality* (15).

relatively important or unimportant accordingly as it is more or less closely related to the basic goals. A desire for an ice cream cone might actually be an indirect expression of a desire for love. If it is, then this desire for the ice cream cone becomes extremely important motivation. If however the ice cream is simply something to cool the mouth with, or a casual appetitive reaction, then the desire is relatively unimportant. Everyday conscious desires are to be regarded as symptoms, as *surface indicators of more basic needs*. If we were to take these superficial desires at their face value we would find ourselves in a state of complete confusion which could never be resolved, since we would be dealing seriously with symptoms rather than with what lay behind the symptoms.

Thwarting of unimportant desires produces no psychopathological results; thwarting of a basically important need does produce such results. Any theory of psychopathogenesis must then be based on a sound theory of motivation. A conflict or a frustration is not necessarily pathogenic. It becomes so only when it threatens or thwarts the basic needs, or partial needs that are closely related to the basic needs (10).

The role of gratified needs. It has been pointed out above several times that our needs usually emerge only when more prepotent needs have been gratified. Thus gratification has an important role in motivation theory. Apart from this, however, needs cease to play an active determining or organizing role as soon as they are gratified.

What this means is that, *e.g.,* a basically satisfied person no longer has the needs for esteem, love, safety, etc. The only sense in which he might be said to have them is in the almost metaphysical sense that a sated man has hunger, or a filled bottle has emptiness. If we are interested in what *actually* motivates us, and not in what has, will, or might motivate us, then a satisfied need is not a motivator. It must be considered for all practical purposes simply not to exist, to have disappeared. This point should be emphasized because it has been either overlooked or contradicted in every theory of motivation I know.[12] The perfectly healthy, normal, fortunate man has no sex needs or hunger needs, or needs for safety, or for love, or for prestige, or self-esteem, except in stray moments of quickly passing threat. If we were to say otherwise, we should also have to aver that every man had all the pathological reflexes, *e.g.,* Babinski, etc., because if his nervous system were damaged, these would appear.

It is such considerations as these that suggest the bold postulation that a man who is thwarted in any of his basic needs may fairly be envisaged simply as a sick man. This is a fair parallel to our designation as "sick" of the man who lacks vitamins or minerals. Who is to say that a lack of love is less important than a lack of vitamins? Since we know the pathogenic effects of love starvation, who is to say that we are invoking value-questions in an unscientific or illegitimate way, any more than the physician does who diagnoses and treats pellagra or scurvy? If I were permitted this usage, I should then say simply that a healthy man is primarily motivated by his needs to develop and actualize his

---

12. Note that acceptance of this theory necessitates basic revision of the Freudian theory.

fullest potentialities and capacities. If a man has any other basic needs in any active, chronic sense, then he is simply an unhealthy man. He is as surely sick as if he had suddenly developed a strong salt-hunger or calcium hunger.[13]

If this statement seems unusual or paradoxical the reader may be assured that this is only one among many such paradoxes that will appear as we revise our ways of looking at man's deeper motivations. When we ask what man wants of life, we deal with his very essence.

IV. SUMMARY

1. There are at least five sets of goals, which we may call basic needs. These are briefly physiological, safety, love, esteem, and self-actualization. In addition, we are motivated by the desire to achieve or maintain the various conditions upon which these basic satisfactions rest and by certain more intellectual desires.

2. These basic goals are related to each other, being arranged in a hierarchy of prepotency. This means that the most prepotent goal will monopolize consciousness and will tend of itself to organize the recruitment of the various capacities of the organism. The less prepotent needs are minimized, even forgotten or denied. But when a need is fairly well satisfied, the next prepotent ("higher") need emerges, in turn to dominate the conscious life and to serve as the center of organization of behavior, since gratified needs are not active motivators.

Thus man is a perpetually wanting animal. Ordinarily the satisfaction of these wants is not altogether mutually exclusive, but only tends to be. The average member of our society is most often partially satisfied and partially unsatisfied in all of his wants. The hierarchy principle is usually empirically observed in terms of increasing percentages of non-satisfaction as we go up the hierarchy. Reversals of the average order of the hierarchy are sometimes observed. Also it has been observed that an individual may permanently lose the higher wants in the hierarchy under special conditions. There are not only ordinarily multiple motivations for usual behavior, but in addition many determinants other than motives.

3. Any thwarting or possibility of thwarting of these basic human goals, or danger to the defenses which protect them, or to the conditions upon which they rest, is considered to be a psychological threat. With a few exceptions, all psychopathology may be partially traced to such threats. A basically thwarted man may actually be defined as a "sick" man, if we wish.

13. If we were to use the word "sick" in this way, we should then also have to face squarely the relations of man to his society. One clear implication of our definition would be that (1) since a man is to be called sick who is basically thwarted, and (2) since such basic thwarting is made possible ultimately only by forces outside the individual, then (3) sickness in the individual must come ultimately from a sickness in the society. The "good" or healthy society would then be defined as one that permitted man's highest purposes to emerge by satisfying all his prepotent basic needs.

4. It is such basic threats which bring about the general emergency reactions.

5. Certain other basic problems have not been dealt with because of limitations of space. Among these are (*a*) the problem of values in any definitive motivation theory, (*b*) the relation between appetites, desires, needs and what is "good" for the organism, (*c*) the etiology of the basic needs and their possible derivation in early childhood, (*d*) redefinition of motivational concepts, *i.e.*, drive, desire, wish, need, goal, (*e*) implication of our theory for hedonistic theory, (*f*) the nature of the uncompleted act, of success and failure, and of aspiration-level, (*g*) the role of association, habit and conditioning, (*h*) relation to the theory of inter-personal relations, (*i*) implications for psychotherapy, (*j*) implication for theory of society, (*k*) the theory of selfishness, (*l*) the relation between needs and cultural patterns, (*m*) the relation between this theory and Allport's theory of functional autonomy. These as well as certain other less important questions must be considered as motivation theory attempts to become definitive.

REFERENCES

1. Adler, A.: *Social interest.* London: Faber & Faber, 1938.
2. Cannon, W. B.: *Wisdom of the body.* New York: Norton, 1932.
3. Freud, A.: *The ego and the mechanisms of defense.* London: Hogarth, 1937.
4. Freud, S.: *New introductory lectures on psychoanalysis.* New York: Norton, 1933.
5. Fromm, E.: *Escape from freedom.* New York: Farrar and Rinehart, 1941.
6. Goldstein, K.: *The organism.* New York: American Book Co., 1939.
7. Horney, K.: *The neurotic personality of our time.* New York: Norton, 1937.
8. Kardiner, A.: *The traumatic neuroses of war.* New York: Hoeber, 1941.
9. Levy, D.M.: Primary affect hunger. *Amer. J. Psychiat.*, 1937, **94**, 643-652.
10. Maslow, A. H.: Conflict, frustration, and the theory of threat. *J. abnorm. (soc.) Psychol.*, 1943, **38**, 81—86.
11. _____: Dominance, personality and social behavior in women. *J. soc. Psychol.*, 1939, **10**, 3—39.
12. _____: The dynamics of psychological security-insecurity. *Character & Pers.*, 1942, **10**, 331—344.
13. _____: A preface to motivation theory. *Psychosomatic Med.*, 1943, **5**, 85—92.
14. _____, & Mittelmann, B.: *Principles of abnormal psychology.* New York: Harper & Bros., 1941.
15. Murray, H. A.: *et al.*: *Explorations in personality.* New York: Oxford University Press, 1938.

16. Plant, J.: *Personality and the cultural pattern.* New York: Commonwealth Fund, 1937.

17. Shirley, M.: Children's adjustments to a strange situation. *J. abnorm. (soc.) Psychol.*, 1942, **37**, 201—217.

18. Tolman, E. C.: *Purposive behavior in animals and men.* New York: Century, 1932.

19. Wertheimer, M.: Unpublished lectures at the New School for Social Research.

20. Young, P. T.: *Motivation of behavior.* New York: John Wiley & Sons, 1936.

21. _____: The experimental analysis of appetite. *Psychol. Bull.*, 1941, **38**, 129—164.

Chapter 7

Adult Life Stages: Growth Toward Self-Tolerance

Roger Gould

The evolution of a personality continues through the fifth decade of life. A person does not possess the full range of his uniqueness after merely passing through adolescence, which is the last stage of mental development that many psychologists officially recognize. The process of formation continues through stages of life that we are just beginning to recognize. I began the research reported here to take a new look at the complex process of change in adulthood.

Although a 20-year-old may feel fully formed and mentally well-equipped to cope with life, that same person at 40 will ask how he managed to get through the last 20 years.

Many a man in his 40s wishes he had not been so blinded by his ambition in his 20s. His need to prove himself deprived him of irreplaceable experiences with his wife and children. "If I had only known then what I know now about what is important in living. It takes such a long time to find out what it is all about."

Many a woman in her 40s wonders why she was so foolish in her 20s. She lived up to the rules of householding and child rearing that were in vogue then, but sees them as unimportant now. "I was young then. I did what the doctor told me. I didn't pick the baby up when he was crying even though I knew I should. If only I had followed my own judgment."

Throughout the years of adulthood, there is an ever-increasing need to win permission from oneself to continue developing, through a process I will touch on later in this article. The direction of change is toward becoming more tolerant of oneself, and more appreciative of the complexity of both the surrounding world and of the mental milieu but there are many things that can block, slow down, or divert that process.

Each role in life can lead to two opposite results in the change process. A role can be an opportunity to come to a more comprehensive understanding of oneself in action or a role can become a simplified definition of the self that does not do justice to the whole complex human being. In that sense, a role that may be vitalizing at one period of life can become justifying at another.

We are many years away from having the experience and the studies necessary for an in-depth understanding of the adult period comparable to our current understanding of childhood and adolescence, and my formulations at this point are at best tentative. A number of other researchers are looking at various aspects of adult growth, and all of these studies are adding to our previously impoverished fund of knowledge about the subject.

ESCAPE FROM DOMINANCE

My colleagues and I began our search for adult life phases by observing and recording patients in group therapy at the UCLA psychiatric outpatient clinic. There were seven age-graded groups, with ranges of 16 to 18, 18 to 22, 22 to 28, 29 to 34, 35 to 43 and 50 and over. Our descriptions were not psychologically elegant. We sought a level of psychological description that would be intelligible to a layman. Most of the observations were both consistent among observers and congruent with common sense, which encouraged us.

We found, for example, that the youngest age group was at a period when escape from parental dominance was the predominant theme of their discussions. This concealed the feelings of dependence and anxiety that resulted from preparing to leave the sanctuary of the family. The future was both distant and unknown to these people. The next age group, those between 18 and 22 years, substituted friends for family, and thus continued to grow independent of their family.

The 22- to 28-year-olds definitely felt that they were the now generation. Now was the time to live, and now was the time to build for the future, both professionally and personally. These people concentrate their energies and will power on becoming competent in the real world, and as they develop self-reliance they make less use of their friends as a substitute for the family.

This assurance about what to do wavered somewhat among the 29- to 34-year-olds, who often were questioning what they were doing and why they were doing it. As they became more self-reflective, this group found deeper strivings that had been put aside during their 20s when building a workable life structure had been the most important task.

The continuing expansion of the personality and life structure continued in a leisurely fashion in the early 30s, but changed to quiet urgency in the 35-to-43 set. Time, once shrugged off as infinite, was now visibly finite and the view was often worrisome.

People between the ages of 43 and 50 had come to terms with time, and with themselves as stable personalities. What is done is done; the die is cast. Children previously cherished as extensions of oneself are now to be respected as individuals as they become young adults. The circle closes, as the adult raises a child who again becomes an adult.

DEATH: A NEW PRESENCE

By 50, there is a mellowing of feelings and relationships. Children are a satisfaction, and parents are no longer the cause of one's personality problems. People of this age seemed to focus on what they have accomplished in half a century, and they were unrushed by the sense of urgency that accompanied the achieving 30s. At the same time, they were more eager to have "human" experiences, such as sharing the joys, sorrows, confusions and triumphs of everyday life rather than searching for the glamor, the glitter, the power or the abstract. Precious moments of contact and deep feeling define the value of being in touch. Death becomes a new presence for this age group.

With these general descriptions in mind, I devised a questionnaire to find the more exact periods during which people underwent a transition, and the nature of the things that concerned them the most. The original age categories were somewhat arbitrary, and the original subjects were those receiving psychiatric care. I wanted to see what age groupings would be distinguishable in the responses to the questionnaire, and whether the generalized sentiments found among the patients would be sustained by specific findings on a small sample of the nonpatient population.

I asked eight medical students to listen to tape recordings of the original patient discussions, and to list the statements about personal feelings that they felt stood out. I then grouped these statements into eight sections, covering relationships to parents, friends, children and spouses, and feelings about their own personality, job, time, and sexual behavior.

Each section had 16 questions. People ranked the questions from most to least applicable to their lives. There were no right or wrong answers, only changes in the importance of particular statements to people of various ages. Questions rose and fell in rank like the tide on a beach, providing a sensitive measure of the times of transition—and the tribulations.

The 524 white, middle-class people who filled out questionnaires had seven distinguishable phases: 16 to 17, 18 to 21, 22 to 28, 29 to 36, 37 to 43, 44 to 50 and 51 to 60. There were approximately 20 people (divided equally by sex) for each year between 16 and 33, and 20 for each three years between 33 and 60, with women disproportionately represented over age 45.

For most questions, the rankings stabilized between the ages of 22 and 29, and remained steady throughout life. Certain questions, however, brought distinctly different responses from adjacent age groups, and it was these questions that defined the phases of adult life.

The responses of the 16- and 17-year-olds were almost identical to the stable patterns of those 22 to 29. The young people are still a part of their families, and they think of themselves more as family members than as individuals. In contrast, the 18- to 22-year-olds responded in a pattern quite distinguishable from that of the age set on either side of them.

As other studies previously showed, people in this age group have a unique psychology and subculture. They are more open to new ideas about the world, and are less repressive. When they get back to the mainstream of adult life in the 20s, they give the same pattern of popular responses that characterize the remainder of the population.

THE SPRING TO THE 40s.

The late 20s are an interesting and active time. Marriage absorbs and reflects many of the stresses and strains, and the statement, "I wish my mate would accept me for what I am as a person" takes a sharp upward excursion between the ages of 28 and 32, while there is decreasing agreement that "For me, marriage has been a good thing." Children, on the other hand, become increasingly important during this time, displacing parents in priority as the person's focus shifts from the generation behind to the one ahead.

There is a clear focus on the family in the 30s. An active social life seems less important, while feelings about one's mate and offspring increase in significance. The 30s are a period of very active psychological change, a gathering of mental muscles with which to spring into the 40s. After age 29, there is a decline in the feeling that "I would be quite content to remain as old as I am now," a harbinger of the feeling in the early 30s that life looks a bit more complex and difficult than it did back in the roaring 20s.

In the early 30s, there is suddenly a feeling that "I don't make enough money to do what I want." Although this statement is undoubtedly true for almost everyone, the significance here is signaled by a sharp increase in the relative importance of this feeling to those in their early 30s. There is also an increasing tendency to feel that parents are the cause of many unsolved, stubborn personality problems that are being faced at this age.

The 40s seem to begin in the late 30s, and I distinguish a series of shared sentiments spanning the ages 37 to 43. In this age period, personal comfort decreases, and marital comfort remains at a low level. Between 40 and 43, there are several temporary departures from previous levels on statements dealing with personal comfort, suggesting that the 40s are an unstable and uncomfortable time. Later in the 40s both friends and loved ones become increasingly important. Children continue to be very important, and there is a sharp rise in regrets for "my mistakes in raising my children."

Money, so bothersome because of its insufficiency in the early 30s, becomes less important, and there is an accompanying feeling that it is "Too late to make any major change in my career." Coupled to the first downward shift in the feeling that "There's still plenty of time to do most of the things I want to do," these responses show a 40s phase of reconciliation of what is with what might have been.

The sharp sense that "My personality is pretty well set" in the 41- to 43-year-old group establishes a dramatic beginning to the 44 to 50 period. In the span from 44 to 50, life settles down. With a slight sigh, there is an acceptance of the new ordering of things. Life is even. Not even better, not even worse, but simply even up.

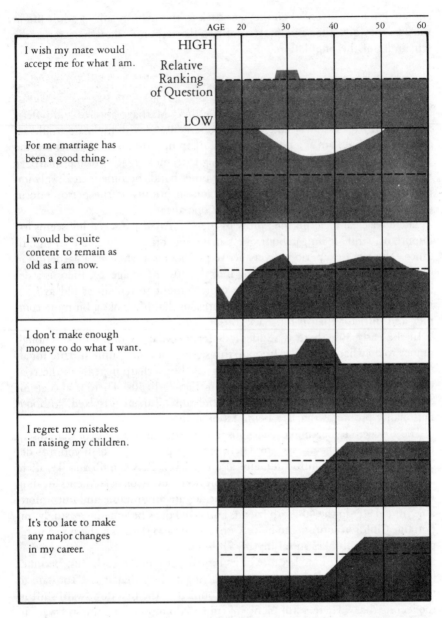

Stability fraught with concern marks the 50s, and the concern is largely about time. With one's allotment of life more than half used up, people respond with increasing pessimism to the statement that "There's still plenty of time to do most of the things I want to do," and with increasing agreement that "I try to be satisfied with what I have and not to think so much about the things I probably won't be able to get." Concerns about health rise, and there is increasing agreement that "I can't do things as well as I used to do."

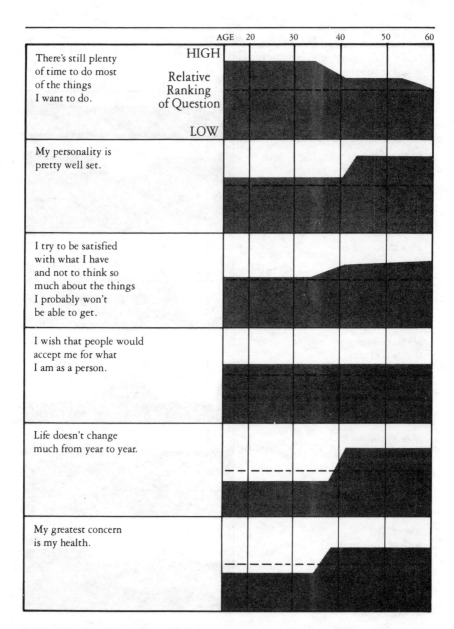

		AGE	20	30	40	50	60
There's still plenty of time to do most of the things I want to do.	HIGH Relative Ranking of Question LOW						
My personality is pretty well set.							
I try to be satisfied with what I have and not to think so much about the things I probably won't be able to get.							
I wish that people would accept me for what I am as a person.							
Life doesn't change much from year to year.							
My greatest concern is my health.							

THE ADULT BUTTERFLY

It is important to realize that the above descriptions are generalizations, reflecting the average of considerable personal variation. While I believe the sequence to be true for the majority of people, the precise ages at which changes occur are a product of an individual's total personality, lifestyle and subculture. How these changes are expressed and dealt with varies considerably from person

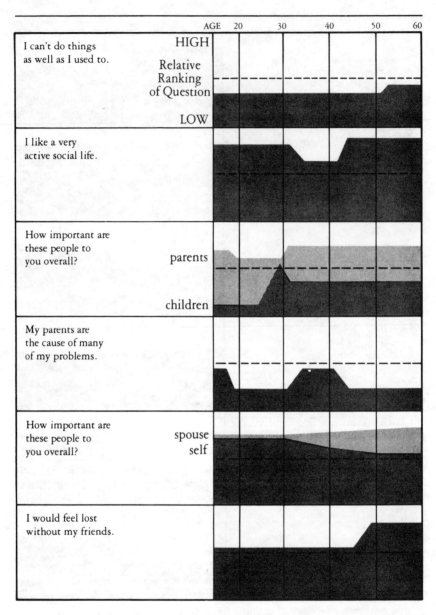

to person; it's what you face, not how you face it, that is the common denominator.

The prevailing concepts of adulthood have obscured not only what is being faced, but also the fact that an adult needs to engage in any kind of continuing growth process at all. Like a butterfly, an adult is supposed to emerge fully formed and on cue, after a succession of developmental stages in childhood. Equipped with all the accouterments, such as wisdom and rationality, the adult supposedly remains quiescent for another half century or so. While children change, adults only age. My research demonstrates a need to overhaul our current view of adulthood, and to recognize that there is a developmental sequence in the early and middle-adult years.

Many researchers have previously pointed out isolated times of change in adult life, such as parenthood or the mid-life crisis. While helpful, none of these studies identifies the progression of phases that might link such changes together.

Yet I feel that there is such a progression. Childhood delivers most people into adulthood with a view of adults that few could ever live up to. A child's idealized image of an adult can become the adult's painful measure of himself. Without an active, thoughtful confrontation of this image, the impressions of childhood will prevail. An adult who doesn't undertake this thinking and confrontation lives out his or her life controlled by the impossible attempt to satisfy the magical expectations of a child's world.

THOUGHTFUL CONFRONTATION

The process of change means coming to new beliefs about oneself and the world. Habitually unorganized beliefs are more felt than thought, yet these beliefs must be thought about before they can be modified by experiences.

Many people hold themselves accountable for being perfect even when they have decided that the limiting conditions of a particular situation made the "perfect" act inappropriate, unwise, unnecessary or impossible. On one hand they believe that the decision that shaped their action was correct, but on the other hand they continue to feel (and on some level believe) that something is wrong with them for not having acted at some arbitrary level of perfection.

The belief that is felt—I should have done the impossible— is often not raised to a high enough level of consciousness to be thought about. The incomplete and inexact form of the thought is usually substituted, "Somehow I should have been able to do it better" and is left dangling, unexamined, and therefore unmodified.

The proper next step in a thoughtful confrontation would be, "I have always felt I should do things perfectly regardless of the circumstances; but this time *I decided* to do things differently for this and this reason." In that statement the conflict between the past and present beliefs are joined and resolution becomes possible between two *operative* and contending beliefs of the self. Neither of these operative beliefs represents mere intellectualized conclusions that are also called beliefs. They are valid and valuable parts of the self that have to be reconciled before a new value can be created that is reflective of the adult experience.

The process of confrontation involves thinking honestly about what one really feels. Modern psychologies have not been of much help in delineating the persistently obscure relationship between feelings and thinking. There has been a tendency to see feeling and thinking as two unconnected realms, yet my observations as a psychoanalyst are that thinking can and does modify feelings. I believe that it is through the constant examination and reformulation of beliefs embedded in feelings that people substitute their own conception of adulthood for their childhood legacy.

This process of thinking through is a cumulative one, and it should really come as no surprise that there are certain similarities in what people experience, and when they experience it. The passing of time sets the stage for several interacting processes that combine to produce the adult life phases I suggest. In addition to substituting an alternate reality for the childhood view, increasing age also brings changes in biological functioning, changes in the ages of one's parents and children, and changes in the cultural expectations about what a person should be doing.

My colleagues and I found that, in addition to the individualized process of changing childhood feelings about adulthood, there were enough experiences common to all adults to make it possible to find similarities in the way these people felt at different ages.

While children mark the passing years by their changing bodies, adults change their minds. Passing years and passing events slowly accumulate, like a viscous wave, eventually releasing their energy and assuming new forms in altered relationships with both time and people. By recognizing the patterns, we may gain some control over the forces by smoothing the transitions and muting the peaks and valleys of adult life phases.

Chapter 8

Motivation versus Hygiene

Frederick Herzberg
Bernard Mausner
Barbara Bloch Snyderman

Let us summarize briefly our answer to the question, "What do people want from their jobs?" When our respondents reported feeling happy with their jobs, they most frequently described factors related to their tasks, to events that indicated to them that they were successful in the performance of their work, and to the possibility of professional growth. Conversely, when feelings of unhappiness were reported, they were not associated with the job itself but with conditions that *surround* the doing of the job. These events suggest to the individual that the context in which he performs his work is unfair or disorganized and as such represents to him an unhealthy psychological work environment. Factors involved in these situations we call factors of *hygiene*, for they act in a manner analogous to the principles of medical hygiene. Hygiene operates to remove health hazards from the environment of man. It is not a curative; it is, rather, a preventive. Modern garbage disposal, water purification, and air-pollution control do not cure diseases, but without them we should have many more diseases. Similarly, when there are deleterious factors in the context of the job, they serve to bring about poor job attitudes. Improvement in these factors of hygiene will serve to remove the impediments to positive job attitudes. Among the factors of hygiene we have included supervision, interpersonal relations, physical working conditions, salary, company policies and administrative practices, benefits, and job security. When these factors deteriorate to a level below that which the employee considers acceptable, then job dissatisfaction ensues. However, the reverse does not hold true. When the job context can be characterized as optimal, we will not get dissatisfaction, but neither will we get much in the way of positive attitudes.

The factors that lead to positive job attitudes do so because they satisfy the individual's need for self-actualization in his work. The concept of

From *The Motivation to Work,* John Wiley & Sons, Inc., New York, ©1959, chapter 12, pp. 113-119. Reprinted by permission of the publisher.

self-actualization, or self-realization, as a man's ultimate goal has been focal to the thought of many personality theorists. For such men as Jung, Adler, Sullivan, Rogers, and Goldstein the supreme goal of man is to fulfill himself as a creative, unique individual according to his own innate potentialities and within the limits of reality. When he is deflected from this goal he becomes, as Jung says, "a crippled animal."

Man tends to actualize himself in every area of his life, and his job is one of the most important areas. The conditions that surround the doing of the job cannot give him this basic satisfaction; they do not have this potentiality. It is only from the performance of a task that the individual can get the rewards that will reinforce his aspirations. It is clear that although the factors relating to the doing of the job and the factors defining the job context serve as goals for the employee, the nature of the motivating qualities of the two kinds of factors is essentially different. Factors in the job context meet the needs of the individual for avoiding unpleasant situations. In contrast to this motivation by meeting avoidance needs, the job factors reward the needs of the individual to reach his aspirations. These effects on the individual can be conceptualized as an actuating approach rather than avoidance behavior. Since it is in the approach sense that the term motivation is most commonly used, we designate the job factors as the "motivators," as opposed to the extra-job factors, which we have labeled the factors of hygiene. It should be understood that both kinds of factors meet the needs of the employee; but it is primarily the "motivators" that serve to bring about the kind of job satisfaction and, as we saw in the section dealing with the effects of job attitudes, the kind of improvement in performance that industry is seeking from its work force.

We can now say something systematic about what people want from their jobs. For the kind of population that we sampled, and probably for many other populations as well, the wants of employees divide into two groups. One group revolves around the need to develop in one's occupation as a source of personal growth. The second group operates as an essential base to the first and is associated with fair treatment in compensation, supervision, working conditions, and administrative practices. The fulfillment of the needs of the second group does not motivate the individual to high levels of job satisfaction and . . . to extra performance on the job. All we can expect from satisfying the needs for hygiene is the prevention of dissatisfaction and poor job performance.

In the light of this distinction, we can account for much of the lack of success that industry has had in its attempts to motivate employees. Let us examine two of the more ubiquitous avenues through which industry has hoped to gain highly motivated employees: human-relations training for supervisors and wage-incentive systems.

As part of this era of human relations, supervisory training directed toward improving the interpersonal relationships between superior and subordinate has been widely incorporated into industrial-relations programs. These programs have been initiated with expectations of bringing about positive job attitudes and, hopefully, increased performance on the job. When we examine the results of our study, we find interpersonal relationships appearing in an exceedingly small number of the high sequences; in only 15 per cent of the low sequences are poor interpersonal relationships with the superior reported. The negligible role which interpersonal relationships play in our data tallies poorly with the assumption basic to most human-relations training programs that the way in which a supervisor gets along with his people is the single most important determinant of morale. Supervisory training in human relations is probably essential to the maintenance of good hygiene at work. This is particularly true for the many jobs, both at rank-and-file and managerial levels, in which modern industry offers little chance for the operation of the motivators. These jobs are atomized, cut and dried, monotonous. They offer little chance for responsibility and achievement and thus little opportunity for self-actualization. It is here that hygiene is exceptionally important. The fewer the opportunities for the "motivators" to appear, the greater must be the hygiene offered in order to make the work tolerable. A man who finds his job challenging, exciting, and satisfying will perhaps tolerate a difficult supervisor. But to expect such programs to pay dividends beyond the effects that hygiene provides is going contrary to the nature of job motivation. In terms of the approach-avoidance concept, the advocates of human relations have suggested that by rewarding the avoidance needs of the individual you will achieve the desired approach behavior. But a more creative design will not emerge from an engineer as a result of fair supervisory treatment. To achieve the more creative design, one or more of the motivators must be present, a task that is interesting to the engineer, a task in which he can exercise responsibility and independence, a task that allows for some concrete achievement. The motivators fit the need for creativity, the hygiene factors satisfy the need for fair treatment, and it is thus that the appropriate incentive must be present to achieve the desired job attitude and job performance.

The failure to get positive returns in both job attitudes and job performance from rewarding the avoidance needs of the individual is most clearly seen in the use of monetary incentives. We have listed salary among the factors of hygiene, and as such it meets two kinds of avoidance needs of the employee. First is the avoidance of the economic deprivation that is felt when actual income is insufficient. Second, and generally of more significance in the times and for the kind of people covered by our study, is the need to avoid feelings of being treated unfairly. Salary and wages are very frequently at the top of the list of factors describing answers to the question, "What don't you like about your job?" in morale surveys. They are at the middle of the list of answers to the question, "What do you want from your job?" We have explained this difference in emphasis by our distinction between factors that lead to job satisfaction and the factors that contribute to job dissatisfaction. Asking people what is important to them in their jobs will bring responses that we have classified as "motivators." The atmosphere of the usual morale survey encourages people to emphasize sources of dissatisfaction.

Where morale surveys have differentiated between dissatisfaction with amount of salary as opposed to the equity of salary, the latter looms as the more important source of dissatisfaction. In two consecutive morale surveys by the senior author in which the employees were requested to illustrate their dissatisfaction or satisfaction with the various items on the morale questionnaire with critical incidents, the comments on the equity of salary greatly outnumbered the comments on the absolute amount of salary. All 1382 employees surveyed were at the supervisory level (21).

How then can we explain the success of the many employee motivational schemes that seem to rely directly on the use of wage incentives and bonuses? Reports on the Lincoln Electric Company of Cleveland, Ohio (37), and the George A. Hormel meat-packing plant at Austin, Minnesota (7), suggest good examples of the efficacy of money incentives for increasing production, job satisfaction, and company loyalty. But let us examine for a moment the nature of these programs and the nature of their success in the light of the findings presented here.

First, there are many other ingredients to these plans which are generally given less attention than they merit, ingredients that combine a large proportion of the factors that we have found to be motivators. The formation of Lincoln's Advisory Board and Hormel's Business Improvement Committee both resulted from attempts to increase job content and job responsibility by giving workers knowledge of, and responsibility for, operations and improvements. Both operate on the theory that the "boss" cannot know everything about all the work processes, that the workers are experts in their fields, and that their knowledge is of great value. Lincoln Electric, which is not unionized, has the additional advantage of being able to advance workers on the basis of merit, not seniority. James E. Lincoln, president of the company, says that "money is of relatively small importance. Beyond enough for our real needs, money itself is valued less for what it will buy than as an evidence of successful skill in achievement (37)." Money thus earned as a direct reward for outstanding individual performance is a reinforcement of the motivators of *recognition* and *achievement*. It is not hygiene as is the money given in across-the-board wage increases.

The Scanlon plan is a system for involving employees of a company in the improvement of production by the distribution of savings in labor costs to all of the personnel of a participating company. This aspect of participation and of increased responsibility is the real secret of whatever success the Scanlon plan and its imitators have achieved. Lincoln Electric is implementing man's natural striving for self-realization. No man wants to be just a cog in a wheel. Lincoln says, "The most insistent incentive is the development of self-respect and the respect of others. Earnings that are the reward for outstanding performance, progress, and responsibility are signs that he is a man among men. The worker must feel that he is part of a worthwhile project and that the project succeeded because his ability was needed in it. Money alone will not do the job."

When incentive systems do not permit any of the motivators to operate, then any increase in performance or in apparent job satisfaction is misleading. For in these instances the removal of a decrement in performance by the elimination of job dissatisfaction is often mistakenly referred to as a positive gain in performance. That voluntary restriction of output is practiced on an enormous scale is common knowledge in industry (26, 27, 58). The existence of a standard of "a fair day's work" has been well documented in systematic studies by industrial psychologists and sociologists as well as industrial engineers. It is likely that poor hygiene will depress performance below the level of "the fair day's work." Correction of this poor hygiene, or the application of monetary incentives not related to motivators, may return performance to the norm. The improvement produced under these circumstances is actually far less than one could obtain were motivators to be introduced.

Are good job attitudes and company loyalty engendered by these incentive plans? The surface answer often seems to be yes. Employees in such companies will report that they like working for their companies, but the "liking" seems to be little more than the absence of disliking, their satisfaction little more than the absence of dissatisfaction. Blum reports on the Hormel packinghouse workers in this regard:

> If I had to summarize workers' feelings about the company in one sentence, I would repeat the words of a worker: "If a man is going to work for anybody else, it's hard to beat Hormel." It is the single most often heard expression in any conversation about the company. I have never heard a worker express an unconditional acceptance of the company as an organization to work for (7).

Are they really saying they like their work? Or are they merely saying that they have found a place to work in which life is not unbearable?

What is the evidence? According to Blum's report, shop talk is deafening by its absence when the work day is over. There seems to be a deliberate effort on the part of the employees to repress any mention of their jobs away from the plant. Contrast this with the unceasing shop talk reported by Walker in his study of steel workers at the National Tube Company of Ellwood City, Pennsylvania (56). His description of their jobs emphasizes the large number of motivators present. They are not running away from their work at the shift bell. They continue to live their jobs at home. The employees of Hormel seem to be psychologically running away from their jobs. Their extra effort, while it increases production, albeit probably not to the level of which they are capable, is not indicative of positive job attitudes. Rather it provides the means for escape from a job toward which their attitudes are little better than neutral. The sooner they finish the job, the sooner they can get away from it; the more money they can earn, the more effective their escape in pleasant living off the job. It is doubtful that the true production potential of these workers is being tapped; it is undeniable that the incentive system, along with other hygienic factors, serves to make their jobs tolerable.

The definition of *hygiene* and *motivation* and the relationship of these complexes of factors to the behavior of men at work has many implications for industrial practice. In the next section we try to explore these implications after setting the findings of our study in an historical background.

REFERENCES

7. Blum, F.A.: *Toward a Democratic Work Process.* New York: Harper, 1953.

21. Herzberg, F.: "An Analysis of Morale Survey Comments." *Personnel Psychol.,* 1954, 7 (2), pp. 267-275.

26. Horsfall, A.B., and C.M. Arensberg: "Teamwork and Productivity in a Shoe Factory." *Hum. Organization,* 1949, 8, pp. 13-25.

27. Hughes, E.C.: "The Knitting of Racial Groups in Industry." *American Sociol. Review,* 1946, 11, pp. 512-519.

37. Lincoln, J.F.: *Lincoln's Incentive System.* New York: McGraw-Hill, 1946.

56. Walker, C.R.: *Steeltown.* New York: Harper, 1950.

58. Whyte, W.F.: *Money and Motivation.* New York: Harper, 1955.

Chapter 9

A Basic Incongruency between the Needs of a Mature Personality and the Requirements of Formal Organization

Chris Argyris

Bringing together the evidence regarding the impact of the formal organizational principles upon the individual, it is concluded that there are some basic incongruencies between the growth trends of a healthy personality and the requirements of the formal organization. If the principles of formal organization are used as ideally defined, employees will tend to work in an environment where (1) they are provided minimal control over their workaday world, (2) they are expected to be passive, dependent, and subordinate, (3) they are expected to have a short time perspective, (4) they are induced to perfect and value the frequent use of a few skin-surface shallow abilities and, (5) they are expected to produce under conditions leading to psychological failure.

All these characteristics are incongruent to the ones *healthy* human beings are postulated to desire. . . . They are much more congruent with the needs of infants in our culture. In effect, therefore, organizations are willing to pay high wages and provide adequate seniority if mature adults will, for eight hours a day, behave in a less than mature manner! *If the analysis is correct, this inevitable incongruency increases as* (1) *the employees are of increasing maturity,* (2) *as the formal structure* (based upon the above principles) *is made more clear-cut and logically tight for maximum formal organizational effectiveness,* (3) *as one goes down the line of command, and* (4) *as the jobs become more and more mechanized* (i.e., take on assembly line characteristics).

As in the case of the personality developmental trends, this picture of formal organization is also a model. Clearly, no company actually uses the formal principles of organization exactly as stated by their creators. There is ample evidence to suggest that they are being modified constantly in actual situations. However, those who expound these principles would probably be willing to defend their position that this is the reason that human relations problems exist; the principles are not followed as they should be.

In the proposed models of the personality and the formal organization, we are assuming the extreme of each in order that the analysis and its results can be highlighted. Speaking in terms of extremes helps us to make the position sharper. In doing this, no assumption is made that all situations in real life are extreme (i.e., that the individuals will always want to be more mature and that the formal organization will always tend to make people more dependent and passive all the time). In fact, much evidence is presented in subsequent chapters to support contrary tendencies.

The model ought to be useful, however, to plot the degree to which each component tends toward extremes and then to predict the problems that will arise. . . .

It is not difficult to see why some students of organization suggest that immature and even mentally retarded individuals would probably make excellent employees. There is little documented experience to support such a hypothesis. One reason for this lack of information is probably the "touchiness" of the subject. Examples of what might be obtained if a systematic study is made may be found in a recent work by Brennan.[1] He cites the Utica Knitting Mill, which made arrangements during 1917 with the Rome Institution for Mentally Defective Girls to employ 24 girls whose mental ages ranged from six to ten years. The girls were such excellent workers that their employment continued after the war emergency ended. In fact the company added forty additional mentally defective girls in another of their plants. The managers praised the subnormal girls highly.

> In several important reports, they said that "when business conditions required a reduction of the working staff," the hostel girls were never "laid off" in disproportion to the normal girls; that they were more punctual, more regular in their habits, and did not indulge in as much "gossip and levity." They received the same rate of pay, and they had been employed successfully at almost every process carried out in the workshops.

In another experiment, the Works Manager of the Radio Corporation Ltd. reported that of five young morons:

> The three girls compared very favourably with the normal class of employee in that age group. The boy employed in the store performed his work with satisfaction. . . . Although there was some doubt about the fifth child, it was felt that getting the most out of him was just a matter of right placement.

In each of the five cases, the morons were quiet, respectful, well-behaved, and obedient. The Works Manager was especially impressed by their truthfulness, and lack of deceit or suppression of the facts. A year later, the same Works Manager was still able to advise that,

In every case, the girls proved to be exceptionally well-behaved, particularly obedient, and strictly honest and trustworthy. They carried out work required of them to such a degree of efficiency that *we were surprised they were classed as subnormals for their age*.[2] Their attendance was good, and their behavior was, if anything, certainly better than any other employee of the same age.

Let us now turn to the literature to see if there are illustrations of the points made regarding the dependence and subordination created by the nature of formal organization and its impact upon the individuals. Unfortunately, there are not many available studies that focus on the impact of the formal organization on the individuals (holding the leadership variable "constant").

Probably the best available evidence of the impact of formal organization based upon unity of command and task specialization is the experimental work on communication by Bavelas[3] and Leavitt,[4] which is confirmed by Heise and Miller[5] and Shaw and Rothchild.[6] They focus on the question—can the structure of certain patterns of communication result in significantly better performance than others? Their results clearly imply that in a structure where one individual has a "central" position in the communications network and thereby is able to control communications, as would an executive in a plant, he will probably be chosen the leader and have the best morale in the group. The individuals who depend upon him (e.g., supervisors) will tend to have lower morale, feel more frustrated, confused, and irritated at others along the network. Guetzkow and Simon confirm these results, and through the use of more refined experimental procedure they show strong evidence to support the hypothesis that of all communications structures tried, the "wheel"[7] created initially the *least* organizational problem for the group, thereby permitting the group to organize itself most quickly in order to solve a particular problem.[8]

Further indirect evidence is provided by Arensberg,[9] who "revisited" the famous Hawthorne Studies. He noted that many of the results reported about the relay assembly experiments occurred *after* the girls were placed in a work situation where they were (1) made "subjects" of an "important" experiment, (2) encouraged to participate in decisions affecting their work, (3) given veto power over their supervisors to the point where, as the girls testify, "we have no boss." Clearly these conditions constitute a sweeping shift in the basic relationship of modern industrial work where the employee is subordinate to people above him.

Bakke's study of the unemployed worker[10] includes much evidence that the workers are clearly aware of the differences in the degree of authority and control manifested by themselves and their boss. His evidence suggests that independently of the personality of the boss, the workers perceived their boss as someone with power to achieve his goals; a power which they did not believe they had. For example, one worker defines the boss as someone who, "When he decides to do something, he can carry it through." Another states, "Some birds have got enough (authority) and stand high enough so that what they say goes . . . and anybody who can do that won't be found very often to be what you might call a worker.''[11]

Blau,[12] in a study of the departmental structure in a federal enforcement agency, reports that even when deliberate attempts were made to minimize the social distance between leaders and subordinates and where leaders tried to use a ''democratic'' approach, the supervisors frequently but inadvertently lapsed into behavior more appropriate to the formal authoritarian relationships with the subordinates. Thus, the impact of the formal structure influences leadership behavior toward being more ''autocratic'' even when there exist informal norms emphasizing a more egalitarian climate and when the leaders consciously try to be more ''democratic.''

Not only do the supervisors ''slip'' into more directive leadership, but the subordinates ''slip'' into dependent, submissive roles even if the supervisor requests their increased participation. As one subordinate states, ''Lots of times, I've differed with the supervisor, but I didn't say anything. I just said, 'Yes,' with a smile, *because he gives the efficiency rating.*'' Blau continues:

> Bureaucratic authority is *not* based on personal devotion to the supervisor or on respect for him as a person but on an adaptation necessitated by his rating power. The *advancement chances of officials and even their chances to keep their civil service jobs depend on the rating they periodically receive from their superior.* . . . The group's insistence that the supervisor discharge his duty of issuing directives—''That's what he gets paid for''—serves to emphasize that their obedience to them does *not* constitute submission to his will but *adherence, on his part as well as theirs, to abstract principles* which they have socially accepted.[13]

In comprehensive reviews of the literature Gibb,[14] Blau[15] and Bierstedt[16] conclude that it is important to differentiate between formal leadership (headship or authority) based upon formal organization and informal leadership (leadership). For example, Gibb states:

> . . . leadership is to be distinguished, by definition, from domination or headship. The principal differentia are these: (i) Domination or headship is maintained through an organized system and not by the spontaneous recognition, by fellow group members, of the individual's contribution to group goals. (ii) The group goal is chosen by the head man in line with his interests and is not internally determined by the group itself. (iii) In the domination or headship relation there is little or no sense of shared feeling or joint action in the pursuit of the given goal. (iv) There is in the dominance relation a wide social gap between the group members and the head, who strives to maintain this social distance as an aid to his coercion of the group. (v) Most basically, these two forms of influence differ with respect to the *source* of the authority which is exercised. The leader's authority is spontaneously accorded him by his fellow group members, the followers. *The authority of*

the head derives from some extra-group power which he has over the members of the group, who cannot meaningfully be called his followers. They accept his domination on pain of punishment, rather than follow. The business executive is an excellent example of a head exercising authority derived from his position in an organization through membership in which the workers, his subordinates, satisfy many strong needs. They obey his commands and accept his domination because this is part of their duty as organization members and to reject him would be to discontinue membership, with all the punishments that would involve.[14]

Carter,[17] in some recent controlled field experiments, points up the importance of the power and status inherent in the formal organizational structure by an interesting study of the behavior of "emergent" vs. "appointed" leaders. He concludes that appointed leaders tend to support their own purposes, defend their proposals from attack, express their own opinions, and argue—all *less* than emergent leaders. Apparently, the data suggests, because the appointed leader feels that he has power and status, he feels less need to defend his position than does an emergent leader.

Fleishman's [18] descriptions of leadership training also point up the degree of dependence and leader-centeredness of a subordinate upon his boss. He reports that subordinates tend to use the same leadership style that their boss tends to use regardless of the training they receive.

Probably no review of the literature would be complete without mentioning the classic work of Max Weber on the study of bureaucracy.[19],[20] It is important to keep in mind that Weber conceived of bureaucracy (formal organization) as "the most efficient form of social organization ever developed."[21] He maintained that bureaucracy was one of the characteristic forms of organization of all modern society, finding wide expression in industry, science, and religion, as well as government.[22] In fact, it may be said that he saw no difference between socialism and capitalism, since the fundamental characteristic of both was (a particular kind of) formal organization. "If Marx said that the workers of the world had nothing to lose but their chains by revolting, Weber contended that they really had nothing to gain."[23] It remained for Merton to try to balance the "rosy" picture that Weber painted about bureaucracy. At the outset of this work, Merton, in clear and consise terms, describes some of the essential conditions of formal organization. Again we note the emphasis made here on the inherent authoritarian power structure of the formal organization which is independent of the leadership pattern of the person holding the power position.

Authority, the power of control which derives from an acknowledged status, inheres in the office and not in the particular person who performs the official role. Official action ordinarily occurs within the framework of pre-existing rules of the organization. The system of prescribed relations between the various offices involves a considerable degree of formality and clearly defined social distance between the occupants of these positions. Formality is manifested by means of a more or less complicated social ritual which symbolizes and supports the "pecking order" of the various offices. Such formality, which is integrated with the distribution of authority within the system, serves to minimize friction by largely restricting (official) contact to modes which are previously defined by the rules of the organization. . .[24]

Charles Walker, Robert Guest, and Arthur Turner have been studying the impact of the assembly line (an example of a highly specialized aspect of organizational structure) and of the management upon the workers. Their findings show the degree and kind of impact of the mass production type of organizational structure upon the employee, independent of the personality of the management. Walker and Guest report that about 90 per cent (of 180) workers dislike their actual job because of its mechanical pacing, repetitiveness, minimum skill requirements, minute subdivision of work, and surface mental attention. Their results show that the degree of dislike for the job increased in proportion to the degree to which the job embodies mass production characteristics[25] and to the degree to which the employees are dependent upon management. These results have been confirmed in another study by the same team.[26]

Turner, in an article based upon the second study mentioned above, expands on the impact of the assembly line. The employees especially dislike the mechanical pacing of the assembly line which (1) decreases their control over their own activities, (2) makes them dependent, subordinate, and passive to a machine process, and (3) leads them to forget quality production and aspire to an acceptable minimum quantity output. Turner[27] points out that the men dislike the necessity to work at a job that requires only a minimum skill, and forces them, through repetitiveness, to continue using only a minimum skill. These findings are understandable since these requirements run counter to the needs of relatively mature human beings. Finally, the characteristics of impersonality and anonymity also inveigh against the needs of "ego integrity" and feelings of self worth.

Indirect evidence comes from two studies of organization reported by the writer. In both organizations the employees' degree of morale with the company increased as the degree of directive leadership decreased. Passive leadership (i.e., leadership that seldom contacts the employees) minimized the pressure from above and permitted the employees to feel more "self-responsible" (i.e., they could be their own boss). Over 91 per cent of the respondents (total group sampled about 300) reported that passive leadership (i.e., "we hardly ever talk with the boss") permits them to be their own boss and thereby reduces the potential pressure from above. However, the same number of employees also reported they still feel pressure from the very way the work and the companies are organized. For example, a bank teller states,

I don't know what I would do if Mr. B. supervised us closely. The pressure would be terrific. As it is, I hardly see him. He leaves me alone and that's fine with me. But don't get me wrong. It isn't that I don't feel I haven't got a boss. I have one. *I know I will always have one, if it's Mr. B or Mr. X.*[28]

Some trade union leaders are aware that the formal organization places the workers in dependent and dissatisfying situations. Many report that the process of management (independent of the personality of the leader) carries with it certain "inevitable" dislikes by the workers, because the workers view management (who represent the formal organization) as the ones who place them in dissatisfying work situations. This may be one reason that many trade union leaders do not aspire to gain political control over the management.

Mr. Green, for example, said, "The line of distinction between the exercise of the rights of labor and of management must be scrupulously observed. The philosophy which some have advanced that labor should join with management in the actual management of the property could not and cannot be accepted."[29] Mr. Murray agrees when he states, "To relieve the boss or the management of proper responsibility for making a success of the enterprise is about the last thing any group of employees would consider workable or even desirable."[30]

The fears implied by these two labor leaders exist as facts in countries like Norway, England, and Holland. The trade union leaders in these countries are partially or indirectly responsible for the economic health of the country (because the party identified with labor has strong political power). It is not uncommon to see trade union leaders "selling" work study, scientific management, and increased productivity to the workers.[31] Many workers feel that their national leaders are closer in outlook with management than with their own members.[32] In short, the American trade union leaders may realize that because of the impact of the nature of formal organization, even if they were perfect administrators, they still would have human problems with the employees.

SUMMARY

On the basis of a logical analysis, it is concluded that the formal organizational principles make demands of relatively healthy individuals that are incongruent with their needs. Frustration, conflict, failure, and short time perspective are predicted as resultants of this basic incongruency.

Empirical evidence is presented to illustrate the rational character of the formal organization and to support the proposition that the basic impact of the formal organizational structure is to make the employees feel dependent, submissive, and passive, and to require them to utilize only a few of their less important abilities.

In the next chapter [of *Personality and Organization*], empirical evidence is amassed to illustrate the existence in the employee of the predicted frustration, conflict, failure, and short time perspective and to show some of the resultants of these factors.

REFERENCES

1. Brennan, Mal: *The Making of a Moron* (New York: Sheed and Ward, 1953), pp. 13-18.

2. Mr. Brennan's emphasis.

3. Bavelas, Alex: "Communication Patterns in Task-Oriented Groups." Chapter X in *The Policy Sciences* (ed.) by D. Lerner and H.L. Lasswell (Palo Alto: Stanford University Press, 1951), pp. 193-202. _____, "A Mathematical Model for Group Structures," *Applied Anthropology,* Vol. VII, 1948, pp. 16-30.

4. Leavitt, H. J.: "Some Effects of Certain Communication Patterns on Group Performance," *Journal of Abnormal Social Psychology,* Vol. 46, 1951, pp. 38-50.

5. Heise, G. C., and Miller, G. A.: "Problem-Solving by Small Groups Using Various Communications Nets," *Journal of Abnormal Social Psychology,* Vol. 46, 1951, pp. 327-335.

6. Shaw, Marvin E., and Rothchild, Gerard H.: "Some Effects of Prolonged Experience in Communication Nets," *Journal of Applied Psychology,* Vol. 40, No. 5, October, 1956, pp. 281-286.

7. A "wheel" structure is similar to the structure that is created by the use of the principles of chain of command and span of control. One individual becomes the "boss" of the structure.

8. However, they also point out that once the other structures "got going," they were as efficient (in terms of time required to achieve the task) as the wheel. Guetzkow, Harold, and Simon, Herbert A.: "The Impact of Certain Communication Nets upon Organization and Performance in Task-Oriented Groups," *Management Science,* Vol. 1, April-July, 1955, pp. 233-250.

9. Arensberg, Conrad M.: "Behavior and Organization: Industrial Studies," (eds.) John H. Rohrer and Musafer Sherif, *Social Psychology at the Crossroads* (New York: Harper, 1951), p. 340.

10. Bakke, E. Wight: *Citizens Without Work, op. cit.,* p. 90.

11. *Ibid.,* p. 91.

12. Blau, Peter M.: *The Dynamics of Bureaucracy* (Chicago: University of Chicago Press, 1955), pp. 167 ff.

13. *Ibid.,* pp. 172-173.

14. Gibb, Cecil A.: "Leadership," in *Handbook of Social Psychology* (ed.), Gardner Lindzey (Reading, Mass.: Addison-Wesley, 1954), pp. 887-920. (Italics mine.)

15. Blau, Peter M.: *Bureaucracy in Modern Society* (New York: Random House, 1956).

16. Bierstedt, Robert: "The Problem of Authority," in Morroe Berger, Theodore Abel, and Charles H. Page (eds.), *Freedom and Control in Modern Society* (New York: Van Nostrand, 1954), pp. 67-81.

17. Carter, Launor: "Leadership and Small Group Behavior," in M. Sherif

and M.O. Wilson (eds.); *Group Relations at the Crossroads* (New York: Harper, 1953), p. 279.

18. Fleishman, Edwin A.: "The Description of Supervisory Behavior," *Journal of Applied Psychology*, Vol. 37, No. 1. Although I was unable to obtain it, E.F. Harris' thesis is also reported to include valuable data. It is entitled, "Measuring Industrial Leadership and Its Implications for Training Supervisors," Ph.D. thesis, Ohio State, 1952. It should be pointed out that Fleishman's study was not limited to the impact of the formal structure. It includes leadership patterns.

19. Weber, Max: *The Theory of Social and Economic Organization*, A.M. Henderson (tr.) and Talcott Parsons (ed.) (New York: Oxford, 1947).

20. For an interesting discussion of Weber's and others' work, see Merton, Robert K., Gray, Ailsa P., Hackey, Barbara, and Selvin, Hanan C.: *Reader in Bureaucracy* (Glencoe, Illinois: The Free Press, 1952).

21. Gouldner, Alvin (ed.): *Studies in Leadership* (New York: Harper, 1950), p. 75.

22. *Ibid.*, p. 57.

23. *Ibid.*, p. 58.

24. Merton, Robert K.: "Bureaucratic Structure and Personality," *Social Forces*, 1940, printed also in *Studies in Leadership, op. cit.*, pp. 67-68.

25. Walker, Charles R., and Guest, Robert H.: *The Man on the Assembly Line* (Cambridge: Harvard University Press, 1952).

26. Personal communication. Publication in progress.

27. Turner, Arthur N.: "Management and the Assembly Line," *Harvard Business Review*, September-October, 1955, pp. 40-48.

28. Argyris, Chris: *Organization of a Bank, op. cit.*, and *Human Relations in a Hospital, op. cit.*

29. *New York Sun*, December, 1954.

30. Lewisohn, Sam: *Human Leadership in Industry* (New York: Harper, 1945).

31. Ruttenberg (one of the originators of the idea of the Guaranteed Annual Wage, while an economist for the CIO Steel Workers and now a plant president) insists that if "pay by the year" becomes effective the employees must take on management responsibilities. *Harper's*, December, 1955, pp. 29-33.

32. Argyris, Chris: *An Analysis of the Human Relations Policies and Practices in England, Norway, Holland, France, Greece, and Germany*, OEEC, Dept. of Management Reports, Paris, France, 1955.

Afterthoughts

The basic definition of management—achieving work through people—carries with it a requirement for knowledge and skills in human motivation—understanding why people work and being able to create the conditions under which they work best. Strictly speaking you cannot motivate another person. You can, however, manage the motivation process by creating an environment and working conditions under which people can pursue their own motives, where motivated behavior is allowed to occur. The ideas presented by Maslow, Gould, Herzberg, and Argyris help to make the task more systematic.

Maslow's "need hierarchy" is most often depicted as a triangle or pyramid as

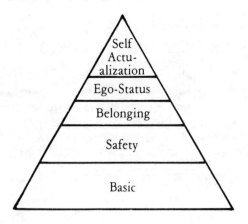

Figure 1.

shown in Figure 1. This is a simple way to visualize the hierarchy and the relationship of one need system to another.

Data collected from over 20,000 employees verify Maslow's original predictions.[1] The data displayed in Figure 2 present a profile of the average strength of each need over the entire research sample.

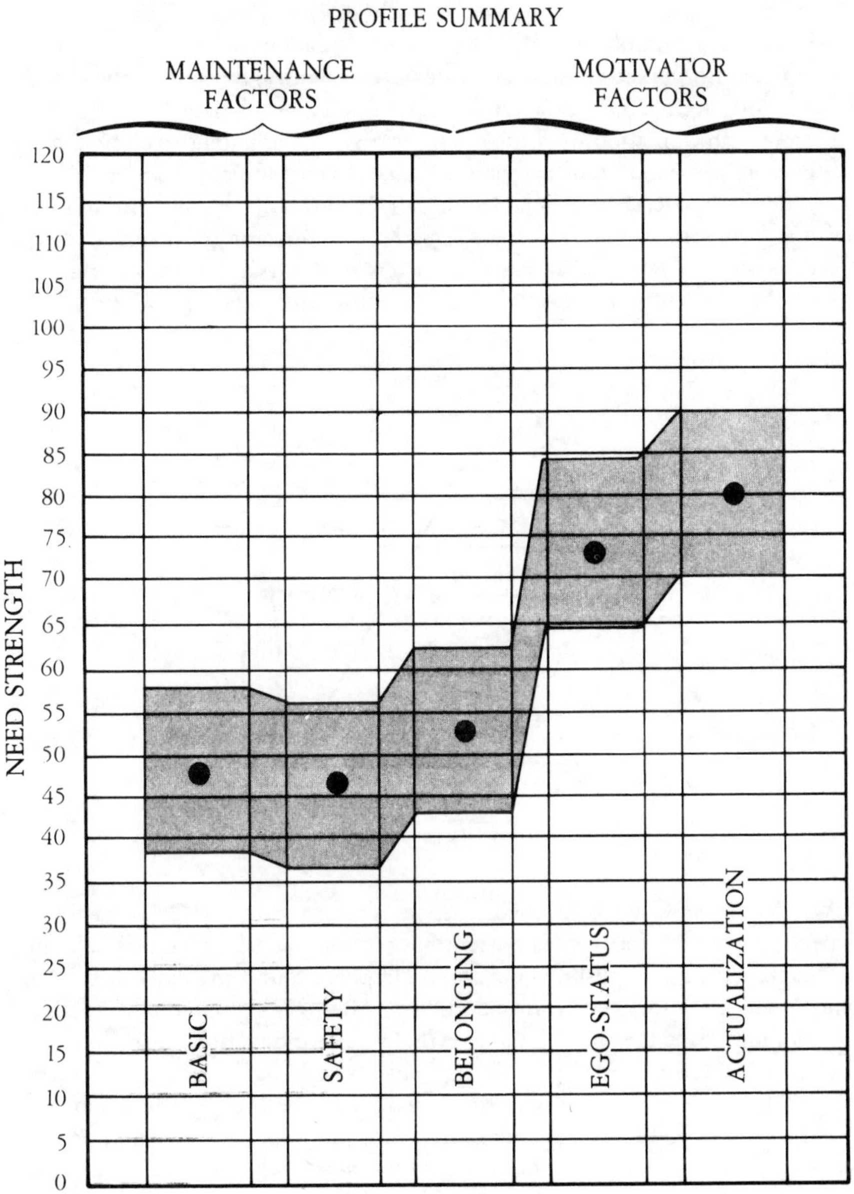

PROFILE SUMMARY

Figure 2.

Several conclusions can be drawn but, for our purposes, it will suffice to say that *needs do exist* as Maslow indicated, they can be measured, and in today's organizations the higher level needs of Belonging, Ego-Status, and Actualization are, in fact, dominant. *The things most people are most concerned about in their work are the needs that most directly affect feelings of self-worth.*

Interestingly, research conducted in such diverse areas as Brazil, Scandinavia[2] and the Republic of China[3] has produced data which indicate that need systems among workers in these areas are nearly identical to those in the United States. Although some managers may attempt to avoid data by the ''we're different'' proclamation, it is becoming increasingly apparent that these need systems are universal despite even cultural and geographic differences.

By depicting Herzberg's model alongside Maslow's, a clear relationship can be seen between the two. Herzberg's model of motivator and hygiene factors overlays on Maslow's model as shown in Figure 3. As it turns out, the two theorists are addressing the same issues but from different angles.

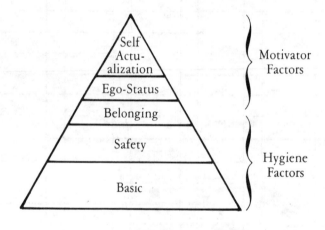

Figure 3.

Whereas Maslow was concerned with the sources of motivated behavior in general, Herzberg focused his attention on those goal objects which are pertinent to the accomplishment of work. Herzberg found that only those goal objects which satisfy needs corresponding to Maslow's Ego-Status, Actualization, and, to some extent, Belonging actually serve motivation on the job. On the other hand, lower level goal objects which satisfy Basic, Safety and superficial Belonging needs have only the potential for easing dissatisfaction, for making work tolerable, and are not sources of work-oriented motivation. *But as Argyris noted, most organizations and those who manage them never raise their sights above these lower level needs.*

With an eye to the need hierarchy, you can classify the related goal objects you make available in your work environment. For example, elementary goal objects such as desks, air conditioning, parking, and reasonable working hours satisfy basic needs; job descriptions, seniority systems, and fringe benefits meet safety needs; company clubs, friendly co-workers, and work groups can be valued goal objects for belonging needs. Beginning with the more significant belonging needs, the goal objects tend to have more psychological impact. Ego needs lead to the pursuit of goal objects such as a special role, praise from respected colleagues, and sharing authority in key organizational matters. Finally, self-actualization needs, the most personal, drive a person to situations or conditions which provide autonomy in decision-making and the time and materials to promote personal growth and development on the job. While classifying the goal objects you offer, keep in mind the implication of Gould's work—the desirability of a particular goal object will vary with the age of the individual.

At this point you might reflect for a moment on *your* approach to motivation. Where do you place the emphasis? What are the needs you emphasize and what messages do you send to your employees? Do they find their work challenging and interesting? Are your employees important individuals that you rely on and do you let them know it—or do you give them the impression they are just cogs in a machine?

Such questions probe, in large measure, your view of the "nature of working man" as described previously by McGregor. Managers with a Theory X view will provide different goal objects than managers holding a Theory Y view. Because of their feelings and attitudes toward their employees, managers with a Theory X orientation will tend to provide only those goal objects that satisfy lower level needs—as if other needs did not exist. The idea of providing goal objects to satisfy higher level needs may seem inappropriate, or a waste of time, or, more probably, may never even occur to them.

Think again, "What message am I sending to my employees by the goal objects I emphasize? What am I telling them about my belief in their potential for growth within our organization? If I structure a work environment containing goal objects related only to the lower level needs, am I not saying, in effect, that I consider my employees to be immature and that growth is improbable? Would not a manager following a Theory Y assumption provide a sufficient amount of goal objects to meet lower level needs but also insure that jobs are designed for sound interpersonal relations, feelings of self-worth and continuing development?"

Controlling the availability of particular types of goal objects on the job is another form of self-fulfilling prophecy. *Worker behavior will be determined for the most part by the goal objects available.* Managers may unconsciously limit behavior in the workplace to striving for a pay check and a benefit package because only those, not pride in workmanship or innovation, are sanctioned as legitimate. The behaviors related to higher level needs, those involving high morale and productivity, will not occur because the absence of goal objects denies their expression. The need is there but not the behavior because there is no opportunity for it to be satisfied.

In these circumstances, employees usually stop looking to the organization as a means of proving their worth and look elsewhere. They involve themselves in outside activities and often devote incredible energy and long hours that the organization literally could have had but failed to use. Management has not created the conditions that would have directed those energies to the benefit of the organization. As Argyris indicated, organizations not structured so as to meet the needs of their employees miss a substantial portion of their potential for productivity.

REFERENCES

1. Hall, Jay and Williams, Martha. "Work Motivation Inventory." The Woodlands, Texas: Teleometrics International, 1980. See normative data.

2. Unpublished research on cross-cultural similarities in the workplace. Teleometrics International, 1980.

3. Singer, Henry A. "AMERICAN, BRITISH AND CHINESE MANAGERS". . .The Hong Kong Connection. Westport, Connecticut: Human Resources Institute Inc.

Section III.

Involvement: The Neglected Factor in Performance

Management's traditional approach to dealing with employees, to providing rewards for performance, has been based on a concept of "economic man": people work to make a living, for survival's sake in a civilized sense. If a manager thinks about work as an act done in the name of food, clothing, shelter, and the like, it follows that rewards should be tangible and immediate—a regular paycheck, and maybe a chance for overtime and bonuses to provide for a good life after working hours.

As the authors in the previous section on motivation stressed, however, most people want more—they want life on the job to be *psychologically* as well as economically rewarding. And what makes for a good life on the job is to be deeply involved in one's work. *Involvement:* It is the wellspring of commitment and creativity which are themselves indispensable dimensions of productivity in organizations, but it is a factor that is often neglected by managers even as they seek top level performance.

When a manager creates opportunities for people to participate in planning their work and making decisions about how it is to be carried out, those people become ego-involved. They sense they have their manager's confidence and respect which enhances their feelings of self-worth. They feel good about themselves, personally powerful and capable, and have positive feelings about their work which we have come to call a sense of ownership. These feelings of energy and commitment allow them to bring all of their talent to bear on the pursuit of innovative strategies and creative alternatives. It is under these circumstances that employees are at their absolute best in accomplishing the work of the organization. And these feelings are the result of involvement—not salaries, bonuses, group insurance plans or paid vacations!

Even when a manager believes that subordinates are capable of contributing valuable insights on how work can best be accomplished, they may still not be involved. Planning, directing, and controlling have been so ingrained as purely managerial functions, that working with subordinates on a peer level seems to smack of permissiveness and to violate the image of the strong leader. However, the most powerful managers, those that have the greatest influence and impact, know that the best use of power is to share it with others.

POWER—A CORE ISSUE
IN INVOLVEMENT

Power is defined, in part, as the "possession of control, authority or influence over others" and, as such, is intrinsic to management. Power is utilized or applied in different ways by different managers, but research has indicated that the most salutary effects come from using power in ways that fall between the extreme poles of a coercive authoritarian approach and a permissive laissez-faire style. The idea is to share the power traditionally associated with management without abnegating responsibilities. Collaboration and joint determination are the watchwords for the most productive use of managerial power.

The first three chapters in this section describe in more specific terms the effective use of power in manager-subordinate relationships. The degree to which power is balanced between the parties will influence feelings of satisfaction and responsibility within the working relationship itself and will significantly enhance its products. When all power is retained by management, the long term results are apt to be worker hostility, absenteeism, and low productivity.

In the first of their two chapters in this section, entitled "How Power Affects Human Behavior," Robert R. Blake and Jane S. Mouton introduce the concept of the power spectrum for mathematically depicting the ratio of power between managers and their subordinates. In laboratory settings they demonstrate three different power styles within a collaborative mode of problem-solving. Each power style has a different impact on both the manager's and subordinates' feelings about the experience.

In their second chapter, "Power Styles Within an Organization," Blake and Mouton contrast the authority-obedience approach to organizational direction with the collaborative mode described in the previous chapter. The former style relies on mechanical rules such as chain of command and span of control while the latter strives for a dynamic system which is responsive to the requirements of a given situation. In laboratory experiments which simulate problem-solving within an entire organization, the two approaches yield marked differences at several levels of management. Furthermore, managers operating within each approach experience dramatically different personal workloads.

The third chapter on power looks at the issue from the manager's point of view. David C. McClelland and David H. Burnham are concerned with the manager's attraction to power and its use in "Power is the Great Motivator." They challenge the frequent criticism that power-seeking managers do so for selfish reasons. In their view the question is not whether a manager should try to acquire the wherewithal to influence others and have a personal impact, but to what end—for personal benefit or for the growth and development of co-workers and the organization.

PARTICIPATION—THE MECHANISM
FOR POWER SHARING

The opening chapters in this section explore the dynamics of power sharing and its ego enhancing effects as measured by positive feelings. The remaining chapters move the issue of involvement forward on several fronts. First, the concept of involvement is made more concrete as power sharing is operationalized through the mechanism of participation. Second, outcome measures shift from positive feelings to productive actions. Finally, the data from laboratory settings are extended to the real world of work.

These particular chapters were selected because each is a classic in behavioral science research in its own right and because collectively they exemplify a key point—*the effects of power sharing through participation have no discernible limits of application.* The data in these chapters are drawn from a diversity of subjects and settings; children, women production workers, and male scientists were studied in after-school hobby clubs, factory, and research center settings. The research spectrum is so broad and the conclusions so complementary that it would be difficult for any manager to claim that any situation or subordinate were so unique that participative practices would not produce similar results.

The research done in this area has been massive and conclusive—those studies presented in the following chapters represent only a small part of the total. Interestingly, however, some "situational" management theorists choose to ignore this evidence and propose that different environments and different types of people require drastically different management approaches. These chapters should serve, in part, to refute that position.

"Leader Behavior and Member Reaction in Three 'Social Climates' " presents pioneering research conducted by Ralph White and Ronald Lippitt in the early 1940's. Their goal was to create working conditions for children corresponding to interaction patterns in democratic, authoritarian, and laissez-faire structures. Within each of the three conditions, they sought to quantify the effects of social atmospheres upon individual and group behavior. White and Lippitt's work confronts the traditional wisdom that tough autocratic structures are essential for high production whereas democratic structures yield higher morale but mediocre performance.

Lester Coch and John R.P. French produced a classic behavioral science case study, "Overcoming Resistance to Change," when they examined the reactions of female machine operators to changing products and procedures at a pajama manufacturing company in Appalacia. They too were interested in the effects of democracy in the workplace, especially its impact on productivity, absenteeism, turnover, and hostility during periods of change. Given the complexity of the problem and its industrial context, the use of such a simple and uncontrolling method as participation seems, in retrospect, as some sort of managerial miracle. Without undue exaggeration, the results achieved can also be termed miraculous.

The impact of participative practices which promote ego enhancement for youths or industrial workers may appear somewhat beside the mark to managers who work with highly educated colleagues whose task it is to create new knowledge rather than manufacture assembly-line products. In university-like atmospheres there is a prevalent belief that the best way to gain high productivity from the highly educated is to stay out of their way. Donald C. Pelz speaks directly to that point in "Some Social Factors Related to Performance in a Research Organization." Pelz studied staff members of a large medical research complex who were all at or near the doctoral level. When high performing scientists were compared with lower performing colleagues, their managers' approach to participation was a deciding factor.

Managers, no matter the level or background of their workers or the nature of the work, can best meet individual and organizational needs by sharing power through participation. They can fulfill their responsibility for control and exert a high level of influence without resorting to authoritarianism and coercion. In short, a manager will find that when people are treated as something of value, as individuals capable of contributing to organizational decision-making and problem-solving, they do in fact become more valuable.

Chapter 10

How Power Affects
Human Behavior

Robert R. Blake
Jane S. Mouton

Power is a central factor in human relationships. Nothing could be more significant for comprehending the human factors which influence the operation of a plant or office than understanding the consequences of different uses of power.

On the one hand, the two person situation characterized by the phrase "supervisor-subordinate" is surrounded by implicit assumptions regarding power. Work direction, supervision, discipline and performance review all involve the use of power. On the other extreme, as soon as the concept of an organization is dealt with, systems of coordination and control such as chain of command, span of control, delegation of authority and so on immediately come to mind. All refer to how social power is distributed to get work done.

By studying the reactions of participants in experiments within the setting of a management development laboratory, we have gathered some interesting information on how people react to the extremes between hard, tight control and the loose rein approach. This chapter describes some of the experiments, sample results and generalizations regarding power use in connection with supervision.

Power Styles in Supervision. Supervision is leadership, and one effective approach to studying leadership is to examine the leadership act—the act of leading. How does a person who is in a position to lead do so? Does he throw his weight around? Does he retain tight control over the subordinate, does he share his power so that they can move jointly, or does he use a loose rein approach? What are the effects on both supervisor and subordinate of various possible approaches?

From *Group Dynamics—Key to Decision Making* by Robert R. Blake and Jane S. Mouton. Copyright ©1961 by Gulf Publishing Company, Houston, Texas, chapter 3, pp. 27-38. Used with permission. All rights reserved.

THE POWER SPECTRUM

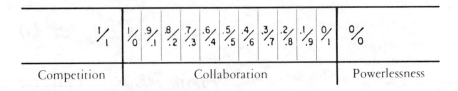

Figure 3.1. **One way of measuring leadership.**

The Power Spectrum. One way of actually measuring leadership is by evaluating the amount of weight an individual exerts on a decision made by himself and a subordinate. This is called the power spectrum. Take, for example, the system where two people work together. At the left side within the collaboration area shown in Figure 3.1 is the situation where the person in the position of leadership actually controls all of the weight on the decision. He receives a weight of 1. On the other hand, the subordinate receives a rating of 0 because he contributes nothing to the outcome. This is known as a 1/0 system of collaboration.

At the opposite extreme is the situation where the person officially designated as the supervisor exerts no weight whatsoever, and as a result the subordinate makes the decision. This is known as the 0/1 condition. The subordinate controls the entire weight exercised in determining the decision.

As shown in Figure 3.1, the distribution of weight between a supervisor and a subordinate can be any ratio between 1/0 and 0/1. It can be .8/.2, or .7/.3, or .5/.5, or .4/.6, and so on. Although the example here involves the power relationship between only two people, it can as well be a single leader and several other people who form the work system. A department head may give no power to his subordinates as a group, or he may share it with them in different ratios, depending on the decision under consideration, and so on.

Competition. The spectrum can be extended so that on the extreme left there is a competitive relation where each person seeks to achieve or retain the total decision-making weight. This situation then is one of contest, with the two competing, each seeking to influence the other, so that as one succeeds, the other fails.

In a capitalistic economic system, this approach to the distribution of economic power is appropriate between organizations, unless an organization gets so strong that it has 1 unit of strength and all others have 0. Then a monopoly situation exists, and that's generally recognized as unhealthy. As long as there are a number of companies, each trying to grow stronger, but with no one getting too much, then the conditions for sound competition are present. The 1/1 competition between companies is healthy as long as they follow legal and ethical rules of competition.

Labor-management relations are intended to form a collaborative system, approaching .5/.5. However, too frequently collaboration breaks down and turns into competition with many of the features of a 1/1 type relationship. The 1/1 labor-management situation is present when the groups themselves are unable to resolve disputes and when it becomes necessary to appeal to arbitration or to resort to strike.

In the case of arbitration both management and labor reduce their power to 0 and raise the power of the arbiter to 1 in order to break the deadlock and to re-establish a working basis. The same is true when it becomes necessary to invoke the Taft-Hartley law to provide a cooling-off period in order to turn away from competition and re-establish collaboration.

Powerlessness. Over on the other end, at the right extreme of Figure 3.1 and labelled "powerlessness," the scale can be extended to a point where there is no weight available to be distributed between individuals or groups. This approaches an 0/0 situation. There are some conspicuous and highly instructive examples of this kind of situation. The Texas City disaster is typical. In that situation, there was no adequately prepared plan to cover the size of the emergency and, for a critical period, individuals were unable to exercise sufficient influence on one another to achieve the coordinated effort necessary for restoring order. The result was that people walked into one another, or away from one another, or parallel, but they were not connected enough to influence each other. They were powerless.

Critical periods, mergers between companies, or between units within a company tend toward 0/0 situations. No one can answer anyone else's questions, old rules no longer apply and people are powerless to influence one another or to get decisions which permit necessary actions. Particularly noteworthy is the reduction in morale that may come about during a merger period when power relations have not yet been re-established.

Demonstrating Relationships. In an applied group dynamics laboratory, participants experience the three power styles, 1/0, .5/.5, and 0/1, in the setting of a supervisor-subordinate relationship. Each supervisor conducts problem-solving conferences with three different subordinates. The task is to rank three sets of 10 different items in their order of importance for improving management, one set being ranked with each of the three subordinates.

Here is one of the three sets, concerning characteristics useful for selecting a middle manager. Differences of opinion between a supervisor and his subordinate provide the basis for interaction.

ITEM

1. Able to grasp structure of organization quickly and use it effectively

2. Able to give clear-cut instructions

3. Able to change own conclusions where proven to be wrong

4. Able to delegate effectively

5. Keeps all parties concerned fully informed on progress and final actions

6. Capable of making fast decisions under time and pressure

7. Able to resist shaping an opinion before all facts are in

8. Goes about decision-making by developing a range of alternatives before coming to a final verdict

9. Capable of seeing appropriate relations among a variety of items

10. Able to grasp instructions and act appropriately in terms of them

One time during the three interactions the supervisor behaves in a 1/0 manner, retaining the power and influencing the outcome as much as possible. In a second pairing he participates in a .5/.5 collaborative manner, rubbing ideas with the subordinate until they achieve a mutually acceptable ranking of the items. On a third occasion he relinquishes all power to his subordinate in a 0/1 manner, avoiding influencing the subordinate's opinions in any way. Subordinates are unaware that the supervisors change their behavior in this manner.

After each interaction, both the supervisor and the subordinate describe their reactions. The leadership scale ranges from a rating of 9 for "The supervisor led completely," (the condition of 1/0 in the power spectrum) to 1 for "The subordinate led completely" (the condition of 0/1). The cohesion scale, "How much satisfaction did you derive from your participation," ranges from 9, "Completely satisfying experience," to 1, "Completely dissatisfying experience."

Another scale measures relations between feelings of responsibility and the way power is distributed. It ranges from 9, "Felt completely responsible for the activity," to 1, "Felt a total lack of responsibility."

The reactions of hundreds of managers to different power ratios are summarized in Figures 3.2 and 3.3. One shows relationships between power distribution and satisfaction. The other relates the power distribution to feelings of responsibility. Let's look at each a little closer.

Power and Satisfaction. The subordinate is dissatisfied when the supervisor leads completely or almost completely. But when he, the subordinate, gains even a small feeling of shared power, his reactions shift from dissatisfaction to moderately satisfying. At the 0/1 end, where he has all the power, his satisfaction reaches its peak and he finds the experience "almost completely satisfying." These trends are shown in Figure 3.2.

The same holds for the supervisor except that it takes a greater amount of power to tip the balance on the side of satisfaction for him. As you see, the highest individual satisfaction is found where one member controls the balance of power, but this satisfaction is at the expense of dissatisfaction by the other.

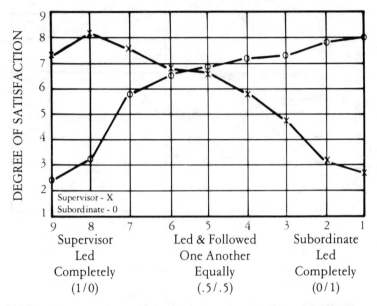

RELATIONSHIP BETWEEN POWER DISTRIBUTION
AND SATISFACTION WITH PARTICIPATION

Figure 3.2. The greater the personal power the greater the satisfaction; but highest overall balance of satisfaction between supervisors and subordinates is when power distribution approaches .5/.5.

In other words, wielding power is a highly satisfying experience, but the cost of wielding power is to destroy the satisfaction of the other person.

The positions in the middle of the power distribution—especially .6/.4 and .5/.5—give the most equal amount of satisfaction for both supervisor and subordinate. The important implication here is that if the 1/0 model of authority-obedience is inappropriately used, it leads, inevitably, to trouble. This means that in normal work situations, you should exercise your power, not in terms of your needs to wield it, but in terms of the needs of the situation. The 1/0 is acceptable if the situation is an emergency. It isn't if people feel they should have a voice in decisions which is being denied them. Something in the neighborhood of .6/.4 or .5/.5 produces the best results, if it is realistic within the framework of an operating situation.

Power and Responsibility. Figure 3.3 shows the relationship between power and feelings of responsibility. The general finding is that feelings of responsibility by both supervisor and subordinate peak at the .5/.5 position on the power spectrum. When the balance of power is in favor of either member of the pair, responsibility on the part of *both decreases*, but the decrease is more rapid for the member who *loses* power. The greater the imbalance, the lower the

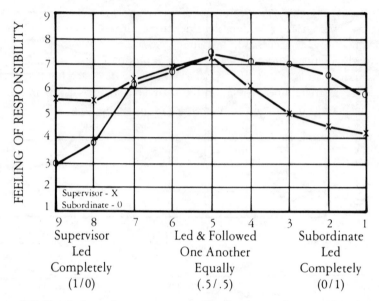

Figure 3.3. Best balance between power distribution and sense of responsibility is around .5/.5.

feelings of responsibility by the person whose power is reduced. Only when power is shared, or when it is close to a joint relationship, do both accept full, or close to full responsibility.

These findings have clear implications for understanding the chronic complaint of many supervisors that "subordinates just aren't responsible—they don't accept the responsibility given them." The suggestion here is that when you see people acting this way, re-examine the power distribution between yourself and your subordinates.

When subordinates feel they have a measure of power or influence, then they willingly accept responsibility. The situation changes from a 1/0 or authority-obedience, to something closer to joint-determination and mutual responsibility with common goals.

Specific Examples of Power Ratios. In the actual work situation, the strategy of how power is used can be analyzed according to the power spectrum, whether the situation involves two people, a small group, two groups or the organization as a whole. The following summaries represent concerted opinions regarding power use by people with years and years of plant experience behind them.

The 1/0 Situation. In a number of cases, leadership is an acceptable 1/0 proposition. Emergency plans and operations must be of a 1/0 character particularly under conditions of danger such as a unit fire where there must be immediate decisions in order to control disaster. Another 1/0 situation would be where a foreman sees and stops a welder from burning in an area where there may be a heavy concentration of flammable vapors.

Another general situation where 1/0 is appropriate is when there is inadequate information or lack of competence on the part of a subordinate. Along these same general lines, a relationship between a supervisor and an untrained man in matters of pure instruction on work direction often is 1/0.

The 0/1 Situation. In many situations, however, an 0/1 type of relationship may prevail—especially as people achieve greater technological skill and as industry moves toward multi-craft supervision. Then the supervisor may no longer be able to direct a more skilled subordinate. The supervisor is rendered powerless relative to the skill of his own subordinate. For example a mechanical supervisor with a background as a pipefitter who has been made responsible for an electrical job must rely heavily on the craftsman for job method decisions.

Frequently immediate action is required and the supervisor is incapable of acting so the subordinate must make the decisions. For example, in the event of an emergency shutdown in pumping gas or oil to tankage, in an oil refinery, the operator decides on a course of action which becomes binding on all concerned.

The 0/1 situation tends to happen also in companies that practice rotation extensively. Here is a chemical engineer who is rotated to Personnel. He doesn't get bogged down in details; he coordinates! He "interprets" broad policy while the Personnel department operates pretty much on an 0/1 level, doing about what it would do even if he weren't there.

Decisions regarding participation in benefit programs also are 0/1 in character. The company provides the opportunity but the man himself is responsible for his own decisions on whether or not he wants to enroll in such a program. Suggestion programs of various sorts also have the same character. You can't direct a person to make suggestions, but you can create the situation in which he takes the personal responsibility for offering his thoughts on new techniques, processes, procedures, etc.

The .5/.5 Situation. A .5/.5 approach, or something close to it, can best be used when there is time for interaction and discussion. By and large in companies where people have been employed 15 to 20 years, it is highly probable that any two layers of supervision are relatively equal to one another in their skills for handling problems. On the ability level they are close to .5/.5.

As the number of layers increases, there may be ability or knowledge differences, but between any two layers it is likely that the subordinate is just about as skillful as his supervisor. Under these conditions, where there is a common goal or where feelings of participation are important, a .5/.5 approach is desirable.

Mutual sharing of decision-making responsibilities between supervisors and subordinates can occur, for example, between department and division heads who meet to determine the best course of action in receiving, storing, and processing of gas or oil. Jointly-determined job assignments, needs for on-the-job training, vacation rules, and schedules also fall in this category.

The .5/.5 is also significant in relations among groups. An example where this approach can be used is in scheduling turnarounds which has an overriding effect on the operation of several departments. For instance, the Mechanical department is involved from the view of equalizing mechanical workload by staggering turnarounds to fit in with manpower availability; supply and distribution are concerned from the standpoint of efficiently carrying out their functions associated with the turnaround. Scheduling a turnaround under .5/.5 conditions is essential as the cooperation and understanding of all parties are necessary to insure success.

Union-management relations many times have a .5/.5 character. True collective bargaining is an example.

In Conclusion. You might summarize the application of the various positions on the power spectrum by saying that as you move away from emergencies into activities where individuals have great personal skills for handling the situation you move from 1/0 toward 0/1. Between these extremes many situations exist where a .5/.5 approach is optimal. However, in addition to the reasons already given such as a high degree of satisfaction and high feelings of responsibility associated with it, a .5/.5 situation is a learning situation par excellence. It means that as people make decisions they are more or less automatically teaching one another. Thus, a plant or office moves toward success in close parallel with the extent to which it teaches people the skills of collaboration when it's desirable—and self-reliance when it's possible.

Chapter 11

Power Styles Within An Organization

Robert R. Blake
Jane S. Mouton

It is quite possible to study an entire organizational unit, such as an office or plant, through applied group dynamics. One approach to this is to contrast the consequences of the two basic power styles which have been shown earlier to be so important for thinking about supervisor-subordinate relations, small group action and intergroup aspects of behavior. We'll briefly review these two theories as applied in analyzing an organization, then take up a description of a typical management development laboratory experimental study of two simulated companies.

Identical in all other respects, one simulated refinery will be operated according to authority-obedience principles, while the other will be run in terms of an integrated goals concept. This segment of a management development laboratory brings into focus two important options available to managerial personnel as the basis for designing the human side of an organization. But first, let's review the two systems.

AUTHORITY-OBEDIENCE BASIS

For Organizational Direction. Over the years, a number of principles have been devised for operating an organization based on the authority-obedience formula. Some of the broader basic rules include prescriptions regarding chain of command, delegation of authority, span of control, and the exception principle. Let's look at each of these more closely.

1. *Chain of Command.* The formal organization chart only works if each

person knows to whom he reports and who reports to him. What is the concept of this chain of command? In the final analysis it is a formal statement of who takes orders from whom. It tells the subservience plan of an organization: A can direct and control the energies of B, B of C, and C is authorized to direct and control D, etc. Further, A is authorized to make decisions which B can't, B can that C can't, and so on down the line, from top to bottom.

If the top man in an organization actually behaved in this fashion, which he often doesn't, if for no other reason than often he doesn't know *what* decisions to make and, therefore, *has* to seek for collaboration, and if all the subordinate levels accepted their pecking order relations, an organization would work perfectly. However, organizations do not work perfectly. Wage people, through unionization, already have enforced on management their refusal to be treated as troops; foremen in many situations are a disgruntled, unhappy and disenfranchised group which tells you the 1/0 formula isn't producing fully effective collaboration.

Chain of command looks good on paper, but in practice it falls far short as an effective system for arousing cooperation when basic economic conditions have resulted in men being released from industrial servitude. Though no company is without an organization chart, the evidence points toward the view that *actual* operations are far different than they would be if the paper organization were to be followed literally.

2. *Span of Control.* A second evidence of the authority-obedience managerial formula is found in ideas about span of control. As interpreted by one company, span of control says: "A man should direct the work of eight others—no more and no fewer."

In another setting, "A vice-president should have four operating divisions reporting to him, etc."

Why should it be so? Is there something magical in the numbers 8 and 4?

Obviously not! It is *only* under a 1/0 formula that these rules of thumb make any sense at all. If a work group is without feelings of responsibility for getting a job done and has to be directed, action-by-action, then a supervisor needs time to do it. Eight may be a reasonable formula for work direction under those circumstances. But if the work group is more or less self-regulating, which means it operates closer to .5/.5, it may function effectively with 5 or 10 or 12 or 20.

Span of control, in other words, is relative to how the *power* to control activity is distributed. Whether or not persons participate with one another in setting goals and in designing appropriate conditions so that members mutually support one another's efforts determines how "close" or how "general" supervision needs to be for the effective coordination of work.

3. *Delegation of Authority.* Delegation of authority strikes at the center of the problem. It says that because the span of a man's control is limited, he can't direct everyone. Therefore, he needs other directors to report to him. But

there is a riddle here. The question is, "How can you delegate your authority, which is like 0/1, and yet retain it by requiring accountability through a reporting system which is 1/0?"

The logic of the system demands that you do it this way. Yet, closer examination suggests that delegation usually is not practiced in the sense described. Where it works most successfully, delegation turns out to be much nearer to collaboration, with supervisor and subordinate co-planning, in order to insure coordination, and then with the subordinate carrying out the implementation. Implementation also may be co-planned at each of the lower levels. The result is that the rule regarding delegation of authority frequently turns out to be a myth when interpreted literally. Practice and theory just don't jibe.

4. *The Exception Principle.* The exception principle states that all matters which are routine and for which policies already have been established can be passed on by subordinates at any given level in the organization. When an exception occurs that is not covered by the rules, the subordinate is to pass it up the line for decision-making.

This widely stated logical rule goes against another sound rule, which is to lower the level of decision-making as deeply as possible into the organization. Indeed, it says that whenever an opportunity occurs for a lower level to make a decision it must refrain from doing so and give the problem to higher supervision! Here again actual practice is different from what is prescribed according to the exception principle.

These four mechanical rules of organization share in common the authority-obedience formulation for running a business. In the extreme, they result in top-level decision-making, middle-level message carrying, and lower level execution. It is because the system isn't working too well that the *pendulum theory,* which sees management endlessly swinging from hard to soft, or the *middle-of-the-road* theory, which says don't push too hard one way or another, have come into prominence.

COLLABORATION BY INTEGRATING INDIVIDUAL AND ORGANIZATIONAL GOALS

As has already been suggested in discussing chain of command, span of control, and so on, exercise of power in a 1/0 manner can create resentment, dissatisfaction, hostility, lack of responsibility and diminished productivity. In addition, if higher level management is primarily concerned with making policy level decisions, and lower level management and the rank-and-file are only concerned with executing a small consequence of each decision, it is likely that the functional goals of lower supervision and of the rank-and-file will be quite different from the goals of higher levels of management.

The fact that the goals of members of the organization at the various levels are different—and frequently antagonistic to one another—can create a major source of conflict within the organization. In order to achieve maximum collaborative effort, according to this view, the managerial job is one of merging a range of goals into an overall plan of operation.

If an organization is operated so that the members of the organization share the desire to collaborate in order to achieve relevant goals, they also should be able to agree on the means for obtaining them. Then an organization can maintain itself at a high level of efficiency even when the organization's goals change, and new problems face it. Why? Because the organization is geared to collaborative goal setting and to attaining maximum effort through mutual understanding at all levels within the organization.

With an increased flow of unbiased communication throughout an entire organization it becomes possible for all management levels to get required feedback concerning the effects of decisions made at any level, and to change, modify and adapt operations according to the requirements of the actual situation of work.

COMPARING SYSTEMS

A final experiment in a management development laboratory[1] places emphasis on the entire organization as a problem-solving system in contrast with focusing on the two person, small group, or intergroup aspects of organizational life. The experience represents a culmination of training for it provides participants the opportunity to test the implications of basic learnings as applied to smaller units of organizational life during the earlier phases of the laboratory.

Simulating a Refinery. The method of approach in investigating problems at this level is to simulate an organization, a refinery in this example, which is working on a stated problem. Laboratory participants are assigned positions within a refinery's organizational hierarchy, with as many levels and functions as possible represented. For example, one person is cast in the role of the general manager. Another becomes the operating superintendent. A third is the administrative superintendent. Department heads of major units, with subordinate levels down to first line foremen, also are assigned. Other individuals are assigned to staff jobs, so that the simulated refinery has a personnel department head, a public relations manager and so on.

When the simulated refinery begins to operate, each of its members is working on some typical refinery problem. For example, a grievance is being dealt with at one level. At another, meetings are being held regarding the planning

1. *Proceedings* of The Human Relations Training Laboratory, 6th Annual Session, Austin, Texas: Department of Psychology, University of Texas, 1960.

of a turnaround. A segment of the Personnel Department is concerned with developing budget recommendations and so on.

After the simulated refinery goes on stream, the manager receives a letter from outside the refinery which alerts him to an emergency which will shortly confront the refinery. The problem usually deals with an important labor-management issue and touches the concerns of every managerial person in some aspect or another. It is the responsibility of the manager to initiate action.

Under these circumstances the authority-obedience approach and the collaborative method of operating a refinery are contrasted with one another. All details of refinery operation are identical except for the rules under which the general manager operates. He acts according to instruction, but all other participants are uninstructed. Under one set of arrangements, the manager operates according to authority-obedience principles, viewing his job as that of making the decision regarding the issue at hand. He usually does so by himself or with the assistant general managers. The remainder of the eight or so hours of time available is spent in pushing the decision down in the organization and gaining acceptance of it as a basis for refinery-wide action.

Under a second set of arrangements the manager operates according to rules of collaboration for handling the issue, seeking to develop an integration of individual and organizational goals. Rather than making the decision, he formulates the *problem* to the assistant managers. Together they develop a plan for involving the entire organization in studying the problem and coming up with ideas, proposals, suggestions and recommendations for handling it.

The remaining hours of the exercise are utilized by the organization in resolving points of view and in communicating upward and downward the various attitudes and feelings of individuals and of groups. The policy to be followed is formulated only after individuals and groups within the organization have had full opportunity to react to the problem and to the issues involved.

Comparison. The two approaches provide the opportunity of studying contrasting organizational styles. In the authority-obedience organization the course of action is to push the *decision* down through the organization and to make it stick as a basis for action. In collaboration, or a common goals organization, the course of action is to push the *problem* down into the organization to get reactions, proposals, and suggestions for handling it moving up and down through the organization. The two approaches provide a dramatic basis for comparison of two alternative methods of decision-making within an organizational structure.

Reactions to the Two Procedures. Reactions of the entire organization at the end of the exercise to the two methods of operation can be summarized as follows:

1. *Participation in the Solution.* Managers and superintendents felt they

participated to a substantial amount in developing the solution under the authority-obedience method of operation; division and department heads an intermediate amount, and the supervisory level felt they contributed almost nothing to the decision.

Under the collaborative system participation is reasonably high at all levels. Collaboration is achieved throughout the organization under the second style but not under the first except for the high degree of participation for the top management group.

2. *Clearness Regarding Refinery Policy.* Under the authority-obedience system, higher level management was quite clear on the refinery policy, but division and department heads and supervisors were less clear, even at the end of the exercise. By comparison, when a collaborative system was employed, all levels from the top to the bottom of the organization were quite clear as to the policy position of the refinery. These differences are particularly striking when it is recognized that both groups spend an identical amount of time working on the problem. A simple interpretation is that people get clearer pictures of the whys and wherefores of things when they think a problem through rather than being given answers.

3. *Practicality of the Solution.* Under the authority-obedience approach the policy achieved was felt to be quite practical by the upper and middle levels. Supervisors, who had not participated very much in formulating the position, regarded it as quite impractical. Under the collaboration system the policy achieved was seen as quite practical by *all* levels of supervision.

Of particular interest is the comparison of the feelings of practicality by the top men under the two styles of organization. The manager and superintendents do *not* feel that sharing decision-making under the collaborative organization leads to an impractical result; indeed, they report feeling the policy is even a little *more* practical than it is felt to be by the manager and superintendents under the authority-obedience formula. Collaborative decision-making, feared by some as a sign of weakness, doesn't seem to produce that result in practice.

4. *Coordination of Parts.* Coordination of effort to solve the problem is not too great at any level in the authority-obedience system. It was seen as moderate to fair from above and a good deal less by those below. Relatively good coordination is sensed at all levels within the collaborative system. Coordination is not lost when the entire organization works on developing a solution but indeed is sensed as higher than under the traditional rules of organization.

The Manager's Role. Striking qualitative observations regarding differences associated with the style of operation of the two organizations can be described. Under the authority-obedience organization, the manager is extremely busy.

His first action is to make the decision by setting the policy for the organization to follow. During the rest of the work period he is busy meeting objections, answering queries by showing how the policy must work, making exceptions for parts of the organization to which his policy does not fit and so on.

The authority-obedience manager is overloaded. He has insufficient time to do the job as he sees it. He is continually harassed by objections from the lower rungs of the organization. This behavior is the same kind of fire-fighting described earlier as a symptom of the failure of modern management to constructively use the resources available.

The manager who operates according to collaborative principles, on the other hand, has extensive free time available as do the assistant managers. This is particularly so during the early phases of the problem-solving while the rest of the organization is working on the solution to the problem. Uncommitted free time is available for planning, for studying other problems, or for investigating a range of technical and human resources of the kind with which senior management should be intimately informed.

A broad distinction has been drawn between two styles of refinery organization. In the first, decision-making is based on power, the formula of authority-obedience. In the second, management effort is based on achieving collaboration between individuals and among groups through bringing about an integration of the goals of the organization with individual ones. Under this second arrangement, power is in the goals toward which people strive more than it is in the authority of individuals to make decisions or to command effort.

Under a pure power system, in other words, the actions of some people are directed through the efforts of others higher on the organizational ladder. Under a pure goals system individuals and groups are pulled toward common action through the involvement in and satisfaction associated with accomplishing goals which are shared. In the latter situation failure to strive is self-defeating. The whole problem of human motivation is seen very differently under the two systems.

In actual organizational life pure power systems are as rare as are pure goal systems as a basis for operation. Most organizations are a mixture, built on some of both or with authority-obedience the more general rule at the bottom level and common goals more typical at the top. Yet if an improved goals system can be achieved at all levels, it is probably healthier than a power system as a basis for organization.

THE STRATEGY OF GOAL-SETTING

By what steps might a manager go about increasing the use of a goals system as the basis for collaboration? This broad question will command a great amount of thinking during the next 25 years of organizational life. The action research model in Figure 8.1 presents the broad outlines of a goals oriented approach to management.

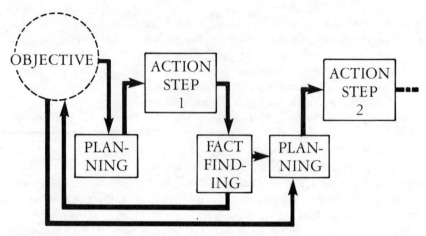

Figure 8.1. This action research model presents broad outlines of a goals-oriented approach to management.

Goals or Objectives. On the left side of the diagram the word "objective" is seen with a circle around it. This is intended to represent a broad, sometimes rough, sometimes vague idea or a general plan to be accomplished. Given changes in the situation, difficulties in predicting the future, or the fact that many situations contain unknowns that cannot be anticipated, any objective or goal is likely to have a tentative, provisional quality. Quite often it is impossible to set up goals that have a final or binding quality, but it is possible to proceed towards a roughly outlined, vague goal in a step-wise manner, with the goal gaining clarity as one moves toward it.

According to what is currently known, the wider the participation in setting goals, the better for action and implementation.

Planning. Given a statement of a goal, a second step is the planning that goes into achieving it. Since goals are tentative, planning has to take place, often more or less in the dark, particularly in the early stages of an operation. Regardless of the conditions, however, planning must occur before a specific action step can be launched.

Taking an Action-Step. The next phase is in taking an action, in moving toward a goal. Given the objective, and a plan for achieving it, action is required to get to it, or closer to it. In the diagram this is shown as "Action-Step 1."

Fact-finding or Feedback Phase. Now comes the critical phase of fact-finding, or feedback. Why is fact-finding so critical in a goals oriented management program? Well, it is because it provides steering data. It gives a measure to evaluate:

1. Progress toward a goal.
2. Adequacy of planning.
3. Quality or effectiveness of any given action step.

Only by fact-finding, in other words, is it possible to know if you're making progress. Fact-finding may demonstrate that the goal is unrealistic, that the plan was poor, or that the action step was unsuccessful. That's why it's so important to pick up measurements whereby you can determine whether or not progress is being made, and what kinds of feelings are being produced.

Much effort in a management development laboratory is placed on data collection and other kinds of fact-finding and feedback as a basis of measuring progress, of clarifying goals, and of evaluating whether action steps are adequate for accomplishing goals.

What kinds of data collection methods seem most useful? Two in particular can be mentioned. One is the 9-point scale system, which ranges over the entire spectrum of possibilities in a situation from completely adequate, or completely good, etc. to completely inadequate, or completely bad, etc. In the 9-point scale system, 5, the middle point, is equivalent to an intermediate amount, an in-between amount, or neutral feelings about whatever it is that is being measured. Scales such as are used in development groups have been shown again and again to have direct utility in measuring performance in many kinds of work situations.

The second is the ranking method, which involves ordering elements in a situation from most to least. The rankings method of fact-finding is excellent wherever it can be satisfactorily applied, for it establishes the order in which people see things.

The 2nd Action Step. Given 1) the facts developed from data and other methods of evaluation, and 2) a reexamination of an original goal to determine whether or not it needs to be modified or changed, new planning for the next action step is now possible.

The step-wise goal-setting method described above is a pretty true picture of how to make sound decisions that can lead to goal accomplishment.

Application. Any manager can use the model described above for thinking about how he works with subordinates when searching for sound connections between individual, group and organizational goals.

Critical in thinking according to the goals system is the question, "Who sets the goals?" Here the general answer is, "Those who must work to achieve them." When a person works to achieve goals he sets for himself either alone or with others, it is likely that one is more fully committed to the actions required in order to make the plan work successfully when one is working to achieve something he wants, rather than doing something he has been told to do.

A Manager is a Trainer. Managers who have sought to employ the action research model with groups who have not been exposed to laboratory training routinely find difficulty in application through failure of others to appreciate the meaning and implications of the method. Such an experience throws into bold relief a general problem confronting any manager who attempts to change and to operate according to a different set of rules than those currently in effect.

The problem is to train individuals and groups to explore, to evaluate, to understand and to feel comfortable with a new set of rules regarding modes of work. The reason is that a manager must train as well as contribute to the maintenance and development of an operation. Unless he trains people in evaluating current rules of operation and new rules that might be employed, massive failures of communication and understanding are inevitable.

Failure to see himself in the role of a trainer results in the inability of others to contribute to the solution of problems. The consequence is that the manager is again thrown back on making the decision himself, frequently in the role of a fire-fighter, overloaded with requirements of decision-making. He is unable to employ others who might legitimately be participating in decision-making.

You might say that a manager who is overloaded with decision-making is a manager who has failed to view training as his legitimate responsibility. First and foremost a manager is a trainer. Without continuous training he remains the victim of his organization rather than its leader!

The ultimate aim of the human side of the organization is to increase the quality of its products, the productivity and satisfaction of its people, and its profit position. This is done by improving the skills of management through continuous, never-ending training for more effective decision-making by individuals working separately, by people who work in pairs, by small groups, between groups and by the entire organization as a decision-making system.

Chapter 12

Power is the
Great Motivator

David C. McClelland
David H. Burnham

Good managers, ones who get the best out of their subordinates and who there-
by produce positive results for their organizations, are the keys to an organiza-
tion's success. It is not surprising then that much research and thought has
gone into trying to define just what motivates a good manager and how to de-
scribe him so that his characteristics can be objectively measured and identified.
In this article, the authors describe a motivation pattern that empirical research
has discovered most good managers share. Good managers are not motivated
by a need for personal aggrandizement, or by a need to get along with subor-
dinates, but rather by a need to influence others' behavior for the good of the
whole organization. In other words, good managers want power. On its own,
however, power can lead to authoritarianism, so it needs to be tempered by ma-
turity and a high degree of self-control. The authors maintain that workshops
can help a manager discover whether he has the correct motivation profile to be
a good manager. If he does, or even if he does not have the correct profile,
workshops can help him become a good or better manager.

What makes or motivates a good manager? The question is so enormous in scope that anyone trying to answer it has difficulty knowing where to begin. Some people might say that a good manager is one who is successful; and by now most business researchers and businessmen themselves know what motivates people who successfully run their own small businesses. The key to their success has turned out to be what psychologists call "the need for achievement," the desire to do something better or more efficiently than it has been done before. Any number of books and articles summarize research studies explaining how the achievement motive is necessary for a person to attain success on his own.[1]

But what has achievement motivation got to do with good management? There is no reason on theoretical grounds why a person who has a strong need to be more efficient should make a good manager. While it sounds as if everyone ought to have the need to achieve, in fact, as psychologists define and measure achievement motivation, it leads people to behave in very special ways that do not necessarily lead to good management.

For one thing, because they focus on personal improvement, on doing things better by themselves, achievement-motivated people want to do things themselves. For another, they want concrete short-term feedback on their performance so that they can tell how well they are doing. Yet a manager, particularly one of or in a large complex organization, cannot perform all the tasks necessary for success by himself or herself. He must manage others so that they will do things for the organization. Also, feedback on his subordinate's performance may be a lot vaguer and more delayed than it would be if he were doing everything himself.

The manager's job seems to call more for someone who can influence people than for someone who does things better on his own. In motivational terms, then, we might expect the successful manager to have a greater "need for power" than need to achieve. But there must be other qualities beside the need for power that go into the makeup of a good manager. Just what these qualities are and how they interrelate is the subject of this article.

To measure the motivations of managers, good and bad, we studied a number of individual managers from different large U.S. corporations who were participating in management workshops designed to improve their managerial effectiveness.

The general conclusion of these studies is that the top manager of a company must possess a high need for power, that is, a concern for influencing people. However, this need must be disciplined and controlled so that it is directed toward the benefit of the institution as a whole and not toward the manager's personal aggrandizement. Moreover, the top manager's need for power ought to be greater than his need for being liked by people.

Now let us look at what these ideas mean in the context of real individuals in real situations and see what comprises the profile of the good manager. Finally, we will look at the workshops themselves to determine how they go about changing behavior.

MEASURING MANAGERIAL EFFECTIVENESS

First off, what does it mean when we say that a good manager has a greater

1. For instance, see my books *The Achieving Society* (New York: Van Nostrand, 1961) and (with David Winte) *Motivating Economic Achievement* (New York: Free Press, 1969).

need for "power" than for "achievement"? To get a more concrete idea, let us consider the case of Ken Briggs, a sales manager in a large U.S. corporation who joined one of our managerial workshops. Some six or seven years ago, Ken Briggs was promoted to a managerial position at corporate headquarters, where he had responsibility for salesmen who service his company's largest accounts.

In filling out his questionnaire at the workshop, Ken showed that he correctly perceived what his job required of him, namely, that he should influence others' success more than achieve new goals himself or socialize with his subordinates. However, when asked with other members of the workshop to write a story depicting a managerial situation, Ken unwittingly revealed through his fiction that he did not share those concerns. Indeed, he discovered that his need for achievement was very high—in fact over the 90th percentile—and his need for power was very low, in about the 15th percentile. Ken's high need to achieve was no surprise—after all, he had been a very successful salesman—but obviously his motivation to influence others was much less than his job required. Ken was a little disturbed but thought that perhaps the measuring instruments were not too accurate and that the gap between the ideal and his score was not as great as it seemed.

Then came the real shocker. Ken's subordinates confirmed what his stories revealed: he was a poor manager, having little positive impact on those who worked for him. Ken's subordinates felt that they had little responsibility delegated to them, that he never rewarded but only criticized them, and that the office was not well organized, but confused and chaotic. On all three of these scales, his office rated in the 10th to 15th percentile relative to national norms.

As Ken talked the results over privately with a workshop leader, he became more and more upset. He finally agreed, however, that the results of the survey confirmed feelings he had been afraid to admit to himself or others. For years, he had been miserable in his managerial role. He now knew the reason: he simply did not want to nor had he been able to influence or manage others. As he thought back, he realized that he had failed every time he had tried to influence his staff, and he felt worse than ever.

Ken had responded to failure by setting very high standards—his office scored in the 98th percentile on this scale—and by trying to do most things himself, which was close to impossible; his own activity and lack of delegation consequently left his staff demoralized. Ken's experience is typical of those who have a strong need to achieve but low power motivation. They may become very successful salesmen and, as a consequence, may be promoted into managerial jobs for which they, ironically, are unsuited. If achievement motivation does not make a good manager, what motive does? It is not enough to suspect that power motivation may be important; one needs hard evidence that people who are better managers than Ken Briggs do in fact possess stronger power motivation and perhaps score higher in other characteristics as well. But how does one decide who is the better manager?

Real-world performance measures are hard to come by if one is trying to rate managerial effectiveness in production, marketing, finance, or research and

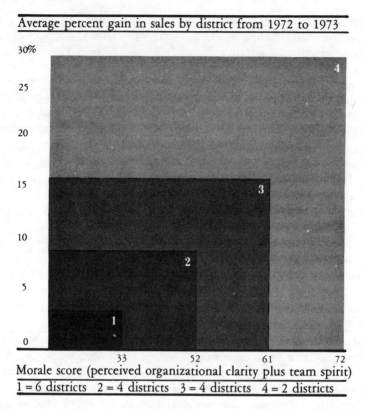

Average percent gain in sales by district from 1972 to 1973

Morale score (perceived organizational clarity plus team spirit)
1 = 6 districts   2 = 4 districts   3 = 4 districts   4 = 2 districts

Exhibit 1. Correlation between morale score and sales performance for a large U.S. corporation.

development. In trying to determine who the better managers were in Ken Brigg's company, we did not want to rely only on the opinions of their superiors. For a variety of reasons, superiors' judgments of their subordinates' real-world performance may be inaccurate. In the absence of some standard measure of performance, we decided that the next best index of a manager's effectiveness would be the climate he or she creates in the office, reflected in the morale of subordinates.

Almost by definition, a good manager is one who, among other things, helps subordinates feel strong and responsibile, who rewards them properly for good performance, and who sees that things are organized in such a way that subordinates feel they know what they should be doing. Above all, managers should foster among subordinates a strong sense of team spirit, of pride in working as part of a particular team. If a manager creates and encourages this spirit, his subordinates certainly should perform better.

In the company Ken Briggs works for, we have direct evidence of a connection between morale and performance in the one area where performance measures are easy to come by—namely, sales. In April 1973, at least three employees from this company's 16 sales districts filled out questionnaires that rated their office for organizational clarity and team spirit. Their scores were averaged and totaled to give an overall morale score for each office. The percentage gains or losses in sales for each district in 1973 were compared with those for 1972. The difference in sales figures by district ranged from a gain of nearly 30% to a loss of 8%, with a median gain of around 14%. *Exhibit 1* shows the average gain in sales performance plotted against the increasing averages in morale scores.

In *Exhibit 1* we can see that the relationship between sales and morale is surprisingly close. The six districts with the lowest morale early in the year showed an average sales gain of only around 7% by years' end (although there was wide variation within this group), whereas the two districts with the highest morale showed an average gain of 28%. When morale scores rise above the 50th percentile in terms of national norms, they seem to lead to better sales performance. In Ken Briggs's company, at least, high morale at the beginning is a good index of how well the sales division will actually perform in the coming year.

And it seems very likely that the manager who can create high morale among salesmen can also do the same for employees in other areas (production, design, and so on), leading to better performance. Given that high morale in an office indicates that there is a good manager present, what general characteristics does he possess?

A Need For Power

In examining the motive scores of over 50 managers of both high and low morale units in all sections of the same large company, we found that most of the managers—over 70%—were high in power motivation compared with men in general. This finding confirms the fact that power motivation is important for management. (Remember that as we use the term "power motivation," it refers not to dictatorial behavior, but to a desire to have impact, to be strong and influential.) The better managers, as judged by the morale of those working for them, tended to score even higher in power motivation. But the most important determining factor of high morale turned out not to be how their power motivation compared to their need to achieve but whether it was higher than their need to be liked. This relationship existed for 80% of the better sales managers as compared with only 10% of the poorer managers. And the same held true for other managers in nearly all parts of the company.

In the research, product development, and operations divisions, 73% of the better managers had a stronger need for power than a need to be liked (or what we term "affiliation motive") as compared with only 22% of the poorer managers. Why should this be so? Sociologists have long argued that, for a bureaucracy to function effectively, those who manage it must be universalistic in applying rules. That is, if they make exceptions for the particular needs of individuals, the whole system will break down.

The manager with a high need for being liked is precisely the one who wants to stay on good terms with everybody, and, therefore, is the one most likely to make exceptions in terms of particular needs. If a male employee asks for time off to stay home with his sick wife to help look after her and the kids, the affiliative manager agrees almost without thinking, because he feels sorry for the man and agrees that his family needs him.

When President Ford remarked in pardoning ex-President Nixon that he had "suffered enough," he was responding as an affiliative manager would, because he was empathizing primarily with Nixon's needs and feelings. Sociological theory and our data both argue, however, that the person whose need for affiliation is high does not make a good manager. This kind of person creates poor morale because he or she does not understand that other people in the office will tend to regard exceptions to the rules as unfair to themselves, just as many U.S. citizens felt it was unfair to let Richard Nixon off and punish others less involved than he was in the Watergate scandal.

Socialized Power

But so far our findings are a little alarming. Do they suggest that the good manager is one who cares for power and is not at all concerned about the needs of other people? Not quite, for the good manager has other characteristics which must still be taken into account.

Above all, the good manager's power motivation is not oriented toward personal aggrandizement but toward the institution which he or she serves. In another major research study, we found that the signs of controlled action or inhibition that appear when a person exercises his or her imagination in writing stories tell a great deal about the kind of power that person needs. [2] We discovered that, if a high power motive score is balanced by high inhibition, stories about power tend to be altruistic. That is, the heroes in the story exercise power on behalf of someone else. This is the "socialized" face of power as distinguished from the concern for personal power, which is characteristic of individuals whose stories are loaded with power imagery but which show no sign of inhibition or self-control. In our earlier study, we found ample evidence that these latter individuals exercise their power impulsively. They are more rude to other people, they drink too much, they try to exploit others sexually, and they collect symbols of personal prestige such as fancy cars or big offices.

Individuals high in power and in control, on the other hand, are more institution minded; they tend to get elected to more offices, to control their drinking, and to want to serve others. Not surprisingly, we found in the workshops

2. David C. McClelland, William N. Davis, Rudolf Kalin, and Erie Warner, *The Drinking Man* (New York: The Free Press, 1972).

that the better managers in the corporation also tend to score high on both power and inhibition.

PROFILE OF A GOOD MANAGER

Let us recapitulate what we have discussed so far and have illustrated with data from one company. The better managers we studied are high in power motivation, low in affiliation motivation, and high in inhibition. They care about institutional power and use it to stimulate their employees to be more productive. Now let us compare them with affiliative managers—those in whom the need for affiliation is higher than the need for power—and with the personal power managers—those in whom the need for power is higher than for affiliation but whose inhibition score is low.

In the sales division of our illustrative company, there were managers who matched the three types fairly closely. *Exhibit 2* shows how their subordinates rated the offices they worked in on responsibility, organizational clarity, and team spirit. There are scores from at least three subordinates for each manager, and several managers are represented for each type, so that the averages shown in the exhibit are quite stable. Note that the manager who is concerned about being liked by people tends to have subordinates who feel that they have very little personal responsibility, that organizational procedures are not clear, and that they have little pride in their work group.

In short, as we expected, affiliative managers make so many ad hominem and ad hoc decisions that they almost totally abandon orderly procedures. Their disregard for procedure leaves employees feeling weak, irresponsible, and without a sense of what might happen next, of where they stand in relation to their manager, or even of what they ought to be doing. In this company, the group of affiliative managers portrayed in *Exhibit 2* were below the 30th percentile in morale scores.

The managers who are motivated by a need for personal power are somewhat more effective. They are able to create a greater sense of responsibility in their divisions and, above all, a greater team spirit. They can be thought of as managerial equivalents of successful tank commanders such as General Patton, whose own daring inspired admiration in his troops. But notice how in *Exhibit 2* these men are still only in the 40th percentile in the amount of organizational clarity they create, as compared to the high power, low affiliation, high inhibition managers, whom we shall term "institutional."

Managers motivated by personal power are not disciplined enough to be good institution builders, and often their subordinates are loyal to them as individuals rather than to the institution they both serve. When a personal power manager leaves, disorganization often follows. His subordinates' strong group spirit, which the manager has personally inspired, deflates. The subordinates do not know what to do for themselves.

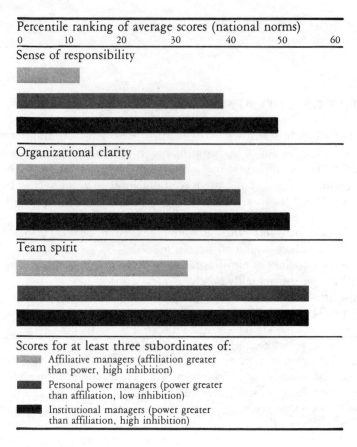

Percentile ranking of average scores (national norms)

Sense of responsibility

Organizational clarity

Team spirit

Scores for at least three subordinates of:

Affiliative managers (affiliation greater than power, high inhibition)

Personal power managers (power greater than affiliation, low inhibition)

Institutional managers (power greater than affiliation, high inhibition)

Exhibit 2. Average scores on selected climate dimensions by subordinates of managers with different motive profiles.

Of the managerial types, the "institutional" manager is the most successful in creating an effective work climate. *Exhibit 2* shows that his subordinates feel that they have more responsibility. Also, this kind of manager creates high morale because he produces the greatest sense of organizational clarity and team spirit. If such a manager leaves, he or she can be more readily replaced by another manager, because the employees have been encouraged to be loyal to the institution rather than to a particular person.

Managerial Styles

Since it seems undeniable from *Exhibit 2* that either kind of power orientation creates better morale in subordinates than a "people" orientation, we must consider that a concern for power is essential to good management. Our findings seem to fly in the face of a long and influential tradition of organizational psychology, which insists that authoritarian management is what is wrong with most businesses in this country. Let us say frankly that we think the bogeyman of authoritarianism has in fact been wrongly used to downplay the importance of power in management. After all, management is an influence game. Some proponents of democratic management seem to have forgotten this fact, urging managers to be primarily concerned with people's human needs rather than with helping them to get things done.

But a good deal of the apparent conflict between our findings and those of other behavioral scientists in this area arises from the fact that we are talking about *motives*, and behaviorists are often talking about *actions*. What we are saying is that managers must be interested in playing the influence game in a controlled way. That does not necessarily mean that they are or should be authoritarian in action. On the contrary, it appears that power motivated managers make their subordinates feel strong rather than weak. The true authoritarian in action would have the reverse effect, making people feel weak and powerless.

Thus another important ingredient in the profile of a manager is his or her managerial style. In the illustrative company, 63% of the better managers (those whose subordinates had higher morale) scored higher on the democratic or coaching styles of management as compared with only 22% of the poorer managers, a statistically significant difference. By contrast, the latter scored higher on authoritarian or coercive management styles. Since the better managers were also higher in power motivation, it seems that, in action, they express their power motivation in a democratic way, which is more likely to be effective.

To see how motivation and style interact, let us consider the case of George Prentice, a manager in the sales division of another company. George had exactly the right motive combination to be an institutional manager. He was high in the need for power, low in the need for affiliation, and high in inhibition. He exercised his power in a controlled, organized way. His stories reflected this fact. In one, for instance, he wrote, "The men sitting around the table were feeling pretty good; they had just finished plans for reorganizing the company; the company has been beset with a number of organizational problems. This group, headed by a hard-driving, brilliant young executive, has completely reorganized the company structurally with new jobs and responsibilities...."

This described how George himself was perceived by the company, and shortly after the workshop he was promoted to vice president in charge of all sales. But George was also known to his colleagues as a monster, a tough guy who would "walk over his grandmother" if she stood in the way of his advancement. He had the right motive combination and, in fact, was more interested in institutional growth than in personal power, but his managerial style was all wrong. Taking his cue from some of the top executives in the corporation, he told people what they had to do and threatened them with dire consequences if they didn't do it.

When George was confronted with his authoritarianism in a workshop, he recognized that this style was counterproductive—in fact, in another part of the study we found that it was associated with low morale—and he subsequently changed to acting more like a coach, which was the scale on which he scored the lowest initially. George saw more clearly that his job was not to force other people to do things but to help them to figure out ways of getting their job done better for the company.

The Institutional Manager

One reason it was easy for George Prentice to change his managerial style was that in his imaginative stories he was already having thoughts about helping others, characteristic of men with the institution-building motivational pattern. In further examining institution builders' thoughts and actions, we found they have four major characteristics:

1. They are more organization-minded; that is, they tend to join more organizations and to feel responsible for building up these organizations. Furthermore, they believe strongly in the importance of centralized authority.

2. They report that they like to work. This finding is particularly interesting, because our research on achievement motivation has led many commentators to argue that achievement motivation promotes the "Protestant work ethic." Almost the precise opposite is true. People who have a high need to achieve like to get out of work by becoming more efficient. They would like to see the same result obtained in less time or with less effort. But managers who have a need for institutional power actually seem to like the discipline of work. It satisfies their need for getting things done in an orderly way.

3. They seem quite willing to sacrifice some of their own self-interest for the welfare of the organization they serve. For example, they are more willing to make contributions to charities.

4. They have a keen sense of justice. It is almost as if they feel that if a person works hard and sacrifices for the good of the organization, he should and will get a just reward for his effort.

It is easy to see how each of these four concerns helps a person become a good manager, concerned about what the institution can achieve.

Maturity

Before we go on to look at how the workshops can help managers to improve their managerial style and recognize their own motivations, let us consider one more fact we discovered in studying the better managers at George Prentice's company. They were more mature. Mature people can be most simply described as less egotistic. Somehow their positive self-image is not at stake in what they are doing. They are less defensive, more willing to seek advice from experts, and have a longer range view. They accumulate fewer personal possessions and seem older and wiser. It is as if they have awakened to the fact that they are not going to live forever and have lost some of the feeling that their own personal future is all that important.

Many U.S. businessmen fear this kind of maturity. They suspect that it will make them less hard driving, less expansion-minded, and less committed to organizational effectiveness. Our data do not support their fears. These fears are exactly the ones George Prentice had before he went to the workshop. Afterward he was a more effective manager, not despite his loss of some of the sense of his own importance, but because of it. The reason is simple: his subordinates believed afterward that he genuinely was more concerned about the company than about himself. Where once they respected his confidence but feared him, they now trust him. Once he supported their image of him as a "big man" by talking about the new Porsche and the new Honda he had bought; when we saw him recently he said, almost as an aside, "I don't buy things anymore."

CHANGING MANAGERIAL STYLE

George Prentice was able to change his managerial style after learning more about himself in a workshop. But does self-knowledge generally improve managerial behavior?

Some people might ask, "What good does it do to know, if I am a manager, that I should have a strong power motive, not too great a concern about being liked, a sense of discipline, a high level of maturity, and a coaching managerial style? What can I do about it?" The answer is that workshops for managers that give information to them in a supportive setting enable them to change.

Consider the results shown in *Exhibit 3*, where "before" and "after" scores are compared. Once again we use the responses of subordinates to give some measure of the effectiveness of managers. To judge by their subordinates' responses, the managers were clearly more effective afterward. The subordinates felt that they were given more responsibility, that they received more rewards, that the organizational procedures were clearer, and that morale was higher. These differences are all statistically significant.

But what do these differences mean in human terms? How did the managers change? Sometimes they decided they should get into another line of work. This happened to Ken Briggs, for example, who found that the reason he was doing so poorly as a manager was because he had almost no interest in influencing others. He understood how he would have to change if he were to do well in his present job, but in the end decided, with the help of management, that he would prefer to work back into his first love, sales.

Ken Briggs moved into "remaindering," to help retail outlets for his

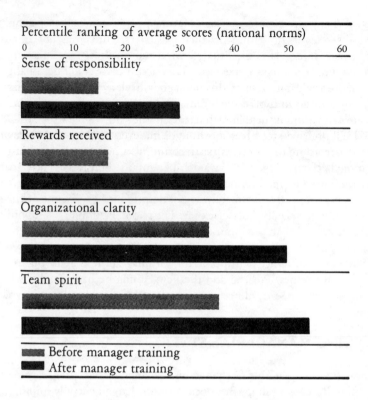

Percentile ranking of average scores (national norms)

Exhibit 3. Average scores on selected climate dimensions by over 50 salesmen before and after their managers were trained.

company's products get rid of last year's stock so that they could take on each year's new styles. He is very successful in this new role; he has cut costs, increased dollar volume, and in time has worked himself into an independent role selling some of the old stock on his own in a way that is quite satisfactory to the business. And he does not have to manage anybody anymore.

In George Prentice's case, less change was needed. He was obviously a very competent person with the right motive profile for a top managerial position. When he was promoted, he performed even more successfully than before because he realized the need to become more positive in his approach and less coercive in his managerial style.

But what about a person who does not want to change his job and discovers that he does not have the right motive profile to be a manager?

The case of Charlie Blake is instructive. Charlie was as low in power motivation as Ken Briggs, his need to achieve was about average, and his affiliation motivation was above average. Thus he had the affiliative manager profile, and, as expected, the morale among his subordinates was very low. When Charlie learned that his subordinates' sense of responsibility and perception of a reward system were in the 10th percentile and that team spirit was in the 30th, he was shocked. When shown a film depicting three managerial climates, Charlie said he preferred what turned out to be the authoritarian climate. He became angry when the workshop trainer and other members in the group pointed out the limitations of this managerial style. He became obstructive in the group process and objected strenuously to what was being taught.

In an interview conducted much later, Charlie said, ''I blew my cool. When I started yelling at you for being all wrong, I got even madder when you pointed out that, according to my style questionnaire, you bet that that was just what I did to my salesmen. Down underneath I knew something must be wrong. The sales performance for my division wasn't so good. Most of it was due to me anyway and not to my salesmen. Obviously their reports that they felt very little responsibility was delegated to them and that I didn't reward them at all had to mean something. So I finally decided to sit down and try to figure what I could do about it. I knew I had to start being a manager instead of trying to do everything myself and blowing my cool at others because they didn't do what I thought they should. In the end, after I calmed down on the way back from the workshop, I realized that it is not so bad to make a mistake; it's bad not to learn from it.''

After the course, Charlie put his plans into effect. Six months later, his subordinates were asked to rate him again. He attended a second workshop to study these results and reported, ''On the way home I was very nervous. I knew I had been working with those guys and not selling so much myself, but I was very much afraid of what they were going to say about how things were going in the office. When I found out that the team spirit and some of those other low scores had jumped from around 30th to the 55th percentile, I was so delighted and relieved that I couldn't say anything all day long.''

When he was asked how he acted differently from before, he said, ''In previous years when the corporate headquarters said we had to make 110% of our original goal, I had called the salesmen in and said, in effect, 'This is ridiculous; we are not going to make it, but you know perfectly well what will happen if we don't. So get out there and work your tail off.' The result was that I worked 20 hours a day and they did nothing.

''This time I approached it differently. I told them three things. First, they were going to have to do some sacrificing for the company. Second, working harder is not going to do much good because we are already working about as hard as we can. What will be required are special deals and promotions. You are going to have to figure out some new angles if we are to make it. Third, I'm going to back you up. I'm going to set a realistic goal with each of you. If you make that goal but don't make the company goal, I'll see to it that you are not punished. But if you do make the company goal, I'll see to it that you will get some kind of special rewards.''

When the salesmen challenged Charlie saying he did not have enough influence to give them rewards, rather than becoming angry Charlie promised rewards that were in his power to give—such as longer vacations.

Note that Charlie has now begun to behave in a number of ways that we found to be characteristic of the good institutional manager. He is, above all, higher in power motivation, the desire to influence his salesmen, and lower in his tendency to try to do everything himself. He asks the men to sacrifice for the company. He does not defensively chew them out when they challenge him but tries to figure out what their needs are so that he can influence them. He realizes that his job is more one of strengthening and supporting his subordinates than of criticizing them. And he is keenly interested in giving them just rewards for their efforts.

The changes in his approach to his job have certainly paid off. The sales figures for his office in 1973 were up more than 16% over 1972 and up still further in 1974 over 1973. In 1973 his gain over the previous year ranked seventh in the nation; in 1974 it ranked third. And he wasn't the only one in his company to change managerial styles. Overall sales at his company were up substantially in 1973 as compared with 1972, an increase which played a large part in turning the overall company performance around from a $15 million loss in 1972 to a $3 million profit in 1973. The company continued to improve its performance in 1974 with an 11% further gain in sales and a 38% increase in profits.

Of course not everyone can be reached by a workshop. Henry Carter managed a sales office for a company which had very low morale (around the 20th percentile) before he went for training. When morale was checked some six months later, it had not improved. Overall sales gain subsequently reflected this fact since it was only 2% above the previous year's figures.

Oddly enough, Henry's problem was that he was so well liked by everybody that he felt little pressure to change. Always the life of the party, he is particularly popular because he supplies other managers with special hard-to-get brands of cigars and wines at a discount. He uses his close ties with everyone to bolster his position in the company, even though it is known that his office does not perform well compared with others.

His great interpersonal skills became evident at the workshop when he did very poorly at one of the business games. When the discussion turned to why he had done so badly and whether he acted that way on the job, two prestigious participants immediately sprang to his defense, explaining away Henry's failure by arguing that the way he did things was often a real help to others and the company. As a result, Henry did not have to cope with such questions at all. He had so successfully developed his role as a likeable, helpful friend to everyone in management that, even though his salesmen performed badly, he did not feel under any pressure to change.

CHECKS AND BALANCES

What have we learned from Ken Briggs, George Prentice, Charlie Blake, and Henry Carter? Principally, we have discovered what motive combination makes an effective manager. We have also seen that change is possible if a person has the right combination of qualities.

Oddly enough, the good manager in a large company does not have a high need for achievement, as we define and measure that motive, although there must be plenty of that motive somewhere in his organization. The top managers shown here have a high need for power and an interest in influencing others, both greater than their interest in being liked by people. The manager's concern for power should be socialized—controlled so that the institution as a whole, not only the individual, benefits. Men and nations with this motive profile are empire builders; they tend to create high morale and to expand the organizations they head.

But there is also danger in this motive profile; empire building can lead to imperialism and authoritarianism in companies and in countries.

The same motive pattern which produces good power management can also lead a company or a country to try to dominate others, ostensibly in the interests of organizational expansion. Thus it is not surprising that big business has had to be regulated from time to time by federal agencies. And it is most likely that international agencies will perform the same regulative function for empire-building countries.

For an individual, the regulative function is performed by two characteristics that are part of the profile of the very best managers—a greater emotional maturity, where there is little egotism, and a democratic, coaching managerial style. If an institutional power motivation is checked by maturity, it does not lead to an aggressive, egotistic expansiveness.

For countries, this checking means that they can control their destinies beyond their borders without being aggressive and hostile. For individuals, it means they can control their subordinates and influence others around them without resorting to coercion or to an authoritarian management style. Real disinterested statesmanship has a vital role to play at the top of both countries and companies.

Summarized in this way, what we have found out through empirical and statistical investigations may just sound like good common sense. But the improvement over common sense is that now the characteristics of the good manager are objectively known. Managers of corporations can select those who are likely to be good managers and train those already in managerial positions to be more effective with more confidence.

Whatever else organizations may be (problem-solving instruments, socio-technical systems, reward systems, and so on), they are political structures. This means that organizations operate by distributing authority and setting a stage for the exercise of power. It is no wonder, therefore, that individuals who are highly motivated to secure and use power find a familiar and hospitable environment in business. [3]

3. From "Power and Politics in Organizational Life," by Abraham Zaleznik, HBR May-June 1970, p. 47.

Chapter 13

Leader Behavior and Member Reaction in Three "Social Climates"

Ralph White
Ronald Lippitt

This investigation was carried out in two different parts: an exploratory experiment and a second, more extensive research. The primary aim of the first study was to develop techniques for creating and describing the "social atmosphere" of children's clubs and for quantitatively recording the effects of varied social atmospheres upon group life and individual behavior. Two degrees of control of group life, labeled "democratic" and "authoritarian," were used as the experimental variables. The second study had a number of purposes. The one most relevant to this report is to examine the effects upon individual and group behavior of three variations in social atmosphere, labeled "democratic," "authoritarian," and "laissez-faire." The actual meaning of the adjectives used to label these social climates is necessarily somewhat different from the meanings attributed to them in political and economic discussions. The accompanying tabulation describes briefly the chief characteristics of these three treatment variations.

In the first study (Experiment I), the same leader met with two clubs. One group was led in a democratic manner, the other in an autocratic style. Both groups had five members, ten years of age. The behavior of the leader and the members was recorded by observers. A fuller description of the experimental plan for this investigation may be found in Lippitt (1).

In the second study (Experiment II), four groups of ten-year-old boys were used. These were also five-member clubs which met after school to engage in hobby activities. The groups were roughly equated on patterns of interpersonal relationships, intellectual, physical, and socio-economic status, and personality characteristics. Four adult leaders were trained to proficiency in the three leadership treatments. The leaders were shifted from club to club every six weeks,

Authoritarian	Democratic	Laissez-faire
1. All determination of policy by the leader	1. All policies a matter of group discussion and decision, encouraged and assisted by the leader	1. Complete freedom for group or individual decision, with a minimum of leader participation
2. Techniques and activity steps dictated by the authority, one at a time, so that future steps were always uncertain to a large degree	2. Activity perspective gained during discussion period. General steps to group goal sketched, and when technical advice was needed, the leader suggested two or more alternative procedures from which choice could be made	2. Various materials supplied by the leader, who made it clear that he would supply information when asked. He took no other part in work discussion
3. The leader usually dictated the particular work task and work companion of each member	3. The members were free to work with whomever they chose, and the division of tasks was left up to the group	3. Complete nonparticipation of the leader
4. The dominator tended to be "personal" in his praise and criticism of the work of each member; remained aloof from active group participation except when demonstrating	4. The leader was "objective" or "fact-minded" in his praise and criticism, and tried to be a regular group member in spirit without doing too much of the work	4. Infrequent spontaneous comments on member activities unless questioned, and no attempt to appraise or regulate the course of events

each one changing his leadership style at the time of this transition. Thus, each club experienced each of the leadership styles under different leaders. All clubs met in the same place and did the same activities with similar materials. The behavior of the leaders and the reactions of the boys were observed during every meeting. The members and their parents were also interviewed concerning

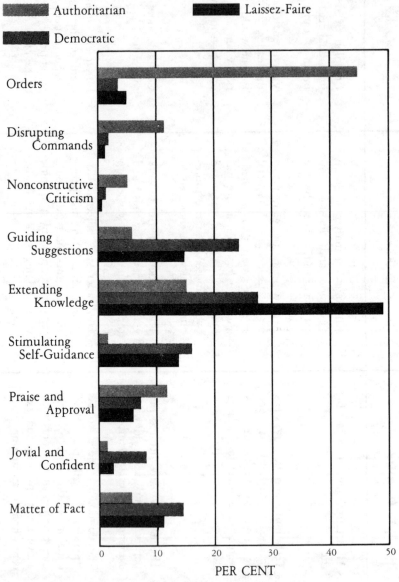

Figure 1. Comparison of behavior of average authoritarian, democratic, and laissez-faire leader.

their feelings about the club in the case of the boys and the nature of parent-child relations in the case of the home visits. A more complete description of the experimental plan for the second study may be found in Lippitt and White (2).

In the following pages we shall first describe in some detail the nature of the leadership behavior typically used in each of the three leader treatments. The second part of this report describes the behavior of the members when under the direction of a leader using each of the variations.

LEADER'S BEHAVIOR

To some extent, the observation of what the leaders actually did was a process of discovery, both for the observer and for the leaders themselves. As we shall see, some of the statistically significant differences in leaders' behavior could not have been directly deduced from our central definitions, although they tend to be consistent with these role definitions. The adult who was faced with the constantly changing problems of leading a group of children found himself doing things which he could never have anticipated he would do. And the unanticipated things which the leader with the predetermined autocratic philosophy did were quite different from the things which he did in the same situations when he changed to the democratic role. The data described the different types of leader-behavior which resulted from the attempts at consistent application of the varying philosophies of leadership represented by the definitions of autocracy, democracy, and laissez-faire.

Figure 1 presents a summary graph of the leader behavior in terms of the percentage of total behavior in each category. These percentages are based upon the grand total of behavior in a given style of leadership over six meetings. All differences concerning leadership behavior which are discussed are statistically significant at the 5% level of confidence or better.

Giving Orders

Statistically, the chief single characteristic of our autocratic leader role, as distinguished from both democracy and laissez-faire, is the giving of orders. Forty-five per cent of the verbal behavior of the autocrats, in contrast to 3% in democracy and 4% in laissez-faire, consisted of this simplest form of the imposition of one human will upon another. Many of these were direct orders or statements in the imperative form:

"Get your work aprons on."[1]

1. The illustrations used throughout this chapter are sample episodes or units of descriptions taken from the continuous research records of the group process.

> "All right, put your brush away."
> "Each of you turn yours over and try on the back."

And many were indirect orders, not in the imperative form, but recognizable as autocratic if given in certain contexts and in certain tones of voice:

> "Now we need some plaster."
> "That should be about two-thirds full."
> "Today we've got to paint and letter the sign."
> "Before we start there's something we have to do. That's to make work aprons."

Such orders clearly correspond to the part of our strict experimental definition of autocratic leadership which calls for "high goal and means control."

Disrupting Commands

A more ambiguous criterion of means and end control is the giving of "disrupting commands"—commands which cut across an expressed wish or on-going activity of a member of the group, and substitute for it some wish of the leader. Such commands represented 11% of the verbal behavior of our autocratic leaders, as contrasted to 1% or less for our democratic and laissez-faire leaders. For example:

> "I want to saw."
> "No, Bill, you and Hamil make another leg." Mr. Bohlen says he wants "two fellows." Fred volunteers, "Let Reilly and me do it." But Mr. Bohlen appoints two others: "I'm going to let Sam and Leonard do this." Mr. Bohlen consistenly refuses to let Fred do what he wants to do—painting on the sign.

The data show that the laissez-faire leaders were consistent in restraining themselves from initiating goals and means.

Non-Objective Criticism And Praise

A third type of behavior which was more characteristic of our autocratic leaders was "non-objective criticism"—criticism which was adverse and personal in character and which did not point objectively toward improvement by suggesting a reason for failure or a way of doing the thing better. Such criticism constituted 5% of the leaders' behavior in our autocratic atmospheres and 1% in the democratic and laissez-faire atmospheres. For example:

"You're not making a sack, you're making an apron."
"No, you can't make it like that. That isn't a good job at all."
"Who was it left the tool box on the floor again?"

Praise was also found more often in the autocrats' behavior (11%) than in that of the democratic (7%) or laissez-faire (5%) leaders. For example:

Fred is doing a nice job of lettering, and Mr. Bohlen compliments him on it—the second compliment he has given him today. "That's the best side view there. But I think I want a front view."
(In democracy) Bill to Mr. Rankin: "Eddie really did a swell job on that, didn't he? I couldn't do as good a job as that."
Mr. Rankin: "Yeah, it's swell."

Different kinds of praise in different contexts can obviously (like different kinds of criticism) have widely different psychological meanings. Yet it is probably significant, from more than one standpoint, that *both* praise and criticism were especially characteristic of our autocratic leaders. From our present standpoint, however, the most interesting implication of the large amount of both praise and criticism is that both suggest an emphasis on *personal evaluation from the leader's standpoint*. Both suggest an emphasis on a status-hierarchy, and both suggest that the leader is setting himself up as chief judge of the status and achievement of the members of the group.

Guiding Suggestions

We come now to the forms of leader-behavior that were more characteristic of democratic or of laissez-faire leadership than of autocratic. For example, as a direct counterpart of the order-giving which was characteristic of the autocratic style, we find "guiding suggestions" to be one of the two most frequent forms of verbal behavior on the part of democratic leaders. It represents 24% of the democratic leaders' behavior, as compared with 6% of the autocrats' behavior. The line between "guiding suggestions" and the indirect type of order-giving is, of course, somewhat difficult to draw. However, the reliability of making this distinction in the coding of the conversation was satisfactory. The way in which we defined "guiding suggestions" can be seen from the following examples, which were classified in this way:

"Did you ever try going the other way—with the grain?"
"That's a knife-sharpener so you can have sharp knives to carve wood with."
Bill holds up his model for Mr. Rankin to see. "That's pretty weak there." Mr. Rankin: "If you don't get it any thinner I think it will be all right."

Mr. Rankin sits down beside Van as he works. "That's good, Van, be-cause if you leave as big a piece as that you can try again."

The distinguishing characteristic in each of these examples is that a given course of action is implicitly or explicitly related to one of the boy's *own* pur-poses. Very similar in psychological meaning is the *clarifying of alternatives,* between which the boys themselves are free to choose (which was included in this same category):

"Motion carried. Now the question is, who wants to be the G-man?" (All speak.) "Should we choose from everybody that wants to be, or just those that haven't had a chance yet?"

And similar, too, is the giving of suggestions by example rather than by pre-cept:

Reilly discovers that Mr. Rankin is making papier-mâché, and stops throwing to join him. He tears up paper too, and so does Fred. Leonard stops throwing. The group is gathered around Mr. Rankin and is listening to him and paying attention.
Bill: "Let's get ready to go home."
Mr. Rankin (picking up a broom): "We don't have much cleaning up to do today."

It should be especially noticed that a very active readiness to give guiding suggestions at precisely those moments when they are appropriate and appre-ciated, and to point out the operating procedure which lies behind the efficient action, was in practice the chief single difference between the democratic and laissez-faire leaders. In laissez-faire such suggestions made up only 14% of the leader's verbal behavior, as compared with 24% in democracy and 6% in autoc-racy.

In other words, democracy (as distinguished from laissez-faire) did not imply freedom alone, i.e., a relatively passive "regard" for the child's welfare, in the sense that the child's desires were not needlessly thwarted. If either individual welfare or group achievement is to be fully attained, the democratic leader took the viewpoint that it is necessary to have also a very *active* respect for those in-dividual desires in the sense of a constant active thinking about how they can best be realized. Only by such full participation in the life of the group can the leader really lead. For instance, the following are examples in which a boy wanted guidance and did not get it. In some situations exactly the same be-havior by the leader—throwing back the question the boy asked—would be a constructive device for stimulating self-guidance. In these situations, however, it seemed to be merely a result of insensitivity to the boy's legitimate needs for goal or means suggestions:

> Reilly: "Where can we put this up?"
> Mr. Rankin: "Where would you like to put it up?"
> Leonard: "How do you cut it?"
> Mr. Rankin: "What do you think? Cut it in the right shape..."

But, at the other extreme, the democratic leader had to avoid overcomplicated suggestions, such as the following, both of which are double-barreled and at least slightly confusing:

> "Who wants to help who to get things finished up?"
> "Have you been thinking about a G-man Club? Do you want a meeting now, fellows?"

The effective use of guiding suggestions seems to depend on timing. The democratic leader had to have a keen sense of awareness of the shifting momentary needs and interests of the boys so that he could make his suggestions at just the moments when they fitted into those interests.

Giving Information

Another major activity of the democratic leader was simply giving information, or extending the knowledge of the members of his group. This constituted 27% of the democratic leaders' behavior, and 15% of the autocratic leaders'. (In laissez-faire it was 49%, which is natural in view of the fact that the laissez-faire leaders' role was explicitly confined very largely to the giving of technical information when asked for it.) Actually the amount of technical information given by the three leader types was not significantly different, even though the proportion was so much greater in laissez-faire. Here are some typical examples of information-giving:

> Finn (holding up orangewood stick): "What's this for?"
> Mr. Rankin: "That's an orangewood stick, and the flat end is for smoothing down this way." (Demonstrates.) "This is more curved here, and you can get a smoother tip of soap because it's narrower than this."
> There is a dispute between the two groups about the ages of the knives....Reilly, Sam and Fred listen to Mr. Rowe talk about the ages of the knives. They are all very much interested.
> (In laissez-faire) Finn (very plaintively): "Why can't we have a crime?"
> Mr. Davis: "I could have a crime for you next week if you wanted me to."

One meaning of information-giving, as compared with either orders or guiding suggestions, is that there is almost no chance of its being a form of social influence or pressure. The information is simply there. The boy can take it or leave it, use it or not use it, depending on his needs at the moment.

Stimulating Self-Direction

Less frequent numerically is a group of leader-behaviors which we have called "stimulating self-direction." This type of behavior was fairly frequent in democracy and almost nonexistent in autocracy; the percentages were, respectively, 16 and 1.2. Although this made up 13% of the behavior of the laissez-faire leaders, this only represented an average of 30 such acts per meeting, as compared with 59 by democratic leaders. The meaning also tended to be quite different. In laissez-faire this type of leadership act tended to be a throwing back of responsibility on the individual member. In the democratic style it was more frequently a teaching of the total group to learn to depend on itself as a group.

One way of stimulating democratic self-direction in setting new goals and choosing means is to inculcate the democratic procedure directly: group decision, majority vote, free discussion with an opportunity for every interested person to have his say, secret ballot when appropriate, delegation of special tasks to committees, minority acceptance of majority decisions, etc. For example:

> Finn: "Guess I'll change the name of our club."
> Bill: "No, it's still the Law and Order Patrol."
> Mr. Rankin: "If the group wants to change the name, they can—if a majority wants."
> Bill: "Eddie should be captain and Van should be a lieutenant-assistant."
> Van: "Hey, that's lower than I am now, and I got a high score!"
> Mr. Rankin: "In an army, the general decides the promotions; but here, even if it is organized like an army, it seems to me the group ought to decide who should get the promotion."
> Bill: "Now you stay out of it and we three will vote." Mr. Rankin steps in to confer with Bill about taking a vote. He gives him a formal wording. "All in favor say aye, opposed, no," etc. (Bill is especially keen on formality and "having things regular.")
> Finn votes for adjournment, and the motion passes. Bill starts to ignore the vote and keep on with the discussion. Mr. Rankin: "All right we don't have any meeting now if the majority votes to adjourn."

It will be noticed that in some of the above examples the role of the democratic adult leader is chiefly one of supporting or bringing to clear expression the feeling of the majority. He is a catalyst, releasing energies that already exist in the group. This was done formally by insisting on a majority when dispute had arisen and backing up the majority with his own prestige. It was also done informally by simply listening to and drawing out the less articulate or less vociferous members of the group. It is also sometimes necessary to support a minority, especially if it is opposed by an even smaller minority. This occurred, for instance, when Finn and Hamil were refusing to accept the arbitrary leadership of Bill. The other two members did not take part in this contest so that it was actually a conflict of two against one.

> Bill: "It's time for our meeting. The second half of our meeting will come to order. Come on boys."
> Hamil: "That's what you think." He and Finn go just outside the burlap curtain surrounding the enclosure, but lift the curtain; it is cooler outside because the moving-picture lights make the enclosure itself very warm.
> Finn: "We'll just listen from out here." Bill doesn't get the response he wants and pouts while he takes up his whittling again.
> Mr. Rankin: "I shouldn't think a good chairman would whittle while the meeting was going on."
> Bill: "Well, I can't get any of the guys to come." Mr. Rankin goes over to the other two and holds up the curtain. Eddie and Van go too so that four of the five boys are gathered at the edge of the enclosure.
> Mr. Rankin: "The meeting is going on over here." (A satisfactory meeting is held, with Bill fully participating, as well as Hamil and Finn.)

The commonest form of stimulating self-direction, however, was simply to follow up a particular boy's ideas, encouraging him to elaborate them and think them through:

> Mr. Rowe: "Let's all sit down and talk it over. Sam suggested glass painting. How does it go, Sam?"
> Sam: "Get a picture under a piece of glass."
> Mr. Rowe: "How would it be if I got a big piece of glass and a big painting? Does the paint come in tubes?"
> Sam: "The stuff in bottles is better."
> Mr. Rowe: "Would everybody like to do it?"
> Reilly: "I'd like to do it."
> Lyman: "I think I'd like to do it."
> Van (in a doubtful tone): "I was thinking of a canoe [for soap carving]."
> Mr. Rankin: "I think a canoe is probably the best idea. Can you see there [picture of canoe model] how almost straight it is for a distance in the middle?"

"Jovial" And "Confiding" Behavior

The last type of conversation that was measured and that significantly distinguished the democratic club atmosphere from the other two is one which, for the want of a better term, has been characterized by the two terms "jovial" and "confiding." It represents the purely social aspect of the leader's behavior and was far more characteristic of our democratic situation than of either autocracy or laissez-faire (8% as compared with less than 1% in autocracy and in laissez-faire). For example:

> Fred talks and laughs with Mr. Rowe—far different from his behavior with Mr. Bohlen.
> There is a very nice relationship between Mr. Rowe and the group....He seems to be having the most fun of all....
> (The acute conflict between Fred and Mr. Bohlen is still fresh in everybody's mind, and on this day Fred is absent. The following topic of conversation is therefore a natural one.) Mr. Rowe: "Does Fred get into much trouble with the teacher?"
> Sam says, "I'll say!" and Lyman adds, "He got sent out of the room two times. He always does something."

This is the clearest instance of a type of behavior which was not consciously planned, but which developed as sort of a by-product of the democratic leader's total relationship to his group, usually by the initiative of group members. It has nothing directly to do with freedom or lack of freedom, but it obviously does have something to do with openness of communication which develops as a result of the relationship created by the other types of leadership behavior described above.

This completes our list of the types of conversation which were statistically analyzed and which clearly differentiated one or more of the three atmospheres. A number of incidental observations can be added, however, which were not statistically analyzed, but which help to round out the picture.

Democratic Criticism And Praise

Although it did not occur frequently enough for statistical comparison, the observer noted that the democratic leaders tended to use praise and criticism in a different way from the autocratic leaders. The democratic leaders recognized that "training in procedures" seemed to mean (*a*) helping individuals to learn the criteria and methods for evaluating their own work without dependence on the adult as well as (*b*) helping the group to learn the methods of mutual support and cooperative operation as a group. This first type of training we find exemplified in such illustrations as:

> Mr. Rankin: "That's good,_____, because if you leave as big a piece

(of soap during soapcarving period) as that you can try again (if the first try fails)."

Leader: "I think that's going to be pretty wobbly (piece of box furniture). Can you guess why I think so?"

Boy: "Maybe because there are so many bent nails and none that go through."

By this type of praise and criticism, the democratic leaders attempted to extend their assigned function of teaching a group procedure for setting goals and means to teaching of criteria and methods for *evaluating* goals and means. This seemed to be a natural part of the same leadership role.

Equalitarian Behavior

It may be worth while also to cull a number of illustrations not falling under any one topic that has already been discussed, but illustrating again, in a variety of ways, some additional implications of respect for own member's goals and means which seem to flow from the leadership patterns that were defined for the leaders. There are, for instance, some egotistical uses of the pronoun "I" by autocratic leaders which are clearly lacking in that sort of respect:

"I'm going to pick out the best one when you get done."

"Guess you'll have to put some more powder in that. I don't like it yet."

By contrast, the democratic leaders often showed equalitarian or even self-effacing behavior, and an absence of concern about their status and dignity. They took off their coats; they sat or squatted instead of standing; they worked just as the boys did and showed that they were enjoying the work just as the boys did. Other illustrations:

Mr. Rowe subordinates himself to the newly elected boy-leader. "What should I do for cleanup, Sam?"

Mr. Rankin, on the first day of democracy in the Law and Order Patrol (after a period of laissez-faire), finds Bill in a position of temporarily revived leadership. He does not challenge this leadership, but helps Bill when he can do so without antagonizing the others.

Bill is administering a test which he has carefully made up on crime-detection agencies in the community, safety rules, etc. Mr. Rankin asks: "Are you testing me too?"

Bill: "No."

Mr. Rankin (with a smile): "I'd probably get the worst grade."

Observer writes: "Another characteristic of the democratic behavior of Rankin is his emotional expressions with the boys—'Oh,' 'Aha'—and his going thoughtfully into everything the children think they want to do.''

On the other hand, the democratic leaders sometimes did not hesitate to accept delegated authority when it was unequivocally handed to them. Mr. Rankin suggests a committee to make up the crime, but the group wants to leave it to him this next time. He agrees.

In other words, the democratic leader's lack of concern about his own dignity was not a blind or compulsive self-effacement; it was a sensitive awareness of and respect for the status needs (own social goals) of the boys in the group as well as of the various other social needs that they might have in this situation.

Role-Changes By The Same Person

Did the four leaders in this experiment actually change their behavior to be consistent with the leadership policy they were supposed to be representing, or did they primarily ''keep on being like themselves'' in each of the three clubs they led? The data clearly reveal that each leader was more like the others in the same role than he was like himself from one role to another. The interviews with each boy, in which the boy compared his leaders, also indicate that the boys were actually reacting to these behavioral differences rather than to other, unchanging aspects of the leader's personalities. Certainly there must have been a core of enduring characteristics which each individual leader took with him from one club to the other. These characteristics probably exerted some influence on the perceptions and reactions of the club members, but these were evidently minor or irrelevant as far as the leader effect on the club life was concerned in the dimensions we have studied.

Summary Of Leader Behavior

We have reviewed the statistical analysis of leader behavior, with illustrations of leader behavior taken from the club records. It is clear that the leaders did behave differently in carrying out their three types of role-assignment. These differences seem to represent consistent behavioral definitions of the three types of leadership policy which we want to compare.

MAJOR DIFFERENCES IN BOYS' BEHAVIOR

The glimpses given above may have conveyed some of the ''feel'' of the atmosphere resulting from the three types of leadership. We will now present the results of the experiments more fully and systematically, in terms of the chief statistical differences between the boys' behavior under autocratic, democratic, and laissez-faire types of leadership. Summary graphs will be found at the end of the chapter. The findings can be grouped under six major generalizations, which are discussed in the remainder of this chapter.

Laissez-Faire Was Not The Same As Democracy

Laissez-faire was less organized, less efficient, and definitely less satisfying than democracy to the boys themselves. Since there is a general tendency to attribute to democracy certain results which are actually results of laissez-faire, it is necessary to make this distinction very clearly before going on to any further thinking about differences between democracy and autocracy. The boys' behavior in laissez-faire differed from their behavior in democracy in the following ways:

1. *Less work was done, and poorer work.* In democracy, the time periods during which there was general absorption in constructive activity or psychological involvement in the work situation represented 50% of the total time; in laissez-faire, 33%. In democracy, the time periods of general out-and-out loafing constituted 0.2% of the total time; in laissez-faire, 5%. And in *quality* of work accomplished, the difference was considerably greater than these figures indicate. The lack of active guiding suggestions in laissez-faire often resulted in disorganization and in failure and setbacks in work, which were discouraging and exasperating. Some outright aggression can be directly attributed to such work failures, as well as much loss of interest in the job that was being done. For instance:

> Eddie and Bill have mixed the plaster-of-Paris before getting the sand and making a print. Mr. Davis doesn't step in to tell them it will soon get hard. Van tries the plaster-of-Paris and finds it quite stiff. Eddie, Bill, and Van finish a handprint and go to pour the plaster-of-Paris, but find it has hardened in the can. Bill pounds at it. Eddie stamps in the sand with his shoe, spoiling the print they had prepared. Finn and Hamil finish some new guns. Everybody is now milling around idly except Bill, who keeps on trying to get the hard plaster-of-Paris out of the can. Horseplay is about to begin.
>
> Fred breaks his cast, is discouraged, goes on and tears up the whole thing. (Later in the same hour, he was the leader in destroying the work of the "Monday gang.")
>
> Fred watches, sitting on a stool he made. A leg falls off. He breaks up the rest of it.

2. *They played more.* Play-minded conversation with other boys was more than 2.5 times as frequent in laissez-faire (33 as compared with 13 in democracy; significant at the 1% level). Pure silliness was included in this category. For instance:

Leonard (hearing the term "orange sticks"): "Orange sticks—pick up sticks."
Ray: "Hooray, hooray—I-O-W-A!"

Democracy Can Be Efficient

Since arguments for autocracy often take the form of claiming that democracy is not efficient enough to accomplish a certain end (such as winning a war, reducing production costs, or educating a child in necessary basic skills), it is of interest to consider the degree of efficiency of the democratic groups in our experiments. Did these groups achieve the ends the boys themselves wanted to achieve?

On the whole, they did. The question is not a simple one, since the boys did not want work achievement to the exclusion of other goals. (And in this respect, of course, the situation was also not comparable with the many situations in which society demands that a certain end be accomplished by methods that are inherently distasteful.) Our clubs were recreational clubs. They were "to have fun," and the boys came to them expecting to have fun through sociability, and probably through occasional good-natured horseplay, as well as through carpentry, painting, and organized crime-games. A respect for the boys' own legitimate goals would perhaps necessitate evaluating "efficiency" as much in terms of the achievement of these social goals as in terms of the achievement of work goals. And certainly from this combined standpoint democracy was decidedly more "efficient" than either autocracy or laissez-faire, since it achieved simultaneously both goals, while autocracy, in the main, achieved only work goals, and laissez-faire achieved (if anything) only social goals. But even from the narrow standpoint of work goals alone, the evidence suggests that in our situation the democratic groups were about *as* efficient as the autocratic ones.

This conclusion is based upon an over-all impression of the observers and experimenters. It is also based on a balancing of certain factors of efficiency which appeared to be more prominent in autocracy and others which appeared to be more prominent in democracy. On the one hand, there was a large quantity of work done in autocracy—or at least, in those autocratic groups in which the reaction to autocracy was a submissive one. In such groups the time periods of general absorption in work constituted 74% of the total time, as compared with 50% in democracy, and 52% in the one instance (in the second experiment) of an aggressive group reaction to autocracy. On the other hand, the amount of genuine interest in work was unquestionably higher in democracy. This was shown by a somewhat larger amount of "work-minded" conversation in democracy (63 such remarks per child as compared with 53 in the aggressive reaction to autocracy and 52 in the submissive reaction). This difference is not significant at the 1% level, but it does strongly suggest that work-mindedness was at least *as* great in democracy as in autocracy. Some illustrations of "work-minded" remarks:

"Let's see, who's got the saw?"
"I'm going to get a chisel to chisel that out with."
"How come some of these pieces are bigger than others?"
"Because they belong to the end of the wing out here."
"I guess all these pieces go together."
"Well this is supposed to stand up straight."

More significantly, the difference in amount of genuine, spontaneous work interest was shown by the difference in the boys' behavior *when the adult leader left the room.* Typically, the boys in democracy kept right on working whether their leader was present or not, while in autocracy when the leader left, the boys stopped working as if glad to be relieved of a task which they "had" to do. In democracy there was a very slight drop in proportion of general work involvement during the leader-out periods—from 50% to 46%. On the other hand, in the one group which reacted aggressively to autocratic leadership, the drop in work involvement was from 52% to 16%, and in the three groups reacting submissively it was from 74% to 29%.

There was, finally, an impression on the part of the experimenters that both work and play showed a higher level of *originality* or creative thinking in the democracies than under either of the other types of leadership. There was a larger amount of creative thinking about the work in progress than in autocracy, and it was more sustained and practical than in laissez-faire.

Autocracy Can Create Much Hostility And Aggression, Including Aggression Against Scapegoats

The word "can" is important here, because this reaction did not always occur. It occurred to a very marked degree in Experiment I, and to some degree in one of the four groups that took part in Experiment II; but the other three groups in Experiment II showed, instead, a "submissive" reaction in which there was significantly *less* overt aggression than in democracy.

The clearest evidence comes from Experiment I. For example:

1. "Dominating ascendance" occurred 392 times in the autocratic group and only 81 times in the democratic group. The category "ascendance" showed no significant difference between the groups (63% of all child-to-child behavior in autocracy, and almost as much—57%—in democracy). But the reason for this apparent similarity was that the term "ascendance" was so broad as to be somewhat meaningless psychologically. When three kinds of ascendance were distinguished, "dominating," "objective," and "friendly" ascendance, it was found that dominating ascendance was highly characteristic of the autocratic

group, while objective and friendly ascendance were characteristic of the democratic group. Some illustrations of dominating ascendance follow.

> "Shut up."
> Two children look in, and Sarah and Jack repulse them with comments of "not wanted."
> "You put them away; you dumped them."
> "Give me some of that paint." (Remarks of this sort are classified as dominating or objective, depending upon context and upon tone of voice. In this case it was classed as dominating.)
> "Get a pan of water, Jack."
> "Why don't you get it yourself?"

Friendly ascendance, on the other hand, occurred 24 times in the autocratic group and 230 times in the democratic group:

> "Let's do coloring."
> "Carry the bottles over there."
> "You've got to get all the cracks filled in."
> "Better fill in your side there."

2. Definite hostility occurred 186 times in the autocratic group and only 6 times in the democratic group. It represented 18% of all the recorded social interactions in the autocratic group, and less than 1% of all the interactions in the democratic group. (This category is included in the larger category of "dominating ascendance.") Some illustrations:

> "You guys haven't got nothing done yet."
> "Hey, you, don't throw water on my hair."
> "Look out, Tom, quit throwing things."
> "Don't start crabbing. I wouldn't talk too much yourself."
> "Oh God, Tom, don't you know anything?"

3. Aggressive demands for attention occurred 39 times in the autocratic group and 3 times in the democratic group. For example:

> Joe (in a loud voice): "I guess this is a mighty fine job I'm doing!"
> Tom: "I'm a lot smarter than you are. Boy-oh-boy, can I ever brag."
> Harry: "I'll say you can."
> Joe: "Sure, I've got three radios; I ought to know."
> All the others: "You have not!"
> Joe: "Oh yes I have."

4. Destruction of own property was conspicuous at the end of the meeting of the autocratic group, and did not occur at all in the democratic group:

Peculiar actions begin after the leader (in the autocratic group) announces that there will be no more meetings. The leader asks Harry and Jack to put more paper on the floor to work on. They put it down and then run and jump on it time and again in a wild manner. The masks are divided out as had been decided by the voting, and Jack immediately begins to throw his around violently, pretending to jump on it. He throws it down again and again, laughing. Ray wants to know if it won't break, then starts to throw his down too. Later Jack and Harry chase each other around the room wildly with streamers of toweling.

5. Scapegoat behavior was conspicuous in the autocratic group, and scarcely occurred at all in the democratic group. "Scapegoat behavior" is here defined as the concentration or polarization of group aggression against a single "innocent" object, i.e., a person or group which does not actually threaten or frustrate the group to an extent comparable with the aggression that occurs. Presumably in this case the autocratic leader was the source of most of the frustration in the autocratic group, yet only a small part of the resulting aggression was directed against him; most of it was directed by the club members against each other. It could therefore be called "displaced aggression." When this displaced aggression is concentrated against a single person, as occurred twice during the course of the meetings of the autocratic group in Experiment I, it can be called "scapegoat behavior."

Autocracy Can Create Discontent That Does Not Appear On The Surface

Less dramatic but more fundamental than the question of aggression is the question of total need satisfaction. Under which major type of leadership is there likely to be more satisfaction of the boys' own needs, and why?

The answer is far from simple. There is no reason to think that democracy is necessarily superior from the standpoint of immediate personal satisfaction. It is a well-established fact that autocracy is often satisfying to some of the needs—the regressive needs, perhaps—of the ruled as well as the rulers. There can be satisfactions in passivity, satisfactions in not having to think, satisfactions in identifying (on an irreal level) with a strong, dominating leader image. On the other hand, it is also obvious, and needs no proof, that autocracy is always frustrating insofar as it imposes barriers to the satisfaction of individual needs. The real problem, then, is to pin down and describe scientifically the specific factors that determine whether, in a given case, the regressive need satisfactions or the frustrations will predominate. Some of the evidence bearing on this point has already been presented. The aggression shown in some of the autocratic groups points to probable frustration—if the frustration-aggression hypothesis has any weight. Also, the lack of spontaneous work interest in autocracy is a relevant fact. If the boys stopped work when the autocrat left the room, it was an indication that they had not been particularly enjoying it when he was in the room. It meant that the work has become merely a task, rather than something to be done with spontaneous zest and enjoyment. In this section, we shall present additional evidence, and in doing so we shall focus on an aspect of the matter which has not hitherto been emphasized: the fact that much of the discontent which existed was not immediately obvious.

The deceptiveness of autocracy in this respect is a fact that needs more emphasis than it has usually received. For example, out of our six autocratic setups (one in Experiment I, and five in Experiment II), five were in some degree deceptive, insofar as the discontent which existed did not show itself to any appreciable extent in protests to the autocrat himself. The evidence that latent discontent did exist in at least some of the other five autocratic situations can be summarized as follows:

1. Four boys actually dropped out, and all of them did so during those autocratic club periods in which overt rebellion did not occur.

2. Of 20 boys who made direct comparisons between their autocratic and democratic leaders, 19 preferred the democratic leader. These comparisons were, of course, made in private interviews with a third person who was not identified in any way with the leader who was being explicitly or implicitly criticized. It was also noticeable that most of the criticisms that did occur were mild and qualified. Nevertheless, when forced to make a choice, their vote was almost unanimous.

3. Discontent in autocracy was occasionally expressed even during the meetings themselves. In Experiment II, the average number of discontented remarks to other boys was 4.4 per meeting in autocracy (aggressive reaction), 2.1 in autocracy (submissive reaction), 3.1 in laissez-faire, and only 0.8 in democracy. The difference between democracy and the submissive reaction to autocracy is significant at the 1% level. Similar, but not as significant statistically, is the difference in number of expressions of discontent directly to the adult leader. In autocracy (aggressive reaction) these averaged 11.1 per meeting; in autocracy (submissive reaction) the average was 2.0; it was 1.5 in laissez-faire and again only 0.8 in democracy. In this case, the difference between democracy and the submissive reaction to autocracy is significant at only the 10% level.

4. "Release" behavior on the day of transition to a freer atmosphere suggested the presence of previous frustration. There were three occasions when a group which had shown the submissive reaction to autocracy came out of this somewhat repressive atmosphere into the freer atmosphere of democracy or laissez-faire. In two of these cases, the first day of freedom was marked by an especially large amount of aggressive behavior (much of it, of course, playful in character). The first explanation that suggests itself is that on these days the boys were "blowing off steam"; discontent in autocracy had led to bottled-up tension, and when the lid was off, the tension discharged itself in a more or less explosive way. Actually, the explanation is probably somewhat more complex than this. On the first day of permissive leadership, the boys apparently still

had the status needs and self-assertive impulses which were frustrated by autocracy, but they no longer felt any great need to inhibit these impulses. They were in the same general situation so that they were reminded of their former frustration, and yet their new freedom contrasted with the old restraint in such a way as to make itself prominent in the psychological field, as if each boy had said to himself, "Aha! *Now* I can do what I've been wanting to do in this club!" On later days the thrill of newfound freedom apparently wore off, and, in addition, the spontaneous interest in work which tended to develop in democracy was stronger on later days than it was at first.

There Was More Dependence And Less Individuality In Autocracy

1. In autocracy, more of the boys' behavior was classified as "submissive" or "dependent." In Experiment I, the number of "submissive" actions toward the adult leader was 256 in autocracy and 134 in democracy. In Experiment II, the number of "dependent" remarks to the leader by each boy averaged 14 in the aggressive reaction to autocracy, 16 in the submissive reaction, 4 in laissez-faire, and 6 in democracy. The difference between democracy and either type of autocracy is significant at the 1% level. Some illustrations:

"Is this O.K.?"
Bill starts to hold up his hand for advice. "Mr. Rowe, shall I paint the bottom of this or not?"

2. Conversation in autocracy was less varied—more confined to the immediate club situation. In Experiment II, the amount of "out-of-field" conversation was significantly less in the submissive reaction to autocracy than in any of the other three group atmospheres. The figures: democracy 14, laissez-faire 13, aggressive reaction to autocracy 12, and submissive reaction 5. The difference between the last figure and any of the other three is significant at the 1% level. Some illustrations of what was called "out-of-field" conversation:

Bill: "Some day I'm going to get me a job at the glass works."
Van: "I wish I could get a job."
Bill: "You should get out and get a job in the newspaper and then work yourself up. That's what I did." (He sells papers on the corner.) "And maybe someday you'll be able to get a good job."
Big conversation about pussy willows; then about places where the boys had traveled.
Leonard: "I saw your girl's picture in the paper, in the Press Citizen. She's fat, boy."
Reilly: "She's not fat, boy. You probably didn't see her."
Leonard: "She is fat. She's not slender."

No figures are available for Experiment I, but the impression of the experimenter is that the same difference held good there also.

3. In the submissive reaction to autocracy there was an absolute (though not a relative) reduction in individual differences in the various behavior categories. The essential fact here is that the total volume of conversation was significantly lowered in the submissive reaction to autocracy, even though the adult did not tell the boys to "keep still" or directly discourage sociability in any way. The mean total amount of recorded child-to-child conversation was 298 in laissez-faire, 220 in democracy, 200 in the aggressive reaction to autocracy, and, in the submissive reaction to autocracy, only 126. The difference between this and the figure for democracy is significant at the 1% level. In other words, there was a sort of general subduedness in the atmosphere, the animal spirits of the boys were damped down, and they kept rather soberly at work. With this reduction in total amount, the range of individual differences in amount of "aggressiveness," or "demands for attention," was correspondingly reduced. Whether this absolute reduction in individual differences has any psychological significance, apart from the general reduction of volume with which it coincided, is a question which we prefer to leave open.

There Was More Group-Mindedness And More Friendliness In Democracy

1. The pronoun "I" was used less frequently. One highly objective approach to the problem of group-mindedness is simply to count the number of times that the members of the group use the pronoun *I* (or *me*, or *mine*) in comparison with the number of times that they use the pronoun *we* (or *us*, or *ours*). Which is more frequent, I-centered remarks such as "I want this," or we-centered remarks such as "We need that"? In Experiment I, this appeared to be a very promising index. In the autocratic group the proportion of singular pronouns in the total of all first person pronouns was 82%, and in the democratic group only 64%. In Experiment II, however, although there was some difference in the same direction, it was not statistically significant.

2. Spontaneous subgroups were larger. In Experiment I, a count was made of the frequency of subgroups representing the highest amount of unity possible in a five-person group (5 and 4-1) and the lowest possible amount of unity (2-1-1-1 and 1-1-1-1-1). The high-unity structures occurred 14 times in the autocratic group and 41 times in the democratic group, while the low-unity structures occurred 41 times in the autocratic group and 19 times in the democratic group. This difference is in spite of, rather than because of, the direct influence of the leader; he exerted his influence in the autocratic group much more often in the direction of higher group unity than in the opposite direction. But in autocracy his direct influence was more than balanced by a strong spontaneous tendency to group fragmentation or disintegration. (In Experiment II, this type of data was not obtained.)

3. "Group-minded" remarks were much more frequent. The "We/I ratio" is atomistic insofar as it deals with words out of context. The word *I*, for instance, may be used in the sentence, "I think we'd better pour in the water now." Here it does not indicate egotism or individualistic competition; in its context it is clearly subordinate to a wholly group-minded idea. More significant than the We/I ratio, therefore, is the number of remarks which were classified as "group-minded." This was done only in Experiment II. The results showed that the highest percentage of group-minded remarks was in laissez-faire—which is paradoxical, in view of the low amount of effective group cooperation in laissez-faire. But an analysis of the actual remarks showed that many of them expressed not the existence of group unity but a *desire* for it:

> "Hey, how about us having a meeting?"
> "Well, we have to do something."
> "Now if we just had a club...."

On the other hand, the contrast between democracy and both forms of autocracy seems to show a genuine difference in effective group-mindedness. The figures are: democracy 18, aggressive reaction to autocracy 7, submissive reaction to autocracy 4. The difference between democracy and each of the others is significant at the 1% level. Some illustrations:

> Finn: "I wish that guy [the "hostile stranger"] would stop telling us stuff and tearing down our work. We won't be able to finish it."
> Eddie: "We're going to vote about it."
> Finn: "We can't leave it here. It's our last day. We're all in charge of this airplane from now on."
> Leonard: "I'll take it home and hang it up."
> Reilly: "You won't if the club doesn't say so."

4. "Friendly" remarks were slightly more frequent. In Experiment I, as we have already noted, "friendly ascendance" occurred 24 times in the autocratic group and 34 times in the democratic group. Similarly, "submissive" behavior of one child to another (which might better have been called "agreeable" or "cooperative" behavior in many cases) occurred 120 times in autocracy and 188 times in democracy. The category of "friendly" behavior was not used in the analysis.

In Experiment II, the category of "friendly" was used, and a slight difference was found in favor of democracy as compared with either form of autocracy, but it was not statistically significant. The figures were: democracy 26, submissive reaction to autocracy 17. The difference between democracy and the submissive reaction was significant at only the 5% level, and the difference between democracy and the other two atmospheres does not even reach the 5% level of significance. It should also be noted that the proportion of friendliness in the total of all conversation was actually larger in the submissive reaction to autocracy than it was in democracy.

How can we account for this surprisingly large amount of mutual friendliness in the submissive reaction to autocracy? It seems likely that the unfriendliness which would naturally result from frustration is here counterbalanced by one or both of two factors: the general atmosphere of moral goodness which the presence of the leader seems to have inculcated (the boys were "on their good behavior"), and perhaps also a sort of drawing-together of the group because of the feeling that "we're all in the same boat." The common experience of being subjected to the same frustrating experience may have created a sort of feeling of comradeship similar to that which has often been described as existing in army groups subjected to a common danger and a common discipline. In our experiments this did not result in any responsible type of group cooperativeness ("group-minded" remarks) but it does seem to have resulted in a certain amount of individual friendliness ("friendly" remarks). Many joking and half-joking remarks are included. For instance:

> Finn: "Well, so long. I'm going to get my hair cut."
> Van: "Look at Finn, he's going to get his head cut off."
> "Now, my fine feathered friend, does this suit you O.K.?" (Friendliness to individual in outgroup.) Finn is over near the box, and Rudy (in the other group) holds up the work he is doing in a friendly manner for Finn to see.
> Finn: "What is it?"
> Rudy: "It's a tin can thing."

5. Mutual praise was more frequent. In Experiment I there were three instances of child-to-child praise in the autocratic group and 16 in the democratic group. In Experiment II praise was not counted as a separate category, but was included in the category of "friendliness." Some instances of its occurrence under democratic leadership:

> Finn: "Well, nice going, Bill—such an idea. You could take a bit more out of that one." (Bill is Finn's archenemy, but Finn is also changeable, and he is now in the best of spirits.)
> Bill (reciprocating, a minute or two later): "Oh, that's good Finn. That's a good idea. Mine's too weak."

> Bill: "Oh, Van, that's coming good."
> Bill (to Mr. Rankin): "Eddie really did a swell job on that, didn't he? I couldn't do as good as that."

6. Friendly playfulness was more frequent. In number of "play-minded" remarks the figures for Experiment II were: laissez-faire 33, democracy 13, submissive reaction to autocracy 8, and aggressive reaction to autocracy 3. The difference between democracy and the submissive reaction is significant at only the 5% level. Here again autocracy may have brought out a paradoxical type of irresponsible we-mindedness. (Illustrations of "play-mindedness" have already been given in differentiating laissez-faire from democracy.)

7. There was more readiness to share group property. This was shown most conspicuously in Experiment I. At the end of the meeting series, each of the two groups was asked to vote, with individual secret ballot, on the question, "What would you like to have done with the masks?" In the autocratic group (in which each child had already identified with one mask), three out of four gave wholly "individualistic" answers: "Give us our masks," and "Let me have mine." In the democratic group, not one of the five regular members gave a completely individualistic answer.

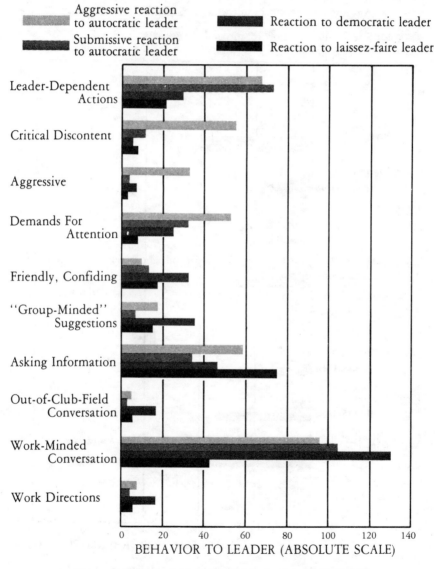

Figure 2. Four patterns of child-to-leader relationship.

SUMMARY

A bird's-eye view of the more important results of Experiment II is given in Figures 2 and 3, which represent, respectively, the boys' behavior toward their leader and toward each other. The chief differences to be noted here are: (*a*) the large number of leader-dependent actions in both reactions to autocracy; (*b*) the large amounts of critical discontent and of aggressive behavior in the aggressive reaction to autocracy; (*c*) the frequency of "friendly, confiding"

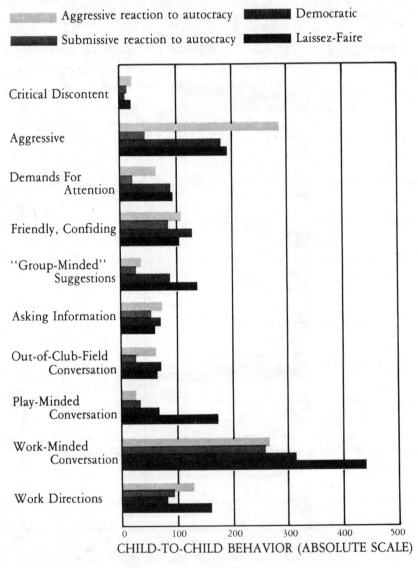

Figure 3. Four patterns of child-to-child relationship.

conversation and of group-minded suggestions in democracy; and (*d*) the contrast between democracy and laissez-faire in work-minded conversation.

Here the following differences should be noticed: (*a*) the large difference between the two reactions to autocracy in amount of aggressive behavior, and the intermediate position of democracy and laissez-faire in this respect; (*b*) the generally subdued atmosphere in the submissive reaction to autocracy, as shown by the small absolute totals of aggressive behavior, attention demands, group-minded suggestions, out-of-club-field conversation, and play-minded remarks; (*c*) the small proportion of group-minded suggestions in both reactions to autocracy; and (*d*) the small amount of play-minded conversation in both reactions to autocracy, and the very large amount in laissez-faire.

Summarizing, then, we can say that the above diagram and several other types of evidence tend to support the following descriptive generalizations.

1. *Laissez-faire was not the same as democracy.*
   (*a*) There was less work done in it, and poorer work.
   (*b*) It was more characterized by play.
   (*c*) In interviews, the boys expressed preference for their democratic leader.
2. *Democracy can be efficient.*
   (*a*) The quantity of work done in autocracy was somewhat greater.
   (*b*) Work motivation was stronger in democracy as shown, for instance, when the leader left the room.
   (*c*) Originality was greater in democracy.
3. *Autocracy can create much hostility and aggression, including aggression against scapegoats.*
   (*a*) In Experiment I, the autocratic group showed more dominating ascendance, much more hostility (in a ratio of 30 to 1), more demands for attention, more destruction of own property, and more scapegoat behavior.
   (*b*) In Experiment II, one of the four clubs showed a similar reaction.
4. *Autocracy can create discontent that does not appear on the surface.*
   (*a*) Four boys dropped out, and all of them did so during autocratic club periods in which overt rebellion did not occur.
   (*b*) Nineteen out of 20 boys preferred their democratic leader.
   (*c*) There was more discontent expressed in autocracy—even when the general reaction was submissive—than in democracy.
   (*d*) "Release" behavior on the day of transition to a freer atmosphere suggested the presence of previous frustration.
5. *There was more dependence and less individuality in autocracy.*
   (*a*) There was more "submissive" or "dependent" behavior.
   (*b*) Conversation was less varied—more confined to the immediate situation.
   (*c*) In the submissive reaction to autocracy, there was an absolute (though not relative) reduction in statistical measures of individual differences.

(*d*) The observers' impression was that in autocracy there is some loss of individuality.
6. *There was more group-mindedness and more friendliness in democracy.*
   (*a*) In Experiment I, the pronoun "I" was used relatively less frequently in the democratic group.
   (*b*) Spontaneous subgroups were larger.
   (*c*) In Experiment II, group-minded remarks were much more frequent in democracy.
   (*d*) Friendly remarks were slightly more frequent.
   (*e*) In Experiment I, mutual praise was more frequent in the democratic group.
   (*f*) In Experiment II, friendly playfulness was more frequent in democracy.
   (*g*) In Experiment I, the democratic group showed more readiness to share group property.

REFERENCES

1. Lippitt, R.: An experimental study of the effect of democratic and authoritarian group atmospheres. *Univ. of Iowa Studies in Child Welfare,* 1940, 16, 43—195.
2. Lippitt, R., & White, R.: The "social climate" of children's groups. In R.G. Barker, J. Kounin, & H. Wright (Eds.), *Child Behavior and Development.* New York: McGraw-Hill, 1943, pp. 485—508.

Chapter 14

Overcoming Resistance
to Change

Lester Coch
John R. P. French, Jr.

It has always been characteristic of American industry to change products and methods of doing jobs as often as competitive conditions or engineering progress dictates. This makes frequent changes in an individual's work necessary. In addition, the markedly greater turnover and absenteeism of recent years result in unbalanced production lines, which again makes for frequent shifting of individuals from one job to another. One of the most serious production problems faced at the Harwood Manufacturing Corporation has been the resistance of production workers to the necessary changes in methods and jobs. This resistance expressed itself in several ways, such as grievances about the piece rates that went with the new methods, high turnover, very low efficiency, restriction of output, and marked aggression against management. Despite these undesirable effects, it was necessary that changes in methods and jobs continue.

Efforts were made to solve this serious problem by the use of a special monetary allowance for transfers, by trying to enlist the cooperation and aid of the union, by making necessary layoffs on the basis of efficiency, etc. In all cases, these actions did little or nothing to overcome the resistance to change. On the basis of these data, it was felt that the pressing problem of resistance to change demanded further research for its solution. From the point of view of factory management, there were two purposes to the research: (*a*) Why do people resist change so strongly? and (*b*) What can be done to overcome this resistance?

Starting with a series of observations about the behavior of changed groups, the first step in the program was to devise a preliminary theory to account for the resistance to change. Then, on the basis of the theory, a real-life action experiment was devised and conducted within the context of the factory

From *Human Relations*, Volume 1, number 4, pp. 512-532. Copyright © 1948 by Tavistock Publications. Reprinted by permission of Plenum Press.

situation. Finally, the results of the experiment were interpreted in the light of the preliminary theory and the new data.

BACKGROUND

The main plant of the Harwood Manufacturing Corporation, where the present research was done, is located in the small town of Marion, Virginia. The plant produces pajamas and, like most sewing plants, employs mostly women. The plant's population is about 500 women and 100 men. The workers are recruited from the rural, mountainous areas surrounding the town, and are usually employed without previous industrial experience. The average age of the workers is 23. The average education is eight years of grammar school.

The policies of the company in regard to labor relations are liberal and progressive. A high value has been placed on fair and open dealing with the employees and they are encouraged to take up any problems or grievances with the management at any time. Every effort is made to help foremen find effective solutions to their problems in human relations, using conferences and role-playing methods. Carefully planned orientation, designed to help overcome the discouragement and frustrations attending entrance upon the new and unfamiliar situation, is used. Plant-wide votes are conducted where possible to resolve problems affecting the whole working population. The company has invested both time and money in employee services such as industrial music, health services, lunchroom, and recreation programs. In the same spirit, the management has been conscious of the importance of public relations in the local community; they have supported, both financially and otherwise, any activity which would build up good will for the company. As a result of these policies, the company has enjoyed good labor relations since the day it commenced operations.

Harwood employees work on an individual incentive system. Piece rates are set by time study and are expressed in terms of units. One unit is equal to one minute of standard work: 60 units per hour equal the standard efficiency rating. Thus, if on a particular operation the piece rate for one dozen is 10 units, the operator would have to produce six dozen per hour to achieve the standard efficiency rating of 60 units per hour. The skill required to reach 60 units per hour is great. On some jobs, an average trainee may take 34 weeks to reach the skill level necessary to perform at 60 units per hour. Her first few weeks of work may be on an efficiency level of 5 to 20 units per hour.

The amount of pay received is directly proportional to the weekly average efficiency rating achieved. Thus, an operator with an average efficiency rating of 75 units per hour (25% more than standard) would receive 25% more than base pay. However, there are two minimum wages below which no operator may fall. The first is the plant-wide minimum, the hiring-in wage; the second is a minimum wage based on six months' employment and is 22% higher than the plant-wide minimum wage. Both minima are smaller than the base pay for 60 units per hour efficiency rating.

The rating of every piece worker is computed every day, and the results are published in a daily record of production which is shown to every operator. This daily record of production for each production line carries the names of all the operators on that line arranged in rank order of efficiency rating, with the highest rating girl at the top of the list. The supervisors speak to each operator each day about her unit ratings. Because of the above procedures, many operators do not claim credit for all the work done in a given day. Instead, they save a few of the piece rate tickets as a "cushion" against a rainy day when they may not feel well or may have a great amount of machine trouble.

When it is necessary to change an operator from one type of work to another, a transfer bonus is given. This bonus is so designed that the changed operator who relearns at an average rate will suffer no loss in earnings after change. Despite this allowance, the general attitudes toward job changes in the factory are markedly negative. Such expressions as, "When you make your units (standard production), they change your job," are all too frequent. Many operators refuse to change, preferring to quit.

THE TRANSFER LEARNING CURVE

An analysis of the after-change relearning curves of several hundred experienced operators rating standard or better prior to change showed that 38% of the changed operators recovered to the standard unit rating of 60 units per hour. The other 62% either became chronically substandard operators or quit during the relearning period.

The average relearning curve for those who recover to standard production on the simplest type of job in the plant is eight weeks long, and, when smoothed, provides the basis for the transfer bonus. The bonus is the percentage difference between this expected efficiency rating and the standard of 60 units per hour.

The relearning period for an experienced operator is longer than the learning period for a new operator. This is true despite the fact that the majority of transfers—the failures who never recover to standard—are omitted from the curve. However, changed operators rarely complain of "wanting to do it the old way" after the first week or two of change, and time and motion studies show few false moves after the first week of change. From this evidence it is deduced that proactive inhibition, or the interference of previous habits in learning the new skill, is either nonexistent or very slight after the first two weeks of change.

An analysis of the relearning curves for 41 experienced operators who were changed to very difficult jobs gives a comparison between the recovery rates for operators making standard or better prior to change, and those below standard prior to change. Both classes of operators dropped to a little below 30 units per hour and recovered at a very slow but similar rate. These curves show a general (though by no means universal) phenomenon: the efficiency rating prior to change does not indicate a faster or slower recovery rate after change.

A PRELIMINARY THEORY OF RESISTANCE TO CHANGE

The fact that relearning after transfer to a new job is so often slower than initial learning on first entering the factory would indicate, on the face of it, that the resistance to change and the slow relearning is primarily a motivational problem. The similar recovery rates of skilled and unskilled operators tend to confirm the hypothesis that skill is a minor factor and motivation is the major determinant of the rate of recovery. Earlier experiments at Harwood by Alex Bavelas demonstrated this point conclusively. He found that the use of group decision techniques on operators who had just been transferred resulted in very marked increases in the rate of relearning, even though no skill training was given and there were no other changes in working conditions (3).

Interviews with operators who have been transferred to a new job reveal a common pattern of feelings and attitudes which are distinctly different from those of successful nontransfers. In addition to resentment against the management for transferring them, the employees typically show feelings of frustration, loss of hope of ever regaining their former level of production and status in the factory, feelings of failure, and a very low level of aspiration. In this respect, these transferred operators are similar to the chronically slow workers studied previously.

Earlier unpublished research at Harwood has shown that the nontransferred employees generally have an explicit goal of reaching and maintaining an efficiency rating of 60 units per hour. A questionnaire administered to several groups of operators indicated that a large majority of them accept as their goal the management's quota of 60 units per hour. This standard of production is the level of aspiration according to which the operators measure their own success or failure, and those who fall below standard lose status in the eyes of their fellow employees. Relatively few operators set a goal appreciably above 60 units per hour.

The actual production records confirm the effectiveness of this goal of standard production. The distribution of the total population of operators in accordance with their production levels is by no means a normal curve. Instead there is a very large number of operators who rate 60 to 63 units per hour, and relatively few operators who rate just above or just below this range. Thus we may conclude that:

Proposition 1. There is a force acting on the operator in the direction of achieving a production level of 60 units per hour or more. It is assumed that the strength of this driving force (acting on an operator below standard) increases as she gets nearer the goal—a typical goal gradient.

On the other hand, restraining forces operate to hinder or prevent her reaching this goal. These restraining forces consist, among other things, of the difficulty of the job in relation to the operator's level of skill. Other things being equal, the faster an operator is sewing the more difficult it is to increase her speed by a given amount. Thus we may conclude that:

Proposition 2. The strength of the restraining force hindering higher production increases with increasing level of production.

In line with previous studies, it is assumed that the conflict of these two opposing forces—the driving force corresponding to the goal of reaching 60 and the restraining force of the difficulty of the job—produces frustration. In such a conflict situation, the strength of frustration will depend on the strength of these forces. If the restraining force against increasing production is weak, then the frustration will be weak. But if the driving force toward higher production, i.e., the motivation is weak, then the frustration will also be weak. Probably both of the conflicting forces must be above a certain minimum strength before any frustration is produced, for all goal-directed activity involves some degree of conflict of this type; yet a person is not usually frustrated so long as he is making satisfactory progress toward his goal. Consequently we assume that:

Proposition 3. The strength of frustration is a function of the weaker of these two opposing forces, provided that the weaker force is stronger than a certain minimum necessary to produce frustration (3).

From Propositions 1, 2, and 3, we may derive that the strength of frustration (a) should be greater for operators who are below standard in production than for operators who have already achieved the goal of standard production; (b) should be greater for operators on difficult jobs than for operators on easy jobs; and (c) should increase with increasing efficiency rating below standard production. Previous research would suggest:

Proposition 4. One consequence of frustration is escape from the field (2).

An analysis of the effects of such frustration in the factory showed that it resulted, among other things, in high turnover and absenteeism. The rate of turnover for successful operators with efficiency ratings above standard was much lower than for unsuccessful operators. Likewise, operators on the more difficult jobs quit more frequently than those on the easier jobs. Presumably the effect of being transferred is a severe frustration which should result in similar attempts to escape from the field.

In line with this theory of frustration and the finding that job turnover is one resultant of frustration, an analysis was made of the turnover rate of transferred operators as compared with the rate among operators who had not been transferred recently. For the year September, 1946, to September, 1947, there were 198 operators who had not been transferred recently; that is, within the 34-week period allowed for relearning after transfer. There was a second group of 85 operators who had been transferred recently; that is, within the time allowed for relearning the new job. Each of these two groups was divided into seven classifications according to their unit rating at the time of quitting. For each classification the percentage turnover per month, based on the total number of employees in that classification, was computed.

The results are given in Figure 1. Both the levels of turnover and the form of the curves are strikingly different for the two groups. Among operators who have not been transferred recently the average turnover per month is about 4½ %; among recent transfers the monthly turnover is nearly 12 %. Consistent with the previous studies, both groups show a very marked drop in the turnover curve after an operator becomes a success by reaching 60 units per hour, or standard production. However, the form of the curves at lower unit ratings is markedly different for the two groups. The nontransferred operators show a gradually increasing rate of turnover up to a rating of 55 to 59 units per hour. The transferred operators, on the other hand, show a high peak at the lowest unit rating of 30 to 34 units per hour, decreasing sharply to a low point at 45 to 49 units per hour. Since most changed operators drop to a unit rating of around 30 units per hour when changed and then drop no further, it is obvious that the rate of turnover was highest for these operators just after they were changed and again much later just before they reached standard. Why?

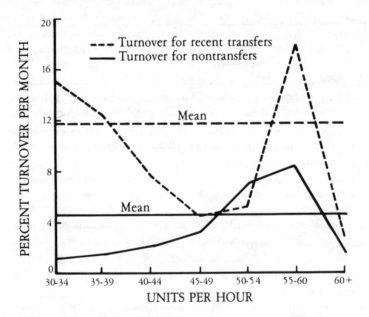

Figure 1. The rate of turnover at various levels of production for transfers as compared with nontransfers.

It is assumed that the strength of frustration for an operator who has not been transferred gradually increases because both the driving force toward the goal of reaching 60 and the restraining force of the difficulty of the job increase with increasing unit rating. This is in line with Propositions 1, 2, and 3, above.

For the transferred operator, on the other hand, the frustration is greatest immediately after transfer when the contrast of her present status with her former status is most evident. At this point, the strength of the restraining forces is at a maximum because the difficulty is unusually great due to proactive inhibition. Then, as she overcomes the interference effects between the two jobs and learns the new job, the difficulty and the frustration gradually decrease and the rate of turnover declines until the operator reaches 45—49 units per hour. Then at higher levels of production the difficulty starts to increase again and the transferred operator shows the same peak in frustration and turnover at 55—59 units per hour.

Though our theory of frustration explains the forms of the two turnover curves in Figure 1, it seems hardly adequate to account for the markedly higher level of turnover for transfers as compared to nontransfers. On the basis of the difficulty of the job, it is especially difficult to explain the higher rate of turnover at 55—59 units per hour for transfers. Evidently, additional forces are operating.

Another factor which seems to affect recovery rates of changed operators is the amount of cohesiveness. Observations seem to indicate that a strong psychological subgroup with negative attitudes toward management will display the strongest resistance to change. On the other hand, changed groups with high cohesiveness and positive cooperative attitudes are the best relearners. Collections of individuals with little or no cohesiveness display some resistance to change, but not so strongly as the groups with high cohesiveness and negative attitudes toward management.

An analysis of turnover records for changed operators with high cohesiveness showed a 4% turnover rate per month at 30 to 34 units per hour, not significantly higher than in unchanged operators, but significantly lower than in changed operators with little or no cohesiveness. However, the acts of aggression are far more numerous among operators with high cohesiveness than among operators with little cohesiveness. Since both types of operators experience the same frustration as individuals but react to it so differently, it is assumed that the effect of the ingroup feeling is to set up a restraining force against leaving the group and perhaps even to set up driving forces toward staying in the group. In these circumstances, one would expect some alternative reaction to frustration rather than escape from the field. This alternative is aggression. Strong cohesiveness provides strength so that members dare to express aggression which would otherwise be suppressed.

One common result in a cohesive subgroup is the setting of a group standard concerning production. Where the attitudes toward management are antagonistic, this group standard may take the form of a definite restriction of production to a given level. This phenomenon of restriction is particularly likely to happen in a group that has been transferred to a job where a new piece rate has been set, for they have some hope that, if production never approaches the standard, the management may change the piece rate in their favor.

A group standard can exert extremely strong forces on an individual member of a small subgroup. That these forces can have a powerful effect on production is indicated in the production record of one presser during a period of 40 days:

In the Group

Days	Efficiency rating
1—3	46
4—6	52
7—9	53
10—12	56

Scapegoating begins

13—16	55
17—20	48

Becomes a single worker

21—24	83
25—28	92
29—32	92
33—36	91
37—40	92

For the first 20 days she was working in a group of other pressers who were producing at the rate of about 50 units per hour. Starting on the 13th day, when she reached standard production and exceeded the production of the other members, she became a scapegoat of the group. During this time her production decreased toward the level of the remaining members of the group. After 20 days the group had to be broken up and all the other members were transferred to other jobs, leaving only the scapegoat operator. With the removal of the group, the group standard was no longer operative, and the production of the one remaining operator shot up from the level of about 45 to 96 units per hour in a period of four days. Her production stabilized at a level of about 92 and stayed there for the remainder of the 20 days. Thus it is clear that the motivational forces induced in the individual by a strong subgroup may be more powerful than those induced by management.

THE EXPERIMENTS

On the basis of the preliminary theory that resistance to change is a combination of an individual reaction to frustration with strong group-induced forces, it seemed that the most appropriate methods for overcoming the resistance to change would be group methods. Consequently, an experiment was designed

(Experiment I) employing three degrees of participation in handling groups to be transferred. The first variation, the control group, involved *no participation* by employees in planning the changes, though an explanation was given to them. The second variation involved *participation through representation* of the workers in designing the changes to be made in the jobs. The third variation consisted of *total participation* by all members of the group in designing the changes. Two experimental groups received the total participation treatment. The four experimental groups were roughly matched with respect to (*a*) the efficiency ratings of the groups before transfer; (*b*) the degree of change involved in the transfer; and (*c*) the amount of cohesiveness observed in the groups.

In no case was more than a minor change in the work routines and time allowances made. The no-participation group, 18 hand pressers, had formerly stacked their work in half-dozen lots on a flat piece of cardboard the size of the finished product. The new job called for stacking their work in half-dozen lots in a box the size of the finished product. The box was located in the same place the cardboard had been. An additional two minutes per dozen was allowed (by the time study) for this new part of the job. This represented a total change of 8.8%.

The group treated with participation through representation, 13 pajama folders, had formerly folded coats with prefolded pants. The new job called for the folding of coats with unfolded pants. An additional 1.8 minutes per dozen was allowed (by time study) for this new part of the job. This represented a total change of 9.4%.

The two total participation groups, consisting of eight and seven pajama examiners, respectively, had formerly clipped threads from the entire garment and examined every seam. The new job called for pulling only certain threads off and examining every seam. An average of 1.2 minutes per dozen was subtracted (by time study) from the total time on these two jobs. This represented a total job change of 8%.

The no-participation group of hand pressers went through the usual factory routine when they were changed. The production department modified the job, and the new piece rate was set. A group meeting was then held in which the group was told that the change was necessary because of competitive conditions, and that a new piece rate had been set. The new piece rate was thoroughly explained by the time-study man, questions were answered, and the meeting dismissed.

The group which participated through representatives was changed in a different manner. Before any changes took place, a group meeting was held with all the operators to be changed. The need for the change was presented as dramatically as possible, showing two identical garments produced in the factory; one was produced in 1946 and had sold for 100% more than its fellow in 1947. The group was asked to identify the cheaper one and could not do it. This demonstration effectively shared with the group the entire problem of the necessity of cost reduction. A general agreement was reached that a savings could be effected by removing the "frills" and "fancy" work from the garment without affecting the folders' opportunity to achieve a high efficiency rating. Management then presented a plan to set the new job and piece rate:

1. Make a check study of the job as it was being done.
2. Eliminate all unnecessary work.
3. Train several operators in the correct methods.
4. Set the piece rate by time studies on these specially trained operators.
5. Explain the new job and rate to all the operators.
6. Train all operators in the new method so they can reach a high rate of production within a short time.

The group approved this plan (though no formal group decision was reached), and chose the operators to be specially trained. A submeeting with the "special" operators was held immediately following the meeting with the entire group. They displayed a cooperative and interested attitude and immediately presented many good suggestions. This attitude carried over into the working out of the details of the new job, and when the new job and piece rates were set the "special" operators referred to the resultants as "our job," "our rate," etc. The new job and piece rates were presented at a second group meeting to all the operators involved. The "special" operators served to train the other operators on the new job.

The total participation groups went through much the same kind of meetings. The groups were smaller, and a more intimate atmosphere was established. The need for a change was once again made dramatically clear. The same general plan was presented by management. However, since the groups were small, all operators were chosen as "special" operators; that is, all operators were to participate directly in the designing of the new jobs, and all operators would be studied by the time-study man. It is interesting to observe that in the meetings with these two groups suggestions were immediately made in such quantity that the stenographer had great difficulty in recording them. The group approved of the plans, but again no formal group decision was reached.

RESULTS

The results of the experiment are summarized in graphic form in Figure 2. The gaps in the production curves occur because these groups were paid on a time-work basis for a day or two. The no-participation group improved little beyond their early efficiency ratings. Resistance developed almost immediately after the change occurred. Marked expressions of aggression against management occurred, such as conflict with the methods engineer, expression of hostility against the supervisor, deliberate restriction of production, and lack of cooperation with the supervisor. There were 17% quits in the first 40 days.

Grievances were filed about the piece rate, but when the rate was checked, it was found to be a little "loose."

The representation group showed an unusually good relearning curve. At the end of 14 days, the group averaged 61 units per hour. During the 14 days, the attitude was cooperative and permissive. They worked well with the methods engineer, the training staff, and the supervisor. (The supervisor was the same person in the cases of the first two groups.) There were no quits in this group in the first 40 days. This group might have presented a better learning record if work had not been scarce during the first seven days. There was one act of aggression against the supervisor recorded in the first 40 days. We should note that the three special representative operators recovered at about the same rate as the rest of their group.

The total participation groups recovered faster than the others. After a slight drop on the first day of change, the efficiency ratings returned to a prechange

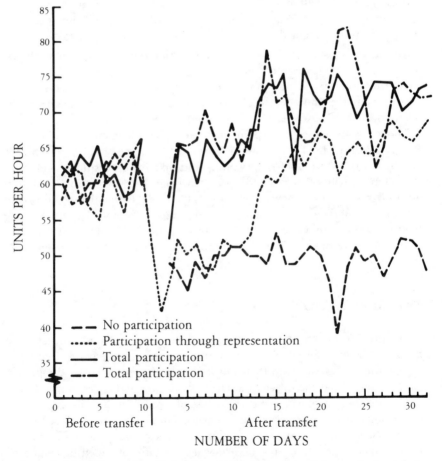

Figure 2. The effects of participation through representation and of total participation on recovery after an easy transfer.

level and showed sustained progress thereafter to a level about 14% higher than the prechange level. No additional training was provided them after the second day. They worked well with their supervisors and no indications of aggression were observed from these groups. There were no quits in either of these groups in the first 40 days.

(A fifth experimental group, composed of only two sewing operators, was transferred by the total participation technique. Their new job was one of the most difficult jobs in the factory, in contrast to the easy jobs for the other four experimental groups. As expected, the total participation technique again resulted in an unusually fast recovery rate and a final level of production well above the level before transfer.)

In the first experiment, the no-participation group made no progress after transfer for a period of 32 days. At the end of this period the group was broken up, and the individuals were reassigned to new jobs scattered throughout the factory. Two and a half months after their dispersal, the 13 remaining members of the original no-participation group were again brought together as a group for a second experiment (Experiment II).

This second experiment consisted of transferring the group to a new job, using the total participation technique. The new job was a pressing job of comparable difficulty to the new job in the first experiment. On the average, it involved about the same degree of change. In the meetings, no reference was made to the previous behavior of the group on being transferred.

The results of the second experiment were in sharp contrast to the first (see Fig. 3). With the total participation technique, the same group now recovered rapidly to their previous efficiency rating and, like the other groups under this treatment, continued on beyond it to a new high level of production. There was no aggression or turnover in the group for 19 days after change, a marked modification of their previous behavior after transfer. Some anxiety concerning their seniority status was expressed, but this was resolved in a meeting of their elected delegate, the union business agent, and a management representative.

INTERPRETATION

The purpose of this section is to explain the drop in production resulting from transfer, the differential recovery rates of the three experimental treatments, the increases beyond their former levels of production by the participating groups, and the differential rates of turnover and aggression.

The first experiment showed that the rate of recovery is directly proportional to the amount of participation, and that the rates of turnover and aggression are inversely proportional to the amount of participation. The second experiment demonstrated more conclusively that the results obtained depended on the experimental treatment rather than on personality factors like skill or aggressiveness, for identical individuals yielded markedly different results in the

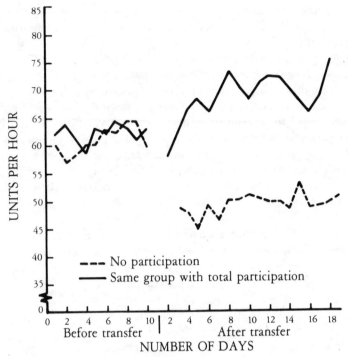

Figure 3. A comparison of the effect of no participation with the total participation procedure on the same group.

no-participation treatment as contrasted with the total-participation treatment.

Apparently total participation has the same type of effect as participation
through representation, but the former has a stronger influence. In regard to
recovery rates, this difference is not unequivocal because the experiment was
unfortunately confounded. Right after transfer, the latter group had insufficient material to work on for a period of seven days. Hence, their slower recovery during this period is at least in part due to insufficient work. In succeeding
days, however, there was an adequate supply of work and the differential recovery rate still persisted. Therefore, we are inclined to believe that participation
through representation results in slower recovery than does total participation.

Before discussing the details of why participation produces high morale, we
shall consider the nature of production levels. In examining the production
records of hundreds of individuals and groups in this factory, one is struck by
the constancy of the level of production. Though differences among individuals
in efficiency rating are very large, nearly every experienced operator maintains a
fairly steady level of production, given constant physical conditions. Frequently the given level will be maintained despite rather large changes in technical
working conditions.

As Lewin has pointed out, this type of production can be viewed as a quasi-
stationary process—in the on-going work the operator is forever sewing new

garments, yet the level of the process remains relatively stationary (3). Thus there are constant characteristics of the production process permitting the establishment of general laws.

In studying production as a quasi-stationary equilibrium, we are concerned with two types of forces: (*a*) forces on production in a downward direction, and (*b*) forces on production in an upward direction. In this situation we are dealing with a variety of both upward forces tending to increase the level of production and downward forces tending to decrease the level of production. However, in the present experiment we have no method of measuring independently all of the component forces either downward or upward. These various component forces upward are combined into one resultant force upward, and the several downward component forces combine into one resultant force downward. We can infer a good deal about the relative strengths of these resultant forces.

Where we are dealing with a quasi-stationary equilibrium, the resultant forces upward and the forces downward are opposite in direction and equal in strength at the equilibrium level. Of course either resultant forces may fluctuate over a short period of time, so that the forces may not be equally balanced at a given moment. However, over a longer period of time, and on the average, the forces balance out. Fluctuations from the average occur, but there is a tendency to return to the average level.

Just before being transferred, all of the groups in both experiments had reached a stable equilibrium level at just above the standard production of 60 units per hour. This level was equal to the average efficiency rating for the entire factory during the period of the experiments. Since this production level remained constant, neither increasing nor decreasing, we may be sure that the strength of the resultant force upward was equal to the strength of the resultant

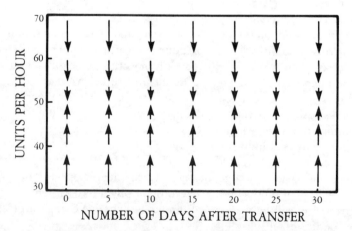

Figure 4. A schematic diagram of the quasi-stationary equilibrium for the no-participation group after transfer.

force downward. This equilibrium of forces was maintained over the period of time when production was stationary at this level. But the forces changed markedly after transfer, and these new constellations of forces were distinctly different for the various experimental groups.

For the no-participation group the period after transfer is a quasi-stationary equilibrium at a lower level, and the forces do not change during the period of 30 days. The resultant force upward remains equal to the resultant force downward, and the level of production remains constant. The force field for this group is represented schematically in Figure 4. Only the resultant forces are shown. The length of the vector represents the strength of the force, and the point of the arrow represents the point of application of the force, that is, the production level and the time at which the force applies. Thus the forces are equal and opposite only at the level of 50 units per hour. At higher levels of production the forces downward are greater than the forces upward, and at lower levels of production the forces upward are stronger than the forces downward. Thus there is a tendency for the equilibrium to be maintained at an efficiency rating of 50.

The situation for the other experimental groups after transfer can be viewed as a quasi-stationary equilibrium of a different type. Figure 5 gives a schematic diagram of the resultant forces for all the participation groups. At any given level of production, such as 50 units per hour or 60 units per hour, both the resultant forces upward and the resultant forces downward change over the

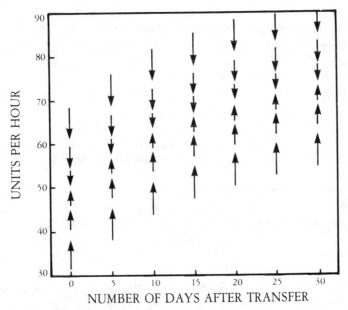

Figure 5. A schematic diagram of the quasi-stationary equilibrium for the experimental group after transfer.

period of 30 days. During this time the point of equilibrium, which starts at 50 units per hour, gradually rises until it reaches a level of over 70 units per hour after 30 days. Yet here again the equilibrium level has the character of a "central force field" where, at any point in the total field, the resultant of the upward and the downward forces is in the direction of the equilibrium level.

To understand how the differences among the experimental and the control treatments produced the differences in force fields represented in Figures 4 and 5, it is not sufficient to consider only the resultant forces. We must also look at the component forces for each resultant force.

There are three main component forces influencing production in a downward direction: (*a*) the difficulty of the job; (*b*) a force corresponding to avoidance of strain; and (*c*) a force corresponding to a group standard to restrict production to a given level. The resultant force upward in the direction of greater production is composed of three additional component forces: (*a*) the force corresponding to the goal of standard production; (*b*) a force corresponding to pressures induced by the management through supervision; and (*c*) a force corresponding to a group standard of competition. Let us examine each of these six component forces.

Job Difficulty. For all operators, the difficulty of the job is one of the forces downward on production. The difficulty of the job, of course, is relative to the skill of the operator. The given job may be very difficult for an unskilled operator but relatively easy for a highly skilled one. In the case of a transfer a new element of difficulty enters. For some time the new job is much more difficult, for the operator is unskilled at that particular job. In addition to the difficulty experienced by any learner, the transferee often encounters the added difficulty of proactive inhibition. Where the new job is similar to the old job, there will be a period of interference between the two similar but different skills required. For this reason a very efficient operator whose skills have become almost unconscious may suffer just as great a drop as a much less efficient operator. Except for the experiment on only two operators, the difficulty of these easy jobs does not explain the differential recovery rates, because both the initial difficulty and the amount of change were equated for these groups. The two operators probably dropped further and recovered more slowly than any of the other three groups under total participation because of the greater difficulty of the job.

Strain Avoidance. The force toward lower production corresponding to the difficulty of the job (or the lack of skill of the person) has the character of a restraining force; that is, it acts to prevent locomotion rather than as a driving force causing locomotion. However, in all production there is a closely related driving force towards lower production, namely, "strain avoidance." We assume that working too hard and working too fast is an unpleasant strain; and corresponding to this negative valence there is a driving force in the opposite direction, namely, towards taking it easy or working slower. The higher the level of production the greater will be the strain and, other things being equal, the stronger will be the downward force of strain avoidance. Likewise, the greater the difficulty of the job, the stronger will be the force corresponding to strain avoidance. But the greater the operator's skill, the smaller will be the strain and the strength of the force of strain avoidance. Therefore:

Proposition 5. The

$$\text{strength of the force of strain avoidance} = \frac{\text{job difficulty x production level}}{\text{skill of operator}}$$

The differential recovery rates of the three experimental groups in Experiment I cannot be explained by strain avoidance because job difficulty, production level, and operator skill were matched at the time immediately following transfer. Later, however, when the experimental treatments had produced a much higher level of production, these groups were subjected to an increased downward force of strain avoidance which was stronger than in the no-participation group in Experiment I. Evidently other forces were strong enough to overcome this force of strain avoidance.

The Goal of Standard Production. In considering the negative attitudes toward transfer and the resistance to being transferred, there are several important aspects of the complex goal of reaching and maintaining a level of 60 units per hour. For an operator producing below standard, this goal is attractive because it means success, high status in the eyes of her fellow employees, better pay, and job security. On the other hand, there is a strong force against remaining below standard because this lower level means failure, low status, low pay, and the danger of being fired. Thus it is clear that the upward force corresponding to the goal of standard production will indeed be strong for the transferee who has dropped below standard.

It is equally clear why any operator who accepts the stereotype about transfer shows such strong resistance to being changed. She sees herself as becoming a failure and losing status, pay, and perhaps the job itself. The result is a lowered level of aspiration and a weakened force toward the goal of standard production.

Just such a weakening of the force toward 60 units per hour seems to have occurred in the no-participation group in Experiment I. The participation treatments, on the other hand, seem to have involved the operators in designing the new job and setting the new piece rates in such a way that they did not lose hope of regaining the goal of standard production. Thus participation resulted in a stronger force toward higher production. However, this force alone can hardly account for the large differences in recovery rate between the no-participation group and the experimental groups; certainly it does not explain why the latter increased to a level so high above standard.

Management Pressure. On all operators below standard the management exerts a pressure for higher production. This pressure is no harsh and autocratic treatment involving threats; rather, it takes the form of persuasion and encouragement by the supervisors. They attempt to induce the low rating operator to improve her performance and to attain standard production.

Such an attempt to induce a psychological force on another person may have several results. In the first place the person may ignore the attempt of the inducing agent, in which case there is no induced force acting on the person. On the other hand, the attempt may succeed so that an induced force on the person exists. Other things being equal, whenever there is an induced force acting on a person, the person will locomote in the direction of the force. An induced force which depends on the power field of an inducing agent—some other individual or group—will cease to exist when the inducing power field is withdrawn. In this respect it is different from an "own" force which stems from a person's own needs and goals.

The reaction of a person to an effective induced force will vary depending, among other things, on the person's relation to the inducing agent. A force induced by a friend may be accepted in such a way that it acts more like an "own" force. An effective force induced by an enemy may be resisted and rejected so that the person complies unwillingly and shows signs of conflict and tension. Thus in addition to what might be called a "neutral" induced force, we also distinguish an *accepted* induced force and a *rejected* induced force. Naturally, the acceptance and the rejection of an induced force can vary in degree from zero (i.e., a neutral induced force) to very strong acceptance or rejection. To account for the difference in character between the acceptance and the rejection of an induced force, we make the following propositions:

Proposition 6. The acceptance of an induced force sets up additional "own" forces in the same direction.

Proposition 7. The rejection of an induced force sets up additional "own" forces in the opposite direction.

The grievances, aggression, and tension in the no-participation group in the first experiment indicate that they rejected the force toward higher production induced by the management. The group accepted the stereotype that transfer is a calamity, but the no-participation procedure did not convince them that the change was necessary, and they viewed the new job and the new piece rates set by management as arbitrary and unreasonable.

The other experimental groups, on the contrary, participated in designing the changes and setting the piece rates so that they spoke of the new job as "our job" and the new piece rates as "our rates." Thus they accepted the new situation and accepted the management-induced force toward higher production.

From the acceptance by the experimental groups and the rejection by the no-participation group of the management-induced forces, we may derive (by Props. 6 and 7 above) that the former had additional "own" forces toward higher production, whereas the latter had additional "own" forces toward lower production. This difference helps to explain the better recovery rate of the participation groups.

Group Standards. Probably the most important force affecting the recovery under the no-participation procedure was a group standard, set by the group, restricting the level of production to 50 units per hour. Evidently this explicit agreement to restrict production is related to the group's rejection of the change and of the new job as arbitrary and unreasonable. Perhaps they had faint hopes of demonstrating that standard production could not be attained and thereby obtain a more favorable piece rate. In any case there was a definite group phenomenon which affected all the members of the group. We have already noted the striking example of the presser whose production was restricted in the group situation to about half the level she attained as an individual. In the no-participation group, we would also expect the group to induce strong forces on the members. The more a member deviates above the standard, the stronger would be the group-induced force to conform to the standard, for such deviations both negate any possibility of management's increasing the piece rate and at the same time expose the other members to increased pressure from management. Thus individual differences in levels of production should be sharply curtailed in this group after transfer.

An analysis was made, for all groups, of the individual differences within each group in levels of production. In Experiment I, the 40 days before change were compared with the 30 days after change; in Experiment II, the 10 days before change were compared to the 17 days after change. As a measure of variability, the standard deviation was calculated each day for each group. The average daily standard deviations before and after change were as follows:

Experiment I	*Before Change*	*After Change*
No participation	9.8	1.9
Participation through representation	9.7	3.8
Total participation	10.3	2.7
Total participation	9.9	2.4

Experiment II		
Total participation	12.7	2.9

There is, indeed, a marked decrease in individual differences within the no-participation group after their first transfer. In fact, the restriction of production resulted in a lower variability than in any other group. Thus, we may conclude that the group standard at 50 units per hour set up strong group-induced forces which were important components in the central force field shown in Figure 4. It is now evident that for the no-participation group the quasi-stationary equilibrium after transfer has a steep gradient around the equilibrium level of 50 units per hour—the strength of forces increases rapidly above and below this level. It is also clear that the group standard to restrict production is a major reason for the lack of recovery in the no-participation group.

The table of variability also shows that the experimental treatments markedly reduced variability in the other four groups after transfer. In the group having participation by representation, this smallest reduction of variability was produced by a group standard of individual competition. Competition among members of the group was reported by the supervisor soon after transfer. This competition was a force toward higher production which resulted in good recovery to standard and continued progress beyond standard.

The total-participation groups showed a greater reduction in variability following transfer. These two groups were transferred on the same day. Group competition developed between the two groups, and this competition, which evidently resulted in stronger forces on the members than did the individual competition, was an effective group standard. The standard gradually moved to higher and higher levels of production, with the result that the groups not only reached but far exceeded their previous levels of production.

Probably a major determinant of the strength of these group standards is the cohesiveness of the group (1). Whether this power of the group over the members was used to increase or to decrease productivity seemed to depend upon the use of participation (4).

Turnover And Aggression

Returning now to our preliminary theory of frustration, we can see several revisions. The difficulty of the job and its relation to skill and strain avoidance has been clarified in Proposition 5. It is now clear that the driving force toward 60 is a complex affair: it is partly a negative driving force corresponding to the negative valence of low pay, low status, failure, and job insecurity. Turnover results not only from the frustration produced by the conflict of these two forces, but also from a direct attempt to escape from the region of these negative valences. For the members of the no-participation group, the group standard to restrict production prevented escape by increasing production, so that quitting their jobs was the only remaining escape. In the participation groups, on the contrary, both the group standards and the additional own forces resulting from the acceptance of management-induced forces combined to make increasing production the distinguished path of escape from this region of negative valence.

In considering turnover as a form of escape from the field, it is not enough to look only at the psychological present; one must also consider the psychological future. The employee's decision to quit the job is rarely made exclusively on the basis of a momentary frustration or an undesirable present situation. She usually quits when she also sees the future as equally hopeless. The operator transferred by the usual factory procedure (including the no-participation group) has, in fact, a realistic view of the probability of continued failure because, as we have already noted, 62% of transfers do fail to recover to standard production. Thus, the higher rate of quitting for transfers as compared to non-transfers results from a more pessimistic view of the future.

The no-participation procedure had the effect for the members of setting up management as a hostile power field. They rejected the forces induced by this hostile power field, and group standards to restrict production developed within the group in opposition to management. In this conflict between the power field of management and the power field of the group, the group attempted to reduce the strength of the hostile power field relative to the strength of their own power field. This change was accomplished in three ways: (*a*) The group increased its own power by developing a more cohesive and well-disciplined group. (*b*) They secured "allies" by getting the backing of the union in filing a formal grievance about the new piece rate. (*c*) They attacked the hostile power field directly in the form of aggression against the supervisor, the time-study engineer, and the higher management. Thus the aggression was derived not only from individual frustration, but also from the conflict between two groups. Furthermore, this situation of group conflict both helped to define management as the frustrating agent and gave the members strength to express any aggressive impulses produced by frustration.

CONCLUSIONS

It is possible for management to modify greatly or to remove completely group resistance to changes in methods of work and the ensuing piece rates. This change can be accomplished by the use of group meetings in which management effectively communicates the need for change and stimulates group participation in planning the changes.

For Harwood's management, and presumably for managements of other industries using an incentive system, this experiment has important implications in the field of labor relations. A majority of all grievances presented at Harwood have always stemmed from a change situation. By preventing or greatly modifying group resistance to change, this concomitant to change may well be greatly reduced. The reduction of such costly phenomena as turnover and slow relearning rates presents another distinct advantage.

Harwood's management has long felt that action research, such as the present experiment, is the only key to better labor-management relations. It is only by discovering the basic principles and applying them to the true causes of conflict that an intelligent, effective effort can be made to correct the undesirable effects of the conflict.

REFERENCES

1. Festinger, L., Back, K., Schachter, S., Kelley, H., & Thibaut, J.: *Theory and experiment in social communication*. Ann Arbor, Mich.: Institute for Social Research, 1950.

2. French, John R.P., Jr.: The behavior of organized and unorganized groups under conditions of frustration and fear. *University of Iowa Studies in Child Welfare*, 1944, **20**, 229-308.

3. Lewin, Kurt: Frontiers in group dynamics. *Human Relations,* 1947, **1**, 5-41.

4. Schachter, S., Ellertson, N., McBride, Dorothy, & Gregory, Doris: An experimental study of cohesiveness and productivity. *Human Relations,* 1951, **4**, 229-238.

Chapter 15

Some Social Factors
Related to Performance
in a Research Organization

Donald C. Pelz

This report will summarize some of the highlights from a study conducted in a large government organization for medical research.[1] The organization employs some three hundred investigators who conduct laboratory research on the frontiers of medical knowledge. The organization is regarded by its employees as having an atmosphere similar to that of a large university. The research is generally of a fundamental rather than applied character, and considerable freedom is allowed the individual investigator.

As part of the study, judgments of individuals' scientific performance were made by panels of investigators. The latter were experienced scientists, non-supervisory as well as supervisory, who were familiar with the work of the others. Where possible, each scientist was evaluated twice, once in comparison with others in his own laboratory or division, and again in comparison with others in the same scientific discipline. A particular individual might be judged by as many as fourteen other scientists, only one or two of whom would have supervisory authority over him. Essentially, this was an evaluation by one's peers. The assessors' judgments were assigned numerical scores from 1 to 9, the scores from different judges were averaged, and where a scientist received both a laboratory and a discipline score the two results were combined.

In our analyses we wanted to study the effects of the social environment on the individual's performance. For this purpose we wanted to reduce variations in performance caused by individual factors such as basic ability, quality of training, or type of experience. It seemed reasonable to assume that such factors would be reflected in the scientist's amount of education and in his job grade.

_Reprinted from _Administrative Science Quarterly_, Vol. I, No. 3 (Dec. 1956), pp. 310-325. Reprinted by permission of the _Administrative Science Quarterly_._

1. The study was financed by the National Institutes of Health, U.S. Public Health Service, and the Department of Health, Education, and Welfare. Additional analysis and writing were made possible by a grant from the Foundation for Research on Human Behavior, Ann Arbor, Michigan. Assisting in the study were Glen Mellinger, Robert C. Davis, and Howard Baumgartel.

The data showed that with increase in grade, there was a definite increase in average performance; and non-Ph.D.'s scored lower than Ph.D.'s of equal rank. By adding or subtracting an appropriate constant, an "adjusted" score for each individual was obtained such that the residual variation still associated with grade or doctoral degree was no greater than 0.4 per cent. In this adjusted measure it seems likely that differences owing to individual factors have been reduced.

SCIENCE VERSUS INSTITUTIONAL VALUES

If social factors can influence a person's scientific achievement, they may do so in part by affecting his motivation toward the work. To study such effects it was first important to determine whether motivational factors have any association with performance.

In a previous study of a government organization administering research grants, Dwaine Marvick[2] demonstrated the significance of certain general motivations or values. He isolated two syndromes labeled the "specialist" and "institutional" orientations. The specialist seeks the approval of a larger circle of peers wherever they may be found; the institutionalist seeks rewards within a localized institution. We wanted to know whether such orientations would relate to scientific performance.

In the present study each scientist filled out a questionnaire, one part of which listed nine factors that might be important in a job. Each person indicated how much personal importance he attached to each factor. A correlational analysis located three items which seemed to represent the specialist or (as we named it) the *science* orientation. Another cluster of items seemed to indicate the *institutional* orientation.[3]

In an analysis of these data, R. C. Davis[4] found that the index of science orientation was significantly related to scientific performance, whereas the index of institutional orientation was not. Furthermore, it appeared that a strong science orientation went with high performance mainly when the institutional

2. D. Marvick, *Career Perspectives in a Bureaucratic Setting* (Ann Arbor: Institute of Public Administration, University of Michigan, 1954).

3. The three science-oriented items were: stress on using present abilities or knowledge, freedom to carry out original ideas, and chance to contribute to basic scientific knowledge. The three institutional-oriented items were: stress on having an important job, association with high-level persons having important responsibilities, and sense of belonging to an organization with prestige in the lay community. The latter cluster might also be labeled a "prestige" orientation. The two indexes were neither positively nor negatively correlated; a person high on one might be either high or low on the other.

4. R.C. Davis, "Factors Related to Scientific Research Performance," in *Interpersonal Factors in Research, Part I* (Ann Arbor: Institute for Social Research, University of Michigan, 1954). See also, R.C. Davis, "Commitment to Professional Values as Related to the Role Performance of Research Scientists" (unpublished doctor's dissertation, University of Michigan, 1956).

orientation was weak; strength of science orientation was not significantly related to performance when the institutional orientation was strong.

Similar results were obtained with data from another study conducted at the Institute for Social Research by S. Lieberman and L. Meltzer[5] as part of the Survey of Physiological Sciences sponsored by the American Physiological Society. In a questionnaire sent to a nation-wide population of physiologists, similar questions about the personal importance of various job factors were asked. Scientific performance was measured in this instance by the number of times each person had been cited in the *Annual Review of Physiology* for the preceding three years. When a parallel index of science orientation was formed, a significant relationship was again found with performance. No relationship was found between the number of citations and the scientist's motivation toward prestige items such as advancement in his profession.

These results raise some provocative questions for research administrators grappling with knotty problems of salaries, titles, and promotion policies. The point to be stressed here, though, is that the index of science orientation does relate to actual performance and thus points toward a way in which performance might be increased. Some results to be given later suggest that science motivations may be affected by the type of leadership in the organization. It may also be possible to raise the level of science motivation through the selection of new personnel or through the kinds of recognition given.

CONTACT WITH SCIENTIFIC COLLEAGUES

A second series of analyses approached the question of whether the style of communication with one's colleagues can raise or depress the level of performance. If so, what is the optimal pattern of such contact? Should a scientist rub elbows daily with his peers or should he be assigned a cubbyhole where he can work without distraction? If frequent contact proves worthwhile, should it be mainly with others of similar background, with whom he can talk the same language, or would he benefit more by the stimulation of ideas from persons of different backgrounds?

To study these questions G. Mellinger[6] used nonsupervisory scientists at a senior level who were mature investigators at civil service grades of GS-12 and higher, with several years of experience.[7] On their questionnaires scientists named up to fifteen people in the organization with whom "some contact is of

---

5. S. Lieberman and L. Meltzer, *The Attitudes and Activities of Physiologists* (Ann Arbor: Survey Research Center, University of Michigan, 1954).

6. G. Mellinger, manuscript prepared for *Interpersonal Factors in Research, Part II* (in process; Ann Arbor: Institute for Social Research, University of Michigan, 1956).

7. In the following data a distinction will be made between senior- and junior-level scientists. They differ in experience and in autonomy and may require different kinds of social environments for high performance.

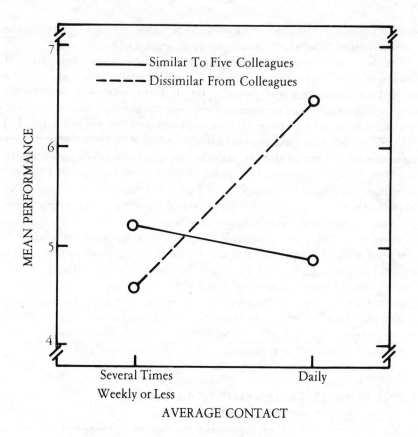

Figure 1. Scientific performance related to similarity to five colleagues in prior employment and to frequency of contact (at senior level).

greatest significance to you in your work," and indicated the frequency of contact with each.

For each respondent we selected the five scientific colleagues he named as most significant, excluding supervisors above him, technical assistants, and administrative personnel. For each colleague we computed a measure of similarity on the science and institutional orientations described above; we averaged these for the five colleagues, and also computed the mean frequency of contact. Figure 1 shows the results when these measures are jointly related to scientific performance.

Among the four possible combinations of frequency and similarity, highest performance is found when scientists have *frequent* contact (more than several times weekly) with colleagues who are on the average *dissimilar* from themselves in values.

Increase in contact is significantly related to performance only if colleagues are on the whole dissimilar from themselves. When colleagues have similar values, more frequent contact is not accompanied by higher performance; there is, in fact, a slight decline.[8]

These findings suggest that scientists benefit by frequent opportunities to exchange ideas with persons having different values. Since the institutionally oriented persons in our study tend to lay stress on improving the nation's health, the results might mean that those who emphasize basic research can benefit from contact with those who stress applied research, and vice versa. The interpretation suggested here is that frequent contact with dissimilar colleagues stimulates higher performance. It might also be argued that abler scientists seek out those of different values. The second interpretation seems to be preferred by some scientists who do not feel that social factors can influence level of performance. The facts are, however (from data not shown here), that the colleagues of abler scientists are on the average just as similar to these scientists as the colleagues of less able scientists are to the less able scientists. It does not look as though the more competent investigators deliberately seek contacts with colleagues of dissimilar values.

Another result in a parallel vein was obtained with a different measure of similarity. On the questionnaire scientists were asked about the kinds of situations in which they had previously worked; most frequently named were government, university, and hospital (including private practice). Depending on the number of such situations that they shared in common, each pair received a high to a low similarity score; and the average similarity between a scientist and his five main colleagues was computed.

The results are shown in Figure 2. We note that highest performance occurs when the senior scientist has frequent contact with five colleagues who are markedly dissimilar from himself in type of previous employment.

Frequency of contact is associated with significantly higher performance only for those scientists whose colleagues are dissimilar from themselves. When colleagues come from similar backgrounds, increase in contact from weekly to daily tends to go with slightly lower performance.

On the other hand, among moderately isolated scientists (who see their colleagues weekly) dissimilarity in previous employment seems to be a handicap; performance is significantly lower in comparison to those having similar colleagues.

It is likely that those who have worked previously in government, university, and hospital situations will develop different views as to the best way of approaching a research problem. Whatever the nature of these differences, it appears that they can encourage high scientific performance, provided there is ample interchange among the individuals. But diverse viewpoints may be a hindrance if they constitute the only contacts of a relatively isolated individual.

Is the similarity illustrated in Figures 1 and 2 the same thing or two different

8. This does not mean that among this group "the fewer contacts the better." Most scientists report average contacts weekly or more often with their colleagues. Among the few isolates who report less than weekly contacts, performance tends to be low.

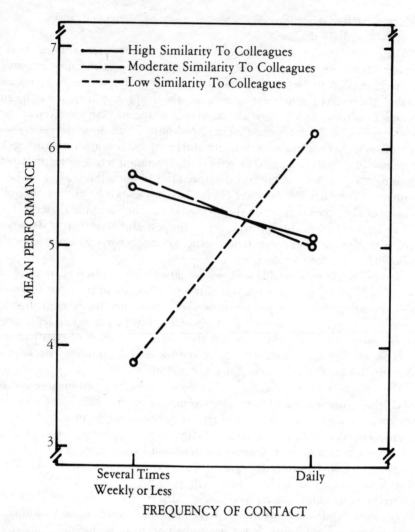

Figure 2. Scientific performance related to similarity in values and to frequency of contact with five main colleagues (at senior level).

things? The correlation between the two similarity measures is in fact slightly negative (-.15) and not statistically significant. It appears that we are dealing with two independent kinds of similarity. What their precise nature is remains a question for future research.

Such results raise the question of scientific discipline. Will scientists benefit from close contact with others in different disciplines? Does organization of laboratories along interdisciplinary "project team" lines give better results than organization into single discipline groups?

In our study we classified each scientist according to the major and minor

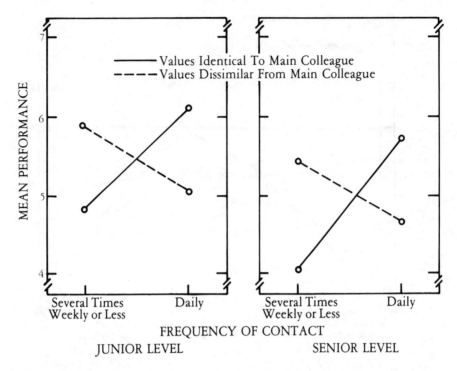

Figure 3. Scientific performance related to similarity in values and to frequency of contact with main colleague.

disciplines he was currently using in his work. These classifications were based in part on the disciplines he named on his questionnaire and in part on the groupings established to assess performance. Similarity scores were assigned, depending on whether scientists had major fields in common, minor fields in common, or no fields in common.

The results of this analysis are not as clear-cut as the previous ones, but they point in a similar direction. In general, senior scientists whose five main colleagues differ from themselves in field of work tend to perform somewhat better; and this tendency is more marked with frequent contact.

The tendencies (according to data not shown here) are also sharper when the colleagues are not equally dissimilar, but vary in their degree of dissimilarity. Thus it appears that for high performance the scientist requires variety in his daily fare. Additional support of this idea will be given below.

CONTACTS WITH SINGLE INDIVIDUALS

The foregoing analyses raised further questions. We have studied contacts with five colleagues; will similar results obtain with the scientist's one most

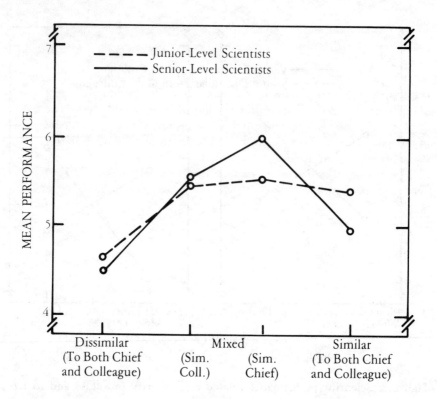

Figure 4. Scientific performance related to similarity of field to that of chief and main colleague.

important colleague? And what about his chief—should the scientist work under a supervisor who is in a different field? To explore such questions we again used frequency of contact and several measures of similarity. The present analysis was extended to junior-level scientists (in civil service grades GS-9 and GS-11, most of whom have doctoral degrees but limited experience) as well as the senior level used previously.

One particularly surprising result emerged, as shown in Figure 3. The measures used are similar to those in Figure 1 except that they refer to the one most significant colleague rather than to an average for five colleagues. The figure demonstrates that high scientific performance is associated with daily contact provided that the scientist's major colleague has *similar* values. By contrast, Figure 1 showed that high performance goes with frequent contact provided that contact is mainly with five colleagues who have *dissimilar* values.

How to reconcile these results? The following view seems plausible: For maximum performance it is helpful to have at least one close colleague with a similar orientation—someone who "talks the same language," with whom the scientist can air his problems and get a sympathetic hearing. But one or two such individuals are enough. To provide the stimulation of new ideas, it is important that the remaining contacts be with people of dissimilar orientation. In short, one kind of environment for high performance is frequent contact with a variety of viewpoints, a few similar, but most of them different.

Other conditions for achieving variety are possible. Consider the relatively isolated scientist who sees his colleagues only once or twice a week. The data from Figures 1 and 3 suggest that in this case his major colleagues should possess different values and the remaining colleagues similar ones. Again the principle of variety is indicated.

The same principle emerges when we examine the relationships of the scientist to both his chief and his major colleague in terms of scientific field. The data in Figure 4 show that scientific performance tends to be higher if the scientist's chief and major colleague are heterogeneous in scientific field—one similar and the other dissimilar. Lower performance occurs when the two are homogeneous—both dissimilar to the scientist or (for senior investigators) both similar.

It does not seem to matter whether the chief plays the role of "confidant" and the colleague that of "stimulator," or vice versa. The important thing is that both roles be provided, especially for senior scientists. The key lies in variety.

LEADERSHIP METHODS OF THE IMMEDIATE CHIEF

What sort of supervision do scientific personnel require for maximum performance? One view commonly held is that the scientific supervisor should do little except keep out of the way of his subordinates. The soundest way to encourage high achievement, according to this philosophy, is to secure good people, give them good equipment and assistants, and then leave them alone. This view arises in part as a protest against the continental tradition of the *Herr Geheimrat,* the professor directing his students, the master his disciples.

Many scientists conceive of leadership in this either/or manner, and do not recognize the existence of a middle ground between domination and isolation. Does such a middle ground of scientific leadership exist, and, if so, how does it affect performance as compared with the extremes?

In the following analyses, measures of supervisory behavior were obtained from the average reports of two or more subordinates. This procedure helps to guard against the possibility that the supervisor is simply adjusting his methods of leadership to the abilities of a particular subordinate.

In this section we shall deal with "small working groups"—two or more investigators who name the same person as their immediate chief. (In terms of the administrative structure, such a group might consist of a unit, a section, or even a small laboratory.)

A major supervisory variable we attempted to measure may be called independence or autonomy from the chief. Two items were used: (1) the percentage of scientists in each group who report that in selecting work problems or in interpreting results they make their *own decisions*; (2) the extent to which they feel the chief's activities and decisions can *influence their work*. With these two items, four patterns of leadership were defined, ranging from "dependence" (subordinates make few decisions, and the chief has considerable influence) to "independence" (subordinates make many decisions on their own, and the chief has little influence). The intermediate categories were "mutual influence" (both subordinates and the chief have much to say) and "separation" (neither subordinates nor the chief have much to say—apparently decisions depend on the nature of the task or on higher chiefs).

The results (not illustrated here) show that performance is slightly higher under an intermediate degree of independence, rather than under full dependence or full independence. Junior scientists (civil service grades GS-9 and GS-11) benefit somewhat more from "mutual influence" between chief and subordinates; senior scientists (GS grades 12 and up) benefit somewhat more from "separation."

It seems plausible that too much independence may deprive the subordinate of the stimulation that a competent chief can provide. On the other hand, too close dependence on the chief may stifle individual initiative. By this line of reasoning, highest performance should result if we can combine the benefits of frequent stimulation with the assurance of freedom for initiative. To test this hypothesis we analyzed not only independence but also amount of contact with the chief.

The results in Figure 5 support the hypothesis that at the junior level performance is highest when independence from the chief is combined with frequent contact with him—when the individual has frequent interaction with the chief, but also has considerable voice in the final decisions. A similar but less striking tendency exists for senior-level scientists (data not shown).

LEADERSHIP FACTORS IN THE LABORATORY CHIEF

The final set of analyses to be reported were conducted by Howard Baumgartel.[9] Studies in industry have indicated that a department head can influence the productivity and morale of employees at several levels under him. Does the same hold true in a research organization? To study this question, Baumgartel analyzed certain measures of the chiefs of twenty laboratories. The latter were basic administrative units ranging in size from six to thirty-three professional investigators, and as many sub-professional assistants. A typical laboratory was subdivided into three or four sections.

9. H. Baumgartel, "Leadership, Motivation and Attitudes in Twenty Research Laboratories" (unpublished doctor's dissertation, University of Michigan, 1955); "Leadership, Motivation and Attitudes in Twenty Research Laboratories" (paper read at American Sociological Society meetings, 1955); and Leadership, Motivations, and Attitudes in Research Laboratories, *Journal of Social Issues*, 12 (1956), no. 2 (in press).

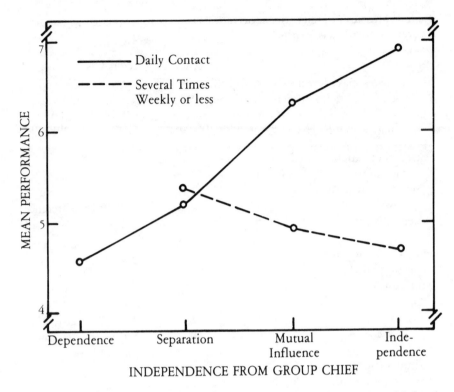

Figure 5. **Scientific performance related to independence from group chief and to contact with chief (at junior level).**

For this analysis it was not possible to use the measure of individual performance as a criterion, since the measure was originally obtained in part by comparing individuals with others in the same laboratory, thus reducing interlaboratory differences. But we have seen above that questionnaire items such as science-oriented values do relate to performance; these and other attitude items were therefore used as criteria.

Baumgartel developed three measures of the laboratory chief. One was an index of the chief's "scientific performance and motivation," based on several intercorrelated items including his own score on performance and his motivation toward the science values. This index measures the extent to which a chief combines both high technical qualifications and strong motivation toward scientific goals.

A second index described patterns of supervision and was similar to the variable of "independence" discussed above. (The latter, in fact, was suggested by Baumgartel's analysis.) Examination of several items revealed three clusters or types: a "directive" type (characterized by high influence by the chief, little freedom for subordinates to make decisions, and moderate frequency of contact between them); a "participatory" type (high influence by the chief plus

Table 1. Measures of scientists' motivations and attitudes related to factors in laboratory chief's leadership.*

Measures from scientists	Leadership factors			
	Perform-ance-and-motivation	Partic., not directive	Partic., not laissez-faire	Role conformity
Science motivations (based on 4 measures)				
Significantly positive	3	1	0	No
Positive	1	2	3	differences
Negative	0	1	1	expected
Sense of progress toward scientific goals (based on 3 measures)				
Significantly positive	2	1	0	No
Positive	1	2	3	differences
Negative	0	0	0	expected
Attitudes toward leadership (based on 8 measures)				
Significantly positive	No	3	3	3
Positive	differences	5	2	5
Negative	expected	0	3	0

*This table summarizes the results of forty-five tests of relationship between leadership factors and scientists' motives and attitudes. (Science motivations were measured in four ways; sense of progress in three ways; and attitudes toward leadership in eight ways.) It was predicted that these relationships would be positive. The table shows the number of tests in which the relationships were positive and negative. A "significantly positive" relationship is a difference in the predicted direction which is large enough to attain the .05 level of confidence (using a one-tailed t test).

considerable freedom for subordinates, and frequent contact); and a "laissez-faire" pattern (little contact, little influence by the chief, and considerable freedom of decision by subordinates).

A third leadership factor was the extent to which the leader's actual methods of making decisions corresponded to the methods preferred by his subordinates. The discrepancy between these two measures constituted an index of "role conformity."

It was predicted that subordinates' motivations toward science values, their sense of progress toward these values, and their attitudes toward leadership would be higher under (a) chiefs with a high index of performance-and-motivation in comparison to a low index; (b) chiefs who used participatory leadership in comparison to those using directive; (c) chiefs who used participatory leadership in comparison to laissez-faire; (d) chiefs who conformed to the role expectations of subordinates in comparison to those not conforming.

A summary of results is given in Table 1. A "positive" relationship is one which conforms to the prediction; a "negative" relationship is one showing no difference, or a difference opposite to prediction.

Of forty-five tests where the direction of relationship was predicted, forty are positive, and sixteen of these are statistically significant at the 5-per-cent level of confidence (using a one-tailed test). Only five results are negative. Thus the data in general support the hypotheses.

Some specific features deserve attention. First, the laboratory chief's own index of performance-and-motivation is more significantly related to his subordinates' motivation and sense of progress than is his pattern of supervisory behavior. In this organization, successful leadership depends not simply on administrative skill but also depends heavily on the leader's personal qualifications and his own motivation toward the task.

Second, there is fairly clear evidence that participatory leadership is more effective than directive leadership (and also slightly better than the laissez-faire pattern).

SUMMARY

In a large government organization conducting basic medical research, the level of individuals' scientific performance is found to be higher under the following conditions:

(1) Strong personal emphasis placed upon science-oriented values of using one's abilities, having freedom to pursue original ideas, and making contributions to basic scientific knowledge;

(2) Frequent (daily) contact with several scientific colleagues who on the average have been employed in settings different from one's own, who stress values different from one's own, and who tend to work in scientific fields different from one's own;

(3) At the same time, frequent contact with at least one important colleague who has similar professional values;

(4) A chief and a major colleague one of whom is in the same scientific discipline and the other in a different one, rather than both similar or both dissimilar;

(5) A chief who gives neither complete autonomy nor excessive direction, but who frequently interacts with subordinates and who also gives them the opportunity to make their own decisions.

In addition to these findings on scientific performance, analyses of scientists' motivations and attitudes in twenty laboratories show that:

(6) Motivation and sense of progress toward scientific goals are stronger under laboratory chiefs who themselves are highly competent and motivated individuals;

(7) Motivations and attitudes also tend to be stronger under laboratory chiefs who employ participatory rather than directive or laissez-faire leadership.

To summarize these findings in a few words, it appears that many scientists may benefit from (a) close colleagues who represent a *variety* of values, experiences, and disciplines, and (b) supervisors who avoid both isolation and domination and who provide frequent stimulation combined with autonomy of action.

Afterthoughts

At this point, you are in a good position to assess the involvement opportunities you now provide for your subordinates. By analyzing your use of power along the lines presented in early chapters, you can determine the likelihood that your organization is receiving the benefits of participation. The issues can be personalized through a series of questions which will indicate where you are in the involvement process and suggest areas where you might restructure social relationships. Readings in the next section will point out specific managerial practices which you may find helpful as a result of your present assessment.

First of all try to form an overall impression of your approach to power. Remember, as McClelland and Burnham stated, seeking out power is a prerequisite managerial act: the crucial issue is what you do with power once it is acquired. Indicate your most preferred way of using power by placing yourself at some point along Blake and Mouton's power spectrum. Do you perceive strong tendencies at either extreme—a 1/0 desire to retain the lion's share or a 0/1 willingness to let subordinates go their own way? A predominant power style at either end of the spectrum precludes effective participation.

You can clarify your initial view of your power style by analyzing the basic system of power and influence you perpetuate in your part of the organization. Ask yourself how closely you adhere to the basic tenets of the authority-obedience formula described by Blake and Mouton—the chain of command, span of control, delegation of authority, and exception principle. Better yet, how do you think your subordinates would answer this question; "How are rules and policies viewed by your manager—as flexible guidelines to be used or as 'holy writ' with which we dare not tamper?"

What will emerge from such probes into the general system of power and influence might be described as the prevailing participative ethic. Although almost subliminal, the participative ethic sends a clear message to everyone about your personal beliefs in the value of participation and thus the value of those who might participate. When the overall system is restricted by preconception and precedent, by a "That's the way we do things—like it or not!" style, involvement opportunities are neither provided by managers nor sought by subordinates.

The involvement process is nowhere more evident than in the decision-making and problem-solving processes in the organization of work. Your analysis at this level will almost complete the picture of involvement in your area. Again ask yourself about normal operating procedures. Who designs individual jobs, establishes priorities and goals, and sets the pace? If your answer is, for the most part, resident experts or staff people with appropriate titles rather than the people who actually do the work, your inclination is more to the authority-obedience model than the desired state of joint determination.

One final question remains to be answered, one that determines whether participation will indeed lead to maximum levels of job satisfaction and productivity. You may invite subordinates to voice their opinions in many areas of decision-making and problem-solving, but what impact do they expect their ideas will have on the organization? If their answer is "not much," your managerial credibility is on the line. Subordinates will become increasingly doubtful of the value of participation per se and your sincerity and honesty in general. Participation demands serious consideration, follow-up and feedback on your part. Without them you create a pseudo-participative system where subordinates learn quickly not to take participative opportunities very seriously and their level of trust in you will be severely threatened. In such a situation it would have been better not to have entered the involvement process in the first place instead of aborting at mid-point and jeopardizing future opportunities.

A final caveat is in order for managers who nod in agreement to involvement in principle, but shake their heads when it comes to putting it in practice. The words that go along with this "yes...but" scenario often sound something like this; "Participation will work for most managers, but my people are chronic complainers who don't want to accept responsibility." If such a refrain sounds at all credible, think back to the leading chapter in this collection by Jay Hall and how a manager's perceptions and practices combine to create self-fulfilling prophecies. The point is that when poor performance is evident the manager may have had an unwitting hand in the situation.

As Blake and Mouton suggest, examine the distribution of power when subordinates act dissatisfied and irresponsible. In all likelihood it will call for redressing the balance of power and for moving to the middle area of joint determination on the power spectrum. It is on this ground that people, despite age, sex, education and the nature of their work are most satisfied, responsible, and productive.

Perhaps it would be useful at this point to remind you as a manager that your attempts to put into effect the precepts of this section may initially meet with resistance on the part of subordinates. Depending on current circumstances, your efforts toward initiating power sharing, participation and democracy in the workplace may be met with skepticism by those who work for you. But who can blame them? To offer to share power with the powerless and to solicit opinions from those whose ideas have previously been ignored represents substantial change and may even elicit a kind of fear based on a misunderstanding of your motives. In any event, you need to be prepared to persevere and to anticipate the cynicism that is likely to occur. It is probable that the greater the resistance that greets you in your attempts toward positive change, the greater the need for the change in the first place.

Section IV.

Interpersonal Competence:
Setting the Standard
for Trust

After reading the chapters on involvement in the last section, a manager may be convinced of its benefits and may even see a number of new opportunities for subordinates to take a greater hand in the affairs of the organization. However, being philosophically in tune with power sharing and participation is not enough to make the promise of higher morale and productivity a reality. As implied in the questions which probed the current level of involvement, managers need a set of interpersonal skills to activate the involvement process. To the degree that the manager is interpersonally competent, subordinates will take advantage of involvement opportunities and consequently the organization will benefit from their increased commitment and creativity.

Chris Argyris has been one of the most vocal proponents of interpersonal competence for managers. According to Argyris, until managers are trusted by their subordinates, are believed to be open and candid and value the same in others, emotional barriers will block closer working relationships. High marks for interpersonal competence depend on how well a manager is seen as:

1. *Owning up to,* or accepting responsibility for one's ideas and feelings.
2. *Being open* to ideas and feelings of others and those from within one's self.
3. *Experimenting* with new ideas and feelings.
4. *Helping others* to own up to, be open to, and to experiment with their ideas and feelings.
5. Accomplishment of these behaviors in such a way that one adds to the norms of individuality (rather than conformity), concern (rather than antagonism), and trust (rather than mistrust).[1]

In short, managers must display trusting behavior so that it will become a standard for others to model.

As useful as Argyris' description is for capturing the spirit of interpersonal competence, it stops short of identifying the specific skills required. Thinking back on the productive use of power and participation can bring the necessary skills into focus. Managers must be able to establish and maintain a collaborative relationship with and among subordinates. To do so calls for a variety of communication skills for sharing information and personal feelings and creating a psychologically safe environment where conflicts can be confronted and used to mutual advantage.

INSURING INVOLVEMENT

In "Interpersonal Style and Corporate Climate: Communication Revisited," Jay Hall stresses that managers set the tone for involvement by the way they interact with others. He uses the Luft-Ingham Johari Window, an information processing model, to describe how managers share their thoughts and feelings and in turn solicit those of others. Hall's research shows that managers' "openness" varies with subordinates, colleagues, and superiors, and thus yields relationships with varying levels of productivity. In addition, managers' interpersonal styles tend to be mirrored by their subordinates: for good or ill managers are largely responsible for the quality of relations in their workgroups.

Providing co-workers with growthful feedback is a core function for every manager but one that often jeopardizes involvement opportunities when either overly critical or cautious. The manager who, in the name of candor, comes down hard on subordinates every time they make a mistake is just as ineffective as one who treads softly, withholding all criticism for fear of hurting their feelings. Phillip G. Hanson points out in "Giving Feedback: An Interpersonal Skill," that extremes of criticism or praise are both inappropriate. To build trust and avoid defensiveness, feedback should be timely, descriptive rather than judgemental, and allow for freedom of choice.

Involvement and harmony are not always synonymous. In fact, allowing more subordinate input in decision making increases the probability of conflict since there are more alternatives available for consideration. However, as Alan C. Filley states in "Personal Styles of Conflict Resolution," conflict in and of itself is neither good nor bad. Whether or not conflict leads to creative problem solving or causes people to withdraw will depend largely on the personal style a manager uses to resolve it.

Most managers are aware of the necessity of managing conflict productively because they have felt the effects of mismanaged conflict. Jerry B. Harvey describes a form of harmony that is just as threatening as cutthroat conflict to the productive ends of involvement. In "The Abilene Paradox: The Management of Agreement," he describes numerous ironic examples where members of organizations agree to take actions they know are not in their best interests. When trust is low and anxiety is high, individuals find it easier to agree, to be good team members, than to create a conflict by exposing their opinions.

Managers need to recognize the facade of agreement and create conditions where everyone involved will feel free to voice their disagreement.

SPECIFIC APPLICATIONS

The final chapters embellish the exposure and feedback dynamics established in the opening chapters by Hall and Hanson. In "How Power Affects Employee Appraisal," Blake and Mouton examine another facet of power sharing for productive involvement. When it comes to performance evaluation the principle of evenly distributed power introduced in their chapters in the previous section is critical. Performance improvement must be a joint effort between subordinate and manager, a give-and-take relationship not an authoritarian tell-and-sell approach. The last chapter, "Systems Maintenance: Gatekeeping and the Involvement Process," the second in this section by Jay Hall, stresses that subordinate participation is contingent on being invited by the manager. Only through active involvement, resulting from the manager's offer to share power, will subordinates experience the positive feelings so necessary for achieving organizational goals.

REFERENCES

1. Argyris, C. *Intervention Theory and Method: A Behavioral Science View.* Reading, Mass.: Addison-Wesley, 1970, p. 40.

Chapter 16

Interpersonal Style and Corporate Climate: Communication Revisited

Jay Hall

High on the diagnostic checklist of corporate health is communication. The ease with which information flows downward, upward, and horizontally is often a major internal indicant of organizational effectiveness; who listens to whom may reveal the real as opposed to the apparent authority structure in a firm; and the proportion of people who consistently fail to get the message is frequently taken as a statistical baseline for predicting the efficiency with which plans will be translated into actions. If sheer volume of spoken and written words is any indication of a topic's perceived importance, then communication would appear to be much on the mind of the average manager. And well it should be, for effective communication underlies both personal and corporate success in the modern world of organizations and the prognosis is less than encouraging. In a recent cross-cultural study,[1] roughly 74 per cent of the managers sampled from companies in Japan, Great Britain, and the United States cited communication breakdown as the single greatest barrier to corporate excellence.

Just what constitutes a problem of communication, however, is less easily agreed upon. Some theorists approach the issue from the vantage point of information bits comprising a message; others speak in terms of organizational roles and positions of centrality or peripherality; still others emphasize the directional flows of corporate data. The result is that more and more people are communicating about communication, while the achievement of clarity, understanding, commitment, and creativity—the goals of communication—becomes more and more limited. At the core of the problem is the fact that "communication breakdown" has become a convenient, and therefore overused, catch-all for diagnosing corporate ills. More often than not, the communication

1. R.R. Blake and Jane S. Mouton, *Corporate Excellence Through Grid Organization Development.* Houston, Texas: Gulf Pu ishing Co., 1968, p. 4.

dilemmas cited by people as the constraints under which they must live and labor are not communication problems at all. They are instead *symptoms* of difficulties at more basic and fundamental levels of corporate life. From a dynamics standpoint—as opposed to a symptomatics perspective—problems of communication in organizations frequently reflect dysfunctions at the level of *corporate climate*. The feelings people have about working where they work or about the work they are doing or about those with whom they work—feelings of impotence, distrust, resentment, insecurity, social inconsequence, and all the other very human emotions of which everyone is capable—not only define the climate which prevails but the manner in which communications will be managed, as well. In speaking to this very point, Blake and Mouton[2] have commented upon an oddity of organizational life: when management is effective and relationships are sound, problems of communication tend not to occur. It is only when relationships among members of the organization are unsound and fraught with unarticulated tensions that one hears complaints of communication breakdown. Thus, the quality of relationships in an organization may dictate to a great extent the level of communication effectiveness achieved, notwithstanding all the more mechanical and obvious influences typically invoked.

INTERPERSONAL STYLES AND THE QUALITY OF RELATIONSHIPS

Consistent with the syllogistic approach pursued so far, the critical factor underlying the quality of relationships in organizations is in need of review. Reduced to its lowest common denominator, the most significant determinant of the quality of relationships is the *interpersonal style* of the parties to a relationship. The learned, characteristic, and apparently preferred manner in which individuals relate to others in the building of relationships—the manner in which they monitor, control, filter, divert, give and seek the information germane to a given relationship—will dictate over time the quality of relationships which exist among people, the emotional climate which will characterize their interactions, and whether or not there will be problems of communication. In the final analysis, individuals are the human links in the corporate network, and the styles they employ interpersonally are the ultimate determinants of what information goes where and of whether it will be distortion-free or masked by interpersonal constraints.

The concept of interpersonal style is not an easy one to harness; yet, if it is to serve as the central mechanism underlying the quality of relationships, the nature of corporate climate, managerial effectiveness, and the level of corporate excellence attainable, it is worthy of analysis. Fortunately, Joseph Luft[3] and

2. *Ibid.* p. 3-5.

3. Joseph Luft, *Of Human Interaction*. Palo Alto, Cal.: National Press Books, 1969, *passim.*

Harry Ingham—two behavioral scientists with special interests in interpersonal and group processes—have developed a model of social interaction which affords a way of thinking about interpersonal functioning, while handling a good deal of the data encountered in everyday living. The *Johari Window,* as their model is called, allows for the identification of several interpersonal styles— their salient features and consequences—and suggests a basis for interpreting the significance of style for the quality of relationships. An overview of the Johari model should help to sharpen the perception of interpersonal practices among managers and lend credence to the contention of Blake and Mouton that there are few communication problems as such, only unsound relationships. At the same time, a normative statement regarding effective interpersonal functioning and, by extension, the foundations of corporate excellence may be found in the model as well. Finally, the major tenets of the model will be found to be testable under practical conditions; and the latter portion of this discussion will be devoted to research on the managerial profile in interpersonal encounters.

The Johari Window: A Graphic Model Of Interpersonal Processes[4]

As treated here, the Johari Window is essentially an information processing model; interpersonal style and individual effectiveness are assessed in terms of information processing tendencies and the performance consequences thought to be associated with such practices. Basically, the model employs a four-celled figure as its format; and it reflects the interaction of two interpersonal sources of information—Self and Others—and the behavioral processes required for utilizing that information. The model, depicted in Figure 1, may be thought of as representing the various kinds of data available for use in the establishing of interpersonal relationships. The squared field, in effect, represents an interpersonal space—the context within which relationships are built. This in turn is partitioned into four regions, with each representing a particular combination

---

4. The author has taken a number of interpretive liberties with the basic provisions of the Johari Awareness model. While it is anticipated that none of these violate the integrity of the model as originally described by Luft, it should be emphasized that many of the inferences and conclusions discussed are those of the author, and Dr. Luft should not be held accountable for any lapses of logic or misapplications of the model in this paper. Notable among the departures from Luft's original work are the following: As treated here, the four regions represent the context of an interpersonal relationship, whereas Dr. Luft employs these to represent the total person in relation to other persons. Exposure and Feedback solicitation are treated here as information processing modes which have purposive characteristics; Luft emphasizes, instead, self-disclosure and feedback from others as critical determinants of personal awareness. Similarly, the prime role of the Self in initiating interpersonal processes receives more emphasis in this presentation than is typically the case. An implicit stimulus-response rationale is invoked in the current treatment to explain the build-up of Others' known data (as triggered responses) in concert with each increment of Exposure by the Self; this underlies the contention that the horizontal and vertical lines move as a total piece, rather than in parts. Finally, the labels applied to the four informational regions are those suggested by the author to best reflect the dynamics occurring in each.

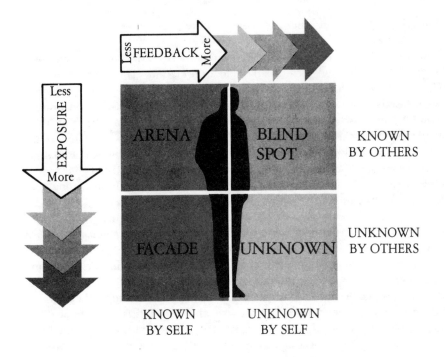

Figure 1. The Johari Window: A model of interpersonal processes.

or mix of relevant information and having special significance for the quality of relationships. To fully appreciate the implications that each informational region has for interpersonal effectiveness, one must consider not only the size and shape of each region but the reasons for its presence in the interpersonal space as well. At the same time, in an attempt to "personalize" the model it is helpful to think of oneself as the *Self* in the relationship for, as will be seen presently, it is what the Self does interpersonally that has the most direct impact on the quality of resulting relationships. In organizational terms, it is how the management-Self behaves that is critical to the quality of corporate relationships.

Reference to Figure 1 will reveal that the two informational sources, Self and Others, have information which is pertinent to the relationship and, at the same time, each lacks information that is equally germane. Thus, there is relevant and necessary information which is *Known by the Self*, while there is equally relevant and necessary information remaining *Unknown by the Self*. By the same token, there are data which bear on the relationship which are *Known by Others* and, conversely, applicable data which are *Unknown by Others*. The Self-Other combinations of known and unknown information make up the four regions within the interpersonal space and, again, these regions serve to characterize the various types and qualities of relationships possible within the Johari framework.

Region I, for example, constitutes that portion of the total interpersonal space which is devoted to mutually held information. This *Known by Self-Known by Others* facet of the interpersonal space is thought to be the part of the relationship which, because of its shared data characteristics and implied likelihood of mutual understanding, controls interpersonal productivity. That is, the working assumption is that productivity and interpersonal effectiveness are directly related to the amount of mutually held information in a relationship. Therefore, the larger Region I becomes, the more rewarding, effective, and productive the relationship will become as well. As the informational context for interpersonal functioning, Region I is called the *Arena*.

Region II, using the double classification approach just described, is that portion of the interpersonal space which holds information *Known by Others* but *Unknown by the Self*. Thus, this array of data constitutes an interpersonal handicap for the Self, since one can hardly understand the behaviors, decisions, or potentials of others if he doesn't have the data upon which these are based. Similarly, others have an advantage to the extent that they know their own reactions, feelings, perceptions, and the like while the Self is unaware of these. Region II—an area of hidden, unperceived information—is called the *Blindspot*. The Blindspot is, of course, a limiting factor with respect to the size of Region I and may be thought of, therefore, as inhibiting interpersonal effectiveness.

Region III may also be considered to inhibit interpersonal effectiveness, but it is due to an imbalance of information which would seem to favor the Self; as the portion of the relationship which is characterized by information *Known by the Self* but *Unknown by Others,* Region III constitutes a protective feature of the relationship for the Self. Data which one perceives as potentially prejudicial to a relationship or which he keeps to himself out of fear, desire for power, or whatever make up the *Facade*. This protective front, in turn, serves a defensive function for the Self. Again, every relationship is thought to have a Facade in it, despite the fact that its information is germane to the relationship at hand. Thus, the question is not one of whether a Facade is necessary but rather how much Facade is required realistically. Put another way, this raises the question of how much conscious defensiveness can be tolerated before the Arena becomes too inhibited and interpersonal effectiveness begins to diminish.

Finally, Region IV constitutes that portion of the relationship which is devoted to material neither known by the self nor by other parties to the relationship. The information in this *Unknown by Self—Unknown by Others* area is thought to reflect psychodynamic data, hidden potentials, unconscious idiosyncrasies, and the data-base of creativity. Thus, Region IV is the *Unknown* area which may become known as interpersonal effectiveness increases.

Summarily, it should be said that the information within all regions can be of any type—feeling data, factual information, assumptions, task skill data, and prejudices—which are *relevant* to the relationship at hand. Irrelevant data are not the focus of the Johari Window concept; just those pieces of information which have a bearing on the quality and productivity of the relationship should be considered as appropriate targets for the information processing practices prescribed by the model. At the same time, it should be borne in mind that the individuals involved in a relationship—particularly the Self—control what and how information will be processed. Because of this implicit personal control aspect, the model should be viewed as an open system which is *dynamic* and amenable to change as personal decisions regarding interpersonal functioning change.

Basic Interpersonal Processes: Exposure And Feedback

The dynamic character of the model, notwithstanding the rather static picture created by its graphic representation, is critical; for it is the movement capability of the horizontal and vertical lines which partition the interpersonal space into regions which gives individuals control over what their relationships will become. More explicitly, the Self can significantly influence the size of his Arena in relating to others by the behavioral processes he employs in establishing relationships. To the extent that one takes the steps necessary to apprise others of relevant information which he has and they do not, he is enlarging his Arena in a downward direction. Within the framework of the model, this enlargement occurs in concert with a reduction of one's Facade. Thus, if one behaves in a non-defensive, trusting, and possibly risk-taking manner with others —sharing pertinent information—he may be thought of as contributing to increased mutual awareness and sharing of data. The process one employs toward this end has been called the *Exposure* process; it entails the open and candid disclosure of one's feelings, factual knowledge, wild guesses, and the like in a conscious attempt to share. Frothy, intentionally untrue, diversionary sharing does not constitute exposure; and, as personal experience will attest, it does nothing to help mutual understanding. The Exposure process is under the direct control of the Self and may be used as a mechanism for building trust and for legitimizing mutual exposures.

The need for mutual exposures becomes apparent when one considers the behavioral process required for enlarging the Arena laterally. As a behavior designed to gain reduction in one's Blindspot, the *Feedback* process entails an active solicitation by the Self of the information he feels others might have which he does not. The active, initiative-taking aspect of this solicitation behavior should be stressed for again the Self takes the primary role in setting interpersonal norms and in legitimizing certain acts within the relationship. Since the extent to which the Self will actually receive the Feedback he solicits is contingent upon the willingness of others to expose their data, the need for a climate of mutual exposures becomes apparent. Control by the Self of the success of his Feedback-seeking behaviors is less direct therefore than in the case of self-exposure. He will achieve a reduction of his Blindspot only with the cooperation of others; and his own prior willingness to deal openly and candidly may well dictate what level of cooperative and trusting behavior will prevail on the part of other parties to the relationship.

Thus, one can theoretically establish interpersonal relationships character-ized by mutual understanding and increased effectiveness—*i.e.*, by a dominant Arena—if he will engage in exposing and feedback soliciting behaviors to an optimal degree. This places the determination of productivity and amount of interpersonal reward—and the quality of relationships—directly in the hands of the Self. In theory this amounts to an issue of interpersonal competence, and in practice it amounts to the conscious and sensitive management of interper-sonal processes.

Interpersonal Styles And Managerial Impacts

While one can theoretically employ Exposure and Feedback processes not only to a great but to a similar degree as well, individuals typically fail to achieve such an optimal practice. Indeed, they usually display a significant *preference* for one or the other of the two processes and tend to overuse one while neglecting the other. This tendency promotes a state of imbalance in interpersonal relationships which, in turn, creates disruptive tensions capable of retarding productivity. Figure 2 presents several commonly used approaches to the employment of Exposure and Feedback processes. Each of these may be thought of as reflecting a basic *interpersonal style*—that is, fairly consistent and preferred ways of behaving interpersonally. As might be expected, each style has associated with it some fairly predictable consequences.

TYPE A. This interpersonal style reflects a minimal use of both Exposure and Feedback processes; it is, in effect, a fairly impersonal approach to interpersonal relationships. The Unknown region dominates under this style; and unrealized potential, untapped creativity, and personal psychodynamics prevail as the sa-lient influences. Such a style would seem to indicate withdrawal and an aver-sion to risk-taking on the part of its user; interpersonal anxiety and safety-seek-ing are likely to be prime sources of personal motivation. Persons who charac-teristically use this style appear to be detached, mechanical, and uncommuni-cative. They may often be found in bureaucratic highly structured organiza-tions of some type where it is possible, and perhaps profitable, to avoid person-al disclosure or involvement. Persons using this style are likely to be reacted to with more than average hostility, since other parties to the relationship will tend to interpret the lack of Exposure and Feedback solicitation pretty much in terms of their own needs and how this interpersonal lack affects need fulfill-ment.

Subordinates whose manager employs such a style, for example, will often feel that his behavior is consciously aimed at frustrating them in their work. The person in need of support and encouragement will often view a Type A manager as aloof, cold, and indifferent. Another individual in need of firm

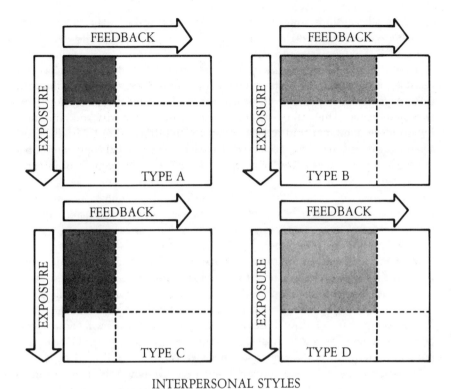

INTERPERSONAL STYLES

Figure 2. Interpersonal styles as functions of exposure use and feedback solicitation.

directions and plenty of order in his work may view the same manager as indecisive and administratively impotent. Yet another person requiring freedom and opportunities to be innovative may tend to see the Type A interpersonal style as hopelessly tradition-bound and as symptomatic of fear and an overriding need for security. Aside from the havoc that may be wrought among those whom one supervises, the use of Type A behaviors on a large scale in an organization reveals something about the climate and fundamental health of that organization. In many respects, interpersonal relationships founded on Type A uses of exposure and feedback constitute the kind of organizational ennui about which Chris Argyris[5] has written so eloquently. Such practices are, in his opinion, likely to be *learned* ways of behaving under oppressive and emasculating policies of the sort which encourage people to act in a submissive and dependent fashion. Organizationally, of course, the result is lack of communication and a loss of human potentials; the Unknown becomes the dominant feature of

5. C. Argyris, *Interpersonal Competence and Organizational Effectiveness*. Homewood, Ill.: Dorsey, 1962, *passim*.

corporate relationships, and the implications for organizational creativity and growth are obvious. This is a *bureaucratic-defensive* interpersonal style.

TYPE B. Under this approach, there is also an aversion to Exposure, but aversion is coupled with a *desire* for relationships not found in Type A. Thus, Feedback is the only process left in promoting relationships and it is much over-used. An aversion to the use of Exposure may typically be interpreted as a sign of basic mistrust of self and others, and it is therefore not surprising that the Facade is the dominant feature of relationships resulting from neglected Exposure coupled with overused Feedback. The style appears to be a probing supportive interpersonal ploy and, once the Facade becomes apparent, it is likely to result in a reciprocal withdrawal of trust by other parties. This may promote feelings of disgust, anxiety, and suspicion on the part of others; such feelings may lead to the manager being treated as a rather superficial person without real substance or as a devious sort with many hidden agenda.

Preference for this interpersonal style among managers seems to be of two types: Some managers committed to a quasi-permissive management may employ Type B behaviors in an attempt to avoid appearing directive. At best, such an approach results in the manager "hiding his light beneath a bushel" since his personal resources are never fully revealed or his opinions aired. Decisions reached on the basis of Type B uses of Exposure and Feedback will consistently be decisions based on less than all the resources available. By way of contrast—but subject to many of the same inadequacies—is the use of Type B behaviors in an attempt to gain or maintain one's personal power in relationships. Weschler, Massarik, and Tannenbaum[6] have observed that many managers engage in a form of behavior which they call "facade-building" as a means of maintaining personal control and an outward appearance of confidence. As these authors have observed and as the Johari model would suggest, however, persons who employ such "close to the vest" practices tend to become isolated from their subordinates and colleagues alike. Lack of trust becomes a major issue, and consolidation of power and promotion of an image of confidence may be the least likely resultants of Type B use in organizations. Very likely, the seeds of distrust and conditions for covert competitiveness—with all that these imply for organizational teamwork—will follow from widespread use of Type B interpersonal practices. This is a *permissive-apprehensive* interpersonal style.

TYPE C. This interpersonal style is based on an overuse of Exposure to the neglect of Feedback. It may well reflect ego-striving and/or distrust of others' competence. The person who uses this style usually feels quite confident of his own opinions and is likely to value compliance from others. The fact that he is often unaware of his impact or of the validity of others' contributions is reflected in the dominant Blindspot which results from this style. Others are likely to feel disenfranchised by one who uses this style; they often feel that he has

---

6. I. Weschler, F. Massarik, and R. Tannenbaum, "The Self in Process: A Sensitivity Training Emphasis", in I. Weschler and E.H. Schein (Eds.) *Issues in Training*. Washington, D.C.: National Training Laboratories, 1962, *passim*.

little use for their contributions or concern for their feelings. As a result, this style often triggers off feelings of hostility, insecurity, and resentment on the part of others. Frequently, others will learn to behave in such a way as to perpetuate the manager's Blindspot by withholding important information or giving only selected feedback; as such, this is a reflection of the passive-aggressiveness and autistic hostility which this style can cause others to experience.

The Type C interpersonal style may be thought of as the one which prompted the French philosopher Rochefoucauld to write: "The reason why so few people are agreeable in conversation is, that each is thinking more of what he is intending to say, than of what others are saying; and we never listen when we are planning to speak." By the same token, it is probably the interpersonal event which has prompted so much interest in "listening" programs around the country. As the Johari model makes apparent, however, the Type C overuse of Exposure and neglect of Feedback is just one of several interpersonal tendencies that may disrupt communications. While hierarchical organizational structure, or centrality in communication nets, and the like may certainly facilitate the use of Type C behaviors by an individual, so can fear of failure, authoritarianism, need for control, and over-confidence in one's own opinions; such traits vary from person to person and limit the utility of communication panaceas. Managers who rely on the style often do so because of a need to demonstrate competence; many corporate cultures require that the manager be *the* planner, director, and controller and many managers behave accordingly to protect their corporate images. Many others are simply trying to be helpful in a paternalistic kind of way; others are, of course, outright dictatorial. Whatever the reason, those who employ the Type C style have one thing in common: their relationships will be dominated by Blindspots and they are destined for surprise whenever people get enough and decide to force feedback on them, solicited or not. This is an *autocratic-complacent* interpersonal style.

TYPE D. Exposure and Feedback processes are used to a great and balanced extent in this style; candor and openness coupled with a sensitivity to others' needs to participate are the salient features of the style. The Arena becomes the dominant feature of the relationship, and productivity may be expected to increase as well. In initial stages, this style may promote some defensiveness on the part of others who are not familiar with honest and trusting relationships; but perseverance will tend to promote a norm of reciprocal candor over time, such that trust and creative potential can be realized.

Among managers, Type D practices constitute an ideal state from the standpoint of organizational effectiveness. Healthy and creative climates result from its widespread use, and the conditions for growth and corporate excellence may be created through the use of constructive Exposure and Feedback exchanges. Type D practices do not give license to clobber, as some detractors might claim; and, for optimal results, the data explored should be germane to the relationships and problems at hand, rather than random intimacies designed to overcome self-consciousness. Trust is slowly built, and managers who experiment with Type D processes should be prepared to be patient and flexible in their relationships. Some managers, as they tentatively try out Type D strategies, encounter reluctance and distrust on the part of others, with the result that they frequently give up too soon, assuming that the style doesn't work. The reluctance of others should be assessed against the backdrop of previous management practices and the level of prior trust which characterizes the culture. Other managers may try openness and candor only to discover that they have uncovered a Pandora's box; a fusilade of hostility and complaints emerge. The temptation of the naive manager is to put the lid back on quickly; but the more enlightened manager knows that when communications are opened up after having been closed for a long period of time, the material which is the most emotionally loaded—*i.e.*, the issues which have been the greatest source of frustration, anger, or fear—will be the first to be discussed. If management can resist its inclination to cut the dialogue short, the diatribe will run its course as the emotion underlying it is drained off, and exchanges will become more problem-centered and future-time oriented. Management intent will have been tested and found worthy of trust, and creative free-wheeling interchanges without the constraint of fear of censure will occur. Organizations built on such practices are those headed for corporate climates and resource utilization of the type necessary for true corporate excellence. The manager—or more precisely, the manager's interpersonal style—may well be the catalyst for this reaction to occur. This is a *collaborative-risk taking* interpersonal style.

Summarily, the Johari Window model of interpersonal processes suggests that much more is needed to understand communication in an organization than information about its structure or one's position in a network. The fact is that people make very critical decisions about what information will be processed or whether it will be processed at all, irrespective of structural and network considerations. People bring with them to organizational settings certain propensities for behaving in certain ways interpersonally. They prefer, if you will, certain interpersonal styles, sharpened and honed by corporate cultures, which significantly influence—if not dictate entirely—the flow of information in organizations. As such, individuals and their preferred styles of relating one to another amount to the synapses in the corporate network which control and coordinate the human system. Central to an understanding of communication in organizations, therefore, is an appreciation of the complexities of those human interfaces which comprise organizations. The work of Luft and Ingham, when brought to bear on management practices and corporate cultures, may lend much needed insight into the constraints unique to organizational life which either hinder or facilitate the processing of corporate data.

RESEARCH ON THE MANAGERIAL PROFILE: THE PERSONNEL RELATIONS SURVEY

As treated here, one of the major tenets of the Johari Window model is that one's use of Exposure and Feedback soliciting processes is a matter of personal decision. Whether consciously or unconsciously, when one employs either process or fails to do so he has decided that such practices somehow serve the goals he has set for himself. Rationales for behaving in a particular way are likely to be as varied as the goals people seek; and they may be in the best sense of honest intent or they may simply represent evasive logic or systems of self-deception. The *purposeful* nature of interpersonal styles remains nevertheless. A manager's style of relating to other members of the organization is never simply a collection of random, unconsidered acts; whether he realizes it or not—or admits it or denies it—his interpersonal style is purposive and is thought to serve either a personal or interpersonal goal in his relationships.

Because of the element of decision and purposive intent inherent in one's interpersonal style, the individual's inclination to employ Exposure and Feedback processes may be assessed. That is, his decisions to engage in open and candid behaviors or to actively seek out the information that others are thought to have may be sampled, and his Exposure and Feedback tendencies thus measured. Measurements obtained may be used, in effect, in determining the individual manager's or, on a broader sample, the organization's Johari Window configuration and the particular array of interpersonal predilections which underlie it. Thus, the Luft-Ingham model not only provides a way of conceptualizing what is going on interpersonally, but it affords a rationale for actually assessing practices which may, in turn, be coordinated to climate and cultural issues in a practical sense.

Hall and Williams have designed a paper-and-pencil instrument for use with managers which reveals their preferences for Exposure and Feedback in their relationships with subordinates, colleagues, and superiors. The *Personnel Relations Survey*[7], as the instrument is entitled, has been used extensively by industry as a training aid for providing personal feedback of a type which serves to "personalize" otherwise didactic theory sessions on the Johari, on one hand, and as a catalyst to evaluation and critique of ongoing relationships, on the other hand. In addition to its essentially training-oriented use, however, the *Personnel Relations Survey* has been employed as a basic research tool for assessing current practices among managers. The results obtained from three pieces of research are of particular interest from the standpoint of their implications for corporate climates and managerial competence.

Authority Relationships And Interpersonal Style Preferences

Using the *Personnel Relations Survey,* data were collected from 1000 managers. These managers represent a cross-section of those found in organizations today; levels of management ranging from company president to just above

7. J. Hall and Martha S. Williams, *Personnel Relations Survey*. The Woodlands, Texas: Teleometrics, Inc., 1967.

first-line supervisor were sampled from organizations all over the United States. Major manufacturing, petroleum, and food producers contributed to the research, as well as a major airline, state and federal governmental agencies, and non-profit service organizations.

Since the *Personnel Relations Survey* addresses the manner in which Exposure and Feedback processes are employed in one's relationships with his subordinates, colleagues, and superiors the data from the 1000 managers sampled reveal something of the patterns which prevail in organizations in terms of downward, horizontal, and upward communications. In addition, the shifting and changing of interpersonal tactics as one moves from one authority relationship to another is noteworthy from the standpoint of power dynamics underlying organizational life. A summary of the average tendencies obtained from managers is presented graphically in Figure 3.

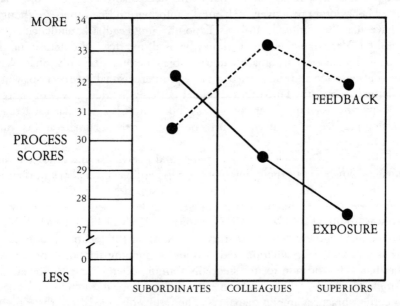

Figure 3. Score plots on exposure and feedback for the "average" manager from a sample of 1000 managers in the United States.

Of perhaps the greatest significance for organizational climates is the finding regarding the typical manager's use of Exposure. As Figure 3 indicates, one's tendency to deal openly and candidly with others is directly influenced by the amount of power he possesses relative to other parties to the relationship. Moving from relationships with subordinates, in which the manager obviously enjoys greater formal authority, through colleague relationships characterized by equal authority positions, to relationships with superiors in which the manager is least powerful, the plots of Exposure use steadily decline. Indeed, a straight linear relationship is suggested between amount of authority possessed by the average manager and his use of candor in relationships.

While there are obvious exceptions to this depiction, the average managerial profile on Exposure reveals the most commonly found practices in organizations; practices which, when taken diagnostically, suggest that the average manager in today's organizations has a number of hang-ups around authority issues which seriously curtail his interpersonal effectiveness. Consistent with other findings from communication research, these data point to power differences among parties to relationships as a major disruptive influence on the flow of information in organizations. A more accurate interpretation, however, would seem to be that it is not power differences as such which impede communication, but the way people *feel* about these differences and begin to monitor, filter, and control their contributions in response to their own feelings and apprehensions.

Implications for overall corporate climate may become more obvious when the data from the Exposure process are considered along with those reflecting the average manager's reliance on Feedback acquisition. As Figure 3 reveals, Feedback solicitation proceeds differently. As might be expected, there is less use of the Feedback process in relationships with subordinates than there is of the Exposure process. This variation on the Type C interpersonal style, reflecting an overuse of Exposure to some neglect of Feedback, very likely contributes to subordinate feelings of resentment, lack of social worth, and frustration. These feelings—which are certain to manifest themselves in the *quality* of subordinate performance if not in production quantity—will likely remain as hidden facets of corporate climate, for a major feature of downward communication revealed in Figure 3 is that of managerial Blindspot.

Relationships at the colleague level appear to be of a different sort with a set of dynamics all their own. As reference to the score plots in Figure 3 will show, the typical manager reports a significant preference for Feedback seeking behaviors over Exposure in his relationships with his fellow managers. A quick interpretation of the data obtained would be that, at the colleague level, everyone is seeking information but very few are willing to expose any. These findings may bear on a unique feature of organizational life; and one which has serious implications for climate among corporate peers. Most research on power and authority relationships suggests that there is the greatest openness and trust among people under conditions of equal power. Since colleague relationships might best be considered to reflect equal if not shared distributions of power, maximum openness coupled with maximum solicitation of others' information might be expected to characterize relationships among management coworkers. The fact that a fairly pure Type B interpersonal style prevails suggests noise in the system. The dominant Facade which results from reported practices with colleagues signifies a lack of trust of the sort which could seriously limit the success of collaborative or cooperative ventures among colleagues. The climate implications of mistrust are obvious, and the present data may shed some light on teamwork difficulties as well as problems of horizontal communication so often encountered during interdepartmental or intergroup contacts.

Interviews with a number of managers revealed that their general tendencies to become closed in encounters with colleagues could be traced to a competitive ethic which prevailed in their organizations. The fact was a simple one: "You don't confide in your 'buddies' because they are bucking for the same job you are! Any worthwhile poop you've got, you keep to yourself until a time when it might come in handy." To the extent that such a one-upmanship ethos prevails in organizations, it is to be expected that more effort goes into facade building and maintenance than is expended on the projects at hand where colleague relationships are concerned.

Superiors are the targets of practices yielding the smallest, and therefore least productive, Arena of the three relationships assessed in the survey. The average manager reports a significant reluctance to deal openly and candidly with his superior while favoring the Feedback process as his major interpersonal gambit; even the use of Feedback, however, is subdued relative to that employed with colleagues. The views from on high in organizations are very likely colored by the interpersonal styles addressed to them; and, based on the data obtained, it would not be surprising if many members of top management felt that their subordinates—*i.e.*, lower level management— were submissive, in need of direction, and with few creative suggestions of their own. Quite aside from the obvious effect such an expectation might have on performance reviews, a characteristic reaction to the essentially Type B style directed at superiors is, on their part, to invoke Type C behaviors. Thus, the data obtained call attention to what may be the seeds of a self-reinforcing cycle of authority-obedience-authority. The long range consequences of such a cycle, in terms of relationship quality and interpersonal style, have been found to be corporate-wide adoption of Type A behaviors which serve to depersonalize work and obscure the potentials of an organization's human resources.

Thus, based on the present research at least, a number of interpersonal practices seem to characterize organizational life which limit not only the effectiveness of communication within, but the attainment of realistic levels of corporate excellence without. The manager's style may set the tone for the organization as a whole.

MANAGERS' INTERPERSONAL STYLE AND SUBORDINATE RECIPROCITY

Both Rensis Likert[8] and Chris Argyris[9] have called attention to the diagnostic significance of organizational climate and the important role it plays in

8. R. Likert, *The Human Organization*. New York: McGraw-Hill, 1967.

9. C. Argyris, *Intervention Theory and Method: A Behavioral Science View*. Reading, Mass.: Addison-Wesley, 1970.

shaping employee motivation and productivity within organizations. Climate—as that array of feelings and cognitions which characterize an organization's personnel regarding their presence and roles in the organization—is seen by both Agryris and Likert as a product of interaction among people. Particular emphasis is placed on the behaviors of managers as they function, wittingly or not, as norm setters in the organization.

In a similar vein, Hall[10] suggested that a reciprocity existed between those who manage and those who are managed so far as interpersonal practices are concerned. In effect, it was suggested that a manager's subordinates—taking their cue from the manager regarding what is appropriate or to be tolerated in the way of interpersonal behaviors—will very likely respond in kind. Thus, those who interact with interpersonally competent managers will over time employ behaviors reflecting interpersonal competence; those who interact with managers less competent interpersonally will, as a result of interpersonal tensions generated by what is perceived to be a normative pressure to adopt imbalanced practices, respond less competently. Such reduced competence may take the form of either a mirroring of managerial actions or of a compensatory set of practices designed to "make up" for the manager's behaviors such that balance may be reestablished and the system maintained. Should such reciprocity be found to characterize subordinate reactions to managerial practices, a significant causal factor underlying the productivity of relationships and the quality of life in organizations might well be identified.

As a test of an implicit reciprocity hypothesis, data were gathered about the interaction of managerial interpersonal practices as reported with the reactions reported by their subordinates. From a subject pool of several hundred male managers, 50 each were selected whose self-reports from the *Personnel Relations Survey* identified them as using one of four archtypical interpersonal styles discussed earlier. These four styles result from differential employment of the Exposure and Feedback processes in relating to one's subordinates. Moreover, they are thought to differ qualitatively in terms of the level of interpersonal competence represented as well as with respect to the climates produced interpersonally.

Thus, the first stage of subject selection amounted to an identification of managerial practices constituting causal factors for interpersonal climates as these were available from managerial self-assessments.

As the second stage of diagnostic data collection, the subordinates of the 50 managers selected as representative of each of the four interpersonal style prototypes were administered the *Management Relations Survey*.[11] The data from the *MRS* may be used either for purposes of subordinate confirmation-disconfirmation of a manager's reported practices or as an indicator of subordinate

10. J. Hall, "Interpersonal Style and the Communication Dilemma: I. Managerial Implications of the Johari Awareness Model." *Human Relations*, 1974, 27 (4): 381-399.

11. J. Hall and Martha S. Williams, *Management Relations Survey*. The Woodlands, Texas: Teleometrics, Inc., 1970.

reactions to perceived managerial practices. In the service of the latter, the *MRS* was used to explore the research question as to whether managers of admittedly different interpersonal predilections elicit significantly different reactive practices from their subordinates. The implicit hypothesis entertained was that differential managerial practices would result in differential and reciprocal practices on the part of subordinates relating to those managers.

The data from the 200 subordinates, taken 50 at a time per group type, were subjected to multiple discriminant function analysis to determine whether the sorting criterion would discriminate among groups with respect to their average use of the Exposure and Feedback processes in relationships with their superiors. In general, the reciprocity hypothesis was supported by the data. The results of the discriminant analysis are summarized in Table 1 below.

Table 1. Summary of group centile means from a discriminant analysis of exposure-feedback use by subordinates of different type managers.

	Management exposure-feedback style			
	A Low/low	B Low/high	C High/low	D High/high
Exposure	27	50	44	67
Feedback	38	48	38	67

The centile scores serve to confirm generally the expectation that the Type D approach, when used by a manager, elicits considerably more effective and productive behaviors from subordinates than do any of the three remaining interpersonal styles. Indeed, the 67 by 67 centile scores on Exposure and Feedback for subordinates of managers using the Type D approach not only appear most effective in terms of overall Arena size, but constitute the only reported reaction to achieve that interpersonal balance deemed important by Argyris.[12]

To the extent that interpersonal style constitutes a critical part of one's more general managerial style, the results obtained from differing managers' subordinates parallel fairly closely the effectiveness order suggested by Likert[13] in his style continuum of System 1 to System 4 practices. Thus, not only do the results

12. C. Argyris, *Ibid.*, 1970.

13. R. Likert, *New Patterns of Management.* New York: McGraw-Hill, 1961.

obtained here seem consistent with the actual or suggested findings from related investigations of managerial impact, but they serve also an important diagnostic issue by confirming generally the reciprocity rationale of interpersonal climate: As a manager sows, it would appear, so does he reap!

INTERPERSONAL STYLE AND ORGANIZATIONAL CLIMATE

As suggested earlier, a major factor in the overall importance of interpersonal style is the effect that style has on the psychological climate in an organization. As an index of how people *feel* about working where and with whom they do, the climate of an organization has direct implications for both morale and productivity. Healthy climates—those characterized by mutual trust and respect, satisfaction, commitment, and pride—enhance both the quality of work life and performance. Unhealthy climates—those marked by distrust, diminished self-esteem, indifference, and frustration—impair both morale and performance. There is good reason to believe that different interpersonal styles promote—perhaps cause—different climates, of varying degrees of health, among those who populate the workplace.

Alfred Marrow[14] spoke directly to this issue when he observed that the use of participative practices by managers cannot occur in a cultural vacuum, that the climate must first be *prepared* for such practices for them to have the desired effect. According to Marrow, for participative practices to work the climate of the organization must be one of mutuality, trust, collaboration, and respect among managers and workers alike. With such thoughts in mind, it might be expected that both the *extent* and *effects* of participative practices among managers— that is, the degree and result of managerial gatekeeping—will differ as a function of the interpersonal style favored by managers. If this were so, it would mean not only that different interpersonal styles have different effects on climate but, as well, that some interpersonal styles have a more salutary effect than others and, as a result, on the prospects for success of any participative practices employed.

This is a testable hypothesis. Data were collected from 833 managers *and* a representative sample of their subordinates to determine the gatekeeping-climate implications of managers' interpersonal styles. Using the *Personnel Relations Survey,* self-assessments of interpersonal style were obtained from managers themselves. Next, using the *Management Relations Survey,* assessments of managers' styles were obtained from some 2,082 of their subordinates. Finally, using the *Personal Reaction Index*[15] —a measure of the degree to which subordinates perceive that their manager has taken steps to involve them in decision making through participative practices and the way they, subordinates,

14. A.J. Marrow, ''The Harwood Organization.'' In A.J. Marrow, D.G. Bowers, & S.E. Seashore (Eds.) *Management by Participation.* New York: Harper & Row, 1967.

15. J. Hall, *Personal Reaction Index.* The Woodlands, Texas: Teleometrics, Inc., 1971.

feel as a result—data were obtained from managers' subordinates about the climate associated with their practices.

Managerial data were separated on the basis of *PRS* scores into four basic interpersonal style groups: those low on both exposure and feedback solicitation (Type A), those low on exposure but high on feedback (Type B), those high on exposure but low on feedback (Type C), and those high on both exposure and feedback solicitation (Type D). The corresponding subordinate reports of managerial use of participative practices and consequent feelings of satisfaction, responsibility, commitment, frustration, and pride were then compared across the four interpersonal styles. This procedure allowed us to (1) determine the climate associated with each style and (2) to test whether different interpersonal styles yield significantly different climates in the workplace.

This basic procedure was repeated using subordinate assessments of managers' interpersonal style gleaned from *MRS* data. We wanted to be sure that managers and subordinates were in basic agreement regarding the manager's interpersonal style so that resulting climate effects might be linked more directly to the effects of style.

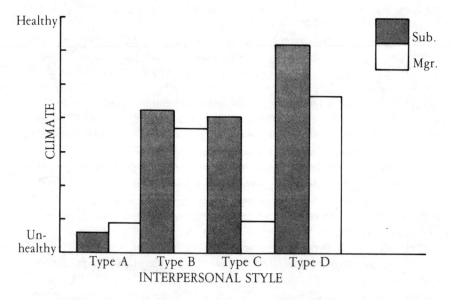

Figure 4. Climate as a function of manager-assessed and subordinate-assessed interpersonal style.

In Figure 4 are portrayed the results obtained from both manager and subordinate assessments of style. As may be clearly seen, different interpersonal styles—whether reported by managers themselves or their subordinates—have substantially different impacts on how people feel in the organization. While the subordinate data are perhaps more pronounced—after all, subordinates are on the receiving end of managerial practices—the implications are the same for managers and workers alike. Type A practices are clearly associated with an unhealthy climate. Type D practices are just as clearly associated with healthy climate effects. Both Types B and C uses of exposure and feedback yield moderately healthy climates; apparently those behaviors which serve to keep people involved—Type B—have more positive climate effects than do those like Type C which serve to close off participation.

These findings would follow from basic theory insofar as climate is concerned, but there is a caveat: while low exposure-high feedback practices were found to yield a more positive climate than either Type A or C practices, they also produced *frustration* ratings which are not apparent in the profiles portrayed. Indeed, closer analyses of the data revealed that Type A and Type B interpersonal styles are equally, and by far the most, frustrating to subordinates.

The main implication for managers and their organizations is that Type D practices—high exposure coupled with high feedback solicitation—clearly yield that kind of healthy climate which is associated with enhanced quality of work life and superior performance. The Type D interpersonal style stands alone as a model of interpersonal competence and the effects we are told to expect from such practices.

CORPORATE CLIMATE AND PERSONAL DECISION

The major thesis of the present discussion has been that interpersonal styles are at the core of a number of corporate dilemmas; communication breakdowns, emotional climates, the quality of relationships, and even managerial practices have been linked to some fairly simple dynamics between people. The fact that the dynamics are simple should not be taken to mean that their management is easy; far from it. But, at the same time, the fact that individuals can and do *change* their interpersonal styles—and thereby set in motion a whole chain of events with corporate significance—should be emphasized. A mere description of one's interpersonal practices has only limited utility, if that is as far as it goes. The value of the Johari Window model lies not so much with its utility for assessing what is but, rather, in its inherent statement of what might be.

Although most people select their interpersonal styles as a *reaction* to what they anticipate from other parties, the key to effective relationships lies in *proaction*; each manager can be a norm-setter in his relationships if he will but honestly review his own interpersonal goals and undertake the risks necessary to their attainment. Organizations can critique their policies—both formal and unwritten—in a search for provisions which serve to punish candor and reward evasiveness while equating solicitation of data from others with personal weakness. In short, the culture of an organization—as well as the personal and corporate philosophies which underlie it—may be thought of as little more than a *decision product* of the human system. The quality of this decision will directly reflect the quality of the relationships existing among those who fashion it.

If the model and its derivations make sense, then corporate relationships and managerial practices based on candor and trust, openness and spontaneity, and optimal utilization of interpersonal resources are available options to every member of an organizational family. As we have seen, power distributions among people may adversely influence the choices they make interpersonally; but the choice is still there, and it is a matter ultimately of personal decision. Type A practices require a breaking out of the corporate womb into which one has retreated; personal experiments with greater Exposure and Feedback, however anxiety producing, may be found in the long run to be their own greatest reward. For the manager locked into Type B behaviors, the task is more simple; he already solicits Feedback to an excellent degree. Needed is enough additional trust in others—whether genuine or forced—to allow a few toe-dipping experiences with Exposure. Others may be found to be less fragile or reactionary than one imagined. Learning to listen is but part of the task confronting managers inclined toward Type C styles; they must learn to seek out and encourage the exposures of others. This new attention to the Feedback process should not be at the expense of Exposure, however; revamping Type C does not mean adopting Type B. As one successfully taps into his own Blindspot, he often wonders how he got along without the data so well for so long; and then he begins to consider how much more effective he might yet become. These are all forms of low-risk high potential yield personal experiments. Whether they will ever be undertaken and their effects on corporate excellence determined, in the final analysis, depends upon the individual; the matter is one of personal decision.

Chapter 17

Giving Feedback:
An Interpersonal Skill

Philip G. Hanson

The process of giving and asking for feedback is probably the most important dimension of laboratory education. It is through feedback that we can learn to "see ourselves as others see us." This, of course, is not an easy task. Effectively giving and receiving feedback implies certain key ingredients: caring, trusting, acceptance, openness, and a concern for the needs of others. Thus, how evaluative, judgmental, or helpful feedback is may finally depend on the personal philosophy of the individuals involved. Nevertheless, giving feedback is a *skill* that can be learned and developed and for which certain useful guidelines exist.

The term "feedback" was borrowed from rocket engineering by Kurt Lewin, a founder of laboratory education. A rocket sent into space contains a mechanism that sends signals back to Earth. On Earth, a steering apparatus receives these signals, makes adjustments if the rocket is off target, and corrects its course. The group can be seen as such a steering mechanism, sending signals when group members are off target in terms of the goals they have set for themselves. These signals—feedback—can then be used by an individual to correct his course. For example, a person's goal may be to become more aware of himself and to learn how his behavior affects others. Information from the group can help him to ascertain whether he is moving toward this goal. If he reacts to criticisms of his behavior by getting angry, leaving the room, or otherwise acting defensively, he will not reach his goal. Group members may help him by saying, "George, every time we give you feedback, you do something that keeps us from giving you further information. If you continue this kind of behavior, you will not reach your goal." If George responds to the "steering" of the group by adjusting his direction, he can again move toward his target. Feedback, then, is a technique that helps members of a group achieve their

Reprinted from: J.E. Jones and J.W. Pfeiffer (Eds.). *The 1975 Annual Handbook for Group Facilitators*. San Diego, Ca. University Associates, 1975. Used with permission.

goals. It is also a means of comparing one's own perceptions of his behavior with others' perceptions.

Giving feedback is a verbal or nonverbal process through which an individual lets others know his perceptions and feelings about *their* behavior. When *soliciting* feedback, an individual is asking for others' perceptions and feelings about *his* behavior. Most people give and receive feedback daily without being aware of doing so. One purpose of laboratory training is to increase the awareness of this process so that it can be engaged in intentionally rather than unconsciously.

INFORMATION-EXCHANGE PROCESS

Between two people, the process of exchange goes something like this: Person A's *intention* is to act in relation to person B, who sees only person A's *behavior*. Between his intention and his behavior comes an encoding process that person A uses to make his behavior congruent with his intentions. Person B perceives person A's behavior, interprets it (a decoding process), and intends to respond. Between person B's intention and his responding behavior an encoding process also occurs. Person A then perceives person B's responding behavior and interprets it. However, if either person's process is ineffective, the receiver may respond in a manner that will confuse the sender. Although the feedback process can help an individual discover whether his behavior is congruent with his intentions, the process focuses on *behavior* rather than on *intentions*. An individual's intentions are private; unless he explains them, other people can only conjecture what those intentions are. One of the most confusing aspects of communication is that people tend to give feedback about other people's *intentions*, rather than their *behavior*. Causing further confusion is the fact that many people perceive behavior as being negatively intended, when in fact it is not. It is often difficult to see that the sender's intentions may not be what they are perceived to be.

RESPONSIBILITY FOR FEEDBACK

In many feedback exchanges, the question of ownership frequently arises: How much responsibility should the giver assume for his behavior and the receiver for his response? If person A behaves so that he evokes a negative response (feedback) from person B, how much ownership should each assume for his part of the interaction? Some people are willing to assume more than their share of the responsibility for another person's responses, while others refuse to own any responsibility for their behavior.

For example, an individual may be habitually late for group meetings and may receive feedback concerning members' negative reactions to this behavior. His response is to point out to the group members their lack of tolerance for individual differences. He says that they are limiting his freedom and that they seem to be investing too much responsibility in him for the group's effectiveness. He states that he wants to be involved in the group, but he does not understand why they need him to be on time.

This situation presents a value dilemma to the group; his observations are accurate, but his behavior is provocative. One clarification of this dilemma is to point out that, while an individual owns only his behavior, the reactions of others inevitably affect him. To the extent that he cares about the others or his relationship with them, he must consider their responses.

Concern for the needs of others as well as one's own is a critical dimension in the exchange of feedback. Ownership or responsibility for one's behavior and the consequences of that behavior overlap between the giver and receiver of feedback. The problem lies in reaching some mutual agreement concerning where one person's responsibility ends and the other's begins.

GUIDELINES FOR USING FEEDBACK

It is possible to minimize a person's defensiveness in receiving feedback and to maximize his ability to use it for his personal growth. Regardless of how accurate feedback may be, if a person cannot accept the information because he is defensive, then feedback is useless. Feedback must be given so that the person receiving it can *hear* it in the most objective and least distorted way possible, *understand* it, and choose to *use* it or *not use* it.

The following guidelines are listed as if they were bipolar, with the second term in each dimension describing the more effective method of giving feedback. For example, in one group George, intending to compliment Marie, says to her, "I wish I could be more selfish, like you." Marie might respond, "Why, you insensitive boor, what do you mean by saying I'm selfish?" George might then get defensive and retaliate, and both people would become involved in the game of "who-can-hurt-whom-the-most." Instead, Marie might give George feedback by stating her position in another way. That is, she could say, "When you said, 'I wish I could be more selfish, like you,' I felt angry and degraded." This second method of giving feedback contains positive elements that the first does not.

Indirect Vs. Direct Expression Of Feelings

When Marie stated that George was an insensitive boor, she was expressing her feelings indirectly. That statement might imply that she was feeling angry or irritated, but one could not be certain. On the other hand, Marie expressed her feelings directly when she said, "I felt angry and degraded." She committed herself, and there was no need to guess her feelings. If Tom says to Andy, "I like you," he is expressing his feelings directly, risking rejection. However, if he says, "You are a likeable person," the risk is less. Indirect expression of feelings is safer because it is ambiguous. Andy might guess that Tom likes him, but Tom can always deny it. If Andy rejects Tom by saying, "I am happy to hear that I am likeable, but I do not like you," Tom can counter, "You are a likeable person, but *I* do not like you." Indirect expression of feelings offers an escape from commitment.

"You are driving too fast" is an indirect expression of feelings. "I am anxious because you are driving too fast" is a direct expression of feelings. Indirect statements often begin with "I feel that..." and finish with a perception or opinion, for example, "I feel that you are angry." This is an indirect expression or perception and does not state what "I" is feeling. Instead, "I am anxious because you look angry" expresses the speaker's feelings directly and also states a perception. People frequently assume that they are expressing their feelings directly when they state opinions and perceptions starting with "I feel that...," but they are not.

Interpretation Vs. Description Of Behavior

In the original example in which Marie said to George, "When you said, 'I wish I could be more selfish, like you,' I felt angry and degraded," Marie was describing the behavior to which she was reacting. She was not attributing a motive to George's behavior, such as "You are hostile," or "You do not like me." When one attributes a motive to a person's behavior one is interpreting that person's *intention*. Since his intention is private and available only to him, interpretation of his behavior is highly questionable. In addition, one person's interpretations probably arise from a theory of personality that may not be shared by the other person. For example, if William is fidgeting in his chair and shuffling his feet, and Walter says, "You are anxious," Walter is interpreting William's behavior. Walter's theory of personality states that when a person fidgets in his chair and shuffles his feet, he is manifesting anxiety. Such a theory interposed between two people may create a distance between them or act as a barrier to understanding. If, instead, Walter *describes* William's behavior, William may interpret his own behavior by saying, "I need to go to the bathroom."

In any event, interpreting another person's behavior or ascribing motives to it tends to put that person on the defensive and makes him spend his energies on either explaining his behavior or defending himself. It deprives him of the opportunity to interpret or make sense of his own behavior and, at the same time, makes him dependent on the interpreter. The feedback, regardless of how much insight it contains, cannot be used.

Evaluative Vs. Nonevaluative Feedback

Effective feedback to George was not accomplished by calling him names such as "insensitive boor" or, in other words, evaluating him as a person. When giving feedback, one must respond not to the personal worth of the person but to his *behavior*. When someone is told that he is "stupid" or "insensitive," it is extremely difficult for him to respond objectively. He may sometimes *act* stupidly or *behave* in an insensitive way, but that does not mean that he is a stupid or insensitive person. Evaluating a person casts one in the role of a judge and places that person in the role of being judged. In addition, a frame of reference or set of values is imposed that may not be applicable to, or shared by, other people. That is, the person making the evaluation assumes that he can distinguish between a "good" person and a "bad" person or between "right" and "wrong," and that if the receiver of the feedback does not exemplify these values, the sender will be unhappy with him.

Response To Evaluative Feedback

It is difficult for anyone to respond to evaluative feedback because it usually offends his feelings of worth and self-esteem. These are core concepts about ourselves that cannot be changed readily by feedback, nor can they be easily interpreted in terms of actual behavior. It is difficult, for example, to point out to an individual the specific behaviors that manifest low self-esteem. If a person is given feedback that he is "stupid," he may not know what *behaviors* to change. It is the person's observable behavior and not his self-esteem that must be responded to when giving feedback.

An additional problem with evaluative feedback is that it often engenders defensiveness. When this occurs, the feedback is not likely to be useful.

General Vs. Specific Feedback

When Marie responded to George by saying, "When you said, 'I wish I could be more selfish, like you,' I felt angry and degraded," she was describing a *specific* behavior. If she had said, "You are hostile," she would have been giving feedback in *general* terms; George might not have known to which behavior she was reacting. The term "hostile" does not specify *what* evoked a response in Marie. If George wanted to change he would not know what behavior to change. However, when the sender is specific, the receiver knows to what behavior the sender is responding, which he can then change or modify. Feedback expressed in general terms, such as "You are a warm person," does not allow the receiver to know what specific behavior is perceived as warm. He cannot expand or build on this feedback until he knows which behavior evoked the response "warm."

Pressure To Change Vs. Freedom Of Choice To Change

When Marie told George that she felt angry and degraded by George's statement, she did not tell him he had to change his behavior. If she or the feedback were important to George, however, he would probably change anyway; if these were not important to him, he might decide not to change. A person should have the freedom to use feedback in any meaningful way without being required to change. When the giver of feedback tells a person to change, he is assuming that he knows the correct standards for right and wrong or good and bad behavior and that the receiver needs to adopt those standards for his own good (or to save the sender the trouble of changing). Imposing standards on another person and expecting him to conform arouses resistance and resentment. The sender assumes that his standards are superior. A major problem in marriages arises when spouses tell each other that they must change their behaviors and attitudes to conform with one or the other partner's expectations and demands. These pressures to change can be very direct or very subtle, creating a competitive, win-lose relationship.

Expression of Disappointment As Feedback

Sometimes feedback reflects the sender's disappointment that the receiver did not meet his expectations and hopes. For example, a group leader may be disappointed that a member did not actualize his potential impact on the group, or a professor may be disappointed in a student's lack of achievement. These situations represent a dilemma. An important part of the sender's feedback is his own feelings, whether they are disappointment or satisfaction; if he withholds these feelings and/or perceptions, he may give the receiver a false impression. If, however, he expresses his disappointment, the receiver may experience this feedback as an indication of personal failure instead of as an incentive to change.

Persistent Behavior

Frequently the complaint is heard that a group member persists in a behavior that others find irritating, despite the feedback he receives. Group members exclaim, "What are we supposed to do? He won't change!" The most the members can do is to continue to confront the offender with their feelings. While he has the freedom not to change, he will also have to accept the consequences of his decision, i.e., other people's continuing irritation at his behavior and their probable punitive reactions. He cannot reasonably expect other group members both to feel positive toward him and to accept the behavior they find irritating. The only person an individual can change is himself. As a by-product of his change, other people may change in relationship to him. As the individual changes, others will have to adjust their behavior to his. No one should be forced to change. Such pressure may produce superficial conformity, but also underlying resentment and anger.

Delayed Vs. Immediate Timing

To be most effective, feedback should, whenever possible, be given immediately after the event. In the initial example of the exchange between George and Marie, if Marie had waited until the next day to give feedback. George might have responded with "I don't remember saying that," or if Marie had asked the other group members later they might have responded with only a vague recollection; the event had not been significant to them, although it had been to Marie.

When feedback is given immediately after the event, the event is fresh in everyone's mind. It is like a mirror of the person's behavior, reflected to him through feedback. Other group members can also contribute their observations about the interaction. There is often, however, a tendency to delay feedback. A person may fear losing control of his feelings, fear hurting the other person's feelings, or fear exposing himself to other people's criticisms. Nevertheless, although the "here-and-now" transactions of group life can often be most threatening, they can also be most exciting and growth producing.

Planned Feedback

An exception to this guideline is the periodic feedback session, planned to keep communication channels open. Staff members in work units or departments may have weekly feedback meetings, or a specific time may be set aside for structured or unstructured feedback sessions in one- or two-week workshops. In these scheduled sessions, participants may cover events occurring since the last session or may work with material generated during their current meeting. For this process to be effective, however, the decision to have these feedback sessions should be reached through a consensus of the participants.

External Vs. Group-Shared Feedback

When feedback is given immediately after the event, it is usually group-shared, so that other members can look at the interaction as it occurs. For example, if group members had reacted to George's statement ("I wish I could be more selfish, like you") by saying, "If I were in your shoes, Marie, I wouldn't have felt degraded" or "I did not perceive it as degrading," then Marie would have had to look at her behavior and its appropriateness. If, on the other hand, group members had supported Marie's feelings and perceptions (consensual validation), her feedback would have had more potency.

Events that occur outside the group ("there-and-then") may be known to only one or two group members and, consequently, cannot be reacted to or discussed meaningfully by other participants. In addition, other group members may feel left out during these discussions. For example, when a group member is discussing an argument he had with his wife, the most assistance group members can provide is to attempt to perceive from his behavior in the group what occurred in that interaction and to share these conjectures with him. Since, in describing the event, the group member's perception is colored by his own bias and emotional involvement, group members may receive a distorted picture of the argument and may not be able to discriminate between fact and fiction. If the argument had occurred in the group, however, group members could have been helpful since they would have shared the event. Then, if the involved group member had begun describing his perceptions of what happened, other group members could have commented on or shared their perceptions of the interaction.

Use Of There-And-Then

In other words, events within the group can be processed by all group members who witness the interaction; they can share their perceptions and feelings about what occurred. This does not mean that group members cannot get *some* value from describing events external to the group and receiving comments from other members. What happens frequently, however, is that the group member describes these events in such a way as to elicit support or confirmation of his own perceptions rather than objective evaluation. Yet this relation of there-and-then events to the here-and-now can often be extremely productive as back-home "bridges." It can also be productive when some members have had long-term relationships with one another. It is important, at these times, to recognize both the necessity and the difficulty of involving other group members in the discussion.

Consistent Perceptions

Shared perceptions of what happens in here-and-now events is one of the primary values of a group. "Group shared" also implies that, ideally, each member has to participate. Frequently a person gets feedback from *one* member in the group and assumes that the rest of the group feels the same. This is not always a correct assumption. Feedback from only one person may present a very private or distorted picture because that person's perceptions of the event may differ from other group members'. When everyone's reactions are given, however, the receiver has a much better view of his behavior. If the group members are consistent in their perception of the receiver, and this disagrees with the receiver's view of himself, then he needs to look more closely at the validity of his self-perceptions. Frequently the fact that people perceive an individual's behavior differently is useful information in itself. Part of each group member's responsibility is to ask for feedback from members who are not responding so that the receiver will know how everyone sees his behavior. The receiver may have to be somewhat aggressive and persistent in seeking this information. Group members may tend to say "me, too" when their feedback is being given by someone else. When *all* the data have been obtained, the receiver is in a better position to make a more effective decision regarding his use of the feedback.

Imposed Vs. Solicited Feedback

In most exchanges, feedback is usually imposed. People give feedback whether it is solicited or not and whether the person is prepared to receive it or not. In addition, the sender's need to give feedback may be much greater than the individual's need to receive it. This is particularly true when the sender is upset about something concerning the potential recipient. In many situations, it is legitimate to impose feedback, particularly when a norm exists for giving as well as for soliciting feedback, or in order to induce a norm of spontaneity. However, feedback is usually more helpful when the person solicits it. Asking for feedback may indicate that the receiver is prepared to listen and wants to know how others perceive his behavior.

In asking for feedback, however, it is important to follow some of the same guidelines as for giving feedback. For example, a person should be specific about the subject on which he wants feedback. The individual who says to the group, "I would like the group to tell me what they think about me" may receive more feedback than he planned. In addition, the request is so general that the group members may be uncertain about where to begin or which behaviors are relevant to the request. In these cases, other group members can help the receiver by asking such questions as "Can you be more specific?" or "About what do you want feedback?" Feedback is a reciprocal process; both senders and receivers can help each other in soliciting and in giving it. Sometimes it is also important to provide feedback on how a person is giving feedback. If a receiver is upset, hurt, or angry, other group members can say to the sender, "Look how you told him that; I would be angry, too" or "What other way could you have given him the same information without evaluating him or degrading him?" It is desirable to give feedback so that the receiver can preserve his self-esteem.

Many people want to know how their behavior is being perceived by others, but they fear the consequences of asking for such information. How easily a person will ask for feedback is related to the amount of trust in the interpersonal relationship. However, people fear that the receiver will use their feedback (particularly negative feedback) to reinforce his negative feelings about himself. Again, it is sometimes difficult for a person to separate his behavior from his feelings of self-worth.

Unmodifiable Vs. Modifiable Behavior

To be effective, feedback should be aimed at behavior that is relatively easy to change. Many individuals' behaviors are habitual and could be described as a personal style developed through years of behaving and responding in certain ways. Feedback on this kind of behavior often is frustrating because the behavior can be very difficult to change.

Feedback on behaviors that are difficult to change may often make the person self-conscious and anxious about his behavior. For example, if the wife of a chain smoker gives him feedback (using all of the appropriate guidelines) about his smoking behavior, it would still be very difficult for him to change. Chain-smoking is a behavior determined by often-unknown causes. The individual may smoke to reduce his tension level; continuous feedback on his smoking behavior may only increase his tension. Consequently, he smokes more to reduce that tension.

Occasionally, in giving feedback, one must determine whether the behavior represents an individual's life style or results from some unknown personality factors. Sometimes it may be helpful first to ask the receiver whether he perceives his behavior as modifiable. Many behaviors can be easily changed through feedback and the person's conscious desire to change his behavior in order to produce a more effective interpersonal style.

Motivation To Hurt Vs. Motivation To Help

It is assumed that the primary motivation of membership in growth groups is to help oneself and others to grow. When an individual is angry, however, his motivation may be to hurt the other person. Frequently, the conflict turns into win-lose strategies in which the goal of the interaction is to degrade the other person. It is difficult when one is angry to consider that the needs of the other person are as important as one's own. Angry feedback may be useless, even when the information is potentially helpful, because the receiver may need to reject the feedback in order to protect his integrity.

Coping With Anger

There are several ways to cope with anger. One is to engage in a verbal or physical attack that frequently increases in intensity. Another method to deal with anger is to suppress it. One consequence of this strategy, however, is that the individual builds internal pressure to the point that he can lose control of his behavior. A third—and better—method is to talk about personal feelings of anger without assigning responsibility for them to the other person. Focusing on personal feelings may frequently encourage other group members to help the individual. In this way the anger dissipates without either viciousness or suppression. Anger and conflict are not themselves "bad." Angry feelings are as legitimate as any other feelings. Conflict can be a growth-producing phenomenon. It is the manner in which conflict or angry feelings are handled that can have negative consequences. Only through surfacing and resolving conflicts can people develop competence and confidence in dealing with these feelings and situations. Part of the benefit derived from growth groups is learning to express anger or to resolve conflicts in constructive, problem-solving ways.

CONCLUSION

The process of giving feedback obviously would be hampered if one attempted to consider *all* of the above guidelines. Some are needed more frequently than others: i.e., feedback should be descriptive, nonevaluative, specific, and should embody freedom of choice. These guidelines can also be used diagnostically. For example, when the person receiving feedback reacts defensively, some of the guidelines have probably been violated. Group members can ask the receiver how he heard the feedback and help the giver assess how he gave it.

Giving feedback effectively may depend on an individual's values and basic philosophy about himself, about his relationships with others, and about other people in general. Certain guidelines, however, can be learned and are valuable in helping people give and receive effective and useful feedback.

Chapter 18

Personal Styles of Conflict Resolution

Alan C. Filley

People learn behavior in different ways. Much learning occurs through trial and error as an individual discovers that one behavior leads to reward or pleasure and another behavior leads to punishment or pain. People also learn behavior by patterning themselves after models. One individual behaves like another because the other seems to have gained reward or satisfaction through a particular behavioral style. Still another method for learning calls for the individual to make a conscious choice regarding behavior. This process involves establishing possible alternative behaviors, determining the likely consequences of those behaviors, computing the odds that the costs or benefits associated with the different behaviors will actually take place, and selection of the best behavior.

The effect of these different methods of learning on supervisory training is illustrated in a study by Couch (1965), who compared incidents from which two groups of supervisors reported that they learned supervisory techniques. One group had a high degree of training related to supervisory practices; the other group had little or no training in such practices. Both groups, it should be pointed out, had the same degree of overall education. Couch's results indicated that both groups learned principally through personal experience. However, the well-trained group learned by reasoning processes and by observation, while the poorly trained group learned by trial and error. The well-trained group gained information from peers, subordinates, and superiors, while the poorly trained group often simply imitated the behavior of an immediate superior. Thus, supervisory training apparently gave the well-trained group the means to analyze information gained through their own experience.

Regardless of the source of learning, however, behavior eventually becomes fixed nd resistant to change; once we are comfortable with a pattern of behavior, there are costs associated with changing a practiced and familiar style. A different style is unfamiliar, perhaps uncomfortable, and might lead to unpredictable outcomes. This chapter focuses on the patterns of behavior which individuals utilize for conflict resolution and provides a model for analyzing the consequences of different styles.[1] In a later chapter we shall address the problem of changing one's pattern of behavior.

STYLES OF CONFLICT

As the axes in Figure 4—1 indicate, there are at least two major concerns in a conflict situation. One concern involves the extent to which an individual wishes to meet his own personal goals. In the present discussion we shall take *goals* to mean either *means* or *ends,* since a person may see his goal as that of doing the task the way he wants to do it or of accomplishing an end which he personally values. Another concern is the extent to which an individual wants to maintain a relationship with another individual or group and to be accepted by that individual or group. For the sake of convenience, in Figure 4—1 concern for personal goals is scaled from 1 to 9, representing the increasing degree of importance in the mind of the individual; similarly, concern for relationships is scaled from 1 (low concern) to 9 (high concern). Given this scaling, we may identify the following approximate types or styles: high concern for personal goals and low concern for relationships (9,1); low concern for personal goals and high concern for relationships (1,9); low concern for personal goals and low concern for relationships (1,1); moderate concern for personal goals and moderate concern for relationships (5,5); and high concern for personal goals and high concern for relationships (9,9). Let us consider each style.

The (9,1) Win-Lose Style—"The Tough Battler"

One who seeks to meet his own goals at all costs, without concern for the needs or the acceptance of others, engages in tough battles. For such an individual, winning or losing is not merely an event; instead, he views losing as reduced status, weakness, and the loss of his self-image. On the other hand, to win gives the (9,1) person a sense of exhilaration and achievement. There is no doubt in his mind that he is right; he stands by his convictions and defends his position, expressing anger and frustration when others do not accede to him. He feels that if there is a winner there must be a loser and that he must be the winner, whatever the cost. The (9,1) person is quite willing to sacrifice

---

1. This chapter is based on Robert R. Blake and Jane S. Mouton, "The Fifth Achievement," *The Journal of Applied Behavioral Science,* Vol. 6, No. 4, 1970, pp. 413-26 and Jay Hall, *Conflict Management Survey,* The Woodlands, Texas: Teleometrics, Inc., 1969.

9

1/9

Differences only serve to drive people apart; their "personal" implications cannot be ignored. Realistically, to differ is to reject. Maximum attention to the needs and desires of others is required if relationships are to endure. Conflict requires self-sacrifice and placing the importance of continued relationships above one's own goals. It is better to ignore differences than to risk open combat by being oversensitive; one must guard against causing irreparable damage to his relationships.

9/9

Differences are a natural part of the human condition. In and of themselves, they are neither good nor bad. Conflict is usually a symptom of tensions in relationships, and should be treated accordingly. When accurately interpreted, they may be resolved and serve to strengthen relationships, rather than to divide. Conflict requires confrontation and objective problem solving, often of a type that goes beyond the apparent needs and opinions of the parties involved. Not only are people brought more closely together when conflicts are worked through, but creativity may be achieved as well.

5/5

Differences should be treated in the light of the common good. At times some parties are obliged to lay aside their own views in the interest of the majority; this allows the relationship to continue to function, however imperfectly, and affords a basis for redress later on. Everyone should have an opportunity to air his views and feelings, but these should not be allowed to block progress. It is never possible for everyone to be satisfied and those who insist on such an unrealistic goal should be shown the error of their way. Resolution requires a good deal of skill and persuasive ability coupled with flexibility.

1/1

Differences simply reflect the more basic attributes which distinguish among people: past experiences, irrational needs, innate limitations and potentials and levels of personal aspirations. As such, they are essentially beyond the influence of others. They constitute necessary evils in human affairs, and one must either accept them or withdraw from human contacts. Impersonal tolerance is the most enlightened approach to handling conflicts.

9/1

Differences are to be expected among people for they reflect the nature of the species: some skills and others have none, and some are right and some are wrong. Ultimately right prevails, and this is the central issue in conflict. One owes it to himself and those who rely on his judgment to prevail in conflicts with others whose opinions and goals are in doubt. Persuasion, power, and force are all acceptable tools for achieving conflict resolution; and most people expect them to be employed.

CONCERN FOR RELATIONSHIP

1 ——————— CONCERN FOR PERSONAL GOALS ———————9

Figure 4-1. A model of conflict management styles. Special permission for reproduction of the material above is granted by the author, Jay Hall, Ph.D., and publisher, Teleometrics International. All rights reserved and no reproductions may be made without express approval of Teleometrics International.

individuals in a group if they refuse to go along with his desires. For him, conflict is a nuisance which occurs only because others do not see the correctness of his own position. He demonstrates to those with whom he disagrees that they are wrong with facts that support his own position.

The (1,9) Yield-Lose Style—"The Friendly Helper"

This type of person overvalues maintenance of relationships with others and undervalues achievement of his own goals. He desires acceptance by others and gives in to their desires where they are in conflict with his own. He is the kind of person who might say, "Well, yes, there are some things I would like to have accomplished, but it's OK, I don't want to make trouble." He feels differences can't be discussed or confronted to any extent without someone getting hurt in the process. Conflict, he feels, grows out of the self-centeredness of individuals and should be avoided in favor of harmony. He seems to feel that anger is bad and that confrontation is destructive; he may try to redirect potential conflict by breaking the tension with humor or suggesting some nonconflictive activity. Mutuality of interests and harmony of relationships are paramount in his approach.

The (1,1) Lose-Leave Style

The person using this style sees conflict as a hopeless, useless, and punishing experience. Rather than undergo the tension and frustration of conflict, the person using the (1,1) style simply removes himself either mentally or physically. Encounters with others are kept as impersonal as possible, and in case of disagreement, the (1,1) person will withdraw. He will comply to avoid disagreement and tension, will feel little commitment to the decision reached, and will not openly take sides in a disagreement among others.

The (5,5) Compromise Style

The basis of this approach is that half a loaf is better than none. One using this style seeks to find a position which allows each side to gain something. The (5,5) person enjoys the maneuvering required to resolve conflict and will actively seek to find some strong middle ground between two extreme positions. He may vacillate between expressing anger and then trying to smooth things over, and may seek to use voting or rules as a way of avoiding direct confrontation on the issues. If he is confronted with a serious disagreement, he will suggest some mechanism for finding a "workable" solution (such as voting or trading) rather than working out the disagreement in order to find the best solution.

The (9,9) Integrative Style—"The Problem Solver"

The individual employing the (9,9) style actively seeks to satisfy his own goals as well as the goals of others. The (9,9) person does not see the two sets of objectives as mutually exclusive and feels that no one's goals need be sacrificed if the appropriate conflict resolution is achieved. The (9,9) person (1) sees conflict as natural and helpful, even leading to a more creative solution if handled properly; (2) evidences trust and candidness with others and recognizes the legitimacy of feelings in arriving at decisions; (3) feels that the attitudes and positions of everyone need to be aired and recognizes that when conflict is resolved to the satisfaction of all, commitment to the solution is likely; (4) sees everyone as having an equal role in resolving the conflict, views the opinions of everyone as equally legitimate; and (5) does not sacrifice anyone simply for the good of the group.

RELATIONSHIP OF CONFLICT STYLES AND OTHER RESEARCH

As just described, Hall (1969) has identified five different behavior styles. Of these five, we shall consider the three which research describes in more detail. They are: (1) the "tough battler," who seeks his own goals and is willing to sacrifice the goals of others; (2) the "friendly helper," who gives in to the goals of others even at the cost of his own desires; and (3) the "problem solver," who seeks to find an outcome that meets both his goals and the goals of others.

Bargaining styles similar to these three have recently been investigated by Cummings and his associates (Cummings et al., 1971; Harnett et al., 1973). They adapted a scale developed to measure personality and attitudes in experimental bargaining situations originated by Shure and Meeker (1965) and correlated the three bargaining styles with four dimensions from the Shure-Meeker questionnaire (Cummings et al., 1972). The personality dimensions in the questionnaire are as follows:

1) Conciliation versus belligerence in interpersonal relations. Conciliators advocate responding to the needy or less fortunate with understanding, help, and friendliness. They admit their own wrongs and are not motivated by revenge.

2) Risk avoidance versus risk taking. Risk avoiders are unadventurous, have a low activity level, and will not expose themselves to dangers or hazardous risks.

3) External versus internal control. Externally controlled persons believe that events are controlled by external forces over which they have no control; that is, by fate or chance.

4) Suspiciousness versus trust. Suspicious persons are characterized by

quasi-paranoid traits of selfishness, projection of hostility, excitability, tenseness, and the lack of trust.

By combining these personality dimensions with various forms of bargaining behavior, we are able to present a typology of such behaviors and the personality correlates of each. Cummings and his associates identified three types of bargainers, the "tough bargainer," the "soft bargainer," and the "equalizer." For our purposes, the "tough bargainer" is equivalent to what we have called the "tough battler" (9,1); the "soft bargainer" is our "friendly helper" (1,9); and the "equalizer" is our "problem solver" (9,9). These three bargaining styles, it will be noted, also exhibit similarities to the Parent, Adult, and Child behaviors described [elsewhere].

Cummings and his associates found that "tough bargainers" were high in internal control, risk taking, and belligerence. The style is unrelated to measures of trust or suspiciousness. The relationships are quite consistent with those posited for the win-lose battlers, since they believe strongly in their own rightness and will do almost anything to avoid losing the battle and destroying their egos.

The win-lose battling style is also consistent with the "Parent" behavior of the transactional analysis model proposed by Eric Berne (1961). The Parent is normative, controlling, and judgmental in his statements and behavior. Like the win-lose battler, he makes sharp distinctions between right and wrong and is unconcerned with the gray area between the two extremes. The Parent thinks in terms of fixed rules and values and will probably elicit either Parent behavior (counter-dependence) or Child behavior (dependence) from those with whom he or she interacts.

The second style to be considered is the helping or yielding approach. The soft bargainer actively seeks acceptance and affiliation with others, and maintains relationships by yielding to the demands or goals of others, since he feels that interpersonal relations are too fragile to withstand direct confrontations on differences. Such a person complies with the wishes of others at the cost of personal goals.

The Cummings data indicate that the soft bargainer is high in external control, low in risk taking, and high in trust. The style is unrelated to conciliation or belligerence. Thus, the soft bargainer might be expected to give in to the demands of others and to avoid the risks of damaging interpersonal relationships. Trust and optimism may help to make this dependent position more tenable.

The soft style reminds us of the "Child" behavior in the transactional analysis model. The Child is subordinate, dependent, and characterized by emotionalism and fantasy. This orientation is certainly antithetical to conflict resolution based on mutual understanding of facts and mutual respect for the needs of others.

The third style to be considered is that of the problem solver, which Hall calls "the dominant style for conflict management." The problem solver believes that his goals and the goals of others are not mutually exclusive, and seeks to maintain the relationship and to meet his own goals by searching for solutions which are mutually acceptable. He believes that more can be achieved with two parties working together than when a single party dominates, and acknowledges the reality of facts and feelings as a necessary ingredient for the resolution of conflict. He deals with others in a trusting, open, and candid way.

There is a problem-solving style, identified by Cummings as that of the "equalizer," which is fact-oriented rather than defeat-oriented and which seeks a fair outcome for both parties. The equalizer is found to be high in internal control, high in trusting behavior, high in conciliation, and unrelated to the measure of risk taking: Other research (Zand, 1972) has shown that trusting behavior is displayed when one does not avoid stating facts, ideas, or feelings that might make him vulnerable to others. One exhibiting trusting behavior does not resist or deflect attempts of others to exert control over him and is responsive to their suggestions. That is, he can work interdependently with others rather than seeking to dominate or to control.

The problem solver is explicitly associated with the "Adult" style in the transactional analysis model. The Adult deals with facts and reality, does not dominate or impose arbitrary rules as does the Parent, and is not involved in fantasy as is the Child. The Adult deals with a problem descriptively and concentrates on giving and receiving information. There is no automatic right or wrong or good or bad but, rather, a need to solve problems objectively.

THE INTERACTION OF DIFFERENT STYLES

The bargaining literature (Cummings et al., 1971) also provides information about the consequences when pairs of different styles interact with each other. Again, we shall focus upon the tough bargainer (or win-lose battler), the soft bargainer (or friendly helper), and the equalizer (or problem solver). As indicated in Table 4-1, the confrontation between two tough battlers most frequently

Table 4-1. Estimated outcomes in dyadic combinations of conflict style in bargaining. Courtesy, Larry L. Cummings, University of Wisconsin.

	Win-lose battler	Friendly helper	Problem solver
Win-lose battler	Stalemate 80%	Battler wins 90%	Battler wins over 50%
Friendly helper	X	Stalemate 80%	Problem solver wins
Problem solver	X	X	Quick agreement

results in a stalemate. As might be expected, the battler dealing with a friendly helper is expected to be the winner; when interacting with the problem solver, the battler wins over 50 percent of the time. Curiously, when two friendly helpers face each other, a stalemate frequently results; when a friendly helper deals with a problem solver, the latter typically wins. Problem solvers interacting with each other deal factually with a perceived problem and arrive quickly at an agreeable solution.

The bargaining literature also suggests what style of conflict resolution is more practical. We might ask whether the problem-solving style is really better on objective grounds, that is, "in the real world." If by "objective" we mean whether or not an agreement is actually reached and whether or not the agreement provides advantages relative to the possible agreements obtained through the use of the other styles, then clearly the problem-solving style is favored.

USING DIFFERENT STYLES

As we indicated [in a previous chapter] effective conflict resolvers rely heavily upon problem solving (9,9) and smoothing (1,9). On the other hand, ineffective conflict resolvers rely upon forcing (9,1) and withdrawal (1,1). Compromise can be used in both effective and ineffective ways. An explanation for these differences in conflict-resolving techniques may lie in the parties' beliefs about whether or not agreement or a mutually beneficial solution is possible. Blake, Mouton, and Shepard (1964) suggest that when the parties believe that agreement is possible and the stakes are high, they will engage in problem solving; on the other hand, if the stakes are low and the consequences of the outcome are not particularly important, they will smooth over the disagreement, yielding if necessary.

In contrast, when the parties do not believe that agreement is possible and the stakes are high, they will engage in win-lose strategies. A party's behavior in this case represents the attitude, "Well, someone has to lose and it isn't going to be me." When the stakes are low, on the other hand, the parties will simply be inactive and leave the outcome to fate. Thus, the behavior which parties exhibit in a situation depends upon several variables: (1) each party's beliefs about the possibility of arriving at an agreement, (2) the objective possibility of finding a win-win solution, and (3) the relative consequences for each party if either or both cannot find a satisfactory solution.

An important element determining whether the parties believe that a mutually acceptable solution is possible is the knowledge of how to arrive at mutually acceptable, integrative solutions. As we pointed out earlier, people will more than likely persist in using methods which are not particularly effective just because they have used them before.

The particular style which *should* be used in a given conflict situation must, of course, depend upon the measures of goodness involved. We have suggested that the problem-solving or integrative style has certain benefits which may make it most desirable. It enhances creativity, promotes understanding, increases the likelihood that both parties will be objectively and subjectively satisfied with the outcome, and provides an aftermath which promotes further trust and cooperation. But it is also time-consuming in most cases and, thus, can be an expensive method. One should have the capacity to use all conflict-resolving styles and to know when they can most effectively be used. Said another way, the styles of conflict resolution are tools—not ends in themselves. They are not particularly good or bad except insofar as they accomplish particular objectives.

Viewed from the perspective discussed above, the tough (9,1) style may be seen either as an end in itself or as a tool. An individual using the (9,1) style as an end says simply that it is "best." An individual using the tough style as a tool says, "These are my objectives and given the likely consequences of using various styles, I will select the tough (9,1) style." For example, if one's objective is to defeat the other party, then one might select the (9,1) style and try to use it as skillfully as possible. Similarly, under certain circumstances, a father or mother might choose to dominate and control small children, in spite of the feelings or attitudes of the children.

In the same way, the helping (1,9) style may be seen either as an end in itself or as a tool. If an individual treats the helping style as an end, that individual is saying that yielding is good, avoiding conflict is good, and/or helping others is good. On the other hand, the helping style, used as a tool, simply leads to certain outcomes which must be evaluated before an individual can decide whether it is best to use this style. For example, a manager may accede to his employees' wishes for a change in working hours because the desire for harmonious relations outweighs the minor inconvenience to himself and because the stakes are so low that problem solving is not warranted.

Finally, the compromise (5,5) style may be seen either as an end in itself or as a tool. Coming about through application of a company's policies and rules, compromise is seen as an end when members of the organization behave out of simple obedience to those policies. In contrast, when the members of an organization say, "The policies and rules of this organization are merely means to certain ends," they view compromise as a tool. An organization's rules are like the traffic signals at busy intersections, they provide predictability of behavior and coordination of effort.

In sum, each of the styles of conflict resolution may be appropriate in different circumstances. Proper conflict-resolving behavior is based on having the skills required for each style and on knowing when each style can most effectively be used.

NOTE ON EXPERIENTIAL LEARNING

A measurement of the personal conflict resolution styles discussed in this chapter has been developed by Jay Hall. The scale measures the extent to which the respondent uses each of the five styles mentioned—win-lose, yield-lose, lose-leave, compromise, and integrative—in hypothetical conflict situations. The survey also measures the extent to which the styles are used in person-to-person conflicts, intragroup conflicts, and intergroup conflicts. The reader may obtain this useful tool by ordering the *Conflict Management Survey,* from Teleometrics International, 2203 Timberloch Place, Suite 104, The Woodlands, Texas 77380.

REFERENCES

Berne, E.: *Transactional Analysis in Psychotherapy.* Grove, 1961.

Blake, R.R., and J.S. Mouton.: "The fifth achievement." *Journal of Applied Behavioral Science* 6 (1970): 413-26.

Blake, R.R., J.S. Mouton, and H.A. Shepard.: *Managing Intergroup Conflict in Industry.* Gulf, 1964.

Couch, P.D.: "Some effects of training and experience on concepts of supervision." Unpublished doctoral dissertation, University of Wisconsin-Madison, 1965.

Cummings, L.L., D.L. Harnett, and O.J. Stevens.: "Risk, fate, conciliation and trust; An international study of attitudinal differences among executives." *Academy of Management Journal* 14 (1971): 285-304.

Cummings, L.L., D.L. Harnett, and S.M. Schmidt.: "International cross-language factor stability of personality: An analysis of the Shure-Meeker Personality/Attitude Schedule." *The Journal of Psychology* 82 (1972): 67-84.

Hall, J.: *Conflict Management Survey.* Teleometrics, 1969.

Harnett, D.L., L.L. Cummings, and W.C. Hamner.: "Personality, bargaining style, and payoff in bilateral monopoly bargaining among European managers." *Sociometry* 36 (1973): 325-45.

Shure, G.H., R.J. Meeker, and E.A. Hansford.: "The effectiveness of pacifist strategies in bargaining games." *The Journal of Conflict Resolution* 9 (1965): 106-17.

Zand, D.E.: "Trust and managerial problem solving." *Administrative Science Quarterly* 17 (1972): 229-39.

Chapter 19

The Abilene Paradox:
The Management
of Agreement

Jerry B. Harvey

The July afternoon in Coleman, Texas (population 5,607) was particularly hot—104 degrees as measured by the Walgreen's Rexall Ex-Lax temperature gauge. In addition, the wind was blowing fine-grained West Texas topsoil through the house. But the afternoon was still tolerable—even potentially enjoyable. There was a fan going on the back porch; there was cold lemonade; and finally, there was entertainment. Dominoes. Perfect for the conditions. The game required little more physical exertion than an occasional mumbled comment, "Shuffle 'em," and an unhurried movement of the arm to place the spots in the appropriate perspective on the table. All in all, it had the makings of an agreeable Sunday afternoon in Coleman—that is, it was until my father-in-law suddenly said, "Let's get in the car and go to Abilene and have dinner at the cafeteria."

I thought, "What, go to Abilene? Fifty-three miles? In this dust storm and heat? And in an unairconditioned 1958 Buick?"

But my wife chimed in with, "Sounds like a great idea. I'd like to go. How about you, Jerry?" Since my own preferences were obviously out of step with the rest I replied, "Sounds good to me," and added, "I just hope your mother wants to go."

"Of course I want to go," said my mother-in-law. "I haven't been to Abilene in a long time."

So into the car and off to Abilene we went. My predictions were fulfilled. The heat was brutal. We were coated with a fine layer of dust that was cemented with perspiration by the time we arrived. The food at the cafeteria provided first-rate testimonial material for antacid commercials.

Some four hours and 106 miles later we returned to Coleman, hot and exhausted. We sat in front of the fan for a long time in silence. Then, both to be sociable and to break the silence, I said, "It was a great trip, wasn't it?"

No one spoke.

Finally my mother-in-law said, with some irritation, "Well, to tell the truth, I really didn't enjoy it much and would rather have stayed here. I just went along because the three of you were so enthusiastic about going. I wouldn't have gone if you all hadn't pressured me into it."

I couldn't believe it. "What do you mean 'you all'?" I said. "Don't put me in the 'you all' group. I was delighted to be doing what we were doing. I didn't want to go. I only went to satisfy the rest of you. You're the culprits."

My wife looked shocked. "Don't call me a culprit. You and Daddy and Mama were the ones who wanted to go. I just went along to be sociable and to keep you happy. I would have had to be crazy to want to go out in heat like that."

Her father entered the conversation abruptly. "Hell!" he said.

He proceeded to expand on what was already absolutely clear. "Listen, I never wanted to go to Abilene. I just thought you might be bored. You visit so seldom I wanted to be sure you enjoyed it. I would have preferred to play another game of dominoes and eat the leftovers in the icebox."

After the outburst of recrimination we all sat back in silence. Here we were, four reasonably sensible people who, of our own volition, had just taken a 106-mile trip across a godforsaken desert in a furnace-like temperature through a cloud-like dust storm to eat unpalatable food at a hole-in-the-wall cafeteria in Abilene, when none of us had really wanted to go. In fact, to be more accurate, we'd done just the opposite of what we wanted to do. The whole situation simply didn't make sense.

At least it didn't make sense at the time. But since that day in Coleman, I have observed, consulted with, and been a part of more than one organization that has been caught in the same situation. As a result, they have either taken a side-trip, or, occasionally, a terminal journey to Abilene, when Dallas or Houston or Tokyo was where they really wanted to go. And for most of those organizations, the negative consequences of such trips, measured in terms of both human misery and economic loss, have been much greater than for our little Abilene group.

This article is concerned with that paradox—the Abilene Paradox. Stated simply, it is as follows: Organizations frequently take actions in contradiction to what they really want to do and therefore defeat the very purposes they are trying to achieve. It also deals with a major corollary of the paradox, which is that *the inability to manage agreement is a major source of organization dysfunction.* Last, the article is designed to help members of organizations cope more effectively with the paradox's pernicious influence.

As a means of accomplishing the above, I shall: (1) describe the symptoms exhibited by organizations caught in the paradox; (2) describe, in summarized case-study examples, how they occur in a variety of organizations; (3) discuss the underlying causal dynamics; (4) indicate some of the implications of accepting this model for describing organizational behavior; (5) make recommendations for coping with the paradox; and, in conclusion, (6) relate the paradox to a broader existential issue.

SYMPTOMS OF THE PARADOX

The inability to manage agreement, not the inability to manage conflict, is the essential symptom that defines organizations caught in the web of the Abilene Paradox. That inability effectively to manage agreement is expressed by six specific subsymptoms, all of which were present in our family Abilene group.

1. Organization members agree privately, as individuals, as to the nature of the situation or problem facing the organization. For example, members of the Abilene group agreed that they were enjoying themselves sitting in front of the fan, sipping lemonade, and playing dominoes.

2. Organization members agree privately, as individuals, as to the steps that would be required to cope with the situation or problem they face. For members of the Abilene group "more of the same" was a solution that would have adequately satisfied their individual and collective desires.

3. Organization members fail to accurately communicate their desires and/or beliefs to one another. In fact, they do just the opposite and thereby lead one another into misperceiving the collective reality. Each member of the Abilene group, for example, communicated inaccurate data to other members of the organization. The data, in effect, said, "Yeah, it's a great idea. Let's go to Abilene," when in reality members of the organization individually and collectively preferred to stay in Coleman.

4. With such invalid and inaccurate information, organization members make collective decisions that lead them to take actions contrary to what they want to do, and thereby arrive at results that are counterproductive to the organization's intent and purposes. Thus, the Abilene group went to Abilene when it preferred to do something else.

5. As a result of taking actions that are counterproductive, organization members experience frustration, anger, irritation, and dissatisfaction with their organization. Consequently, they form subgroups with trusted acquaintances and blame other subgroups for the organization's dilemma. Frequently, they also blame authority figures and one another. Such phenomena were illustrated in the Abilene group by the "culprit" argument that occurred when we had returned to the comfort of the fan.

6. Finally, if organization members do not deal with the generic issue—the inability to manage agreement—the cycle repeats itself with greater intensity. The Abilene group, for a variety of reasons, the most important of which was that it became conscious of the process, did not reach that point.

To repeat, the Abilene Paradox reflects a failure to manage agreement. In fact, it is my contention that the inability to cope with (manage) agreement, rather than the inability to cope with (manage) conflict is the single most pressing issue of modern organizations.

OTHER TRIPS TO ABILENE

The Abilene Paradox is no respecter of individuals, organizations, or institutions. Following are descriptions of two other trips to Abilene that illustrate both the pervasiveness of the paradox and its underlying dynamics.

Case No. 1: The Boardroom.
The Ozyx Corporation is a relatively small industrial company that has embarked on a trip to Abilene. The president of Ozyx has hired a consultant to help discover the reasons for the poor profit picture of the company in general and the low morale and productivity of the R&D division in particular. During the process of investigation, the consultant becomes interested in a research project in which the company has invested a sizable proportion of its R&D budget.

When asked about the project by the consultant in the privacy of their offices, the president, the vice-president for research, and the research manager each describes it as an idea that looked great on paper but will ultimately fail because of the unavailability of the technology required to make it work. Each of them also acknowledges that continued support of the project will create cash flow problems that will jeopardize the very existence of the total organization.

Furthermore, each individual indicates he has not told the others about his reservations. When asked why, the president says he can't reveal his "true" feelings because abandoning the project, which has been widely publicized, would make the company look bad in the press and, in addition, would probably cause his vice-president's ulcer to kick up or perhaps even cause him to quit, "because he has staked his professional reputation on the project's success."

Similarly, the vice-president for research says he can't let the president or the research manager know of his reservations because the president is so committed to it that "I would probably get fired for insubordination if I questioned the project."

Finally, the research manager says he can't let the president or vice-president know of his doubts about the project because of their extreme commitment to the project's success.

All indicate that, in meetings with one another, they try to maintain an optimistic facade so the others won't worry unduly about the project. The research director, in particular, admits to writing ambiguous progress reports so the president and the vice-president can "interpret them to suit themselves." In fact, he says he tends to slant them to the "positive" side, "given how committed the brass are."

The scent of the Abilene trail wafts from a paneled conference room where the project research budget is being considered for the following fiscal year. In the meeting itself, praises are heaped on the questionable project and a unanimous decision is made to continue it for yet another year. Symbolically, the organization has boarded a bus to Abilene.

In fact, although the real issue of agreement was confronted approximately eight months after the bus departed, it was nearly too late. The organization failed to meet a payroll and underwent a two-year period of personnel cut-backs, retrenchments, and austerity. Morale suffered, the most competent technical personnel resigned, and the organization's prestige in the industry declined.

Case No. 2: The Watergate.
Apart from the grave question of who did what, Watergate presents America with the profound puzzle of why. What is it that led such a wide assortment of men, many of them high public officials, possibly including the President himself, either to instigate or to go along with and later try to hide a pattern of behavior that by now appears not only reprehensible, but stupid? (*The Washington Star and Daily News,* editorial, May 27, 1973.)

One possible answer to the editorial writer's question can be found by prob-ing into the dynamics of the Abilene paradox. I shall let the reader reach his own conclusions, though, on the basis of the following excerpts from testimony before the Senate investigating committee on ''The Watergate Affair.''

In one exchange, Senator Howard Baker asked Herbert Porter, then a mem-ber of the White House staff, why he (Porter) found himself ''in charge of or deeply involved in a dirty tricks operation of the campaign.'' In response, Por-ter indicated that he had had qualms about what he was doing, but that he ''...was not one to stand up in a meeting and say that this should be stopped. ...I kind of drifted along.''

And when asked by Baker why he had ''drifted along,'' Porter replied, ''In all honesty, because of the fear of the group pressure that would ensue, of not being a team player,'' and ''...I felt a deep sense of loyalty to him [the Presi-dent] or was appealed to on that basis.'' (*The Washington Post,* June 8, 1973, p. 20.)

Jeb Magruder gave a similar response to a question posed by committee counsel Dash. Specifically, when asked about his, Mr. Dean's, and Mr. Mit-chell's reactions to Mr. Liddy's proposal, which included bugging the Water-gate, Mr. Magruder replied, ''I think all three of us were appalled. The scope and size of the project were something that at least in my mind were not en-visioned. I do not think it was in Mr. Mitchell's mind or Mr. Dean's, although I can't comment on their states of mind at that time.''

Mr. Mitchell, in an understated way, which was his way of dealing with diffi-cult problems like this, indicated that this was not an ''acceptable project.'' (*The Washington Post,* June 15, 1973, p. A14.)

Later in his testimony Mr. Magruder said, ''... I think I can honestly say that no one was particularly overwhelmed with the project. But I think we felt that this information could be useful, and Mr. Mitchell agreed to approve the project, and I then notified the parties of Mr. Mitchell's approval." (*The Washington Post,* June 15, 1973, p. A14.)

Although I obviously was not privy to the private conversations of the principal characters, the data seem to reflect the essential elements of the Abilene Paradox. First, they indicate agreement. Evidently, Mitchell, Porter, Dean, and Magruder agreed that the plan was inappropriate. ("I think I can honestly say that no one was particularly overwhelmed with the project.") Second, the data indicate that the principal figures then proceeded to implement the plan in contradiction to their shared agreement. Third, the data surrounding the case clearly indicate that the plan multiplied the organization's problems rather than solved them. And finally, the organization broke into subgroups with the various principals, such as the President, Mitchell, Porter, Dean, and Magruder, blaming one another for the dilemma in which they found themselves, and internecine warfare ensued.

In summary, it is possible that because of the inability of White House staff members to cope with the fact that they agreed, the organization took a trip to Abilene.

ANALYZING THE PARADOX

The Abilene Paradox can be stated succinctly as follows: Organizations frequently take actions in contradiction to the data they have for dealing with problems and, as a result, compound their problems rather than solve them. Like all paradoxes, the Abilene Paradox deals with absurdity. On the surface, it makes little sense for organizations, whether they are couples or companies, bureaucracies or governments, to take actions that are diametrically opposed to the data they possess for solving crucial organizational problems. Such actions are particularly absurd since they tend to compound the very problems they are designed to solve and thereby defeat the purposes the organization is trying to achieve. However, as Robert Rapaport and others have so cogently expressed it, paradoxes are generally paradoxes only because they are based on a logic or rationale different from what we understand or expect.

Discovering that different logic not only destroys the paradoxical quality but also offers alternative ways for coping with similar situations. Therefore, part of the dilemma facing an Abilene-bound organization may be the lack of a map—a theory or model—that provides rationality to the paradox. The purpose of the following discussion is to provide such a map.

The map will be developed by examining the underlying psychological themes of the profit-making organization and the bureaucracy and it will include the following landmarks: (1) Action Anxiety; (2) Negative Fantasies; (3) Real Risk; (4) Separation Anxiety; and (5) the Psychological Reversal of Risk and Certainty. I hope that the discussion of such landmarks will provide harried organization travelers with a new map that will assist them in arriving at where they really want to go and, in addition, will help them in assessing the risks that are an inevitable part of the journey.

ACTION ANXIETY

Action anxiety provides the first landmark for locating roadways that bypass Abilene. The concept of action anxiety says that the reason organization members take actions in contradiction to their understanding of the organization's problems lies in the intense anxiety that is created as they think about acting in accordance with what they believe needs to be done. As a result, they opt to endure the professional and economic degradation of pursuing an unworkable research project or the consequences of participating in an illegal activity rather than act in a manner congruent with their beliefs. It is not that organization members do not know what needs to be done—they do know. For example, the various principals in the research organization cited *knew* they were working on a research project that had no real possibility of succeeding. And the central figures of the Watergate episode apparently *knew* that, for a variety of reasons, the plan to bug the Watergate did not make sense.

Such action anxiety experienced by the various protagonists may not make sense, but the dilemma is not a new one. In fact, it is very similar to the anxiety experienced by Hamlet, who expressed it most eloquently in the opening lines of his famous soliloquy:

> To be or not to be; that is the question:
> Whether 'tis nobler in the mind to suffer
> The slings and arrows of outrageous fortune
> Or to take arms against a sea of troubles
> And by opposing, end them?. . .
> (*Hamlet,* Act III, Scene ii)

It is easy to translate Hamlet's anxious lament into that of the research manager of our R&D organization as he contemplates his report to the meeting of the budget committee. It might go something like this:

> To maintain my sense of integrity and self-worth or compromise it, that is the question. Whether 'tis nobler in the mind to suffer the ignominy that comes from managing a nonsensical research project, or the fear and anxiety that come from making a report the president and V.P. may not like to hear.

So, the anguish, procrastination, and counterproductive behavior of the research manager or members of the White House staff are not much different from those of Hamlet; all might ask with equal justification Hamlet's subsequent searching question of what it is that:

...makes us rather bear those ills we have than fly to others we know not of. (*Hamlet,* Act III, Scene ii)

In short, like the various Abilene protagonists, we are faced with a deeper question: Why does action anxiety occur?

NEGATIVE FANTASIES

Part of the answer to that question may be found in the negative fantasies organization members have about acting in congruence with what they believe should be done.

Hamlet experienced such fantasies. Specifically, Hamlet's fantasies of the alternatives to current evils were more evils, and he didn't entertain the possibility that any action he might take could lead to an improvement in the situation. Hamlet's was not an unusual case, though. In fact, the "Hamlet syndrome" clearly occurred in both organizations previously described. All of the organization protagonists had negative fantasies about what would happen if they acted in accordance with what they believed needed to be done.

The various managers in the R&D organization foresaw loss of face, prestige, position, and even health as the outcome of confronting the issues about which they believed, incorrectly, that they disagreed. Similarly, members of the White House staff feared being made scapegoats, branded as disloyal, or ostracized as non-team players if they acted in accordance with their understanding of reality.

To sum up, action anxiety is supported by the negative fantasies that organization members have about what will happen as a consequence of their acting in accordance with their understanding of what is sensible. The negative fantasies, in turn, serve an important function for the persons who have them. Specifically, they provide the individual with an excuse that releases him psychologically, both in his own eyes and frequently in the eyes of others, from the responsibility of having to act to solve organization problems.

It is not sufficient, though, to stop with the explanation of negative fantasies as the basis for the inability of organizations to cope with agreement. We must look deeper and ask still other questions: What is the source of the negative fantasies? Why do they occur?

REAL RISK

Risk is a reality of life, a condition of existence. John Kennedy articulated it in another way when he said at a news conference, "Life is unfair." By that I believe he meant we do not know, nor can we predict or control with certainty, either the events that impinge upon us or the outcomes of actions we undertake in response to those events.

Consequently, in the business environment, the research manager might find that confronting the president and the vice-president with the fact that the project was a "turkey" might result in his being fired. And Mr. Porter's saying that an illegal plan of surveillance should not be carried out could have caused his ostracism as a non-team player. There are too many cases when confrontation of this sort has resulted in such consequences. The real question, though, is not, Are such fantasized consequences possible? but, Are such fantasized consequences likely?

Thus, real risk is an existential condition, and all actions do have consequences that, to paraphrase Hamlet, may be worse than the evils of the present. As a result of their unwillingness to accept existential risk as one of life's givens, however, people may opt to take their organizations to Abilene rather than run the risk, no matter how small, of ending up somewhere worse.

Again, though, one must ask, What is the real risk that underlies the decision to opt for Abilene? What is at the core of the paradox?

FEAR OF SEPARATION

One is tempted to say that the core of the paradox lies in the individual's fear of the unknown. Actually, we do not fear what is unknown, but we are afraid of things we do know about. What do we know about that frightens us into such apparently inexplicable organizational behavior?

Separation, alienation, and loneliness are things we do know about—and fear. Both research and experience indicate that ostracism is one of the most powerful punishments that can be devised. Solitary confinement does not draw its coercive strength from physical deprivation. The evidence is overwhelming that we have a fundamental need to be connected, engaged, and related and a reciprocal need not to be separated or alone. Everyone of us, though, has experienced aloneness. From the time the umbilical cord was cut, we have experienced the real anguish of separation—broken friendships, divorces, deaths, and exclusions. C.P. Snow vividly described the tragic interplay between loneliness and connection:

> Each of us is alone; sometimes we escape from our solitariness, through love and affection or perhaps creative moments, but these triumphs of life are pools of light we make for ourselves while the edge of the road is black. Each of us dies alone.

That fear of taking risks that may result in our separation from others is at the core of the paradox. It finds expression in ways of which we may be unaware, and it is ultimately the cause of the self-defeating, collective deception that leads to self-destructive decisions within organizations.

Concretely, such fear of separation leads research committees to fund projects that none of its members want and, perhaps, White House staff members to engage in illegal activities that they don't really support.

THE PSYCHOLOGICAL REVERSAL OF RISK AND CERTAINTY

One piece of the map is still missing. It relates to the peculiar reversal that occurs in our thought processes as we try to cope with the Abilene Paradox. For example, we frequently fail to take action in an organizational setting because we fear that the actions we take may result in our separation from others, or, in the language of Mr. Porter, we are afraid of being tabbed as "disloyal" or are afraid of being ostracized as "non-team players." But therein lies a paradox within a paradox, because our very unwillingness to take such risks virtually ensures the separation and aloneness we so fear. In effect, we reverse "real existential risk" and "fantasied risk" and by doing so transform what is a probability statement into what, for all practical purposes, becomes a certainty.

Take the R&D organization described earlier. When the project fails, some people will get fired, demoted, or sentenced to the purgatory of a make-work job in an out-of-the-way office. For those who remain, the atmosphere of blame, distrust, suspicion, and backbiting that accompanies such failure will serve only to further alienate and separate those who remain.

The Watergate situation is similar. The principals evidently feared being ostracized as disloyal non-team players. When the illegality of the act surfaced, however, it was nearly inevitable that blaming, self-protective actions, and scapegoating would result in the very emotional separation from both the President and one another that the principals feared. Thus, by reversing real and fantasied risk, they had taken effective action to ensure the outcome they least desired.

One final question remains: Why do we make this peculiar reversal? I support the general thesis of Alvin Toffler and Philip Slater who contend that our cultural emphasis on technology, competition, individualism, temporariness, and mobility has resulted in a population that has frequently experienced the terror of loneliness and seldom the satisfaction of engagement. Consequently, though we have learned of the reality of separation, we have not had the opportunity to learn the reciprocal skills of connection, with the result that, like the ancient dinosaurs, we are breeding organizations with self-destructive decision-making proclivities.

A POSSIBLE ABILENE BYPASS

Existential risk is inherent in living, so it is impossible to provide a map that meets the no-risk criterion, but it may be possible to describe the route in terms that make the landmarks understandable and that will clarify the risks involved. In order to do that, however, some commonly used terms such as victim, victimizer, collusion, responsibility, conflict, conformity, courage, confrontation, reality, and knowledge have to be redefined. In addition, we need to explore the relevance of the redefined concepts for bypassing or getting out of Abilene.

• *Victim and victimizer.* Blaming and fault-finding behavior is one of the basic symptoms of organizations that have found their way to Abilene, and the target of blame generally doesn't include the one who criticizes. Stated in different terms, executives begin to assign one another to roles of victims and victimizers. Ironic as it may seem, however, this assignment of roles is both irrelevant and dysfunctional, because once a business or a government fails to manage its agreement and arrives in Abilene, all its members are victims. Thus, arguments and accusations that identify victims and victimizers at best become symptoms of the paradox, and, at worst, drain energy from the problem-solving efforts required to redirect the organization along the route it really wants to take.

• *Collusion.* A basic implication of the Abilene Paradox is that human problems of organization are reciprocal in nature. As Robert Tannenbaum has pointed out, you can't have an autocratic boss unless subordinates are willing to collude with his autocracy, and you can't have obsequious subordinates unless the boss is willing to collude with their obsequiousness.

Thus, in plain terms, each person in a self-defeating, Abilene-bound organization *colludes* with others, including peers, superiors, and subordinates, sometimes consciously and sometimes subconsciously, to create the dilemma in which the organization finds itself. To adopt a cliche of modern organization, "It takes a real team effort to go to Abilene." In that sense each person, in his own collusive manner, shares responsibility for the trip, so searching for a locus of blame outside oneself serves no useful purpose for either the organization or the individual. It neither helps the organization handle its dilemma of unrecognized agreement nor does it provide psychological relief for the individual, because focusing on conflict when agreement is the issue is devoid of reality. In fact, it does just the opposite, for it causes the organization to focus on managing conflict when it should be focusing on managing agreement.

• *Responsibility for problem-solving action.* A second question is, Who is responsible for getting us out of this place? To that question is frequently appended a third one, generally rhetorical in nature, with "should" overtones, such as, Isn't it the boss (or the ranking government official) who is responsible for doing something about the situation?

The answer to that question is no.

The key to understanding the functionality of the no answer is the knowledge that, when the dynamics of the paradox are in operation, the authority figure—and others—are in unknowing agreement with one another concerning the organization's problems and the steps necessary to solve them. Consequently, the power to destroy the paradox's pernicious influence comes from confronting and speaking to the underlying reality of the situation, and not from one's hierarchical position within the organization. Therefore, any organization member who chooses to risk confronting that reality possesses the necessary leverage to release the organization from the paradox's grip.

In one situation, it may be a research director's saying, "I don't think this project can succeed." In another, it may be Jeb Magruder's response to this question of Senator Baker:

> If you were concerned because the action was known to you to be illegal, because you thought it improper or unethical, you thought the prospects for success were very meager, and you doubted the reliability of Mr. Liddy, what on earth would it have taken to decide against the plan?

Magruder's reply was brief and to the point:

> Not very much, sir. I am sure that if I had fought vigorously against it, I think any of us could have had the plan cancelled. (*Time,* June 25, 1973, p. 12.)

• *Reality, knowledge, confrontation.* Accepting the paradox as a model describing certain kinds of organizational dilemmas also requires rethinking the nature of reality and knowledge, as they are generally described in organizations. In brief, the underlying dynamics of the paradox clearly indicate that organization members generally know more about issues confronting the organization than they don't know. The various principals attending the research budget meeting, for example, knew the research project was doomed to failure. And Jeb Magruder spoke as a true Abilener when he said, "We knew it was illegal, probably, inappropriate." (*The Washington Post,* June 15, 1973, p. A16.)

Given this concept of reality and its relationship to knowledge, confrontation becomes the process of facing issues squarely, openly, and directly in an effort to discover whether the nature of the underlying collective reality is agreement or conflict. Accepting such a definition of confrontation has an important implication for change agents interested in making organizations more effective. That is, organization change and effectiveness may be facilitated as much by confronting the organization with what it knows and agrees upon as by confronting it with what it doesn't know or disagrees about.

REAL CONFLICT AND PHONY CONFLICT

Conflict is a part of any organization. Couples, R&D divisions, and White House staffs all engage in it. However, analysis of the Abilene Paradox opens up the possibility of two kinds of conflict—real and phony. On the surface, they look alike, but, like headaches, have different causes and therefore require different treatment.

Real conflict occurs when people have real differences. ("My reading of the research printouts says that we can make the project profitable." "I come to the opposite conclusion.") ("I suggest we 'bug' the Watergate." "I'm not in favor of it.")

Phony conflict, on the other hand, occurs when people agree on the actions they want to take, and then do the opposite. The resulting anger, frustration, and blaming behavior generally termed "conflict" are not based on real differences. Rather, they stem from the protective reactions that occur when a decision that no one believed in or was committed to in the first place goes sour. In fact, as a paradox within a paradox, such conflict is symptomatic of agreement!

GROUP TYRANNY AND CONFORMITY

Understanding the dynamics of the Abilene Paradox also requires a "reorientation" in thinking about concepts such as "group tyranny"—the loss of the individual's distinctiveness in a group, and the impact of conformity pressures on individual behavior in organizations.

Group tyranny and its result, individual conformity, generally refer to the coercive effect of group pressures on individual behavior. Sometimes referred to as Groupthink, it has been damned as the cause for everything from the lack of creativity in organizations ("A camel is a horse designed by a committee") to antisocial behavior in juveniles ("My Johnny is a good boy. He was just pressured into shoplifting by the kids he runs around with").

However, analysis of the dynamics underlying the Abilene Paradox opens up the possibility that individuals frequently perceive and feel as if they are experiencing the coercive organization conformity pressures when, in actuality, they are responding to the dynamics of mismanaged agreement. Conceptualizing, experiencing, and responding to such experiences as reflecting the tyrannical pressures of a group again serves an important psychological use for the individual: As was previously said, it releases him from the responsibility of taking action and thus becomes a defense against action. Thus, much behavior within an organization that heretofore has been conceptualized as reflecting the tyranny of conformity pressures is really an expression of collective anxiety and therefore must be reconceptualized as a defense against acting.

A well-known example of such faulty conceptualization comes to mind. It involves the heroic sheriff in the classic Western movies who stands alone in the jailhouse door and singlehandedly protects a suspected (and usually innocent) horsethief or murderer from the irrational, tyrannical forces of group behavior —that is, an armed lynch mob. Generally, as a part of the ritual, he threatens to blow off the head of anyone who takes a step toward the door. Few ever take the challenge, and the reason is not the sheriff's six-shooter. What good would one pistol be against an armed mob of several hundred people who *really* want to hang somebody? Thus, the gun in fact serves as a face-saving measure for people who don't wish to participate in a hanging anyway. (''We had to back off. The sheriff threatened to blow our heads off.'')

The situation is one involving agreement management, for a careful investigator canvassing the crowd under conditions in which the anonymity of the interviewees' responses could be guaranteed would probably find: (1) that few of the individuals in the crowd really wanted to take part in the hanging; (2) that each person's participation came about because he perceived, falsely, that others wanted to do so; and (3) that each person was afraid that others in the crowd would ostracize or in some other way punish him if he did not go along.

DIAGNOSING THE PARADOX

Most individuals like quick solutions, ''clean'' solutions, ''no risk'' solutions to organization problems. Furthermore, they tend to prefer solutions based on mechanics and technology, rather than on attitudes of ''being.'' Unfortunately, the underlying reality of the paradox makes it impossible to provide either no-risk solutions or action technologies divorced from existential attitudes and realities. I do, however, have two sets of suggestions for dealing with these situations. One set of suggestions relates to diagnosing the situation, the other to confronting it.

When faced with the possibility that the paradox is operating, one must first make a diagnosis of the situation, and the key to diagnosis is an answer to the question, ''Is the organization involved in a conflict-management or an agreement-management situation?'' As an organization member, I have found it relatively easy to make a preliminary diagnosis as to whether an organization is on the way to Abilene or is involved in legitimate, substantive conflict by responding to the Diagnostic Survey shown in the accompanying figure. If the answer to the first question is ''not characteristic,'' the organization is probably not in Abilene or conflict. If the answer is ''characteristic,'' the organization has a problem of either real or phony conflict, and the answers to the succeeding questions help to determine which it is.

In brief, for reasons that should be apparent from the theory discussed here, the more times ''characteristic'' is checked, the more likely the organization is on its way to Abilene. In practical terms, a process for managing agreement is called for. And finally, if the answer to the first question falls into the ''characteristic'' category and most of the other answers fall into the category ''not characteristic,'' one may be relatively sure the organization is in a real conflict situation and some sort of conflict management intervention is in order.

COPING WITH THE PARADOX

Assuming a preliminary diagnosis leads one to believe he and/or his organization is on the way to Abilene, the individual may choose to actively confront

---

Organization Diagnostic Survey

Instructions: For each of the following statements please indicate whether it IS or IS NOT characteristic of your organization.

---

1. There is conflict in the organization.

2. Organization members feel frustrated, impotent, and unhappy when trying to deal with it. Many are looking for ways to escape. They may avoid meetings at which the conflict is discussed, they may be looking for other jobs, or they may spend as much time away from the office as possible by taking unneeded trips or vacation or sick leave.

3. Organization members place much of the blame for the dilemma on the boss or other groups. In "back room" conversations among friends the boss is termed incompetent, ineffective, "out of touch," or a candidate for early retirement. To his face, nothing is said, or at best, only oblique references are made concerning his role in the organization's problems. If the boss isn't blamed, some other group, division, or unit is seen as the cause of the trouble: "We would do fine if it were not for the damn fools in Division X."

4. Small subgroups of trusted friends and associates meet informally over coffee, lunch, and so on to discuss organizational problems. There is a lot of agreement among the members of these subgroups as to the cause of the troubles and the solutions that would be effective in solving them. Such conversations are frequently punctuated with statements beginning with, "We should do..."

5. In meetings where those same people meet with members from other subgroups to discuss the problem they "soften their positions," state them in ambiguous language, or even reverse them to suit the apparent positions taken by others.

6. After such meetings, members complain to trusted associates that they really didn't say what they wanted to say, but also provide a list of convincing reasons why the comments, suggestions, and reactions they wanted to make would have been impossible. Trusted associates commiserate and say the same was true for them.

7. Attempts to solve the problem do not seem to work. In fact, such attempts seem to add to the problem or make it worse.

8. Outside the organization individuals seem to get along better, be happier, and operate more effectively than they do within it.

---

the situation to determine directly whether the underlying reality is one of agreement or conflict. Although there are, perhaps, a number of ways to do it, I have found one way in particular to be effective—confrontation in a group setting. The basic approach involves gathering organization members who are key figures in the problem and its solution into a group setting. Working within the context of a group is important, because the dynamics of the Abilene Paradox involve collusion among group members; therefore, to try to solve the dilemma by working with individuals and small subgroups would involve further collusion with the dynamics leading up to the paradox.

The first step in the meeting is for the individual who "calls" it (that is, the confronter) to own up to his position first and be open to the feedback he gets. The owning up process lets the others know that he is concerned lest the organization may be making a decision contrary to the desires of any of its members. A statement like this demonstrates the beginning of such an approach:

> I want to talk with you about the research project. Although I have previously said things to the contrary, I frankly don't think it will work, and I am very anxious about it. I suspect others may feel the same, but I don't know. Anyway, I am concerned that I may end up misleading you and that we may end up misleading one another, and if we aren't careful, we may continue to work on a problem that none of us wants and that might even bankrupt us. That's why I need to know where the rest of you stand. I would appreciate any of your thoughts about the project. Do you think it can succeed?

What kinds of results can one expect if he decides to undertake the process of confrontation? I have found that the results can be divided into *two* categories, at the technical level and at the level of existential experience. Of the two, I have found that for the person who undertakes to initiate the process of confrontation, the existential experience takes precedence in his ultimate evaluation of the outcome of the action he takes.

• *The technical level.* If one is correct in diagnosing the presence of the paradox, I have found the solution to the technical problem may be almost absurdly quick and simple, nearly on the order of this:

"Do you mean that you and I and the rest of us have been dragging along with a research project that none of us has thought would work? It's crazy. I can't believe we would do it, but we did. Let's figure out how we can cancel it and get to doing something productive." In fact, the simplicity and quickness of the solution frequently don't seem possible to most of us, since we have been trained to believe that the solution to conflict requires a long, arduous process of debilitating problem solving.

Also, since existential risk is always present, it is possible that one's diagnosis is incorrect, and the process of confrontation lifts to the level of public examination real, substantive conflict, which may result in heated debate about technology, personalities, and/or administrative approaches. There is evidence that such debates, properly managed, can be the basis for creativity in organization-al problem solving. There is also the possibility, however, that such debates cannot be managed, and substantiating the concept of existential risk, the person who initiates the risk may get fired or ostracized. But that again leads to the necessity of evaluating the results of such confrontation at the existential level.

• *Existential results.* Evaluating the outcome of confrontation from an existential framework is quite different from evaluating it from a set of technical criteria. How do I reach this conclusion? Simply from interviewing a variety of people who have chosen to confront the paradox and listening to their responses. In short, for them, psychological success and failure apparently are divorced from what is traditionally accepted in organizations as criteria for success and failure.

For instance, some examples of success are described when people are asked, "What happened when you confronted the issue?" They may answer this way:

> I was told we had enough boat rockers in the organization, and I got fired. It hurt at first, but in retrospect it was the greatest day of my life. I've got another job and I'm delighted. I'm a free man.

Another description of success might be this:

> I said I don't think the research project can succeed and the others looked shocked and quickly agreed. The upshot of the whole deal is that I got a promotion and am now known as a "rising star." It was the high point of my career.

Similarly, those who fail to confront the paradox describe failure in terms divorced from technical results. For example, one may report:

> I didn't say anything and we rocked along until the whole thing exploded and Joe got fired. There is still a lot of tension in the organization, and we are still in trouble, but I got a good performance review last time. I still feel lousy about the whole thing, though.

From a different viewpoint, an individual may describe his sense of failure in these words:

> I knew I should have said something and I didn't. When the project failed, I was a convenient whipping boy. I got demoted; I still have a job, but my future here is definitely limited. In a way I deserve what I got, but it doesn't make it any easier to accept because of that.

Most important, the act of confrontation apparently provides intrinsic psychological satisfaction, regardless of the technological outcomes for those who attempt it. The real meaning of that existential experience, and its relevance to a wide variety of organizations, may lie, therefore, not in the scientific analysis of decision making but in the plight of Sisyphus. That is something the reader will have to decide for himself.

THE ABILENE PARADOX AND THE MYTH OF SISYPHUS

In essence, this paper proposes that there is an underlying organizational reality that includes both agreement and disagreement, cooperation and conflict. However, the decision to confront the possibility of organization agreement is all too difficult and rare, and its opposite, the decision to accept the evils of the present, is all too common. Yet those two decisions may reflect the essence of both our human potential and our human imperfectability. Consequently, the choice to confront reality in the family, the church, the business, or the bureaucracy, though made only occasionally, may reflect those "peak experiences" that provide meaning to the valleys.

In many ways, they may reflect the experience of Sisyphus. As you may remember, Sisyphus was condemned by Pluto to a perpetuity of pushing a large stone to the top of a mountain, only to see it return to its original position when he released it. As Camus suggested in his revision of the myth, Sisyphus' task was absurd and totally devoid of meaning. For most of us, though, the lives we lead pushing papers or hubcaps are no less absurd, and in many ways we probably spend about as much time pushing rocks in our organizations as Sisyphus did in his.

Camus also points out, though, that on occasion as Sisyphus released his rock and watched it return to its resting place at the bottom of the hill, he was able to recognize the adsurdity of his lot, and for brief periods of time, transcend it.

So it may be with confronting the Abilene Paradox. Confronting the absurd paradox of agreement may provide, through activity, what Sisyphus gained from his passive but conscious acceptance of his fate. Thus, through the process of active confrontation with reality, we may take respite from pushing our rocks on their endless journeys and, for brief moments, experience what C.P. Snow termed "the triumphs of life we make for ourselves" within those absurdities we call organizations.

SELECTED BIBLIOGRAPHY

Chris Argyris in *Intervention Theory and Method: A Behavioral Science View* (Addison-Wesley, 1970) gives an excellent description of the process of "owning up" and being "open," both of which are major skills required if one is to assist his organization in avoiding or leaving Abilene.

Albert Camus in *The Myth of Sisyphus and Other Essays* (Vintage Books,

Random House, 1955) provides an existential viewpoint for coping with absurdity, of which the Abilene Paradox is a clear example.

Jerry B. Harvey and R. Albertson in "Neurotic Organizations: Symptoms, Causes and Treatment," Parts I and II, *Personnel Journal* (September and October, 1971) provide a detailed example of a third-party intervention into an organization caught in a variety of agreement-management dilemmas.

Irving Janis in *Victims of Groupthink* (Houghton-Mifflin Co., 1972) offers an alternative viewpoint for understanding and dealing with many of the dilemmas described in "The Abilene Paradox." Specifically, many of the events that Janis describes as examples of conformity pressures (that is, group tyranny) I would conceptualize as mismanaged agreement.

In his *The Pursuit of Loneliness* (Beacon Press, 1970), Philip Slater contributes an in-depth description of the impact of the role of alienation, separation, and loneliness (a major contribution to the Abilene Paradox) in our culture.

Richard Walton in *Interpersonal Peacemaking: Confrontation and Third Party Consultation* (Addison-Wesley, 1969) describes a variety of approaches for dealing with conflict when it is real, rather than phony.

Chapter 20

How Power Affects
Employee Appraisal

Robert R. Blake
Jane S. Mouton

A study of the dynamics of power shows clearcut connections between the power distribution between supervisor and subordinate and their relative feelings of satisfaction and responsibility.

Performance appraisal is another facet of supervisor-subordinate relations. It would be inappropriate to regard it as a separate class of events distinguishable from other relationships that connect supervisors and subordinates. This is only a forewarning which says that in the interests of consistency, if for no other reason, a supervisor can't act one way in the context of work and in a contradictory fashion in counseling a subordinate.

In a management development laboratory, participants experience and compare the ratings and the goals method of performance evaluation. As you will see, the ratings method is a 1/0 power relation because all the decisions are entirely in the hands of the supervisor. On the other hand, a goals approach goes in the direction of a .5/.5 power distribution because both members of the pair are collaborating in a common search for solutions to problems. When you come right down to it, it's the difference between a "tell and sell" and a "give and take" situation.

The Experiment. Here is how an employee performance appraisal is handled in a group dynamics laboratory. However, you would do well to remember these principles whenever you are being evaluated or when you are evaluating the work performance of another employee.

Each participant is cast either as a ficticious supervisor named Bob Hayes or as Fred Winters his subordinate. Then they are briefed on how Fred Winters has been operating in his position. They are also instructed on how to conduct the

From *Group Dynamics — Key to Decision Making* by Robert R. Blake and Jane S. Mouton. Copyright ©1961 by Gulf Publishing Company, Houston, Texas, chapter 4, pp. 39-49. Used with permission. All rights reserved.

277

typical ratings type of performance appraisal. Each participant receives a rating form characteristic of that used by many organizations.

The goals method is described also, and a sample interview outline provided. Then each supervisor conducts two performance review interviews, one according to a ratings approach and one using the goal-setting procedure, each with a different subordinate.

The supervisor, Bob Hayes, is a department head. Four general foremen report to Bob. In turn each general foreman has three or four division foremen reporting to him. One general foreman, Fred Winters, is new in his job. Fred tends to run his division full speed ahead without much forethought for the scheduling needs of or available resources in other divisions. Certain heads in the other divisions have pointed this out to Bob and expressed the feeling that Fred is difficult to work with.

Fred's attitudes also are reflected among his subordinates. For example, his division foremen are hardhitting, energetic people. They leave little room for supervisors in supporting divisions to take any initiative in contributing to the solutions of common problems.

Bob Hayes is well-adjusted to the organization and sensitive to its demands. His counseling problem is to aid Fred to integrate his efforts into the organization more effectively.

Fred, on the other hand, is particularly proud of his achievements. He is pleased with the caliber of his division foremen and with the cooperation they give him. He has a strong relationship with these men and has achieved substantial economic gains in unit operations. He feels he has flexibility in running his section full speed ahead without committing himself to much more than day-to-day planning.

The Ratings Approach. For the ratings interview Bob Hayes fills in a rating scale concerning Fred's performance. A typical item includes *adaptability* in which Fred's ability to meet new conditions and to execute new assignments is rated on a scale ranging from, "highly versatile, meets new situations readily," through, "adjusts with sufficient ease for good performance," to, "fails to adjust." Others include *job knowledge, punctuality, cooperation, ingenuity, judgment, economy, supervisory skill,* and so on. Thus having rated him, Bob calls Fred in to discuss his strong and weak points and to indicate steps he thinks Fred should take to improve his performance.

The Goals Approach. Under the goals approach, a week in advance Bob and Fred agree on the areas of performance that they want to talk through. They agree to come together with a diagnosis of the situation and with some well defined goals which, if acceptable, will forward the situation. Both have thought about it, and each has come up with some ideas in the areas of planning, interdepartmental relations, development of subordinates, self-improvement, and administrative efficiency. Both have suggestions, but they are by no means identical even though they overlap at some points.

In the area of administrative efficiency, for example, Bob feels Fred ought to free his division foremen and avoid getting so involved in their work details. He also thinks Fred should give more attention to problems at the interdepartment level.

Fred, on the other hand, feels he should strive to further reduce operating costs by another three percent during the next six-month period. During the interview they both work toward establishing mutually acceptable goals from their individual suggestions and toward a time schedule for achieving them.

Half of the supervisors use the ratings performance appraisal method first and the other half use the goals first. Thus in the course of the session each person, whether supervisor or subordinate, has the opportunity of contrasting the two approaches to performance appraisal. After each appraisal is complete both supervisor and subordinate express their feelings toward the two kinds of interviews.

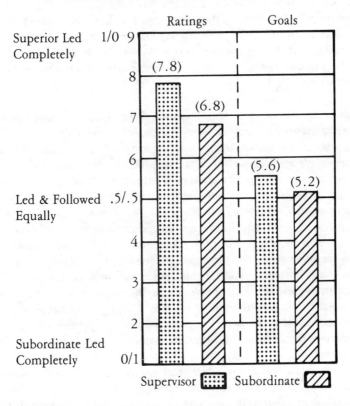

POWER DISTRIBUTION IN TWO
APPROACHES TO PERFORMANCE REVIEW

Figure 4.1. Leadership is more equally distributed between the supervisor and subordinate under goals approach than under ratings approach.

Distribution of Power. The ratings approach has been characterized as a more or less 1/0 type of interview, with the supervisor telling the subordinate what he needs to do to change. The goals approach is on a more .5/.5 basis with emphasis on attaining a mutually acceptable set of goals through joint participation. Figure 4.1 demonstrates that the ratings approach is experienced by both the supervisor and the subordinate as being under the control of the supervisor, or close to a 1/0 power distribution. The goals approach results in leadership being more readily distributed, approaching a .5/.5 give-and-take relationship.

What do these results mean? Supervisors are not instructed to act in a 1/0 manner when using the ratings system, nor are they coached to use a .5/.5 approach in the goals system. Rather the systems themselves contain the power assumptions. In the ratings case, it is extremely difficult to evaluate a subordinate and bring him into a discussion of the ratings without exercising power in a 1/0 direction. Too frequently, what starts out as a 1/0 ratings interview, ends up as a 1/1 fight. By comparison, in the goals system, the inclination is to examine the problems at hand in a give-and-take way without feeling that the supervisor is judging and that the subordinate is being judged.

If for no other reason than the results reported here, personnel heads or line supervisors should be wary of the flowery language describing ratings systems contained in current management textbooks. Textbooks too often tell "how to do it" and remain silent with regard to the dynamics of the relationship hidden in the method.

Teamness. Casting these results against those from the power spectrum experiment presented in Chapter 3 we anticipate that the goals system will arouse a greater sense of teamness than the rating system. The data for evaluating the teamness angle are presented in Figure 4.2. As you see, teamness is at a minimum, verging on a feeling of separateness between the pair in the ratings interview, whereas both supervisor and subordinate report a relatively high sense of teamness under the goals approach.

These results mean that the ratings method tends to separate people; that is, it pushes them apart and makes them feel individualistic and distinctive rather than as members of a team. The goals approach, by comparison, pulls them together with both searching for solutions to common problems.

If collaboration between supervisor and subordinate is the objective, it is clear that the ratings method does not contribute to it. Rather than producing collaboration, it tends to produce competition and defensiveness. It is equally apparent that the goals system fosters joint thinking and coordination of effort.

Satisfaction. Parallel reactions are apparent in connection with satisfaction as is shown in Figure 4.3. Both superior and subordinate have a neutral feeling for performance appraisal under the ratings approach—it is neither satisfying nor dissatisfying. In the goals approach, however, the appraisal is very satisfying not only to the supervisor but to the subordinate as well. The most logical

SENSE OF TEAMNESS BETWEEN
SUPERVISORS AND SUBORDINATES

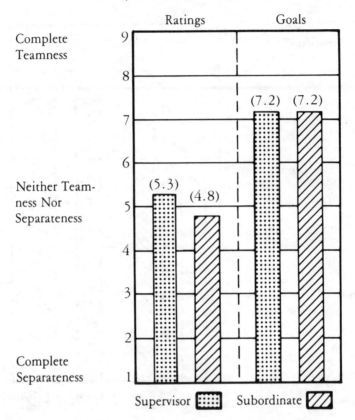

Figure 4.2. **Teamness is higher for both supervisors and subordinates under goals approach than under ratings approach.**

generalization then, is that when a supervisor and a subordinate work together in the pursuit of common goals they find satisfaction in the effort expended. Here again, the comparison of results establishes unequivocally that a relationship based on goals accomplishments produces a healthier and more collaborative basis of association than does the classical ratings method.

Responsibility for Change. Also consistent with reactions to the power spectrum, under the ratings approach, are the feelings of responsibility associated with power imbalance. This conclusion is based on results shown in Figure 4.4. Here we have the ironic situation where the supervisor feels *responsibility* for the subordinate to change *but the subordinate doesn't.*

Here is a paradox of the first class. It says that under the ratings approach the subordinate who is being counseled to change feels little responsibility for

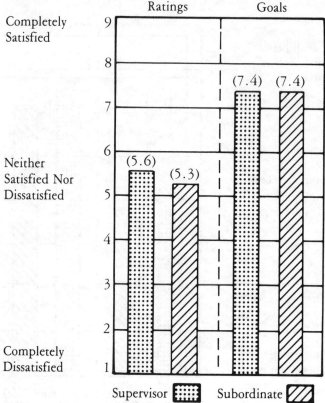

Figure 4.3. Satisfaction is higher for both supervisors and subordinates under goals approach than under ratings approach.

doing so while the supervisor who is counseling for change feels a great deal of responsibility for the subordinate to shift his behavior. What could be more frustrating than a situation in which a supervisor feels responsibility for a subordinate with the subordinate feeling reduced responsibility for his own behavior?

On the other hand, both supervisor and subordinate feel a moderately high degree of responsibility for change when the goals approach is used. This finding is particularly significant, for it says that responsibility of the subordinate flows with his sense of power to influence the definition of his own situation. Another way of saying it is that a supervisor cannot dictate responsibility for change. In the final analysis he can only create the conditions under which responsibility is experienced!

Thus, the power spectrum tells the story. When power is shared, as it is in a

RESPONSIBILITY FOR CHANGE
FELT UNDER TWO APPROACHES
TO PERFORMANCE REVIEW

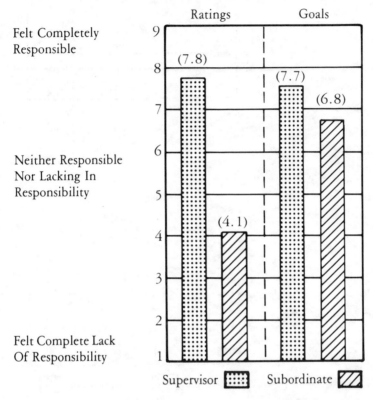

Figure 4.4. **Both supervisors and subordinates feel moderately high responsibility for change under goals approach; only the supervisor feels responsible under ratings approach.**

.5/.5 situation, the basis for control is *mutual* effort, not *directed* effort. Mutuality of interests generates joint responsibility, whether on the battle lines or on the workbench!

Overview. This concrete application of power theory to a specific two-person relationship says that the way a supervisor thinks of himself and utilizes the power available to him in working with subordinates makes a lot of difference. Used one way, he gets one set of results; used another, he gets a different set. Every man has to decide which way to go, but the results here are sufficiently dramatic to a person's thinking if he is using a ratings system of the kind described.

If you want constructive results that lead to satisfaction, teamness and feelings of responsibility in your subordinates, move in the direction of a .5/.5 goal-setting relationship. The data say that you have to make a choice—you can go either way—tell-and-sell or give-and-take. It's an important choice.

Chapter 21

Systems Maintenance: Gatekeeping and the Involvement Process

Jay Hall

Organizations and groups—just as other mechanisms incorporating and relying upon a number of interdependent parts for success—require maintenance. Indeed, the individuals who comprise any sort of organized effort may be thought of as constituting the moving parts of a social vehicle. The organization, the group, or the two-person encounter which is convened for the purpose of accomplishing movement toward some goal is just as dependent upon the effective intermeshing of its related parts as is an automobile or jet aircraft. Too often the need for coordination and relating of resources is ignored by members of organizations; and a paradox is that, while most people are extremely mindful of the maintenance needs of mechanical systems, they de-emphasize or deny such requirements in the case of human systems. Yet experience with faulty committee actions or interdepartmental conflicts will attest to the fact that human systems too may sputter and misfire.

LOVE, WORK, AND GATEKEEPING

It was Sigmund Freud who observed nearly sixty years ago that, in the final analysis, there are only two realities: love and work. While Freud based his conclusions on the data of observation filtered through an exceptional intuitive system, research in the social sciences has confirmed many of his tenets. The love-work dichotomy has perhaps received stronger support than any other of his ideas; for, again and again, experimental results have fallen into and concerned what may be more accurately termed task and social-emotional categories of behavior. Essentially, most of the research on human systems has concerned the attempts of individuals to reconcile and integrate their task and social-emotional needs in the accomplishment of objectives. Out of these major areas of group effort have evolved the functions called task and maintenance which are designed to sustain movement toward objectives, on one hand, and to maintain the moving system, on the other. Since maintenance is the focus of the present discussion, primary attention will be given to it in the interest of more effective organizational and group functioning.

The interfaces requiring maintenance in human systems are numerous. So too are the types of maintenance functions which might be performed. Of perhaps the greatest significance for an enduring system and its need for effective implementation of goal-directed decisions is the Gatekeeping function. The Gatekeeping function, first identified by Kurt Lewin[1,2] in his classic studies of attitude change and subsequent behavioral conformity, addresses the flow of information and patterns of interaction in groups and organizations. As such, it is concerned with insuring the conditions for shared participation among parties to the enterprise. Succinctly, *it is the assumption of responsibility for others' levels of participation; it is the active solicitation of contributions from other members and it is the providing of support and reinforcement, as well as the creating of openings, for others to become involved.* Its objective is one of involvement; and involvement, in turn, is one of the cornerstones of contemporary approaches to attitude change and effective management. Thus, the Gatekeeping function may be thought of as the primary mechanism for achieving the organizational effects that are associated with involvement. These effects it will be discovered have significant implications for the manner in which human systems function.

Gatekeeping and its involvement consequences are relevant to organizational performance because they affect the way people *feel* about the decisions which govern their actions and their roles under those decisions. At the same time, the mechanism and its effects constitute an area of human interaction that most people have considered very little. Indeed, the notion that people should be actively involved in the making of decisions that affect them—not to mention the corollary that someone should take active responsibility for eliciting participation from everyone—flies in the face of more traditional assumptions about group and organizational functioning.

RESEARCH ON THE EFFECTS OF INVOLVEMENT AND NONINVOLVEMENT

A paradox exists regarding involvement as a systems maintenance tool. On one hand, the involvement premise has a foreign ring for many managers because it is less expedient and runs counter to the managerial image of director, controller, and decision maker. More than one has dismissed both the Gatekeeping function and its involvement consequences as little more than managerial permissiveness. On the other hand, data from basic research in the behavioral sciences are quite clear on the point that people who have been actively involved in the shaping of organizational ventures tend to be more satisfied with their roles in the system and to exhibit to a greater extent what many managers describe as "loyalty to the firm." Thus, the intuitive role-prescribed perceptions of many individuals in the workaday world of organizations do not jibe with the conclusions resulting from more objective empirical research. A knowledge gap is further compounded by an attitudinal gap in too many instances.

Because of the philosophical and underlying attitudinal issues surrounding Gatekeeping and involvement as management tools, the average manager requires something more than a list of selected readings to nudge his awareness of the cause-and-effect significance of his Gatekeeping practices and the feeling concomitants generated among those whom he manages. To *experience* the phenomenon seems to be the key to awareness, particularly when one's experience can be reviewed in the light of a systematic data feedback. The author has designed an action exercise to afford such a structured experience; and perhaps a discussion of the exercise and its results will shed greater light on the effects of involvement and noninvolvement than is possible otherwise.

The Gatekeeping Exercise

Wanted was an analogue of the typical situation in which members of a human system are at work on a task of relevance to the system and in which the participation of some members is contingent upon the Gatekeeping behaviors of others. In addition, it was thought that an awareness of this contingency on the part of potentially silent members would more closely approximate the conditions commonly encountered in organizations where, for example, a subordinate's participation is directly contingent upon being invited by his superior. Therefore, a simple group discussion format was employed as the basis of the exercise, and discussion topics were assigned which were known to be highly relevant to group members. (It has since been found that the topic need not be particularly germane for the involvement dynamics to make themselves felt.) One or two group members were asked, without the knowledge of other members, to play a group role during the exercise. Their roles were quite simple and, on the surface at least, easily maintained. Succinctly, they were asked to play the role of *silent members* throughout the discussion *unless* someone noticed their plight and extended a direct invitation to join in and participate. In effect, these instructions amounted to the creation of a silent member in each group who was at once aware of his own silence and the contingency of any participation upon the Gatekeeping efforts of other members. It should be stressed that all that was required for members thus instructed to participate was a direct question regarding what they thought, whether they were in agreement, how they were feeling, or the like. When this happened, silent members were obliged to join in and voice any opinions they might have on the topic under discussion. Thus, a very simple and straightforward analogue of commonly encountered situations—regardless of system size and numbers—was created artificially for purposes of studying (1) the reactions of people either involved or uninvolved, and (2) the extent to which participating members would spontaneously undertake Gatekeeping functions for the system.

Since it was also expected that there would be naturally silent members in groups and that they might have different feelings about noninvolvement than instructed silent members (as Vroom's[3] data might suggest), half the groups studied were typically autonomous with no instructed members. Groups were asked to work for anywhere from fifteen to forty-five minutes; it was later determined that amount of time spent did not significantly affect the results obtained. Apparently, the involvement dynamic is quickly aroused and persists for a considerable duration. At the conclusion of group discussions, a reaction form was distributed to members which they were asked to fill out anonymously, indicating as honestly as possible their feelings about the session which had just ended. A sample of the reaction form is presented as *Exhibit I*. In addition to the earlier instructions about their roles, silent members were also asked to indicate that they had been instructed by placing an "S" on their reaction forms while filling them out.

Questions on the reaction form covered the range of feelings that individuals might experience during group discussion and particular emphasis was placed on sampling those feelings thought to be most affected by involvement-noninvolvement. Question 1 represented a control question critical to the exercise, for it was directed at the perception of the respondent as to how much he had participated; that is, it indirectly assessed the extent to which his opinions had been solicited by other group members. On the basis of one's response to this question alone, he was treated either as an active participator and potential Gatekeeper or as a relatively silent member of the system. Anyone scoring "6" or higher on a possible 9-point scale was considered to be a participator; while those scoring "5" or below were considered to be silent members, irrespective of whether they indicated by an "S" that they were instructed.

The data were therefore separated into three groups for analysis: (1) potential Gatekeepers and high participators, (2) instructed silent members, and (3) uninstructed silent members. Once these groupings were achieved, the data from the remaining five questions on the reaction form were compared as a function of amount of involvement. Essentially, the reactions of Gatekeepers may be interpreted as reflecting the effects of higher than average involvement, while the reactions of silent members—either instructed or not—may be interpreted as reflecting the effects of noninvolvement.

Summary Of Obtained Results

Of approximately 400 people involved in the study, roughly two-thirds reported active participation and were counted as Gatekeepers. Approximately

1. *To what extent did you partici-pate in making the decisions reached by your group?*

I participated:

9 Completely
8 Quite a lot
7 A little more than moderately
6 Moderately
5 Neither very much nor very little
4 Less than expected
3 Moderately less than expected
2 Quite a lot less than expected
1 Not at all

2. *How satisfied did you feel with the amount and quality of your parti-cipation in reaching a joint decision?*

I felt:

9 Completely satisfied
8 Quite satisfied
7 Moderately satisfied
6 A little more satisfied than dissatis-fied
5 Neither very satisfied nor very dis-satisfied
4 A little more dissatisfied than satis-fied
3 Moderately dissatisfied
2 Quite dissatisfied
1 Completely dissatisfied

3. *How much responsibility for making the decision work would you feel?*

I would feel:

9 Completely responsible
8 Quite responsible
7 Moderately responsible
6 A little more responsible than not responsible
5 Neither very responsible nor very irresponsible
4 A little more irresponsible than re-sponsible
3 Moderately irresponsible
2 Quite irresponsible
1 Completely irresponsible

4. *How committed do you feel to the decision your group made?*

I feel:

9 Completely committed
8 Quite committed
7 Moderately committed
6 A little more committed than un-committed
5 Neither very committed nor very uncommitted
4 A little more uncommitted than committed
3 Moderately uncommitted
2 Quite uncommitted
1 Completely uncommitted

5. *How much frustration did you feel during the work on the decision?*

I felt:

9 Completely frustrated
8 Quite frustrated
7 Moderately frustrated
6 A little more frustrated than ap-proving
5 Neither very frustrated nor very ap-proving
4 A little more approving than frus-trated
3 Moderately approving
2 Quite approving
1 Completely approving

6. *How good was the decision your group made?*

It was:

9 The best possible
8 Quite good
7 Moderately good
6 A little more good than bad
5 Neither very good nor very bad
4 A little more bad than good
3 Moderately bad
2 Quite bad
1 The worst possible

Exhibit 1. Personal Reaction Index

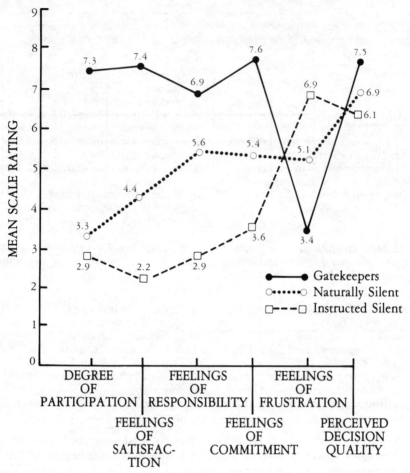

Figure 1. Summary of data from 400 participants in the Gatekeeping exercise.

100 instructed silent members reported that they were allowed to remain throughout the discussion period; and about 40 naturally silent members reported low participation without instructions to that effect. Those instructed silent members who were subsequently involved by their groups reflected this fact in answering the first question, and their data were pooled with those of other participating members. The results obtained are summarized in *Table 1* and presented graphically in *Figure 1*.

Again, in reviewing the data, the reactions of Gatekeepers can be interpreted in terms of the *effects of involvement,* while the reactions of Silent Members would seem to reflect the *effects associated with failure to involve* (or to become involved). As such, some important consequences of intra-group behavior are illuminated. First, the difference in the degree to which Gatekeepers and Silent Members felt they were able to participate is interesting in two respects: (1) the

Table 1. Reactions of Gatekeepers and Silent Members.*

	Degree of participation	Amount of satisfaction derived from participation	Feelings of responsibility for making decisions	Degree of commitment to decision	Amount of frustration experienced	Appraisal of decision quality
Potential Gatekeepers	7.3	7.4	6.9	7.6	3.4	7.5
Naturally Silent Members	3.3	4.4	5.6	5.4	5.1	6.9
Instructed Silent Members	2.9	2.2	2.9	3.6	6.9	6.1

*Based on 9-point scale

obviously lower degree of perceived involvement which characterized instructed and naturally Silent Members (average *2.9* and *3.3* as compared with the Gatekeeper average of *7.3*) gives some indication as to just how attentive group members are to the participation-needs of others and (2) the higher Gatekeeper score raises a question as to whom was soliciting their opinions if no one was soliciting the opinions of Silent Members. Differences on this scale may reflect a tendency on the part of people to feel that because they *are* talking they have been encouraged to talk. Similarly, the failure of Gatekeepers to involve Silent Members would seem to reflect dramatically the effects of ''allowing everyone to participate'' versus ''encouraging and facilitating the participating of everyone.'' Coupled with the results of the remaining scales, the data argue for a less passive orientation than ''allowing'' others to participate.

The scales reflecting satisfaction, feelings of responsibility, and commitment to the decision are seen to differ systematically for Gatekeepers and Silent Members as a direct function of the degree to which individuals were involved and participating in the decision-making session. A not too tenuous generalization is readily apparent from these data: *a positive relationship exists between the amount of participation an individual experiences and his feelings of satisfaction, responsibility and commitment.* Put another way, this simply says that people value and tend to support what they help create.

Scale Number 5, a measurement of the amount of frustration experienced, reveals another important by-product of Gatekeeping behavior. People who have not been involved and encouraged to participate experience much greater frustration during the course of group discussion than do those who, for one reason or another, participate actively. Gatekeepers produced average ratings of 3.4 on frustration as compared with those of 6.9 and 5.1 for instructed and naturally Silent Members, respectively. The fact that feelings of frustration on the part of a few or many of a group's members can seriously impair the system's performance needs little discussion. Thus, the implication is that if frustration—either overt or covert—is to be reduced via a ''talking it out'' process, it is often necessary for someone to assume the responsibility for seeing that everyone is encouraged and has an opportunity to voice his feelings.

The last scale, an appraisal of the quality of the group's decision, raises another interesting and potentially critical issue for human systems. Many members feel that if a decision reached is logically sound it will meet with acceptance and support. Taking the results of scale number 6 and viewing them in the light of the other scale results indicates that this is not so. Gatekeepers quite naturally rate the decisions they were active in producing quite high; an average rating of 7.5 out of a possible 9 is reported. Surprisingly, so do both natural and instructed silent members, with ratings of 6.9 and 6.1, respectively; but their reactions to the decision on dimensions other than perceived quality differ radically. Thus, the assumption often held by people that logically derived decisions need no other defense would seem tenuous. Indeed, the data from silent members say, in effect, "We have heard your arguments, and they are sound. On the basis of the facts—which we all heard and assessed— the decision you reached is a good one. But don't expect me to be satisfied with it, feel responsible for its success, or be committed to it." The feeling tones associated with noninvolvement would seem to overshadow the logical appeal of decision content. The data from the exercise clearly reveal a paradox of human systems: *what may be logically acceptable is not necessarily psychologically acceptable*. Involvement speaks to the psychological level of functioning. A group dynamics axiom is that all persons directly affected by a decision should be involved in the making of that decision if more than logical certification is desired. This, in the final analysis, is the message of the Gatekeeping Exercise and the objective of the effectively functioning human system.

CAUSES AND SYMPTOMS OF THE FAILURE TO INVOLVE

At the risk of redundancy, it may prove worthwhile to underscore the three major themes developed thus far: (1) people who are actively involved in the planning of their own activities and in the making of decisions by which they will be directly affected tend to experience more positive feelings toward such activities; (2) since the feelings people have of personal responsibility, commitment, satisfaction, and lack of frustration often have predictive significance in determining how they will perform, the effects associated with involvement are desirable from an organizational point of view; and (3) Gatekeeping is the function which will most likely create the conditions for people becoming involved. Laying aside for the moment many of the personal views of man or hoary assumptions about efficient organizational functioning which individuals may hold, the involvement process may be reviewed in terms of its opposite effects—that is, from a consideration of the symptoms of noninvolvement—and from a cause-and-effect vantage point regarding the failure of individuals to perform the Gatekeeping function required for involvement.

Common Symptoms Of Noninvolvement

The failure of individuals either to be or become involved results in many of the system breakdowns which plague human groups. The consequences run the gamut of resistance to change and rebellion to indifference and overcompliance. Lack of involvement is hardly ever cited by the uninvolved person as the reason for his consequent behavior. Often, to admit (assuming that one is consciously aware of his own feelings in the matter) that the extent to which he was involved was inadequate and, therefore, led to no binding commitments on his part requires a skill and candor not possessed by many. Rather than reporting objectively on the feelings being experienced, most people react to noninvolvement by either acting out their feelings or by displacing their aggressions onto more available persons or situations. The indirect and unfocused nature of acting out behavior and the misleading and diversionary effect of displaced blame not only serve to obscure the involvement-noninvolvement dynamics which are actually operating, but lend themselves to interpretive fantasies on the part of potential Gatekeepers trying to make sense of apparently inconsistent behavior. Thus, one must deal out of necessity with symptoms.

Generally speaking, the symptoms of noninvolvement appear as indifference and uncooperative activities. The uninvolved person may appear, and indeed be, bored; he frequently will engage in peripheral kinds of action, designed to take the group off on a tangent or merely to kill time. Uninvolved individuals frequently appear as self-centered and unconcerned with the well-being of the system. They may actually work counter to the objectives of the system and, after a prolonged period of noninvolvement, they may even resist attempts to get them involved. Operationally, such behaviors show up in a lack of conformity to apparently agreed upon plans and in a dearth of follow-through effort during the implementation phases of work. In its extreme form, apathy induced by noninvolvement may even cause the individual to forego membership in the system; the result is an elegant case of the self-fulfilling prophecy as far as the system's potential Gatekeepers are concerned.

In a more practical context, the consequences of noninvolvement may take a number of forms with which people in many walks of life are familiar. How often, for example, have people given every indication that they approved a plan and its implications for them only to default on their own responsibilities under the plan at a later time? How often has a manager, enthusiastic about and proud of the strategy he has personally developed, felt that he has persuaded others of his logic only to discover that, despite a good bit of head-nodding from others, he is the only one really committed? How often has the skilled salesman waxed eloquent about the virtues of his product and apparently made his sale, complete with customer signature on the dotted line, only to find later that the client has "reconsidered"? Finally, how common has it become for entire political systems to be challenged and their basic tenets to be disregarded by those for whom the system exists and by whom it was ostensibly created? These fairly common examples are all symptomatic of misapplied involvement strategies. It is very likely that the failures to follow up, the reluctance to get on board, or the changes of mind depicted may all be traced to a lack of involvement on the part of those to whom the message was being pitched. Members of human systems may be momentarily awed by the eloquence of presentation or swamped and befuddled by the mass of data presented them to the extent that they appear to comprehend and accept; but when the smoke clears they too often see things in a different light—their own light—and may, in addition, have a number of negative feelings about their relatively passive-receptive roles in the process. The conditions are created for system failure during implementation periods, and only symptoms will exist as the causal factors. Symptoms, of course, are themselves effects and not causes; for the causes, we must look elsewhere to those who are potential Gatekeepers in the system.

Causal Factors In The Failure To Involve

The working assumption underlying the present discussion is that people fail to involve others rather than that people fail to get involved. While it is certainly true that some people do not care to be involved and that others are threatened by and therefore resist involvement, this is not the case with the broad spectrum of individuals one encounters in human systems. Therefore, the perspective employed here is essentially one of defaulted Gatekeeping behavior, its causes and consequences. At least five general factors—all reflecting attitudes or needs of potential Gatekeepers—bear the brunt of failures to involve others. These are, briefly, (a) the content versus process dilemma in human systems; (b) the perception that each is free to do as he pleases and, therefore, personally responsible for himself in the system; (c) what might be termed leadership fallacies; (d) interpretive fantasies of Gatekeepers confronted with the symptoms of noninvolvement; and (e) the subtleties of positive projection. Each of these will be discussed in an attempt to present the position and plight of a system's Gatekeepers.

(a) *Content versus process as the focal point of efforts.* By and large, individuals are more sensitive to and interested in the substantive, intellectual, task-related issues that a human system is working on than in the manner in which it is working. Put another way, it would appear that the *content* of group or organizational work is of greater concern than is the *process* whereby the work will be accomplished. Content is usually roughly equivalent to the system's production; and performance output is always a formidable criterion with which systems are concerned. Beyond its performance significance, however, the content facet of human encounters has a seductive quality all its own, such that the rich array of opinions and counter-opinions, logic and illogic, real and contrived statistical supports which make up content have a way of preempting the attention of people from any awareness of *how* they are working together. Issues of who is doing what to whom, or of the impact that one is having on others go begging. Involvement and its incumbent Gatekeeping function, being essentially process issues, also go begging. To return to the vehicular analogy used earlier, content may be equated with the fuel supply of the human system; some fuel or content issue is required for movement to occur. By the same token, process may be equated with the gear system or combustion design of the system; for smooth intermeshing and finely tuned timing are required for optimal functioning. While it would be ridiculous for one to attempt to remedy a malfunctioning engine simply by adding fuel time and again, that is in essence what people seem inclined to do when human systems malfunction. Rather than exploring the nature of the ongoing process, most people simply modify and add more content. Thus, one aspect of human systems that predisposes potential Gatekeepers to ignore their requisite function while seeing to their own participation is the sheer seductiveness of content per se. In the attempt to get one's own ideas across and to influence the direction of thought, the individual tends to forget that not everyone is either as interested or aggressive as he is. Moreover, the content may be so rich and the process so subtle that there is virtually no awareness of how many or who is or is not participating. Insensitivity, not malicious intent, becomes the causal factor of interest where content and process collide.

(b) *The freedom presumption.* A second causal factor underlying defaulted Gatekeeping is the presumption, peculiar to our culture, that everyone is *free* to participate. Lip service to the democratic process and an almost obsessive pronouncement of equality in groups often lead members of human systems to believe that if anyone has something to say he will. Each is free to speak his piece, and if he does not, the inference is either that he has nothing to say or is in basic agreement with whatever has gone before. While inferences such as these may be accurate and while it is certainly hoped that everyone is free to speak his mind, the case for participation is not so simple as might be imagined. The prevailing ground rules may afford freedom, in a normative sense; but psychological freedom is something else again. To feel free of constraint, at ease, and capable of differing with the prevailing flow is a luxury that not all members of human systems can afford. Indeed, one study has shown that the probability that an idea will actually be expressed is a direct function of its perceived commonality. People more often say what they have reason to believe others already think and with what they will agree. Similarly, Asch's[4] classic studies of conformity have demonstrated clearly that people will modify their contributions to coincide with prevailing thought, even when it is objectively inaccurate. Given such common barriers to candor, the notion that anyone who has something to say will always volunteer his opinions is a tenuous one at best. Nevertheless, many potential Gatekeepers share in the perception of freedom, and leave participating up to the individual on the basis of this. Realistically, one cannot be sure how free a person feels to participate or whether he is in agreement or simply without opinion unless he actively tests out his perception. The test in most cases constitutes Gatekeeping behavior. A final point might be made with respect to the effect of power differences on one's feelings of freedom to participate. A number of studies have shown that any imbalance of power affects the willingness of people to participate; particularly in situations in which such participation might be construed as an attempt to influence. Lippitt, Polansky, Redl, and Rosen,[5] for example, have reported that those members of the system who have more power do feel free to participate; those with less power not only feel less free, but will address their comments only to other less powerful members when they do participate. Summarily it would appear that the lack of freedom which conformity-pressures, aversions to conflict, and power imbalances can create at the level of psychological functioning is sufficient to both refute the freedom ethic in groups and to underscore the need for someone to create openings for otherwise silent members via the Gatekeeping process. Pockets of silence may be the ultimate consequences of presumed freedom.

(c) *Leadership fallacies and membership roles.* In addition to the power dynamics already discussed, a number of other factors surrounding leadership in human systems may serve to undermine the Gatekeeping function. These may be assigned to (1) the values and assumptions which the individual holds about his role as leader, and (2) the values and assumptions groups hold about the leadership role. Consider first the individual's conception of leadership. In many instances, leadership is seen as the prize for effective functioning in the system. As such, it is actively sought after and courted to the extent that individuals so motivated disenfranchise other members by their own efforts to influence group thinking. Behaviors reflecting not too subtle ego-strivings and power needs often disrupt human systems, while their perpetrators revel in the knowledge that they have dominated the group. Individuals who act on the basis of such a value system also frequently proceed on the basis of an assumption that persuasiveness is the key to effective leadership. Implicit in this assumption is a complementary notion that most people have few ideas of their own and can therefore be directly influenced by the skillfully presented persuasive appeal. Not to mention an implication of gullibility which is inherent in the persuasive approach, another facet that limits its utility is the fact that roughly only thirty percent of the people are really influenced by such an approach. The previously cited work of Asch[6] on conformity as well as that of Hovland[7] and his Yale attitude study group suggest that a relatively small percentage of people respond as the persuasive speaker anticipates. Thus, the needs and strategies of some members of human systems not only interject procedural noise into the system, but they lead to behaviors which are in direct opposition to effective Gatekeeping practices.

A parallel issue may be found at the group level of leadership values. Possibly because of folklore and our own history, groups seem to place a good deal of emphasis on the leader role. One of the first things most groups do upon convening is elect a leader. An unfilled leader role constitutes an intolerable void in the life of most groups. Without getting too enmeshed in the relative value of leaderless group functioning, it should be pointed out that research on the topic strongly suggests that emergent rather than formally fixed leadership is the earmark of effective groups. Of greater significance for the involvement process and Gatekeeping, however, is the fact that too often members feel that having elected a leader to watch over them, they are free of process responsibilities. Gatekeeping, as well as all other task and maintenance functions, become the purview of the leader. Not only is one person seriously limited in performing the critical functions for a system from the standpoint of sheer numbers, but he is equally limited by his own conception of the leadership role. Should, for example, the reins of the system be turned over to an ego-striving individual like the one described previously, pluralistic ignorance would be the order of the day and the system would perform accordingly. Similarly, a leader devoted to parliamentary procedure very likely would not attend to the flow of participation in such a way as to gain optimal involvement, since the focus would be more on control than upon commitment. Therefore, as a third causal factor leading to unmet Gatekeeping responsibilities is the cumulative effect of individual and group fallacies around the issue of leadership in human systems.

(d) *Interpretive fantasies and silent members.* A fourth factor leading to abdication of one's Gatekeeping function is the tendency of active members to *interpret* the silence of noninvolved members without bothering to check with them on the accuracy of their interpretations. The result of such tendencies is usually one of imputing to silent members motives and feelings which they in all probability are not experiencing. It is commonly reported, for example, that when potential Gatekeepers do happen to notice the silence of a fellow member, they are inclined to explain away the silence according to some implicit rule of rational behavior: "He's probably got a headache," or "He's probably awfully tired not to be joining in." The variations on the theme are numerous, but the implications for Gatekeeping are the same; no need to interfere in the private lives or feelings of people who obviously have their own reasons for not becoming involved. The imputative nature of potential Gatekeepers' interpretations of silence flows from the symbolic and diffuse nature of the acting out behaviors often employed by uninvolved members.

This point was alluded to earlier in the discussion. Of prime significance is the self-reinforcing cycle which may now begin to operate unless it is broken by effective Gatekeeping. Failure to Gatekeep, for any of the reasons already presented, may create conditions for noninvolvement; in turn, noninvolvement may lead to the expressive non-verbal communication of frustrations experienced by silent members which lead, sequentially, to inferences of fatigue, illness, and the like and decisions not to bother the silent member. Thus, potential Gatekeepers may be caught in a psychodynamic fallacy—i.e., the tendency to explain observed behaviors as caused by a person's own dynamics—at the attitudinal level, and self-fulfilling prophecies—i.e., adopting behaviors personally which elicit from others predicted reactions—at the level of operations. Systems so predicated eventually succumb to ennui.

(e) *Positive projection and the participatory boomerang.* The very positive feelings associated with participation and involvement have already been discussed at length. What might be added is that these feelings are often quite powerful; so much so that those who have become involved and claimed the emotional rewards of commitment and satisfaction often *project* their own positive feelings onto other members. In effect, the involved member frequently ends the encounter not only elated himself, but quite sure that others are equally elated. No one, for example, may feel that a session has gone quite as well as the lecturer who has done all the participating or the manager who has made the report or the salesman whose presentation has accounted for ninety percent of the client contact time. The assumption that one's legitimately acquired positive feelings are shared makes one vulnerable and, at the same time, further obscures the need for Gatekeeping efforts. Potential Gatekeepers who allow their own enthusiasm to spill over onto others may be laying the groundwork for a participatory boomerang; that is, again, there is no substitute for checking out the validity of one's perceptions—good or bad —if one is really interested in avoiding surprises of the type that accompany disconfirmed expectations. Speaking metaphorically, it may well be that personal participation is the carbon monoxide of group systems; while what one consumes may seem to be the staff of life, its by-products may be poisoning the environment in which others must live as well. Gatekeeping helps clear the air.

By way of summary, it might be said that the failure of individuals to Gatekeep and thereby to aid others in becoming involved is due to a lack of procedural awareness coupled with a lack of interpersonal skills of the type required for making others feel at ease and capable of candor. Add to these basic lapses in interpersonal competence such attributes as autistic thinking, egocentric power drives, false assumptions about the nature of people in human systems and of systems per se, plus a dash of insensitivity to the needs of others and one has all the ingredients for inept Gatekeeping behavior. It should be recalled in the light of such an incriminating summary that the emphasis has been placed on the *unconscious* determinants of defaulted Gatekeeping; the picture is even less pleasant if one considers the conscious determinants of poor Gatekeeping such as dogmatic belief systems that never invite disconfirmation or the will to power which leads one to keep others silent and submissive. While several pages could be devoted to purposeful avoidance of Gatekeeping, in the final analysis only extreme personality types would be depicted. The present discussion does not concern extremes of behavior, but rather the very common behaviors of men of good will. There are no black-hatted members so much as there are blindfolded members where the Gatekeeping process is concerned. A subgoal of this discussion has been to strip away as many of the filters and blinders as possible so that those interested in the effective functioning of human systems might better serve those systems.

FACETS OF EFFECTIVE GATEKEEPING

A good deal of attention has been given to causes of unmet Gatekeeping responsibilities. In many respects, the emphasis is appropriate because the preponderance of behaviors fall in that category. At the same time, this discussion would be less than constructive if the more positive aspects of competent Gatekeeping behavior were ignored. It is perhaps a hopeful sign that the facets of effective Gatekeeping can be discussed in roughly half the space devoted to faulty Gatekeeping.

To say that effective Gatekeeping is simply the reverse of faulty Gatekeeping would be an oversimplification; but in many respects this is essentially the case. The working assumption of the effective Gatekeeper is that he cannot tell at a distance what others are feeling or thinking; so he works actively at determining where they are with respect to the ongoing process. The effective Gatekeeper resists becoming seduced by the flow of content and strives for the participant-observer role; he participates, but he also observes the effects of his participation on others as well as what the pattern of interaction is in the system. He is procedurally sensitive. At the same time, the effective Gatekeeper is selfish from a system performance standpoint; he covets the resources available in the system, and is willing to take a personal role in getting these out in the open for group review. He distrusts silence on the part of the few and, more importantly, he distrusts his own ability to interpret silence accurately. Finally, the effective Gatekeeper is as concerned with the long-range issue of member commitment as he is with the more short-term goal of task accomplishment; for he recognizes that commitment has implications not only for the follow-through necessary for task performance, but for the system's capacity for holding appeal for its membership as well. Personal commitment is, after all, the most effective control mechanism available. Gatekeepers may or may not be sensitive and they may or may not possess emphatic awareness; what they do have in common is a fairly realistic perception that systems require the best that people have to offer and that there is no way of knowing what this is unless conditions are created for the display of wares.

Operationally, effective Gatekeeping may take many forms. It may appear as quasi-reflective utterances in responding to tentative contributions from members on the brink of silence. It may be directed at the feeling levels of silent members when it appears that they are troubled by the prevailing content. It may be confronting in the case of bored or detached members; and it may simply entail an inquiry as to whether someone agrees or can add to what has gone before. The multitudinous faces of silence require a multitude of Gatekeeping responses. The one common facet of Gatekeeping practices is that they are all active. Nothing is inferred or taken for granted; waiting and passivity only feed the conditions for a silent membership and make noninvolvement all the easier. Thus, the effective Gatekeeper is an active solicitor of opinions and feelings, a creator of openings, and a lender of support. The manner in which he does this is considerably less important than the fact that he is trying to do it. Finally, it should be said that the effective Gatekeeper has a preventative rather than corrective orientation; he works at maintaining the system so that members do not become lost to silence in the first place, rather than waiting to reclaim them after the fact.

SUMMARY OBSERVATIONS

Gatekeeping and the involvement process have been treated as essentially system *maintenance* issues. From the standpoint of their theoretical and operational significance for human systems, this perspective is accurate. In a larger sense, however, the function and its dynamic objective have task implications that risk being overlooked. In the final analysis, anything which helps the system better accomplish its mission may be thought of as task related. The fact that Gatekeeping—and maintenance activities in general—address the feelings and attitudes of a system's members doesn't mean that by any stretch of the imagination such functions are by nature softhearted or irrelevant to the system's production goals. While many people equate any concern for the climate of the system or the feelings of its members with indecisiveness and a loss of direction in the service of impractical humanism, reality suggests that systems which have taken care of these facets of their working arrangement satisfactorily typically are better able to take care of the other. Collins and Guetzkow,[8] two social psychologists, have pointed out in their analysis of decision-making group performance that the major task confronting group members is that of successfully integrating task and social-emotional factors. Similarly, this line of reasoning is evident in the work of Blake and Mouton[9] and Likert[10] in management, and in the research of Herbert Kelman[11] on attitude change.

Indeed, the message which is central to this discussion is that involvement and its Gatekeeping requisite have applicability across the whole spectrum of human interaction. Whether one is a manager, a salesman, an agent of change, or simply an interested parent or member of a community group, involvement constitutes a major tool for use in insuring commitment, feelings that the enterprise is meaningful, and the ever important inclination to follow up one's words with affirmative action.

REFERENCES

1. Lewin, K.: "Group Decision and Social Change." In G.E. Swanson, T.M. Newcomb, and E.L. Hartley (Eds.), *Readings in Social Psychology.* (2nd ed.) New York: Holt, 1952.

2. Lewin, K., and Lippitt, R.: "An Experimental Approach to the Study of Autocracy and Democracy: A Preliminary Note." *Sociometry,* Vol. 1, pp. 292-300.

3. Vroom, V.H.: "Some Personality Determinants of the Effects of Participation." *Journal of Abnormal Social Psychology,* Vol. 59, 1959, pp. 322-327.

4. Asch, S.E.: "Effects of Group Pressure upon the Modification and Distortion of Judgment." In H. Guetzkow (Ed.), *Groups, Leadership, and Men.* Pittsburgh: Carnegie Press, 1951.

5. Lippitt, R., Polansky, N., Redl, F., and Rosen, S.: "The Dynamics of Power: A Field Study of Social Influence in Groups of Children." In E.E. Maccoby, T.M. Newcomb, and E.L. Hartley (Eds.), *Readings in Social Psychology.* (3rd ed.) New York: Holt, 1958.

6. Asch, S.E.: *op. cit.*

7. Hovland, C.I., Campbell, E.H., and Brock, T.: "The Effects of 'Commitment' on Opinion Change Following Communication." In C.I. Hovland *et al, The Order of Presentation in Persuasion.* New Haven: Yale University Press, 1957.

8. Collins, B.E., and Guetzkow, H.: *A Social Psychology of Group Processes for Decision-making.* New York: Wiley, 1964.

9. Blake, R.R., and Mouton, J.S.: *The Managerial Grid.* Houston: Gulf Publishing, 1964.

10. Likert, R.: *The Human Organization.* New York: McGraw-Hill, 1967.

11. Kelman, H.C.: "Compliance, Identification, and Internalization." *Journal of Conflict Resolution,* Vol. 2, 1958, pp. 51-60.

Afterthoughts

The manager's interpersonal competence is the mechanism for activating the involvement process, for capitalizing on opportunities for subordinates to share power and participate in decisions which affect their quality of work and work-life. As the focal point for collaboration, the manager sets a standard for interpersonal trust for all group members and must continually strive to create an atmosphere where participation is a satisfying and productive experience for all concerned. Therefore, it is quite likely that the first step toward the goal of an interdependent team is the individual manager's personal development.

The Johari Window offered by Jay Hall in the first chapter is a useful conceptual model for reflecting on your personal use of exposure and feedback. An over-reliance on either dimension results in blindspots or facades—barriers to sharing needed information—which severely limit the quality of relationships. Only a generous and balanced use of both processes results in the kind of candor and openness which Argyris noted as the hallmark of interpersonal competence. Remember—your interpersonal style—one that facilitates involvement or cuts it short—will be adopted by your subordinates and come to characterize the entire workgroup.

Within Hanson's chapter is an important caveat about the feedback dimension described by Hall which reflects a shortcoming in interpersonal communications of our society at large. When asked for our viewpoint, an uncritical description is called for, but instead we often render a judgement. This tendency to criticize evokes defensiveness from those who solicit feedback and diverts attention and energy away from solving the problem at hand. In Johari Window terms the size of the Arena, the area which controls interpersonal productivity, will be diminished if the feedback you give makes a subordinate experience personal failure rather than gain new insights for continued improvement. The motivation behind our giving feedback is to help, not hurt, but we can defeat our purpose and stifle involvement in our rush to express our opinions.

Conflict is the likely consequence of an increased airing of opinions in a large Arena, but it need not be a threat to continued involvement. Indeed, as we shall see in the next section, conflict is a prime ingredient in group productivity. The key determinant of whether conflict proves to be dysfunctional to involvement is the manager's personal style in resolving it. Conflict must be confronted and resolved in a problem solving manner.

Filley describes a number of personal styles for resolving conflicts which impact on the involvement process. For example, the "tough battler" promotes win-lose confrontations where the losers quickly learn to disengage and avoid future bouts. The price of involvement paid in bruised feelings becomes too costly. On the other hand the "problem solver" maintains mutual respect and equality in the midst of conflict so that in the end all parties are satisfied with the outcome and relationships remain intact. You should not avoid conflict, ignore or smooth it over, but win-lose competition is inappropriate when the goal is win-win collaboration.

Harvey extends Filley's guidance for dealing with overt conflict by warning that you should not be deceived just because all is quiet on all fronts. Covert conflict, conflict that is masked by apparent agreement, can be just as detrimental. When subordinates seem to be overly playing the role Filley described as "the friendly-helper," the "yield-lose style," it is time for you to probe deeper to see if agreement is based only on a fear of rocking the boat.

Every manager required to use a standard evaluation instrument, be it a check-list or a more intricate numerical rating system, should be disturbed by Blake and Mouton's findings on employee appraisal. Such standardized evaluation techniques disrupt power sharing and produce lower levels of satisfaction than do individualized, mutually developed systems. The point is that one-sided evaluation with the manager in the lead can do serious damage to an otherwise productive relationship. Even though you may be forced to use a standard form, most likely you are not prohibited from building upon this tell-and-sell approach and creating a more give-and-take exchange which is compatible with your other involvement practices.

The data Hall presents in the final chapter points out the need for constant vigilance to maintain the benefits accrued from the involvement process. Participation must be encouraged constantly for continuing commitment—you must be sure the gate is always open to participation and, if necessary, subordinates may have to be ushered into the interpersonal arena. It is more than a matter of "allowing everyone to participate;" it is "encouraging and facilitating the participation of everyone." The success of the involvement process may well hinge on how often you ask a few simple questions—"What do you think?" "How do you feel about that?"—and do not accept silence as an answer.

Section V.

Group Dynamics:
The Setting for Competence

Many of the principles presented up to this point, from basic assumptions about individual productivity and working conditions to involvement strategies and interpersonal skills, come together in an applied way under the rubric of group dynamics. Groups are a dominant feature of organizational life—the team, task force, or committee is the predominant form of corporate interaction. It is in such settings that many managers will apply for the first time principles drawn from several managerial models. And the results in terms of group performance will be a significant measure of their competence.

A knowledge of group dynamics can help a manager maximize a group's capacity for excellence and avoid its well-publicized shortcomings. For years traditionalists have criticized groups as being detrimental to individualism and for the mediocre quality of their products. Everyone has heard the old saw about the camel being a horse put together by a committee. Much of this criticism, however, has been laid to rest by such observers as Dorwin Cartwright and Ronald Lippitt[1] and Douglas McGregor.[2] After surveying the available research, Cartwright and Lippitt observed that there were indeed potential liabilities inherent in group work but all were controllable. In much the same vein, McGregor concluded that there is nothing inherently good or inherently bad about groups—quite simply they function as their members make them function. More specifically, groups function the way their *managers* make them function.

MANAGING GROUP PRODUCTIVITY

Jay Hall takes up the issue of productivity in "Managing for Group Effectiveness" and presents solid evidence of what can ultimately be achieved through collaborative interaction. When managers insure the participation of other group members and allow them to utilize their interpersonal skills for sharing data and resolving differences, decisions will not only be of superior quality but will have the support necessary for implementation. Following chapters provide additional insights about the influence of group settings and how groups must be maintained to function competently.

Group settings have a powerful impact on individual behavior. In "Group Decision and Social Change," Kurt Lewin describes several studies which articulate the relationships between individuals and groups and which tell how social change occurs. Experiments conducted by Lewin and others indicate that, contrary to what might be expected, it is easier to change individuals in a group setting than it is to change an individual alone. Ironically, many practitioners of the behavioral sciences have inadvertently misinterpreted Lewin's position and direct their efforts at changing "groups." What Lewin says is that groups are a vehicle for change not a target for change. It is individuals who change, albeit more easily in a group setting. It is also apparent that certain techniques for change have much better chances for lasting success than others, and the manager who would be a change agent must understand the what, how and why of these techniques.

In their chapter, "Functional Roles of Group Members," Kenneth D. Benne and Paul Sheats delineate the roles individuals assume within groups with the intent of training members to improve group functioning. The diversity of roles implies that group-centered behavior is not an act-alike think-alike matter as critics claim. Ironically, one difficulty in developing group performance is getting members to expand their range of roles rather than forcing them to pursue a limited number of conventional behaviors. The emphasis in this chapter is on teaching individuals how to function effectively as group members rather than as group leaders, and the role-playing format employed should be of substantial value to managers.

Irving L. Janis adds to the understanding of group influence and techniques for diagnosing and treating group dysfunction in "Groupthink." He warns that groups with extreme esprit de corps are often poor at decision-making and problem-solving because members' needs to conform to the group impede their ability to function effectively. Some of the greatest disasters in our country's history have resulted from faulty group interaction—Vietnam, the Bay of Pigs, and Pearl Harbor. When stakes get high, stress on group members increases. Under these circumstances there is a tendency for group members to suppress their individual doubts and to charge on with single-minded purpose and narrow vision, considering few alternatives, ignoring non-supportive data, and harboring an illusion of invulnerability. Whether this occurs in high government office, the boardroom, or on the line in the assembly plant, disaster is inevitable.

To insure proper group functioning and to increase effectiveness, Leland P. Bradford and his colleagues provide practical guidelines in "How to Diagnose Group Problems." Managers need to pay constant attention to both how well the group is accomplishing its task and how well its members are working together. The authors provide over seventy indicators of group dysfunction relating to conflict, apathy, and inadequate decision-making. Analysis of these problem indicators by the group will point to practical solutions for improving group efficiency.

Managers should approach groups with optimism and caution. They are more powerful as sources for individual and corporate good than most managers realize, but like any power source they can suddenly become malevolent if not monitored closely. Maximizing the group's potential for constructive action is the responsibility for all group members, but the manager is in the best position to insure individual integrity, high quality products, and the continuing development of the group as a competent entity.

REFERENCES

1. Cartwright, Dorwin and Lippitt, Ronald. "Group Dynamics and the Individual." *International Journal of Group Psychotherapy, Vol.* 7, 1957, pp. 86-103.

2. McGregor, Douglas. *The Human Side of Enterprise.* New York: McGraw-Hill, 1967.

Chapter 22

Managing for Group Effectiveness

Jay Hall

To deny the very existence of groups used to be a common practice among managers. If one wanted to rattle the executive chain, all he needed was to suggest that many organizational decisions might more profitably be made by executive groups or manager-subordinate teams. Heresy! When aggressive independence and one-upsmanship were the trademarks of the executive on the move, to even hint that some form of committee action or coordination might be appropriate was a direct attack on all that was corporately holy.

Most managers have mellowed a bit by now; technology has become more complex and national goals have shifted. Lunar travel has opened the door for the project team and social critique has brought forth the task force. Most recently, word has come from several major corporations that the course of their organizational affairs is jointly determined by three to five top ranking executives...a committee...that heretofore maligned group credited with producing the camel while trying to build a horse! Fortunately, we are beginning to get back in touch with reality, to recognize that the issue is not *whether* to use groups in the decision process but *how* to use them effectively. By whatever name they are known, decision-making sessions involving two or more people are *group* decision events and subject to exactly the same processes which govern any productive human assembly.

While some suggest that too few of an organization's critical decisions are made in groups to warrant special attention, psychologist Bernard Bass has estimated that well over 74% may be made by sitting groups.[1,2] It's really immaterial *how many* occur within formal group settings. Regardless of how other decisions are reached, if the one at hand is important, we want it to be as creative, productive, and qualitatively sound as possible...and this frequently involves some form of group deliberation.

I favor the view that *most* decisions are made in settings which, although neither consciously intended nor recognized as such, possess all the dynamics of group problem-solving sessions. The casual consultation between manager and colleague which leads to a decision product...the chance exchange of information between boss and subordinate which produces a decision to take new action...the spontaneous coffee-break discussion of pertinent issues...these are all group decision sessions; they require enlightened management for optimum effectiveness.

Douglas McGregor's cogent analysis[3] bears repeating. *Groups function as their members make them function.* In organizations, groups also function as the *manager* makes them. An aware manager is an invaluable group member and obviously, it behooves him to learn as much as he can about group dynamics. As in most organizational instances, the manager strongly influences the operation of groups under his purview. But so many years have been spent denying the existence of groups and then defending against their formal inclusion in organization theory, most managers are ill-equipped to use the group vehicle effectively. Although *groups* of people decide upon and do most of an organization's work, they are perhaps the least understood factor in the corporate body.

But much is known about groups, their potentials and limitations, and about the conditions for effective *vs.* ineffective group functioning. Information about individual contributions, techniques of decision making, their effects on individual thinking and decision adequacy are available. It is perhaps a measure of the gap between the social scientist's productivity and the "practical" concerns of managers that, while no other area of human enterprise has received quite so much research attention as *group performance*, many managers are abysmally ignorant of the resultant social technology.

This need not be the case. To gain insight into the action steps necessary for effectiveness—an awareness of what is possible—merely requires a review of some salient features of group dynamics research. Drawing from my own and others' research in the area, we can lay out guidelines for group effectiveness, but it is up to the manager to put them to work; it is he who must supply the energy.

EXECUTIVE ACTION VERSUS GROUP DECISION

Traditional organizational values favor individual action and accountability. Often the most successful executive is the most self-sufficient, but individualism is a loaded issue in decision making: here we must challenge the "lone wolf" manager.

Research using decision tasks which are quantifiable shows that the *numerical average* of individual decisions *is superior to more than half* of the individual decisions which make up that average.[4] The axiom that "two heads are better than one" reflects this notion that the *probability* of obtaining a good decision is increased by using more people to make it; extreme judgments tend to cancel each other so that neither extremely good nor extremely bad judgments are reflected in the final decision. If the distribution of individual scores were normal, *i.e.*, if it followed the familiar bell curve, 50% of the individual scores would be better and 50% would be worse than the average score as shown in Figure 1:

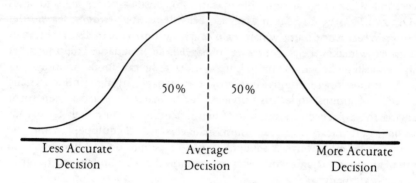

Figure 1. A normal distribution of individual decision products.

However, the discovery that the average decision is *superior* to more than half of the individual scores tells us that the distribution of individual scores is *not* what we might think. It is actually skewed in the direction of less accuracy; more than half of the individual decisions fall toward the inaccurate end of the scale as shown in Figure 2:

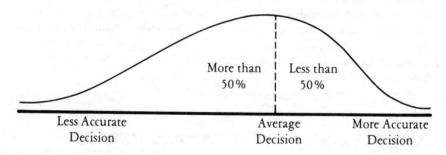

Figure 2. The negatively skewed distribution of individual decision products.

We see that, in terms of what we can expect on the basis of probabilities, an individual decision will be less accurate than a numerical average of a number of individual decisions *at least* 51% of the time...even in the face of executive expertise. The practical meaning of this fact is that if, from a group of top level executives we were to randomly choose *one* person's decision as the final position we would have *less* than a 50-50 chance of reaching the best decision possible.

Statistical averaging is group decision making in that more than one individual is taken into account, but group members need not have had contact with one another. Simple examples are decisions based on secret ballot counts or a majority of privately expressed preferences. An increase in decision adequacy, above and beyond that attributable to statistical considerations, seems to occur in groups when the decision makers actively discuss the pertinent issues. Decisions produced by groups which *interact* are most often better than the average of individual decisions. Moreover, the *manner* in which members interact is particularly important; the kind of decision making *procedure* employed by the group exerts significant influence on the quality of the final product...we all know that in some mismanaged situations, two heads are simply *more* than one.

Research in this area usually compares three kinds of decisions: (1) those made by individuals and/or a minority faction of the group, (2) those based on the support of a majority of the group members and (3) decisions based on equal support and agreement of the total group membership. The methods involved may be termed the *Minority Control Technique,* the *Majority Vote Technique,* and the *Democratic Technique.*

While it is difficult to find any of these procedures in their pure form, even under controlled conditions, we know that each has a different cause and effect relationship to group performance. Probabilities, as we discussed above, are loaded against the single individual making as good a decision as one reached by a greater percentage of the group membership...even when the individual is the leader or highest in the administrative hierarchy. The same is true for a small minority. Decisions resulting from the Minority Control Technique are usually less than adequate; the fewer the persons contributing to the decision, the more the final decision depends on individual competence. Remember, more than half of the individuals will be less accurate than the statistical average. Thus, chance works against the Minority Control Technique which is most often used to short-circuit conflict, overcome group inertia, and save time. Especially favored when there are power differences among members, the technique flies in the face of probability.

Superior to the Minority Control Technique in terms of decision adequacy, the Majority Vote Technique relies on the combined effects of statistical and interaction contributions. Since at least some interaction involving a majority of the group is necessary, many of the positive effects accruing from interaction are reflected in the final decision, but a portion of the benefits are still missing ...the outvoted minority is unable to exert its influence. As a rule, this mechanical technique is used to reduce or avoid altogether the conflict which results from differences of opinion. Unfortunately, those who are most accurate in their personal judgments often are most divergent from the prevailing view; it is difficult to determine in the heat of deliberations which members are simply off target and which possess genuinely unique and creative insights. Too often, we are too willing to forfeit our best resources in order to protect ourselves against our worst. This is the Achilles heel of majority rule.

The Democratic Technique represents a pattern of interaction designed to salvage all resources to the group, not just those which "sound on target." As an approach in which all group members share equally in the outcome, no decision becomes final which cannot meet with the general approval of each and every member. For this reason, the technique seems difficult to use and requires a fairly sophisticated understanding of conflict dynamics, interpersonal sensitivity, and the distribution and use of internal group power. It is definitely not designed to avoid conflict or bow to power and, because of this, has often been discounted by more autocratic managers as unfeasible. Research indicates, however, that the Democratic Technique results in better decisions than either Minority Control or Majority Vote[5], and we shall see later that it is neither impractical nor unworkable.

Figure 3 shows the relationship between the utilization of group resources and the probable adequacy of the end decision product, capturing the essence of the argument in favor of group decision making:

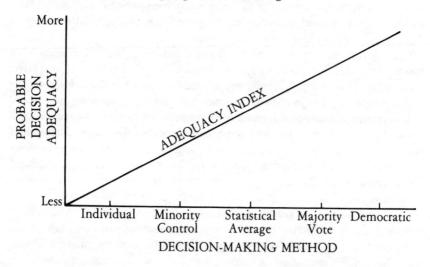

Figure 3. **The relative adequacy of different methods for utilizing group resources in decision making.**

In a nutshell, the adequacy of group-produced decisions reflects the contributions of *both* statistical and interaction effects. Because of sheer probability, using a group to reach a decision rather than depending on a single individual provides some degree of insurance that a more adequate decision will be reached. Interaction increases decision quality and the *type* of interaction determines the extent to which the group decision will benefit.

Managers are justifiably concerned about the quality of the decisions for which they will be held accountable, and we have found that they may take steps to insure decision quality by submitting the problem which requires a decision to the appropriate group *and then managing the ensuing interaction* consistent with the principles of effective action.

A MODEL OF GROUP ACTION

In group deliberations we have all seen one dominant member who, at the expense of others, presses consistently for closure and task completion. Monopolizing the group's air time, running roughshod over more tentative members, taking exception to disagreement and mustering personal attacks on those who remain unpersuaded, such task-oriented individuals value expertise and expediency over all else. And too, in the same group, there is invariably someone who tries to keep things from getting too personal or completely out of hand; skirting conflicts in favor of neutral topics, using humor and coffee break suggestions to alleviate tension, feigning agreement to promote peace and looking for the point of minimum disagreement, he seeks to serve the social needs of the group and promote a climate which will insure its continuation. Many groups operate according to such emergent role dictates, but they are not effective. They do, however, display the perennial symptoms of the group dilemma: the need to manage both task and social dynamics.

Barry Collins and Harold Guetzkow[6] have summarized an exhaustive review of group dynamics research in a model of group functioning. The model presented in Figure 4 identifies two major considerations for group effectiveness: to overcome the obstacles pertaining to the group's task goals and environment and to solve the problems flowing from the social system which characterizes the interaction.

To be effective, a group must find ways of successfully integrating task (A) and social-emotional (B) activities which have been triggered by the group's task requirements (1) and the interpersonal maneuverings which occur as the group gears itself for work (2). An interplay is set in motion between members' task-oriented behaviors and those responsive to interpersonal demands. Behaviors which serve only the task at hand may trigger difficulties at the interpersonal level; purely interpersonal contributions, despite their utility for maintaining the group as an entity, frequently leave task requirements to go begging. Neither facet may be ignored.

Achieving the necessary *integration* of task and social-emotional behaviors, not to mention an equal appreciation of both, is one of the major dilemmas confronting groups. It is also the single most difficult challenge facing individuals who want to manage for group effectiveness. Human proclivities often seem to contradict integrative logic. Indeed, some people have very definite preferences for either the task or the social domain; intuitively at least, they function on just one plane. R. F. Bales[7], after extensive study of hundreds of

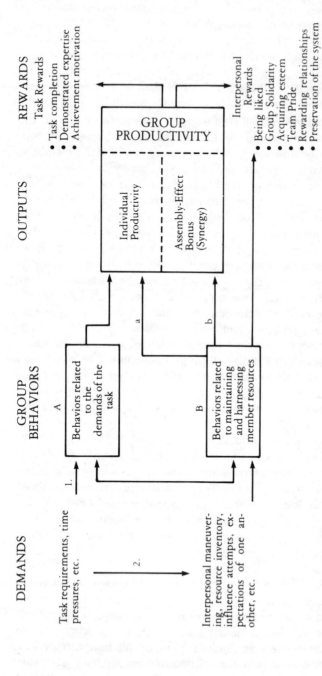

Figure 4. Working model of the decision-making group from B.E. Collins and H. Guetzkow: *A Social Psychology of Group Processes for Decision-Making*, John Wiley & Sons, 1964. (Reprinted by permission of the publisher.) Task demands trigger off (1) behaviors aimed at task completion and (2) interpersonal transactions aimed at gearing the system for action. An interplay is set in motion between (A) behaviors related to task and (B) behaviors related to interpersonal demands. A serves "Individual Productivity," directly, which in turn contributes to "Group Productivity." B serves both (a) Individual Productivity and (b) the achievement of Synergy, which in turn contribute to Group Productivity. Group Productivity is coordinated to the nature of the rewards accrued; these may be both, either-or, or neither task and interpersonal, depending on the nature of Group Productivity.

problem solving groups, concluded that virtually every group puts forth a Task Expert and a Social Expert and members align their contributions somewhere along task *vis-à-vis* social dimensions. Only rarely did he find an individual sensitive to and inclined to serve both concerns, causing him to label such a person "the Great Man" member. While my own research with the *Group Encounter Survey*[8,9], an index of decision style, has revealed that members' predispositions to behave in the service of task-social-integrative goals are rooted in quite different personality dynamics, other research, as we shall see later, reveals that such influences may be overcome through training so that all become capable of jointly serving task and social demands effectively.

The manager is more often than not the overseer of the group process, and it is essential for him to realize that *integrative behaviors can be learned.* His task in the search for group effectiveness is to make sure that a systematic and empirically valid ground rule prevails in his groups, rather than some dictate spawned from personal needs or left over from student government days replete with Robert's Rules of Order.

For the manager interested in optimal returns from the investment of group time, the objective must be one of achieving the integration called for by Collins and Guetzkow. Their model is explicit: group productivity is a joint function of individual task productivity and the synergistic effects which the group achieves out of its own deliberations. Only rarely does synergy occur if the group has failed to integrate its task and interpersonal processes. For this reason, the Collins-Guetzkow model ties individual productivity and synergy to the manner in which members *behave* interpersonally (B).

We must bear in mind that task demands differ from group to group and from organization to organization, that the kinds of expertise and knowledge required at the task level of functioning are for the most part problem specific. However, in the interpersonal network, the behaviors of people in groups are essentially the same regardless of group, organization, task or expertise. They reflect the human condition and amount to the one universal factor in group dynamics. They lend themselves to the construction of decision guidelines of the type required by those seeking to optimize.

We intend to propose just such a tested decision rule—a generic guideline which applies equally to groups of scientists, financial analysts, community volunteers and employees regardless of their technological background. The manager's objective becomes one of achieving the kind and quality of interaction among group members which will result in an integration of the group's task and social-emotional goals. A state of complementarity must be established wherein members serve task demands best by serving their own and others' social-emotional needs effectively.

Such a state requires behaviors and decision-making rules which differ from the social imperatives typically encountered in group settings; the effective group is filled with discordant notes and proceeds with its rules in grand disarray, giving the outward appearance of anything but an effectively functioning mechanism. Managing group effectiveness, therefore, also requires a tolerance for disorder if not a mistrust of pervasive harmony in human encounters. The ground rules set forth in this chapter should leave the concerned manager with definable options, specifiable causes and effects.

THE FOUR C'S OF GROUP EFFECTIVENESS

I am inclined to view group effectiveness as a function of *commitment, conflict, creativity* and *consensus*. Other approaches notwithstanding, a practical distillation of the research strongly suggests that commitment level and how it is achieved, conflict and how it is resolved, creativity and whether it emerges, and consensus as a decision rule incorporating all the former underlie and distinguish the effective group.

Commitment Via Involvement As A Social-Emotional Control

When members are basically indifferent to the group, when they are sluggish about following up on group decisions, they are exhibiting the most significant symptom of the ineffective group: lack of commitment. The enlightened manager recognizes such low levels of commitment to be the result of poor Gatekeeping within the group. Commitment, that highly personal feeling of attraction, belonging and ownership of the group ethos, is the force which holds a group together; it is a matter of feeling responsible for the well-being of the group and for taking the action steps required to implement group decisions and to achieve their attendent goals. In short, commitment is that psychological state which serves as an internalized guideline for each individual and manifests itself collectively in the form of concerted group effort. It cannot be achieved by coercion, persuasion, duplicity or unconditional positive regard. Commitment is self-generating and the natural consequence of involvement.

In discussing managerial Gatekeeping,[10] we focused on the desirability and importance of participation within the organization. In the decision-making group, effective Gatekeeping serves a number of functions from helping to operationalize egalitarian values via widespread interaction to insuring more uniform participation so that member resources are used to the best advantage. Figure 5 depicts the dramatic growth in commitment level, as a function of increased involvement.

Member participation and involvement enhance commitment to the group and its products, at the same time increasing the likelihood that members will see the group as a source of important social rewards. Employees are then more inclined to follow words with definitive action in support of group goals. Commitment, therefore, is a *control mechanism* for the manager at the social-emotional level—not in the usual sense of externally imposed controls, but in terms of internalized personal guidance systems which members use as a basis for relating to, and on behalf of, the group.

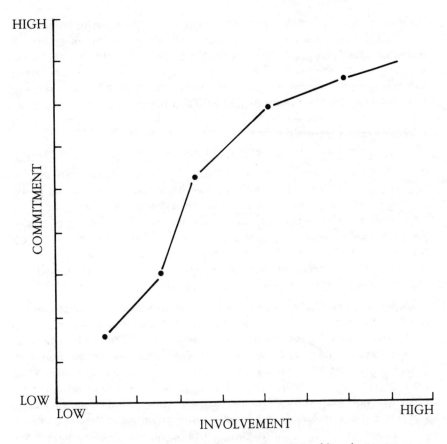

Figure 5. Growth of commitment as a function of involvement.

In the effective group, every member—not just the leaders or elected parliamentarians—attends to others' needs for involvement as well as his own. There is a sensitivity to silence; lack of participation is taken as anything but agreement. To create openings for others to enter deliberations, to prod retrenched members, and to support the tentative are social imperatives. As commitment is pursued, however, we must expect to encounter—indeed, unleash—difficulties at the task level.

Conflict And It's Task-Emotional Significance

With widespread and freewheeling participation comes a vast array of divergent ideas and values. Disagreement about definitions of and strategies for reaching goals, interpersonal grievances, and collisions of values begin to surface. Latent conflict comes to the level of group awareness and must be openly dealt with; it is welcomed, even sought out by the effective group. Conflicts and their underlying causes are prognostic for the quality of group performance. Many groups pay lip service to the participative ethic but are unwilling to deal with the emerging conflict. The effective group, on the other hand, values heightened interaction as much for its conflict surfacing properties as for its social-emotional contributions. The *meaning* which conflict holds for group members and the *manner* in which it is handled distinguish effective from ineffective group functioning.

To the effective group, conflict indicates that there is less than optimal sharing of the group frame of reference; it is treated as a symptom of unarticulated rationales or latent feelings from which, once verbalized, the group may profit. Getting to the bottom of conflicts, drawing out deviant opinions to be tested for feasibility and seriously attending to far-out insights usually spark a reappraisal of group thinking—group positions are revised and performance enhanced. The effective group has a tolerance for conflict; to "clear the air," differences are encouraged and worked through, increasing the likelihood that end products will reflect the contributions of all.

Ineffective groups, on the other hand, tend to view conflict as inherently unhealthy; emergent differences either frustrate the group's need for expediency or threaten the social fabric of member relationships. There is often an unarticulated feeling that speedy resolution of task demands is a sine qua non of effective functioning and anything, particularly a dissenting point of view, which frustrates closure is seen as detrimental to the group. At the same time, there is often a pervasive expectancy that relationships among members are so tenuous and fragile that they cannot stand the strain of prolonged differences without risking a disruption of the entire group. As a result, many groups have developed skillful ground rules for suppressing, smoothing over, tabling or circumventing altogether any conflict which does emerge. One group may have an unofficial "peace-maker" while another invokes the sanctity of majority rule, encouraging its minority to acquiesce, implying that "your time will come." Most frequently, the topic under discussion is simply abandoned in favor of a less controversial issue. In any event conflicts remain unresolved, to fester and perhaps worsen over time, while member commitment and task performance deteriorate.

My colleagues and I have explored the treatment of conflict at both the individual and group levels. Not only are suppressive, withdrawal and compromising conflict resolving strategies associated at the individual level with dysfunctional personality traits, such approaches also seriously deter functioning at the group level. Consequently, there is slim chance that the group will find itself wholeheartedly committed to an excellent decision product. More than likely, it will end up halfheartedly committed to an inferior product, virtually uncommitted to a questionable product or moderately committed to mediocrity. Groups which allow their concern for harmony to preempt their concern for the task, those in which the contributions of only a small but articulate minority are allowed to override the ideas and feelings of the majority are not managing conflict; they are being managed by it. The same may be said of compromise. Groups which prefer to engage in any of these practices, or see them as the only options available, are less than effective.

In 1966 Martha Williams and I conducted a study of decision making in *ad hoc* and established executive groups which yielded graphic support for the critical nature of conflict management.[11] Not only did we find established groups superior in performance to *ad hoc* groups, we found the bulk of their superiority to occur when groups had a high potential for conflict.

In both research and consultative settings we use a group decision-making task in which average or pooled individual scores may be taken as a base line for assessing group performance following discussion. By measuring the pre-discussion resources available to a group, computing the accuracy of the average individual decision and comparing this with the final group discussion-produced decision we can assess a group's decision-making skills. Changes in quality from pre- to post-discussion products are taken as an indication of the effect group

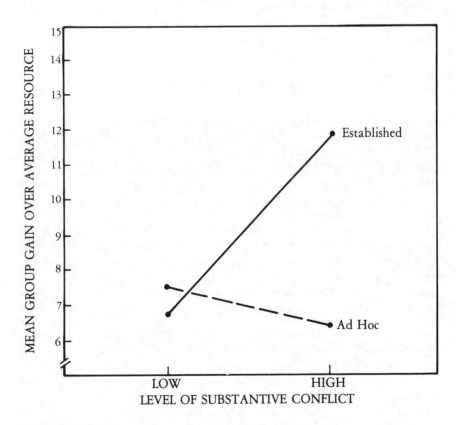

Figure 6. Mean gain-loss scores for established and ad hoc groups as a function of level of substantive conflict.

discussion has had on performance. In addition, the content of the decision task may be statistically analyzed to indicate the degree of inherent conflict potential.

In our study, established groups, with their time-tested intragroup norms and activated skills, excelled under conditions of high conflict, while the temporarily convened *ad hoc* groups literally went to pieces as depicted in Figure 6. The decisions reached by *ad hoc* groups are not only impeded by conflict, but limited by the quality of their pre-discussion resources; groups with a good knowledge base did pretty well, those lacking in task expertise not so well. *No such limiting effect* was apparent in established groups; they improve *most* when their initial resources are least good. Moreover, established groups profit, while *ad hoc* groups appear to suffer, from judgments fostered by the discussion.

We began to see that conflict and its management have, in addition to their expected impact on social-emotional functioning, rather startling implications for task performance. Indeed, it began to appear that *conflict in groups constitutes a necessary pre-condition for the awakening of creative insights.* The management of conflict then becomes the determining factor in whether or not creativity potential is capitalized upon.

Creativity From The Springboard Of Conflict

The initial results of our study prompted us to examine more closely group performance under high conflict conditions. We found in both type groups that the more diverse the pre-discussion individual decisions, the greater the tendency for groups to produce and incorporate in their final decisions judgments not held previously by any member; *i.e., emergent judgments.* While there is no appreciable difference between *ad hoc* and established groups as far as the *frequency* of emergent judgments under conflict conditions is concerned, there is definitely a difference in the *quality* of such decisions. Judgments produced by *ad hoc* groups are consistently inferior to the average individual resource available; by contrast, those fashioned by established groups are consistently superior to such resources. This dramatic qualitative difference is portrayed in Figure 7. Differences in decision quality are pronounced under conditions of high conflict, while low conflict exerts relatively little influence.

It seems that established groups, with a history of interaction and a relatively stable basis of social-emotional ties, sieze upon conflict and see it as an opportunity for creative problem solving. *Ad hoc* groups, on the other hand, appear to feel that conflict is a serious threat to the continuation of the group; they seek out and incorporate decisions about which no one feels strongly one way or another, thereby completing the task while dispatching the conflict with little risk of offense. Their final decision, of course, lies somewhere between pure compromise and a lose-lose resolution strategy; task performance is certainly

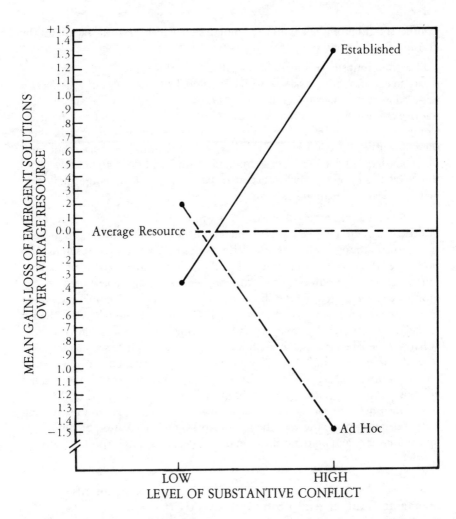

Figure 7. Quality of emergent judgments as a function of amount of conflict in established and ad hoc groups.

affected adversely and there is good reason to expect commitment to suffer as well.

There are many standing committees and ongoing executive conclaves in modern organizations which function like our *ad hoc* groups. Mismanagement prevents that final coalescence which characterizes the effective group and conflicts are skirted as threats to the social fabric of the executive suite. Since there is a certain appeal and comfort associated with the familiar, conflict may so intimidate members that they resist reevaluating opinions. But, according to Kelley and Thibaut,[12] individuals are likely to re-examine personal assumptions *only* when they become aware that their opinions differ from others'.

Conflict should promote a tentative opinion state which, in turn, facilitates the decision flexibility necessary for creativity.

Effective groups have a learned tolerance of conflict and see it as an opportunity to enhance both task and social-emotional functioning rather than as a personal issue with ego-maintenance properties. Disagreement retains its substantive essence, and does not degenerate to emotion-laden issues of right *vs.* wrong or me *vs.* you. Effective groups seem to recognize intuitively that where there is conflict there is a need for a closer examination of existing inputs and for more data. Out of such re-examinations and additions frequently come those "aha!" insights which, once articulated, have a compelling quality of logic and lead to creativity as well.

So it is that a group may *create* insights which, despite their zero probability of occurrence, are reviewed and ultimately incorporated into the group decision. When groups manage conflict effectively, they not only measurably improve over their base line resources, but they often outperform their *best* resource, creating resources above and beyond anything represented in the group. We have touted the possibility of tapping the collective unknown when interpersonal competence is at a high level; Collins and Guetzkow[13] called it the assembly effect bonus and others have termed it the synergistic effect.[14] Whatever the label, it is that end product of the creative process which is higher in quality than could have been predicted from any of the member resources; it is due to a unique marriage of existing and emergent resources such that the net effect is greater than either the sum of individual efforts or talents of the most skilled member. The synergistic effect is equally available to all groups; its realization depends upon the way the group works, on the creation of conditions for commitment and on the utilization of conflict as a springboard to creativity.

Consensus As A Decision Rule For Achieving Commitment, Managing Conflict And Promoting Creativity

As cited at the outset, group effectiveness appears to be coordinated with commitment and the way it is achieved, conflict and the way it is managed, and creativity and whether it emerges. Underlying and facilitating these three factors are group norms which set the group's performance goal and prescribe the strategy for reaching that goal. Synthesizing our own and numerous other research findings, Dr. Williams and I found that groups perform most effectively when:

1. Democratic or "collaborative" leadership is employed so that:
    a. the interpersonal climate will be relatively free of power-based constraints;
    b. all members feel that they share equally in opportunities for influencing the direction of group effort;

   c. there is opportunity for "emergent" leadership based on relevant expertise and group needs.

2. Flexible patterns of communication are used so that:
   a. all members are able to participate equally and at will;
   b. minority opinions are encouraged and, consequently, more likely to be voiced.

3. A cooperative problem-solving approach to discussion is employed rather than a competitive "win-lose" approach, so that:
   a. disagreements may be viewed as substantive rather than affective and, therefore tolerated;
   b. individuals become more sensitive to the ideas and reactions of others.

4. Members deal openly and candidly with one another so that:
   a. "hidden agendas" or personal needs do not distort the handling of the task;
   b. feelings of resistance or doubt can be discussed and resolved at the time they are experienced, rather than remaining latent barriers to commitment.

5. Decision techniques which favor a sharing of responsibility via a protection of individual rights are used, rather than techniques which place the responsibility clearly in the hands of but a portion of the group membership, so that:
   a. all share equally the burden of performing the necessary task and social-maintenance functions required by the above actions;
   b. all members feel a sense of responsibility for group success.

Such conditions provide for that integration deemed so important by Collins and Guetzkow. Not only is the group able to capitalize upon the cancellation-of-individual-errors effect, it also gains the opportunity to explore emergent and creative insights as well. It is better able to meet task demands because equal participation and flexible communication patterns foster an increased number of resources. Interpersonal and group maintenance issues can now receive greater attention because there is an implicit need to guard against conformity, dominance, withdrawal, etc.

Guided by the combined wisdom reflected in previous research, we undertook additional studies to identify the *behavioral contributions* needed to create the conditions for group effectiveness.[15] The ultimate objective was to operationalize the behaviors, to formulate a prescriptive decision rule. Our first study involved two weeks of laboratory training in group dynamics for thirty groups—ten each composed of college students, business executives, and hospitalized neuropsychiatric patients. The training was an intervention technique to make the subjects aware of the forces operating in groups and to render them at least somewhat philosophically committed to achieving the conditions for group effectiveness. The performance of these groups on a decision-making task was compared with that of thirty untrained control groups representing the same three populations. As we expected, the trained groups significantly out-performed their untrained counterpart groups in every major area of group functioning.

In addition, 50% of the trained groups out-performed their best individual resource; the remaining groups did not differ significantly from the best individual decision score. Only 13% of the untrained groups achieved such a synergistic effect, and the rest performed significantly less well than their highest members. The most dramatic support for a conscious attempt to use effective process is the fact that the ten trained neuropsychiatric groups outperformed the ten untrained groups composed of business executives in spite of the superiority of the executives' pre-discussion resources. Trained NP groups made up their initial resource deficit and, in final decision quality, surpassed the untrained executives by an accuracy margin of about 25%!

We confirmed some data-based inferences by observation and found that members of trained groups *behave* quite differently from those of untrained groups in a number of ways...they resist pressures to converge and agree prematurely...they promote discussion and conflict when there is none apparent... they actively press for involvement of the total group...they studiously avoid mechanical rules such as majority vote or bargaining to resolve differences... and above all else, they firmly expect their group to excel at its task. Untrained groups for the most part pursue just the opposite path.

On the basis of these observations, it became possible to think in prescriptive terms regarding member contributions in the service of effective group functioning. First, a decision rule identified as *consensus* was postulated: *No judgment may be incorporated into the group decision until it meets at least with the tacit approval of every member.* This is not a ground rule of unanimity, wherein each person is in total agreement; it means that one can "live with" the judgment or is at least willing to try it out. As a minimal condition for group movement, our operational definition of consensus is facilitated by the following prescribed behaviors:

1. Avoid arguing for your own position. Present it as lucidly and logically as possible, but be sensitive to and consider seriously the reactions of the group in any subsequent presentations of the same point.

2. Avoid "win-lose" stalemates in the discussion of opinions. Discard the notion that someone must win and someone must lose in the discussion; when impasses occur, look for the next most acceptable alternative for all the parties involved.

3. Avoid changing your mind only in order to avoid conflict and to reach agreement and harmony. Withstand pressures to yield which have no

objective or logically sound foundation. Strive for enlightened flexibility; but avoid outright capitulation.

4. Avoid conflict-reducing techniques such as the majority vote, averaging, bargaining, coin-flipping, trading out and the like. Treat differences of opinion as indicative of an incomplete sharing of relevant information on someone's part, either about task issues, emotional data, or "gut-level" intuitions.

5. View differences of opinion as both natural and helpful rather than as a hindrance in decision making. Generally, the more ideas expressed, the greater the likelihood of conflict will be; but the richer the array of resources will be as well.

6. View initial agreement as suspect. Explore the reasons underlying apparent agreements; make sure people have arrived at the same conclusions for either the same basic reasons or for complementary reasons before incorporating such opinions into the group decision.

7. Avoid subtle forms of influence and decision modification; e.g., when a dissenting member finally agrees, don't feel that he must be "rewarded" by having his own way on some subsequent point.

8. Be willing to entertain the possibility that your group can achieve all the foregoing and actually excel at its task; avoid doomsaying and negative predictions for group potential.

Such a decision rule increases the probability that all resources available to the group as well as new discussion-stimulated insights will in fact surface.

In physiology, the term *consensus* refers to information gained by combining the data from more than one sense. For instance, taste in conjunction with smell yields a third quality which we call flavor. So it is in the current sense. If several of our points sound perilously close to compromise, we must keep in mind that neither taste nor smell yields to the other in producing flavor; flavor is a combined function of and qualitatively different from each. By the same token when viewed from the perspective of a group's total membership, all of the above listed behaviors set in motion a series of checks and balances which yield uniform participation, flexibility, acceptable (if not optimal) levels of commitment, confronting and working-through approaches to conflict and increased likelihood of creativity—all consistent with the consensual objective.

Moreover, the consensus decision rule embodies most of the principles embedded in the structure of management competence. Gatekeeping behaviors, in keeping with the best sense of involvement and the participative ethic are implicit in its instructions. The candid sharing of facts and feelings, concurrent sensitivity to others' needs to contribute and the probing resource-seeking behaviors which comprise interpersonal competence are well represented. Shared power is insured, thus creating conditions for joint deliberation among all members. Checks and balances limit ego striving, deal with comfort seeking, prevent conformist ingratiation and appeal to needs for challenge and creative enterprise. Traditional conflict and agreement management issues are addressed operationally. The practical thrust of much of our emerging social technology is summarized in the consensus prescription.

In a study to test the utility of the consensus technique, W.H. Watson and I asked sixteen groups of executives to perform the NASA Moon Survival decision task according to its provisions.16 We compared the instructed groups' performance with that of sixteen uninstructed executive groups who were left to their own intuitive devices in dealing with the task. In general, the instructed groups reported little difficulty in adhering to the decision rules of consensus, while uninstructed groups generally relied on a majority rule approach. In terms of decision quality, instructed groups produced superior decisions; in

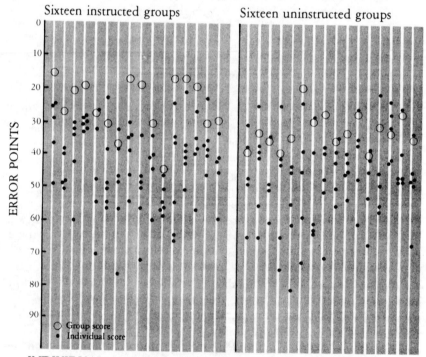

INDIVIDUAL AND GROUP SCORES. Given Group-Decision instructions, 75 per cent of groups did better than their best individuals. Only 25 per cent of uninstructed groups improved on the scores of their best members. Best possible score is 0, worst is 112.

Figure 8. Summary of group and individual performances.

terms of creativity, 75% of the instructed groups outperformed their best individual resource while this effect was achieved by only 25% of the uninstructed groups. A content analysis of group products revealed that the major portion of instructed group superiority could be traced to the quality of judgments which *emerged* from group discussion in spite of their zero probability of occurrence. This is creativity exemplified. Our results are summarized in the scatter plot presented in Figure 8.

Paul Nemiroff and Don King,[17] of Purdue University, replicated our study in 1975, adding a new dimension to further test the efficacy of the consensus rule. Using the same task and decision instructions, they composed their experimental groups according to the degree of self-orientedness of group members. Self-orientedness is recognized to be dysfunctional to group process because of its individualistic properties and self-centered goal seeking potentials; as a rather serious "interpersonal obstacle" one would expect it to limit idea sharing in groups and to contribute to impulse driven win-lose conflicts.

Nemiroff and King expected self-orientedness to be too strong a personality influence to overcome with simple consensus decision rules. They gave consensus instructions to one half of the groups high in self-orientedness and the other half were not instructed; by the same token, half of the low self-oriented groups received instruction and the rest were uninstructed. Nemiroff and King discovered the power of the consensus decision rule.

As in the Hall and Watson study,[18] groups with consensus instructions outperformed uninstructed groups on all measures of group effectiveness. The uninstructed groups used almost twice as much bargaining and trading and, according to self-reports and third party observations, relied significantly on majority rule. Moreover, 72% of the consensus groups achieved synergy as compared with only 33% of the uninstructed groups in spite of the effects of a counterproductive personality trait. Groups of high *versus* low self-orientedness *differed significantly only in the absence of consensus instructions* and then primarily in terms of the decision processes they employed; the effect of this was found to impact group synergy.

In Figure 9, we have plotted the average synergy scores for instructed *vs.* uninstructed groups as a function of self-orientation. The facilitative effect of the consensus decision rule for both personality groups is obvious as, by way of contrast, is the degree of interference of personality effects in the absence of such a guideline. While self-oriented instructed groups did less well than their selfless counterparts, *both instructed groups* achieved synergy. When left to their own devices, self-oriented groups do not even come close to their best resource while those low in this trait approach but fail to reach the output potential of their best resource. If we recall that self-orientedness is reinforced and conditioned by many "lone wolf" corporate cultures, such data serve to re-emphasize the advisability of adopting the consensus decision rule.

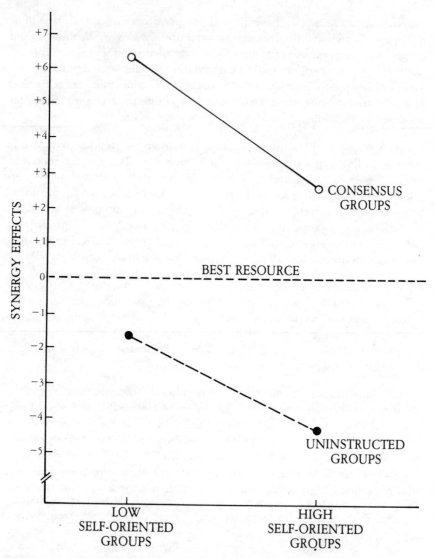

Figure 9. The effects of consensus instructions on creativity in groups composed of either self-centered or more collaborative people.

EXECUTIVE ACTION RECONSIDERED

Studies of the type discussed have been replicated numerous times in training seminars and in actual organizational decision-making sessions. I have witnessed the making of major corporate decisions according to the constraints of the consensus rule and invariably the outcomes have been superior to the initial inclinations of group members.

In one instance, a particularly courageous Executive Vice President held his staff and colleagues to a consensual ground rule in the choice of a new plant location in Europe; vastly different rationales for site priorities came to light and the final emergent decision saved a truly considerable sum. In another and most unlikely case, a small company in need of a huge crane and not able to bear the retail expense, assembled a group of its own engineers who were, employing the consensus rules, able to design and build it.

Model assembly procedures have been worked out by the automotive industry on the basis of consensus and mental patients have administered their own ward government according to the process. The process works when managers have the courage to apply it.

But there are always pressures to the contrary. As we noted at the outset, traditional organization theory is founded on a premise of accountability and control. The modern manager is perhaps more aware of this than anyone else, for it is he who is held accountable for both the performance of those he manages and the quality of the decisions underlying that performance. Quite rightly he is concerned that the decisions influencing him and his employees be the best decisions possible. Consensus represents a form of insurance that decisions will in fact be of a superior nature, even when the manager might feel more comfortable going it alone.

It is axiomatic that good decisions badly implemented are for naught. This is a commitment phenomenon and one that is aptly controlled for in the consensus process. In the final analysis the personal and private decisions which individuals subscribe to will dictate and guide their attempts at implementation. Kelly and Thibaut[19] have described the group decision process from the vantage point of the individual member as composed of (1) the formation of a personal private judgment, followed by (2) public discussion and varying expressions of personal views, resulting in (3) a public subscription to a collective "group" decision, ending in (4) a personal reformulation and subscription to a final private judgment. It is this latter decision phase over which the manager has least control but upon which he is most dependent for the success of his enterprise. If his employees, for example, buy in to the ostensible decision content of the manager's or group's decision, good implementation will likely follow. If on the other hand they are really unpersuaded, less than optimal follow-up can be expected. Neither coercion nor appeasement will prove successful in upgrading either the quality or commitment associated with those private final decisions to which group members cling in their work. But consensus does.

Because we recognized the potential for the "hidden" pitfalls residing in peoples' phase 4 processes, we decided to explore the effects of the consensus process in group encounters on individual post-discussion private judgments. Do they *really* subscribe to the superior decisions produced from the group deliberations or do they tend to regress to their own initially held private opinions? The answer to this question obviously has a lot to say about executive apprehensions over accountability.

We studied only twelve groups composed of 65 people. These groups were first asked to render individual decisions, then group decisions according to consensus followed by a third final private decision. Insofar as group performance was concerned, we found our usual consensus-related effects: groups improved significantly over their average base line decision adequacy and 67% — eight out of twelve—achieved synergy. Our interest this time, however, lay with the 65 individuals and we paid particular attention to the quality of their pre- as compared to their post-discussion decision accuracies. Our results were comforting. All but four of the 65 individual managers increased their personal private decision accuracy after the consensus experience...and significantly so. An average increase of 37% in individual decision accuracy was recorded for the 65 managers and even the most accurate members shared this bonus. In effect, not only were members found to subscribe in private to the essence of the group-produced decision, but in some instances they improved to a point superior to the group; in short, managers were smarter regarding the task at hand when they finished the consensus session than they were when they began it!

In the final analysis, it is the manager who will decide whether he wishes to take advantage of the benefits described in these pages. In many respects the issue becomes an exercise in trust...a trust of the capabilities and resources possessed by others and faith in the process designed to unleash these so that they might be incorporated in a decision product. In other respects, the issue is one of managerial competence for it is the manager who must manage for group effectiveness. The social technology exists and it has been demonstrated to work. The decision to *use* the technology is perhaps the only one the manager must truly make alone.

REFERENCES

1. Bass, B.M., McGregor, D.W., and Walters, J.L.: Selecting foreign plant sites: Economic, social and political considerations. Unpublished manuscript, 1976.

2. Bass, B.M.: Group decisions. In "Comments," *American Psychologist*, 1977, pp. 230-231.

3. McGregor, D.: *The Human Side of Enterprise*. New York: McGraw-Hill, 1967.

4. Gurnee, H.: A comparison of collective and individual judgments of fact. *Journal of Experimental Psychology*, 1937, *21*, pp. 106-112.

5. Barnlund, D.C.: A comparative study of individual, majority, and group judgment. *Journal of Abnormal Social Psychology*, 1959, *58*, pp. 55-60.

6. Collins, B., and Guetzkow, H.: *A Social Psychology of Group Processes for Decision-making*. New York: Wiley, 1964.

7. Bales, R.F.: The equilibrium problem in small groups. In T. Parsons, R.F. Bales, and E.A. Shils, *Working Papers in the Theory of Action*. Glencoe, Ill.: Free Press, 1953.

8. Hall, J., O'Leary, V., and Williams, M.S.: The decision-making grid: A

model of decision making styles. *California Management Review,* 1964 (winter), pp. 43-53.

9. Hall, J., and Williams, M.S.: Personality and group encounter style: A multivariate analysis of traits and preferences. *Journal of Personality and Social Psychology,* 1971, *18*(2), pp. 163-172.

10. Hall, J.: *Systems Maintenance: Gatekeeping and the Involvement Process.* The Woodlands, Texas: Teleometrics International, 1969.

11. Hall, J., and Williams, M.S.: A comparison of decision-making performances in established and ad hoc groups. *Journal of Personality and Social Psychology,* 1966, *3*(3), pp. 214-222.

12. Kelly, H.H., and Thibaut, J.W.: Experimental studies of group problem solving and process. In G. Lindzey (Ed.), *Handbook of Social Psychology.* Cambridge, Mass: Addison-Wesley, 1954, pp. 746-747.

13. Collins, B., and Guetzkow, H.: *Op. cit.*

14. Hall, J., and Watson, W.H.: The effects of a normative intervention on group decision-making performance. *Human Relations,* 1970, *23*(4), pp. 299-317.

15. Hall, J., and Williams, M.S.: Group dynamics training and improved decision making. *Applied Behavioral Science,* 1970, *6*(1), pp. 39-68.

16. Hall, J., and Watson, W.H.: *Op. cit.*

17. Nemiroff, P., and King, D.: Group decision-making performance as influenced by consensus and self-orientation. *Human Relations,* 1975, *28*(1), pp. 1-21.

18. Hall, J., and Watson, W.H.: *Op. cit.*

19. Kelly, H.H., and Thibaut, J.W.: *Op. cit.*

Chapter 23

Group Decision and Social Change

Kurt Lewin

The following experiments on group decision have been conducted during the last four years. They are not in a state that permits definite conclusions. But they show the nature of the problems and the main factors concerned. They also indicate the type of concepts to which the attempt to integrate cultural anthropology, psychology, and sociology into one social science may lead.

Scientifically the question of group decision lies at the intersection of many basic problems of group life and individual psychology. It concerns the relation of motivation to action and the effect of a group setting on the individual's readiness to change or to keep certain standards. It is related to one of the fundamental problems of action-research, namely, how to change group conduct so that it would not slide back to the old level within a short time. It is in this wider setting of social processes and social management that group decision should be viewed as one means of social change.

SOCIAL CHANNELS AND SOCIAL PERCEPTION

The meaning and the over-all effect of a group decision depends upon the nature of the process itself, and upon the position of the group, within the total social field. In regard to these broader questions we will consider two aspects of social steering, namely, steering through gatekeepers and the function which reality perception should have.

From *Readings In Social Psychology,* Third Edition, by Editorial Committee Eleanore E. Maccoby, Theodore M. Newcomb, and Eugene L. Hartley. Copyright 1947, 1952, ©1958 by Holt, Rinehart and Winston, Inc. Reprinted by permission of Holt, Rinehart and Winston.

Channels, Gates, And Gatekeepers

Food Habits and Food Channels. The first experiment on group decision was part of a larger study on food habits. Its main objective was a comparison of different ethnic and economic groups in a midwestern town. The favorite family food was studied, what food was considered essential, what main frame of reference and values guided the thinking of these groups about foods, and what authorities were seen as standing behind these standards and values. Children at different ages were included to indicate the process of acculturation of the individual in regard to food. Since this study was part of a larger problem of changing food habits in line with war needs, we were interested in including an attempt to bring about some of the desired changes at least on a small scale.

The data acquired give considerable insight into the existing attitudes and practices of the various groups. However, in this, as in many other cases, such data about a present state of affairs do not permit many conclusions in regard to how to proceed best to bring about a change. Should one use radio, posters, lectures, or what other means and methods for changing efficiently group ideology and group action? Should one approach the total population of men, women, and children who are to change their food habits, or would it suffice and perhaps be more effective to concentrate on a strategic part of the population? Obviously the housewife plays some particular role in food habits. What are the underlying assumptions?

Food which comes to the family table is likely to be eaten by someone in the family since little is thrown away. If this is correct, to consider methods of changing family food habits we have first to ask: how does food come to the table?

Food comes to the table through different channels, such as the Buying Channel or the Gardening Channel.[1] After the food has been bought, it might be placed in the icebox or put in the pantry to be either cooked later or prepared directly for the table (Fig. 1). Similarly, the food moves through the garden channel in a step-by-step fashion.

To understand what comes on the table we have to know the forces which determine what food enters a channel. Whether food enters the channel to the family table or not is determined in the buying situation. The buying situation can be characterized as a conflict situation. Food 1 (Fig. 1) might be attractive, that is, the force (fP,EF) toward eating is large but at the same time the food might be very expensive and therefore the opposing force (fP,SpM) against spending money is large too. Food 2 might be unattractive but cheap. In this case the conflict would be small. The force toward buying might be composed of a number of components, such as the buyer's liking for the food, his knowledge of his family likes and dislikes, or his ideas about what food is "essential."

---

1. For quantitative data, see K. Lewin, "Forces Behind Food Habits and Methods of Change," *Bull. Nat. Res. Coun.*, 1943, CVIII, 35-65.

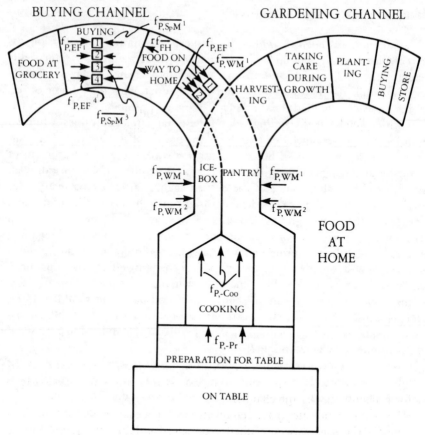

Figure 1. Channels through which food reaches the family table.

The opposing forces might be due to the lack of readiness to spend a certain amount of money, a dislike of lengthy or disagreeable form of preparation, unattractive taste, lack of fitness for the occasion, etc. Food is bought if the total force toward buying becomes greater than the opposing forces (Food 3) until the food basket is filled. Food of type 1 can be called conflict food.

It is culturally significant that the average conflict rating is considerably higher in the middle group (7.44) than in the high (4.35) or the low economic group (5.62). This conflict is probably the result of the greater discrepancy between the standards this group would like to keep up and their ability to do so in a situation of rising prices.

In comparing the conflict rating of different foods for the same group, one finds that meat stands highest for the low group, whereas it is second for the middle and third for the high economic group. That probably means that the conflict between "like" and "expense" in the low group is most outspoken for meat. The high conflict rating of vegetables for the high and middle economic group is probably an expression of the fact that vegetables are desirable as health food but not well liked and not easily prepared. The rates are:

Food	High group	Middle group	Low group
Vegetables	.89	1.44	.57
Milk	.70	.89	.33
Meat	.65	1.28	.95
Butter	.30	.94	.67
Fruits	.43	.94	.62
Potatoes	...	.33	.76

The Gate. It is important to know that once food is bought some forces change its direction. Let us assume the housewife has finally decided to buy the high conflict Food 1. The force against spending money, instead of keeping the food out of the channel, will then make the housewife doubly eager not to waste it. In other words, the force (fP, WM) against wasting money will have the same direction as the force toward eating this food or will have the character of a force against leaving the channel.

This example indicates that a certain area within a channel might function as a "gate": The constellation of the forces before and after the gate region are decisively different in such a way that the passing or not passing of a unit through the whole channel depends to a high degree upon what happens in the gate region. This holds not only for food channels but also for the traveling of a news item through certain communication channels in a group, for movements of goods, and the social locomotion of individuals in many organizations. A university, for instance, might be quite strict in its admission policy and might set up strong forces against the passing of weak candidates. Once a student is admitted, however, the university frequently tries to do everything in its power to help everyone along. Many business organizations follow a similar policy. Organizations which discriminate against members of a minority group frequently use the argument that they are not ready to accept individuals whom they would be unable to promote sufficiently.

The Gatekeeper. In case a channel has a gate, the dominant question regarding the movements of materials or persons through the channel is: who is the gatekeeper and what is his psychology?

The study of the high, middle, and low groups, as well as of a group of Czechs and of Negroes in a midwestern town, revealed that all channels except gardening were definitely controlled by the housewife.

We can conclude from this that changes of food habits in the family finally depend on changes of the psychology of the housewife in the buying situation. Changes of the attitudes and desires of children and husbands will affect actual food habits only to the degree they affect the housewife.

Similar considerations hold for any social constellation which has the character of a channel, a gate, and gatekeepers. Discrimination against minorities will not be changed as long as the forces are not changed which determine the decisions of the gatekeeper. Their decision depends partly on their ideology, that is, the system of values and beliefs which determines what they consider to be "good" or "bad," partly on the way they perceive the particular situation. This latter point will be considered more closely by discussing problems of planning.

Planning, Fact-Finding, And Execution

Planning usually starts with something like a general idea. For one reason or another it seems desirable to reach a certain objective. Exactly how to circumscribe this objective and how to reach it is frequently not too clear. The first step, then, is to examine the idea carefully in the light of the means available. Frequently more fact-finding about the situation is required. If this first period of planning is successful, two items emerge: an "over-all plan" of how to reach the objective and a decision in regard to the first step of action. Usually this planning has also somewhat modified the original idea.

The next period is devoted to executing the first step of the over-all plan. In highly developed fields of social management, such as modern factory management or the execution of a war, this second step is followed by certain fact-findings. For example, in the bombing of Germany a certain factory may have been chosen as the first target after careful consideration of various priorities and of the best means and ways of dealing with this target. The attack is pressed home and immediately a reconnaissance plane follows with the one objective of determining as accurately and objectively as possible the new situation (Fig. 2).

This reconnaissance or fact-finding has four functions: It should evaluate the action by showing whether what has been achieved is above or below expectation. It should serve as a basis for correctly planning the next step. It should serve as a basis for modifying the "over-all plan." Finally, it gives the planners a chance to learn, that is, to gather new general insight, for instance, regarding the strength and weakness of certain weapons or techniques of action.

The next step again is composed of a circle of planning, executing, and reconnaissance or fact-finding for the purpose of evaluating the results of the second step, for preparing the rational basis for planning the third step, and for perhaps modifying again the over-all plan.

Rational social management, therefore, proceeds in a spiral of steps each of which is composed of a circle of planning, action, and fact-finding about the result of the action.

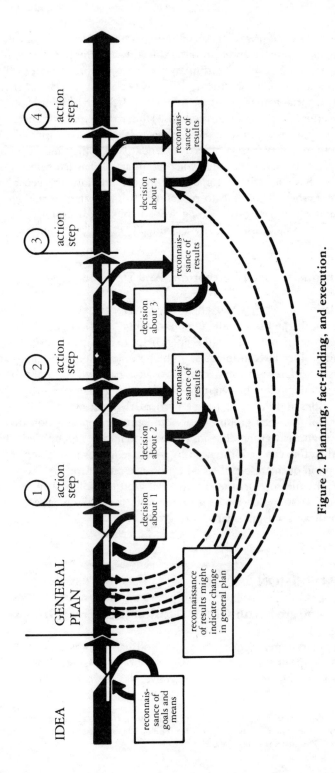

Figure 2. Planning, fact-finding, and execution.

In most social areas of management and self-management of groups, such as conducting a conference and committee meeting, family life, or the improvement of intergroup relations within and between nations, we are still lacking objective standards of achievement. This has two severe effects: (1) People responsible for social management are frequently deprived of their legitimate desire for reconnaissance on a realistic basis. Under these circumstances, satisfaction or dissatisfaction with achievement becomes mainly a question of temperament. (2) In a field that lacks objective standards of achievement, no learning can take place. If we cannot judge whether an action has led forward or backward, if we have no criteria for evaluating the relation between effort and achievement, there is nothing to prevent us from coming to the wrong conclusions and encouraging the wrong work habits. Realistic fact-finding and evaluation is a prerequisite for any learning.

Social Channels, Social Perception, And Decision

The relation between social channels, social perception and decisions is methodologically and practically of considerable significance.

The theory of channels and gatekeepers helps to define in a more precise way how certain "objective" sociological problems of locomotion of goods and persons intersect with certain "subjective" psychological and cultural problems. It points to sociologically characterized places, such as gates in social channels, where attitudes and decisions have a particularly great effect.

The relation between group decision and pre- and post-action diagnosis is twofold: (1) group decision depends partly upon how the group views the situation and therefore can be influenced by a change in this perception. (2) A correct perception of the result of social action is essential for the decision of the next step. The measurement of the effect of group decisions is in line with the need for objective evaluation as a prerequisite for making progress in social management and self management of groups.

GROUP DECISION

Lecture Compared With Group Decision (Red Cross Groups)

A preliminary experiment in changing food habits[2] was conducted with six Red Cross groups of volunteers organized for home nursing. Groups ranged in size from 13 to 17 members. The objective was to increase the use of beef

---

2. The studies on nutrition discussed in this article were conducted at the Child Welfare Research Station of the State University of Iowa for the Food Habits Committee of the National Research Council (Executive Secretary, Margaret Mead).

hearts, sweetbreads, and kidneys. If one considers the psychological forces which kept housewives from using these intestinals, one is tempted to think of rather deep-seated aversions requiring something like psychoanalytical treatment. Doubtless a change in this respect is a much more difficult task than, for instance, the introduction of a new vegetable such as escarole. There were, however, only 45 minutes available.

In three of the groups attractive lectures were given which linked the problem of nutrition with the war effort, emphasized the vitamin and mineral value of the three meats, giving detailed explanations with the aid of charts. Both the health and economic aspects were stressed. The preparation of these meats was discussed in detail as well as techniques for avoiding those characteristics to which aversions were oriented (odor, texture, appearance, etc.). Mimeographed recipes were distributed. The lecturer was able to arouse the interest of the groups by giving hints of her own methods for preparing these "delicious dishes," and her success with her own family.

For the other three groups Mr. Alex Bavelas developed the following procedure of group decision. Again the problem of nutrition was linked with that of the war effort and general health. After a few minutes, a discussion was started to see whether housewives could be induced to participate in a program of change without attempting any high-pressure salesmanship. The group discussion about "housewives like themselves" led to an elaboration of the obstacles which a change in general and particularly change toward sweetbreads, beef hearts, and kidneys would encounter, such as the dislike of the husband, the smell during cooking, etc. The nutrition expert offered the same remedies and recipes for preparation which were presented in the lectures to the other groups. But in these groups preparation techniques were offered after the groups had become sufficiently involved to be interested in knowing whether certain obstacles could be removed.

In the earlier part of the meeting a census was taken on how many women had served any of these foods in the past. At the end of the meeting, the women were asked by a showing of hands who was willing to try one of these meats within the next week.

A follow-up showed that only 3 percent of the women who heard the lectures served one of the meats never served before, whereas after group decision 32 percent served one of them (Fig. 3).

If one is to understand the basis of this striking difference, several factors may have to be considered.

1. *Degree of Involvement.* Lecturing is a procedure in which the audience is chiefly passive. The discussion, if conducted correctly, is likely to lead to a much higher degree of involvement. The procedure of group decision in this experiment follows a step-by-step method designed (*a*) to secure high involvement and (*b*) not to impede freedom of decision. The problem of food changes was discussed in regard to "housewives like yourselves" rather than in regard to themselves. This minimized resistance to considering the problems and possibilities in an objective, unprejudiced manner, in much the same way as such

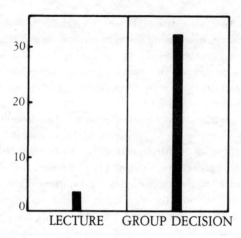

Figure 3. Percentage of individuals serving type of food never served before, after lecture and after group decision.

resistance has been minimized in interviews which use projective techniques, or in a socio-drama which uses an assumed situation of role playing rather than a real situation.

2. *Motivation and Decision.* The prevalent theory in psychology assumes action to be the direct result of motivation. I am inclined to think that we will have to modify this theory. We will have to study the particular conditions under which a motivating constellation leads or does not lead to a decision or to an equivalent process through which a state of "considerations" (indecisiveness) is changed into a state where the individual has "made up his mind" and is ready for action, although he may not act at that moment.

The act of decision is one of those transitions. A change from a situation of undecided conflict to decision does not mean merely that the forces toward one alternative become stronger than those toward the other alternative. If this were the case, the resultant force should frequently be extremely small. A decision rather means that the potency of one alternative has become zero or is so decidedly diminished that the other alternative and the corresponding forces dominate the situation. This alternative itself might be a compromise. After the decision people may feel sorry and change their decision. We cannot speak of a real decision, however, before one alternative has become dominant so far as action is concerned. If the opposing forces in a conflict merely change so that the forces in one direction become slightly greater than in the other direction, a state of blockage or extremely inhibited action results rather than that clear one-sided action which follows a real decision.

Lecturing may lead to a high degree of interest. It may affect the motivation of the listener. But it seldom brings about a definite decision on the part of the listener to take a certain action at a specific time. A lecture is not often conducive to decision.

Evidence from everyday experience and from some preliminary experiments by Bavelas in a factory indicate that even group discussions, although usually leading to a higher degree of involvement, as a rule do not lead to a decision. It is very important to emphasize this point. Although group discussion is in many respects different from lectures, it shows no fundamental difference on this point.

Of course, there is a great difference in asking for a decision after a lecture or after a discussion. Since discussion involves active participation of the audience and a chance to express motivations corresponding to different alternatives, the audience might be more ready "to make up its mind," that is, to make a decision after a group discussion than after a lecture. A group discussion gives the leader a better indication of where the audience stands and what particular obstacles have to be overcome.

In the experiment on hand, we are dealing with a group decision after discussion. The decision, itself, takes but a minute or two. (It was done through raising of hands as an answer to the question: Who would like to serve kidney, sweetbreads, beef hearts next week?) The act of decision, however, should be viewed as a very important process of giving dominance to one of the alternatives, serving or not serving. It has an effect of freezing this motivational constellation for action. We will return to this point later.

3. *Individual versus Group.* The experiment does not try to bring about a change of food habits by an approach to the individual, as such. Nor does it use the "mass approach" characteristic of radio and newspaper propaganda. Closer scrutiny shows that both the mass approach and the individual approach place the individual in a quasi-private, psychologically isolated situation with himself and his own ideas. Although he may, physically, be part of a group listening to a lecture, for example, he finds himself, psychologically speaking, in an "individual situation."

The present experiment approaches the individual as a member of a face-to-face group. We know, for instance, from experiments in level of aspiration[3] that goal setting is strongly dependent on group standards. Experience in leadership training and in many areas of re-education, such as re-education regarding alcoholism or delinquency,[4] indicates that it is easier to change the ideology and social practice of a small group handled together than of single individuals. One of the reasons why "group carried changes" are more readily brought about seems to be the unwillingness of the individual to depart too far from group standards; he is likely to change only if the group changes. We will return to this problem.

One may try to link the greater effectiveness of group decision procedures to the fact that the lecture reaches the individual in a more individualistic fashion

3. K. Lewin, "Behavior and Development as a Function of the Total Situation" in L. Carmichael (ed.), *Manual of Child Psychology* (New York: John Wiley, 1946), pp. 791-844.

4. K. Lewin and P. Grabbe (eds.), "Problems of Re-education," *J. Soc. Issues,* (August) 1945, 1, No. 3.

than group discussion. If a change of sentiment of the group becomes apparent during the discussion, the individual will be more ready to come along.

It should be stressed that in our case the decision which follows the group discussion does not have the character of a decision in regard to a group goal; it is rather a decision about individual goals in a group setting.

4. *Expectation.* The difference between the results of the lectures and the group decision may be due to the fact that only after group decision did the discussion leader mention that an inquiry would be made later as to whether a new food was introduced into the family diet.

5. *Leader Personality.* The difference in effectiveness may be due to differences in leader personality. The nutritionist and the housewife who did the lecturing were persons of recognized ability, experience, and success. Still, Mr. Bavelas, who led the discussion and subsequent decision, is an experienced group worker and doubtless of unusual ability in this field.

To determine which of these or other factors are important, a number of systematic variations have to be carried out. To determine, for instance, the role of the decision as such, one can compare the effect of group discussion with and without decision. To study the role of group involvement and the possibility of sensing the changing group sentiment, one could introduce decisions after both, lecture and discussion, and compare their effects.

The following experiments represent partly analytical variations, partly repetitions with somewhat different material.

Lecture Versus Group Decision (Neighborhood Groups)

Dana Klisurich, under the direction of Marian Radke, conducted experiments with 6 groups of housewives composed of 6-9 members per group. She compared the effect of a lecture with that of group decision. The topic for these groups was increasing home consumption of milk, in the form of fresh or evaporated milk or both.[5]

The procedure followed closely that described above. Again there was no attempt at high-pressure salesmanship. The group discussion proceeded in a step-by-step way, starting again with "what housewives in general might do" and only then leading to the individuals present. The lecture was kept as interesting as possible. The knowledge transmitted was the same for lecture and group decision.

A check-up was made after two weeks and after four weeks. As in the previous experiments, group decision showed considerably greater effectiveness, both after two weeks and after four weeks and for both fresh and evaporated milk (Figs. 4 and 5). This experiment permits the following conclusions:

1. It shows that the greater effectiveness of the group decision in the first

5. M. Radke and D. Klisurich, Experiments in Changing Food Habits. Unpublished manuscript.

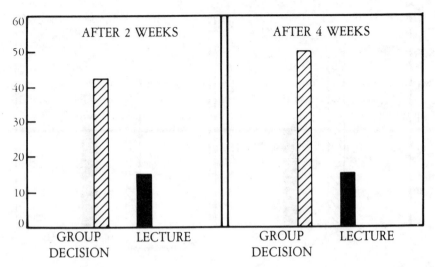

Figure 4. Percentage of mothers reporting an increase in the consumption of fresh milk.

experiment is not merely the result of the personality or training of the leader. The leader was a lively person, interested in people, but she did not have particular training in group work. She had been carefully advised and had had a try-out in the group decision procedure. As mentioned above, the leader in lecture and group decision was the same person.

2. The experiment shows that the different effectiveness of the two procedures is not limited to the foods considered in the first experiment.

3. It is interesting that the greater effectiveness of group decision was observable not only after one week but after two and four weeks. Consumption after group decision kept constant during that period. After the lecture it showed an insignificant increase from the second to the fourth week. The degree of permanency is obviously a very important aspect of any changes in group life. We will come back to this point.

4. As in the first experiment, the subjects were informed about a future check-up after group decision but not after the lecture. After the second week, however, both groups knew that a check-up had been made and neither of them was informed that a second check-up would follow.

5. It is important to know whether group decision is effective only with tightly knit groups. It should be noticed that in the second experiment the groups were composed of housewives who either lived in the same neighborhood or visited the nutrition information service of the community center. They were not members of a club meeting regularly as were the Red Cross groups in the first experiment. On the other hand, a good proportion of these

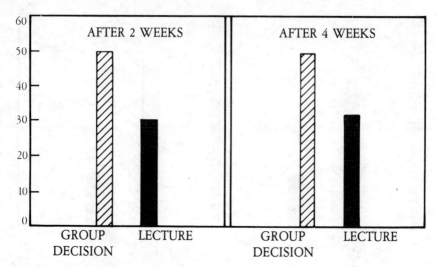

Figure 5. Percentage of mothers reporting an increase in the consumption of evaporated milk.

housewives knew each other. This indicates that decision in a group setting seems to be effective even if the group is not a permanent organization.

Individual Instruction Versus Group Decision

For a number of years, the state hospital in Iowa City has given advice to mothers on feeding of their babies. Under this program, farm mothers who have their first child at the hospital meet with a nutritionist for from 20-25 minutes before discharge from the hospital to discuss feeding. The mother receives printed advice on the composition of the formula and is instructed in the importance of orange juice and cod liver oil.

There had been indication that the effect of this nutrition program was not very satisfactory. An experiment was carried out by Dana Klisurich under the direction of Marian Radke to compare the effectiveness of this procedure with that of group decision.[6]

With some mothers individual instruction was used as before. Others were divided into groups of six for instruction on and discussion of baby feeding. The manner of reaching a decision at the end of this group meeting was similar to that used in the previous experiments. The time for the six mothers together was the same as for one individual, about 25 minutes.

After two weeks and after four weeks, a check was made on the degree to

6. M. Radke and D. Klisurich, Experiments in Changing Food Habits. Unpublished manuscript.

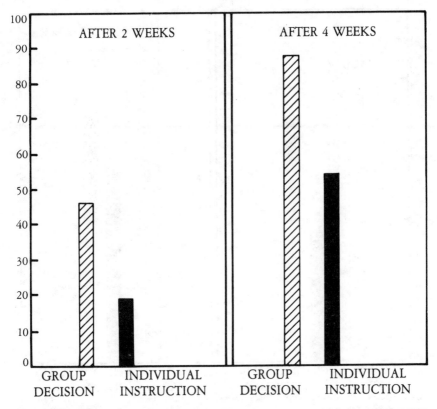

Figure 6. Percentage of mothers following completely group decision or individual instruction in giving cod liver oil.

which each mother followed the advice on cod liver oil and orange juice. Figures 6 and 7 show the percentage of individuals who completely followed the advice. The group decision method proved far superior to the individual instruction. After four weeks every mother who participated in group decision followed exactly the prescribed diet in regard to orange juice.

The following specific results might be mentioned:

1. The greater effect of group decision in this experiment is particularly interesting. Individual instruction is a setting in which the individual gets more attention from the instructor. Therefore, one might expect the individual to become more deeply involved and the instruction to be fitted more adequately to the need and sentiment of each individual. After all, the instructor devotes the same amount of time to one individual as he does to six in group decision. The result can be interpreted to mean either that the amount of individual involvement is greater in group decision or that the decision in the group setting is itself the decisive factor.

2. Most of the mothers were not acquainted with each other. They returned

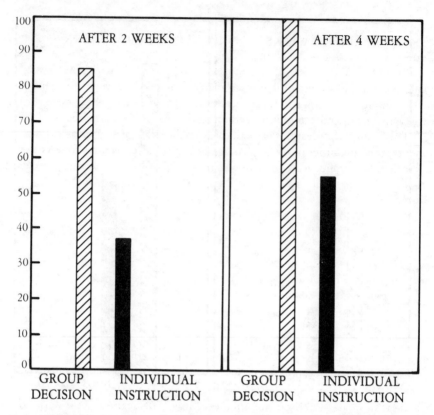

Figure 7. Percentage of mothers following completely group decision or individual instruction in giving orange juice.

to farms which were widely separated. Most of them had no contact with each other during the following four weeks. The previous experiment had already indicated that the effectiveness of group decision did not seem to be limited to well-established groups. In this experiment the absence of social relations among the mothers before and after the group meeting is even more clearcut.

3. The data thus far do not permit reliable quantitative, over-all comparisons. However, they point to certain interesting problems and possibilities. In comparing the various experiments concerning the data two weeks after group decision, one finds that the percentage of housewives who served kidneys, beef hearts or sweetbreads is relatively similar to the percentage of housewives who increased the consumption of fresh milk or evaporated milk or of mothers who followed completely the diet of cod liver oil with their babies. The percentages lie between 32 and 50. The percentage in regard to orange juice for the baby is clearly higher, namely, 85 percent. These results are surprising in several respects. Mothers are usually eager to do all they can for their babies. This may explain why a group decision in regard to orange juice had such a strong effect.

Why, however, was this effect not equally strong on cod liver oil? Perhaps, giving the baby cod liver oil is hampered by the mothers' own dislike of this food. Kidneys, beef hearts, and sweetbreads are foods for which the dislike seems to be particularly deep-seated. If the amount of dislike is the main resistance to change, one would expect probably a greater difference between these foods and, for instance, a change in regard to fresh milk. Of course, these meats are particularly cheap and the group decision leader was particularly qualified.

4. The change after lectures is in all cases smaller than after group decision. However, the rank order of the percentage of change after lectures follows the rank order after group decision, namely (from low to high), glandular meat, fresh milk, cod liver oil for the baby, evaporated milk for the family, orange juice for the baby.

The constancy of this rank order may be interpreted to mean that one can ascribe to each of these foods—under the given circumstances and for these particular populations—a specific degree of "resistance to change." The "force toward change" resulting from group decision is greater than the force resulting from lecture. This leads to a difference in the amount (or frequency) of change for the same food without changing the rank order of the various foods. The rank order is determined by the relative strength of their resistance to change.

5. Comparing the second and the fourth week, we notice that the level of consumption remains the same or increases insignificantly after group decision and lecture regarding evaporated or fresh milk. A pronounced increase occurs after group decision and after individual instruction on cod liver oil and orange juice, that is, in all cases regarding infant feeding. This seems to be a perplexing phenomenon if one considers that no additional instruction or group decision was introduced. On the whole, one may be inclined to expect weakening effect of group decision with time and therefore a decrease rather than an increase of the curve. To understand the problems involved, it is essential to formulate the question of condition of social change on a more theoretical level.

Quasi-Stationary Social Equilibria And The Problem Of Permanent Change

1. *The Objective of Change.* The objective of social change might concern the nutritional standard of consumption, the economic standard of living, the type of group relation, the output of a factory, the productivity of an educational team. It is important that a social standard to be changed does not have the nature of a "thing" but of a "process." A certain standard of consumption, for instance, means that a certain action—such as making certain decisions, buying, preparing, and canning certain food in a family—occurs with a certain frequency within a given period. Similarly, a certain type of group relations means that within a given period certain friendly and hostile actions and

reactions of a certain degree of severity occur between the members of two groups. Changing group relations or changing consumption means changing the level at which these multitude of events proceed. In other words, the "level" of consumption, of friendliness, or of productivity is to be characterized as the aspect of an ongoing social process.

Any planned social change will have to consider a multitude of factors characteristic for the particular case. The change may require a more or less unique combination of educational and organizational measures; it may depend upon quite different treatments or ideology, expectation and organization. Still, certain general formal principles always have to be considered.

2. *The Conditions of a Stable Quasi-stationary Equilibrium.* The study of the conditions for change begins appropriately with an analysis of the conditions for "no change," that is, for the state of equilibrium.

From what has been just discussed, it is clear that by a state of "no social change" we do not refer to a stationary but to a quasi-stationary equilibrium; that is, to a state comparable to that of a river which flows with a given velocity in a given direction during a certain time interval. A social change is comparable to a change in the velocity or direction of that river.

A number of statements can be made in regard to the conditions of quasi-stationary equilibrium. (These conditions are treated more elaborately elsewhere.[7])

(A) The strength of forces which tend to lower that standard of social life should be equal and opposite to the strength of forces which tend to raise its level. The resultant of forces on the line of equilibrium should therefore be zero.

(B) Since we have to assume that the strength of social forces always shows variations, a quasi-stationary equilibrium presupposes that the forces against raising the standard increase with the amount of raising and that the forces against lowering increase (or remain constant) with the amount of lowering. This type of gradient which is characteristic for a "positive central force field"[8] has to hold at least in the neighborhood of the present level (Fig. 8).

(C) It is possible to change the strength of the opposing forces without changing the level of social conduct. In this case the tension (degree of conflict) increases.

3. *Two Basic Methods of Changing Levels of Conduct.* For any type of social management, it is of great practical importance that levels of quasi-stationary equilibria can be changed in either of two ways: by adding forces in the desired direction, or by diminishing opposing forces. If a change from the level L_1 to L_2 is brought about by increasing the forces toward L_2, the secondary effects should be different from the case where the same change of level is brought about by diminishing the opposing forces.

7. K. Lewin, "Frontiers in Group Dynamics: Concept, Method and Reality in Social Science; Social Equilibria and Social Change," *Human Relations*, I,1, June, 1947, pp. 5-42.

8. *Ibid.*

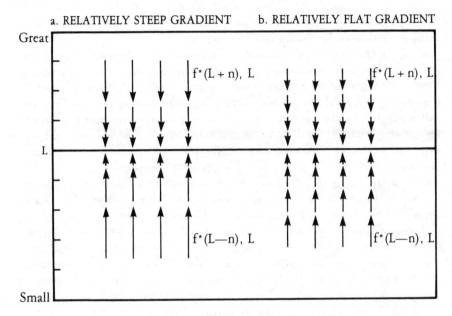

Figure 8. Gradients of resultant forces (f*).

In both cases the equilibrium might change to the same new level. The secondary effect should, however, be quite different. In the first case, the process on the new level would be accompanied by a state of relatively high tension; in the second case, by a state of relatively low tension. Since increase of tension above a certain degree is likely to be paralleled by higher aggressiveness, higher emotionality, and lower constructiveness, it is clear that as a rule the second method will be preferable to the high pressure method.

The group decision procedure which is used here attempts to avoid high pressure methods and is sensitive to resistance to change. In the experiment by Bavelas on changing production in factory work (as noted below), for instance, no attempt was made to set the new production goal by majority vote because a majority vote forces some group members to produce more than they consider appropriate. These individuals are likely to have some inner resistance. Instead a procedure was followed by which a goal was chosen on which everyone could agree fully.

It is possible that the success of group decision and particularly the permanency of the effect is, in part, due to the attempt to bring about a favorable decision by removing counterforces within the individuals rather than by applying outside pressure.

The surprising increase from the second to the fourth week in the number of mothers giving cod liver oil and orange juice to the baby can probably be explained by such a decrease of counterforces. Mothers are likely to handle their first baby during the first weeks of life somewhat cautiously and become more ready for action as the child grows stronger.

4. *Social Habits and Group Standards.* Viewing a social stationary process as the result of a quasi-stationary equilibrium, one may expect that any added force will change the level of the process. The idea of "social habit" seems to imply that, in spite of the application of a force, the level of the social process will not change because of some type of "inner resistance" to change. To overcome this inner resistance, an additional force seems to be required, a force sufficient to "break the habit," to "unfreeze" the custom.

Many social habits are anchored in the relation between the individuals and certain group standards. An individual P may differ in his personal level of conduct (L_P) from the level which represents group standards (L_{Gr}) by a certain amount. If the individual should try to diverge "too much" from group standards, he would find himself in increasing difficulties. He would be ridiculed, treated severely and finally ousted from the group. Most individuals, therefore, stay pretty close to the standard of the groups they belong to or wish to belong to. In other words, the group level itself acquires value. It becomes a positive valence corresponding to a central force field with the force $f_{P,L}$ keeping the individual in line with the standards of the group.

5. *Individual Procedures and Group Procedures of Changing Social Conduct.* If the resistance to change depends partly on the value which the group standard has for the individual, the resistance to change should diminish if one diminishes the strength of the value of the group standard or changes the level perceived by the individual as having social value.

This second point is one of the reasons for the effectiveness of "group carried" changes[9] resulting from procedures which approach the individuals as part of face-to-face groups. Perhaps one might expect single individuals to be more pliable than groups of like-minded individuals. However, experience in leadership training, in changing of food habits, work production, criminality, alcoholism, prejudices, all indicate that it is usually easier to change individuals formed into a group than to change any one of them separately.[10] As long as group standards are unchanged, the individual will resist changes more strongly the farther he is to depart from group standards. If the group standard itself is changed, the resistance which is due to the relation between individual and group standard is eliminated.

6. *Changing as a Three-step Procedure: Unfreezing, Moving, and Freezing of a Level.* A change toward a higher level of group performance is frequently short lived: after a "shot in the arm," group life soon returns to the previous level. This indicates that it does not suffice to define the objective of a planned change in group performance as the reaching of a different level. Permanency of the new level, or permanency for a desired period, should be included in the

---

9. N. R. F. Maier, *Psychology in Industry* (Boston: Houghton Mifflin Co., 1946).

10. K. Lewin and P. Grabbe (eds.) *op. cit.*

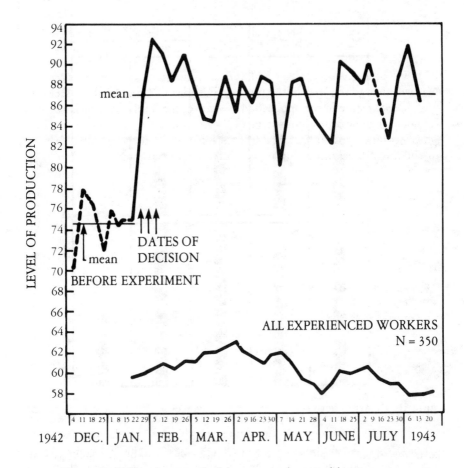

Figure 9. Effect of group decision on sewing-machine operators.

objective. A successful change includes therefore three aspects: unfreezing (if necessary) the present level L_1, moving to the new level L_2, and freezing group life on the new level. Since any level is determined by a force field, permanency implies that the new force field is made relatively secure against change.

The "unfreezing" of the present level may involve quite different problems in different cases. Allport[11] has described the "catharsis" which seems to be necessary before prejudices can be removed. To break open the shell of complacency and self-righteousness, it is sometimes necessary to bring about deliberately an emotional stir-up.

Figure 9 presents an example of the effect of three group decisions of a team

11. G. W. Allport, "Catharsis and the Reduction of Prejudice" in K. Lewin and P. Grabbe (eds.), *op. cit.*, 3-10.

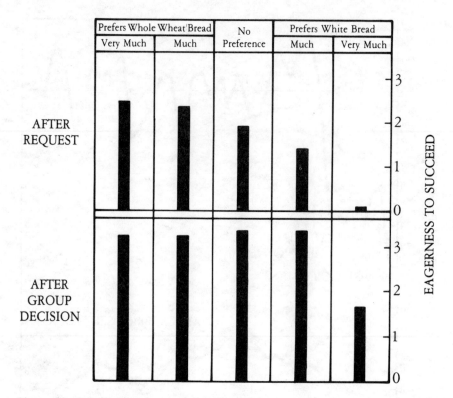

Prefers Whole Wheat Bread		No	Prefers White Bread	
Very Much	Much	Preference	Much	Very Much

Figure 10. Relation between own food preferences and eagerness to succeed.

in a factory reported by Bavelas[12] which illustrates an unusually good case of permanency of change measured over nine months.

The experiments on group decision reported here cover but a few of the necessary variations. Although in some cases the procedure is relatively easily executed, in others it requires skill and presupposes certain general conditions. Managers rushing into a factory to raise production by group decisions are likely to encounter failure. In social management as in medicine there are no patent medicines and each case demands careful diagnosis.

One reason why group decision facilitates change is illustrated by Willerman.[13] Figure 10 shows the degree of eagerness to have the members of a students' eating cooperative change from the consumption of white bread to whole wheat. When the change was simply requested the degree of eagerness varied greatly with the degree of personal preference for whole wheat. In case of group decision the eagerness seems to be relatively independent of personal preference; the individual seems to act mainly as a "group member."

12. N. R. F. Maier, *op. cit.*

13. K. Lewin "Forces Behind Food Habits...," *op. cit.*

SUMMARY

Group decision is a process of social management or self management of groups. It is related to social channels, gates and gatekeepers; to the problem of social perception and planning; and to the relation between motivation and action, and between the individual and the group.

Experiments are reported in which certain methods of group decision prove to be superior to lecturing and individual treatment as means of changing social conduct.

The effect of group decision can probably be best understood by relating it to a theory of quasi-stationary social equilibria, to social habits and resistance to change, and to the various problems of unfreezing, changing and freezing social levels.

Chapter 24

Functional Roles of Group Members

Kenneth D. Benne
Paul Sheats

THE RELATIVE NEGLECT OF MEMBER ROLES IN GROUP TRAINING

Efforts to improve group functioning through training have traditionally emphasized the training of group leadership. And frequently this training has been directed toward the improvement of the skills of the leader in transmitting information and in manipulating groups. Little direct attention seems to have been given to the training of group members in the membership roles required for effective group growth and production. The present discussion is based on the conviction that both effective group training and adequate research into the effectiveness of group training methods must give attention to the identification, analysis, and practice of leader *and* member roles, seen as correlative aspects of over-all group growth and production.

Certain assumptions have undergirded the tendency to isolate the leadership role from membership roles and to neglect the latter in processes of group training. 1) "Leadership" has been identified with traits and qualities inherent within the "leader" personality. Such traits and qualities can be developed, it is assumed, in isolation from the functioning of members in a group setting. The present treatment sees the leadership role in terms of functions to be performed within a group in helping that group to grow and to work productively. No sharp distinction can be made between leadership and membership functions, between leader and member roles. Groups may operate with various degrees of diffusion of "leadership" functions among group members or of concentration of such functions in one member or a few members. Ideally, of course, the concept of leadership emphasized here is that of a multilaterally shared responsibility. In any event, effectiveness in the leader role is a matter of

From *Journal of Social Issues*, Vol. IV, No. 2 (1948), pp. 41-49. Reprinted by permission of the Society for Psychological Study of Social Issues.

leader-member relationship. And one side of a relationship cannot be effectively trained in isolation from the retraining of the other side of that relationship. 2) It has been assumed that the "leader" is uniquely responsible for the quality and amount of production by the group. The "leader" must see to it that the "right" group goals are set, that the group jobs get done, that members are "motivated" to participate. On this view, membership roles are of secondary importance. "Membership" is tacitly identified with "followership." The present discussion assumes that the quality and amount of group production is the "responsibility" of the group. The setting of goals and the marshalling of resources to move toward these goals is a group responsibility in which all members of a mature group come variously to share. The functions to be performed both in building and maintaining group-centered activity and in effective production by the group are primarily member roles. Leadership functions can be defined in terms of facilitating identification, acceptance, development and allocation of these group-required roles by the group. 3) There has frequently been a confusion between the roles which members enact within a group and the individual personalities of the group members. That there are relationships between the personality structures and needs of group members and the range and quality of group membership roles which members can learn to perform is not denied. On the contrary, the importance of studies designed to describe and explain and to increase our control of these relationships is affirmed. But, at the level of group functioning, member roles, relevant to group growth and accomplishment, must be clearly distinguished from the use of the group environment by individuals to satisfy individual and group-irrelevant needs, if clear diagnosis of member-roles required by the group and adequate training of members to perform group-required roles are to be advanced. Neglect of this distinction has been associated traditionally with the neglect of the analysis of member roles in group growth and production.

A CLASSIFICATION OF MEMBER ROLES

The following analysis of functional member roles was developed in connection with the First National Training Laboratory in Group Development, 1947. It follows closely the analysis of participation functions used in coding the content of group records for research purposes. A similar analysis operated in faculty efforts to train group members in their functional roles during the course of the laboratory.[1]

The member-roles identified in this analysis are classified into three broad groupings.

(1) *Group task roles.* Participant roles here are related to the task which the

---

1. A somewhat different analysis of member-participations, in terms of categories used by interaction observers in observation of group processes in the First National Training Laboratory, is described in the *Preliminary Report* of the laboratory, pages 122-132. The number of categories used by interaction observers was "directed primarily by limitations of observer load."

group is deciding to undertake or has undertaken. Their purpose is to facilitate and coordinate group effort in the selection and definition of a common problem and in the solution of that problem.

(2) *Group building and maintenance roles.* The roles in this category are oriented toward the functioning of the group as a group. They are designed to alter or maintain the group way of working; to strengthen, regulate and perpetuate the group as a group.

(3) *Individual roles.* This category does not classify member-roles as such, since the "participations" denoted here are directed toward the satisfaction of the "participant's" individual needs. Their purpose is some individual goal which is not relevant either to the group task or to the functioning of the group as a group. Such participations are, of course, highly relevant to the problem of group training, insofar as such training is directed toward improving group maturity or group task efficiency.

GROUP TASK ROLES

The following analysis assumes that the task of the discussion group is to select, define and solve common problems. The roles are identified in relation to functions of facilitation and coordination of group problem-solving activities. Each member may of course enact more than one role in any given unit of participation and a wide range of roles in successive participations. Any or all of these roles may be played at times by the group "leader" as well as by various members.

a. The *initiator-contributor* suggests or proposes to the group new ideas or a changed way of regarding the group problem or goal. The novelty proposed may take the form of suggestions of a new group goal or a new definition of the problem. It may take the form of a suggested solution or some way of handling a difficulty that the group has encountered. Or it may take the form of a proposed new procedure for the group, a new way of organizing the group for the task ahead.

b. The *information seeker* asks for clarification of suggestions made in terms of their factual adequacy, for authoritative information and facts pertinent to the problem being discussed.

c. The *opinion seeker* asks not primarily for the facts of the case but for a clarification of the values pertinent to what the group is undertaking or of values involved in a suggestion made or in alternative suggestions.

d. The *information giver* offers facts or generalizations which are "authoritative" or relates his own experience pertinently to the group problem.

e. The *opinion giver* states his belief or opinion pertinently to a suggestion made or to alternative suggestions. The emphasis is on his proposal of what should become the group's view of pertinent values, not primarily upon relevant facts or information.

f. The *elaborator* spells out suggestions in terms of examples or developed meanings, offers a rationale for suggestions previously made and tries to deduce how an idea or suggestion would work out if adopted by the group.

g. The *coordinator* shows or clarifies the relationships among various ideas and suggestions, tries to pull ideas and suggestions together or tries to coordinate the activities of various members or sub-groups.

h. The *orienter* defines the position of the group with respect to its goals by summarizing what has occurred, points to departures from agreed upon directions or goals, or raises questions about the direction which the group discussion is taking.

i. The *evaluator-critic* subjects the accomplishment of the group to some standard or set of standards of group functioning in the context of the group task. Thus, he may evaluate or question the "practicality," the "logic," the "facts" or the "procedure" of a suggestion or of some unit of group discussion.

j. The *energizer* prods the group to action or decision, attempts to stimulate or arouse the group to "greater" or "higher quality" activity.

k. The *procedural technician* expedites group movement by doing things for the group—performing routine tasks, e.g., distributing materials or manipulating objects for the group, e.g., rearranging the seating or running the recording machine, etc.

l. The *recorder* writes down suggestions, makes a record of group decisions, or writes down the product of discussion. The recorder role is the "group memory."

GROUP BUILDING AND MAINTENANCE ROLES

Here the analysis of member functions is oriented to those participations which have for their purpose the building of group-centered attitudes and orientation among the members of a group or the maintenance and perpetuation of such group-centered behavior. A given contribution may involve several roles and a member or the "leader" may perform various roles in successive contributions.

a. The *encourager* praises, agrees with and accepts the contribution of others. He indicates warmth and solidarity in his attitude toward other group members, offers commendation and praise and in various ways indicates understanding and acceptance of other points of view, ideas and suggestions.

b. The *harmonizer* mediates the differences between other members, attempts to reconcile disagreements, relieves tension in conflict situations through jesting or pouring oil on the troubled waters, etc.

c. The *compromiser* operates from within a conflict in which his idea or position is involved. He may offer compromise by yielding status, admitting his error, by disciplining himself to maintain group harmony, or by "coming halfway" in moving along with the group.

d. The *gatekeeper and expediter* attempts to keep communication channels open by encouraging or facilitating the participation of others ("we haven't got the ideas of Mr. X yet,'' etc.) or by proposing regulation of the flow of com-munication (''why don't we limit the length of our contributions so that everyone will have a chance to contribute?'', etc.)

e. The *standard setter* or *ego ideal* expresses standards for the group to at-tempt to achieve in its functioning or applies standards in evaluating the qual-ity of group processes.

f. The *group-observer* and *commentator* keeps records of various aspects of group process and feeds such data with proposed interpretations into the group's evaluation of its own procedures.

g. The *follower* goes along with the movement of the group, more or less passively accepting the ideas of others, serving as an audience in group discus-sion and decision.

"INDIVIDUAL" ROLES

Attempts by ''members'' of a group to satisfy individual needs which are ir-relevant to the group task and which are non-oriented or negatively oriented to group building and maintenance set problems of group and member training. A high incidence of ''individual-centered'' as opposed to ''group-centered'' participation in a group always calls for self-diagnosis of the group. The diag-nosis may reveal one or several of a number of conditions—low level of skill-training among members, including the group leader; the prevalence of ''authoritarian'' and ''laissez faire'' points of view toward group functioning in the group; a low level of group maturity, discipline and morale; an inappropri-ately chosen and inadequately defined group task, etc. Whatever the diagnosis, it is in this setting that the training needs of the group are to be discovered and group training efforts to meet these needs are to be defined. The outright ''suppression'' of ''individual roles'' will deprive the group of data needed for really adequate self-diagnosis and therapy.

a. The *aggressor* may work in many ways—deflating the status of others, ex-pressing disapproval of the values, acts or feelings of others, attacking the group or the problem it is working on, joking aggressively, showing envy toward another's contribution by trying to take credit for it, etc.

b. The *blocker* tends to be negativistic and stubbornly resistant, disagree-ing and opposing without or beyond ''reason'' and attempting to maintain or bring back an issue after the group has rejected or by-passed it.

c. The *recognition-seeker* works in various ways to call attention to himself, whether through boasting, reporting on personal achievements, acting in un-usual ways, struggling to prevent his being placed in an ''inferior'' position, etc.

d. The *self-confessor* uses the audience opportunity which the group setting provides to express personal, non-group oriented, ''feeling'', ''insight'', ''ideology'', etc.

e. The *playboy* makes a display of his lack of involvement in the group's processes. This may take the form of cynicism, nonchalance, horseplay and other more or less studied forms of "out of field" behavior.

f. The *dominator* tries to assert authority or superiority in manipulating the group or certain members of the group. This domination may take the form of flattery, of asserting a superior status or right to attention, giving directions authoritatively, interrupting the contributions of others, etc.

g. The *help-seeker* attempts to call forth "sympathy" response from other group members or from the whole group, whether through expressions of insecurity, personal confusion or depreciation of himself beyond "reason."

h. The *special interest pleader* speaks for the "small business man", the "grass roots" community, the "housewife", "labor", etc., usually cloaking his own prejudices or biases in the stereotype which best fits his individual need.

THE PROBLEM OF MEMBER ROLE REQUIREDNESS

Identification of group task roles and of group building and maintenance roles which do actually function in processes of group discussion raises but does not answer the further question of what roles are required for "optimum" group growth and productivity. Certainly the discovery and validation of answers to this question have a high priority in any advancing science of group training and development. No attempt will be made here to review the bearing of the analyzed data from the First National Training Laboratory in Group Development on this point.

It may be useful in this discussion, however, to comment on two conditions which effective work on the problem of role-requiredness must meet. First, an answer to the problem of optimum task role requirements must be projected against a scheme of the process of group production. Groups in different stages of an act of problem selection and solution will have different role requirements. For example, a group early in the stages of problem selection which is attempting to lay out a range of possible problems to be worked on, will probably have relatively less need for the roles of "evaluator-critic", "energizer" and "coordinator" than a group which has selected and discussed its problem and is shaping to decision. The combination and balance of task role requirements is a function of the group's stage of progress with respect to its task. Second, the group building role requirements of a group are a function of its stage of development—its level of group maturity. For example, a "young" group will probably require less of the role of the "standard setter" than a more mature group. Too high a level of aspiration may frustrate a "young" group where a more mature group will be able to take the same level of aspiration in its stride. Again the role of "group observer and commentator" must be carefully adapted to the level of maturity of the group. Probably the distinction between "group" and "individual" roles can be drawn much more sharply in a relatively mature than in a "young" group.

Meanwhile, group trainers cannot wait for a fully developed science of group training before they undertake to diagnose the role requirements of the groups with which they work and help these groups to share in such diagnosis. Each group which is attempting to improve the quality of its functioning as a group must be helped to diagnose its role requirements and must attempt to train members to fill the required roles effectively. This describes one of the principal objectives of training of group members.

THE PROBLEM OF ROLE FLEXIBILITY

The previous group experience of members, where this experience has included little conscious attention to the variety of roles involved in effective group production and development, has frequently stereotyped the member into a limited range of roles. These he plays in all group discussions whether or not the group situation requires them. Some members see themselves primarily as "evaluator-critics" and play this role in and out of season. Others may play the roles of "encourager" or of "energizer" or of "information giver" with only small sensitivity to the role requirements of a given group situation. The development of skill and insight in diagnosing role requirements has already been mentioned as an objective of group member training. An equally important objective is the development of role flexibility, of skill and security in a wide range of member roles, on the part of all group members.

A science of group training, as it develops, must be concerned with the relationships between the personality structures of group members and the character and range of member roles which various personality structures support and permit. A science of group training must seek to discover and accept the limitations which group training per se encounters in altering personality structures in the service of greater role flexibility on the part of all members of a group. Even though we recognize the importance of this caution, the objective of developing role flexibility remains an important objective of group member training.

METHODS OF GROUP MEMBER TRAINING

The objectives in training group members have been identified. Some of the kinds of resistances encountered in training group members to diagnose the role requirements of a group situation and to acquire skill in a variety of member roles have been suggested. Before analyzing briefly the methods used for group member training in the First National Training Laboratory, a few additional comments on resistances to member training may be useful. The problem of group training is actually a problem of re-training. Members of a training group have had other group experiences. They bring to the training experience attitudes toward group work, more or less conscious skills for dealing with leaders and other members, and a more or less highly developed rationale of group processes. These may or may not support processes of democratic operation in the training group. Where they do not, they function as resistances to retraining. Again, trainees are inclined to make little or no distinction between the roles they perform in a group and their personalities. Criticism of the role a group member plays is perceived as criticism of "himself." Methods must be found to reduce ego-defensiveness toward criticism of member roles. Finally, training groups must be helped to make a distinction between group feeling and group productivity. Groups which attain a state of good group feeling often perceive attempts to diagnose and criticize their level of productivity as threats to this feeling of group warmth and solidarity.

(1) Each Basic Skill Training group in the Laboratory used self-observation and diagnosis of its own growth and development as a primary means of member training.

a. Sensitization to the variety of roles involved in and required by group functioning began during the introduction of members to the group. In one BST group, this early sensitization to member role variety and role requiredness began with the "leader's" summarizing, as part of his introduction of himself to the group, certain of the member roles in which he was usually cast by groups and other roles which he found it difficult to play, even when needed by the group. He asked the group's help in criticizing and improving his skill in those roles where he felt weakest. Other members followed suit. Various members showed widely different degrees of sensitivity to the operation of member roles in groups and to the degree of their own proficiency in different roles. This introduction procedure gave the group a partial listing of member roles for later use and supplementation, initial self-assessments of member strengths and weaknesses and diagnostic material concerning the degree of group self-sophistication among the members. The training job had come to be seen by most members as a re-training job.

b. A description of the use of training observers in group self-evaluation sessions is given [elsewhere]. At this point, only the central importance which self-evaluation sessions played in member training needs to be stressed. Research observers fed observational data concerning group functioning into periodic discussions by the group of its strengths and weaknesses as a group. Much of these data concerned role requirements for the job the group had been attempting, which roles had been present, which roles had probably been needed. "Individual" roles were identified and interpreted in an objective and non-blaming manner. Out of these discussions, group members came to identify various kinds of member roles, to relate role requiredness to stages in group production and in group growth and to assess the range of roles each was able to play well when required. Out of these discussions came group decisions concerning the supplying of needed roles in the next session. Member commitments concerning behavior in future sessions also came out of these evaluations. These took the form both of silent commitments and of public commitments in which the help of the group was requested.

c. Recordings of segments of the group's discussion were used by most Basic Skill Training groups. Groups listened to themselves, diagnosed the member and leader functions involved and assessed the adequacy of these.

(2) Role-played sessions in each group, although they were pointed content-wise to the skills of the change-agent, offered important material for the diagnosis of member roles and of role-requiredness. These sessions offered an important supplement to group self-diagnosis and evaluation. It is easier for members to get perspective on their participation in a role-played episode of group process than it is on their own participation in a "real" group. The former is not perceived as "real". The role is more easily disengaged for purposes of analysis and evaluation from the person playing the role. Ego-defensiveness toward the role as enacted is reduced. Role-playing sessions also provided practice opportunity to members in a variety of roles.

(3) Practice by group members of the role of *observer-commentator* is especially valuable in developing skill in diagnosing member roles and in assessing the role requirements of a group situation. In several groups, each member in turn served as observer, supplementing the work of the research observers in evaluation sessions. Such members worked more or less closely with the anecdotal observer for the group on skill-problems encountered. Practice opportunity in the *observer-commentator* role was also provided in clinic group meetings in the afternoon.

SUMMARY

Training in group membership roles requires the identification and analysis of various member roles actually enacted in group processes. It involves further the analysis of group situations in terms of roles required in relation both to a schema of group production and to a conception of group growth and development. A group's self-observation and self-evaluation of its own processes provides useful content and practice opportunity in member training. Practice in enacting a wider range of required roles and in role flexibility can come out of member commitment to such practice with help from the group in evaluating and improving the required skills. Member training is typically re-training and resistances to re-training can be reduced by creating a non-blaming and objective atmosphere in group self-evaluation and by using role-playing of group processes for diagnosis and practice. The training objectives of developing skill in the diagnosis of group role requirements and developing role flexibility among members also indicate important research areas for a science of group training.

Chapter 25

Groupthink

Irving L. Janis

"How could we have been so stupid?" President John F. Kennedy asked after he and a close group of advisers had blundered into the Bay of Pigs invasion. For the last two years I have been studying that question, as it applies not only to the Bay of Pigs decision-makers but also to those who led the United States into such other major fiascos as the failure to be prepared for the attack on Pearl Harbor, the Korean War stalemate and the escalation of the Vietnam War.

Stupidity certainly is not the explanation. The men who participated in making the Bay of Pigs decision, for instance, comprised one of the greatest arrays of intellectual talent in the history of American Government—Dean Rusk, Robert McNamara, Douglas Dillon, Robert Kennedy, McGeorge Bundy, Arthur Schlesinger Jr., Allen Dulles and others.

It also seemed to me that explanations were incomplete if they concentrated only on disturbances in the behavior of each individual within a decision-making body: temporary emotional states of elation, fear, or anger that reduce a man's mental efficiency, for example, or chronic blind spots arising from a man's social prejudices or idiosyncratic biases.

I preferred to broaden the picture by looking at the fiascos from the standpoint of group dynamics as it has been explored over the past three decades, first by the great social psychologist Kurt Lewin and later in many experimental situations by myself and other behavioral scientists. My conclusion after poring over hundreds of relevant documents—historical reports about formal group meetings and informal conversations among the members—is that the groups that committed the fiascos were victims of what I call "groupthink."

"GROUPY." In each case study, I was surprised to discover the extent to which each group displayed the typical phenomena of social conformity that are regularly encountered in studies of group dynamics among ordinary citizens. For example, some of the phenomena appear to be completely in line with findings from social-psychological experiments showing that powerful social pressures are brought to bear by the members of a cohesive group whenever a dissident begins to voice his objections to a group consensus. Other phenomena are reminiscent of the shared illusions observed in encounter groups and friendship cliques when the members simultaneously reach a peak of "groupy" feelings.

Above all, there are numerous indications pointing to the development of group norms that bolster morale at the expense of critical thinking. One of the most common norms appears to be that of remaining loyal to the group by sticking with the policies to which the group has already committed itself, even when those policies are obviously working out badly and have unintended consequences that disturb the conscience of each member. This is one of the key characteristics of groupthink.

1984. I use the term groupthink as a quick and easy way to refer to the mode of thinking that persons engage in when *concurrence-seeking* becomes so dominant in a cohesive ingroup that it tends to override realistic appraisal of alternative courses of action. Groupthink is a term of the same order as the words in the newspeak vocabulary George Orwell used in his dismaying world of *1984.* In that context, groupthink takes on an invidious connotation. Exactly such a connotation is intended, since the term refers to a deterioration in mental efficiency, reality testing and moral judgments as a result of group pressures.

The symptoms of groupthink arise when the members of decision-making groups become motivated to avoid being too harsh in their judgments of their leaders' or their colleagues' ideas. They adopt a soft line of criticism, even in their own thinking. At their meetings, all the members are amiable and seek complete concurrence on every important issue, with no bickering or conflict to spoil the cozy, "we-feeling" atmosphere.

KILL. Paradoxically, soft-headed groups are often hard-hearted when it comes to dealing with outgroups or enemies. They find it relatively easy to resort to dehumanizing solutions—they will readily authorize bombing attacks that kill large numbers of civilians in the name of the noble cause of persuading an unfriendly government to negotiate at the peace table. They are unlikely to pursue the more difficult and controversial issues that arise when alternatives to a harsh military solution come up for discussion. Nor are they inclined to raise ethical issues that carry the implication that *this fine group of ours, with its humanitarianism and its high-minded principles, might be capable of adopting a course of action that is inhumane and immoral.*

NORMS. There is evidence from a number of social-psychological studies that as the members of a group feel more accepted by the others, which is a central feature of increased group cohesiveness, they display less overt conformity to group norms. Thus we would expect that the more cohesive a group becomes, the less the members will feel constrained to censor what they say out of fear of being socially punished for antagonizing the leader or any of their fellow members.

In contrast, the groupthink type of conformity tends to increase as group cohesiveness increases. Groupthink involves nondeliberate suppression of critical thoughts as a result of internalization of the group's norms, which is quite different from deliberate suppression on the basis of external threats of social punishment. The more cohesive the group, the greater the inner compulsion on the part of each member to avoid creating disunity, which inclines him to believe in the soundness of whatever proposals are promoted by the leader or by a majority of the group's members.

In a cohesive group, the danger is not so much that each individual will fail to reveal his objections to what the others propose but that he will think the proposal is a good one, without attempting to carry out a careful, critical scrutiny of the pros and cons of the alternative. When groupthink becomes dominant, there also is considerable suppression of deviant thoughts, but it takes the form of each person's deciding that his misgivings are not relevant and should be set aside, that the benefit of the doubt regarding any lingering uncertainties should be given to the group consensus.

STRESS. I do not mean to imply that all cohesive groups necessarily suffer from groupthink. All ingroups may have a mild tendency toward groupthink, displaying one or another of the symptoms from time to time, but it need not be so dominant as to influence the quality of the group's final decision. Neither do I mean to imply that there is anything necessarily inefficient or harmful about group decisions in general. On the contrary, a group whose members have properly defined roles, with traditions concerning the procedures to follow in pursuing a critical inquiry, probably is capable of making better decisions than any individual group member working alone.

The problem is that the advantages of having decisions made by groups are often lost because of powerful psychological pressures that arise when the members work closely together, share the same set of values and, above all, face a crisis situation that puts everyone under intense stress.

The main principle of groupthink, which I offer in the spirit of Parkinson's Law, is this: *The more amiability and esprit de corps there is among the members of a policy-making ingroup, the greater the danger that independent critical thinking will be replaced by groupthink, which is likely to result in irrational and dehumanizing actions directed against outgroups.*

SYMPTOMS. In my studies of high-level governmental decision-makers, both civilian and military, I have found eight main symptoms of groupthink.

1. *Invulnerability.* Most or all of the members of the ingroup share an *illusion* of invulnerability that provides for them some degree of reassurance about obvious dangers and leads them to become overoptimistic and willing to take extraordinary risks. It also causes them to fail to respond to clear warnings of danger.

The Kennedy ingroup, which uncritically accepted the Central Intelligence

Agency's disastrous Bay of Pigs plan, operated on the false assumption that they could keep secret the fact that the United States was responsible for the invasion of Cuba. Even after news of the plan began to leak out, their belief remained unshaken. They failed even to consider the danger that awaited them: a worldwide revulsion against the U.S.

A similar attitude appeared among the members of President Lyndon B. Johnson's ingroup, the "Tuesday Cabinet," which kept escalating the Vietnam War despite repeated setbacks and failures. "There was a belief," Bill Moyers commented after he resigned, "that if we indicated a willingness to use our power, they [the North Vietnamese] would get the message and back away from an all-out confrontation. . . . There was a confidence—it was never bragged about, it was just there— that when the chips were really down, the other people would fold."

A most poignant example of an illusion of invulnerability involves the ingroup around Admiral H. E. Kimmel, which failed to prepare for the possibility of a Japanese attack on Pearl Harbor despite repeated warnings. Informed by his intelligence chief that radio contact with Japanese aircraft carriers had been lost, Kimmel joked about it: "What, you don't know where the carriers are? Do you mean to say that they could be rounding Diamond Head (at Honolulu) and you wouldn't know it?" The carriers were in fact moving full-steam toward Kimmel's command post at the time. Laughing together about a danger signal, which labels it as a purely laughing matter, is a characteristic manifestation of groupthink.

2. *Rationale.* As we see, victims of groupthink ignore warnings; they also collectively construct rationalizations in order to discount warnings and other forms of negative feedback that, taken seriously, might lead the group members to reconsider their assumptions each time they recommit themselves to past decisions. Why did the Johnson ingroup avoid reconsidering its escalation policy when time and again the expectations on which they based their decisions turned out to be wrong? James C. Thompson Jr., a Harvard historian who spent five years as an observing participant in both the State Department and the White House, tells us that the policymakers avoided critical discussion of their prior decisions and continually invented new rationalizations so that they could sincerely recommit themselves to defeating the North Vietnamese.

In the fall of 1964, before the bombing of North Vietnam began, some of the policymakers predicted that six weeks of air strikes would induce the North Vietnamese to seek peace talks. When someone asked, "What if they don't?" the answer was that another four weeks certainly would do the trick.

Later, after each setback, the ingroup agreed that by investing just a bit more effort (by stepping up the bomb tonnage a bit, for instance), their course of action would prove to be right. *The Pentagon Papers* bear out these observations.

In *The Limits of Intervention*, Townsend Hoopes, who was acting Secretary of the Air Force under Johnson, says that Walt W. Rostow in particular showed a remarkable capacity for what has been called "instant rationalization." According to Hoopes, Rostow buttressed the group's optimism about being on the road to victory by culling selected scraps of evidence from news reports or, if necessary, by inventing "plausible" forecasts that had no basis in evidence at all.

Admiral Kimmel's group rationalized away their warnings, too. Right up to December 7, 1941, they convinced themselves that the Japanese would never dare attempt a full-scale surprise assault against Hawaii because Japan's leaders would realize that it would precipitate an all-out war which the United States would surely win. They made no attempt to look at the situation through the eyes of the Japanese leaders—another manifestation of groupthink.

3. *Morality.* Victims of groupthink believe unquestioningly in the inherent morality of their ingroup; this belief inclines the members to ignore the ethical or moral consequences of their decisions.

Evidence that this symptom is at work usually is of a negative kind—the things that are left unsaid in group meetings. At least two influential persons had doubts about the morality of the Bay of Pigs adventure. One of them, Arthur Schlesinger Jr., presented his strong objections in a memorandum to President Kennedy and Secretary of State Rusk but suppressed them when he attended meetings of the Kennedy team. The other, Senator J. William Fulbright, was not a member of the group, but the President invited him to express his misgivings in a speech to the policymakers. However, when Fulbright finished speaking the President moved on to other agenda items without asking for reactions of the group.

David Kraslow and Stuart H. Loory, in *The Secret Search for Peace in Vietnam,* report that during 1966 President Johnson's ingroup was concerned primarily with selecting bomb targets in North Vietnam. They based their selections on four factors—the military advantage, the risk to American aircraft and pilots, the danger of forcing other countries into the fighting, and the danger of heavy civilian casualties. At their regular Tuesday luncheons, they weighed these factors the way school teachers grade examination papers, averaging them out. Though evidence on this point is scant, I suspect that the group's ritualistic adherence to a standardized procedure induced the members to feel morally justified in their destructive way of dealing with the Vietnamese people—after all, the danger of heavy civilian casualties from U.S. air strikes was taken into account on their checklists.

4. *Stereotypes.* Victims of groupthink hold stereotyped views of the leaders of enemy groups: they are so evil that genuine attempts at negotiating differences with them are unwarranted, or they are too weak or too stupid to deal effectively with whatever attempts the ingroup makes to defeat their purposes, no matter how risky the attempts are.

Kennedy's groupthinkers believed that Premier Fidel Castro's air force was so ineffectual that obsolete B-26s could knock it out completely in a surprise attack before the invasion began. They also believed that Castro's army was so weak that a small Cuban-exile brigade could establish a well-protected beachhead at the Bay of Pigs. In addition, they believed that Castro was not smart enough to put down any possible internal uprisings in support of the exiles.

They were wrong on all three assumptions. Though much of the blame was attributable to faulty intelligence, the point is that none of Kennedy's advisers even questioned the CIA planners about these assumptions.

The Johnson advisers' sloganistic thinking about "the Communist apparatus" that was "working all around the world" (as Dean Rusk put it) led them to overlook the powerful nationalistic strivings of the North Vietnamese government and its efforts to ward off Chinese domination. The crudest of all stereotypes used by Johnson's inner circle to justify their policies was the domino theory ("If we don't stop the Reds in South Vietnam, tomorrow they will be in Hawaii and next week they will be in San Francisco," Johnson once said). The group so firmly accepted this stereotype that it became almost impossible for any adviser to introduce a more sophisticated viewpoint.

In the documents on Pearl Harbor, it is clear to see that the Navy commanders stationed in Hawaii had a naive image of Japan as a midget that would not dare to strike a blow against a powerful giant.

5. *Pressure.* Victims of groupthink apply direct pressure to any individual who momentarily expresses doubts about any of the group's shared illusions or who questions the validity of the arguments supporting a policy alternative favored by the majority. This gambit reinforces the concurrence-seeking norm that loyal members are expected to maintain.

President Kennedy probably was more active than anyone else in raising skeptical questions during the Bay of Pigs meetings, and yet he seems to have encouraged the group's docile, uncritical acceptance of defective arguments in favor of the CIA's plan. At every meeting, he allowed the CIA representatives to dominate the discussion. He permitted them to give their immediate refutations in response to each tentative doubt that one of the others expressed, instead of asking whether anyone shared the doubt or wanted to pursue the implications of the new worrisome issue that had just been raised. And at the most crucial meeting, when he was calling on each member to give his vote for or against the plan, he did not call on Arthur Schlesinger, the one man there who was known by the President to have serious misgivings.

Historian Thomson informs us that whenever a member of Johnson's ingroup began to express doubts, the group used subtle social pressures to "domesticate" him. To start with, the dissenter was made to feel at home, provided that he lived up to two restrictions: 1) that he did not voice his doubts to outsiders, which would play into the hands of the opposition; and 2) that he kept his criticisms within the bounds of acceptable deviation, which meant not challenging any of the fundamental assumptions that went into the group's prior commitments. One such "domesticated dissenter" was Bill Moyers. When Moyers arrived at a meeting, Thomson tells us, the President greeted him with, "Well, here comes Mr. Stop-the-Bombing."

6. *Self-censorship.* Victims of groupthink avoid deviating from what appears to be group consensus; they keep silent about their misgivings and even minimize to themselves the importance of their doubts.

As we have seen, Schlesinger was not at all hesitant about presenting his strong objections to the Bay of Pigs plan in a memorandum to the President and the Secretary of State. But he became keenly aware of his tendency to suppress objections at the White House meetings. "In the months after the Bay of Pigs I bitterly reproached myself for having kept so silent during those crucial discussions in the cabinet room," Schlesinger writes in *A Thousand Days.* "I can only explain my failure to do more than raise a few timid questions by reporting that one's impulse to blow the whistle on this nonsense was simply undone by the circumstances of the discussion."

7. *Unanimity.* Victims of groupthink share an *illusion* of unanimity within the group concerning almost all judgments expressed by members who speak in favor of the majority view. This symptom results partly from the preceding one, whose effects are augmented by the false assumption that any individual who remains silent during any part of the discussion is in full accord with what the others are saying.

When a group of persons who respect each other's opinions arrives at a unanimous view, each member is likely to feel that the belief must be true. This reliance on consensual validation within the group tends to replace individual critical thinking and reality testing, unless there are clear-cut disagreements among the members. In contemplating a course of action such as the invasion of Cuba, it is painful for the members to confront disagreements within their group, particularly if it becomes apparent that there are widely divergent views about whether the preferred course of action is too risky to undertake at all. Such disagreements are likely to arouse anxieties about making a serious error. Once the sense of unanimity is shattered, the members no longer can feel complacently confident about the decision they are inclined to make. Each man must then face the annoying realization that there are troublesome uncertainties and he must diligently seek out the best information he can get in order to decide for himself exactly how serious the risks might be. This is one of the unpleasant consequences of being in a group of hardheaded, critical thinkers.

To avoid such an unpleasant state, the members often become inclined, without quite realizing it, to prevent latent disagreements from surfacing when they are about to initiate a risky course of action. The group leader and the members support each other in playing up the areas of convergence in their thinking, at the expense of fully exploring divergencies that might reveal unsettled issues.

"Our meetings took place in a curious atmosphere of assumed consensus," Schlesinger writes. His additional comments clearly show that, curiously, the consensus was an illusion—an illusion that could be maintained only because the major participants did not reveal their own reasoning or discuss their idiosyncratic assumptions and vague reservations. Evidence from several sources makes it clear that even the three principals—President Kennedy, Rusk and McNamara—had widely differing assumptions about the invasion plan.

8. *Mindguards.* Victims of groupthink sometimes appoint themselves as mindguards to protect the leader and fellow members from adverse information that might break the complacency they shared about the effectiveness

and morality of past decisions. At a large birthday party for his wife, Attorney General Robert F. Kennedy, who had been constantly informed about the Cuban invasion plan, took Schlesinger aside and asked him why he was opposed. Kennedy listened coldly and said, ''You may be right or you may be wrong, but the President has made his mind up. Don't push it any further. Now is the time for everyone to help him all they can.''

Rusk also functioned as a highly effective mindguard by failing to transmit to the group the strong objections of three ''outsiders'' who had learned of the invasion plan—Undersecretary of State Chester Bowles, USIA Director Edward R. Murrow, and Rusk's intelligence chief, Roger Hilsman. Had Rusk done so, their warnings might have reinforced Schlesinger's memorandum and jolted some of Kennedy's ingroup, if not the President himself, into reconsidering the decision.

PRODUCTS. When a group of executives frequently displays most or all of these interrelated symptoms, a detailed study of their deliberations is likely to reveal a number of immediate consequences. These consequences are, in effect, products of poor decision-making practices because they lead to inadequate solutions to the problems under discussion.

First, the group limits its discussions to a few alternative courses of action (often only two) without an initial survey of all the alternatives that might be worthy of consideration.

Second, the group fails to reexamine the course of action initially preferred by the majority after they learn of risks and drawbacks they had not considered originally.

Third, the members spend little or no time discussing whether there are non-obvious gains they may have overlooked or ways of reducing the seemingly prohibitive costs that made rejected alternatives appear undesirable to them.

Fourth, members make little or no attempt to obtain information from experts within their own organizations who might be able to supply more precise estimates of potential losses and gains.

Fifth, members show positive interest in facts and opinions that support their preferred policy; they tend to ignore facts and opinions that do not.

Sixth, members spend little time deliberating about how the chosen policy might be hindered by bureaucratic inertia, sabotaged by political opponents, or temporarily derailed by common accidents. Consequently, they fail to work out contingency plans to cope with foreseeable setbacks that could endanger the overall success of their chosen course.

SUPPORT. The search for an explanation of why groupthink occurs has led me through a quagmire of complicated theoretical issues in the murky area of human motivation. My belief, based on recent social psychological research, is that we can best understand the various symptoms of groupthink as a mutual effort among the group members to maintain self-esteem and emotional equanimity by providing social support to each other, especially at times when they share responsibility for making vital decisions.

Even when no important decision is pending, the typical administrator will begin to doubt the wisdom and morality of his past decisions each time he receives information about setbacks, particularly if the information is accompanied by negative feedback from prominent men who originally had been his supporters. It should not be surprising, therefore, to find that individual members strive to develop unanimity and esprit de corps that will help bolster each other's morale, to create an optimistic outlook about the success of pending decisions, and to reaffirm the positive value of past policies to which all of them are committed.

PRIDE. Shared illusions of invulnerability, for example, can reduce anxiety about taking risks. Rationalizations help members believe that the risks are really not so bad after all. The assumption of inherent morality helps the members to avoid feelings of shame or guilt. Negative stereotypes function as stress-reducing devices to enhance a sense of moral righteousness as well as pride in a lofty mission.

The mutual enhancement of self-esteem and morale may have functional value in enabling the members to maintain their capacity to take action, but it has maladaptive consequences insofar as concurrence-seeking tendencies interfere with critical, rational capacities and lead to serious errors of judgment.

While I have limited my study to decision-making bodies in Government, groupthink symptoms appear in business, industry and any other field where small, cohesive groups make the decisions. It is vital, then, for all sorts of people—and especially group leaders—to know what steps they can take to prevent groupthink.

REMEDIES. To counterpoint my case studies of the major fiascos, I have also investigated two highly successful group enterprises, the formulation of the Marshall Plan in the Truman Administration and the handling of the Cuban missile crisis by President Kennedy and his advisers. I have found it instructive to examine the steps Kennedy took to change his group's decision-making processes. These changes ensured that the mistakes made by his Bay of Pigs ingroup were not repeated by the missile-crisis ingroup, even though the membership of both groups was essentially the same.

The following recommendations for preventing groupthink incorporate many of the good practices I discovered to be characteristic of the Marshall Plan and missile-crisis groups:

1. The leader of a policy-forming group should assign the role of critical evaluator to each member, encouraging the group to give high priority to open airing of objections and doubts. This practice needs to be reinforced by the leader's acceptance of criticism of his own judgments in order to discourage members from soft-pedaling their disagreements and from allowing their striving for concurrence to inhibit critical thinking.

2. When the key members of a hierarchy assign a policy-planning mission to any group within their organization, they should adopt an impartial stance instead of stating preferences and expectations at the beginning. This will encourage open inquiry and impartial probing of a wide range of policy alternatives.

3. The organization routinely should set up several outside policy-planning

and evaluation groups to work on the same policy question, each deliberating under a different leader. This can prevent the insulation of an ingroup.

4. At intervals before the group reaches a final consensus, the leader should require each member to discuss the group's deliberations with associates in his own unit of the organization—assuming that those associates can be trusted to adhere to the same security regulations that govern the policymakers—and then to report back their reactions to the group.

5. The group should invite one or more outside experts to each meeting on a staggered basis and encourage the experts to challenge the views of the core members.

6. At every general meeting of the group, whenever the agenda calls for an evaluation of policy alternatives, at least one member should play devil's advocate, functioning as a good lawyer in challenging the testimony of those who advocate the majority position.

7. Whenever the policy issue involves relations with a rival nation or organization, the group should devote a sizable block of time, perhaps an entire session, to a survey of all warning signals from the rivals and should write alternative scenarios on the rivals' intentions.

8. When the group is surveying policy alternatives for feasibility and effectiveness, it should from time to time divide into two or more subgroups to meet separately, under different chairmen, and then come back together to hammer out differences.

9. After reaching a preliminary consensus about what seems to be the best policy, the group should hold a "second-chance" meeting at which every member expresses as vividly as he can all his residual doubts, and rethinks the entire issue before making a definitive choice.

HOW. These recommendations have their disadvantages. To encourage the open airing of objections, for instance, might lead to prolonged and costly debates when a rapidly growing crisis requires immediate solution. It also could cause rejection, depression and anger. A leader's failure to set a norm might create cleavage between leader and members that could develop into a disruptive power struggle if the leader looks on the emerging consensus as anathema. Setting up outside evaluation groups might increase the risk of security leakage. Still, inventive executives who know their way around the organizational maze probably can figure out how to apply one or another of the prescriptions successfully, without harmful side effects.

They also could benefit from the advice of outside experts in the administrative and behavioral sciences. Though these experts have much to offer, they have had few chances to work on policy-making machinery within large organizations. As matters now stand, executives innovate only when they need new procedures to avoid repeating serious errors that have deflated their self-images.

In this era of atomic warheads, urban disorganization and ecocatastrophes, it seems to me that policymakers should collaborate with behavioral scientists and give top priority to preventing groupthink and its attendant fiascos.

Chapter 26

How to Diagnose
Group Problems

Leland P. Bradford
Dorothy Stock
Murray Horwitz

A group has two things in common with a machine or with any organism anywhere.

1. *It has something to do.*
2. *It must be kept in running order to do it.*

These twin functions require continual attention. Groups show their concern for the first—their specific jobs, goals, activities—by establishing procedures, rules of order, expected leadership responsibilities. But sometimes the rules a group sets up for itself fail to take into account its maintenance needs. When this happens the group finds itself bogging down.

The importance of the maintenance function is immediately recognized in other situations. Airliners require the services of maintenance crews as well as navigators. An automobile, a sewing machine, a typewriter, or a whistling peanut wagon that has no care paid to its upkeep soon begins to break down.

We can't, of course, carry the analogy too far. Among the important ways in which groups differ from machines, consider this: A new machine has its peak of efficiency at the beginning of its life. A new group, on the other hand, is likely to be more inept and less efficient at the beginning than it is later. If it is healthy, a group grows and changes, becoming more cohesive, more productive, more capable of helping its individual members in specific ways. The problem of maintenance, therefore, is inseparable from the process of growth.

This article will analyze the causes and symptoms of some common problems that interfere with group growth and productivity, and describe some methods of diagnosis.

Reproduced by special permission from *Group Development*, Selected Reading Series One, by Leland P. Bradford, Dorothy Stock, and Murray Horwitz, pp. 37-50, 1961, NTL Institute for Applied Behavioral Science.

GROUP PROBLEMS

Three of the most common group problems are:
1. Conflict or fight
2. Apathy and nonparticipation
3. Inadequate decision-making.

FIGHT—we don't necessarily mean a heavyweight bout. Fight here means disagreement, argumentation, the nasty crack, the tense atmosphere, conflict. Some ways in which fight can be expressed are:
   a) members are impatient with one another
   b) ideas are attacked before they are completely expressed
   c) members take sides and refuse to compromise
   d) members disagree on plans or suggestions
   e) comments and suggestions are made with a great deal of vehemence
   f) members attack one another on a personal level in subtle ways
   g) members insist that the group doesn't have the know-how or experience to get anywhere
   h) members feel the group can't get ahead because it is too large or too small
   i) members disagree with the leader's suggestions
   j) members accuse one another of not understanding the real point
   k) members hear distorted fragments of other members' contributions.
The following are several possible reasons for such fight behavior:

1. *The group has been given an impossible job and members are frustrated because they feel unable to meet the demands made of them.* This frequently happens when the group is a committee of a larger organization. Perhaps the committee has a job which is impossible because it doesn't have enough members. Or perhaps the job is impossible because it is ambiguous—the task for the committee has not been clearly defined by the larger group. (Under these circumstances the committee has no way of knowing to what extent alternative plans are appropriate or will be acceptable to the larger group.) For whatever reason, an impossible task can easily produce frustration and tension among the members of a group, and this may be expressed in bickering and attack.

2. *The main concern of members is to find status in the group.* Although the group is ostensibly working on some task, the task is being used by the members as a means of jockeying for power, establishing alignments and cliques, or trying to suppress certain individuals or cliques. Under such circumstances certain members may oppose one another stubbornly on some issue for reasons which have nothing to do with the issue. Or there may be a lot of attack on a personal level which is intended to deflate and reduce the prestige of another member. This kind of power struggle may involve the leader. If it does, the attack will include him, perhaps in the form of refusing to understand or to follow his suggestions (if members can show that the leader is not a good leader, then he should be deposed).

3. *Members are loyal to outside groups of conflicting interests.* This can happen when the members of a committee are each representing some outside organization. They have an interest in getting a job done within the committee but they also have a loyalty to their own organization. This situation creates conflicts within each individual so that he doesn't know whether he should behave as a member of this committee or as a member of another group. His behavior may be inconsistent and rigid and his inner confusion may burst out as irritation or stubbornness. His loyalty to his own organization may make him feel that he has to protect its interests carefully, keep the others from putting something over on him, be careful not to give more than he gets. This may lead to a refusal to cooperate, expressions of passive resistance, etc.

4. *Members feel involved and are working hard on a problem.* Members may frequently express impatience, irritation, or disagreement because they have a real stake in the issue being discussed. They fight for a certain plan because it is important to them—and this fight may take the form of real irritation with others because they can't "see" or won't go along with a suggestion which—to the member—is obviously the best one. As long as there is a clearly-understood goal and continuing movement on a problem, this kind of fight contributes to good problem-solving.

These are not intended to be *all* the possible reasons for fight behavior, but they are some, and they are quite different from one another. The obvious question arises: How can a member or leader tell which diagnosis is appropriate to a specific situation? If the fourth situation obtains, then fight is operating in the service of work and should not worry a group. If fight is interfering with getting things done on the work task, as it is in the other three situations, then it is important to know which description fits the group so that the underlying causes can be attacked.

The solution to this diagnostic problem lies in the need to understand the context in which the symptom has occurred. That is, one cannot understand fight, or any other symptom, by looking at the symptom only. It is necessary to broaden one's view and look at the syndrome—all the other things which are going on in the group at the same time.

Let's re-examine our four descriptions of symptoms, this time in terms of possible diagnoses:

IF
—every suggestion made seems impossible for practical reasons,
—some members feel the committee is too small,
—everyone seems to feel pushed for time,
—members are impatient with one another,
—members insist the group doesn't have the know-how or experience to get anywhere,
— each member has a different idea of what the committee is supposed to do,

—whenever a suggestion is made, at least one member feels it won't satisfy the larger organization.

THEN

—the group may have been given an impossible job and members are frustrated because they feel unable to meet the demands made of them, or the task is not clear or is disturbing.

IF

—ideas are attacked before they are completely expressed,
—members take sides and refuse to compromise,
—there is no movement toward a solution of the problem,
—the group keeps getting stuck on inconsequential points,
—members attack one another on a personal level in subtle ways,
—there are subtle attacks on the leadership,
—there is no concern with finding a goal or sticking to the point,
—there is much clique formation,

THEN

—the main concern of members may be in finding status in the group. The main interest is not in the problem. The problem is merely being used as a vehicle for expressing interpersonal concerns.

IF

—the goal is stated in very general, non-operational terms,
—members take sides and refuse to compromise,
—each member is pushing his own plan,
—suggestions don't build on previous suggestions, each member seeming to start again from the beginning,
—members disagree on plans or suggestions,
—members don't listen to one another, each waiting for a chance to say something,

THEN

—each member is probably operating from a unique, unshared point of view, perhaps because the members are loyal to different outside groups with conflicting interests.

IF

—there is a goal which members understand and agree on,
—most comments are relevant to the problem,
—members frequently disagree with one another over suggestions,
—comments and suggestions are made with a great deal of vehemence,
—there are occasional expressions of warmth,

—members are frequently impatient with one another,
—there is general movement toward some solution of the problem,

THEN
—probably, members feel involved and are working hard on a problem. The fight being expressed is constructive rather than destructive in character and reflects real interest on the part of members.

APATHY—an apathetic membership is a frequent ailment of groups. Groups may suffer in different degrees from this disease. In some cases members may show complete indifference to the group task, and give evidences of marked boredom. In others, apathy may take the form of a lack of genuine enthusiasm for the job, a failure to mobilize much energy, lack of persistence, satisfaction with poor work.

Some ways in which apathy may be expressed:

a) frequent yawns, people dozing off
b) members lose the point of the discussion
c) low level of participation
d) conversation drags
e) members come late; are frequently absent
f) slouching and restlessness
g) overquick decisions
h) failure to follow through on decisions
i) ready suggestions for adjournment
j) failure to consider necessary arrangements for the next meeting
k) reluctance to assume any further responsibility.

A commonly held idea is that people require inspirational leadership in order to maintain a high level of interest and morale and to overcome apathy. An outgrowth of this belief is the prescription of pep talks which, unfortunately, have only momentary effects, if any, and become less and less effective the more often they are used. To overcome or prevent apathy, we must treat the causes rather than the symptoms.

Here are some of the common reasons for apathy:

1. *The problem upon which the group is working does not seem important to the members, or it may seem less important than some other problem on which they would prefer to be working.* The problem may be important to someone. Perhaps to some outside part, perhaps to the total organization of which the group is a part, perhaps to the group leader, or even to a minority of the members. But it fails to arouse positive feelings or "involvement" on the part of the apathetic members.

Sometimes problems will be considered because of tradition. Again, members may find it difficult to express themselves freely enough to call for reconsideration of an unsatisfactory group goal. Sometimes, in organizational settings, problems are assigned, and the members haven't enough information to judge why the problem is important, except that "somebody upstairs" thinks it is. Again, the problem may be important to the leader or to some dominant member, and the group is coerced by these individuals into working on the problem as if it were really its own. In all of these cases the members will feel that they have had no part in initiating the problem, but that it has been imposed upon them. The basic feature of such imposed, "meaningless" tasks is that they are not related to the present needs of the members.

2. *The problem may seem important to members, but there are reasons which lead them to avoid attempting to solve the problem.* If members both desire to achieve the goal and fear attempting to achieve it, they are placed in a situation of conflict which may lead to tension, fatigue, apathy. Where subordinates feel they will be punished for mistakes, they will avoid taking action, hoping to shift responsibility to someone higher up the line of organizational authority. Similar fears, and similar desires to avoid working on particular problems, may stem from hostile feelings to other individuals, or to subgroups within the group. Sometimes the group atmosphere is such that members avoid exposing themselves to attack or ridicule, and feel insecure, self-conscious or embarrassed about presenting their ideas.

3. *The group may have inadequate procedures for solving the problem.* Inadequacies in procedure arise from a variety of sources. There may be lack of knowledge about the steps which are necessary to reach the goal. There may be poor communication among members within the group based on a failure to develop mutual understanding. There may be a poor coordination of effort so that contributions to the discussion are made in a disorganized, haphazard way, with a failure of one contribution to build upon previous ones. Members may not have the habit of collecting facts against which to test decisions, so that decisions turn out to be unrealistic and unrealizable.

4. *Members may feel powerless about influencing final decisions.* Although none of the apathy-producing conditions described above exists, it is possible that any decisions they arrive at are "meaningless." If the decisions will have no practical effects, the activity of problem-solving becomes only an academic exercise. Examples of this may be found in committees within an organization which are assigned some job, where members feel that their recommendations will get lost somewhere up the line. Or, perhaps they may feel that the top personnel in the organization are pretending to be "democratic," and are only making a show of getting participation, but will in all likelihood ignore their suggestions. In such cases groups tend to operate ritualistically, going through the required motions, without involvement.

The same effect may occur if within the group there is a domineering leader, who is recognized by other members as making all the decisions. Again it is pointless for the members to invest their emotional energy in attempting to create solutions to their problem. Apathy may also arise because individual members are passed by while a smoothly functioning subgroup forces quick decisions, not giving the slower members opportunity to make decisions. Status differences within the group will frequently have the same effect. People with lower status may find it difficult to get an opportunity to be heard by other members, with the result that they come to feel that their contributions will have little effect upon the outcome.

5. *A prolonged and deep fight among a few members has dominated the group.* Frequently two or three dominant and talkative members of a group will compete with one another or with the leader so much that every activity in the group is overshadowed by the conflict. Less dominant members who feel inadequate to help solve the conflict become apathetic and withdraw from participation.

In considering these five types of causes for apathy, it seems clear we have to direct our attention to underlying conditions, rather than symptoms. Measures which are taken directed at the symptom itself—pep-talks, for example, may be completely off the mark. It should also be borne in mind that while a single explanation may largely account for the apathetic behavior, this is not necessarily the case. Any of the suggested reasons may apply, in any combination, and in varying degrees. To determine whether a given reason applies to a particular group situation, it is sometimes helpful to look for the set of symptoms, the syndrome—which may be associated with each cause. Not all the symptoms under each set need be present to indicate that the disease is of a given type, but if several can be observed, it is probably a good bet that the particular diagnosis applies.

IF
—questions may be raised about what's really our job, what do *they* want us to do,
—members fail to follow through on decisions,
—there is no expectation that members will contribute responsibly, and confused, irrelevant statements are allowed to go by without question,
—members wonder about the reason for working on this problem,
—suggestions are made that we work on something else,
—the attitude is expressed that we should just decide on anything, the decision doesn't really matter,
—members seem to be waiting for a respectable amount of time to pass before referring the decision to the leader, or to a committee,
—members are inattentive, seem to get lost and not to have heard parts of the preceding discussion,
—suggestions frequently "plop," are not taken up and built on by others,
—no one will volunteer for additional work,

THEN
—the group goal may seem unimportant to the members.

IF

—there are long delays in getting started, much irrelevant preliminary conversation,

—the group shows embarrassment or reluctance in discussing the problem at hand,

—members emphasize the consequences of making wrong decisions, imagine dire consequences which have little reference to ascertainable facts,

—members make suggestions apologetically, are over-tentative, and hedge their contributions with many *if's* and *but's*,

—solutions proposed are frequently attacked as unrealistic,

—suggestions are made that someone else ought to make the decision—the leader, an outside expert, or some qualified person outside the group,

—members insist that we haven't enough information or ability to make a decision, and appear to demand an unrealistically high level of competence,

—the group has a standard of cautiousness in action,

—numerous alternative proposals are suggested, with the group apparently unable to select among them,

THEN

—members probably fear working toward the group goal.

IF

—no one is able to suggest the first step in getting started toward the goal,

—members seem to be unable to stay on a given point, and each person seems to start on a new tack,

—members appear to talk past, to misunderstand one another, and the same points are made over and over,

—the group appears to be unable to develop adequate summaries, or restatements of points of agreement,

—there is little evaluation of the possible consequences of decisions reached, and little attention is given to fact-finding or use of special resources,

—members continually shift into related, but off-target, tasks,

—complaints are made that the group's job is an impossible one,

—subgroups continually form around the table, with private discussions held off to the side,

—there is no follow-through on decisions or disagreement in the group about what the decisions really were,

—complaints are made that you can't decide things in a group anyway, and the leader or somebody else should do the job,

THEN

—the group may have inadequate problem-solving procedures.

IF
- —the view is expressed that someone else with more power in the organization should be present in the meeting, that it is difficult to communicate with him at a distance.
- —unrealistic decisions are made, and there is an absence of sense of responsibility for evaluating consequences of decisions,
- —the position is taken that the decision doesn't really matter because the leader or someone outside the group isn't really going to listen to what we say,
- —there is a tendency to ignore reaching consensus among members, the important thing being to get the leader to understand and listen,
- —the discussion is oriented toward power relations, either within the group, jockeying to win over the leader, or outside the group, with interest directed toward questions about who really counts in the organization,
- —doubts are voiced about whether we're just wasting our efforts in working on this program,
- —members leave the meeting feeling they had good ideas which they didn't seem to be able to get across,

THEN
- —members feel powerless about influencing final decisions.

IF
- —two or three members dominate all discussion, but never agree,
- —conflict between strong members comes out no matter what is discussed,
- —dominant members occasionally appeal to others for support, but otherwise control conversation,
- —decisions are made by only two or three members,

THEN
- —a conflict among a few members is creating apathy in the others.

INADEQUATE DECISION-MAKING—getting satisfactory decisions made is often a major struggle in the group. These problems are discussed in detail in the article "Decisions...Decisions...Decisions!"...* Here is a list of common symptoms of inefficient decision-making.

IF
- —the group swings between making too rapid decisions and having difficulty in deciding anything,
- —the group almost makes the decision but at the last minute retreats,
- —group members call for definition and redefinition of minute points,
- —the discussion wanders into abstraction,

*By Robert R. Blake and Leland P. Bradford, *Adult Leadership*, Vol. II, No. 7, December, 1953.

THEN
>—there has been premature calling for a decision, or the decision is too difficult, or the group is low in cohesiveness and lacks faith in itself.

IF
>—the group has lack of clarity as to what the decision is,
>—there is disagreement as to where consensus is,
>—a decision is apparently made but challenged at the end,
>—group members refuse responsibility,
>—there is continued effort to leave decision-making to leader, subgroup or outside source,

THEN
>—the decision area may be threatening to the group, either because of unclear consequences, fear of reaction of other groups, or fear of failure for the individuals.

IMPROVING GROUP EFFICIENCY

Today guided missiles have a feedback mechanism built into them that continuously collects information about the position of the target in relation to the flight of the missile. When the collected information indicates a shift of the target or a discrepancy in the arc of flight of the missile, the feedback mechanism corrects the flight of the missile.

Most houses with central heating today have a small feedback mechanism, called a thermostat. When the information collected by it indicates the temperature is below a certain point, the mechanism signals the furnace to turn itself on. When information collected by the thermostat indicates that the temperature is too high, it signals the furnace to stop.

Groups need to build in feedback mechanisms to help in their own steering. Such a process of feedback calls for collecting information on the discrepancy between what the group wants to do (its target) and what it is doing (reaching its target) so that it can make corrections in its direction.

DIAGNOSIS AND FEEDBACK

Human beings, and therefore groups, not only need continuous self-correction in direction but also (and here they differ from machines) need to learn or grow or improve. Collecting adequate data and using this information to make decisions about doing things differently is one of the major ways of learning.

There are three basic parts to the process of changing group behavior:
1. Collecting information
2. Reporting the information to the group
3. Making diagnoses and decisions for change.

WHO SHOULD DIAGNOSE?

If a member of a group strives to improve his own behavior in the group so that he can make more useful contributions, he will need to make his own personal observations and diagnoses about the group and about his behavior in it. Each member has this individual responsibility.

If the group as a whole is to make decisions about changing its procedures or processes, then the entire group must assume responsibility for collaborative diagnoses of its difficulties and its effectiveness. If the leader takes over this function, he continues to direct and dominate the group—leading them like sheep. If only the leader analyzes group difficulties and acts upon them, only he learns. Similar problems arise if diagnosis is left to any group member; he may too readily use this job to steer the group in the direction he desires.

Each member and the leader may guide and encourage the group toward diagnosis, but the responsibility for self-steering and the opportunities to learn and to grow must remain with the group if it is to improve its operational effectiveness.

COLLECTING INFORMATION

While analysis and evaluation of information and decisions about what to do should be carried out by the total group, the collecting of information may be delegated. A number of patterns of delegation are possible.

1. The leader, serving also as observer, can report to the group certain pertinent observations he has made about problems and difficulties of group operation. However, although the leader may have more experience with groups, to add the function of observer to his leadership responsibilities complicates his job and also tends to create greater dependency upon him.

   But when the group is unfamiliar with the process of observation, the leader may play an informal observer role for a few meetings, gradually getting other group members to assume this function.

2. The group may appoint one of its members, perhaps on a rotating basis, to serve as group observer, with the task of noting the manner in which the group works. While a group loses a member as far as work on its task is concerned, it can gain in the growth and improvement of the group.

   Frequently there is a leader-team made up of a discussion leader and observer. The leader and observer work together in behalf of the group, one helping to guide the group and making procedural suggestions, the other watching how it works.

   When a leader-team is formed, it makes possible team planning for each meeting. Between meetings the leader-observer team can look back at the past meeting from two vantage points, and look forward to the next meeting.

3. A third method calls for all group members to be as sensitive as they can, while participating actively, to the particular problems the group faces. Although in mature groups members may raise a question about group procedures or maintenance at any time as a normal contribution to the discussion, in new groups the leader may start a discussion looking at how the group has worked and what its problems are. This may occur at some time during the discussion, when the group has bogged down, or during the last fifteen minutes to half an hour as an evaluation of the entire meeting.

WHAT INFORMATION TO COLLECT?

Because of the many group problems and the many causes of these problems there is a wide range of information that a group may need at different points in time. General questions such as these may help get started:

1. What is our goal? Are we "on" or "off the beam"?
2. Where are we in our discussion? At the point of analyzing the problem? Suggesting solutions? Testing ideas?
3. How fast are we moving? Are we bogged down?
4. Are we using the best methods of work?
5. Are all of us working or just a few?
6. Are we making any improvement in our ability to work together?

In any observation of a group more can be seen than can possibly be used for steering, corrective or growth purposes. The following questions may help guide an observer in collecting data about a group.

1. What basic problems does the group seem to have for which information is needed?
2. What is most important or pertinent information? What information will lead the group into stray paths?
3. What is the essential minimum of material the group needs?

METHODS OF OBSERVATION

Just as there are many areas of information about group behavior, so there are many possible guides and scales for observation. Frequently groups develop such scales to fit their particular needs. Three techniques of observation are given, each useful for collecting a different kind of information.

1. *WHO TALKS TO WHOM*

The number of lines made by the observer on [the following] form indicates the number of statements made in a fifteen-minute period—20. Four of these were made to the group as a whole, and so the arrows go only to the middle of

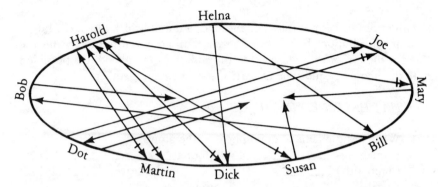

the circle. Those with arrows at each end of a line show that the statement made by one person to another was responded to by the recipient.

We see that one person, Harold, had more statements directed toward him than did anyone else and that he responded or participated more than anyone else. The short lines drawn at the head of one of the pair of arrows indicates who initiated the remark. Harold, the leader, in other words had remarks directed at him calling for response from four other people.

2. WHO MAKES WHAT KINDS OF CONTRIBUTIONS*

Member No.	1	2	3	4	5	6	7	8	9	10
1. Encourages										
2. Agrees, accepts										
3. Arbitrates										
4. Proposes action										
5. Asks suggestion										
6. Gives opinion										
7. Asks opinion										
8. Gives information										
9. Seeks information										
10. Poses problem										
11. Defines position										
12. Asks position										
13. Routine direction										
14. Depreciates self										
15. Autocratic manner										
16. Disagrees										
17. Self-assertion										
18. Active aggression										
19. Passive aggression										
20. Out-of-field										

*Based upon observation categories discussed in *Interaction Process Analysis* by Robert F. Bales. Cambridge, Mass.: Addison-Wesley Press, 1950.

This record makes possible the quick rating not only of who talked, but the type of contribution. Individuals in the group are given numbers which are listed at the top of the columns. At the end of a time period it is possible to note the frequency and type of participation by each member.

3. *WHAT HAPPENED IN THE GROUP*

1. What was the general atmosphere in the group?
   Formal_____ Informal_____
   Competitive_____ Cooperative_____
   Hostile_____ Supportive_____
   Inhibited_____ Permissive_____
   Comments: _____

2. Quantity and quality of work accomplished
   Accomplishment: High_____ Low_____
   Quality of Production: High_____ Low_____
   Goals: Clear_____ Vague_____
   Methods: Clear_____ Vague_____
                           Flexible_____ Inflexible_____
   Comments: _____

3. Leader behavior
   Attentive to group needs_____
   Supported others_____
   Concerned only with topic_____ Took sides_____
   Dominated group_____ Helped group_____
   Comments: _____

4. Participation
   Most people talked_____ Only few talked_____
   Members involved_____ Members apathetic_____
   Group united_____ Group divided_____
   Comments: _____

This form can be used as a checklist by an observer to sum up his observations, or it can be filled out by all group members to start an evaluation discussion. Forms 1 and 2 can be used only by a full-time observer.

REPORTING INFORMATION TO THE GROUP

The second step is feeding back pertinent information to the entire group. Whether the information is collected and reported by the leader or by the observer, it is very easy to hurt the group rather than help it. The following cautions are particularly pertinent in reporting to the group.

1. Be sensitive to what information the group is ready to use—what will be most helpful to the group now, rather than what was the most interesting point observed.
2. Don't "avalanche" the group with information. If too much information is given it can't be used. Select only two or three observations which will stimulate thinking and discussion. Let the group ask for more information as it needs it.
3. Don't praise the group too much. Learning doesn't take place by being told only when we are "on the beam." Mentioning accomplishments is desirable as it helps difficulties get honestly faced.
4. Don't punish or preach or judge. The observer can't play the role of God. He says, "It was interesting that participation was less widespread today than yesterday." He doesn't say, "Some of you dominated the discussion today."
5. It is easier to discuss role behavior than people's behavior. "What role did the group need filled at that time," rather than, "That behavior is bad."
6. Go lightly on personality clashes. It is usually better to discuss what helped and what hindered the whole group.

EVALUATING INFORMATION AND DECIDING ABOUT CHANGE

The third stage is diagnosis from the information reported and the consideration of what the group and its members will do differently in the future. Usually this has a number of steps.

1. The members assess the observations, relate them to their experiences, test to see whether they agree with the report.
2. The group examines the reasons. What caused a thing to happen? Could we have recognized it earlier?
3. The group moves to a decision of what to do. What can be done in future similar circumstances? What can individual members do earlier to help? What methods or procedures should be changed? What new directions sought?

This stage is the crucial one if the group is to benefit from its feedback activities. Unless the members are able to gain new insights into the functioning of the group, and are able to find new ways of behaving, the group will not improve its processes and continue in its growth and development.

It is very easy for the time of the discussion to be consumed by the first two steps in this procedure. The leader, as well as the members, needs to be sensitive to this danger and encourage the group to move into the third step of decision. Although the decisions which are made may be quite simple, agreement on future action sets up common expectations for the next meeting and gives a point to the evaluation.

Afterthoughts

Several authors made the analogy between a group and a mechanical system to convey the idea that, to insure success, attention must be given to how well the group members are interacting as well as to how well the group is achieving its purpose. The analogy can be carried a step further to highlight your role as a manager in group effectiveness. In automotive terms you must act as the design engineer and master mechanic, not just the driver, to keep the group on track and moving at peak efficiency. Each of the preceding chapters offered special knowledge and skills for you to perform these group management tasks.

When group members learn to play roles and adopt certain rules of group functioning, the group as a whole can become so competent that its capacity for creative problem solving can surpass its most knowledgeable and talented member. That is part of Hall's message in the first chapter—the quality of decisions made by individuals is usually surpassed by consensual deliberations. The other part of his message is that the highest levels of group effectiveness can only be achieved when you bring the philosophy, knowledge, and skills presented in the first four sections to bear within the workgroup.

Hall attributed four characteristics to the effective group—commitment, conflict, creativity, and consensus. As stressed throughout preceding chapters, you must believe that the capacity for competent work is widespread before even entertaining the notion of a collaborative enterprise. Only then are you likely to share power through participative practices and utilize your interpersonal skills to engage group members and to make conflict a springboard to creativity. Without applying models for managerial competence within the framework of consensus decision-making, synergy, the fruitful result of pooled resources, will be a desirable but unattainable goal.

As Lewin described, change is a three-step process of unfreezing, moving and refreezing—of breaking down and replacing old behaviors and subsequently reinforcing the desired way of acting. We tend to think of such a process as occurring in a one-on-one coaching and counseling or performance appraisal session. However, involvement and commitment are key forces in change and the small group is the most potent setting. In situations where privacy and confidentiality are not restraining factors, the message is clear—do no attempt to bring about change with a divide and conquer strategy; instead unite and collaborate.

Although Benne and Sheats made their observations on group functioning more than thirty years ago, their basic assertion still holds true—more attention is paid to group leader skills than member roles. Instead of looking at groups from only the viewpoint of leadership, a variety of member roles and responsibilities needs to be designed into their processes.

You have an important function in helping the group design its basic system of interaction. First of all, the group must be aware of the task and maintenance roles which contribute to group effectiveness and those which only serve individual needs, for example to grandstand or gain sympathy. Next they must be able to determine where the group is in the problem-solving process to select appropriate roles. Obviously, the group would be better served by an *elaborator* than by an *evaluator-critic* in the early phases of generating alternatives. Finally, and not so obviously, the group must be aware of its maturity, its own stage of development. A group which has just been established and is characterized by tentative interpersonal communications is more in need of a *standard setter* and *encourager* to increase the use of exposure and feedback than a *compromiser* to resolve differences.

Once you have helped group members learn the roles they should play at particular moments, you need to insure that this new awareness will continue to be brought to bear on the way the group conducts its affairs. Benne and Sheats suggest that a specific person be assigned the role of *group-observer*—someone who does not actively participate but instead notes critical incidents relating to task and interaction patterns. By rotating the *group-observer* role, all members become sensitive to factors related to maintaining effectiveness. Thus the process leading to group effectiveness which you initiate will be assimilated into the group.

Douglas McGregor[1] said that the common characteristic of all effective groups is that they are self-conscious about their own operation. The *group-observer* role is in direct service of that characteristic, and Bradford and his colleagues help to make it fully operational. To play the role to its fullest, the observer should be on the lookout for the seventy symptoms of group dysfunction—behaviors which might go unnoticed by those deeply involved in the task.

Observing and recording these symptoms is the first of three steps in the diagnosis-remediation cycle. The data are then presented to the group by the observer and the rules for giving feedback cited for interpersonal competence apply again—avoid the kind of criticizing or preaching which puts people on the defensive. Once the data have been discussed the group needs to decide on what actions are warranted. As Bradford indicates, you may have to push for a decision at this point since there is a tendency to recycle back into the feedback-discussion phase.

If the group continues to be self-conscious by following the guidelines offered by Benne and Sheats and Bradford, it should mature and become more effective over time. Even though a group gets better with age, there is a barrier to continued development, a liability related to age which is difficult to detect because it is largely an unconscious phenomenon. As Janis warns, "group-think" involves the nondeliberate, often unconscious, suppression of critical thoughts as a result of the internalization of group norms—group members begin to believe they can do no wrong.

Janis offers another set of symptoms of group dysfunction to be placed along-side Bradford's. Whereas Bradford's symptoms relate to individual behavior, Janis' eight symptoms apply to the group as a whole. The group must check itself to see, for example, if it is developing a "holier than thou" attitude regarding its adversaries or pressuring individual group members to put aside their disagreement and become good team players. If the symptoms of group-think are present in your group, try Janis' strategies to restore critical thinking. Set up independent task forces on the same issue, encourage internal devil's advocates, and invite external experts in for the express purpose of challenging the group's thinking.

These chapters have shown that the group can be an outstanding decision-making and problem-solving body when you manage it properly. Another point needs to be stressed in closing lest you be left with the impression that the group is being presented as the *sole* means to corporate excellence. Group work, concensus decision-making per se, should not be seen as a way of life, but a desirable alternative when you are concerned about high levels of commitment and a quality product.[2,3] When across-the-board support is necessary to put an idea into action and no single person has full knowledge of the matters at hand, the rules of consensus have proven to be the most productive means. At other times when there are few barriers to implementation and the best alternative is readily apparent, the manager may well go it alone in decision-making.

REFERENCES

1. McGregor, Douglas. *The Professional Manager.* New York: McGraw-Hill, 1967.

2. Maier, Norman R. F. *Problem Solving Discussions and Conferences: Leadership Methods and Skills.* New York: McGraw-Hill, 1963.

3. Vroom, V.H. and Yetton, Philip. *Leadership and Decision Making.* Pittsburg: University of Pittsburg, 1973.

Section VI.

Managerial Competence: Putting Models to the Test

Beginning with managerial philosophy in the first section and continuing through selections on motivation, involvement, interpersonal competence and group dynamics, the readings and editorial comments have focused on how a manager could better serve the interests of the organization and its members. But what about the manager? Altruism is commendable, but it is also fair for a manager to ask, "If I really put to use what has been suggested—what happens to my career? What's in it for me?" These questions have been ignored in some management development efforts, and consequently, the potential benefits of any innovative practices have been limited. As Hall and Donnell[1] note, "we are convinced that gaps of application and theory vis-a-vis practice will persist so long as executives are unsure of the consequences for themselves and their own achievement."

The question of career achievement for the manager who would apply the managerial practices suggested up to this point is answered in the final section. The six chapters explore managerial success from a practical point of view. What is it that successful managers do that accounts for their achievement? The answers contained in these chapters show that there is nothing magical about managerial success; it is the result of *behaving* in ways that any manager can learn.

One point needs clarification. Managerial success will be addressed in terms of *competence*, not merely *effectiveness*. Competence calls for a sustained high level of performance emanating from a set of well-knit values and positive beliefs about people and work. Effectiveness, on the other hand, is value free and is concerned with technique rather than principle. A manager concerned only with effectiveness could sanction any action which would resolve the immediate issue, accomplish the task at hand. Such a manager is pragmatic and amoral, and will not experience the level of success enjoyed by the competent manager.

EMERGING PATTERNS OF MANAGEMENT

In the mid 1950's Rensis Likert detected a new method of management emerging from a decade of research on organization and leadership. He examines those findings in "Patterns in Management." Before looking to the implications of the research data, he notes the contributions made by two major influences on management thought, "scientific management" and the "human relations movement." Both approaches have contributed to industrial performance but neither is fully adequate in and of itself.

Scientific management orients managers to production-centered concerns while human relations turns them to employee-centered thinking. But which yields the best results? Likert's preliminary findings indicated that employee-centered managers achieved greater productivity as long as they recognized that getting the job done was an equally important responsibility. Pushing for production alone led to a high level of work completed, but was offset by increasing costs related to scrap loss, grievances, work stoppages, and the like.

As Likert looked to the future, he called for a new management theory which would integrate scientific management and human relations in such a way that productivity and morale were of equal concern. Understanding the individual's motivation to work in more than economic terms would be key to achieving the simultaneous focus. He admitted at the time that he did not know exactly what was necessary to put the new theory into practice. However, he believed that research over the next decade would further refine and operationalize his contention that production and employee concerns were not only compatible but must receive equal attention from the manager.

In the 1960's Likert was able to fill in the pattern of successful managers. As described in "An Integrating Principle and an Overview," high producing managers, unlike low producers, tended to emphasize participation and the informal group in such a way that their units became highly coordinated, highly motivated, cooperative social systems. Subordinates within high producing units saw their managers as friendly, confident in the subordinates' ability, supportive, and demanding of high performance. Apparently the managers recognized their subordinates' need for influence and a feeling of accomplishment and pursued the principle of supportive relationships. The principle can be used as an organizing concept to harness all the energy and talent available in the work group.

Likert was confident in his findings but knew additional research would yield further evidence in support of integrating concerns for both people and production in the workplace. Robert R. Blake and Jane S. Mouton extended Likert's work throughout the 1960's. In "The Developing Revolution in Management Practices," Blake and Mouton present the Managerial Grid, a novel conceptual model for exploring further the facets of managerial success. The Grid provides a way of depicting different styles which can be used to achieve production through people. Managers who are able to maintain a high level of concern for both people and production use the most constructive style called "team management." The style and its component behaviors clearly reflect the integrated concerns of the high producing managers Likert observed.

Being able to characterize managers by their basic style leaves one question that needs to be answered before probing deeper into the dynamics of managerial success. To paraphrase a bewildered Sigmund Freud, "Women! What do they want?" Freud often spoke of the need for work but limited his conclusions to males. From all reports women remained somewhat of an enigma to Freud, but Susan Donnell and Jay Hall have been able to analyze their needs and abilities insofar as women as managers are concerned.

The title of Donnell and Hall's research report reflects their findings, "A Significant Case of No Significant Differences." Their investigation involved almost one thousand female managers who were matched and compared with the same number of male counterparts. Dimensions selected for comparison included managerial philosophy, motivation, participative practices, interpersonal competence, and managerial style. After all the data were analyzed, female managers differed from male managers in only two of forty-three ways. Basically, women administer the management process just as men do and their achievement will result from the same behavior.

MANAGERIAL STYLE, COMPETENCE, AND ACHIEVEMENT

Jay Hall's investigations, culminating in one of the largest studies of managerial behaviors and achievement ever undertaken, offer a comprehensive view of the ingredients of managerial success. The last three chapters interface: first, Hall synthesizes the elements of managerial style offered by several of the major behavioral science theorists of the past twenty-five years; second, he isolates those managerial behaviors which predict success; and finally, he puts wise words and optimistic predictions to the test as he indentifies the front-runners in a field of sixteen thousand managers.

In "Management Synthesis: An Anatomy of Managerial Style," Hall recognizes the contributions of such luminaries as Maslow, Herzberg, Blake and Mouton and others, but notes their tendency to proceed as if they were each alone if the field. He uses the Managerial Grid as an integrating device to show how managers behave within different style areas and how their behaviors impact on subordinates. The results are not the product of heady speculation. Seventeen hundred managers and more than three thousand of their subordinates provided the data base.

In "Managerial Competence: Working Productively with Most of the People Most of the Time," Hall extends the findings from his synthesis research. By using a statistical technique called a "hit" table, each major Grid style is evaluated as to the absence or presence of perspectives and skills critical to competence. The degree of competence inherent in the five managerial styles ranges from being right on target with most people over ninety percent of the time to the other extreme where a manager will be mistaken eighty-five percent of the time. Such a dramatic range of predicted success is well worth looking at closely for every manager concerned with achieving as high a level of competence as possible.

The variety of conceptual models and managerial practices presented throughout this volume are put to the test by Hall in the final chapter, "To Achieve or Not: The Manager's Choice." He confronts the "data-less" certainty that pop management literature presents, such as winning through intimidation, being an OK boss, or managing according to the situation at hand, by rigorously pursuing two questions: "First, who are our achieving managers? Second, what do they do to distinguish themselves from their less achieving cohorts?

The portrait that emerges of high achieving managers mirrors what the behavioral science theorists have suggested for twenty-five years. The most successful, competent managers work within a structure wherein people are valued as much as production, candor is common, and participation is the norm. Moreover, their success is contagious. High achievers are motivated by higher order needs in the workplace and convey these needs to their subordinates in such a way that they too adopt the same pursuits and experience the same success—*truly achieving managers produce achievers.* Competence is rewarding for managers as well as their fortunate subordinates. Hall's final words are provocative—today's low achievers can move up the competence ladder if they make the choice to change.

REFERENCES

1. Hall, Jay and Donnell, Susan M. "Managerial Achievement: The Personal Side of Behavioral Theory." *Human Relations, Vol. 32,* 1974, pp. 77-101.

Chapter 27

*Patterns in
Management*

The time has come to examine the findings that are now emerging from research on organization and leadership and to ask what are the implications of these findings for the development and training of those who will occupy positions of executive leadership in the next decade or two.

In trying to look into the future, it will be useful to consider historical trends as well as to examine the general pattern that is emerging from research findings. Two important trends have resulted in significant improvement in industrial performance and are exercising a major influence on current management practices. It will be of value to examine these trends, the character of their contribution, and the problems which they are creating.

"SCIENTIFIC MANAGEMENT"

The first of the two trends to be examined began almost a century ago. This was the earlier of the two and is the one which has had by far the greater influence upon both management practices and industrial productivity. I refer to the whole movement in which Frederick W. Taylor and his colleagues provided pioneering leadership. In discussing this trend, for purposes of brevity, I shall use the term "scientific management" to refer to this whole movement and related developments.

Generally speaking, the very great improvements in productivity brought about by scientific management have resulted from the elimination of waste. Functionalization, work simplification, motion study, analysis of work flow,

Reprinted, by permission of the publisher, from "Patterns in Management" by Rensis Likert, in *Strengthening Management for New Technology: Organization-Automation, Management Development,* General Management Series No. 178, ©1955 by American Management Association, Inc., pp. 32-51. All rights reserved.

standardization, and so on, have all resulted in simpler work cycles with the elimination of much waste motion and effort. They have also reduced the amount of learning required. Similarly, the establishment of clear-cut and specific goals and the creation of well-defined channels of communication, decision making, and control have contributed to better productivity. But associated with these gains have been serious problems and adverse effects.

The setting of production goals through the use of time standards often has been accompanied by a higher level of expected productivity and increased pressure on the workers to produce more. Workers resented and resisted this, and the "speed-up" was and still is a major source of conflict and bitterness. Moreover, workers and supervisors often resented an industrial engineer's providing evidence that they had been stupid when he showed that a much simpler and easier way of doing the work was possible. Another aspect of this method of managing which caused resentment was the view that workers could contribute nothing of value to the organization of their jobs and to the methods of work to be used. As Henry Ford expressed it, "All that we ask of the men is that they do the work which is set before them."[1]

These and similar adverse effects of scientific management were recognized more and more clearly during the second, third, and fourth decades of this century. The "speed-up" and "efficiency engineering" were the source of much hostility on the part of workers and supervisors. The resentment and hostilities manifested themselves in a variety of ways. They resulted in widespread restriction of output, even under incentive pay, and in a demand for protection through unions which led to the Wagner Act.

HUMAN RELATIONS TREND

The second trend which I wish to examine started at the end of the First World War when a few business leaders and social scientists began to appreciate the consequences of these and similar problems which accompanied the use of the scientific management approach. More general recognition of these problems, however, was brought about dramatically by the famous Western Electric studies. In the mid-twenties the National Research Council arranged with the Massachusetts Institute of Technology for Vannevar Bush and Joseph Barker to study the effect of different amounts of illumination, ventilation, and rest periods upon the production of industrial workers. They conducted this research in the Hawthorne plant of the Western Electric Company. After a few years of experimentation it became clear that morale and motivation factors were so important that they were completely obscuring the effect of the illumination, ventilation, and fatigue factors being studied. Bush then withdrew, suggesting that the morale factors were important and should be studied by

1. H. Pord and S. Crowther, *Today and Tomorrow* (New York: Doubleday, 1926).

social scientists, whereupon Elton Mayo and his colleagues undertook the research which resulted in their famous reports.[2]

These studies showed conclusively and quantitatively that workers were responding to scientific management methods by restricting production to levels which the workers felt were appropriate. Moreover, incentive methods of payment, either individual or group, did not prevent this restriction. These studies also showed that the workers had developed an "informal organization" which differed from the "formal" or organization-chart organization. Through this informal organization, workers exercised an important influence upon the behavior of themselves and their colleagues, often effectively countermanding the orders given officially through the formal organization. The Western Electric studies also showed that when the hostilities, resentments, suspicions, and fears of workers were replaced by favorable attitudes, a substantial increase in production occurred. The results showed that unfavorable attitudes exert an appreciable restraining influence upon productivity.

Mathewson,[3] Houser,[4] and others in a modest number of studies during the thirties showed that conditions existing in the Western Electric Company were relatively widespread. Morale and motivational factors were found to influence production. Restriction of output was common, and "informal organizations" were found to exist in most of the companies studied.

EMERGING PATTERN

During the past decade this second trend, which might be called the human relations trend, has gained greater impetus. The volume of research is still small but growing. The findings are consistent with the earlier studies and have important implications for the future trend of management theories and practices.

Some of the relevant parts of the pattern of results emerging from this more recent research can be shown by presenting a few findings from studies conducted by the Institute for Social Research. Since 1947 we have been conducting a series of related studies[5] seeking to find what kinds of organizational structure and what principles and methods of leadership and management result in the highest productivity, least absence, lowest turnover, and the greatest

2. E. Mayo, *The Human Problems of an Industrial Civilization,* Harvard Business School, Division of Research, 1946 (first printing by the Macmillan Co., 1933); F.J. Roethlisberger and W.J. Dickson, *Management and the Worker* (Cambridge: Harvard University Press, 1939).

3. S.B. Mathewson, *Restriction of Output among Unorganized Workers* (New York: The Viking Press, 1931).

4. J.D. Houser, *What People Want from Business* (New York: McGraw-Hill Book Co., Inc., 1938).

5. Generous support from the Office of Naval Research, the Rockefeller Foundation, and the companies and agencies involved have made this research possible.

job satisfaction.6 Studies have been conducted or are under way in a wide variety of organizations. These include one or more companies in such industries as the following: public utilities, insurance, automotive, railroad, electric appliances, heavy machinery, textiles, and petroleum.7 Studies also have been made in government agencies.8

In general, the design of the studies has been to measure and examine the kinds of leadership and related variables being used by the best units in the organization in contrast to those being used by the poorest. In essence, these studies are providing management with a mirror by measuring and reporting what is working best in industry today.

Briefly stated, some of the findings which are relevant for this discussion follow.

Orientation of Supervision. When foremen are asked what they have found to be the best pattern of supervision to get results, a substantial proportion, usually a majority, will place primary emphasis on getting out production. By this they mean placing primary emphasis on seeing that workers are using the proper methods, are sticking to their work, and are getting a satisfactory volume of work done. Other supervisors, whom we have called employee-centered, report that they get the best results when they place primary emphasis on the human problems of their workers. The employee-centered supervisor endeavors to build a team of people who cooperate and work well together. He tries to place people together who are congenial. He not only trains people to do their present job well but tends to train them for the next higher job. He is interested in helping them with their problems on the job and off the job. He is friendly and supportive, rather than punitive and threatening.

6. "A Program of Research on the Fundamental Problems of Organizing Human Behavior" (Ann Arbor: Institute for Social Research, University of Michigan, 1946).

7. L. Coch and J. French, "Overcoming Resistance to Change," *Human Relations,* Vol. 1, 1948, pp. 512-32; R. Kahn and D. Katz, "Leadership Practices in Relation to Productivity and Morale," a chapter in D. Cartwright and A. Zander (eds.), *Group Dynamics Research and Theory* (Evanston: Row, Peterson and Company, 1953); D. Katz and R. Kahn, "Human Organization and Worker Motivation," a chapter in *Industrial Productivity,* Industrial Relations Research Association, 1952; D. Katz and R. Kahn, "Some Recent Findings in Human Relations Research," a chapter in E. Swanson, T. Newcomb, and E. Hartley (eds.), *Readings in Social Psychology* (New York: Henry Holt and Co., 1952); D. Katz, N. Maccoby, G. Gurin, and L. Floor, *Productivity, Supervision and Morale among Railroad Workers* (Ann Arbor: University of Michigan Press, 1951); D. Katz, N. Maccoby, and N. Morse, *Productivity, Supervision and Morale in an Office Situation, Part I* (Ann Arbor: University of Michigan Press, 1950); F. Mann and H. Baumgartel, *Absences and Employee Attitudes in an Electric Power Company,* Institute for Social Research, 1953; F. Mann and H. Baumgartel, *The Supervisor's Concern with Costs in an Electric Power Company,* Institute for Social Research, 1953; F. Mann and J. Dent, *Appraisals of Supervisors and Attitudes of Their Employees in an Electric Power Company,* Institute for Social Research, 1954; N. Morse, *Satisfactions in the White-Collar Job* (Ann Arbor: University of Michigan Press, 1953); S. Seashore, *Group Cohesiveness in the Industrial Work Group* (Ann Arbor: University of Michigan Press, 1955).

8. E. Jacobson and S.E. Seashore, "Communication Practices in Complex Organizations," *The Journal of Social Issues,* Vol. VII, No. 3, 1951; D. Marvick, *Career Perspectives in a Bureaucratic Setting* (Ann Arbor: Institute of Public Administration, University of Michigan Press, 1954).

NUMBER OF FIRST-LINE SUPERVISORS

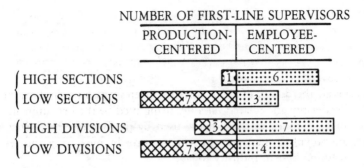

Exhibit 1. "Employee-centered" supervisors are higher producers than "production-centered" supervisors.

Higher levels of management, in discussing how they want their foremen to supervise, tend to place more emphasis on the production-centered approach as the best way to get results than do foremen.[9] Workers, on the other hand, tend to place less.

But which orientation yields the best results? A variety of studies in widely different industries show that supervisors who are getting the best production, the best motivation, and the highest levels of worker satisfaction are employee-centered appreciably more often than production-centered.[10] This is shown in Exhibit 1.

There is an important point to be added to this finding: Those employee-centered supervisors who get the best results tend to recognize that getting production is also one of their major responsibilities.

Closeness of Supervision. Related to orientation of supervision is closeness of supervision. Close supervision tends to be associated with lower productivity and more general supervision with higher productivity. This relationship, shown in Exhibit 2, holds for workers and supervisors.[11]

Low productivity, no doubt, at times leads to closer supervision, but it is clear also that it causes low productivity. In one of the companies involved in this research program it has been found that switching managers of high- and low-production divisions results in the high-production managers' raising the productivity of the low-production divisions faster than the former high-production divisions slip under the low-production managers. Supervisors, as they are shifted from job to job, tend to carry with them and to maintain their habitual attitudes toward the supervisory process and toward their subordinates.

Closeness of supervision is also related to the attitudes of workers toward

9. E.A. Fleishman, "Leadership Climate, Human Relations Training, and Supervisory Behavior," *Personnel Psychology*, Vol. 6, No. 3, 1953.

10. D. Katz, N. Maccoby, and N. Morse, *Productivity, Supervision and Morale in an Office Situation, Part I, op. cit.*

11. *Ibid.*

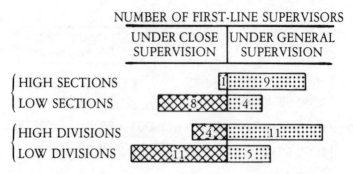

Exhibit 2. **Low-production section heads are more closely supervised than are high-production heads.**

their supervisors. Workers under foremen who supervise closely have a less favorable attitude toward their boss than do workers who are under foremen who supervise more generally.

EXPERIMENT DESCRIBED

These results which have just been presented on closeness of supervision and on employee-centered supervision were among those found early in the series of studies conducted by the Institute. They led to an experiment which I should like to describe briefly.

As we have seen, the research findings indicate that close supervision results in lower productivity, less favorable attitudes, and less satisfaction on the part of the workers; while more general supervision achieves higher productivity, more favorable attitudes, and greater employee satisfaction. These results suggest that it should be possible to increase productivity in a particular situation by shifting the pattern of the supervision so as to make it more general. To test this we conducted an experiment involving 500 clerical employees.[12]

Very briefly, the experiment was as follows: Four parallel divisions were used, each organized the same as the others, each using the same technology and doing exactly the same kind of work with employees of comparable aptitude. In two divisions, the decision levels were pushed down, and more general supervision of the clerks and their supervisors was introduced. In addition, the managers, assistant managers, supervisors, and assistant supervisors of these two divisions were trained in group methods of leadership.[13] The experimental changes in these two divisions will be called Program I.

12. N. Morse, E. Reimer, and A. Tannenbaum, "Regulation and Control in Hierarchical Organizations," *The Journal of Social Issues,* Vol. VII, No. 3, 1951.

13. Methods developed by the National Training Laboratory in Group Development were drawn upon heavily in this training.

In order to provide an effective experimental control on the changes in supervision which were introduced in Program I, the supervision in the other two divisions was modified so as to increase the closeness of supervision and move the decision levels upward. This will be called Program II. These changes were accomplished by a further extension of the scientific management approach. One of the major changes made was to have the jobs timed by the methods department and standard times computed. This showed that these divisions were overstaffed by about 30 per cent. The general manager then ordered the managers of these two divisions to cut staff by 25 per cent. This was to be done by transfers and by not replacing persons who left; no one, however, was to be dismissed.

Productivity in all four of the divisions depended upon the number of clerks involved. The work was something like a billing operation; there was just so much of it, but it had to be processed as it came along. Consequently, the only way in which productivity could be increased was to change the size of the work group. The four divisions were assigned to the experimental programs on a random basis, but in such a manner that a high- and low-productivity division was assigned to each program.

The experiment at the clerical level lasted for one year. Several months were devoted to planning prior to the experimental year, and there was a training period of approximately six months just prior to the experimental year. Productivity was measured continuously and computed weekly throughout the period. Employee and supervisory attitudes and related variables were measured just before and after the experimental year.

Productivity Reflected in Salary Costs. Exhibit 3 shows the changes in salary

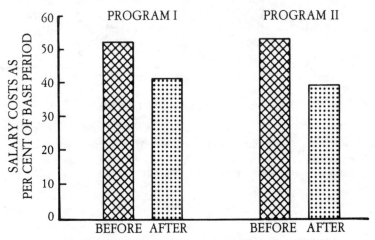

Exhibit 3. Change in productivity.

costs which reflect the changes in productivity that occurred. As will be observed, Program II, where there was an increase in the closeness of supervision, increased productivity by about 25 per cent. This, it will be recalled, was a result of direct orders from the general manager to reduce staff by that amount.

Exhibit 3 shows, furthermore, that a significant increase in productivity was achieved in Program I, where supervision was modified so as to be less close. The increase in productivity in Program I was not so great as in Program II but, nevertheless, was a little more than 20 per cent. One division in Program I increased its productivity by about the same amount as each of the two divisions in Program II. The other division in Program I, which historically had been the poorest of all of the divisions, did not do so well.

Productivity and Workers' Responsibility. Although both programs were alike in increasing productivity, they were significantly different in the other changes which occurred. The productivity increases in Program II, where decision levels were moved up, were accompanied by shifts in an adverse direction in attitudes, interest, and involvement in the work and related matters. The opposite was true in Program I. Exhibit 4, for example, shows that when more general supervision is provided, as in Program I, the employees' feeling of re-

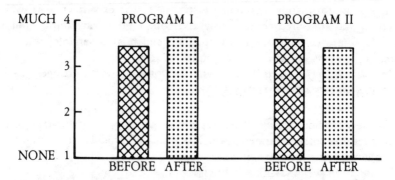

Exhibit 4. Employees' feeling of responsibility to see that work gets done.

sponsibility to see that the work gets done is increased. In Program II, however, this responsibility decreased. In Program I, when the supervisor was away, the employees kept on working. When the supervisor was absent in Program II, the work tended to stop.

Effect of Employee Attitudes. Exhibit 5 shows how the programs changed in regard to the workers' attitudes toward their superiors. In Program I all the shifts were favorable; in Program II all the shifts were unfavorable. One significant aspect of these changes in Program II was that the girls felt that their superiors were relying more on rank and authority to get the work done. In general, the shifts were greatest, both favorable in Program I and unfavorable in Program II, for those relationships which other studies have shown to be the

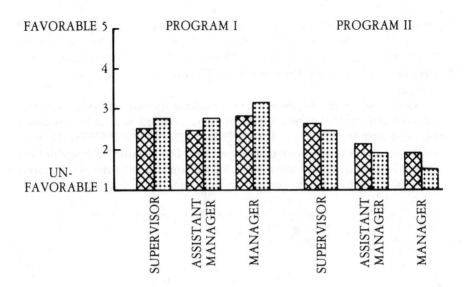

FAVORABLE 5

PROGRAM I

PROGRAM II

UN-
FAVORABLE 1

SUPERVISOR

ASSISTANT
MANAGER

MANAGER

SUPERVISOR

ASSISTANT
MANAGER

MANAGER

Exhibit 5. Satisfaction with superiors as representatives.

most important in influencing behavior in the working situation. A number of other measures of attitudes toward superiors all showed similar shifts: favorable in Program I and unfavorable in Program II.

FUNDAMENTAL CONCLUSION

This very brief description of this experiment, I hope, has made clear the pattern of results. Both experimental changes increased productivity substantially. In Program I this increase in productivity was accompanied by shifts in a favorable direction in attitudes, interests, and perceptions. The girls became more interested and involved in their work, they accepted more responsibility for getting the work done, their attitudes toward the company and their superiors became more favorable, and they accepted direction more willingly. In Program II, however, all these attitudes and related variables shifted in an unfavorable direction. All the hostilities, resentments, and unfavorable reactions which have been observed again and again to accompany extensive use of the scientific management approach manifested themselves.

This experiment with clerical workers is important because it shows that increases in productivity can be obtained with either favorable or unfavorable shifts in attitudes, perceptions, and similar variables. Further application of classical methods of scientific management substantially increased productivity, but it was accompanied by adverse attitudinal reactions upon the part of the workers involved. With the other approach used in the experiment, a substantial increase in productivity was also obtained, but here it was accompanied by shifts in attitudes and similar variables in a favorable direction. A fundamental conclusion from this experiment and other similar research is that direct pressure from one's superior for production tends to be resented, while group pressure from one's colleagues is not.[14]

PRESSURE FOR PRODUCTION

Keeping in mind these results, let us look at another chart. The solid line in Exhibit 6 shows the relation between the amount of pressure a worker feels from his foreman for production and the productivity of the worker. Productiv-

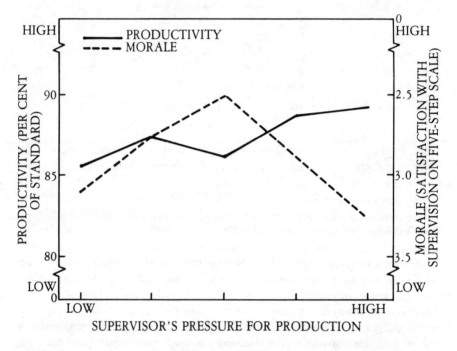

Exhibit 6. The relation of productivity and morale to supervisor's pressure for production.

ity is measured, and shown in the chart, as a percentage of standard; i.e., jobs are timed, standards are set, and production is then expressed as a percentage of standard. As will be observed, the chart shows that greater pressure from the supervisor is associated with higher production. The differences in production from low pressure to high pressure are not great, but they are large enough to be important in any highly competitive industry.

The broken line in Exhibit 6 shows the relationship between amount of

14. L. Coch and J. French, *op. cit.*

pressure the worker feels from his supervisor and his attitude toward his super-visor. In interpreting this curve, it is important to keep in mind that a worker's attitude toward his supervisor has a major influence upon all his other attitudes toward his work and his work situation, as well as his motivations toward his work. Little interest in production on the part of the supervisor, a laissez-faire point of view, is associated both with low production and with a less favorable attitude toward the supervisor. Workers who experience an average amount of pressure from their supervisors express the most favorable attitude toward them, while those workers who report feeling the greatest pressure from their supervisors have the least favorable attitude of all workers toward their super-visors. Direct pressure for production, here as in the clerical experiment, is as-sociated with hostility, resentment, and unfavorable attitudes on the part of workers.

Exhibit 6 is based on several thousand workers and shows relationships which we have found also in other studies. In some situations the production curve drops slightly with high levels of pressure from the supervisor for production. But the general picture seems to be that relatively high pressure for production is associated with fairly good production but with relatively unfavorable atti-tudes.

HIGH COST

Available evidence indicates that a substantial proportion of workers general-ly are working under conditions like those shown in Exhibit 6. Only a fraction of all workers, of course, are working at present under high levels of pressure from their supervisors. But the probabilities are that when competition gets tough for a company, and costs must be cut, an attempt will be made to cut them by increasing the pressure for production. The accompanying conse-quences of this increased pressure are clear, as shown by Exhibit 6 and by the clerical experiment.

A similar situation exists with regard to decentralization. Decentralization is generally viewed as one way of pushing decisions down and providing more general supervision. But, when the decentralization involves basing the compensation of the man in charge of the decentralized unit largely on the earnings shown by this unit, increased pressure on subordinates often occurs. Substantial earnings over the short run can occur from supervising subordinates more closely and putting more pressure on them to increase production and earnings. But the adverse effects both on subordinates and on workers can be predicted. If current reports are correct, the staffs of some decentralized units are genuinely unhappy over the pressure which they are experiencing. Trained engineers as well as non-supervisory employees are leaving, even for jobs that pay less.

Thus, though the scientific management approach has clearly demonstrated its capacity to get high production, this productivity is obtained at a serious cost. People will produce at relatively high levels when the techniques of production are efficient, the pressures for production are great, the controls and inspections are relatively tight, and the economic rewards and penalties are sufficiently large. But such production is accompanied by attitudes which tend to result in high scrap loss, lowered safety, higher absence and turnover, increased grievances and work stoppages, and the like. It also is accompanied by communication blocks and restrictions. All these developments tend to affect adversely the operation of any organization. Restricted communications, for example, tend to result in decisions based on misinformation or a lack of information.

INITIATIVE AND PARTICIPATION

In considering the strengths and weaknesses of the scientific management approach and how to deal with them, I believe that there is an important long-range trend to keep in mind. Supervisors and managers report in interviews that people are less willing to accept pressure and close supervision than was the case a decade or two ago. For example, one supervisor said:

> Girls want to and do express themselves more today than when I started to work. In the past, girls were more cringing and pliable, but not now. We get a great many girls who have had no restraints at home, and we have to do the teaching.

The trend in America generally, in our schools, in our homes, and in our communities is toward giving the individual greater freedom and initiative. There are fewer direct, unexplained orders in schools and homes, and youngsters are participating increasingly in decisions which affect them. These fundamental changes in American society create expectations among employees as to how they should be treated. These expectations profoundly affect employee attitudes, since attitudes depend upon the extent to which our experiences meet our expectations. If experience falls short of expectations, unfavorable attitudes occur. When our experience is better than our expectations, we tend to have favorable attitudes. This means, of course, that if expectations in America are changing in a particular direction, experience must change in the same direction or the attitudinal response of people to their experiences will be correspondingly influenced.

In my opinion, the cultural changes occurring in the United States will, in the next few decades, make people expect even greater opportunities for initiative and participation than is now the case.

POSSIBLE ADVANTAGES

There are important advantages to be gained if the resources of the scientific

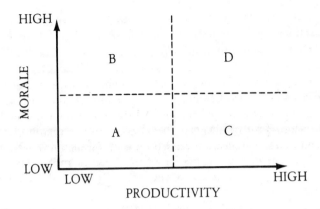

Exhibit 7. Schematic relationship between morale and productivity.

management approach and the human relations approach can be combined. These are illustrated schematically in Exhibit 7, which shows the relation between morale and production.

On the basis of a study I did in 1937,[15] I believed that morale and productivity were positively related; that the higher the morale, the higher the production. Substantial research findings since then have shown that this relationship is much too simple. In our different studies we have found a wide variety of relationships. Some units have low morale and low production; they would fall in Area A on the chart. Other units have fairly good morale and low production; these fall in Area B. Still others have fairly good production but low morale; these fall in Area C. Finally, other units have both high morale and high production and fall in Area D on the chart.

Units with low morale and low production (Area A) tend to have supervision which is laissez-faire in character and in which the leadership function has been abandoned to all intents and purposes. Units which fall in Area B and have fairly good morale but poor production tend to have supervisors who try to keep people "happy." These supervisors are often found in companies in which human relations training programs have been introduced and emphasized.

Some supervisors in these companies interpret the training to mean that the company management wants them to keep employees happy; therefore, they work hard to do so. The morale of these workers is essentially complacent in character. The result is a nice "country club" atmosphere. Employees like it, and absence and turnover are low; but, since little production is felt to be expected, the workers produce relatively little.

Into Area C, of course, fall those units which have technically competent supervision that is pressing for production. Area D includes those units which

15. R. Likert and J. Willits, *Morale and Agency Management* (Hartford: Life Insurance Agency Management Association, 1940).

have a kind of supervision which results in high production with high morale, high satisfactions, and high motivation. Here the nature of the morale can be characterized as "the will to achieve."

INTEGRATED APPROACH

Most of us would agree, I believe, that the kind of supervision which we desire is that which is represented by Area D. It is my further belief that this kind of supervision represents an integration of the scientific management and human relations approach which has not yet been fully achieved and about which we know relatively little.

What will be required for the resources of these two approaches to be integrated fully and effectively? I am not sure that I know the answer to this question, but I should like to suggest a way of coping with it which I believe has real promise. Fundamentally, what I wish to propose is that the major resources of human relations research be focused upon what experience and research have shown to be the major weakness in the scientific management approach.

The tremendous contribution which scientific management and related management theories have made to increasing production and to improved organizational performance provides adequate evidence as to the great power of the basic concepts involved. These concepts include emphasis on such processes as the following:

1. The elimination of waste and inefficiency through functionalization, work simplification, and related processes.
2. The establishment of specific work goals.
3. The measurement of work accomplished and the continual examination of the extent to which the specified goals are being achieved.
4. Coordinated and clear-cut channels of control, communication, and decision making.

IMPORTANCE OF MOTIVATION

The critical weaknesses in the scientific management approach, of course, are the resentments, hostilities, and adverse motivational and attitudinal reactions which it tends to evoke. In my judgment, these hostilities and unfavorable attitudes stem from powerful motives which the scientific management approach has ignored in its over-all conceptualization and in the day-to-day operating procedures which it has developed. Although the scientific management approach has ignored these powerful motives, it has not been able to avoid the substantial impact of their influence in daily operations.

The fundamental cause, therefore, of the adverse motivational reactions produced by the scientific management approach is the inadequate motivational assumption upon which it is based. It assumes, as classical management and economic theories do generally, that all persons are simple economic men.[16] More specifically, the underlying motivational assumption upon which scientific management is based is that it is only necessary to buy a man's time and he will then do willingly and effectively everything which he is ordered to do. Management textbooks emphasize authority and control as the foundation of administration. They either take for granted the power to control or hold that "the relationship of employer and employee in an enterprise is a contractual obligation entailing the right to command and the duty to obey."[17]

The critical weakness of the scientific management approach occurs at precisely the point where the human relations research approach has its greatest strength: motivation. The great power of human relations research findings is in the understanding and insight which they provide as to:

1. The character and magnitude of the powerful motivational forces which control human behavior in working situations.
2. The manner in which these forces can be used so that they reinforce rather than conflict with one another.

MODIFIED THEORY CALLED FOR

The fundamental problem, therefore, is to develop an organizational and management theory, and related supervisory and managerial practices for operating under this theory, which will make use of the tremendous resources of the scientific management concepts while fully utilizing in a positive and reinforcing manner the great power of all the major motivational forces which influence human behavior in working situations. To develop this organizational and management theory will be slow, complex, and difficult work. The motives upon which this modified theory should be based include:

1. All the economic motives.
2. All the ego motives including the desires for status, recognition, approval, sense of importance and personal worth, etc.
3. The desire for security.
4. The desire for new experiences.

Human relations research is yielding concepts which appear to be important tools in deriving a modified theory of management. For example, the research

16. The gross inadequacy of this assumption with regard to the behavior of people as consumers has been amply demonstrated. See, e.g., Katona, *Psychological Analysis of Economic Behavior* (New York: McGraw-Hill, 1951), or Klein, Katona, Lansing, and Morgan, *Contributions of Survey Methods to Economics* (New York: Columbia University Press, 1954).

17. J.D. Millett, *Management in the Public Service* (New York: McGraw-Hill, 1954); C. O'Donnell, "The Source of Managerial Authority," *Political Science Quarterly*, Vol. 67, 1952, p. 573.

findings have clearly demonstrated that there is no set of specific supervisory practices which is the right or best way to supervise. A way of supervising which may yield the best results in one specific situation may produce poor results in a different situation.[18] The behavior of the superior is not the only variable which determines the subordinate's response. The subordinate's response is also determined by what he has learned to expect. Consequently, the response of the subordinate to the behavior of the supervisor will be influenced by the "culture" of the plant or organization and the expectations of the subordinate. To help superiors meet the problems created by this major finding, human relations research is providing evidence as to general principles which can serve as guides to the most appropriate way to supervise in a given situation. Moreover, it is also providing rapid and efficient methods of measuring what the culture and expectations are in any given plant or unit.

CURRENT THINKING AND PRACTICE

The modified theory of management and the supervisory and managerial practices which can be derived, theoretically, when adequate motivational assumptions are used differ in important respects from the theory and practices commonly employed today. For example, with regard to methods of supervision, the current pattern of thinking and practice is in terms of a man-to-man pattern; each superior deals with each subordinate on a man-to-man basis. From a theoretical point of view, however, supervising each work group primarily as a group rather than relying on the man-to-man pattern should result in an appreciable improvement in performance. It is significant that there is an important and increasing body of research findings which indicate that group methods of supervision result in higher productivity, greater job satisfaction, and greater motivation than are obtained with the man-to-man pattern.

In discussing this particular derivation with a director of industrial relations a few months ago, I was impressed by his comment that top management in many of our most successful corporations implicitly recognize the value and power of group methods of supervision themselves and are using it in the top levels of their corporations. Apparently, these company officers recognize the value of group methods of supervision and use these methods personally. They have not generalized these methods, however, as standard operating procedures and extended them and related practices throughout the organization.

The available research findings, nevertheless, indicate that high group loyalty has an important influence upon performance at all levels in the organization. The data show that high group loyalty coupled with high production goals in the work group results in high productivity, accompanied by high job satisfaction and a feeling of working under little pressure. The data also show

18. D. Pelz, "Influence: A Key to Effective Leadership in the First Line Supervisor," *Personnel*, Vol. 29, 1952.

that in the work groups with high group loyalty there is better communication between supervisors and ·men and each has a better understanding of the other's points of view.

FURTHER DERIVATIONS

Much more could be said about group methods of supervision and recent research findings bearing upon the importance of group loyalty. I hope, however, that this illustrates the kind of theoretical derivation of managerial practices that can be made, based upon more adequate motivational assumptions. Similar derivations can be made as to the manner in which selection, training, work simplification, functionalization, job evaluation, communication, compensation, decentralization, union-management relations, and so on, can and should be carried out so as to achieve the best all-around performance. In each case, the derivations that will be made are likely to point to procedures which will differ significantly from the practices now generally accepted.

Obviously, managerial and supervisory practices which are derived theoretically are bound to show some operational "bugs" or inadequacies when tested in operating situations. It is essential, therefore, to test and improve these derived practices in pilot or small-scale operations just as is done with any new process in chemistry or engineering. In these pilot projects it will be essential to have the full cooperation and participation of all those unions which represent the workers involved.

THE IMPLICATIONS

What are the implications of these developments for management and executive training? First, the proposed pilot projects offer a unique opportunity for training. Learning by doing has always been an effective training process. Consequently, I believe that one of the best ways to develop those persons who will become executives in the coming decades will be to have them play a major part now in conducting pilot projects.[19] These pilot projects would be devoted to testing and refining the improved supervisory and managerial practices which can be derived theoretically from available research findings.

A second major implication to be drawn is that important changes are occurring in the management and organizational theory and in the supervisory processes now being used by American industry. Managers and supervisors are in the process of developing and refining new theory and principles and improved practices. But, unfortunately, this is being done the hard and costly

19. R. Likert and R. Lippitt, "The Utilization of Social Sciences," a chapter in L. Festinger and D. Katz (eds.), *Research Methods in the Behavioral Sciences* (New York: Dryden Press, 1953), pp. 581-646; *Training in Human Relations,* report of a seminar conducted by the Foundation for Research on Human Behavior, Ann Arbor, 1955.

way, the trial-and-error way. Every research project dealing with supervision and leadership shows how the most able supervisors and managers are struggling in company after company with trial-and-error methods to discover how to improve their supervision.

It is possible to wait for this trial-and-error process gradually to evolve and to make clear what the new organization and management theory and processes will be. It would be faster and much more efficient to use the power of systematic research and experimentation to accelerate their discovery and refinement.

In my judgment, those companies which support and cooperate in research to discover improved processes of management and to train their personnel will have a distinct advantage over companies which do not. Those which support research will discover at an earlier date the principles and practices which the successful companies of the future will be using and in which their own developing executives and managers should be trained. They will not experience the tragedy and cost of obsolete management.

Chapter 28

An Integrating Principle
and an Overview

Rensis Likert

The managers whose performance is impressive appear to be fashioning a better system of management. [Earlier] two generalizations were stated based on the available research findings:

The supervisors and managers in American industry and government who are achieving the highest productivity, lowest costs, least turnover and absence, and the highest levels of employee motivation and satisfaction display, on the average, a different pattern of leadership from those managers who are achieving less impressive results. The principles and practices of these high-producing managers are deviating in important ways from those called for by present-day management theories.

The high-producing managers whose deviations from existing theory and practice are creating improved procedures have not yet integrated their deviant principles into a theory of management. Individually, they are often clearly aware of how a particular practice of theirs differs from generally accepted methods, but the magnitude, importance, and systematic nature of the differences when the total pattern is examined do not appear to be recognized.

Based upon the principles and practices of the managers who are achieving the best results, a newer theory of organization and management can be stated. An attempt will be made in this chapter to present briefly some of the over-all characteristics of such a theory and to formulate a general integrating principle which can be useful in attempts to apply it.

There is no doubt that further research and experimental testing of the

From *New Patterns of Management*, McGraw-Hill Book Company, Inc., New York, 1961, chapter 8, pp. 97-106. Reprinted by permission of the publisher.

theory in pilot operations will yield evidence pointing to modifications of many aspects of the newer theory suggested in this volume. Consequently, in reading this and subsequent chapters it will be well not to quarrel with the specific aspects of the newer theory as presented. These specifics are intended as stimulants for discussion and as encouragement for experimental field tests of the theory. It will be more profitable to seek to understand the newer theory's general basic character and, whenever a specific aspect or derivation appears to be in error, to formulate more valid derivations and propositions.

Research findings indicate that the general pattern of operations of the highest-producing managers tends to differ from that of the managers of mediocre and low-producing units by more often showing the following characteristics:

A preponderance of favorable attitudes on the part of each member of the organization toward all the other members, toward superiors, toward the work, toward the organization—toward all aspects of the job. These favorable attitudes toward others reflect a high level of mutual confidence and trust throughout the organization. The favorable attitudes toward the organization and the work are not those of easy complacency, but are the attitudes of identification with the organization and its objectives and a high sense of involvement in achieving them. As a consequence, the performance goals are high and dissatisfaction may occur whenever achievement falls short of the goals set.

This highly motivated, cooperative orientation toward the organization and its objectives is achieved by harnessing effectively all the major motivational forces which can exercise significant influence in an organizational setting and which, potentially, can be accompanied by cooperative and favorable attitudes. Reliance is not placed solely or fundamentally on the economic motive of buying a man's time and using control and authority as the organizing and coordinating principle of the organization. On the contrary, the following motives are all used fully and in such a way that they function in a cumulative and reinforcing manner and yield favorable attitudes:

The ego motives. These are referred to throughout . . . as the desire to achieve and maintain a sense of personal worth and importance. This desire manifests itself in many forms, depending upon the norms and values of the persons and groups involved. Thus, it is responsible for such motivational forces as the desire for growth and significant achievement in terms of one's own values and goals, i.e., self-fulfillment, as well as the desire for status, recognition, approval, acceptance, and power and the desire to undertake significant and important tasks.

The security motives.

Curiosity, creativity, and the desire for new experiences.

The economic motives.

By tapping all the motives which yield favorable and cooperative attitudes, maximum motivation oriented toward realizing the organization's goals as well as the needs of each member of the organization is achieved. The substantial decrements in motivational forces which occur when powerful motives are pulling in opposite directions are thereby avoided. These conflicting forces exist, of course, when hostile and resentful attitudes are present.

The organization consists of a tightly knit, effectively functioning social system. This social system is made up of interlocking work groups with a high degree of group loyalty among the members and favorable attitudes and trust between superiors and subordinates. Sensitivity to others and relatively high levels of skill in personal interaction and the functioning of groups are also present. These skills permit effective participation in decisions on common problems. Participation is used, for example, to establish organizational objectives which are a satisfactory integration of the needs and desires of all members of the organization and of persons functionally related to it. High levels of reciprocal influence occur, and high levels of total coordinated influence are achieved in the organization. Communication is efficient and effective. There is a flow from one part of the organization to another of all the relevant information important for each decision and action. The leadership in the organization has developed what might well be called a highly effective social system for interaction and mutual influence.

Measurements of organizational performance are used primarily for self-guidance rather than for superimposed control. To tap the motives which bring cooperative and favorable rather than hostile attitudes, participation and involvement in decisions is a habitual part of the leadership processes. This kind of decision-making, of course, calls for the full sharing of available measurements and information. Moreover, as it becomes evident in the decision-making process that additional information or measurements are needed, steps are taken to obtain them.

In achieving operations which are more often characterized by the above pattern of highly cooperative, well-coordinated activity, the highest producing managers use all the technical resources of the classical theories of management, such as time-and-motion study, budgeting, and financial controls. They use these resources at least as completely as do the low-producing managers, but in quite different ways. This difference in use arises from the differences in the motives which the high-producing, in contrast to the low-producing, managers believe are important in influencing human behavior.

The low-producing managers, in keeping with traditional practice, feel that the way to motivate and direct behavior is to exercise control through authority. Jobs are organized, methods are prescribed, standards are set, performance goals and budgets are established. Compliance with them is sought through the use of hierarchical and economic pressures.

The highest-producing managers feel, generally, that this manner of functioning does not produce the best results, that the resentment created by direct exercise of authority tends to limit its effectiveness. They have learned that better results can be achieved when a different motivational process is employed. As suggested above, they strive to use all those major motives which have the potentiality of yielding favorable and cooperative attitudes in such a way that favorable attitudes are, in fact, elicited and the motivational forces are mutually reinforcing. Motivational forces stemming from the economic motive are not then blunted by such other motivations as group goals which restrict the quantity or quality of output. The full strength of all economic, ego, and other motives is generated and put to use.

Widespread use of participation is one of the more important approaches employed by the high-producing managers in their efforts to get full benefit from the technical resources of the classical theories of management coupled with high levels of reinforcing motivation. This use of participation applies to all aspects of the job and work, as, for example, in setting work goals and budgets, controlling costs, organizing the work, etc.

In these and comparable ways, the high-producing managers make full use of the technical resources of the classical theories of management. They use these resources in such a manner, however, that favorable and cooperative attitudes are created and all members of the organization endeavor to pull concertedly toward commonly accepted goals which they have helped to establish.

This brief description of the pattern of management which is more often characteristic of the high-producing than of the low-producing managers points to what appears to be a critical difference. The high-producing managers have developed their organizations into highly coordinated, highly motivated, cooperative social systems. Under their leadership, the different motivational forces in each member of the organization have coalesced into a strong force aimed at accomplishing the mutually established objectives of the organization. This general pattern of highly motivated, cooperative members seems to be a central characteristic of the newer management system being developed by the highest-producing managers.

How do these high-producing managers build organizations which display this central characteristic? Is there any general approach or underlying principle which they rely upon in building highly motivated organizations? There seems to be, and clues as to the nature of the principle can be obtained by reexamining some of the [previous] materials. . . . The research findings show, for example, that those supervisors and managers whose pattern of leadership yields consistently favorable attitudes more often think of employees as "human beings rather than just as persons to get the work done." Consistently, in study after study, the data show that treating people as "human beings" rather than as "cogs in a machine" is a variable highly related to the attitudes and motivation of the subordinate at every level in the organization. . . .

The superiors who have the most favorable and cooperative attitudes in their work groups display the following characteristics:

The attitude and behavior of the superior toward the subordinate as a person, *as perceived by the subordinate,* is as follows:

He is supportive, friendly, and helpful rather than hostile, He is kind but firm, never threatening, genuinely interested in the well-being of subordinates and endeavors to treat people in a sensitive, considerate way. He is just, if not generous. He endeavors to serve the best interests of his employees as well as of the company.

He shows confidence in the integrity, ability, and motivations of subordinates rather than suspicion and distrust.

His confidence in subordinates leads him to have high expectations as to their level of performance. With confidence that he will not be disappointed, he expects much, not little. (This, again, is fundamentally a supportive rather than a critical or hostile relationship.)

He sees that each subordinate is well trained for his particular job. He endeavors also to help subordinates be promoted by training them for jobs at the next level. This involves giving them relevant experience and coaching whenever the opportunity offers.

He coaches and assists employees whose performance is below standard. In the case of a subordinate who is clearly misplaced and unable to do his job satisfactorily, he endeavors to find a position well suited to that employee's abilities and arranges to have the employee transferred to it.

The behavior of the superior in directing the work is characterized by such activity as:

Planning and scheduling the work to be done, training subordinates, supplying them with material and tools, initiating work activity, etc.

Providing adequate technical competence, particularly in those situations where the work has not been highly standardized.

The leader develops his subordinates into a working team with high group loyalty by using participation and the other kinds of group-leadership practices summarized [earlier].

THE INTEGRATING PRINCIPLE

These results and similar data from other studies (Argyris, 1957; March & Simon, 1958; Viteles, 1953) show that subordinates react favorably to experiences which they feel are supportive and contribute to their sense of importance and personal worth. Similarly, persons react unfavorably to experiences which are threatening and decrease or minimize their sense of dignity and personal worth. These findings are supported also by substantial research on personality development (Argyris, 1957; Rogers, 1942; Rogers, 1951) and group behavior (Cartwright & Zander, 1960). Each of us wants appreciation, recognition, influence, a feeling of accomplishment, and a feeling that people who are important to us believe in us and respect us. We want to feel that we have a place in the world.

This pattern of reaction appears to be universal and seems to be the basis for the general principle used by the high-producing managers in developing their highly motivated, cooperative organizations. These managers have discovered that the motivational forces acting in each member of an organization are most likely to be cumulative and reinforcing when the interactions between each individual and the others in the organization are of such a character that they convey to the individual a feeling of support and recognition for his importance and worth as a person. These managers, therefore, strive to have the interactions between the members of their organization of such a character that each member of the organization feels confident in his potentialities and believes that his abilities are being well used.

A second factor, however, is also important. As we have seen [previously], an individual's reaction to any situation is always a function not of the absolute character of the interaction, but of his perception of it. It is how he sees things that counts, not objective reality. Consequently, an individual member of an organization will always interpret an interaction between himself and the organization in terms of his background and culture, his experience and expectations. The pattern of supervision and the language used that might be effective with a railroad's maintenance-of-way crew, for example, would not be suitable in an office full of young women. A subordinate tends also to expect his superior to behave in ways consistent with the personality of the superior. All this means that each of us, as a subordinate or as a peer or as a superior, reacts in terms of his own particular background, experience, and expectations. In order, therefore, to have an interaction viewed as supportive, it is essential that it be of such a character that the individual himself, in the light of his experience and expectations, sees it as supportive. This provides the basis for stating the general principle which the high-producing managers seem to be using and which will be referred to as the *principle of supportive relationships*. This principle, which provides an invaluable guide in any attempt to apply the newer theory of management in a specific plant or organization, can be briefly stated: *The leadership and other processes of the organization must be such as to ensure a maximum probability that in all interactions and all relationships with the organization each member will, in the light of his background, values, and expectations, view the experience as supportive and one which builds and maintains his sense of personal worth and importance.*

THE PRINCIPLE OF SUPPORTIVE RELATIONSHIPS AS AN ORGANIZING CONCEPT

This general principle provides a fundamental formula for obtaining the full potential of every major motive which can be constructively harnessed in a working situation. There is impressive evidence, for example, that economic motivations will be tapped more effectively when the conditions specified by the principle of supportive relationships are met (Katz & Kahn, 1951; Krulee,

1955). In addition, as motives are used in the ways called for by this general principle, the attitudes accompanying the motives will be favorable and the different motivational forces will be cumulative and reinforcing. Under these circumstances, the full power from each of the available motives will be added to that from the others to yield a maximum of coordinated, enthusiastic effort.

The principle of supportive relationships points to a dimension essential for the success of every organization, namely, that the mission of the organization be seen by its members as genuinely important. To be highly motivated, each member of the organization must feel that the organization's objectives are of significance and that his own particular task contributes in an indispensable manner to the organization's achievement of its objectives. He should see his role as difficult, important, and meaningful. This is necessary if the individual is to achieve and maintain a sense of personal worth and importance. When jobs do not meet this specification they should be reorganized so that they do. This is likely to require the participation of those involved in the work in a manner suggested in subsequent chapters.

The term "supportive" is used frequently in subsequent chapters and also is a key word in the principle of supportive relationships. Experiences, relationships, etc., are considered to be supportive when the individual involved sees the experience (in terms of his values, goals, expectations, and aspirations) as contributing to or maintaining his sense of personal worth and importance.

The principle of supportive relationships contains within it an important clue to its effective use. To apply this general principle, a superior must take into consideration the experience and expectations of each of his subordinates. In determining what these expectations are, he cannot rely solely on his observations and impressions. It helps the superior to try to put himself in his subordinate's shoes and endeavor to see things as the subordinate sees them, but this is not enough. Too often, the superior's estimates are wrong. He needs direct evidence if he is to know how the subordinate views things and to estimate the kinds of behavior and interaction which will be seen by the subordinate as supportive. The superior needs accurate information as to how his behavior is actually seen by the subordinate. Does the subordinate, in fact, perceive the superior's behavior as supportive?

There are two major ways to obtain this evidence. In a complex organization it can be found by the use of measurements of the intervening variables . . . It can also be obtained by the development of work-group relationships, which not only facilitate but actually require, as part of the group building and maintenance functions, candid expressions by group members of their perceptions and reactions to the behavior of others. . . .

THE CENTRAL ROLE OF THE WORK GROUP

An important theoretical derivation can be made from the principle of supportive relationships. This derivation is based directly on the desire to achieve and maintain a sense of personal worth, which is a central concept of the principle. The most important source of satisfaction for this desire is the response we get from the people we are close to, in whom we are interested, and whose approval and support we are eager to have. The face-to-face groups with whom we spend the bulk of our time are, consequently, the most important to us. Our work group is one in which we spend much of our time and one in which we are particularly eager to achieve and maintain a sense of personal worth. As a consequence, most persons are highly motivated to behave in ways consistent with the goals and values of their work group in order to obtain recognition, support, security, and favorable reactions from this group. It can be concluded, therefore, that *management will make full use of the potential capacities of its human resources only when each person in an organization is a member of one or more effectively functioning work groups that have a high degree of group loyalty, effective skills of interaction, and high performance goals.*

The full significance of this derivation becomes more evident when we examine the research findings that show how groups function when they are well knit and have effective interaction skills. Research shows, for example, that the greater the attraction and loyalty to the group, the more the individual is motivated (1) to accept the goals and decisions of the group; (2) to seek to influence the goals and decisions of the group so that they are consistent with his own experience and his own goals; (3) to communicate fully to the members of the group; (4) to welcome communication and influence attempts from the other members; (5) to behave so as to help implement the goals and decisions that are seen as most important to the group; and (6) to behave in ways calculated to receive support and favorable recognition from members of the group and especially from those who the individual feels are the more powerful and higher-status members (Cartwright & Zander, 1960). Groups which display a high level of member attraction to the group and high levels of the above characteristics will be referred to . . . as *highly effective groups*. These groups are described more fully [elsewhere].

As our theoretical derivation has indicated, an organization will function best when its personnel function not as individuals but as members of highly effective work groups with high performance goals. Consequently, management should deliberately endeavor to build these effective groups, linking them into an over-all organization by means of people who hold overlapping group membership (Figure 1). The superior in one group is a subordinate in the next group, and so on through the organization. If the work groups at each hierarchical level are well knit and effective, the linking process will be accomplished well. Staff as well as line should be characterized by this pattern of operation.

The dark lines in Figure 1 are intended to show that interaction occurs between individuals as well as in groups. The dark lines are omitted at the lowest level in the chart in order to avoid complexity. Interaction between individuals occurs there, of course, just as it does at higher levels in the organization.

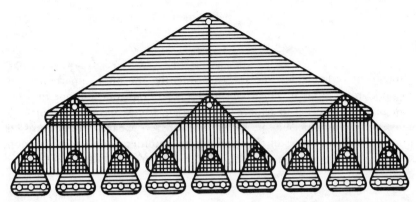

Figure 1. The overlapping group form of organization. Work groups vary in size as circumstances require although shown here as consisting of four persons.

In most organizations, there are also various continuing and *ad hoc* committees, committees related to staff functions, etc., which should also become highly effective groups and thereby help further to tie the many parts of the organization together. These links are in addition to the linking provided by the overlapping members in the line organization. Throughout the organization, the supervisory process should develop and strengthen group functioning. This theoretically ideal organizational structure provides the framework for the management system called for by the newer theory.

REFERENCES

Argyris, C.: *Personality and Organization.* New York: Harper, 1957.

Cartwright, D., & Zander, A. (Eds.): *Group Dynamics: Research and Theory* (2d ed.). Evanston, Ill.: Row, Peterson, 1960.

Katz, D. & Kahn, R.L.: Human Organization and Worker Motivation. In L. Reed Tripp (Ed.), *Industrial Productivity.* Madison, Wis.: Industrial Relations Research Association, 1951, pp. 146-171.

Krulee, G.K.: The Scanlon Plan: Co-operation Through Participation. *J. Business, University of Chicago,* 1955, **28** (2), 100-113.

March, J.G., & Simon, H.A.: *Organizations.* New York: Wiley, 1958.

Rogers, C.R.: *Counseling and Psychotherapy.* Boston: Houghton Mifflin, 1942.

Rogers, C.R.: *Client-centered Therapy.* Boston: Houghton Mifflin, 1951.

Viteles, M.S.: *Motivation and Morale in Industry.* New York: Norton, 1953.

Chapter 29

The Developing Revolution in Management Practices

Robert R. Blake
Jane Srygley Mouton

A searching inquiry regarding conventional practices of management is underway. Traditional ways of deploying people to achieve production are being challenged. This examination of many so-called tested and true, yet antiquated, assumptions about managerial behavior which have evolved from "rule of thumb" and "seat of pants" efforts of the past has been impelled by the impact of developments in the behavioral sciences.

The significance of advances made in behavioral sciences during the past decade parallels important strides over the past fifty years in the physical sciences. In the latter, creation of new products, development of new processes, and design of new procedures has resulted in a dramatic transformation of technical aspects of work. The implications of the advent of the behavioral sciences for improvement in the management of people engaged in work are no less than have been and will continue to be as great as the implications of physical sciences regarding new approaches to the technical side of work and productivity.

A SCIENCE OF MANAGEMENT

A most striking consequence of these developments is that a science of management is replacing what only a short time span ago was referred to as the "art of managing." The art of managing people of the immediate past era was something that people either had or did not have. Whether an individual did or did not have it, one basic assumption prevailed. It was that the man who *was* skillful in the art of management couldn't teach it to others, and the person who was not, probably could not learn it no matter how he tried.

From the *Training and Development Journal*, July 1962. Copyright 1962 by the American Society for Training and Development. Reprinted by special permission of the authors and publisher.

The science of management now taking shape is based on two related considerations. On the one hand, research in the behavioral sciences has produced a body of systematic knowledge regarding the consequences of various conditions of human interaction during the performance of both mental and physical work. On the other, new training techniques developed over the past fifteen years now make it practical to teach individuals to use this body of systematic behavioral science knowledge regarding the nature of human conduct in the practice of management. In other words, an applied science of management, founded on systematic techniques, is now at hand.

Over the past decade, particularly in the last five years, a number of America's major corporations have been investigating intensively the implications and consequences for organization improvement that are contained in these concepts and teaching methods. Now is the time for description of theory and technique and for initial evaluation.

Results to date are most encouraging.

In some situations union-management conflict has been relieved and restored to conditions of cooperation and problem-solving.[1] Mutual suspicion and distrust between operating departments and the staff groups intended to serve them has been reduced in others. Disturbed relationships between headquarters and the plants reporting to them also have been corrected through experimental applications of behavioral science concepts.[2] The theory and training methods to be described have been successfully employed to perfect team effectiveness by bringing about more effective decision-making among the management of large industrial organizations.[3] Most interesting is the fact that with only small adaptation, the same concepts of management and techniques of training have been used at operating levels to aid people, who for a decade had been classified as untrainable, to learn how to handle complicated chemical units and electronic equipment.[4] Best judgment available indicates positive profit improvement results from these behavioral science application ventures.

What is being said, then, is this. A revolution in the behavioral sciences is producing a science of management. Simultaneously a revolution in training technology is producing the techniques by which managerial personnel can learn principles of human behavior in such a concrete way as to permit their application in a manner consistent with theoretical specifications in the context of work.

OVERVIEW

I would like to delve more deeply into these important matters in three separate sections of this presentation. The first deals with the basic theory of modern management practices which underlies the remarks made above. I refer to the *Managerial Grid* ® which is a systematic statement describing nine theories of how production through people is accomplished. The most satisfactory theory of production-people integration, entitled team management, is presented here. Each and all of these theories are found in application in management situations today. The *Grid* theory is basic for appreciating the shift from any one management *style* to the application of management *science*. Having completed this presentation, attention then is turned to an examination of the training techniques by which a sound applied science of team management can be taught. Then, I want to indicate what I believe to be the broader implications for the future of this developing revolution in management practices.

I—THE MANAGERIAL GRID: CONDITIONS OF INTERACTION BETWEEN PRODUCTION AND HUMAN RELATIONSHIPS

The Managerial Grid, shown in Figure 1, offers a schematic behavioral science framework for comparing nine theories of interaction between production and human relationships.

The horizontal axis represents *concern for production.* The vertical axis indicates *concern for relationships* among those engaged in production. Each is expressed as a nine-point scale with the one end representing minimum concern and the nine end representing maximum interest. Before going on, however, a word needs to be said about *concerns for* as variables reflecting attitudes underlying the organization of people into production units. The variables do not necessarily reflect *how much* production is obtained or the degree to which human relationship needs are *actually* met. Rather, emphasis here is placed on the degree of *concern for,* because action is based on underlying attitudes which dictate what those actions should or will be.

By orienting these two variables at right angles to one another, nine theories regarding possible relationships between concern for production and concern for relationships can be evaluated. Emphasis is placed on the corners and the midpoint of the grid to bring out the various ways in which production and human relationships interact. While these extreme positions are to be found in pure form only rarely in the production settings of today, nonetheless, many situations are rather close approximations of one or the other of the pure conditions.

Theories in Which Concern for Production and Concern for Relationships are Seen to be in Conflict

Three theories rest on the notion that production requirements and human relations needs essentially are in basic opposition. The logic of the argument rests on two assumptions. One is that the way to achieve production is to push in such a way as to violate people and treat them with suspicion. The other is that if people are treated "nicely," that is in a friendly sociable manner in the work situation, there will be soldiering, dragging of feet and shirking. In other words, it is impossible to obtain high production on the easy notion that people

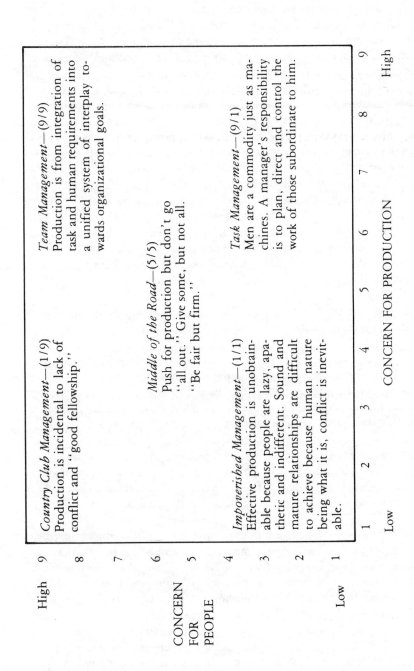

Country Club Management—(1/9)
Production is incidental to lack of conflict and "good fellowship."

Team Management—(9/9)
Production is from integration of task and human requirements into a unified system of interplay towards organizational goals.

Middle of the Road—(5/5)
Push for production but don't go "all out." Give some, but not all. "Be fair but firm."

Impoverished Management—(1/1)
Effective production is unobtainable because people are lazy, apathetic and indifferent. Sound and mature relationships are difficult to achieve because human nature being what it is, conflict is inevitable.

Task Management—(9/1)
Men are a commodity just as machines. A manager's responsibility is to plan, direct and control the work of those subordinate to him.

CONCERN FOR PEOPLE

High 9
8
7
6
5
4
3
2
Low 1

CONCERN FOR PRODUCTION

1   2   3   4   5   6   7   8   9
Low   High

Figure 1. The Managerial Grid

will respond to trust with trust. This is the kind of attitude that says that *concerns for production and concerns for relationships* are in essential conflict with one another; attainment of either one means the other must be sacrificed.

Task Management: The 9/1 Approach to the Production-Human Relations Interaction. The lower right hand corner where 9, high concern for production, intersects 1, low concern for people, represents an approach referred to as *Task Management.* Here the primary concern is for output of the enterprise with people being viewed in terms of their contribution to production. This theory is based on the notion that a manager's central responsibilities are to plan, direct and control the actions of subordinates in such a manner as to achieve the production objectives of the enterprise. Subordinates are expected to react with compliance to various plans, directions and controls placed upon them. The situation is one of authority and obedience with respect to production. Need for understanding and agreement among those engaged in production is not given serious consideration. According to 9/1, a job is a job and someone has to do it. Like machines, people are seen as production tools. They are obligated to comply and execute what they have been told to do.

A 9/1 supervisor questioned by a subordinate reflected his managerial attitude in the following manner.

> "These are your instructions. Do it, and don't give me any lip. If there's anything I detest, it's insubordination."

At lower levels, concern for production may be easily thought of in terms of actual *output.* The results of concern for production at the managerial levels, in terms of decision-making and policy formulation, are just as critical as units of output are among operators. The following kind of advice which was given to managers in the middle levels is characteristic of a 9/1 orientation.

> "For an executive to challenge orders, directions and instructions, policy and procedures, rules and regulations, etc., smacks of insubordination or lack of cooperation. It shows his failure to understand the need for decisions at higher levels and for direction and control of operations."

Under the 9/1 theory, people should comply with job procedures, specifications, rules and policies which are demanded of them by the more rational organization. Therefore, heavy emphasis is placed on quantifying the efforts and procedures concerned with output. One focus is on measuring the requirements of a job, simplifying it to the maximum degree possible and then training individuals one-by-one to perform the operations according to "scientific" standards. An additional consideration involves intensively evaluating the "fit" between the individual's capacity and requirements for doing the job. The basis of concern for people is that of designing the operations and the work place to minimize effort and fatigue, while obtaining maximum output.

Another important assumption of 9/1 is the sharp and definite division drawn between the planning and the execution of work. Planners plan and doers do. The relationships between those who plan and those who do is on the strictest concepts of authority and obedience. Management exercises authority, in the extreme, over the slightest motions of the doer. The person who performs the operations is obligated to oblige, in the sense of doing what and how he is told.

Management effort can be so perfect as to anticipate an individual's physical needs under a condition of obedience and to prescribe the best conditions of his work in such a way as his participation can only be in the compliant doing. As a result of this authority and obedience basis for cooperation much resistance is generated. Rather than increasing productivity, which clearly is possible under this managerial approach, it may actually be reduced by those who execute the operations in order to avoid being taken advantage of.

The managerial thinking of 9/1 management focuses mostly on the production side. Even here, because of the separation of planning and doing, very little provision for the psychological needs of meaningfulness in work are provided. Meaningfulness for those who plan stems from the challenging mental effort remaining. For those who are planned for, however, the job becomes one of mechanical obedience to another's format. Thus, 9/1 fails to regard needs for meaningfulness of effort. In addition, through the exercise of power via the authority and obedience model, mutual trust, which leads to a sense of personal worth, has been essentially eliminated as a consideration.

An assumption concerning relationships which is basic to 9/1 management, is that the productive unit is the man, and that the dominant relationship in work is the supervisor-subordinate pairs. The effort is to isolate individuals for working arrangements in order to prevent social relationships or human interaction from interfering with work. The assembly line and the concept of the one-man gang are two familiar procedures for accomplishing this aim. The effectiveness of the informal work group in slowing down production under 9/1 management has been amply documented.

Under these circumstances of a 9/1 orientation tensions among people who are with one another arise in the course of production. When people with ideas seek a way to express them and needs for personal worth and mature human interactions are denied, resistance and conflicts arise. Conflict itself implies a faulty relationship between production needs and human relationships requirements.

As tension erupts, it is necessary to make an effort to deal with it in some manner. The basis of conflict management in 9/1 is mostly in terms of suppression. The phrases "If you don't like it, lump it" or "Yours is not to question why, yours is but to do or die" are indicative of a 9/1 approach. Conflict is suppressed by the person in the position of authority. Most systems based on 9/1 provide a rich assortment of *disciplinary* arrangements which can be taken against the individual who fails to obey. If people fail to comply with the obedience requirement, they are seen as troublemakers or weaklings or resistant people. Unfortunately, however, disciplinary action all too frequently fails to correct the cause of the conflict. The sources of the conflict therefore remain essentially unrelieved.

Another symptom of difficulty associated with 9/1 management, particularly on the production axis, is seen in the richness of creative techniques employed by people who are related around the production activity in order to slow production down to a low and sometimes to a disturbing unacceptable level. When this happens, it is clear that the creativity of which people are capable is not being used to enhance production. Rather, the capacity for creative and innovative thinking is being used in ways which are detrimental to work. The 9/1 theory tends, then, to be associated with unsound human relationships among those within the production setting who should be operating in an integrated manner.

The 1/9 Orientation to the Production-Relationship Interaction. The country club approach to production, 1/9 is in many respects the reverse of the 9/1 style. The 1/9 appears contradictory to the very purpose for which an industrial situation is organized, since it places key emphasis on relationships and offers little concern for production.

The approach starts from the opposite end in the sense that relationships among people are seen to be all important, and direct concern for production is minimal. The goal of 1/9 in other words, is to achieve harmonious relationships, without particular regard for the effect on production results. A comfortable or slack work tempo can be maintained within the framework of a happy, secure, social atmosphere.

It is necessary to understand two circumstances in order to appreciate how 1/9 can become an organizational way of life. The first has to do with the history of competitive economics within the plant. Many settings, where profit is on a fixed contract cost plus basis or where there is an acute market shortage and quasi monopolistic conditions exist, constitute situations favorable to the appearance of a 1/9 managerial approach. Under any of these circumstances, the manufacturer can return a profit without being truly effective because there is little or no pressure from competition. As a result, it becomes unattractive to make efficiency moves that spread anxiety and that lead to conflict. It is simpler to take the easy way out and to let things go as they are. Such a decision is negative from the standpoint of genuine production, but it favors the development or maintenance of good relationships. Such relationships, however, are not sound in a basic sense. The point being made here, in other words, is that there are situations where competition pressures are so weak that a profit can be returned without genuinely using or creating the conditions under which people can make an effective contribution to it. As a result, the term ''country club'' has been used to refer to this approach.

Where results didn't turn out so well as they might, a 1/9 supervisor is likely to express his lack of concern for production in the following manner.

>   ''Don't take it too hard, we all make mistakes. Maybe we'll have better luck next time.''

Rather than focusing on the job itself, or the way in which it was done, he assumes that contented people will produce as well as contented cows, if they are given the chance.

Executives also are aware of the need to "be nice" under the 1/9 approach to management. A 1/9 manager whose decision was not looked upon favorably describes his way of proceeding:

> "I withdrew my decision to keep harmony, but followed-up on a 'soft sell' basis. You've got to keep making peace with people at all levels by winning allies for your cause."

Not only is the 1/9 managerial theory ineffective in the sense of achieving high output but it is also unlikely to achieve any meaningful human relations gains.

With respect to actual planning and work direction, the 1/9 manager frequently adopts one of two modes of dealing with subordinates, who, of necessity, are looking to him to establish conditions of work. One procedure commonly is described as "I try to lead, rather than push." The assumption is that people should be shown, rather than commanded. They should be supported and aided in their work efforts, in the sense of doing for them those difficult parts of the job for which the supervisor has more technical knowledge rather than allowed or expected to struggle for themselves. Under these conditions people should be willing followers. Other techniques are those of the "soft sell" or pseudo-participation approaches in which the order becomes either a request or the subordinate is led to see the error in his own thinking through gentle persuasion by the supervisor. These and other approaches can be typified by the "be nice" school of thought.

Although work is likely to be planned in an undivided manner, as is true in 9/1, the use of the "group" as a basis for social interaction is frequent in 1/9. Here, members of the work unit get together with the primary goal that of providing good relations among people. Sharing of information, discussing issues that arise for recommended action, family dinners and parties, and so on are all used as means to achieving harmony and happiness by letting people know that management is interested in them as people. However, the best way of understanding the 1/9 approach is to return to the concept of conflict. For some individuals, conflict between themselves and others or even conflicts in which they are not directly involved, except as observers, are experienced as intolerable—something which must be avoided at all costs. The result is that a 1/9 individual tends to operate in such a way as to take whatever actions he can to maintain harmony and to prevent the eruption of conflict in relationships. The actions that he takes as a consequence of this orientation are frequently detrimental to production and seen as "soft" by more production-minded people.

There are many subtle ways in which surface harmony can be maintained and the open appearance of disruptive conflict avoided. One way is to separate those who argue and disagree so that they don't have the opportunity to come into contact with one another. In this way conflict is avoided, even though the advantages that come from the clash of ideas may be thrown out by such a gesture. Another way is to pour oil on troubled waters. In this way, conflict is smoothed over even though the problem remains underneath the surface. A third is to act in such a way that the conditions of interaction among people are summarized through generalizations and abstractions that are of such a high level that everyone can agree with them, even though the abstraction or con- clusion or summary fails to come to grips with the basic problem. Finally, it fre- quently is possible to table a decision until tensions reduce, or other issues be- come more pressing.

The quotations below are ones typical of country club management. The "be nice" approach, which smothers conflict or which seeks to avoid the conditions that will produce it, can lead to a situation of harmony on the relationship side, but a result is that production requirements can simultaneously suffer severely. While the 1/9 manager is seen as a likeable fellow, a good Joe, and a big brother, who is prepared to make his subordinates happy and satisfied regard- less of production costs, nonetheless 1/9 fails to achieve an integration of rela- tionships among people around the requirements of production. Therefore, it also fails to marshal the creative and innovative thinking needed regarding how production can best be accomplished. Not only is the 1/9 approach ineffective in the sense of achieving high output, but it is also unlikely to achieve any last- ing human relation gains since conflict and frustration are not in any realistic manner dealt with and relieved, but rather they are smoothed over or avoided.

The point wants reemphasis here that the production/human relations inter- action in which little or no emphasis is placed on getting production through people but rather emphasis is placed on achieving good relationships by not upsetting the apple cart and creating the conditions under which needed changes actually are effected is no way to get a job done. Nonetheless, the 1/9 approach is far more common than would be expected on casual examination of how people are integrated in the context of production.

The 1/1 Position. The lower left hand corner of Figure 1 is entitled "im- poverished management." The reason is that neither the attainment of pro- duction nor of sound relationships are positive values. 1/1 deemphasizes both. It is an "ostrich" situation where the goal is that of "staying out of trouble" by avoiding involvement in thinking or in feelings. In terms of production re- quirements, the individual does enough to keep an appearance of effort, but his actual contribution is little.

Under the 1/1 orientation the following remarks are typical of a person in the lower levels of an organization.

> "My goal is to keep my nose clean. The best way to do it is to shoot for minimum output. I do enough to get by and to keep people off my back."

Within the executive level, a 1/1 orientation can be found under the circumstances where a person has been repeatedly passed by or has reached the highest level possible in the company. Rather than looking elsewhere, he adjusts in the work setting by minimal performance, seeking satisfaction elsewhere.

> "The work isn't too bad. We like the town; we have a comfortable house. You might say that I'm *marking time* until my retirement."

With respect to the problem of conflict, rather than suppressing conflict as in the 9/1 situation, or smothering it as in 1/9, the goal of a 1/1 manager is to *avoid* conflict by avoiding involvement. When actually faced with conflict, though, the 1/1 approach is to withdraw by such means as ignoring it, postponing confrontation or ultimately leaving the situation.

The 1/1 managerial style is certainly not prevalent. A factory operated under 1/1 circumstances would be unable to stay in business very long. On the other hand, numerous *individuals* relate to the organization in a 1/1 manner and are able to survive for long periods of time. This is particularly so in production situations that have become bureaucratic in nature and where "no one is ever fired."

In some respects 1/1 is an unnatural condition. It is a situation of personal defeat that an individual "comes to," rather than "beginning with." 1/1 as a way of relating to an organization represents a system of failure for the individual and for the organization. It is failure of the organization to integrate individual production efforts with sound relationships and failure for the individual who has accepted defeat and withdrawn his involvement to the degree that even criticism carries no prick.

Five "Mixed" Theories

Five additional approaches represent combinations or "mixes" of the 9/1 and 1/9 positions already discussed. All in one way or another stem from the notion that concern for production and concern for human relationship are in irreconcilable conflict and therefore are not subject to any true integration. Yet, the two concerns must, in some manner or other, be combined within a single organizational setting.

The 5/5 Position. In the center of the *Managerial Grid* is the "middle-of-the road" theory. The same underlying assumptions regarding the impossibility of achieving high production under conditions of high concern for human relationships exists. The 9/1 theory of work planning and control is maintained. Nonetheless, the necessity for avoiding disruptive effects of poor relationships also is recognized in action consequences. The 5/5 theory is middle of the road in that the managerial organization is "push enough to get acceptable production, but yield to the degree necessary to develop or to maintain morale." As a 5/5 supervisor would say,

> "Look, all we want is a fair day's work for a fair day's pay. We know a fellow gets tired. Put out as much as you can, but don't kill yourself. Try to maintain a steady pace that's fair to the company, but that treats you right, too."

Balancing getting the job done with some concern for what people basically "want," also applies higher up the managerial ladder. For example, a 5/5 manager does not *command* as does the 9/1 manager.

> "I don't just *tell* my people what to do. I always try to remember to give the reason why. Of course, it takes a little longer to do it this way, but people basically resent being told what to do."

When the happy medium is achieved, too much production is not expected as people recognize that one must be flexible and "give." Under 5/5 it is believed that by clever string pulling, management can prevent either of the two *concerns* from blocking the satisfactory attainment of the other.

In a number of respects it would appear that the majority of present day organizations have abandoned the severe 9/1 separation between "planning" on the one hand and "doing" on the other and have tended over time to gravitate toward the 5/5 position. Restoration or maintenance of "good" relations among people engaged in work have been obtained through a 1/9 approach. The shift is not a healthy one since 5/5 retains important elements of the theory of work direction contained in 9/1 with the theory of human relations, or 1/9 added to it. It does not "solve" the problem. Rather, a "live and let live" situation is created under which the real problem is muted. In a 5/5 organization the "balance" between output and morale is sought for in connection with work. As a 5/5 manager said, "Maintenance of man is just as important as maintenance of machines."

Paternalism. Paternalism is another more or less stable "mix" of two anchor positions. Paternalistic organizations also tend to push for output in a 9/1 way. In time, the feelings of arbitrariness and alienation take on disturbing proportions. Additional steps are taken to "satisfy" or to correct negative human relations resulting from it. While 9/1 production controls are retained, concern for people is expressed through "taking care of them" in a 1/9 fashion. Organizational members are "given" many fine things—good pay, excellent benefits programs, recreational facilities, retirement programs and even low cost housing. These are not made available however, to acknowledge contribution to output but rather, at best, to gain respect and, at worst, to get subservience.

The mood of paternalism is caught in the following quotation. A supervisor, 20 minutes before the break of work, called one of his men over and said,

> "Joe, you've put in a good day's work and finished all your assignments. Go over to the smoking shack and have yourself a butt."

A paternalistic executive tends to retain tight control in work matters, but to be benevolent and kindly in a personal way. In other words, he treats his junior executives as part of his managerial "family." On the one hand, he encourages them to take initiative and to be responsible. On the other, he is unable to truly delegate and frequently is heard to characterize a succession of subordinates in this way.

> "My assistant won't accept responsibility. He's a bright, capable fellow with plenty of knowhow, but he checks and double checks everything he does with me. He will not take the ball and run. It's difficult to see how he'll ever get to the top of the ladder."

The work situation approaches 9/1 conditions in terms of direction and control, but it is coupled with the 1/9 style of concern for the well being of people. The reward for subordinates' complying with direction, control and push in work is security, happiness and "being taken care of" in terms of financial and social security.

Although paternalism has failed repeatedly to solve problems of getting production through the involvement of people, it is still a rather widespread attitude underlying much organizational thinking.

Wide-Arc Pendulum Theory. The wide-arc pendulum theory is one way of combining the 9/1 and the 1/9 positions in a temporal manner. When tightening up for increased output occurs, as often happens under thin profit margins or recession conditions, production pressure is applied in a manner consistent with 9/1 attitudes. At this point in time the organization would truly be described as 9/1. As a result, relationships can become so disturbed that production suffers. The organization feels forced to ease off and increase its concern for the thoughts, feelings and attitudes of people in a 1/9 manner. The negative results from 9/1 then start a pendulum swing. For a subsequent period of time the organization could validly be described as 1/9. When a degree of confidence has been restored, a tightening up occurs to regain losses in production suffered during the previous pendulum swing towards 1/9.

One of the best times for viewing wide-arc pendulum dynamics is before and after a certification election in companies that want to preserve an independent union which is challenged by an international union. Supervisors say,

> "The signal is out. Management wants to insure that the present union will win the forthcoming representation election. For the next few months, let up on the tough stuff. Ease up on washup time and the coveralls and gloves policy. Show an interest in people. Find out what's griping them. Take whatever actions are required to help the wage man recognize that management is interested in him."

Cracking down to get efficiency and then easing off to restore confidence and then pushing for increased production again is the pendulum swing from hard to soft to hard, etc.

Counterbalancing. Counterbalancing is another way of applying 9/1 and 1/9 simultaneously. Again, the line organization is operated in the direction of 9/1 principles of getting production. However, an antidote is supplied within the structure of the organization for 9/1 attitudes which result in suppressing negative feelings of the kind that can fester and smoulder and that eventually can erupt with devastating effects on production. The antidote or safety valve is the *personnel* function which is designed as a 1/9 counterforce to relieve the conflict and tension generated from the line organization's pressures for production. A strong 1/9 personnel department is intended as a balancing weight where gripes and grievances can be aired and where corrective action can be obtained. Thus, both 9/1 and 1/9 attitudes are present in a "cold war" state of co-existence between two parts of the organization, with the line seeing personnel as hopelessly "soft" and personnel's viewing the line as hopelessly "hard-nosed."

The Two-Hat Theory. The two-hat theory of management occurs when considerations of production are viewed independently from concerns for people, but both are deemed of significance. Under this arrangement, rather than a split occurring within branches of the organization, the separation is maintained in the thinking of those responsible for overall policy and planning. For example, in a two-hat organization it is likely that one day a week, say on Monday, the top group gets together to consider issues concerned with efficient company operation. Then on another day, say Wednesday, the same group meets again, this time to review problems of people. The actions relative to production taken on Monday, though they may have deep implications for the problems that appear on Wednesday, [are] not considered in the context of their possible impact on relationships. The same is true when difficulties on the human side of the enterprise are encountered. Production aspects are held or tabled until the appointed time. Again, the basic assumption is that it is impossible to achieve an integration between production and relationships so that high production is obtained under conditions of satisfying relationships.

Review

All the styles above accept conflict between concerns for production and concern for people as more or less inevitable. Each deals with the assumed basic contradiction in a different way. The 9/1 and 1/9 two-hat and pendulum theories are "either or" in that the emphasis at any one point in time is *either* on production *or* on people. 5/5 paternalism and counterbalancing are efforts to achieve some sort of reconciliation between the two by using some of each simultaneously. The "ostrich" dynamic of 1/1, where involvement in the situation has been withdrawn can, under certain conditions, aid an individual to escape conflict by "hiding" from it. Under the 1/1 approach, the manager does the minimum.

The ways for bringing about some kind of connectedness between concerns for production and concerns for relationships above can be regarded as indications of what more or less skillful practitioners of the "art of management" achieve. None can be accepted as healthy, in the sense of representing a sound basis of operational life. The critical question now is, what is the managerial theory based on the application of behavioral science concepts in the context of work? This question can now be dealt with.

Integrating Production And Human Relationships: The 9/9 Position

The final position in Figure 1 is "team management." The team concept is based on the interdependence of people engaged in work activities. The productive unit is not viewed as an individual working in isolation of others whose output is added to the overall total of the unit. Rather, the building block of a 9/9 situation is the team. The word *team* emphasizes the concept of unity of effort of individuals in the work group, of interdependence between members, of "team play," and of "moving together." Team leadership avoids the blunder of person-centeredness. Individuals are seen, not one-by-one as separate entities, but team management recognizes relationships of members with one another since all are embedded and interconnected with one another in the context of production. As a result, attitudes toward achieving production in the 9/9 situation are vastly different than under any of the other theories mentioned above.

Certain distinctions for gaining an appreciation of 9/9 team effort can be made by drawing comparisons between 9/1 concepts and 9/9 on the one hand and 1/9 concepts and 9/9 on the other. Planning of work is one way in which constrasts can be drawn. In the 9/1 situation responsibility for planning tends to be centralized, with the responsibility of those who execute the work being that of following the instructions they receive. The goal of 9/9 management is to arouse participation and to get involvement in planning, so that all who share concerns for production can find the opportunity to think through and to develop a basis of effort which reflects the best thinking of all.

Team participation is not for social purposes or to "maintain morale as an end in itself, nor does the team concept provide a cloak of anonymity within which inadequate performance can be buried or hidden. Rather, sound interpersonal relations are seen as the *best* way to achieve or to maintain production at peak levels. It is accepted as a given fact that people interact with one another in a context of production, and that feelings and emotions arise. As production problems are thought through, interpersonal feelings affect thinking and vice versa. Conflict is one result. The reason is that when a number of people interact around problems of production, it is likely that different points of view regarding how to solve production problems will develop. People have intense feelings about their own points of view. Conflict, in other words, is bound to appear. An important problem of 9/9 is concerned with how conflict around conditions of production is to be dealt with.

The sound way of conflict management as viewed from the 9/9 position is an approach which offers an opportunity for conflict to be relieved or "worked through" rather than to be suppressed, smothered, denied or avoided. As a result, one of the critical managerial skills present under 9/9 circumstances is the skill of bringing protagonists into relation with one another such that they can work through their differences and points of view rather than separating them as might be true in 1/9 or punishing them as might be true in 9/1.

9/1 managers are likely, under superficial examination, to see 9/9 as soft because it makes strenuous efforts to arouse participation of people and involve their creative and innovative thinking in the solutions of problems. The involvement and participation are what a 9/1 manager may see as weak. On the other hand, a 1/9 manager is likely to see a 9/9 operation as hard, for the reason that it places key emphasis on production. That is, the basis of interrelationships among people is that of achieving the goal of the organization, namely that of production. Furthermore, conflict is not avoided or played down as a 1/9 manager might do, but is actively dealt with.

Finally, it may be possible to give further clarification to the concept of 9/9 management by considering the psychological needs of people for the opportunity to apply mental effort in the attainment of production. This basic psychological need must also be considered in the context of the other and equally important need, namely that of establishing sound and mature relationships among people, which can be characterized as ones of mutual trust, mutual support, pleasure and satisfaction. The position stated here is that thinking through problems of production is most possible when individuals are related in such a manner that there is trust and mutual support, rather than distrust, suspicion, and tension. The interaction of production and people under 9/9 is one which takes advantage of the capacities of individuals to think creatively and innovatively by creating the conditions under which the relationships among people are centered on and conditioned by the need for solving problems of production.

Now with broad theory of production-people relationships before us we can turn to a new question. The question is, "How can a manager learn the skills needed to apply 9/9 management practices in everyday situations?"

II—THEORY AND TRAINING TECHNIQUES FOR LEARNING THE SCIENCE OF MANAGEMENT

To this point emphasis has been placed on theories of management with a brief evaluation given as to the consequences in application of employing any one in the effort to achieve production.

The second critical issue now can be examined in greater detail. The question is, "How is it possible for managers to learn the science of management described above under the 9/9 anchor position?"

Many of you have either read or heard about or else have participated in laboratory training. Much of both a praiseworthy and of a derogatory nature has been said and written regarding it. Over the fifteen year period now drawing to a close, it has persisted and gained in force and character as an approach to training of great impact, application and implication.

Though some descriptions of it make it appear mystical, laboratory training is not difficult to understand. Perhaps the best way to characterize its critical components is to compare the meaning of laboratory, as applied in the human context, to the meaning of laboratory as applied in the physical, biological and earth sciences.

As is widely recognized, the teaching of biological or physical sciences out of a textbook, without direct laboratory experiments to clarify and make concrete the principles involved, would be unheard of in today's universities. The reason is that a great gap is recognized to exist between principles and practice *unless* an individual is provided opportunity to learn to apply principles to practical, concrete circumstances. In chemistry an intriguing laboratory experiment is concerned with solving for an unknown. In biology the student has an opportunity, perhaps for the first time, to see and feel and examine and to understand a frog or a fish from a systematic or scientific point of view. It is the same in physics where students come face-to-face with gravity, magnetism and electricity through concrete laboratory experiments. In geology he has an opportunity to see rocks as something produced by forces of nature rather than simply as something to be picked up and thrown. What I am saying is that physical and biological earth sciences have come to a high state of usefulness *because* teachers of the natural and biological sciences have correctly recognized the great gap between theory and application where scientific concepts are formulated only in verbal ways and no effort is made to aid an individual to understand their meaning through use and application.

The same strategy of thinking about how to make theory and principle concrete to the individual is behind human laboratory training. One not only learns principles of behavior in a human laboratory, but also one has the opportunity to experiment, to try out, to test, to examine, to evaluate and to understand when a behavioral science principle is being correctly applied and when it is being inappropriately violated. Human laboratory training then, provides an opportunity for the student-manager to experiment with behavior under controlled conditions just as any "student" in a physical or biological laboratory follows in the footsteps of physical and biological scientists by performing miniature experiments.

But the remarks above are only practical ways of talking about the human laboratory teaching approach to behavioral science management. The teaching theory itself, which is also a behavioral science theory, can be characterized as a cycle of events under the title of Dilemma-invention-feedback-generalization theory of learning[5] as described below in more detail.

Dilemma. The strategy of experimentation in a human laboratory begins with a dilemma. A dilemma occurs whenever, for a given situation, there is no sound basis for selecting among a range of alternatives, or else there appears to be no satisfactory course of action whatsoever. Furthermore, habitual actions based on past behavior are ineffective as a basis for proceeding. Traditional, "second nature," kinds of behavior don't apply; custom offers no solution. In other words, a person doesn't know what to do. The goal of the teacher or trainer in the human laboratory setting is to create just [such] situations since they contain the key to learning: a dilemma.

What do people confronted with a dilemma do? Do they begin to experiment or to invent? The answer, true almost without exception, is "No." The *immediate* reaction is to try out *older* methods of behaving with which one already is secure or else to get guidance as to what to do from an "expert." In this way, the anxiety so invariably associated with not knowing what to do can be avoided. In the human laboratory then, anticipated first reactions by participants to a dilemma are to try traditional ways of responding. These "frozen behaviors" are ones based on more or less automatic assumptions so deeply rooted that most individuals are unaware of making them. They define the true meaning of second nature. But, as said above, tradition or habit are not adequate to solve the dilemma at hand.

Invention. Only when conventional or traditional ways of dealing with a dilemma have been tried—*unsuccessfully*—are conditions appropriate for the emergence of inventive action. Now people are ready to think, to discard old and unworkable notions, to experiment, and to explore new ways of reacting to determine if *they* will work. If they do not work better, they also may be rejected or modified, or a struggle to apply traditional ways of solving the dilemma may reoccur, until new and more adequate ways of responding eventually are proposed, applied and evaluated.

The period when old behavior is being abandoned and when new behavior has yet to be invented to replace it is an "unfrozen" period, at times having some of the aspects of an emotional crisis. It is a period surrounded by uncertainty, confusion, anxiety, and frequently, of conflict. If people have to work together under human laboratory conditions to invent an acceptable course of action, there is likely to be criticism, attack, withdrawal, flight or defensiveness. Rather than trying to eliminate such reactions as barriers to learning, the goal is to use such reactions in order to learn to understand what produces them. This is part of what a human laboratory is!

Another way of dealing with a training dilemma is to look backward to trace the steps that led to the present impasse. By doing so, it may be possible to spot points at which the present dilemma could have been avoided and also to develop a clear perception of what is required if the situation is to be solved. Such an approach enriches understanding of how history may be constructively used to understand future situations.

Thinking of an inventive kind, thinking that contains proposed solutions for a dilemma with which members were unacquainted in their prior experience, may occur with or without a prior period of involving the reconstruction of history kind of thinking. Propositions presented call for experimentation; they have to be tried to see if they will work in this particular human laboratory situation. Very commonly situations are proposed as a quasiexperimental maneuver, "Let's try this 9/9 alternative for 30 minutes and then shift to a 9/1 orientation to see which of the two works better." An act of comparison is inventive behavior for now people are *reaching* for solutions in the "here-and-now," rather than invoking tradition or acting from "memory," or appealing to an "authority," or grasping for straws. They are acting in a self-directing inventive manner, not in an historically rooted or an outer-directed fashion.

Both retrospective thinking and inventive thinking are highly important to experience if human laboratory learning is to take place. Without one or the other, or both, people are likely to continue along conventional lines even though they are inappropriate and ineffective for dealing with the problem at hand. Then participants are likely to learn little from the experiences they encounter.

Feedback. Fullest learning from the dilemma-invention cycle occurs when two additional types of actions are taken. One is *feedback*, the process by which members acquaint one another with their own characteristic ways of feeling and reacting in a dilemma-invention situation. Feedback aids in evaluating the consequences of actions that have been taken as a result of the dilemma situation. Such reactions and feelings may be in the area of thinking, or feeling, or motivation. They may be centered on personal behavior aimed at telling an individual what he is doing that "blocks" problem-solving or experimenting or, in a more general way, how to devise methods and procedures for experimenting. Feedback also may be centered on actions which hinder or contribute to effective group problem solving. True feedback of this sort is extremely hard to come by outside of the human laboratory setting.

Generalization. The final step in the dilemma-invention cycle is *generalizing* about the total sequence of events that occurred in solving the dilemma in order to get a comprehensive picture of the "common case." When this is done, people are searching to determine the extent to which behavior observed under human laboratory conditions applies in dealing with outside situations. If generalization is not attempted, the richness of dilemma-invention learning is "lost." It is in the generalization phase that Grid theory supplies a rich conceptual system for integrating experience into a framework of more general understanding.

Summary. The theory of learning basic to the human laboratory approach to learning about human factors is that when faced with a dilemma a person experiments; he invents, devises and tests methods out on himself; he gets feedback and he generalizes, leading to new and different ways of reacting. Translated into daily operations, then, the purpose of the laboratory in human training is to create dilemmas that lead to learning to apply the invention-feedback-generalization cycle outlined above.

The next question is, "How is the dilemma-invention-feedback-generalization theory of learning carried out in a laboratory training program which is designed to aid a manager to apply behavioral science concepts in work?

Under laboratory conditions, participants study their *own* behavior under various conditions that contain Grid theory elements such as 9/1, 5/5, 1/1, 1/9, etc. But, rather than diagnosing, analyzing, proposing actions, observing consequences, and evaluating the behavior of someone else, the subject matter is the manager's examination of his own grid-based actions, reactions, feelings and attitudes as they are produced through interaction with others, who also are behaving according to grid theory positions.

The role of the behavioral science trainer in the human laboratory setting is that of creating dilemmas. That is, to produce contrasting experiences through which managers are able to invent, devise, seek out and select new or different ways of behaving, try them out, test their consequences for getting the job done through various feedback procedures and then formulate relevant generalizations from a Grid theory point of view.

III—TECHNIQUES OF HUMAN LABORATORY TRAINING

It would be incorrect to leave the description of a human laboratory at this point. Most of you will immediately equate what I am saying with labels such as "Bethel," and "Arden House," and this would not be entirely appropriate. While these training situations are indeed critically important in the development of human laboratory training, they by no means tell the whole story. A little history will help to place developments in context.

In 1947 in Connecticut, Lewin, Bradford, Benne, Lippitt, Horwitz, and others[6] entered into a novel experiment. An effort was made to understand some of the characteristics of intergroup relations of the kind that separate religious groupings of people. In 1948, the same group developed a human laboratory concerned with more general problems of behavior at Bethel, Maine. In the middle 1950s a similar human laboratory was developed at Arden House for a more highly selected occupational group, those responsible for industrial management. A laboratory for key executives was inaugurated a few years later.

During this period other laboratory centers were developing too. The Western Training Laboratory[7] came into prominence as did one developed in Texas and referred to as the Human Relations Training Laboratory. Others were in the New England area, in Chicago, and in other places about the country. More recently human laboratory ventures have been launched in Europe, the Far East, the Caribbean and other places in the world.

But all of the human laboratories described above were based on another notion about human learning which also is undergoing revolution and change at this time. The notion is that learning of principles of behavior in a human laboratory is *best* accomplished by bringing individuals together, who are *strangers* to one another, to learn together. Participants for human laboratory training traditionally have been "sent to a laboratory," away from the company setting, to be exposed to behavioral science knowledge among other strangers. When people from the same management team are subjected to this type of laboratory training, such as one person going to Arden House, another being at WTL and a third proceeding through a similar program at HRTL, the result is somewhat *mechanical*. The reason for this result is that each may be learning essentially identical things, but when they return there has been no basis provided for them to digest what they have learned and to discover what they need to understand in common if they are to use the training as the basis for team effort. Thus, stranger training prevents achievement of the kind of mutual support and increased interpersonal understanding required by team management as described in Part I under 9/9.

As a result, in 1957, a step toward creating in-company human laboratory training in which the content was tailored to the specific needs of organization members was taken. In this step participants were selected and scheduled to participate so that people with "cousin" relationships in the company network trained together.

In one selection procedure, called the horizontal slice, people at the same organizational level but from different components of the organization are brought together as the unit for training. In this approach, care is taken to separate bosses and their subordinates as well as to separate peers who work for the same boss. Alternatively, a diagonal slice of the organization is scheduled for training. Representatives from different levels in the hierarchy are included in the laboratory program so that it is possible for them to rub shoulders with and to gain perspective concerning the points of view of others lower and higher in the same hierarchy. However, since the slice is diagonal, people at different levels come from different work groups so that actual boss-subordinate pairings or subordinates who are peers of one another are not thrown together.

By using the horizontal or diagonal slice concept, however, program designers insure that *teams* of people who work together *will not* learn to work together more effectively under human laboratory conditions. By committing this error, important contributions to improving team effectiveness of the 9/9 variety frequently are blocked.

When program designers are asked, "Why separate the boss from his subordinates?" their reply often is, "If the bosses were here, the subordinates wouldn't feel free to talk openly. The subordinate's future lies in his boss's hands, and he would be afraid to reveal himself in his 'true light.'"

The next obvious question to program designers is, "Why not train subordinates together who have brother relationships because they work for the same boss?" The answer springs from a similar logic, "People who work for the same boss are competing for advancement and pay. The tendency is for each to engage in 'one-upsmanship' and to seek to put himself in a more favorable light relative to others. These negative side effects from competition are reduced when people from different family work groups are brought together." Such a decision avoids coming to grips with 9/1 win-lose competitiveness; one of the key purposes of human laboratory learning is thereby forfeited.

The inability to talk openly with one's boss and competitiveness with one's peers are critical 9/1 kinds of problems in working relationships. Training programs built around both the horizontal and diagonal slice today insure that these barriers to 9/9 team action will be preserved.

The Alternative Approach: Train the Team as a Unit

What are the implications of the alternative approach in which the unit for training is the team? The first step is for individual members of the team to train together to perfect the skills needed in discharging their work responsibilities more effectively. In football, for example, critical learning is associated with actual scrimmage where a team perfects its communication, control and decision-making skills. Scrimmage is not what each specialist trained by himself does, but rather each of the specialists, in terms of his own job description, blends his effort with team effort to achieve success. In addition to scrimmage, a coach uses chalk talks to explore the internal strategies of plays and to gain understanding of what each individual needs to contribute to support effective team action. Finally, specialized coaching may be provided team members to increase individual skills so that each person can make a more effective personal contribution to team operation.

The same thinking as described above should be applied when the goal is improving total management of an industrial organization through human laboratory training. Team training is accomplished by setting up human laboratory training programs, where Tom, Dick and Harry train *together* in their family work groups. The content of the laboratory program is built around Tom, Dick and Harry's having the opportunity to explore concepts involved in their work as a team and to investigate interpersonal and group difficulties in their own relationships which are preventing team action of the 9/9 variety, particularly barriers to team effectiveness that are related to the faulty or [immature] management of conflict, as required according to 9/9. In this way, they can study the managerial theories being practiced among themselves which are related to existing problems of the organization and of its operation. This approach to learning focuses on training together the people in the *organization* who must work together.

Getting Integrated Effort Through Mobilizing Team Effort

Companies where team training has been carried out agree that more effective team action is the result and the conclusion has been confirmed experimentally.[8] Problems of the people-production relationships which are major stumbling blocks to increased organizational effort and profits can be effectively dealt with. The barriers which stunt personal growth and activity on the one hand (9/1) and which divert an individual's energies from organization problem solving on the other (1/9 or 1/1) are reduced through team laboratory training. These same people can tackle and solve the "hot" issues of organizational performance from which they had previously been shying away, because they have learned to work together in something approaching a 9/9 manner.

SUMMARY

Although the story does not end here it can be concluded at this point for now by briefly summarizing what has been said.

Two significant developments of the past 15 years have been joined together. They are exerting a powerful influence on American industrial life. One influence is the advent of the behavioral sciences as an applied area of knowledge which can be usefully employed in improving management practices. The Grid theory presented in Part I is a summation of much of the relevant behavioral science work regarding conditions for effective production-people integration.

The second aspect is of equal importance. Just as knowledge of physical, biological and earth sciences is relatively less useful until one learns to apply it to concrete situations, so it is with respect to behavioral science knowledge of management processes.

The simple knowing, in an intellectual way, is less than sufficient as the basis for effectively applying the knowledge in concrete situations of application. Laboratory training is what makes the difference. Laboratory training is what permits translation from pure concept to practical application. Human laboratory training makes it possible for practice to become theoretical! Team training meets the requirements of 9/9 Grid theory as the most adequate basis yet described through behavioral science research for achieving effective production-people integration.

What are the implications of these developments of the past 15 years?

In our view, the implications are no less than are the similar implications which can be drawn from present day applications of the physical, biological and earth sciences. A general trend is under way in which the operation of society, at an ever increasing pace, is being transformed and brought into line with basic and systematic understanding of the appropriate conditions of human behavior. These include the conditions of commitment and involvement, the conditions that produce creative thinking, and the conditions of introducing meaningful direction and acceptable control into human activities: in a word, 9/9. As a result, action is based on understanding and agreement, rather than on compliance or subservience. The implications for a more mature production-oriented society are obvious.

Where the trend may end is not easy to say. The implications are great, and the significance over the long term is difficult to fully comprehend at this time.

REFERENCES

1. Blake, R.R. & Mouton, J.S. "Union-Management Relations: From Conflict to Collaboration." *Personnel,* Vol. 38, 1961.

2. Blake, R.R. & Mouton, J.S. "Headquarters-Field Training for Organizational Improvement." *Journal of the ASTD,* March, 1962.

3. Blake, R.R. & Mouton, J.S. "How Executive Team Training Can Help You and Your Organization." *Journal of the ASTD,* Jan. 1962.

4. Bidwell, A.C., Farrell, J.J. & Blake, R.R. "Team Job Training—A New Strategy for Industry." *Journal of the ASTD,* Oct. 1961.

5. Mouton, J.S. & Blake, R.R. "The Instrumented Laboratory." NTL Reading Series. Research in Human Relations Training, in press.

6. Bradford, Leland. "Explorations in Human Relations Training." Washington, D.C., National Training Laboratory for Group Development, 1954.

7. Weschler, Irving & Reisel, Jerome. "Inside a Sensitivity Training Group." Industrial Relations Monograph No. 4, Los Angeles: Institute of Industrial Relations, University of California.

8. Argyris, Chris. *Interpersonal Competence and Organizational Effectiveness.* Homewood, Ill., Richard D. Irwin, Inc., 1962.

Chapter 30

Management Synthesis: An Anatomy of Managerial Style

Jay Hall

While models per se may serve some worthwhile integrative functions, too often they obscure the underlying complexities they were designed to explain. Models sometime tend to supplant the richness of complexity with the false comforts of simplicity. When they do this, they impede rather than facilitate understanding. This poses a real problem for so complex an issue as managerial behavior. Even though some managerial models are quite sound, as far as they go, most do not go far enough. Knowing, for example, whether a manager is autocratic, task-oriented, or interpersonally competent is inadequate without real insight into the *operational* components implied and the *consequences* associated with various practices. By the same token, it does little good to identify one's managerial style unless some appreciation can be gained of the various practices which make up that style and the impact it has on subordinates.

Unfortunately, theorists themselves often do not contribute to a manager's comprehensive understanding of the implications of their models. As each becomes more and more enamored of his own unique representation of events, resulting models sometimes assume a property of functional autonomy; they become energized and persist beyond and apart from the research concerns and practical considerations which gave rise to their development.

Models were never meant to supplant the research findings they summarize. But given the seductive appeal of simplicities, models are often accepted because of their conceptual attractiveness rather than on their theoretical or research supported merits. One of the strengths of *valid* theories, however, is that they not only generate practical hypotheses, they tend to *converge*. They lend themselves to integration and synthesis with proper research effort. Such an effort toward synthesis, incorporating the contributions of the several behavioral science models which have been presented in previous chapters of this volume, is the focus of this chapter.

The goal of the research reported here is to counter the tendency toward idiosyncratic model building by using a data base to highlight how various well-known behavioral models do in fact relate to each other. In doing so it assumes that the reader is familiar with the currently prominent models offered by Robert Blake and Jane Mouton,[1] Douglas McGregor,[2] Abraham Maslow,[3] Frederick Herzberg,[4] and Joe Luft and Harry Ingham.[5]

THE SYNTHESIS RESEARCH PROJECT

Because of a growing discomfort with the apparently fragmented and mutually exclusive nature of management theory development, a research project was aimed at obtaining an empirical integration of those models currently enjoying prominence among managers and behavioral scientists. Such a data-based project, tempered by statistical rigor, demanded that two difficult conditions be met: first, the number of managers studied must be large enough to lend an acceptable range of confidence to the findings and, second, multiple measurements must be obtained from each manager.

With the help of colleagues in business, industry, government and service organizations, reasonably complete data on over 1,700 managers were obtained over a two-year period. Measurements ran the gamut of managerial surveys and indices and, because of the executive development setting in which data were collected, information came from subordinates as well as from their managers, a unique research bonus. In brief, a manager's dominant style was identified, *i.e.,* the style of management most preferred according to managers' self-reports and confirmed by their subordinates' appraisals, and then such factors of the management process as theory of mankind, involvement strategies, motivational practices, and interpersonal competence were studied relative to different managerial styles. Moreover, information about that usually obscured domain of subordinate reactions to managerial practices and resulting feelings was available in the subordinate data.

The results appear on a model-by-model basis. The five management styles depicted by Blake and Mouton to identify and categorize managers of different persuasions will be compared with respect to the principles enunciated by McGregor, Maslow, Herzberg, Luft and Ingam and others. Since these theorists address issues and practices inherent in management but not typically treated in depth under the style rubric, the synthesis becomes an *anatomy of management style.*

Managerial Beliefs

A manager's personal theory about the nature of those who work is the foundation upon which he or she builds a set of practices described in the

Managerial Grid. *Differences in management style are rooted in basic differences in belief systems;* the theoretical argument is that the behaviors which are labeled 9/9 flow from basic beliefs and expectations regarding others which are fundamentally different, for example, from the beliefs and expectations leading to 9/1 or 5/5 practices.

Hard data are preferred over speculation in such analyses. Information from 1,685 managers was available regarding[6] (1) their most preferred management style and (2) their appraisal of an employee group which reflected McGregor's *negative Theory X* or *positive Theory Y* beliefs regarding human nature and the motivation to work.[7] Thus, it was possible to assess managers' style preferences in the light of their X-Y beliefs, thereby gaining insight into the relationship between the two models. Several research questions arose: Are differences in management style really couched in differences in X-Y beliefs as McGregor has suggested? If so, in what ways do those preferring different styles differ in X-Y orientation? And, is a manager's belief apparent from his or her practices?

The data were subjected to statistical analysis to identify the dimensions along which selected groups most differ. As anticipated, the analysis yielded evidence of highly significant differences among style groups in terms of their subscription to X-Y values. The nature of the differences may best be appreciated when the results are viewed in graphic form. Figure 1 shows that

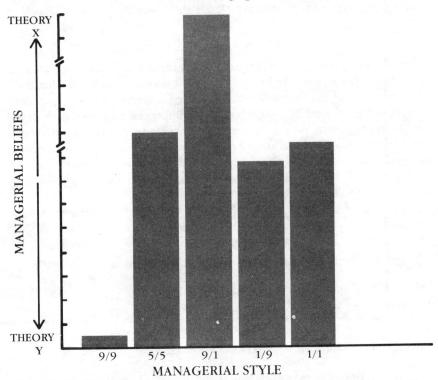

Figure 1. Managerial beliefs as a function of style.

substantial differences in belief systems characterize the five management styles. A bipolar X-Y dimension emerged from the statistical analysis and those scoring high on Theory X are toward the top and those scoring high on Theory Y fall toward the bottom. As might be expected, managers most preferring the 9/1 style show the greatest reliance on Theory X values. Those favoring the 5/5 style also lean heavily toward a Theory X value system along with the individuals identified as favoring 1/1. By way of contrast, 9/9-oriented managers are the lone occupants of the space characterizing strong Theory Y orientation.

Of surprise to some perhaps is the finding that managers of a 1/9 persuasion reveal a substantial *Theory X* value system. The 1/9 style has confused people, because a certain ambivalence surrounds it. Foss, for example, erred in an all too common direction when he concluded that Theory X corresponds to *Concern for Production* and Theory Y to *Concern for People*.[8] According to this logic, 1/9 behaviors should be just as Theory Y-based as 9/9. Foss, like many others, simply imposed a relationship where none existed: 1/9 management does *sound* Theory Y because of its preoccupation with social relationships, therefore it must be Theory Y!

As Blake points out, however, there are many forms of "concern" and the 9's in 1/9 and 9/1 are different in character from those in 9/9. It is one thing to have a high concern for people and their need for autonomy and personal achievement but quite another to have a high concern for people because of a

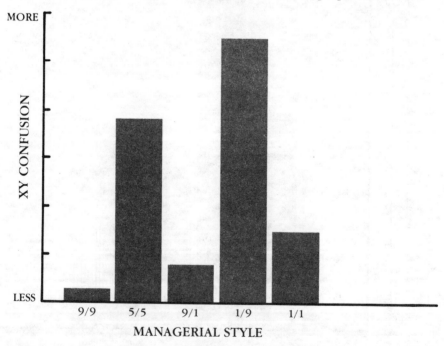

Figure 2. Belief consistency—XY confusion—as a function of managerial style.

belief in their helplessness as creatures in an oppressive system. Obviously, a maximum concern on the human dimension must be analyzed for the *type* of concern as well as the amount to differentiate between Theory X and Theory Y beliefs.

The statistical analysis yielded a second dimension of interest: X-Y confusion or how well one's beliefs fit together to form a coherent basis for managing. As shown in Figure 2, the consistency of beliefs underlying each style can be measured from a pure, authentic philosophy to one which is mixed or pretentious. Both the 5/5 and 1/9 management groups are strongly characterized by X-Y confusion. These essentially Theory X managers exhibiting high X-Y confusion *appear* through words and actions to be something other than Theory X oriented. The beauty of the discriminant analysis technique employed, however, is that it can strip away the more ostensible trappings of style and bore in on the significant core components. In the present case—words, self-images, and protestations to the contrary notwithstanding—the result is the unmasking of both 5/5 and 1/9 management groups: Philosophically confused but with their values quite firmly rooted in Theory X suppositions. Indeed, although both the 9/1 and 1/1 groups are equally if not more committed to Theory X tenets, they are straightforward and unequivocal about it; their belief structure is simple and neither is very high on the X-Y dimension. The same may be said for the 9/9 group's commitment to a Theory Y stance.

In effect three management styles—9/1, 1/1, and 9/9—are "pure" in the sense that they are direct expressions of basic and uncontaminated beliefs about the nature of those who work. In this respect, each is an *authentic* management style insofar as managerial practices are reflections of personal intent and interpersonal values. It is likely that the subordinates of those so disposed have a good idea of what to expect from them. They may or may not like such managers, but at least they know where the managers stand!

On the other hand, managers embracing either the 5/5 or 1/9 style appear to lack such authenticity; the X-Y confusion serves to disarm or divert attention from the basic Theory X values underlying both styles. Both in word and deed, the 5/5 and 1/9 styles are *indirect* expressions of their advocates' basic beliefs about others. To be sure there are qualitative differences, but they are obscured by X-Y smokescreens.

Those who most prefer the 5/5 style employ what can be considered the classic defense of Western Man, namely *compartmentalization*. With their cultural background of democratic values, some individuals find it difficult to *profess* straightforward Theory X beliefs even when they feel they accurately represent practical realities. One way of coping with the managerial doublebind is to pay verbal homage to one while pursuing actions consistent with the other, to confine each to its appropriate mental compartment. When individuals adopt such a political posture but can see no discrepancy whatsoever between their espoused values and their subsequent acts, compartmentalization exists. So it is that those preferring the 5/5 style might espouse fairly accurate Theory Y tenets such as "People are more committed and will support those ideas they have a hand in producing," and follow them with Theory X action plans like, ". . .So that means we've got to find some way to make our people think this was their idea!" While the philosophical assumption embraced is in keeping with the participative ethic of Theory Y, the action is rooted in pure Theory X expectations; the underlying premise is that people are gullible enough to be sold on ideas not truly their own.

Those preferring the 1/9 style are characterized by a different set of defensive reactions to different conflicts. The conflict evidenced by the 1/9's X-Y confusion is less one of philosophic versus practical reality than one stemming from an incompatibility between managers' personal needs in relating to those they manage and the task demands inherent in the managerial role per se. There is *role* conflict implicit in adherence to the 1/9 style; that is, neither the needs of such managers nor their beliefs about the nature of workers permit them to discharge comfortably what they perceive to be the onerous chores associated with management: planning, directing, controlling, evaluating performance, and the like.

Just as Blake has explained that the 9s in 1/9 and 9/9 are not the same, the Theory X to which the 9/1 manager subscribes is not the same as that influencing those disposed to 1/9 management. Indeed, while the 9/1 style posits a "them versus me" form of *displacement* in appraising others' traits, the *projective* quality underlying the 1/9 style promotes a "we" set of considerations. It is "we" who must protect ourselves from organizational oppression.

This readiness to identify with others is one of the factors which often makes the 1/9 style appear similar to the 9/9 style; but the *nature* of the identity is critical. The 1/9 "we-ness" is not founded on an assumption of shared healthy, goal-seeking, expressive traits which characterized the 9/9 style so much as on an assumption of shared fragility and vulnerability. The manager sees himself and others as easily hurt, readily open to exploitation, and utterly dependent on the whims of others with greater power. People are given little credit for their resiliency or innate coping strengths; they need to be protected and comforted. The manager, in need of someone he can depend on for support, behaves as one who can be depended on for support. Not only is such a stance difficult to maintain where task accomplishment and production are valued highly, it is also difficult to admit to anyone, including oneself, that such considerations dominate one's choice of managerial style. Consequently, the 1/9 X-Y confusion takes the form of *rationalization*: a semi-conscious attempt to gloss over discrepancies and explain away troublesome misgivings by reciting a veritable litany of counter values. So it is that those employing the 1/9 style often *appear* to be the only ones in an organization who truly care about the growth, feelings, morale, and strivings of others. As the data reveal, in spite of what the 1/9 style might *appear* to represent, it is rooted in Theory X, obscured by contrived behaviors.

Finally, and most noteworthy, over 70% of the managers who displayed a clear preference for a particular style in this study subscribed to some variant of

Theory X thinking. This is a sobering finding as we begin to consider the action components of management.

Differences in the choice of managerial style, rooted in basic differences in beliefs about the nature of mankind, are significant in ways which go beyond the statistical sense of the word. In the light of significant attitudinal differences involving X-Y dynamics, the next question is, "What are the action components and desirability of their consequences of the various managerial styles?" It is logical in light of different managerial beliefs to expect quite different behaviors from stylistically different managers in the realm of involvement strategies, interpersonal competence, and motivational policies. And indeed there are differences.

Management Style and the
Participative Ethic

Providing opportunities for people to participate in making decisions which directly affect their work is not only consistent with humanistic values gaining prominence in management thought but is a technique for achieving heightened ego-involvement as well.[9,10] The *returns* expected by a manager from participatory practices will vary according to his view of others' capacity to contribute and desire to be involved. As noted in the previous discussion, theories regarding the nature of those who work differ from style to style and it is probable that application of the participative ethic does also.

To test this assumption and to determine the extent to which managers attempt to involve their subordinates in decision making, an involvement index[11] was administered to the 2,161 subordinates of 831 managers. The index assesses not only the degree of participation enjoyed by people in shaping the nature of their work, but their reactions to prevailing conditions in terms of satisfaction and frustration. An average of 2.6 subordinates per manager were sampled. Once managers were grouped according to dominant style preference, the subordinate data for each manager were averaged; thus the measurements employed reveal the way a manager's subordinates *on the average* view his involvement strategy and consequently feel in the performance of their work.

Involvement effects differ significantly among managers differing in style preference. By far the most significant dimension detected was an index of the amount of participation encouraged—or allowed—by each group of managers. As might be expected in the light of previous discussion, managers of a "people" orientation do substantially more gatekeeping, more actively pursue the opinions of others. By and large, those managers with less concern for the human facets of work were reported to use fewer involvement strategies. Figure 3 displays the amount of participation reported by subordinates of managers using each of the five styles.

Sheer amount of participation, however, does not fully capture the essence of

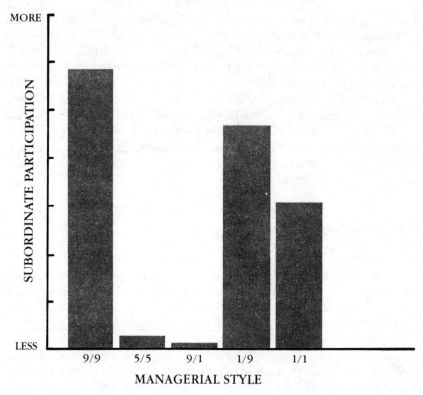

Figure 3. Subordinate participation as a function of managerial style.

involvement dynamics. The *quality* of participative opportunities must be considered, for it is in this domain that the feeling tones underlying sustained commitment are to be found. If opportunities to participate in decision making are confined to unimportant issues or if there is little management follow-up on those decisions produced under participative conditions, subordinates may interpret their opportunities for participation as little more than lip-service to values not really held. Subordinates will be frustrated. Needless to say, subordinate reactions in such instances will be something less than healthy ego-involvement and, indeed, trust between manager and subordinate may become totally undermined.

A second point of trend level significance illumines the interplay between the amount of participation afforded under a given style of management and the feelings of pride *vis a vis* frustration experienced by subordinates under each style. This dimension serves as an index of the healthiness of the climate in the organization. As Figure 3 revealed, participation opportunities are most frequent under managers subscribing to either 9/9 or 1/9 management; managers disposed to 5/5, 9/1, and 1/1 practices, on the other hand, appear to make little use of this involvement strategy. Such results are congruent with theory. Resulting climates are less harmonic, however, as shown in Figure 4.

The most noteworthy aspect of Figure 4 contrasts the climates resulting from participation under 9/9 and 1/9 managers. While subordinates of 9/9 managers report high levels of involvement leading to feelings of pride in accomplishment and minimal frustration, those who work for 1/9 managers report serious levels of frustration in tandem with no pride to speak of despite fairly desirable levels of involvement. The effects under 1/9 participation are just as

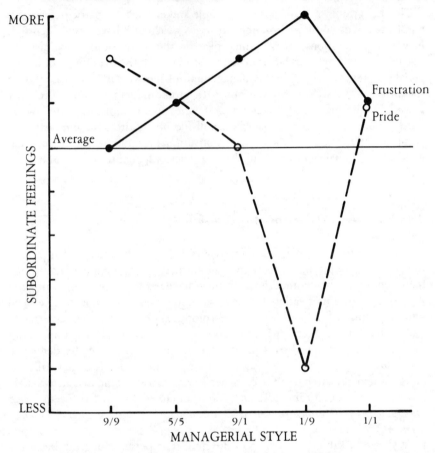

Figure 4. Climate effects associated with five different managerial styles.

counterproductive as those under 9/1 non-participation. In all likelihood, the source of this unhealthy climate lies in involving subordinates in trivial matters or a dearth of follow-up on significant decisions where their input has been solicited. Due to a misapplication of the participative ethic, subordinates expect something other than what occurs and frustration follows. Other styles—the 5/5 and 1/1 approaches—do not differ notably with respect to climate; their relative neglect of participation yields moderate levels of both frustration and pride. It is noteworthy that only the 9/9 style evinces those positive effects associated with truly collaborative practices.

Managerial Style and the
Motivational Process [12,13]

The way groups of managers view people and employ the participative ethic and consequent employee reactions in terms of climate have been discussed. Now several questions emerge which bear on the motivational dynamics implicit in the findings thus far. It makes sense to extend the hypotheses of managerial differences to include the management of motives; managers preferring the different grid styles very likely approach subordinate motivation differently as well. Do they have different personal theories about employee goal-striving? Furthermore, how does a manager's use of incentives affect the motivation of employees? Do managers fulfill their motivational prophecies and, if so, what is the motivational significance of the 9/9 style compared to, for example, the 9/1?

The Manager's Theory of Motivation

In order to further link managerial style with the way in which managers seek to encourage subordinate productivity, information was obtained from 1,667 managers about the manner in which they managed the motivational process. Assessments via a motivational index[14] yielded scores on each of the five need systems postulated by Maslow: creature comfort, safety, belonging, ego-status, and actualization. Score strength served as a measure of the importance ascribed to a given need by a manager and, consequently, of the degree to which it is emphasized in the day-to-day management of his or her subordinates. When the strengths for each need system were compared across style groups, highly significant differences were obtained for all five needs: *each management style group professed an idiosyncratic approach to the management of motives.*

As shown in Table 1, managers of different style persuasions send drastically different messages to their subordinates regarding what they deem important and feasible from a motivational standpoint. Those managers given to 1/1 practices clearly send the message that maintenance-hygiene factors are most important. Perhaps these are the only factors which they feel they can control or, having strong Theory X beliefs, they may think these are the factors which most concern their subordinates. These managers attach major importance to *creature comfort* and *safety* incentives; it is likely that they administer such peripheral factors according to some motivational formula found in their personnel manuals. These data shed light on the low participation-moderate

Table 1. Style practices in the Management of Motives.*

NEEDS	MANAGERS' MANAGEMENT OF MOTIVES				
	9/9	5/5	9/1	1/9	1/1
BASIC	39	**55**	**55**	**51**	**62**
SAFETY	45	**52**	**68**	41	**60**
BELONGING	**51**	47	28	**57**	44
EGO-STATUS	**54**	**54**	**61**	42	43
ACTUALIZATION	**59**	48	44	**51**	39

*Tabled values reflect percentile scores derived from a normative sample of 5,281 managers. Bold type denotes needs receiving major emphasis.

frustration-pride paradox of subordinates under 1/1 noted earlier. *Avoidance* dynamics are stressed under 1/1 management; to avoid dissatisfaction, the manager emphasizes and becomes preoccupied with the impersonal concerns of the work environment—all neatly spelled out in prearranged policy. The subordinate's participation would be superfluous; he is not particularly needed to help with lighting, heating, and cleaning problems.

Managers favoring the 1/9 style promote a slightly different set of motivational practices. Like the 1/1 manager they are preoccupied with providing creature comforts but *claim* to also promote belonging and actualization. Keeping in mind the high frustration and diminished pride experienced by subordinates of 1/9 managers, it is safe to assume the quality of opportunities to meet these needs is quite low. Belonging might be pursued by "awfulizing" about the job in a group setting, a cathartic but none too satisfying an activity. Lip service is probably given to personal growth and testing one's potential but the 1/9 manager does not follow through and provide the means to that worthy end.

The 5/5 and 9/1 managerial postures both manifest motivational practices which, at best, are designed to frustrate subordinates. Both reflect approaches founded on Theory X (note the maintenance emphasis of both) and reveal a mismanagement of motivational dynamics which results in an approach-avoidance conflict.

For example, the 5/5 group is characterized by a joint emphasis on *ego-status* (growth) and *creature comfort* (maintenance) incentives. These needs are basically incompatible; progression to an *ego-status* level is highly unlikely until lower level needs have been adequately satisfied. The subordinate under 5/5 management therefore becomes something of a Pushmi-Pullyu, exhorted to take pride in competence (an *approach* mechanism) and constantly reminded of the importance of peripheral factors in the work setting (an *avoidance* mechanism).

The 9/1 style's practices are in many respects even more insidious. While extolling the virtue of striving for recognition and other *ego-status* incentives, managers favoring 9/1 report an even greater reliance on *safety-security* incentives. The convoluted message—not lost on subordinates— is one of, "Give me your best effort...but if you value your job, don't screw up" or the old Sales Management chestnut, "We're having a contest: whoever wins gets to keep his job!"

Once again only 9/9 managers emerge as emphasizing motivational values consistent with behavioral theory: they attach major importance to social and expressive motivators. Most characteristic is their attention to *actualization* incentives, followed in order of emphasis by *ego-status* and *belonging;* all possess approach properties. Managerial emphasis under 9/9 is on constructive contributions to one's organization and the satisfaction of needs deemed by Maslow and Herzberg to lie at the core of human gratification. If the 9/9 style is deficient motivationally, it may be so in the relatively low emphasis attached to maintenance-hygiene factors; it is not clear from the data whether these are simply deemed less significant than higher needs or if they are so de-emphasized that their replenishment requirements are ignored. If the latter is the case, even the 9/9 group will encounter motivational difficulties from time to time.

So it is that managers espousing different styles differ in their conceptions of and approaches to the management of motives. Of equal importance is to discover the effects of the various practices on subordinate motivation. Do subordinates persist and pursue the goals most characteristic of mature adults or do they learn to internalize, to adopt, organizational values and managerial preachments? The data indicate that in many cases the power of managerial prophecies to shape subordinate expectations and behavior may have been underestimated.

Prophecies Fulfilled: Subordinate Needs Under Different Management Styles

With another index of motivation,[15] data were collected from over 4,500 subordinates of managers representing the five grid styles and averaged for each manager, giving a generalized motivational index for each style. Statistical analysis revealed that subordinates differ significantly on each need system from style to style.

A summary of the scores for subordinates' experienced needs is presented in Table 2. When the data are compared with those in Table 1, the subordinate profiles reflect strong indications of managerial influence. Not only do

Table 2. Experienced needs of subordinates' grouped according to their managers' styles.*

NEEDS	SUBORDINATES' WORK MOTIVATION				
	9/9	5/5	9/1	1/9	1/1
BASIC	42	45	49	45	46
SAFETY	47	47	**56**	52	**56**
BELONGING	**53**	49	43	**53**	**53**
EGO-STATUS	49	**53**	52	45	44
ACTUALIZATION	**54**	**54**	49	49	48

*Tabled values reflect percentile scores derived from a normative sample of 20,452 individuals. Bold type denotes needs receiving major emphasis.

subordinate profiles differ significantly from management style to management style, they differ in ways consistent with the motivational practices of those styles.

The most obvious and encouraging evidence of managerial prophecies fulfilled is found among the subordinates of 9/9-oriented managers. As their scores in Table 2 show, these subordinates report that their major motivational concerns lie with *belonging* and *actualization*. Managers employing the 9/9 style most strongly promote the motivators which, according to Herzberg, underlie work satisfaction and enhanced performance; their subordinates espouse the same values. Moreover, these subordinates value social motivators more than *ego* incentives, suggesting that the latter are less important than their managers think. This reflects some of the effects associated with psychological maturation, facilitated by the manager's strong emphasis on actualizing potentials. It is known that people become less egocentric and more altruistic as they gain more and more experience with *actualization* opportunities. Consequently, managers favoring 9/9 succeed in implementing their motivational theories; so do managers of other persuasions but with less fortunate results.

The approach-avoidance dilemma created by 9/1 manager's practices is internalized and openly manifested by their subordinates. These managers press for *ego-status* in tandem with *safety-security* strivings and their subordinates are primarily motivated by those same concerns. It is difficult to imagine a more enervating and tension-filled climate. Encouraged, even pushed, to demonstrate competence and seek out opportunities for gaining recognition, subordinates are constantly reminded of the prescribed manner in which they must work and the consequence of mistakes. Ego satisfactions require taking risks while security demands just the opposite. And yet this is the message relayed by managers and, judging from subordinate reports, it comes through loud and clear. Under 9/1 management, no foundation exists on which to build a joint enterprise or collaborative effort; both *ego* and *security* needs epitomize self-centeredness. Using a divide and conquer strategy, these managers' prophecies, too, are fulfilled.

Strong support for prophetic fulfillment was also obtained from the subordinates of managers disposed to 1/9 and 1/1 practices. Slight variations are evident for the two groups in Table 2, but these may be subordinates' attempts to assert themselves in the face of the two passive managerial styles. In the case of subordinates under 1/9 treatments, their managers' preoccupation with *belonging* is noted, accompanied by an almost equally strong concern for *safety* and *security* rather than the *creature comforts* touted by management. Subordinates frankly do not trust their managers and are apprehensive and preoccupied with the avoidance of risk-taking. They are afraid to move without structure, work descriptions, and some assurance of long-range maintenance; *i.e.*, insecurity prevails. If the 1/9 management of motives is interpreted as a form of overprotection and dependency training, then the reactions of subordinates are quite characteristic of dependent employees. The subordinate's development in his or her work may be regressive and the actualization touted by 1/9 managers is not only notably lacking, it is extremely unlikely.

The same regressive implications appear in the 1/1 approach to motivation. The subordinates of managers favoring this style report their major motivational preoccupation to be maintenance of *safety* and *security* as their managers have emphasized. When managers and subordinates agree on the importance of safety-seeking there likely is a slavish maintenance of the status quo: Learn the rules, apply them diligently, keep your nose clean and you'll still be around after the next reduction-in-force! Once again, subordinates reflect managerial perceptions of the world of work.

Finally, there is the 5/5 style and its motivational accoutrements. It is puzzling that the subordinates of managers disposed to the 5/5 style report the healthy motivational profiles depicted in Table 2. Statisticians may claim this to be caused by a mathematical phenomenon called regression toward the mean. However, 5/5 managers may show little surprise, claiming these results are exactly those they are striving for. Whether subordinates fail to read the motivational message of the 5/5 style, obscured as it is by X-Y compartmentalization, or whether they simply ignore its import while marching to their own beats, they appear to prosper motivationally. Whatever the reason, the data show that in spite of the managerial emphasis on *creature comfort, safety,* and *ego-status* needs, heavy on hygiene factors, the subordinates of managers favoring 5/5 purport to experience needs which, in order of importance, are quite similar to those reported by the subordinates of managers employing the 9/9 style. Such data point up one of the ironies of the 5/5 style: the right effects, albeit achieved for the wrong reasons, tend to reinforce 5/5 practices and further convince the manager that he or she is on target. However, motivation is only a part of the management process and one should not forget the less than healthy climate created by 5/5 managers as well as the shortcomings in interpersonal competence which will be pointed out in the next section.

The data from the management of motives study are quite sobering. In four of five instances the results represent straightforward examples of motivational self-fulfilling prophecies. The congruence between managerial interpretations of motivational needs and subsequent subordinate strivings speaks eloquently of the powerful role played by managers in defining the nature of the work-place for those they manage. This is one of the most potent yet least researched aspects of management.

It has been well over two decades since Chris Argyris alerted managers *and* social scientists to the discrepancies between organizational values and the needs of individuals who comprise organizations.[16] Argyris' point was not that there is an *inherent* discrepancy (like that propounded by a Theory X view), but that managers view workers' capabilities in such a limited and reductive way that organizations *appear* to require such superficial, primitive skills and behaviors that, to fit in, workers must become something less than they truly are. Motivation is a subtle facet of management; yet the motivational effects associated with the 9/1, 1/9, and 1/1 managerial styles not only confirm Argyris' interpretation, they attest to the inordinate power of managers to alter realities for their employees so that they, the employees, over time internalize and don the behavioral trappings ascribed to them by management. This is brainwashing on a more massive and subtle scale than perhaps ever encountered, and it is occuring within many organizations on a daily basis.

Management Style and Interpersonal Competence

Concerned with the apparent discrepancy between organizations' espoused values and the needs and capabilities of the workforce, Argyris searched for ways to solve the problem by effectively integrating individual and organiza-tional dynamics. While Blake and Mouton hit upon 9/9 management as their preferred mechanism, Argyris cited the critical role of *interpersonal compe-tence:* the manager's willingness to deal openly and candidly with others, to own up to ideas and feelings while remaining sensitive to others' participative needs and potential contributions, and accomplishing this in such a way that the problem-solving climate is preserved and strengthened.[17]

The Luft-Ingham Johari Window model[18] is an excellent format for assessing a manager's level of interpersonal competence. As with several other behavioral science models enjoying prominence, however, the interpersonal model often appears as an *alternative* to managerial style treatments or philosophic orien-tations. But, the capacity for dealing with others competently is not an alter-native to the global issue of style preference, nor is it separable from style considerations. Style and level of interpersonal competence are part and parcel of the total managerial process, but they are not the same dynamically.

In general, interpersonal behavior is a factor which might be expected to vary as a function of managerial style. An investigation of the *interpersonal dynamics* of managerial style may illuminate that critical point at which managerial intent is translated into action. Managers may well differ in their capacity for transacting effectively with others in ways which are consistent with the other values and theories characterizing their various styles.

Using a survey[19] to obtain self-reports from managers and a companion survey[20] to gather subordinate views of interpersonal practices, appraisals were collected for 1,646 managers and 4,259 of their subordinates. Analyses reveal that, according to both ratings, the level of interpersonal competence does indeed vary with managerial style; highly significant differences are to be found in the way managers of different persuasions use exposure and feedback-solicitation.

The amount of exposure and feedback-solicitation employed affects the overall size *and* shape of the interpersonal space called the Arena in the Luft-Ingham Johari Window model. In this known-by-self/known-by-others area, an area of shared data and mutual understanding, size is equated with the quantitative productivity of resulting relationships, while shape implies the prevailing interpersonal climate. The management style groups in this study reflect both size (productivity) and shape (climate) differences.

Statistical analysis yields a dimension which may be taken as an index of overall interpersonal competence, capturing the net effect of exposure and feedback practices. Figure 5 portrays both the self-rating and average subordinate ratings. As the graphs clearly show, managers and their subordinates sense vast differences in management's interpersonal behaviors. Managers given to 9/9 employ practices which rank highest in interpersonal competence. Least competent in both appraisals are those favoring 1/1 management. Of some surprise is the disclosure by managers and their subordinates alike, that the 9/1 management group is judged second in interpersonal competence to the 9/9 group, followed by 5/5 and 1/9 groups.

In some respects, the positioning of 9/1 and 1/9 groups might appear to be reversed. The competence index underlines some of the ironies of organizational life: while those who really care very little about the well-being of their subordinates (9/1) are seen as interpersonally effective, those who look most to others for support and are most geared to giving in kind (1/9) are seen as virtually inept interpersonally. It is not totally unexpected that 9/1 managers' self-ratings yield a picture of competence, but it is surprising that their subordinates, frustrated with non-involvement and stultified motivationally, produce appraisals of above average interpersonal effectiveness. By the same token, it is not unexpected that managers in the 1/9 group are somewhat self-effacing, presenting themselves in a way signaling reduced competence. But the fact that subordinates judge 1/9 management incompetent interpersonally bears more thought.

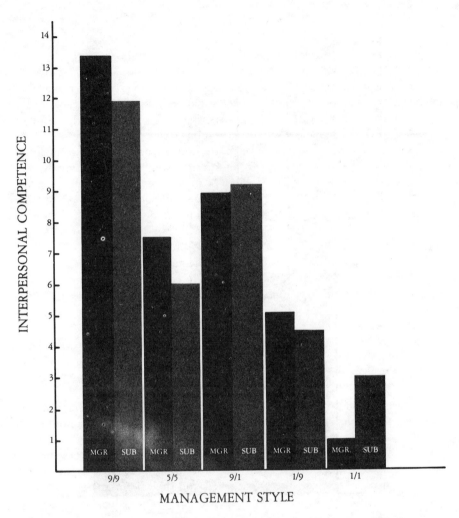

Figure 5. Self and others appraisals of managers' interpersonal competence as a function of management style.

Persons embracing the 1/9 style employ interpersonal practices which are in the best tradition of non-directive Rogerian techniques. Such techniques are favored by counselors and therapists as a means to giving interpersonal support, of demonstrating caring, so as to make others feel more comfortable and self-accepting. Whether or not such a posture is effective in a clinical setting, the current data imply that the workplace is *not* appropriate for such behaviors; managers are seen as less competent for it.

Certainly such interpersonal competence differences among managers of five people-production persuasions are not lost on subordinates; their practices reflect what they perceive to be ''appropriate'' behaviors for relating with their

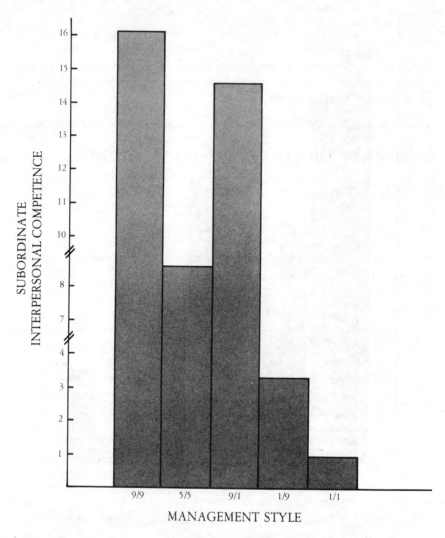

Figure 6. Subordinate interpersonal competence as a function of the manager's style of management.

managers. So there are normative or culture-shaping issues associated with style which are also important.

In general, subordinates mirror or complement their managers' practices, thus filtering managerial practices down through the organizational layers. As a test of this phenomenon and of the long-range effects and potential efficacy of the interpersonal practices employed by various managerial groups, information was gathered about subordinate profiles as well. The results are presented graphically in Figure 6.

Subordinates of each management style tend to behave interpersonally in much the same way as do their managers. Thus, subordinates too differ in terms of their levels of competence and these differences are traceable to the normsetting influences of managerial practices. So it is that *organizational cultures perpetuate themselves according to the prevailing managerial behaviors rather than formally tested principles.*

SUMMARY OF THE SYNTHESIS RESEARCH PROJECT

Persuaded of the utility of each theoretical development and convinced of the existence of complementarity and overlap among models, in the Synthesis Project we attempted to gain a more complete and data-based picture of each management style and provide a much needed integration of theory. For too long, managers have had only the jargon and armchair inferences of style, with too little valid and useable information about the practices and values involved.

In presenting the results on a model-by-model basis, however, some of the desired sense of integration may have been lost. By way of summary therefore, the salient facets which characterize each managerial style from the Blake and Mouton grid are presented below. These summary capsules may be approached as statements of ingredients which make up each style and may serve as guideposts to anyone seeking clarification or aspiring to change his or her style.

The 9/9 style is rooted in a pure form of *Theory Y* thought.
- These managers, characterized by maximum concerns for both production and people, capitalize on the *involvement strategy*. Their subordinates report *high levels of participation and pride with decision products.*
- In their management of motives, 9/9-oriented managers assume that their subordinates are the typical mature and healthy adults described by Maslow and Herzberg, primarily concerned with *higher level needs*; their subordinates respond in kind and are most preoccupied with *actualization, belonging, and ego-status.*
- According to managers and subordinates alike, the *interpersonal competence* of 9/9 management is the *greatest* of all those studied; high, balanced and uniform reliance on exposure and feedback processes is reported. Finally, subordinates employ these *same* interpersonal practices, thus promulgating *collaborative-risk taking* values throughout the organization.

The 5/5 style flows from essentially *Theory X* thought somewhat obscured by a *compartmentalized* version of *X-Y confusion.*
- Managers use *involvement strategies* to a *limited* extent, but subordinates are *moderately comfortable* with this state of affairs.

- Managers disposed to 5/5 assume that subordinate motivation lies primarily in concern for *creature comfort, safety* and *ego-status* needs. Subordinates, however, appear unaffected by such motivational emphases; they are most concerned with the motivator factors deemed most important by Herzberg and Maslow.
- Both managers and their subordinates report *average interpersonal competence.*

The 9/1 style is rooted in an essentially pure *Theory X* view of mankind.
- *Little* use is made of *involvement strategies* and subordinates react to this deprivation with feelings of *high frustration and little pride of accomplishment.*
- Motivationally, 9/1 devotees stress *safety-security, creature comfort,* and *ego-status* pursuits. Their prophecy is fulfilled; subordinates report like concerns.
- An *autocratic* interpersonal style characterizes 9/1 management; subordinates, however, rate both their managers and themselves quite competent interpersonally.

The 1/9 style follows a view of mankind which is essentially *Theory X,* strongly glossed over by X-Y *confusion* which takes the form of *rationalization.*
- While a *substantial* amount of *participative activity* is reported, subordinates are *lacking in pride* and *frustrated.*
- The 1/9 approach to motivation flows from an assumption that subordinates are most concerned with *actualization, belonging* and *creature comfort* needs; this is a somewhat peculiar supportive maintenance view and subordinates respond by being most concerned with *social* and *safety* needs.
- Managers using a 1/9 style are judged to have *low interpersonal competence* by their subordinates. Moreover, subordinates tend to behave with equal incompetence in their relationships.

The 1/1 style is a manifestation of fairly pure *Theory X* thought.
- While some use is made of *involvement strategies,* subordinate reactions suggest that these are superfluous.
- Motivational assumptions are in keeping with Herzberg's hygiene theory of motivation; *creature comfort* and *safety* needs are most emphasized by 1/1 management. Subordinates are concerned with *safety* and *belongingness,* consistent with their managers' emphasis on lower level dissatisfiers.
- In terms of relative *interpersonal competence,* 1/1 oriented managers are the *least* competent of all and influence their subordinates to be essentially incompetent interpersonally.

Hopefully, the results of this project will serve to reaffirm the interdependency among theories of the human side of the enterprise and recapture some of the richness of those complexities which emerge when an empirical multi-model view of the management process is taken. In addition to promoting an integration which should prove helpful in understanding more clearly the implications of management style per se, the present study serves to underscore the tremendous capacity for management's behavior to set norms and influence practices within an organization. Whether for good or ill, managers occupy positions of enormous, yet unarticulated power to shape the quality of organizational life and to determine the organization's movement toward its goals of production and achievement.

The results from the Synthesis Project enumerate the several ways a manager might seek to use this "power" and, by inference, shed light on the various options open to him or her. Hopefully these results will serve as palatable food for thought as managers come to give more conscious consideration to their choices of management style. Now at least they may appreciate what each entails and how it affects the lives of those it touches.

References

1. Blake, R.R., & Mouton, J.S.: *The Managerial Grid.* Houston: Gulf Publishing, 1964.

2. McGregor, D.: *The Human Side of Enterprise.* New York: McGraw-Hill, 1967.

3. Maslow, A.: *Personality and Motivation.* New York: Harper, 1954.

4. Herzberg, F.: *Work and the Nature of Man.* New York: Wiley, 1966.

5. Luft, J.: *Of Human Interaction.* Palo Alto, California: National Press, 1962.

6. Hall, J., Harvey, J. & Williams, M.S.: *Styles of Management Inventory.* The Woodlands, Texas: Teleometrics International, Inc., 1963.

7. Hall, J.: *The Harwood Dilemma: A Case Study of Management Practices.* In *Models for Management Seminar.* The Woodlands, Texas: Teleometrics International, Inc., 1970.

8. Foss, Laurence: "Managerial Strategy for the Future: Theory Z Management." In D. Hellriegel and J.W. Slocum (Eds.), *Management in the World Today.* Reading, Massachusetts: Addison-Wesley, 1975, pp. 412-444.

9. Coch, L., & French, J.R.P.: "Overcoming Resistance to Change." *Human Relations,* Vol. 1, No. 4, 1948, p. 512.

10. Marrow, A.J., Bowers, D.G., and Seashore, S.E.: *Management by Participation.* New York: Harper & Row, 1967.

11. Hall, J.: *Personal Reaction Index.* The Woodlands, Texas: Teleometrics International, Inc., 1971.

12. Maslow, A.: *op. cit.*

13. Herzberg, F.: *op. cit.*

14. Hall, J.: *Management of Motives Index.* The Woodlands, Texas: Teleometrics International, Inc., 1973.

15. Hall, J., & Williams, M.S.: *Work Motivation Inventory*. The Woodlands, Texas: Teleometrics International, Inc., 1967.

16. Argyris, C.: *op. cit.*

17. Argyris, C.: *Interpersonal Competence and Organizational Effectiveness*. Homewood, Illinois: Dorsey Press, 1962.

18. Luft, J.: *op. cit.*

19. Hall, J. & Williams, M.S.: *Personnel Relations Survey*. The Woodlands, Texas: Teleometrics International, Inc., 1967.

20. Hall, J., & Williams, M.S.: *Management Relations Survey*. The Woodlands, Texas: Teleometrics International, Inc., 1970.

Chapter 31

Men and Women as Managers:
A Significant Case of No
Significant Differences

Susan Donnell
Jay Hall

Since the early seventies, more and more women have been entering the labor force with definite aspirations of upward mobility. And there is no doubt about it—they have a far greater chance of realizing their ambitions than did their mothers or even their elder sisters. No longer is it a "given" that men make decisions and women make coffee. But there does seem to be a tacitly agreed upon assumption that women differ from men in administering the management process—no one is quite sure *how*, but many *know* the difference is there and few are terribly optimistic about women's managerial capabilities.

This pessimism is reflected in the kinds of questions researchers have asked: Do women fear success?[1,2] Are they really equipped to play the corporate game?[3] Do they even possess the characteristics thought to be required for the managerial role?[4,5] What do top level executives think about women in management?[6,7] How do men feel about working for women?[8] Is the need to influence others, when found in female managers, detrimental to subordinate satisfaction?[9] Who or what is responsible for the stereotypical notion that female managers are less competent than males?[10]

Clinical sensitivity is not needed to detect the note of apprehension in such research themes. There have been other, less applied and more scientifically based studies, but even they address such emotionally loaded topics as stereotypes,[11,12] prejudice,[13] and role conflict[14] insofar as women in management are concerned.

So organizations find themselves faced with a dilemma: apprehensive about women's capacity for handling managerial chores without doing damage to employee morale and organizational health, they must nevertheless conform to EEO requirements in hiring and promotion practices. The pressure is on. There

A similar version of this chapter under the same title appears in *Organizational Dynamics*, 1980, Vol. 8, No. 4. Copyright ©1980, Jay Hall.

are those who point out that although women comprise almost half of the work force, only 18% of the managerial complement is female.[15] They fuss about the fact that the median income of female managers is only half that of male managers. They complain that women total only 2.3% of all managers making more than $25,000 per year. And they even make noise about sexist prejudice!

It would be foolish to claim the issue of women in management is not a loaded one. But it need not be if we adopt a more scientific perspective. Neither researchers nor organizations have ever, for example, concerned themselves with the question of whether men *in general* make good managers, so why should college students continue to be studied and men continue to be asked how they feel about women in management in an attempt to discover whether women *in general* might make good managers? The more critical question is whether women whose career choice is management do in fact manage differently from their male counterparts. There is reason to expect they do not,[16] but few studies have addressed this point directly. The two or three serious attempts to evaluate differences between male and female managers either deal with only one dimension of the management process[17] or examine only a small group in one organization.[18]

Most research involving women in management has been done with attitude surveys and opinion polls, and the results have been less than overwhelmingly favorable to women. In fact such research may have served to entrench stereotypical thinking rather than to dispel it. The point is, until there are reliable data on differences between male and female managers, all the agonizing may well be premature. What is needed more than anything at this juncture of the male *vs* female managerial dilemma are some facts—facts about how men and women compare in administering the management process. Although we do not delude ourselves that this type of data-based information will do away with either anxiety or prejudice, we do believe it will provide a more enlightened reference point for organizational decisions than do stereotypical or wishful thinking.

We believe the time has come to end the debate and political posturing in favor of a little less exciting but more enduring hard work: a scientific investigation of the broad spectrum of managerial practices of males and females. If there are differences, let them reveal themselves; if there are none, let this fact be known. But at least let us be guided by some valid and usable information as we make our choices in the future.

Toward this end, we have studied nearly 2,000 individuals over the past two years. We have systematically compared the practices of 950 female managers with those of 966 male managers. Our studies have been *exploratory*—we began the process with no hypotheses; we sought neither to confirm nor to disconfirm any preconceptions. On the other hand, we have remained frankly *comparative* in our approach; we were particularly careful to assure that whatever differences we might find could be attributed to sex rather than, for instance, age or achievement. We have been conscientiously *evaluative*; we looked for indicators of managerial competence in both male and female managers.

SCOPE OF THE STUDY

For any evaluative comparison of managers to be at all meaningful—much less valid—two conditions must be met. First the comparative dimensions should relate to and be valid indicators of managerial competence. For example, in our review of previous research we found one study[19] which concluded that women are perhaps better suited for management than men—they excel in six of eight aptitudes wherein sex differences have been found, including finger dexterity. Interesting? Perhaps. Relevant? Hardly. Second, and equally important, the individuals studied should be truly comparable. We would expect only biased results if we compared the managerial practices of female supervisors with those of male chief executive officers. Accordingly, we used only tested and reliable indicators of managerial achievement and we studied only those females who had matched counterparts in the male comparison group. So far as we know this is the first truly stringent attempt to present empirical facts with which to address the gender dilemma as it relates to managerial competence.

The Dimensions Of Managerial Achievement

In planning our study of male and female managers, we used five dimensions of managerial achievement which had served us so well in other studies.[20,21] Briefly we can identify our comparative dimensions as: (1) *managerial philosophy*—the beliefs and values which underlie and shape the individual's approach to the management process; (2) *motivational dynamics*—the manager's own motivational needs, the way these affect his or her management of incentives, and the consequent effects on subordinate motivation; (3) *participative practices*—the degree to which subordinates feel their managers are sensitive to their needs to become involved and the degree to which they feel their managers take direct actions to include them in decision-making; (4) *interpersonal competence*—the sheer ability to deal honestly and effectively in managerial transactions; and finally (5) *managerial style*—the simultaneous attention to and concern for the people/production interface which is the final outward expression of all the foregoing dimensions. Our male-female study, therefore, amounts to five studies in one, with males and females being compared according to a total social technology of managerial achievement.

Selecting And Matching Male And Female Managers

As we have already mentioned, we strongly felt a comparison of managers on the basis of sex should weed out any factors which might bias our findings. This concern led us to use what statisticians call a *matched sample* approach to the selection of managers for the study. In a matched sample design, individuals in one group are matched with individuals in their comparison group on factors which are relevant to the research objectives.

Because we were studying managers within an organizational context, we selected several factors commonly used by organizations themselves in making value judgements. We matched male and female data according to age, rank in the organization, organizational type and number of people supervised. Although we attempted to match on all four categories, we accepted two of the four as a match as long as one of the two was either age or rank.

The Department of Labor[22] reports 18% of all managers to be women, but female data comprise only 3% of our total data file. We utilized all available female data and the preponderance of male data provided a broad selection for careful matching. Scores for more than one measure were available for 14.7% of the females and some were matched with one male on one measure and a different male on another, thus accounting for the difference in total numbers of male and female subjects. For each measure however, the male and female groups were equal and matched.

On subordinate appraisals, an average of 2.6 subordinates rated each manager and for each manager the average subordinate rating was used in the statistical analysis. In all, we analyzed data from 950 female managers and 966 male managers.

A Representative Sample

Tables 1, 2 and 3 summarize the distribution of the 1,916 individuals according to sex, age, organizational rank and organizational type. The female group is similar to others which have been reported. A recent survey,[23] for instance, found the most substantial increase in female employment among the 25-34 year olds which constitute 36.5% of our group. Consistent with USDL figures, 3.5% of the females in our study are in top management and almost one third are employed in human services traditionally considered "women's work."

Incidentally, the rationale for categorizing organizational types comes from the USDL's *Occupational Outlook Handbook*[24] and places individuals describing their organization as research and development, engineering, technical, *etc.*, into *science and technology*. Those in *manufacturing* come from organizations involved in the actual production of durable and non-durable goods; *semi-public* personnel work in organizations providing transportation, communications and public utilities. *Sales* people are from firms responsible for the ultimate transfer of goods to the consumer, and those involved with the management and protection of money are included in *finance*, which encompasses insurance and real estate as well as banking and finance firms. Individuals

Table 1. Age Profile Of The Sample (N = 1916)

AGE	FEMALE				MALE			
	Single Measure	Multiple Measure	Age-Group Total	Percent of Total N	Single Measure	Multiple Measure	Age-Group Total	Percent of Total N
20-24	64	6	70	7.4	58	5	63	6.5
25-29	176	30	206	21.7	172	33	205	21.2
30-34	115	26	141	14.8	132	27	159	16.4
35-39	108	23	131	13.8	109	24	133	13.8
40-44	100	12	112	11.8	97	12	109	11.3
45-49	87	16	103	10.8	86	16	102	10.6
50-54	71	11	82	8.6	77	11	88	9.1
55-59	36	5	41	4.3	38	6	44	4.6
60 and over	9	2	11	1.2	11	2	13	1.3
Not specified	44	9	53	5.6	41	9	50	5.2
Total	810	140	950	100%	821	145	966	100%

Table 2. Organizational Rank Profile Of The Sample (*N* = 1916)

ORGANIZATIONAL RANK	FEMALE				MALE			
	Single Measure	Multiple Measure	Rank-Group Total	Percent of Total *N*	Single Measure	Multiple Measure	Rank-Group Total	Percent of Total *N*
Top	25	8	33	3.5	28	7	35	3.6
Upper	92	19	111	11.7	86	21	107	11.1
Middle	330	38	368	38.7	361	40	401	41.5
Lower	181	37	218	22.9	192	41	233	24.1
Supervisory	125	30	155	16.4	119	32	151	15.6
Not specified	57	8	65	6.8	35	4	39	4.1
Total	810	140	850	100%	821	145	966	100%

Table 3. Organizational Type Profile Of The Sample (*N* = 1916)

ORGANIZATIONAL TYPE	FEMALE				MALE			
	Single Measure	Multiple Measure	Type-Group Total	Percent of Total *N*	Single Measure	Multiple Measure	Type-Group Total	Percent of Total *N*
Science & Technology	41	2	43	4.5	56	9	65	6.7
Manufacturing	124	25	149	15.7	196	43	239	24.7
Semi-public	37		37	3.9	27		27	2.8
Sales	76	17	93	9.8	56	7	63	6.5
Finance	82	24	106	11.2	108	25	133	13.8
Human Service*	280	29	309	32.5	205	6	211	21.8
Government	59	41	100	10.5	63	55	118	12.2
Law Enforcement	38		38	4.0	44		44	4.6
Military	13		13	1.4	13		13	1.4
Other	60	2	62	6.5	53		53	5.5
Total	810	140	950	100%	821	145	966	100%

*Human Service sub-grouping:

Education	9.4% of females	7.3% of males
Health Care	8.4% of females	3.5% of males
Social Work	14.7% of females	10.9% of males

dealing in non-tangible amenities reflecting the goals of an affluent society (education, health and social service) comprise the *human service* group. All federal, state and municipal government workers are included in *government* with the exception of *law enforcement* and the *military*.

Because we know our comparative dimensions are sensitive to differences in managerial achievement, we divided males and females into high, average and low achievement groups. We used a variation of Benjamin Rhode's *Managerial Achievement Quotient (MAQ)*[25] which takes into consideration the individual's potential upward mobility within the organization, present rank and age. Each individual in the study was grouped according to a statistical transformation of his or her *MAQ*, and because both age and rank are required to compute the *MAQ*, individuals whose age or rank data were not available were not included in the achievement analyses.

Data Analysis

Each of our testing surveys yields more than one score. For instance, there are five scales on our motivational surveys and each of an individual's five scores tells us his or her need level for a particular incentive; the way the five need scores combine gives us an overall motivational profile of that individual. To analyze the data, we chose a statistical technique called multivariate analysis of variance which allowed us to group individuals by sex and by achievement and to take into consideration the overall combination of scores on a particular measurement. With respect to motivation, this technique enables us to say whether there are differences in the groups' overall motivational profiles, and whether the differences are attributable to sex or to achievement or to a combination of the two.

When we found differences attributable to sex or to sex by achievement, we used another technique called discriminant function analysis to better define the nature of the differences. For example, it is possible for men and women to have significantly different motivational profiles and for all of the difference to be accounted for by their different self-actualization needs, or for the difference to be accounted for by the difference between average male and female achievers on several need scales. We should point out that it is also possible for groups to differ on one of the need scales but *not* to differ motivationally because that particular need does not carry enough weight when all five needs are taken into consideration. And, primarily concerned with overall behavior patterns, we did not in most cases carry our investigation this far unless we found overall differences in the first place.

So in the results sections, when we discuss *overall* differences, we mean men and women differ on a total behavioral profile. When we discuss *discrete* differences, we mean for instance, average male and female achievers differ on a particular need scale. And when we discuss differences at all, unless otherwise noted, we mean we are at least 97% sure these differences could not have occurred by chance—the differences are *statistically* significant.

In summary, our investigation of managerial practices, as reported by male and female managers and several subordinates of each manager, proceeded according to rigorous research constraints. Working with matched pairs of male and female managers, we made our comparisons on the basis of known and reliable indicators of managerial competence. We controlled for the possible contamination of achievement effects. We conducted five separate studies and, as a final precaution against the kinds of spurious conclusions all too characteristic of the male-female comparison issue, we engaged the services of an objective third party statistician to analyze the data.[26] With confidence and in good faith, we can report results which should do much to dispel the myths of an earlier time and to reassure organizations faced with EEO anxieties.

STUDY I: MANAGERIAL PHILOSOPHY

Most experts on behavior agree that the way we *think* about other people determines the way we treat them. Research has shown the interpersonal values we hold, the assumptions we make about others' intentions, and our own self-concepts—all factors also involved in managerial philosophy—influence in very significant ways the nature of the interpersonal transactions in our daily lives.

Douglas McGregor[27] first called attention to the importance of these same processes as the guiding factors underlying managerial practices. Combined with their attitudes about power and control, managers' assumptions about subordinate intent and competence shape their overall philosophy of management and, as a result, determine many of their managerial acts. McGregor maintained that each managerial act stems from the manager's assumptions about the nature of the people who populate the workplace. Ultimately, these assumptions and their related practices determine the character of the organization.

Most managers are familiar with McGregor's portrayal of contrasting managerial beliefs: Theory X and Theory Y. Theory X reflects a reductive and pessimistic position wherein the manager sees the labor force as basically lazy, in need of direction and control, having little desire for responsibility, not very creative, and motivated primarily by survival and security needs. Theory Y reflects a more positive set of integrative and developmental beliefs wherein the manager assumes employees enjoy work, are creative and seeking of responsibility, and are motivated by higher order needs for challenge and variety. McGregor believed management practices grounded in Theory Y facilitate organizational objectives by encouraging employee growth and development, whereas a Theory X posture reduces managerial, subordinate and organizational growth and potential.

To discover how male and female managers compare on managerial belief structure, we administered the *Managerial Philosophies Scale (MPS)*[28] to 239 male and 239 female managers. The two *MPS* scores indicate the strength of an individual's subscription to both Theory X and Theory Y philosophies. The Theory X scale correlates positively with general measures of authoritarian-ism[29] and is the scale of the *MPS* which differentiates between achievement groups—it is not the amount of their Theory Y subscription which relates to managers' competence, but the amount of their subscription to Theory X be-liefs.

We found no significant overall differences between males and females in managerial philosophy. However, there was some "not quite significant" evi-dence that prompted us to investigate for discrete differences. And we found low and average achieving females showing significantly lower subscription to Theory X beliefs than do low and average achieving males, whereas high achieving males and females do not differ at all. In other words, low and aver-age achieving females have a less negative attitude about people and their rea-sons for working than do their counterparts among male managers.

We noticed another interesting, though not significant trend when the groups were compared by achievement level. For males, the Theory X scores were ordered so that low achievers scored highest, then average achievers, and high achievers scored lowest. But the female achievement pattern was reversed: low achievers scored lowest and high achievers scored highest on the Theory X dimension.

We can only speculate about the underlying reasons for females' reversal of the achievement pattern. It may be that high achieving women of the seven-ties, compared with their lower achieving sisters, do indeed view the world of work and its populace as an arena wherein people are not to be trusted and where direction and control are warranted. It may be that in accordance with the stereotypical attitude which holds women to be the weaker sex and in con-junction with the outdated notion that good management involves strong di-rection and control, the comparatively authoritarian female has been rewarded as seeming "more like a man" and therefore a manager more worthy of ad-vancement. It may be that the high achieving females in our study have achieved at such interpersonal expense that like Margaret Hennig and Anne Jardim's group[30] of female executives who feel they have "mortgaged their personal lives" for success, they have adopted an "iron maiden" stance. On the other hand and more probably, it may be that low and moderate achieving females are simply exhibiting a higher achieving philosophy than their rank in the organization would predict—remember, high achieving females do not dif-fer from high achieving males in Theory X subscription. Whatever the reason for the trend, it is well to keep in mind that too strong a Theory X posture has been found to be counterproductive to achievement in today's organizations.

This digression serves only to point out an anomalous trend which is not sta-tistically significant but which may be an area for consideration in executive training for both sexes. For our purpose of studying sex differences in manage-ment personnel, the noteworthy finding remains: *there are no differences in*

personal values or managerial philosophy between male and female managers.
If there are sex differences in administering the management process, we must
look beyond the issue of managerial philosophy.

STUDY II: THE MOTIVATION TO WORK

McGregor believed assumptions posited in a Theory X or a Theory Y posture
have a direct bearing on the issue of work motivation. Each individual, manager and subordinate alike, brings his or her own motivational needs to the
workplace. We know the incentives which managers themselves pursue affect
not only the way they perform personally, but their ideas about what motivates
others. We also know managers cannot inject employees with motivation. The
best they can do is to accurately identify subordinate needs, and then to effectively channel subordinate activities toward organizational goals. Most importantly, we know managers, by their actions and by the values they promote, influence subordinate expectations about the world of work. Therefore, in order
to comprehensively measure male-female motivational phenomena in the
workplace, we must examine (1) the motivational profiles of the managers
themselves, (2) the managers' approach to employee motivation and (3) the
motivational profiles of their subordinates.

Our approach to the study of motivational dynamics is based on a synthesis
of Abraham Maslow's need-hierarchy concept[31] and Frederick Herzberg's hygiene-motivator theory.[32] Maslow suggested there are five basic need systems
which account for most of human behavior. They are arranged in a hierarchy
ranging from those which promote the most primitive and immature behaviors
to those which elicit the most civilized and mature behaviors. A natural growth
trend allows individuals to experience an awareness of, and therefore to be motivated by, each of the need systems in ascending order. An individual's progression through this hierarchy is something like climbing a ladder one rung at
a time: to be aware of the next rung and to experience a need to step on it
imply the individual has successfully negotiated the lower rung. Thus the
natural progression from need to need occurs only to the extent that each lower
need has received adequate satisfaction.

The lower level needs—basic, safety and, to some extent, belonging—underlie a preoccupation with what Herzberg called hygiene, or maintenance, factors. Similarly, the higher level needs—ego-status and self-actualization—underlie a preoccupation with what Herzberg labeled motivators. Only motivators
are related to job satisfaction; only when people have the opportunity to display their competence, to be innovative and creative in their work, to satisfy
their upper level needs, will they experience job satisfaction. On the other
hand, maintenance factors are the repository of the seeds of job dissatisfaction;
without adequate pay, clean and safe working conditions, and some fringe
benefits, there will probably be dissatisfaction. But even the provision for these

lower level needs—even higher pay, better working conditions and more fringe benefits—can never insure that people will be satisfied in their work.

Personal Work Motivation Among Male And Female Managers

To study motivation in the workplace we used two surveys. The first, the *Work Motivation Inventory (WMI)*,[33] is a measure of personal need systems and is equally applicable to managers and their subordinates. The *WMI* yields five need scores which combine to give a two-dimensional motivational profile. The social dimension encompasses self-centered (safety and ego-status) *vis-á-vis* other-directed (belonging and actualization) concerns; the work incentives dimension encompasses hygiene (basic and safety) *vis-á-vis* motivator (ego-status and actualization) concerns. It was administered to 136 matched pairs of managers to assess their own basic, safety, belonging, ego and self-actualization needs in the workplace.

There were overall differences in the motivational profiles of male and female managers. The women reported lower basic needs and higher needs for self-actualization. Compared to males, female managers are more concerned with opportunities for growth, autonomy and challenge, and less concerned with work environment, pay, and strain avoidance. And contrary to popular belief, females do not have a greater need to "belong" than do males. Further analysis revealed that the male-female differences in personal motivation occur primarily among average achievers; the profiles of high achievers did not differ, nor did those of low achievers.

Thus, there are sex differences in managerial work motivation and the differences favor the female manager. *Females, scoring higher on both the social and work incentives dimensions, exhibit what we know to be a more mature and higher achieving motivational profile than do males.* Whether this effect carries over into their management of the motivational process for others was our next focus.

The Management Of Motives By Males And Females

To tap the managers' theories about what motivates others, we administered our second motivational survey, the *Management of Motives Index (MMI)*[34] which utilizes the same five need scales. When the scores of 168 male and 168 female managers were analyzed, no overall differences between the sexes or on sex by achievement were found. Apparently *males and females approach the management of incentives in pretty much the same way,* emphasizing the same goals and promoting the same values. Given the similarities of approach to motivation of male and female managers, we should expect their subordinates to be motivationally alike as well.

Work Motivation Among The Subordinates Of Male And Female Managers

We used the *WMI* again, this time to examine the motivational profiles of 336 subordinates of females and 336 subordinates of males. *We found no overall differences in subordinates' motivational profiles.* However the discrete investigation showed that, like their managers, subordinates of females have lower basic needs than do subordinates of males.

Once more we are faced with anomalies. Other studies[35] have found no evidence that different incentives more effectively motivate one sex than the other. The fact that females in our study show higher needs for self-actualization than males may, according to Maslow, indicate these women are not being so challenged by their jobs as are their male counterparts. Their lower basic need concern might indicate a lack of "bread winner" pressure among females; however, their subordinates also reported low basic needs and their subordinates are not necessarily female. A more probable explanation might be that the much talked about issue of "equal pay for equal work" is not, for females at least, tied to a basic need for adequate food and shelter, but tied to ego and actualization gratification. If this is so, organizations had best take heed! Hell hath no fury....

Differences in the managers' motivational profiles coupled with the *lack* of differences in their management of subordinate motivation is not consistent with our findings in other studies that managers tend to "motivate" others as a function of their own needs.[36] Although the motivational profiles of the managers themselves differ as a function of sex, male and female managers apparently gear their management practices in the same fashion to address the needs of subordinates. And the sex of the manager apparently has no bearing on subordinate need profiles.

On the basis of these findings we have every reason to expect more of female managers than we have in the past; they are presently neither so challenged by their jobs as they might be nor so challenged as they would like to be. And of equal significance for the focus of this study, we may expect no more and no less from the subordinates of female managers than we do from those of male managers.

STUDY III: PARTICIPATION AND CLIMATE

A manager's philosophical view of his or her subordinates and their motivational aspirations undoubtedly influences that manager's choice of options regarding subordinate participation in work-related decisions. Participative management has received increased attention in recent years and is yet another yardstick for measuring managerial acumen.

The effectiveness of the participative approach was first demonstrated in the now classic studies at the Harwood Manufacturing Company. [37,38] Beset with production slowdown and employee turnover after every design change, management of this Virginia pajama factory as a last resort encouraged its predominantly female, eighth grade-educated workers to form work teams and decide for themselves the best way to effect required changes. They were eminently successful and Harwood moved ahead in the pajama game by eventually buying out its competitors.

The major thrust of participative management is one of joint participation in the making of work-related decisions; the technique is based on the belief that people directly affected by a decision will be more satisfied with and committed to the outcome of the decision if they have participated in making it. Because we have found no overall differences in male and female belief structure and because males and females address subordinate motivation in essentially the same fashion, we might expect no differences in the participative emphases of male and female managers.

To test this facet of managerial achievement, we studied 474 subordinate personnel by administering the *Personal Reaction Index (PRI)*. [39] The six scales of the *PRI* measure the degree of subordinate participation in, satisfaction with, felt responsibility for, commitment to, frustration about, and perceived quality of work-related decisions. These six combine to reflect a subordinate ego-involvement index which in turn implies the kind of work climate subordinates perceive their manager to be creating.

Analysis of the scores of 234 subordinates of females and 240 subordinates of males revealed no overall differences in subordinate ego-involvement as a function of either manager sex alone or sex by achievement. And there were no subordinate differences attributable to managerial sex on any of the six scales. As with the motivational process, *male and female managers employ participative practices in a similar fashion and obtain similar results from their subordinates.* Male and female managers lay the groundwork for essentially the same kind of work climate; perhaps a valid reason for stereotyping and apprehension about female managers can be found in that most basic of organizational arenas—interpersonal relations.

STUDY IV: INTERPERSONAL COMPETENCE

As an evaluative dimension, participative management does not stand alone in the management process any more than does either managerial belief structure or the management of motives. Its effectiveness depends on the climate of interpersonal concern and mutual trust created by the manager, and this varies with the quality of the manager-subordinate relationship. Chris Argyris [40] theorized that this quality is born of the level of interpersonal competence brought to the relationship by the *manager*; and the manager's level of interpersonal competence depends upon the way he or she behaves in relating to others.

In terms of the *Johari Window* model developed by Joseph Luft and Harry Ingham,[41] interpersonal competence may be thought of as depending on maximum utilization of two behavioral processes: the *exposure* process and the *feedback* process. Exposure is purposeful sharing of relevant information; it consists of the open and candid expression of feelings, factual knowledge, and guesses in a conscious attempt to share. The exposure process is controlled by the individual and its use builds trust and legitimizes mutual exposures; extraneous and diversionary sharing is not part of the process and does nothing to help mutual understanding. The feedback process involves active solicitation of information from others; it is not so much under the control of the individual as is the exposure process because others have to be willing to divulge their information. And others' willingness to cooperate is influenced by the individual's previous willingness to deal openly and candidly.

To determine the interpersonal practices of male and female managers, we administered the *Personnel Relations Survey* (PRS)[42] to 442 matched pairs of managers. The *PRS* is based on the *Johari Window* model and measures the manager's use of the exposure and feedback processes with three different groups: superiors, colleagues and subordinates.

When we analyzed the six resulting scores, we found overall differences between male and female managers in their use of the interpersonal processes. However, the differences were role specific: no differences were found in interpersonal practices with superiors or with subordinates, and no differences were found between the sexes when broken into achievement groups. *The entire difference lay in the females' lower willingness to share relevant data with their colleagues.*

The issue of collegiality and communication has been raised before. Sandy Albrecht[43] has reported that female scientists are not sought out by, nor do they seek out, their male colleagues, and there have been several calls for immediate programs aimed at improving interpersonal communication in the workplace between the sexes. Our finding that female managers do not utilize the exposure process with their colleagues so much as males do is confirming evidence of interpersonal noise at the peer level.

If we look further, we find there is also evidence of interpersonal noise at the subordinate level—and it is not of the females' making. The *Management Relations Survey* (MRS)[44] is designed as a companion training tool to the *PRS*. In its first section, subordinates assess their managers' interpersonal practices, and in its second section, subordinates report on their own use of interpersonal processes with these same managers. We administered it to 428 subordinates of 185 females and to 504 subordinates of 185 males. *Subordinates report their managers' interpersonal practices do not differ according to sex or to sex by achievement.* But assessing their own practices with those same managers in the second section of the *MRS*, *subordinates of females reported they solicit less feedback from their managers than did the subordinates of male managers.* Where does the interpersonal problem lie?

Virginia Schein's studies[45] indicate that both males and females equate the managerial role with male personality traits. Therefore, although we do not know the sex of the subordinates in this case, we may still infer the presence of stereotypical attitudes when subordinates report soliciting less feedback from their female managers. In essence, these subordinates are saying, in spite of the fact their managers do not behave differently depending on sex, they themselves relate differently to male managers than they do to female managers. There is evidence in research on stereotyping that it decreases as specific information is garnered about the individual women in the workplace. So time may serve to quiet some of the subordinate noise. But for now we might wonder whether this interpersonal noise is loud enough to affect the females' method of interfacing the people / production issues so vital to managerial competence.

STUDY V: MANAGEMENT STYLE

A study of management behaviors would not be complete without addressing the task-centered, as well as the interpersonal, climate, motivational and philosophical facets of the organization. The relationship between the level of interpersonal competence and the preferred manner of managing the people / production interface has been confirmed, and we have linked management style preference with managerial achievement.[46] Indeed, the construct of style includes the whole cluster of behaviors already discussed; it represents the manager's preferred, consistent approach to the tasks and the people under his or her purview.

With the *Styles of Management Inventory (SMI)*,[47] based on the popular Blake-Mouton managerial grid model,[48] we are able to assess a manager's values and practices concerning task and social demands. The *SMI* generates five scores. Each score represents the degree of the individual's adherence to one of the five styles inherent in the grid model: 9/9 (maximum concern for both task and people), 5/5 (moderate concern for both), 9/1 (maximum concern for task at the expense of people), 1/9 (maximum concern for people at the expense of task), and 1/1 (minimum concern for both). A comparison of the five scores indicates the manager's preferred style.

The *SMI* was administered to 227 matched pairs of managers and there were no overall differences in management style preference. *Male and female managers do not differ in the way they manage the organization's technical and human resources;* they view and handle the production / people interface in the same way and are apparently not unduly hampered by the differences in interpersonal competence we found in Study IV.

Nor were any overall differences found when 320 subordinates of 119 female managers and 334 subordinates of 119 male managers assessed their managers' style preferences on the *Management Appraisal Survey (MAS)*.[49] Utilizing the same five scales, *subordinates' appraisals simply confirmed their managers' own reports regarding management style; there were no overall differences in subordinates' perceptions of the management styles preferred by males and females.*

Once again however, as was the case with managerial belief structure, we noticed some trend differences worthy of digression. Although no sex differences were found in overall style preference, either according to the managers themselves or according to their subordinates, there were discrete differences. Males, according to self-reports, scored lower than females on the 1/9 and 1/1 scales. Subordinate appraisals partially confirmed the managers' reports by rating males higher than females on 9/1 behaviors and lower on 1/9 behaviors.

Lacking subordinate confirmation, the female managers' self-reported tendency to resort more often to a "hands off" stance (indicated by their higher 1/1 scores) may be taken as more a self-image effect than an actual behavioral difference. By the same token, subordinates' rating their male managers higher on the autocratic 9/1 scale may reflect only a stereotypical "halo effect," especially in light of the fact that manager self-assessments do not agree.

More important is the agreement of manager and subordinate reports regarding females' higher employment of the "country club" stance of the 1/9 approach. We know from our own research that such an approach arises from the same philosophical base as the 9/1 approach which subordinates reported being more prevalent in male managers; they both are based on the assumption that people cannot take care of and direct themselves and neither approach is considered high achieving—in fact our research has shown the two styles are about equally effective or, more accurately, ineffective.

We need to place these findings in perspective however, so we avoid creating confusion where no more is needed. The discrete effects involving male "9/1-ism" and female "1/9-ism" pertain to what Robert Blake and Jane Mouton have identified as *back-up-style* [50] —the style a manager most likely resorts to when the most preferred is not working. So we may say that our results indicate that under stress males are more likely to adopt a 9/1 stance as their back-up strategy whereas female managers will behave in a more 1/9 fashion. Under stress, males are more likely to become dictatorial and females are more likely to become conciliatory.

For purposes of this study it is most important that we emphasize that *there is no overall sex difference in management style preference.* The discrete differences we've noted only point to areas to be considered in management training for both sexes.

SUMMING UP

What does it all mean? We've reviewed five different studies involving almost 2,000 people compared on a total of 43 different scales. We have studied matched pairs and controlled for level of managerial achievement. And after all is said and done we have detected a total of *two* overall differences between male and female managers. One of these, involving managerial work motivation, favors females: their work motivation profiles are more "achieving" than those of their male counterparts. The other difference, pertaining to interpersonal competence, favors the male managers: they are more open and candid with their colleagues than are females. Add to these the more titillating than significant anomalies of differing back-up style preferences and we are left with one conclusion: *women, in general, do not differ from men, in general, in the ways in which they administer the management process.*

Managers themselves and their subordinates concur. It seems we can no longer explain away the disproportionately low numbers of women in management by the contention that women practice a different brand of management than men. Whereas this may amount to "good news" in some quarters, we ought not be prematurely elated by discovering that women manage just like men do. Carolyn Sherif[51] has pointedly called attention to the fact that all is not necessarily well in today's male-oriented management activities.

We, of course, view management in its more global aspects: the important issue to us is how an individual manages in relation to achievement criteria. Individual achievement and organizational health ultimately depend upon the way management is practiced. And we now see that the way management is practiced is not related to the sex of the manager—the issue is *generic* rather than gender-bound.

REFERENCES

1. Horner, M.S.: "Sex Differences in Achievement Motivation and Performance in Competitive and Non-competitive Situations." Unpublished doctoral dissertation, University of Michigan, 1968.

2. Horner, M.S., & Walsh, M.R.: "Psychological Barriers to Success in Women." In R.B. Kundsin (Ed.), *Women and Success: The Anatomy of Achievement.* New York: William Morrow and Co., 1974, 138.

3. Hennig, M., & Jardim, A.: *The Managerial Woman.* Garden City, New York: Anchor Press, 1977.

4. Schein, V.E.: "The Relationship Between Sex Role Stereotypes and Requisite Management Characteristics." *Journal of Applied Psychology,* Vol. 57, No. 2, 1973, 95.

5. Schein, V.E.: "Relationships Between Sex Role Stereotypes and Requisite Management Characteristics Among Female Managers." *Journal of Applied Psychology,* Vol. 60, No. 3, 1975, 340.

6. Bowman, G.W., Worthy, N.B., & Greyser, S.A.: "Are Women Executives People?" *Harvard Business Review,* Vol. 43, 1965, 52.

7. Bass, B.M., Krusell, J., & Alexander, R.H.: "Male Managers' Attitudes Toward Working Women." *American Behavioral Scientist,* Vol. 15, 1971, 77.

8. *Ibid.*

9. Bartol, K.M.: "Male versus Female Leaders: The Effect of Leader Need for Dominance on Follower Satisfaction." *Academy of Management Journal,* Vol. 17, 1974, 225.

10. Goetz, T.E., & Herman, J.B.: *Effects of Supervisors and Subordinates Sex on Productivity and Morale.* Presented at the 84th Annual Convention of the American Psychological Association, 1976.

11. Rosen, B., & Jerdee, T.H.: "Sex Stereotyping in the Executive Suite." *Harvard Business Review,* March-April, 1974, 45.

12. Ilgen, D.R., & Terborg, J.R.: "Sex Discrimination and Sex-role Stereotypes: Are They Synonymous? No!" *Organizational Behavior and Human Performance,* Vol. 14, 1975, 154.

13. Terborg, J.R., Peters, L.H., & Ilgen, D.R.: "Organizational and Personal Correlates of Attitudes Toward Women as Managers." *Academy of Management Journal,* 1977.

14. Sheehey, G.: *Passages: Predictable Crises of Adult Life.* New York: Bantam, 1976.

15. *Handbook on Women Workers.* U.S. Department of Labor, 1975.

16. Jacklin, C.N., & Maccoby, E.E.: "Sex Differences and Their Implications for Management." In F.E. Gordon and M.H. Strober (Eds.), *Bringing Women into Management.* New York: McGraw-Hill, 1975.

17. Herrick, J.S.: "Female Executives and Their Motives." In D.O. Jewell, (Ed.), *Women in Management: An Expanding Role.* Publishing Services Division, School of Business Administration, Georgia State University, 1977.

18. Day, D.R., & Stogdill, R.M.: "Leader Behavior of Male and Female Supervisors: A Comparative Study." *Personnel Psychology,* Vol. 25, 1972, 361.

19. "Women May Be More than Equal." *Training,* September, 1976, 7.

20. Hall, J.: "To Achieve or Not: The Manager's Choice." *California Management Review,* Vol. 18, No. 4, 1976.

21. Hall, J., & Donnell, S.M.: "Managerial Achievement: The Personal Side of Behavioral Theory." *Human Relations,* Vol. 32, No. 1, 1979.

22. *Handbook on Women Workers. op.cit.*

23. VanDusen, R.A., & Sheldon, E.B.: "The Changing Status of American Women: A Life Cycle Perspective." In D.O. Jewel (Ed.), *Women and Management An Expanding Role,* Publishing Services Division, School of Business Administration, Georgia State University, 1977.

24. *Occupational Outlook Handbook.* U.S. Department of Labor, 1976.

25. Hall, J., & Donnell, S.M.: *op. cit.*

26. Poynor, H.: Poynor Associates, Los Angeles.

27. McGregor, D.: *The Human Side of Enterprise.* New York: McGraw-Hill, 1960.

28. Jacoby, J., & Terborg, J.R.: *Managerial Philosophies Scale.* The Woodlands, Texas: Teleometrics International, Inc., 1975.

29. Jacoby, J., & Terborg, J.R.: *Development and Validation of Theory X*

and Y Scales for Assessing McGregor's Managerial Philosophies. The Woodlands, Texas: Teleometrics International, Inc., 1975.

30. Hennig, M. & Jardim, A.: *op. cit.*
31. Maslow, A.: *Personality and Motivation.* New York: Harper, 1954.
32. Herzberg, F.: *Work and the Nature of Man.* New York: Wiley, 1966.
33. Hall, J., & Williams, M.S.: *Work Motivation Inventory.* The Woodlands, Texas: Teleometrics International, Inc., 1967.
34. Hall, J.: *Management of Motives Index.* The Woodlands, Texas: Teleometrics International, Inc., 1973.
35. Herrick, J.S.: *op. cit.*
36. Hall, J., & Donnell, S.M.: *op. cit.*
37. Coch, L., & French, J.R.P.: "Overcoming Resistance to Change." *Human Relations,* Vol. 1, No. 4, 1948, 512.
38. Marrow, A.J., Bowers, D.G., & Seashore, S.E.: *Management by Participation.* New York: Harper & Row, 1967.
39. Hall, J.: *Personal Reaction Index.* The Woodlands, Texas: Teleometrics International, Inc., 1971.
40. Argyris, C.: *Interpersonal Competence and Organizational Effectiveness.* Homewood, Illinois: Dorsey Press, 1962.
41. Luft, J.: *Of Human Interaction.* Palo Alto, California: National Press, 1969.
42. Hall, J., & Williams, M.S.: *Personnel Relations Survey.* The Woodlands, Texas: Teleometrics International, Inc., 1967.
43. Albrecht, S.: "Informal Interaction Patterns of Professional Women." In M. Gerrard, J.S. Oliver, and M. Williams (Eds.), *Women in Management.* Human Services Monograph Series, School of Social Work, University of Texas, 1976, 67.
44. Strober, M.H.: "Bringing Women Into Management: Basic Strategies." In F.E. Gordon and M.H. Strober (Eds.), *Bringing Women into Management.* New York: McGraw-Hill, 1975, 77.
45. Schein, V.E.: *op. cit.*
46. Hall, J., & Donnell, S.M.: *op. cit.*
47. Hall, J., Harvey, J.B., & Williams, M.S.: *Styles of Management Inventory.* The Woodlands, Texas: Teleometrics International, Inc., 1963.
48. Blake, R.R., & Mouton, J.S.: *The Managerial Grid.* Houston: Gulf Publishing Company, 1964.
49. Hall, J., Harvey, J.B., & Williams, M.S.: *Management Appraisal Survey.* The Woodlands, Texas: Teleometrics International, Inc., 1970.
50. Blake, R.R., & Mouton, J.S.: *op. cit.*
51. Sherif, C.W.: "On Becoming Collegial While Being Woman." In M. Gerrard, J.S. Oliver, and M. Williams (Eds.), *Women in Management.* Human Services Monograph Series, School of Social Work, University of Texas, 1976.

Chapter 32

Managerial Competence: Working Productively With Most of the People Most of the Time

Jay Hall

In recent years managers have become more concerned about personal effectiveness and legitimately so since career progress is rightfully tied to ability. How well managers are able to accomplish the objectives for which they are accountable, the degree to which they do so in a cost-effective manner, how their practices affect the willingness and ability of those they manage to perform productively—all of these are related to effectiveness. In addition, such considerations most often serve as evaluation criteria for managerial performance per se.

Managers move up or out on the basis of how well they have administered the managerial process. Knowing this, most managers are legitimately preoccupied with finding the best way they can to accomplish work through others. But most managers are ambivalent, both eager and dubious, in contemplating new managerial technologies: maybe at last they will hit upon the fail-safe solution to their career progress; but what if it does not work? What if a change to some new, less comfortable and familiar approach is not for the better? What if their current style is the best they are capable of, even if it does not always produce the desired effect? The issue of managerial effectiveness is not without some attending trauma.

The synthesis study described in this volume sheds light on the topic of managerial effectiveness. First of all, it has become clear that there are several distinctly different social technologies of management, several internally consistent approaches to management, each with its own unique cause-effect properties. But, and this is the unexpected bonus, the synthesis data also afford a basis for evaluating the relative effectiveness of the various technologies which emerged. For the manager concerned about personal effectiveness, our findings provide choice points for future action.

What Is Effective Management?

The whole issue of managerial performance is loaded—emotionally and factually. Managers are expected to be effective, but the guideposts to effectiveness are often inconsistent or lacking altogether. As treated in the literature, managerial effectiveness appears to be one part data, several parts personal bias, and several more parts pure emotion. In the final analysis, it is impossible to talk about managerial effectiveness unless it is defined. Even so this does not solve the problem entirely. Pragmatists define effectiveness as whatever approach seems to work in a given situation; humanists define it as any approach that promotes growth, raises consciousness, and gratifies personal impulse; shareholders view it in terms of top dollar earnings per share; and more than a few managers define it in terms of personal power and control. And yet most managers and those they manage agree on one point—they want to be effective.

The fundamental consideration in assessing the effectiveness of any approach to management lies in specifying the goal to be served. If getting a certain amount of work out within a certain period of time is the objective—regardless of quality, cost, morale, absenteeism, or turnover—then any given style of management could be thought of as effective so long as the work arrives before the deadline. By the same token, if effectiveness is judged only in terms of being liked by subordinates—again regardless of other considerations—some other approach might be deemed effective. But no one lives in such a simple world. Simplistic definitions of managerial effectiveness yield simplistic results: they are short-lived; they only treat symptoms; they fail to generalize; they ignore the greater proportion of reality. And they are often disastrous because they isolate managers from their true impacts as they become more distant from the real complexities of organizational life.

The Competence Alternative

If an effectiveness criterion leads to simplistic and expedient ideas and practices, perhaps a more encompassing set of criteria based on the idea of *competence* would be more profitable. Competence implies a modal view, one which takes into account not the extremes of performance and other improbable considerations but, rather, a definition which addresses the broad range of managerial events and personalities which managers are most likely to encounter in their work. Hence, a modal definition of managerial competence, based on those most frequent occurrences and concerns of management, would encompass *those practices which work with most of the people most of the time.* Such a definition not only generalizes across organizational situations, but lends itself to verification along empirical lines as well. *Competent management is an approach to managing others which seeks to make optimal use of available resources in meeting organizational objectives on a sustained basis.*

Three key phrases appear in the definition of managerial competence:

optimal implies the best of which people are capable; *available* means those resources typically at the manager's disposal for meeting the organization's goals; and *sustained* means over the long haul, not just for fleeting moments, as people go about their work. This assumes a typical management situation where objectives are neither so ill-defined nor exotic as to require extra special considerations and personnel are average, neither extraordinary nor chronically subcaliber. Rather the concern is with day-to-day effectiveness on the important but common issues and events where most managers spend 99% of their time.

It may be more stimulating to inject a moment of drama into the otherwise mundane world of management by focusing as many writers do on improbable dilemmas and make-or-break decisions, but to do so would simply misportray management as most managers know it. Management is not always exciting. But this does not mean it is easy or unimportant. Competent management is very likely the single most important ingredient contributing to organizational well-being, despite its workaday place in the total scheme of things.

If personal competence is achieved at the daily level of performance, more dramatic instances may be handled with even greater aplomb. How can this be done? The answer is given throughout this book of readings. If theory and supporting research are correct, the answer begins with the following conditions under which people will optimize—remembering that people are our most varying and costly available resource—and what the manager might do to facilitate the existence of such conditions:

Most people work at their highest level when they find meaning and challenge in their work, when they are able to derive a sense of personal identity from doing what they do and doing it well, when they enjoy a sense of community, mutual respect and reliance, and are free of the distractions caused by deprivations or undue sensitivity to peripheral considerations surrounding their work.

Most people put forth their best efforts when they enjoy a sense of dominion over their work, when their ideas and feelings are incorporated into the design and procedures governing the work, and when they have a sense of generative involvement in the accomplishment of objectives.

Most people, to perform at their best level, require opportunities for interchange and collaborative comparisons with those with whom they work—superior, co-worker, and subordinate—so that understanding of the tasks at hand is enhanced while reservations, anxieties, and related misgivings are worked through as well; the resulting climate enables people to address their work more directly without distracting apprehensions about failure or internal noises stemming from unexpressed feelings or opinions.

Most people put forth their best efforts when they see themselves as—and indeed are—collaborators in the enterprise before them; when their needs and objectives are met by achieving the goals of their organization (or their part of it) and these are attended to via an assurance of a problem-solving posture under which all contribute to and participate in generating solutions, most people are willing to give whatever effort is required.

These effects have been confirmed time and again both in basic research and in ongoing organizations. The intention here is not to prove again the veracity of such statements; the literature is compelling. More important is the fact that for such conditions to exist, as known from data, managers must behave in particular ways.

From research with subordinate personnel, for example, we know that the manager—both in outlook and practices—greatly influences the extent to which such conditions and consequent predilections will characterize the work force. In fact, simply by reviewing the practice-effect insights gained from this research, specific managerial acts can be identified which are likely to result in those desirable circumstances where most people put forth their best efforts most of the time. A behavioral equation is: *if we have some idea of the effects we wish to obtain and reliable information about the various effects which stem from a number of diverse practices, we can then reduce this information to a statement of which practices evoke which effects.*

A review of earlier chapters on managerial expectations, motivation, gatekeeping, interpersonal competence, management styles, and the synthesis of all these—with the emphasis on data rather than on theory—reveals that the managerial practices with the highest probability of creating the conditions under which people will perform at their highest levels are the following:

Positive Prophecies   Management acts which are founded in an unfragmented, internally consistent, Theory Y view of the nature of those people who populate the work place, i.e., practices based on an anticipation that people are both capable and desirous of doing well.

Meaningful Work   Approaches to employee motivation which take into consideration employee self-esteem, potential for growth and capacities for both finding and responding constructively to positive stimulations accruing from the nature of work and the context within which it is imbedded; i.e., major managerial emphasis on the belonging, ego, and actualization needs of people in both design and administration of work processes.

Involvement   Managerial recognition of the power and significance of ego-involvement on the part of employees and its dependence on managerial Gatekeeping for release into the workflow, i.e., management practices which harness the energies, both physical and psychological, which characterize that generative involvement to which most people aspire in the doing of the organization's work.

Inter- Competent management of the face-to-face relationships which
personal characterize any coordinated activity; i.e., practices which pro-
Competence mote owning up to personal ideas and feelings, sharing these
openly with pertinent parties, being receptive to and encouraging others to do the same so that an interpersonal climate free of
power and performance constraints prevails.

Combined, of course, such acts amount to a total social technology of competent management in which motivator-seeking behavior is supported, participative techniques are used via sustained Gatekeeping practices, and wherein a
strong personal reliance on both exposure and feedback-solicitation processes is
combined with encouragement for others to do the same. Such acts constitute a
set of criteria for evaluating the various technologies which emerged from the
synthesis research project. Those management styles which meet the most
criteria may be deemed the most competent...the ones which work best with
most of the people most of the time.

PREDICTING COMPETENCE

A check list of critical managerial attributes and practices can be used to
evaluate each style of management...both in terms of the degree to which
managers themselves profess to employ the various practices *and* the extent to
which their subordinates report the effects as demonstrated by their own practices and attitudes. Information is available from some 2,000 managers and
over 3,500 of their subordinates. Rearranging the results from the synthesis research in a more simple format reveals an estimate of the competence of each
managerial style described by Blake and Mouton in their managerial grid
model.

Competence Criteria

Clearly, an estimate of competence should proceed according to behavioral
criteria on one hand and probability theory on the other, noting what managers do and how this impacts on their subordinates. This is consistent with the
view that managers' expectations regarding employee potential and performance affect both their own behaviors toward subordinates and subsequent subordinate behaviors in relating to managers and in doing the work of the organization. Therefore, parameters of competence include: (1) whether or not the
manager operates from a set of Theory Y expectations regarding those who
populate the workplace; (2) the consistency and internal congruity of personal
beliefs; (3) the degree to which the manager attends to and emphasizes those
constructive incentives most characteristic of mature adults, viz, belongingness,
ego status, and actualization; (4) the extent to which, in turn, subordinates

respond in kind by exhibiting responsive potential to those same higher level and most constructive needs; (5) the degree to which subordinates report that they enjoy participative opportunities of the type found to be important in the incidence of ego involvement and commitment; (6) managerial estimates of their interpersonal competence as it reflects a reliance on and employment of both exposure and feedback processes in relating to others in the workplace; and, finally, (7) the level of interpersonal competence which their subordinates report as characterizing their practices in relating to managers.

Decision Rules

Statisticians often use a technique called a "hit" table in making predictive estimates of the type required to assess management competence. The notion is that in predicting an outcome, one is primarily interested in accuracy or the number of "hits" obtained as opposed to the number of misses. By using a very similar procedure, it is possible to estimate the probable competence of the five management styles studied in the synthesis research. A point system is first established for measuring "hits" on competence criteria. For example, should a manager report a reliance on a well-knit Theory Y belief system he or she should be credited with a one point hit for "managerial beliefs" and a one point hit for "belief consistency." But what if another manager exhibited strong evidence of a well-knit Theory X orientation? He or she should at least receive a one point hit for the authenticity and clarity of beliefs but no points for the Theory X view. No points are given for X-Y confusion. When scoring multifaceted criteria, as in the case of motivational dynamics, weighted points are given for hits on each of three potentially important need systems.

By employing such a system, the proportion of actual hits to possible hits across the seven parameters of competence may be taken as an index of probable managerial competence. When this type logic is applied to the data from the synthesis research, different estimates of competence result for the five management styles described by Blake and Mouton. The results of the hit analysis indicate that the basic technologies underlying each of the grid styles differ dramatically in overall managerial competence.

RESULTS

Table 1 contains a summary of the hit analysis of each of the Blake and Mouton managerial styles. The point system employed is indicated for each component. And the estimated competence for each style—expressed in terms of probabilities—is given as the proportion of *obtained* to *possible* total points. A close study of these data, coupled with a review of the findings from the synthesis research, will give a clearer and fuller depiction of each style than previously available—just what a given style entails, where it is more or less in accord

Table 1. "Hit" analysis of style competence.

FACTORS / STYLE	MANAGERIAL BELIEFS — X (0)	Y (1)	BELIEF CONSISTENCY — Inconsistent (0)	Consistent (1)	INVOLVEMENT PRACTICES — Participation (1) / Climate (1)	MANAGEMENT OF MOTIVES — Belonging (1) / Ego (2) / Self-Actualization (3)	WORK MOTIVATION — Belonging (1) / Ego (2) / Self-Actualization (3)	MANAGER'S INTERPERSONAL COMPETENCE (5)	SUBORDINATE'S INTERPERSONAL COMPETENCE (5)	PROBABLE COMPETENCE Hits/Total	%
Available "Hit" Points	0	1	0	1	1 / 1	1 / 2 / 3	1 / 2 / 3	5	5		
9/9		1/1		1/1	2/2	6/6	4/6	5/5	5/5	24/26	92
5/5		0/1		0/1	1/2	2/6	5/6	3/5	3/5	14/26	54
9/1		0/1		1/1	0/2	2/6	2/6	4/5	4/5	13/26	50
1/9		0/1		0/1	1/2	4/6	1/6	2/5	2/5	10/26	38
1/1		0/1		1/1	0/2	0/6	1/6	1/5	1/5	4/26	15

with behavioral principles, and its impact on subordinate characteristics and practices.

The 9/9 Style: 92% Competent

The 9/9 style is rooted in a fairly pure form of *Theory Y* thought. These managers, characterized by maximum concerns for both production and people, *capitalize* on the *involvement strategy*. Their subordinates report *high levels of participation, satisfaction* and *commitment* to decision products. In their management of motives, 9/9-oriented managers assume that their subordinates are the typical mature and healthy adults described by Maslow and Herzberg, primarily concerned with *higher level needs*; their subordinates respond in kind and are most preoccupied with *actualization* and *belongingness*, although less preoccupied with *ego-status* gratifications than might be expected. According to managers and subordinates alike, the *interpersonal competence* of 9/9 management is the *greatest* of all those studied; high, balanced and uniform reliance on exposure and feedback processes is reported irrespective of power differences. Finally, subordinates employ these *same* interpersonal practices, thus promulgating *collaborative-risk taking* values throughout the organization.

The 5/5 Style: 54% Competent

The 5/5 style flows from essentially *Theory X* thought somewhat obscured by a *compartmentalized* version of X-Y confusion. Managers use *involvement strategies* to a *limited* extent, but subordinates are *moderately satisfied* with this state of affairs. Managers disposed to 5/5 assume that subordinate motivation lies primarily in a concern for *creature comfort, safety* and *ego-status* needs. Subordinates, however, appear unaffected by such motivational emphases; they are most concerned with the motivator factors deemed most important by Herzberg and Maslow. Both managers and their subordinates report an *average interpersonal profile*. The practices of 5/5 management are limited interpersonally; subordinates reflect the same, limited competence practices.

The 9/1 Style: 50% Competent

The 9/1 style is rooted in an essentially pure Theory X view of mankind. *Little* use is made of *involvement strategies* and subordinates react to this deprivation with feelings of *high frustration*. Motivationally, 9/1 devotees stress *safety-security, creature comfort* and *ego-status* pursuits. Their prophecy is fulfilled; subordinates report like concerns. An *autocratic-complacent* interpersonal profile characterizes 9/1 management; subordinates, however, rate both their managers and themselves quite competent interpersonally.

The 1/9 Style: 38% Competent

Those favoring the 1/9 style harbor views of mankind which are essentially *Theory X*, glossed over by *X-Y Confusion* which takes the form of *rationalization.* While a *substantial* amount of *participative activity* is reported, none of its salutary effects on climate are realized; subordinates are *dissatisfied* and *frustrated.* The 1/9 approach to motivation flows from an assumption that subordinates are most concerned with a strange mix of *actualization, belonging* and *creature comfort* needs; this is primarily a supportive maintenance view and subordinates respond by being most concerned with *social* and *safety* needs. Managers' use of the 1/9 *permissive-apprehensive* profile results in judgments of *low interpersonal competence* from their subordinates. Moreover, subordinates tend to behave with equal incompetence in their relationships.

The 1/1 Style: 15% Competent

The 1/1 management style is a manifestation of fairly pure *Theory X* thought. While moderate use is made of *involvement strategies,* subordinate reactions suggest that these are superfluous. Motivational assumptions are in keeping with Herzberg's hygiene theory of motivation; *creature comfort* and *safety* needs are most emphasized by 1/1 management. Subordinates are concerned with *safety* and *belongingness,* consistent with their managers' emphasis on lower level dissatisfiers. In terms of relative *interpersonal competence,* 1/1 oriented managers are the *least* competent of all, pictured by themselves and subordinates alike with *bureaucratic-defensive* profiles. Their subordinates are also essentially incompetent interpersonally.

The results of the hit analysis of the components of managerial styles are revealing in several ways. Of primary interest, of course, is the portrayal gained of each style's *relative* competence. The 9/9 style clearly emerges as a quantum improvement in competence potential when compared to other styles. In addition, the strengths and weaknesses of a given style emerge more clearly when it is analyzed in terms of its basic components. Indeed, some perhaps unexpected characteristics become apparent, particularly when managerial self-assessments are then compared with subordinate reports. For example, the 9/1 style—obviously deficient in its management of employee motivation—emerges as considerably more competent than the 1/9 style which, while more competent in its attention to employee motives, has a less competent motivational impact on subordinates. The reason for this motivational anomaly can very likely be traced to the substantial differences obtained in interpersonal competence: both managers and their subordinates report greater competence on the part of the 9/1 style as compared to 1/9 interpersonal practices. These and other effects are captured by the hit analysis.

REFLECTIONS

From these findings managers can gain insight into the choices available to them. Whether one's personal career progress is the most important concern or

the well-being of subordinate personnel or the viability of the total organization, the message inherent in these data is clear: the 9/9 style is vastly superior
to all other styles in its potential for attaining the best efforts from most of the
people most of the time.

Also of interest is the picture which emerges from the data of what Blake and
Mouton have called the "statistical 5/5" approach. Variously called contingency management or situational leadership, approaches to management which
favor the use of all styles, depending on the situation, emerge as about 50%
competent. This, incidentally, is a "best case" percentage and necessarily assumes that managers are able to correctly identify each situation for what it is
and confront it appropriately. If, however, managers are less than totally objective and permit their "lenses" to distort their view of a given situation, as
Egon Brunswik suggests they do, then it is not realistic to assume that situational management will be competent even half the time.

While managers may prefer any number or combination of styles, they
should choose these honestly and in terms of their probable consequences: one
cannot obtain 9/9 results with other than 9/9 practices, regardless of intent or
neo-behavioral reasoning. Each style is fixed in terms of both its component
factors and its effects; no amount of rationalizing or theorizing can change this
basic fact. Like it or not certain practices yield their own respective results.
Therefore, while every manager is free to manage as he or she chooses, working
productively with most of the people most of the time—i.e., managing competently may only be accomplished in a particular way. Now, at least, the
choices and consequences are clear. The rest is up to the manager.

Chapter 33

To Achieve or Not:
The Manager's Choice

Jay Hall

Historically, ours has been an achievement-oriented culture. Our national archives fairly burst with the exploits of rugged men of purpose who tamed the frontier and moved mountains so that trains might run, and captains of industry who rose from the stockroom to the Boardroom in less time than it takes to mature medium-term bonds. Our ego-ideals have been leaders of men and we have recited until we believe the litany of leadership: plan, direct, control, organize, decide, win!

The need to achieve permeates our daily lives—all about us, we see books on how to succeed without really trying—or advertisements aimed precisely at our very human desire to grow, to somehow become better than we are. We have all, to some extent, been targeted for miracle cures for our frustrations; nowhere are proffered ''solutions'' more prevalent than in the field of management. Indeed, today's management literature is not unlike a smorgasbord from which each manager can choose according to his own appetite. . .winning through intimidation, being an OK boss, how to avoid groupthink, and even how to say no convincingly.

Unfortunately, the effect on actual achievement is something less than that of a good placebo. By relying on counter-productive rules of success, the modern manager in a hurry to succeed risks being stopped cold in his tracks. The problem is that most of the game plans turn out to have been conceived in a vacuum; they are, by and large, highly intuitive and subjective pronouncements of what should and should not be done. They are long on inspiration but stingy where proof is concerned. But achievement, and one's need to feel that he can achieve, is a serious matter; it deserves better treatment.

Those who have been stifled by the air of data-less certainty surrounding many a management office or bruised by running into the invisible walls of orthodoxy founded on unsupported organizational myths may agree that the time has come to collect data rather than spin personally gratifying or corporately profitable yarns. Many of us have become increasingly curious—if not frankly contentious—about managerial achievement. Who are our achieving managers? What do they do to distinguish themselves from their less achieving cohorts? We need less speculation and more hard data about the achieving condition.

That's what this article is about: a systematic investigation of the achieving condition conducted according to the rules of scientific inquiry, tempered by the demands of rigorous statistical procedures. We have recently completed a five year research project on managerial achievement. We studied over 16,000 managers in the process and we discovered a number of factors which significantly distinguish those who achieve managerially from those who fail to do so. Our research was a partisan effort: because we believe in focusing on things people can do something about, our studies were confined to the *behaviors* managers employ in administering the management process. Our findings are clear-cut and straightforward: those who excel managerially behave differently than do those of only average or low achievement. In these differences lie the choice points for managers confronted with career planning. I would like to share our findings and, perhaps in the process, lay open some alternatives for those contemplating achievement.

THE ACHIEVING MANAGER RESEARCH PROJECT

To be honest, our project began initially on a serendipitous note. We did not set out to prove anything or, for that matter, to study achievement. The nature of our business, in which we apply behavioral science technologies to organizational dynamics, is such that we routinely collect data on management groups from many different types of organizations, from all levels of management. These data concern the values, practices and day-to-day behavioral modes of those who make organizations function the way they do. It occurred to us that we were in a prime position to explore any number of heretofore unresearched relationships between managerial practices and other phenomena and, because of its obvious importance, we addressed ourselves to a systematic study of factors responsible for managerial achievement.

We adopted as our major objective in the Achieving Manager Project the isolation of the behavioral traits which not only appear to characterize achievers, but to distinguish them from other managers. We opted for one of the most basic and frequently encountered research procedures known to the social sciences, comparisons of groups *identified* as different on the basis of objective criteria and *thought* to be different in terms of several other dimensions. We were already busy collecting data on those dimensions we anticipated to underlie group differences; we needed a selection criterion which would allow us to categorize managers according to achievement level.

IDENTIFYING THE ACHIEVING MANAGER:

The Managerial Achievement Quotient

Achievement does not easily lend itself to measurement. Yet for our project we needed an achievement index that was objective and reflected the bench marks subjectively used as reference points by managers themselves. An obvious approach would be to confine ourselves to a study of those who have made it up the corporate ladder. Such an exemplary-case criterion, rooted solely in organizational rank, was rejected as an oversimplification on two grounds. First, rank attainment cannot be evaluated without some consideration of the manager's age; the issue of *potential* for achievement is at stake and it is obscured by a pure rank criterion. Second, we wanted information about managers who are not achievers; insight into counterproductive factors or ones which simply fail to work is just as important as data about factors responsible for achievement. Our search began, therefore, with a review of pertinent techniques for assessing managerial achievement which account for the effects of rank, age and varying levels of achievement status.

A Formula For Measuring Achievement

We found that Blake and Mouton[1] conducted a study of managerial style and career accomplishment in which they used an achievement index developed by Dr. Benjamin Rhodes: the *Managerial Achievement Quotient* or MAQ possesses all the properties of concern to us. Affording an evaluation of an individual's career progress in light of his chronological age much as the IQ ratio provides for assessments of one's mental age relative to his actual age, the MAQ takes into account such practical considerations as the number of career moves necessary to reach the top of an organization, the age span most germane to career planning and the time in grade.

The Blake and Mouton study was conducted within a single firm, allowing for considerable control over, for instance, the number of levels comprising the organization's hierarchy and other features which differ from organization to organization. We desired an index with more generic application so that, through broader sampling, we might guard against any uncontrolled effects traceable to unique organizational cultures; our research plan called for the study of more than fifty different organizations. We adopted a variation of the basic MAQ which reflects our research aims more realistically. As an index of managerial achievement, therefore, we chose:

$$MAQ = \frac{5(6 - \text{Rank})}{\text{Age}} \times 100$$

In the numerator of our revised formula, *5* is a constant progression factor—the time in grade per number of career moves available if one were to spend his work life in an eight-level organization—which reflects potential mobility upward in the absence of any other forces such as politics, chance, etc. Also in the numerator, the quantity (*6 - Rank*) amounts to a rank index obtained by assigning numerical values of 1 to 5 to organizational levels ranging from top (L1) to non-management (L5) and subtracting from the correction factor of 6.

In the denominator, age (20 to 50 years) represents a seniority index: the time, given a more or less standard entry age of twenty, in which an individual might advance from lowest to highest organizational levels if advancement were purely mechanical. Finally, we use the constant multiplier of *100* to eliminate decimals.

Normative Data Base For The MAQ

So that we might have confidence both in the selection mechanism and in the cutoff points we chose to identify individuals of high, average and low managerial achievement, we collected the necessary biographical data for computing the MAQ on a base sample of 5,451 managers. All organizational levels, from non-management supervisory personnel to Chief Executive Officer, ages from 19 to 64 and 26 different types of organizations were represented. MAQ raw scores for this group ranged from 9 to 109.5. The average manager in this base sample had an MAQ of 39.4; he was approximately 38 years old and occupied a middle (L3) management position, a profile corresponding to that found in most organizations.

Raw scores were transformed to standard scores, affording a control for bias and allowing us to categorize managers with *standardized* MAQs of 60 or above as High Achievers, 41 to 59 as Average Achievers and those with 40 or below as Low Achievers. Finally, we conducted a number of pilot studies to determine the sensitivity and discriminant power of the index. Our results confirmed the standardized MAQ as a robust and reliable indicator of managerial achievement.

We were ready for the most important part of our research, that of finding out how managers high in achievement differ from lower achievers in administering the management process; or, as Blake and Mouton phrased it, to discover the factors *responsible* for managerial achievement.

FACTORS IN MANAGERIAL ACHIEVEMENT

The work of several prominent behavioral theorists guided us in our study of managerial achievement as a function of behavioral factors. The issues pursuant to managerial effectiveness which have stemmed from behavioral theory and research essentially concern motivation, the participative ethic, interpersonal competence and managerial style. These areas have been the purview primarily of individuals like Maslow[2], Herzberg[3], McGregor[4], Marrow et al[5], Argyris[6], Likert[7] and Blake and Mouton[8]. Not only have they supplied most of the recorded examples of behavioral science applications to managerial and organizational dynamics, they have been most prescriptive as well. To follow their lead in investigating the factors responsible for managerial achievement, therefore, seems both natural and desirable from the standpoint of testing the validity of prescriptive rules.

As a point of logical departure, we assessed the relationship of managerial achievement to personal belief structures, the bedrock assumptions on which a manager builds his practices. Next, we focused on managerial *and* subordinate motivational phenomena, and followed with an investigation of managers' employment of the participative ethic and its related involvement effects, as reported by their subordinates. Then, the issue of interpersonal competence, as reported by managers themselves and judged by their subordinates, was explored. And finally managerial style, that cluster of behaviors resulting from all the former, was studied as a predictor of managerial achievement.

In all, over 12,000 managers (all males) were studied in the Achieving Manager Project. All organizational levels, the full range of pertinent ages and over fifty actual organizations were represented. In each research instance, managers were assigned to High, Average or Low Managerial Achievement groups on the basis of their standardized MAQ scores. We found, I think, not only what distinguishes the achiever from the non-achiever but a basis for exemplary management as well.

MANAGERIAL ACHIEVEMENT AND
PERSONAL BELIEFS

Douglas McGregor[9] has maintained that every managerial act rests on fundamental assumptions, generalizations, and hypotheses about the nature of the people who populate the world of work. The personal assumptions or "cosmologies" management holds about controlling its human resources determine the whole character of the enterprise. McGregor posits two views for comparative emphasis: Theory X and Theory Y, examples of a pessimistic and reductive view of those human resources under the manager's purview as compared to a set of developmental and integrative beliefs.

Insofar as managerial achievement is concerned, it is McGregor's position that management philosophically based in Theory Y addresses itself to the dynamic potentials for growth and internal control of personnel, facilitating better accomplishment of organizational objectives and encouraging the growth of subordinates at the same time; on the other hand, subscription to a Theory X view is evinced in mechanistic thinking and a preoccupation with the use of external controls which limit growth and reduce organizational potential. If this is a valid position and if the manager's subscription to a reductive, vis-à-vis a developmental set of beliefs about the nature of his human resources does indeed affect the quality of his management, achievers should be found to differ from nonachievers along the dimensions of managerial belief. Study I was undertaken to investigate the relevance of personal belief systems for managerial achievement.

The *Managerial Philosophies Scale*[10] was employed to ascertain the strength of managers' subscriptions to Theory X and Theory Y generalizations about the nature of the human resources comprising their organizations. The MPS was administered to 676 managers, representing the full range of organizational rank from 14 different types of organizations. Subjects were then assigned to achievement groups on the basis of their standardized MAQ scores: 156 Low Achievers, 421 Average Achievers, and 99 High Achieving managers. A strong subscription to Theory X beliefs appeared to be a major characteristic of Low Achieving managers, with such beliefs decreasing in strength from Low through Average to High Achieving groups.

The linear nature of the relationship between belief in reductive propositions regarding an organization's human resources and the level of managerial achievement attained is portrayed graphically in Figure 1. As the plot of centroid scores reveals, High Achieving Managers differ from their Average and Low Achieving colleagues primarily in terms of their relative lack of subscription to Theory X and, it is inferred, allegiance to alternative beliefs. In brief, the results best serve to illustrate the counterproductive impact of reductive views on managerial achievement; as McGregor would have us expect, adherence to Theory X suppositions regarding those who populate one's work environment is associated with lower levels of managerial achievement.

Of some interest is the fact that the obverse proposition to the effect that reliance on a Theory Y view facilitates managerial accomplishment fails to receive support. Managerial achievement appears in the present instance to be a negatively accelerated function of strength of subscription to the reductive and delimiting beliefs comprising Theory X and not much else. This may be an oversimplification of the results, however.

McGregor[11] made explicit his view that X and Y are independent cosmologies, not polar opposites, and that one does not become an advocate of Theory Y simply by moving away from Theory X. The total profile requires analysis. It would appear from our results that the X to Y ratio holds some diagnostic merit. In the present case, an inspection of the X and Y means reveals that the High Achieving groups fall well below the standardized mean for Theory X subscription while scoring equally above the mean for its Theory Y

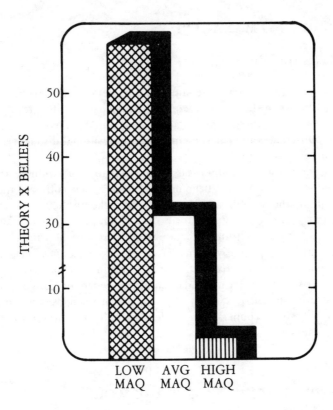

Figure 1. Level of managerial achievement as a function of strength of subscription to Theory X beliefs.

orientation. No such clear preference was evident among Average and Low Achievers. Indeed, from our results, Low and Average Achievers display something akin to what Meyers[12] has called a Traditional View: Theory X tempered by human relations training or, perhaps, social desirability effects. Thus, the present results appear more suggestive than definitive; they point up the significant negative relationship between a Theory X subscription and managerial achievement and they suggest, moreover, that a more critical consideration might well be the degree of subordination of Theory X beliefs to Theory Y assumptions as a precursor to achievement.

We might say that the MPS data reveal more about failure to achieve than they do about achievement per se. Nevertheless, our results indicate that managerial cosmologies, as a part of the existing social technology of management, do distinguish among managers of differing achievement. And, consistent with McGregor's position, it may be expected that managers of differing achievement will be found as well to embrace different approaches to the interaction components of management.

THE ACHIEVING MANAGER:

What Makes Him Run?

Do most managers aspire to the same goals in an organization, but perceive different pathways to their attainment? Or do managers differ regarding the reasons they work and then employ practices best suited to attain their different objectives? Differences in achievement imply motivational differences, not so much in amount as in kind.

While a good deal of thought has been given to motivation in the work place, the dominant thrust has been one of better understanding—and therefore managing—the subordinate personnel who make up the great majority of any work force. Implicit in such a focus is an assumption that managers—by virtue of occupying key slots in the organization—are somehow immune to the mundane world of work motivation. Yet, given differences in managerial performance, one must realize that managers are not above a "motivational analysis" and probably also differ in fundamental ways where needs, goals and personal drives are concerned. We can trace a manager's achievement to motivation just as we can the cooperativeness, dependability and overall productivity of his employees.

MANAGERIAL ACHIEVEMENT AND WORK MOTIVATION

One Man's Ceiling Is Another Man's Floor

To test this notion that our three groups differ with respect to the need profiles which make up "motivation," we administered the Hall and Williams *Work Motivation Inventory*[13] (WMI) to 1,265 managers. Based on a synthesis of the *need hierarchy* concept developed by Abraham Maslow[14] and the *hygiene-motivator* theory of Frederick Herzberg[15], the WMI assesses the factors most important to an individual in making decisions about and/or seeking satisfactions from his work. Five scores are generated from the instrument, each reflecting one of the five need systems Maslow postulated to characterize human motivation, *i.e.*, *basic creature comfort, safety, belongingness, ego-status* and *self-actualization*. The *creature comfort* and *safety* needs, particularly, underlie a preoccupation with the incentives Herzberg has labeled *hygiene* or *maintenance* factors. *Ego-status* and *actualization* needs are linked to motivator incentives. So, the WMI yields both a *need* and a *hygiene-motivator* profile.

The higher a given score, the stronger the represented need and, as a result, the more the individual is motivated to pursue satisfaction of that particular need. Many of his behaviors and feelings, therefore, can best be understood in terms of his *hygiene*-seeking vis-à-vis *motivator*-seeking tendencies. The rationale, simply put, is that the individual primarily concerned with and motivated by *safety* and *security* needs will neither value the same incentives nor employ the same behaviors to attain his objectives as will the individual essentially motivated by an *ego-status* need; while the former is striving to *avoid* dissatisfaction, the latter is seeking to attain satisfaction. To the extent that both the form and quality of managerial behaviors can be traced to motivational dynamics, any differences found in a motivational analysis will prove significant for managerial performance in general and for achievement in particular. And differences there are!

Having sorted the 1,265 managers into their respective achievement groups, we ran a comparison of their WMI profiles. Substantial differences, in a statistical sense, were found between the motivational profiles of the three groups, revealing that the manager's own needs do indeed affect the level of achievement he will realize in his organization.

Briefly, the need for *self-actualization* is the dominant motivational influence for High Achievers, while Average Achievers are most driven by *ego-status* needs. According to the WMI norms available, these two groups are substantially above the average in their respective need strengths and emerge as *motivator* seekers.

Low achievers, on the other hand, are caught up in a peculiar kind of double bind: at one and the same time they are most preoccupied with gaining satisfaction for *basic creature comfort* and *ego-status* needs. As Maslow has told us, it is highly unlikely that higher order needs, such as *ego-status,* will emerge until lower order needs like *creature comfort* have been adequately satisfied. When higher order needs arise in conjunction with lower order needs, as with Low Achievers, it therefore appears that we have a crisis of motivation in which neither *motivator* nor *hygiene* needs are being very well met.

We will return to this issue; for the moment, suffice it to say that managers differing in achievement have markedly different motivational profiles and pursue quite different incentives. Very likely, their practices differ too. Particularly, we would expect High, Average and Low Achieving managers to be characterized by different approaches to employee motivation. If this is the case, we reasoned, more serious implications than those initially apparent come into play. How do these groups of managers deal with the motivational processes within their organizations? What, then, are the motivational consequences among the organization's personnel? We conducted two more studies of motivational phenomena to answer these questions.

ACHIEVEMENT AND THE MANAGEMENT OF MOTIVES:

High Achievers Challenge While Low Achievers Comfort

It is generally accepted that motivation is something the person brings with him to the organization, that managers cannot motivate their employees in any injective sense of the word. The best a manager can hope for is to accurately identify the incentives under his control which coincide with subordinate needs. He may then be able to harness the more constructive and contributive motives of his subordinates, thereby channeling those subordinates' activities toward the doing of the organization's work.

On the other hand, we know that the manager can greatly influence subordinate expectations and views of organizational reality by his actions and by the values he promulgates on behalf of the organization. Employee motives are probably some joint function of what they bring with them to the organization and the conditioning effects achieved by their managers as they mediate rewards and emphasize the practical utility of the organization's various incentives.

The manager's view of motivation—of what is important to his subordinates and of what is possible in the way of satisfactions within the organization—is a critical component of the motivational process. Depending upon his view, the manager can create conditions for need satisfaction coincidental to desired performance or he may frustrate and block needs along with the expression of the very skills of which his subordinates are most proud.

In effect, the manager's *personal theory* of motivation becomes a powerful force in the work place, shaping and facilitating subordinates' expression of some need-related behaviors while blocking or denying that of others. Given the various need profiles which characterize High, Average and Low Achievers, we felt that managers differing in achievement are likely to have different "theories" about the motivational process. And indeed they do; the manager's view of the motivational process and the incentives he emphasizes in his management of that process differ greatly for the three groups.

The *Management of Motives Index*[16] (MMI), a companion piece to the WMI designed for use with managers, was administered to 664 individuals. As with the WMI, the MMI yields a score for each of the five need systems having *hygiene-motivator* significance; each score is an index of how much the manager emphasizes that particular need in his management of others. In mediating reality for their subordinates, High, Average and Low Achievers place significantly different emphases on four of the need systems. Moreover, these managers manage the motivational process for others *primarily as a function of their own needs!*

High Achievers place major emphasis on the *actualization, belonging* and *ego-status* needs comprising the *motivator* package, paying only average attention to *hygiene* factors. Low Achievers, on the other hand, virtually ignore *motivators* while stressing the importance of *creature comfort* and particularly *safety* and *security* issues having *hygiene* significance. Average Achievers stress *ego-status*, giving adequate attention to the actualization needs of their subordinates, essentially promoting *motivator* seeking among those they manage. As we expected, managerial achievement is linked to the motivational climate one creates for his subordinates as well as to personal striving.

Now the critical question. How does all this affect subordinates? If a manager's employees hear and heed his motivational message, the issue is broadened and goes beyond the mere consideration of his *personal* achievement to encompass the well-being of others, not to mention the probable success of their pursuit of organizational objectives. Argyris has cautioned us not to underestimate the power of the managerial self-fulfilling prophecy.

MANAGERIAL ACHIEVEMENT AND THE FULFILLING OF MOTIVATIONAL PROPHECIES

To determine whether the effects of a manager's unique management of motives were strong enough to significantly influence the need profiles of his subordinates, we administered the WMI to over 3,500 subordinates of 1,291 managers. These subordinate data were separated according to the achievement rating of their managers and comparisons were run across the five need strengths. There are highly significant differences between the need profiles of High Achieving managers' subordinates and those of both Average and Low Achievers. Subordinates definitely hear and adopt as their own their manager's motivational message; managers create subordinates in their own image and the image definitely differs as a function of the manager's level of achievement.

To appreciate just how potent managerial prophecies about motivation are in our organizations, one has only to compare the need profiles of High, Average and Low Achievers with those of their subordinates. The statistical technique employed to analyze our data allows for simplifying the inputs from several sources so that we may obtain a distilled, concise and penetrating summary statement of differences. Dimensions along which achievement groups most differ are identified and give us a graphic depiction of the nature and degree of differences among groups. In this case, the dimensions are identical for managers and their subordinates and, as Figure 2 indicates, they allow for the creation of four motivational realms, each a unique portrayal of the need profile of those who fall into it.

The dimensions which emerge from our analysis indicate the degree to which managers and their subordinates are: (1) *maintenance-seeking* or *motivator-seeking* and (2) either *self-centered* or *other-directed* in their orientations to attaining need satisfaction. It is readily apparent that subordinates occupy matrix positions similar to those occupied by their managers and, moreover, managers of different achievement levels and their subordinates occupy vastly different positions as well.

Low Achievers are *self-centered maintenance seekers;* their subordinates display the same, we may assume conditioned, need properties. High Achievers are best characterized as *other-directed motivator-seekers* and so are their

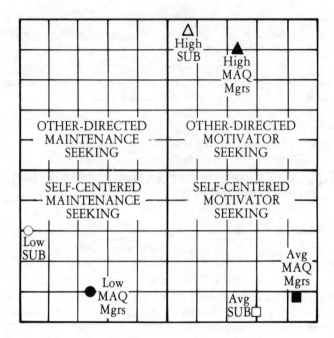

Figure 2. Motivational profiles of High, Average, and Low Achieving managers and their subordinates.

subordinates. Average Achievers are also *motivator-seeking,* but the nature of their quest is qualitatively different from that of High Achievers in that it is *self-centered*; their subordinates are also *self-centered motivator-seekers.*

Thus are motivational prophecies fulfilled. Not only does personal motivation affect a manager's achievement level, so does his perception of the motivational process and his consequent practices in the management of motives. Indeed, in what appears to be a causal fashion, a manager's achievement is directly linked to the motivational profile of his subordinates. A sobering thought is inferred: *the needs and quality of motivation characterizing a manager's subordinates may say more about the manager than about his subordinates.*

PARTICIPATIVE MANAGEMENT AND MANAGERIAL ACHIEVEMENT

Drawing on Kurt Lewin's action research strategy, Al Marrow, John R.P. French and their colleagues first demonstrated the efficacy of a participative approach to management in their studies of the Harwood Manufacturing Corporation[17,18]. Their subsequent application of participative techniques to

Harwood's acquisition of the Weldon Corporation is a modern day classic of applied behavioral science. Marrow and his colleagues have probably done more than any others to advance participative management as a viable and feasible technique for organizational effectiveness, but no one before has directly linked the technique to individual career accomplishment and managerial achievement.

We have seen that there is reason to expect such a relationship. Participative management is founded on the belief that people directly affected by a decision should participate in making that decision; the emphasis is on *joint* decision making about events which have future implications for the parties involved, and over which they can realistically exert influence. One has to be a manager to fully appreciate what a bone of contention such a work ethic can become; there are few who are neutral about the issue of participation. Originally embraced as a mechanism for countering the unilateral decision structure and authoritarian values often found in traditional organization theory, the participative ethic also positively affects loyalty and creativity. Now we find that it distinguishes between those who achieve managerially and those who do not.

To research the relationship between participative management practices and managerial achievement, we focused on subordinates; it is they, we felt, who are best equipped to report on their managers' use of participative practices and those all important feelings which they, the subordinates, experience as a result. We administered the *Personal Reaction Index*[19] to over 2,000 subordinates of 731 managers. The PRI, used extensively for training and research purposes, assesses the degree to which the manager allows a subordinate to participate and encourages him to influence work-related decisions. In addition, it gauges the amount of job satisfaction, sense of personal responsibility, commitment, pride in work and frustration experienced as a consequence of participation. Combined, the scales reflect an *involvement index* implying the kind of work *climate* a given manager creates.

Our results are presented graphically in Figure 3. Low Achievers, as reported by their subordinates, make minimal use of participative practices; Average Achievers make only slightly greater use. High Achievers, according to their subordinates, not only employ far and away greater amounts of the technique, but so much so that participative methods may be said to be a major characteristic of the High Achieving approach to management.

Of equal importance are the climate implications suggested in Figure 3. Our significance dimension is comprised of both participative opportunity data and *feeling* data. Only subordinates of High Achievers report the kind of satisfaction, commitment and pride in work that characterizes the work force of healthy organizations. Low Achievers, and to some extent Average Achievers, employ practices which result in repressive and frustrating circumstances typically found in neurotic organizations.

So the manager's use of participative practices also emerges as a factor

EGO — INVOLVEMENT VIA PARTICIPATION

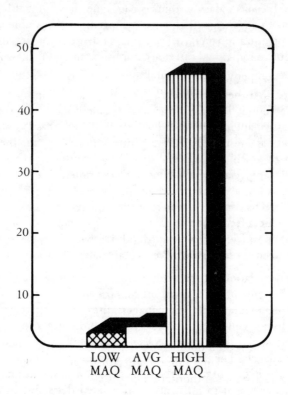

Figure 3. Subordinate ego-involvement as a function of the participative management practices of High, Average, and Low Achieving Managers.

responsible for managerial achievement, but it does not stand alone any more than did management of the motivational process. According to Marrow, we may expect its effectiveness to vary with the amount of mutual confidence found in the manager-subordinate relationship. In other words, to quote Marrow, participative management will only be successful when ". . .employees and managers are trusting and open, and problems can be approached in a spirit of joint inquiry and a consensus worked out."

The stage must be set and a conducive climate prepared for participative management to succeed. Level of *interpersonal competence*, the management dynamic most stressed by Chris Argyris[20], determines the nature of the climate within which participation is proffered. There is, therefore, ample reason to expect managerial achievement to be affected by the managerial level of interpersonal competence.

ACHIEVEMENT VIA INTERPERSONAL COMPETENCE:

Managing The Interplay Among Ideas, Feelings And Norms

Interpersonal competence plays a vital role in the successful use of participative methods. Argyris has enumerated the outcomes of interpersonal competence: (1) greater awareness of relevant problems among parties to the problem-solving relationship, (2) increased problem-solving accuracy in that problems remain solved and (3) decreased likelihood for the problem-solving process to be negatively affected in any way.[21]

A manager involved in building and maintaining relationships with his subordinates achieves interpersonal competence through such behaviors as *owning up* to or accepting responsibility for his ideas and feelings, *being open* to his own thoughts and sentiments and those of others, *experimenting* with new ideas and feelings and *helping others* to own up, be open to and experiment with their concepts and attitudes. When he can accomplish these practices in such a way that norms of individuality, interpersonal concern and mutual trust are engendered, we may call that manager interpersonally competent.

Argyris has found that the required behaviors differ in their contribution to competence *and* in the frequency of their occurence. For example, owning up to ideas is fairly common among managers, but it is not a strong predictor of competence. Actually it is a double-edged sword; an excessive preoccupation with his own ideas and feelings causes many a manager to forego participative methods in favor of more authoritarian practices. On the other hand, being open with others, willing to experiment with ideas and feelings as one helps others do the same, is an extremely potent predictor for competence but it is rare among managers. Implied, of course, is the fact that managers differ in the degree to which they perform all functions and, hence, in interpersonal competence.

The *Personnel Relations Survey*[22], based on the Luft-Ingham Johari Window[23] model of interpersonal processes, has proven to be an excellent device for assessing levels of interpersonal competence. In our investigation of achievement via competence, therefore, we first administered the PRS to 1,691 managers to discover how they handle interpersonal processes in relationships with their subordinates, colleagues and superiors. Not content with self reports alone, we administered a PRS companion piece—the two part *Management Relations Survey*[24]—to 1,884 subordinates who were asked to appraise their managers' practices in Part I and, in Part II, to reveal their own practices in relating to those managers.

As Figure 4 shows, the differences in level of interpersonal competence are substantial between the managerial groups. Moreover, subordinate appraisals of competence level for the three groups are almost identical to those provided by managers themselves.

Not only do we find that level of interpersonal competence is directly bound

INTERPERSONAL COMPETENCE

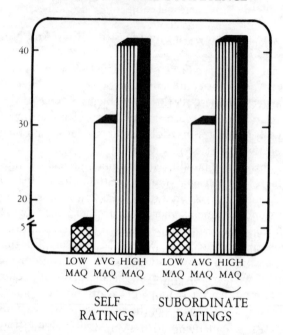

Figure 4. Ratings of interpersonal competence for High, Average, and Low Achieving managers as given by managers themselves and their subordinates.

to level of managerial achievement, but the link is so public and obvious that subordinates confirm it and report that their own interpersonal competence varies as a function of that evinced by their managers; they are well aware of the interplay. Competence and its norm-setting properties, as predicted by Argyris, is a powerful factor in determining the manager's career accomplishment and in shaping the nature and quality of subordinate practices as well.

The agreement between managers' and subordinates' reports is particularly noteworthy for it means that the behavioral messages sent by many managers come through loud and clear to subordinates who internalize them as their own. As with motivational dynamics, the competence of one's subordinates is a direct reflection of his managerial achievement status.

But what about the organization's achievement of its production goals? What do the data have to say about that reality? Argyris has tied interpersonal competence of the executive system to organizational effectiveness, but how is competence linked with the management of technical, as well as interpersonal, facets of the enterprise? We have found in other studies that the level and type of interpersonal competence exhibited by managers coincides in predictable ways with their preferred manner for managing the people-production interface in their organizations. It now appears, by logical extension, that managerial style may also be linked to managerial achievement in much the same way that both are joined to interpersonal competence. If this is so, we just might lay to rest some of those arguments about the merits of "ideal" style vis-à-vis situational or contingency approaches.

ACHIEVEMENT AND STYLE:

The Manager's Choice

Because under a style rubric we can bring together and subsume so many complex, peripheral facets of a given process, the construct of *style*—an individual's preferred, relatively consistent approach to certain situations—has found acceptance as an analytic tool in discussions of decision making, leadership, sales and management. Style incorporates a whole cluster of behaviors and values which assume true operational significance only when they are considered in conjunction.

One of the more popular treatments of management style has been the managerial grid articulated by Blake and Mouton[25], an elaboration of the work of Rensis Likert[26], Fleischman[27] and others. With their model, we can account for those influences underlying an individual's selection of managerial behaviors: his values concerning task and social demands. We locate in the grid a manager's style as a function of his characteristic concerns; then we describe it in terms of the actual behaviors he is likely to employ in the service of such concerns. Production vis-à-vis people emphases serve as the point of departure for identifying the managerial styles and their attendant practices. The beauty of the model is that it brings together and explains, under a single unifying rationale, what appear to be vastly different approaches to management. Equally important is the grid's affordance of a very workable, evaluative framework in terms of assessment as well as prediction of managerial effectiveness.

Obviously, the managerial grid seemed to us a perfect vehicle for exploring the relationship of style to managerial achievement; two assessment instruments based on its format, the *Styles of Management Inventory*[28] and the *Management Appraisal Survey*[29], were used to identify most preferred styles. In the first instance, managers gave self reports and in the second case their subordinates evaluated them. The SMI was administered to 1,878 managers and the MAS was given to the subordinates of over 2,000 managers. In both instances, we find managerial style significantly tied to managerial achievement.

Those managers identified as High Achievers, according to their own reports, emphasize an *integration* of production-people issues, avoiding those impersonal and bureaucratic practices most favored by Low Achievers. Average Achievers are not distinguished by such clear choices, but by their aversion to any management style devoted to maintaining the human system. In general, we found that managers' self reports are more suggestive than definitive,

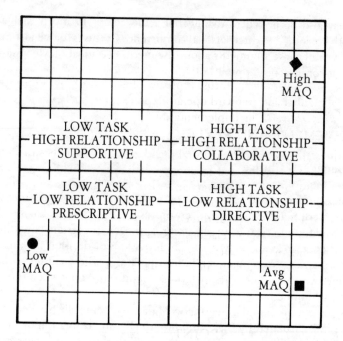

Figure 5. The relationship of managerial style to managerial achievement.

despite the statistical significance of the differences, and again we turned to those on the receiving end.

In Figure 5 we present graphically the two dimensional nature of our results. The subordinate appraisals of their managers' practices are much more revealing; they flesh out and define the nature of differences only implied in the managers' self reports. Consistent with the grid model and numerous pieces of social research, we find two dimensions reflecting task and social demands; their existence allows us to assess managerial achievement as a joint function of *task* and *relationship* emphases.

By orienting the task dimension at right angles to that of relationship, we are able to construct a grid-like model in which four general approaches or "styles" of management are defined: Low Task-Low Relationship, High Task-Low Relationship, Low Task-High Relationship and High Task-High Relationship. Such qualitative labels capture the general focus of a given style; whether or not the style corresponds to a Blake 9/9 or a Likert System 4 is far less important than the fact that the style of High Achievers is different from that of Average or Low Achievers.

As the MAQ data plots in Figure 5 reveal, subordinates say their High Achieving managers are High Task-High Relationship oriented; in essence, a *collaborative* and participative managerial style typifies High Achievers. Average Achieving managers are placed by their subordinates in the style quadrant denoting a High Task-Low Relationship focus; they are so preoccupied with production goals that they give minimal attention to the dynamics of those who must ultimately do the work, *i.e.*, they are *directive* and self-authorizing. Finally, we find that Low Achieving managers employ practices pursuant to a Low Task-Low Relationship focus. Probably rooted in cultural imperatives, the personnel manual and standard operating procedures, such a style is mechanical and *prescriptive* in its implementation.

So it is that one's achievement is linked to his choice of management style. While there are undoubtedly cultural mandates and subtle incentives for managing in one way as opposed to another, our data reveal a *generic* basis for achievement. Our High Achievers and their less fortunate cohorts came from numerous organizations and cultural settings; it is perhaps a commentary on organizational mythology that those managers who achieve are most characterized by a High Task-High Relationship management style. The issue as I see it is not so much a matter of fitting one's style to the organization as a matter of choosing whether or not to achieve. Would that the solution were so simple.

POINT AND COUNTERPOINT:

Now For The Achievement Paradox

The portrait of the Achieving Manager which emerges from our study is that of an individual employing an integrative style of management, wherein people are valued just as highly as accomplishment of production goals...wherein candor, openness, sensitivity and receptivity comprise the rule in interpersonal relationships rather than its exception...wherein participative practices are favored over unilaterally directive or lame duck prescriptive measures. Moreover, from a motivational standpoint the Achieving Manager needs to find meaning in his work and strives to afford such meaning to others. Higher order, constructive incentives are his motivational preoccupations, while his less achieving comrades remain mired in fantasies of defense and self-preservation.

But the results of our study go beyond an impressionistic, ill-defined treatment of the achieving condition; their statistical level of confidence is such that we may say with assurance that if a manager is more concerned about factors that are peripheral to his work than he is about the nature of the work itself, if he is under wraps, secretive, unconfronting and insensitive in his relationships with others; if his subordinates, while mirroring his motives and interpersonal practices, reap none of the rewards associated with that sense of proprietorship which participation affords, and if the manager remains more concerned about procedures and precedence than about productivity and the quality of life in his organization *there is a significant probability that he is a Low Achiever*. But, given a willingness to change, he need not remain so.

We are just as secure in our observation that to achieve, a manager must employ achieving practices and eschew self-serving, defensive self-authorized techniques. He must first embrace that collaborative stance which flows from the view that work—his own and that of his subordinates—is the source of challenge, meaning and opportunity for self-expansion. Through his practices he must acknowledge that his subordinates, as people at work, possess interests and expertise and he must create openings for their expression and incorporation into the work flow. He must be receptive to innovation, sensitive to the dynamics of relating and willing to take risks. And finally, ever conscious of his role of norm setter, the manager who would achieve must look to his subordinates for his reflection: *truly achieving managers produce achievers*. The data could not be more clear.

Yes, But...

It is noteworthy that, in most major respects, the behaviors of Achieving Managers coincide with the very ones the behaviorist school might "prescribe." For the past several years, the literature has been filled with such prescriptive entreaties authored by behavioral scientists and aimed at practicing managers. However, there have also been more than a few rebuttals aimed at the same group, authored by those of a different persuasion. These detractors more often than not dismiss the contributions of psychologists, sociologists and cultural anthropologists as being impractical for an organizational world filled with excruciating pressures for production, or as the theoretical ramblings of well-intentioned but appallingly naive spokesmen for the "soft sciences." Al Marrow[30], a psychologist and Chief Executive Officer of Harwood, has commented at length on managers' resistance to behavioral science concepts; even when these theories are successfully applied, managers remain unpersuaded—the paradoxical failure of success!

Non-behavioral consultants meanwhile, going for the soft underbelly, are quick to undermine the "foreign" field which intrudes. Charles Bowen[31], CEO of a major management consulting firm, has suggested that there is an aura of fantasy surrounding most of the ideas and methods for upgrading managerial performance within a behaviorist framework; all that is needed for management development is an atmosphere in which managers can make hard decisions and make them right. That's putting realism into management development...or is it? What could be more realistic or practical than career accomplishment? And that's what we're talking about.

The Achieving Managers in our study are individuals who, compared to their management cohorts, are excelling in their managerial roles and making major contributions to their organizations. And we have discovered that these same individuals embrace philosophies and practices fully consistent with the erstwhile impractical prescriptions of those maligned purveyors of soft science "who never had to make a payroll!"

The irony is that in this day when the medium is the message, many managers are more receptive to magic elixirs of success: "cute" treatments of mundane phenomena found in any human organization, grossly oversimplified versions of personal success formulae, popularly packaged and dispensed over the counter with no prescription necessary. Charm schools, rules for making it up the organization, encounter groups, computer games, key principles for avoiding incompetence...they all sell. But where is the proof? How do these *really* relate to managerial achievement? Managers might profitably ask such questions. Of prime importance in our study of achievement is the fact that we are able to speak from data rather than from intuition; we are bound by our results rather than by our prejudices.

WHO SHALL ACHIEVE, THE DILETTANTE OR THE DOER?

A related issue is raised by those pragmatists who ask, "Why should we invest time, energy and money to learn more about something that every business administration student picks up on his way to the real world?" Well....if *everyone* already knows the jargon of the human side of enterprise, *someone* isn't putting his knowledge to work. Achieving Managers account for only 13% of all the managers we studied. It seems, as Marvin Weisbord[32] has observed, that there exists a vast gap between managers' glib concept- and name-dropping and their creative use of science-based theories to improve the management of their organizations. And yet, from a purely selfish point of view, it must occur to some managers that a *few* of their colleagues are doing something about putting theory into practice. These individuals we have identified as Achieving Managers, but in their organizations they may simply be called the movers: those who, through some uncanny streak of luck, just happen to get ahead.

Dreaming Of Things That Never Were...

The results of the Achieving Manager Research Project may, upon reflection, be seen to address the future, the prospect not of how things are but of what they may become. Chris Argyris[33] has pointedly referred to the capacity of people to go either way—toward growth or toward stagnation. And it is this theme which emerges most strongly from a study of managerial achievement. *Managers* have a choice. They may decide which way they will go—toward growth and achievement or toward stagnation and accommodation—just as surely as they decide where to live or what career to pursue.

The High Achiever's approach to management can result in not only sweet dreams of success, but true excellence—be it in a small firm, one of *Fortune's 500* or the Oval Office. And each of us has the option of becoming an Achieving

Manager because the manager's achievement may be traced to the behaviors he employs. If we would make one impression, let it be this: managerial achievement does not depend upon the existence of personal traits and extraordinary skills unique to outstanding individuals; it depends instead on the manner in which the manager *behaves* in conducting organizational affairs, on the values he holds regarding personal and interpersonal potentials, all of which can be learned. *The key to becoming an Achieving Manager is to learn to behave like one.*

REFERENCES

1. Blake, R.R., & Mouton, J.S.: *The Managerial Grid.* Houston: Gulf Publishing Company, 1964, 225-246.
2. Maslow, A.: *Personality and Motivation.* New York: Harper, 1954.
3. Herzberg, F.: *Work and the Nature of Man.* New York: Wiley, 1966.
4. McGregor, D.: *The Human Side of Enterprise.* New York: McGraw-Hill, 1960.
5. Marrow, A.J., Bowers, D.G., & Seashore, S.E.: *Management by Participation.* New York: Harper & Row, 1967.
6. Argyris, C.: *Personality and Organization.* New York: Harper & Row, 1957.
7. Likert, R.: *The Human Organization.* New York: McGraw-Hill, 1967.
8. Blake, R.R., & Mouton, J.S.: *op. cit.,* 1964.
9 .McGregor, D.: *op. cit.,* 1960.
10. Jacoby, J. & Terborg, J.R.: *Managerial Philosophies Scale.* The Woodlands, Texas: Teleometrics International, Inc., 1975.
11. McGregor, D.: *Professional Manager.* New York: McGraw-Hill, 1967.
12. Myers, M.S.: "Conditions for Manager Motivation." *Harvard Business Review,* January-February, 1966.
13. Hall, J., & Williams, M.S.: *Work Motivation Inventory.* The Woodlands, Texas: Teleometrics International, Inc., 1967.
14. Maslow, A.: *op. cit.,* 1954.
15. Herzberg, F.: *op. cit.,* 1966.
16. Hall, J.: *Management of Motives Index.* The Woodlands, Texas: Teleometrics International, Inc., 1968.
17. Coch, L., French, J.R.P.: "Overcoming Resistance to Change." *Human Relations,* Vol 1, No. 4, 1948, 512-532.
18. Marrow, A.J., et al.: *op. cit.,* 1967.
19. Hall, J.: *Personal Reaction Index.* In Models for Management seminar. The Woodlands, Texas: Teleometrics International, Inc., 1971.
20. Argyris, C.: *Interpersonal Competence and Organizational Effectiveness,* Homewood, Illinois: Dorsey, 1962.
21. *ibid.*

22. Hall, J. & Williams, M.S.: *Personnel Relations Survey*. The Woodlands, Texas: Teleometrics International, Inc., 1967.

23. Luft, J.: *Of Human Interaction*. Palo Alto: National Press Books, 1969.

24. Hall, J. & Williams, M.S.: *Management Relations Survey*. The Woodlands, Texas: Teleometrics International, Inc., 1970.

25. Blake, R.R., & Mouton, J.S.: *op. cit.*, 1964.

26. Likert, R.: *New Patterns of Management*. New York: McGraw-Hill, 1961.

27. Fleischman, E.A., Harris, E.F., Burt, H.E.: *Leadership and Supervision in Industry*. Columbus, Ohio: Bureau of Educational Research, Ohio State University, 1955.

28. Hall, J., Harvey, J.B., & Williams, M.S.: *Styles of Management Inventory*. The Woodlands, Texas: Teleometrics International, Inc., 1963.

29. Hall, J., Harvey, J.B., & Williams, M.S.: *Management Appraisal Survey*. The Woodlands, Texas: Teleometrics International, Inc., 1970.

30. Marrow, A.J.: *The Failure of Success*. New York: AMACOM, 1972.

31. Bowen, C.P.: "Let's put realism into management development." *Harvard Business Review:* July-August, 1973, 81-87.

32. Weisbord, M.R.: "What, Not Again! Manage People Better?" *Think,* January-February, 1970.

33. Argyris, C.: A Few Words in Advance. In, Marrow, A.J. (Ed.) *The Failure of Success*. New York: AMACOM, 1972.

Afterthoughts

The final section should need very few editorial comments to prompt afterthoughts. From Likert to Hall, the models for management which comprise the structure of competence are those closely linked to today's most successful managers. As stressed throughout the final chapters, each manager has a clear choice of paths and full knowledge of where the chosen path will lead. At the beginning of this volume I urged you to read well and choose wisely. Now, at that choice point for managerial competence or less, I ask you to consider this— If you want to be an achieving manager, *act like one!*